LIQUIDITY ANALYSIS AND MANAGEMENT

LIQUIDITY ANALYSIS AND MANAGEMENT

George W. Gallinger
Arizona State University

P. Basil Healey
Wilfrid Laurier University

ADDISON-WESLEY PUBLISHING COMPANY

Reading, Massachusetts □ Menlo Park, California
Don Mills, Ontario □ Wokingham, England □ Amsterdam
Sydney □ Singapore □ Tokyo □ Madrid □ Bogotá
Santiago □ San Juan

Library of Congress Cataloging-in-Publication Data

Gallinger, George W.
  Liquidity analysis and management.

  Bibliography: p.
Includes index.
1. Cash management.   2. Corporations—Finance.
I. Healey, P. Basil.   II. Title.
HG4028.C45G34   1987   658.1'5244   86–3322
ISBN 0–201–10518–7

Reprinted with corrections, June 1987

Preface

Financial managers conduct their business in an environment that requires frequent decisions to be made to direct economic activities that create economic value for shareholders. The academic literature is replete with theoretical discussion and models pertaining to long-term value-enhancing decisions. Unfortunately, the same cannot be said for short-term financial decision management, more commonly referred to as working capital management. The purpose of this book is to make a small contribution to help alleviate this deficiency.

Short-term financial management has different focuses than those of long-term financial decision making. The first difference is the shorter time dimension. Short-term financial management is concerned with day-to-day operating decisions. The strategic issues of dividend policy, long-term investments, and capital structure are primarily the province of long-term financial management. A second difference is that short-term financial management has a stronger accounting orientation than does long-term financial management — an emphasis that is prevalent in this book.

Traditionally, short-term financial management has been referred to as (net) working capital management — the management of current assets and current liabilities. The duration of these assets and liabilities is considered to be a year or less. The objective when one is managing these short-lived assets and liabilities is the maintenance of adequate *liquidity* to meet obligations as they come due. Since the emphasis is on liquidity, we prefer to think of working capital management as *liquidity management*. Liquidity management is a more descriptive and accurate title of the responsibilities associated with short-term financial decisions.

Analysis of liquidity requires understanding of cash flows — both *to* the business and *from* the business. This chore may seem simple enough.

Unfortunately, these flows can become very difficult to understand under accrual accounting concepts. The primary purpose of accrual accounting is to match expenses with revenues generated in the normal operations of the business. The emphasis is on satisfactory estimation of profits, *not* cash flows. However, the accrual accounting exercise of determining profits affects the balance sheet and the overall financial condition of the firm. The opportunity for management to select from a number of generally accepted accounting principles for recording inventories, tax liabilities, and contra accounts, for example, requires financial statement analysts to conduct a thorough analysis if they are to understand the quality of the earnings and the true liquidity of the company. Unfortunately, most books in finance ignore many of the accounting issues that affect liquidity. Although no statement is made for the reason, the implication is that the untangling of anything other than the simplest accrual accounting complexities more properly belongs with the accountants.

We agree that the accounting functions should be left to the accountants. However, if financial analysts are to understand financial statements, they must be willing to learn more accounting. When they do, they should have a better appreciation of the relationship between economic value and the accountant's historical cost value — and, subsequently, of corporate liquidity and the financial condition of the firm.

Objective

The objective of this book is to reconsider traditional analytical techniques and to investigate new approaches to the liquidity management decision process. The tools of analysis cross the disciplines of accounting, economics, finance, and mathematics. The emphasis is on everyday operations of the firm from a financial perspective. Long-term financial management topics such as dividend policy, optimal capital structure, and capital budgeting decisions are discussed only in terms of their significance to liquidity management. A number of topics discussed in various academic and practitioner journals, but not generally included in financial management books, are examined here. A partial list of these topics includes off–balance sheet financing, variance analysis models, improved liquidity indicators, and hedging techniques. The topics examined in this book should both broaden and deepen your understanding of liquidity management.

Coverage

This book is divided into four sections: (1) foundations, (2) techniques of liquidity analysis, (3) management of specific net working capital accounts, and (4) some related issues.

Part I consists of the first two chapters. Chapter 1 is an overview of liquidity management and introduces an important concept that must be understood: "how to go broke while making a profit." Chapter 2 provides the microeconomic foundations for a better understanding of liquidity management. Much of the chapter is devoted to the concept of marginal analysis since it is clearly the proper decision-making tool. The latter part of the chapter relates economic principles to financial statements to show the close relationship between economics and accounting.

Part II includes Chapters 3 through 6. These chapters discuss financial statement analysis and closely related topics for understanding liquidity. Chapter 3 presents liquidity analysis from a traditional perspective. Limitations of commonly used ratios are discussed. Off–balance sheet financing is examined in Chapter 4. This topic is important to liquidity since many treasurers are under pressure to find techniques that provide necessary financing but, at the same time, financing that does not cause the balance sheet to decline in quality. Chapters 5 and 6 examine techniques that provide improved estimates of liquidity requirements and associated risks over those provided by traditional ratio analysis.

Part III pertains to the management of specific assets and liabilities and consists of Chapters 7 through 18. Cash management is the first topic discussed. This area is an extremely important one within liquidity management since all investable resources flow through the cash accounts. The topics discussed here integrate with inventory, accounts receivable, and accounts payable concepts discussed in later chapters. Chapter 7 provides an overview of the importance of cash management and techniques available for moving cash. Chapter 8 examines forecasting cash balances and determining the appropriate level of cash to maintain.

Accounts receivable management is examined in the next four chapters. Chapter 9 shows how credit terms can be established in a wealth maximization framework. Chapter 10 discusses models for forecasting outstanding receivable balances and bad debts. Techniques for determining who to extend credit to are examined in Chapter 11. Chapter 12 indicates how an effective monitoring system can be established for controlling accounts receivable. Together, these four chapters provide more sophistication for managing receivables than generally exists in practice. This sophisticated management is important because outstanding receivables simply represent uncollected sales. Until collection occurs, the sale is meaningless, since no cash has been realized.

Inventory management is discussed in Chapters 13 through 15. Inventory is usually given little attention in financial management books. This situation is unfortunate, since inventory comprises about 40–60 percent of most manufacturing firms' assets. Chapter 13 examines the numerous accounting methods available for valuing inventories. This material is important because of the direct effect that different accounting schemes have on ratio analysis and operating cash flows. Chapter 14 discusses the relevance of cost minimization models to liquidity management. Analysis of outstanding inventory balances is discussed in Chapter 15.

The next three chapters pertain to financing management. Accounts payable management is discussed in Chapter 16. For many firms accounts payable represents the largest single conduit for cash outflow. The main focus of this chapter is on monitoring techniques. Chapter 17 examines asset-based financing. Whenever secured financing becomes difficult to obtain, management turns to using corporate assets as collateral for loans. Hedging strategies, using futures and options, are discussed in Chapter 18. Hedging can be thought of as a form of financing because it allows management to lock in prices or returns. Hedging results in less volatility and thus is a valuable tool for liquidity management.

The final section of the book, Part IV, consists of two chapters. Chapter 19 discusses bankruptcy and reorganization. Of course, if management thoroughly understands the concepts discussed in the first 18 chapters, it will never need to become involved with the material examined in Chapter 19. The last chapter is a summary. It is intended to provide a useful review of the multifaceted nature of liquidity management. You might find it useful to read Chapter 20 first and then make repeated reference to it as you progress through the book. This procedure should enable you to better understand and appreciate the role of liquidity management.

Appendixes are found throughout the book. We have tried to place involved mathematical material — or material that is important but can be ignored without affecting the continuity of the discussion — in appendixes.

An extensive bibliography of selected readings is found at the end of the book.

Features

The outstanding features of this book are as follows:

- □ Examples are used throughout to clarify and summarize concepts and techniques.
- □ Key concepts are listed at the end of each chapter.
- □ Extensive questions and problems are provided for student assignments.
- □ Shortcomings of traditional techniques are revealed.
- □ Up-to-date coverage is given of all topics.
- □ The breadth and depth of topics discussed is better than that of any competitors' books.
- □ The discussion is consistently related to liquidity and the wealth-maximizing criteria.

An important unifying feature of this book is the use of W. T. Grant Company in numerous examples throughout the book. Prior to its bankruptcy and subsequent liquidation, W. T. Grant was a major retailer in the United States. W. T. Grant's annual reports and 10-K reports, along with articles published in *Business Week* magazine and *The Wall Street Journal*, provide ample evidence of a management team that had very little understanding of liquidity management.

Who Should Read This Book

This book is intended for both business students and business professionals. In the academic environment it is aimed at senior-level undergraduate and MBA students majoring in either finance or accounting. The book is appropriate either as a primary text for a lecture and problem-solving course or as a reference text in a case course. Students who study this book should be in a position to immediately contribute to the daily management of corporate liquidity. This book is also intended for treasurers, controllers, finance directors, budget analysts, and business consultants involved in liquidity analysis. People in these positions may learn new techniques as well as improve their understanding of existing techniques.

There are some minimum prerequisites if the reader is to enjoy the benefits we feel can be gained from this book. These prerequisites are as follows:

☐ An understanding of introductory finance and accounting. Knowledge of intermediate accounting will help in certain areas, although it is not necessary.

☐ A basic working knowledge of high school algebra. If you are willing to learn some matrix algebra and elementary calculus, you will obtain a better appreciation of some of the models we discuss.

☐ A willingness to have some of your preconceptions about finance challenged. We show that various ratios discussed in many finance books are questionable tools. We also show that to understand finance, at least as it pertains to liquidity management, you must have a better understanding of accounting.

Acknowledgments

Many people have been involved in this book. At the proposal and/or manuscript stages we benefited from the encouragement and insightful criticisms of William Beranek of the University of Georgia, Russel P. Boisjoly of the University of Lowell, Michael D. Carpenter of the University of Kentucky, Thomas E. Copeland of the University of California, Los Angeles, Richard Norgaard of the University of Connecticut, Keith V. Smith of

Purdue University, and John Stowe of the University of Missouri. A special thanks is owed to our undergraduate students who were subjected to using our many drafts as texts. Their criticisms have greatly improved the final product. Frank T. Griggs and Joo-hyun Kim, doctoral students at Arizona State University, and Chris Maziarz, an MBA student at Wilfrid Laurier University, helped on various facets of the manuscript. Their contribution is appreciated.

We are particularly indebted to Stephen Dane, publisher of the Business and Decision Science Division of Addison-Wesley, and to Ruth Peterson, Steve's administrative assistant, for helping to overcome some early problems and to bring this book to the market. We also want to extend special thanks to Michael D. Joehnk and Glenn A. Wilt, Jr., both of Arizona State University. Mike was always available when we needed advice. During the numerous early drafts of the manuscript, Glenn unselfishly gave us access to a microcomputer he kept in his office.

Lastly, we thank our wives for their patience while we devoted the many hours it takes to see a project of this nature to completion.

Undoubtedly, there are still some errors that have not been eliminated (the fault lies with the coauthor). We encourage you to bring any errors, differences of opinion, or topics you feel should be included to our attention. We hope that our labors have minimized any serious distractions. We feel that the topics discussed in this book can be readily transferred to practice. This book is not meant to be one of those that is fine in theory but not in practice. Enjoy your reading!

G. W. Gallinger
P. B. Healey

Contents

PART III □
Management of Net Working Capital Accounts

CHAPTER 7 □
Overview of Cash Management   193

LIQUIDITY ANALYSIS AND MANAGEMENT

PART I □

Foundations of
Liquidity Analysis

CHAPTER 1 □
Introduction to Liquidity Management

Liquidity management is the allocation of liquid resources *over time* to meet resource needs for payment of obligations due and for various investments that management undertakes to maximize shareholder wealth. This definition emphasizes the dynamic nature of liquidity management, that is, the providing of resources at times when they are needed and the control of various financial risks, especially that of insolvency.

Liquidity management is frequently thought to be synonymous with *working capital management* — the management of current assets and current liabilities. Such a view may fail to adequately capture the true nature of liquidity management. Liquidity management includes the management of current assets and liabilities as well as the management of noncurrent assets and liabilities, the financing of company growth, the effect of creative financing, and so on. The importance of these factors to the creation of value for shareholders is evident in all firms.

History is replete with examples of good and bad management. Periods of economic recession are generally perceived to be times of liquidity problems. However, periods of economic prosperity have also proven to be burdens to prudent liquidity management. Economic growth, whether inflationary or real, drains cash. Participating in a strong market is exciting, but keeping up with the pace requires cash. Even if real market growth is zero, inflation may consume limited financial resources almost as quickly as real growth. The failure of management to provide adequate liquid resources to finance growth objectives and meet liabilities as they come due has been as common a cause of business failure as have economic recessions.

Perhaps the most important fundamental change that has occurred in economies of the Western world since World War II is government legislation influencing the availability and cost of money. Governmental objectives of reduced unemployment and a high standard of living with a minimal amount of inflation have produced such a strong consumer and social demand for goods and services that businesses and governments have been hard-pressed to satisfy it, even while utilizing all available credit.

Figure 1.1 provides an indication of how the increased demands for credit have been reflected in the rising cost of money over the past 25 years. Formerly, increasing costs of money generally reduced the demand for credit when growth and speculation became excessive. However, in recent years cost has been less significant than the availability of funds in controlling the demand for money — as evidenced by credit restrictions in the mid 1960s and by a latent interest in the use of credit controls in highly inflationary periods.

Corporate financial managers must learn to live with relatively expensive and limited supplies of money under various economic conditions. Their role has become more important in determining corporate policy and direction. It is the responsibility of not only the chief financial officer but also the treasurer, controller, credit manager and all other financial

FIGURE 1.1
Supply and Cost of Funds

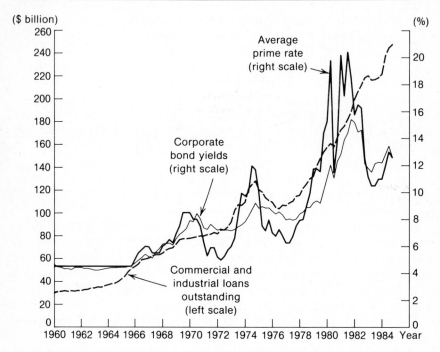

Source: Data from *Federal Bulletins* and issues of *Survey of Current Business*.

personnel to seek ways to make more effective use of corporate cash resources in order to satisfy the heavy cash demands of the corporation
during growth periods as well as during recessions. Furthermore, financial
personnel need to play a significant role in improving the rate of return
on corporate assets by recycling underutilized liquid resources into expanding assets or temporarily investing them in the money markets until they
are needed to support corporate operations designed to satisfy company
objectives.

Corporate Objectives

The discipline of economics defines the firm as a profit- or *wealth-maximizing
entity* dealing in markets of varying degrees of competition. The definition
has remained virtually unchanged for 200 years, although it causes some
concern in that economic profits are often confused with accounting profits.
This definition is discussed in more detail later in this chapter. But what
if management has other motives, such as maximizing sales or size, growth
or market share, or its own survival or peace of mind? Do these operating
goals conflict with the goal of wealth maximization? A good case can be
made that these other objectives are consistent with the goal of wealth
maximization. However, is it right to assume that if a conflict between
objectives arises, managers will act to maximize the market value of the
owners' equity in the firm?

This question is one for which economists have not yet been able to
supply a completely satisfactory answer. Management is generally considered to perform in a manner that will result in maximizing its utility. It
is usually assumed that sufficient additional processes of control or motivation exist to remove any conflicts between the individual and corporate
criterion functions of the managers. Examples of such processes are incentive bonus and stock option schemes that make management's compensation
a direct function of stockholders' compensation, or at the other extreme,
sanctions, such as stockholder proxy revolts or outside takeover bids, that
can be invoked or threatened to remove a management failing to act in
the best interests of the owners.

In an effort to minimize shareholder dissatisfaction, management often
resorts to paying a cash dividend. Since dividends erode the liquidity reserves
needed in furthering other corporate interests, management will try to
keep the outflow as low as possible, minimizing increases and postponing
them as long as possible in the hope that corporate investments will result
in equity appreciation for investors to offset lost dividend income. Management gets a substantial assist here from income tax law, which tends to
transfer the stockholders' attention to capital gains and shifts the source
of the gain from the company itself to the capital market.

Objective of Liquidity Management

Although differences may exist about which corporate objectives management should follow, unanimity generally prevails about the objective of liquidity management. The objective is a supportive one: to provide for the adequate availability and safekeeping of corporate funds under varied economic conditions in order to help achieve the desired corporate objective of shareholder wealth maximization.

Liquidity management has generally been considered relatively unimportant to any of the firm's objectives, particularly to the value maximization objective. The theoretical finance literature has virtually ignored liquidity management in the valuation process. Considerable effort has been expended to develop rules of thumb and ratios to guide management in maintaining adequate liquidity. This treatment has been rationalized on the basis of a difference in the nature of current assets and fixed assets. Current assets are considered relatively liquid, and they are closely related in that each component of current assets is constantly transformed into another (from cash to inventories to receivables to cash) in a relatively short period of time. Fixed assets, in contrast, have limited marketability and are recovered over an extended period of time, and thus they are considered more important to the valuation process.

Such a view of the irrelevance of liquidity management to value maximization is shortsighted, since short-term assets and liabilities have a direct influence on the firm's value. When these assets and liabilities are varied, future profitability and risk of the firm are often affected, other things being constant. Excessive investment in current assets ties up capital that can be productively used elsewhere. The firm may have to assume undue risk if the present level of cash cannot be justified, inventory cannot be sold, accounts receivable cannot be collected, or any combinations of these items exist. If such investments are financed with debt, the financial risk of the firm will likely increase. But too little investment can also be expensive and risky. If the firm does not maintain, or is unable to generate, a satisfactory level of funds, it is likely to become insolvent and may be forced into bankruptcy.

The most fundamental objective of liquidity management is to ensure corporate solvency. Thus from a liquidity perspective value maximization is secondary to survival. However, the two goals are closely related.

Solvency is a dynamic concept and is a function of the allocation of resources, the rate of conversion of assets into cash, the profitability of the firm, and the firm's creditworthiness and debt-paying ability. The word *solvency* has two meanings. One is important in a theoretical sense, the other in a practical sense. The first is often indicated by saying *actual solvency*, the second by *technical solvency*.

In the general, theoretical sense solvency is a state in which the market value of the assets of a firm exceed its debts or in which cash inflows exceed required cash outflows such as interest payments, debt amortizations, leases, salaries, taxes, accounts payable, and so on. Asset values must be sufficiently great to meet all creditor claims. This notion of (actual) solvency, however, is of almost no use in practice. The fact that asset values exceed liabilities can be determined actually only by the sale of the assets. Such a means for testing solvency cannot be used by an ongoing business. No other means for estimating asset values is fully dependable, and hence none indicates with precision whether a firm is actually solvent. In practice, action is based on a condition of technical insolvency.

It is this second meaning of the word that is operational and is used throughout this text. A business is said to be (technically) solvent if it pays its obligations as they fall due. In this sense determining whether the business is solvent is easy. Deciding whether there are obligations, whether they are due, and whether they are paid can be done with readily available facts. For example, the judicial tests for deciding whether a firm is bankrupt are based on this concept of solvency.

The key issues in liquidity management are how much to invest in each component of current assets and current liabilities and how to manage these investments effectively and efficiently in order to minimize insolvency risk. In the allocation of financial resources many complex decisions must be made. The appetite for cash is voracious in even the most efficient firm, but management does not seek to hold cash, for idle cash is unprofitable cash. Hence as soon as cash is received, it should be committed elsewhere — for example, in the expansion of the firm, in its income-earning activities, in the distribution of dividends, and in the payment of creditors. Managers will, however, tend to limit the outflow of cash to creditors for two reasons: First, they can use the cash more profitably within the business. Second, since short-term trade credit finance is usually considered interest-free, they will not pay it off until it is due. Therefore, one would expect to see current liabilities maintained at the maximum level compatible with the firm's debt-paying ability and need for cash funds.

Since the ability to pay obligations in cash is the criterion of solvency, the manner in which a firm holds its assets may be more crucial than a favorable net working capital position, that is, the balance between current assets and current liabilities. At the extreme the conclusion is that with perfect conditions the firm will have no current assets on hand on any one day and will always be operating in part with resources supplied by creditors. Thus the accepted notion of *net working capital* as the difference between the current assets and the current liabilities has little relevance to operating efficiency and liquidity management. The important question concerning liquidity is the ability of the firm to pay in the future, not how much net working capital, profit, or even cash it has at present.

Profits Versus Funds

The objective of the firm often mentions profit maximizing, whereas the objective of liquidity management emphasizes funds. Therefore one must be aware of the difference between profits and funds.

Accounting Profits

One of the dominant concerns in accounting is to develop and apply a consistent, logical procedure for estimating profit in some arbitrarily chosen time period. One may think of profit conceptually as that value that could be withdrawn from the firm over some period without curtailing the financial commitment to the company — in other words, as the addition to the value of the company as a result of its operations, minus the value used in the operations.

The determination of profit would present no difficulties if it were measured from the beginning of the firm's life to the day it goes out of business. In this case the company's debts would be paid off, and the value remaining over the amount the owners had committed to the business would represent the profit for the period — assuming, of course, that no nonwage payments had been made to the owners.

In these circumstances determining profit would present no problem. The amount could be measured with precision. But two things are wrong with this picture. First, most businesses do not begin with the idea of going out of business at the end of some definite period. Most are initiated with the hope of operating in perpetuity. Second, financial data must be current to be useful. Investors cannot wait until the firm goes out of business to know whether additions have been made to their wealth (the firm operated at a profit) or capital was consumed (the firm operated at a loss). For financial data to be utilized, estimates of additions or subtractions to wealth over a period shorter than the life of the business must be made: annually, quarterly, monthly, or over some shorter period, depending on the needs of management and investors.

Since measuring true profit, with precision, over any period less than the life of the company is not possible, accountants are forced to estimate profit. For the shorter period they must, in effect, make assumptions about what the future will hold, assumptions that may or may not prove true.

In most businesses some assets will be used over a period greater than the arbitrary accounting period. The amount of revenues and the amount of costs that can properly be assigned to the period are a matter of judgment. Much of the technical logic of accounting is associated with rules for assigning revenues and costs to arbitrary accounting periods. In an accounting sense *profit is defined as the amount by which realized revenue for a period exceeds the historical cost of the assets used up to obtain the revenue.*

This provisional concept of profit measurement allows periodic estimates to be made of the results of operations on the company's resources.

Even though the determination of profit for periods shorter than the life of the business enterprise involves judgments and cannot be accomplished with precision, the generally accepted accounting principles (GAAP) that guide this estimate still point toward the basic concept of profit as a surplus of, or accretion to, resources committed to the firm: an amount, in effect, that could be distributed as dividends without curtailing the earnings base of the firm. Hence profit to the accountant is a residual concept based on the identification of explicit costs. It is owner-oriented, static, and historical. It can be manipulated by using combinations of generally accepted accounting principles, which include methods of depreciation, inventory valuation, capitalization versus expensing techniques, the accounting treatment for the investment tax credit, or the use of acquisition accounting in merger negotiations.

Economic Profits

The derivation of accounting profit leaves much to be desired for managerial decision making. Economic costs are vital considerations in this process. Economists and accountants use what appear to be identical definitions of profit. Profit is a firm's total revenues minus its total costs. However, economists think of total costs in terms of *economic costs,* or *opportunity costs,* which encompass both explicit and implicit costs. Accountants often fail to include in total costs many of the implicit costs incurred by a business. Implicit costs are the opportunity costs of the resources the firm's owners make available for production without direct outlays of cash. Examples include the value of the entrepreneur's labor, the interest that could be earned on the owner's assets if they were not tied up in the business, and the cost of equity capital used to finance the business. Also, economic profits are a cash flow concept. Thus an economist would expense all capital projects and research and development, while an accountant would often depreciate them over a longer period of time.

Rational decision making should be based on economic costs and profits. But to identify all implicit costs and assign a value to them is often difficult. So that we can operationalize the economist's definition of profit, the *profit objective of the firm is defined here as being the maximization of residual income,*[1] which is reconcilable to the net present value technique (as shown in the Appendix). And since the net present value model is equivalent to the economist's marginal revenue – marginal cost model, the residual in-

---

[1] Ezra Solomon was an early advocate of residual income in his book *The Theory of Financial Management* (New York: Columbia University Press, 1963).

come approach is logically consistent with the wealth maximization objective. General Electric Company, for example, utilizes the residual income model in determining executive incentive compensation bonuses.

Residual income (RI) is defined as the excess of the after-tax net operating income, $NOI(1 - t)$, less the dollar opportunity cost of invested funds $(k \times I)$, that is,

$$RI = NOI(1 - t) - k \times I. \tag{1.1}$$

Invested funds (I) represent the average amount of both net working capital and fixed assets committed to the firm's operations. The percent opportunity cost (k) of these funds is the rate required by a prudent investor to compensate her or him for the risk associated with the (average) investment. The weighted average cost of capital of the firm may be used as an approximation of k.

Adjusting net operating income for a required dollar return on investment requires management to acknowledge that funds tied up in investments have an opportunity cost associated with them. Management must cover all costs, not just those costs that appear on the income statement, if investors are to be adequately compensated for risk. Unfortunately, investment opportunity costs are things accountants do not measure when they organize the firm's financial statements.

Funds

Profit is generally perceived by most people as being the appropriate barometer for measuring a firm's success. Such a view often fails to ascertain the *quality of the earnings* (a concept that is discussed further in Chapter 3). For example, if a credit sale is made, the records will show a profit (assuming the selling price exceeds costs) and the creation of an account receivable. However, the profit is not recognized in a true economic (i.e., cash flow) sense until the receivable is actually collected. However, to wait for the economic profit is contrary to the accountant's matching and realization principles. This aspect of timing is the basis for the difference between profits and funds, or funds flow.

The concept of *funds flow* is vitally important in the managing of a business. Management is concerned with allocating resources and controlling flows in such a way that they are used optimally to maximize the long-run market value of the company. In the short run inflows and outflows of funds must be balanced so that sufficient cash (i.e., liquidity) is on hand to meet demands by creditors. In this context the main interest centers on funds as net liquidity resources. In short, managing cash is more important than earning an adequate profit. Earning a good profit does not necessarily guarantee adequate funds flow when needed. *Waiting too long to turn profit into cash reduces the value of the profit.*

Funds may be derived from the firm's operations, from funds advanced by creditors, from new investment by owners, or from the sale of assets. One of the central duties of the financial manager is to manage (i.e., to control and manipulate) funds flows to ensure that the firm will always have adequate funds on hand to meet demands for payment. These demands may originate externally (i.e., from creditors), or they may arise internally (i.e., from within the firm itself to take advantage of favorable investment opportunities that will require the outlay of funds).

In relation to liquidity management funds flow management is defined as the process involved in the attempt to ensure that financial resources are both obtained and used profitably and effectively for the best accomplishment of the objectives of the firm. Chapter 6 will define funds flow more specifically, but for now the important issue is that the financial manager cannot pay bills with profit or with working capital. Bills must be paid with cash, and *a high level of profit does not automatically ensure that adequate funds will be on hand at the right time to meet these demands for payment.* However, even in the (temporary) absence of profit or net working capital, management may be able to acquire funds: by borrowing, by selling assets, by using funds provided by the tax shield associated with the recovery of value tied up in existing assets (i.e., depreciation), or by new contributions of funds from owners.

ILLUSTRATION 1.1: Profits Versus Funds

About three decades ago *Business Week* magazine ran an article entitled "How to Go Broke While Making a Profit." It is summarized in Exhibit 1.1 to emphasize the significant difference between profits and funds flow.

EXHIBIT 1.1
How to Go Broke . . . While Making a Profit

As the year started, Mr. Jones of the ABC Co. was in fine shape. His company made widgets — just what the consumer wanted. He made them for $.75 each, sold them for $1. He kept a 30 day supply in inventory, *paid his bills promptly,* and billed his customers 30 days net. Sales were right on target, with the sales manager predicting a steady increase. It felt like his lucky year, and it began this way:

Jan. 1: Cash $1,000, inventory $750, receivables $1,000, equity $2,750.

In January, he sold 1,000 widgets; shipped them at a cost of $750; collected his receivables — winding up with a tidy $250 profit and his books looked like this:

Feb. 1: Cash $1,250, inventory $750, receivables $1,000, equity $3,000.

This month sales jumped, as predicted, to 1,500. With a corresponding step-up in production to maintain his 30 day inventory, he made 2,000 units at a cost of $1,500.

All receivables from January sales were collected. Profit so far: $625. Now his books looked like this:

Mar. 1: Cash $750, inventory $1,125, receivables $1,500, equity $3,375.

March sales were even better: 2,000 units.

Collections: on time. Production, to adhere to his inventory policy: 2,500 units. Operating result for the month: $500 profit. Profit to date: $1,125. His books:

Apr. 1: Cash $375, inventory $1,500, receivables $2,000, equity $3,875.

In April, sales jumped another 500 units to 2,500 — and Jones patted his sales manager on the back. His customers were paying right on time. Production was pushed to 3,000 units, and the month's business netted him $625 for a profit to date of $1,750. He took off for Florida before he saw the accountant's report:

May 1: Cash $125, inventory $1,875, receivables $2,500, equity $4,500.

May saw Jones' company really hitting a stride — sales of 3,000 widgets, production of 3,500 and a five month profit of $2,500. But, suddenly, he got a phone call from his treasurer: "Come home! We need money!" His books had caught up with him:

June 1: Cash $0, inventory $2,250, receivables $3,000, equity $5,250.

He came home — and hollered for his banker.

Source: Reprinted from the April 28, 1956 issue of *Business Week* by special permission, © 1956 by McGraw-Hill, Inc.

Table 1.1, which lists the sources and uses of funds, captures the critical interactions and relationships between profits and funds.

The message of this illustration is clear: Profits are wonderful, but liquidity is critical.   □

TABLE 1.1
How to Go Broke . . . While Making a Profit
Sources and Uses of Funds Analysis

| | Beginning of | | | | | |
	Feb.	Mar.	Apr.	May	June	*Total*
Sources of funds:						
Profits	$ 250	$375	$500	$625	$750	$2500
Uses of funds:						
Receivables	$ 0	$500	$500	$500	$500	$2000
Inventories	0	375	375	375	375	1500
Total	$ 0	$875	$875	$875	$875	$3500
⟨Increase⟩/decrease in cash	⟨$ 250⟩	$500	$375	$250	$125	$1000
Cash balance	$1250	$750	$375	$125	$ 0	

Summary

The basic economic objective of managing a firm is to maximize the wealth of the shareholders. Maximizing wealth of shareholders means to follow production, marketing, and financial policies that cause the common stock share price to increase. Most discussions of share price maximization pay little, if any, attention to liquidity management. The implicit assumption is that sufficient funds exist, or can be secured, to ensure that the firm meets its obligations. Such an assumption is difficult to accept in any practical sense. The purpose of this book is to address liquidity management in a wealth-maximizing context.

If managers are to manage liquidity, they must understand the difference between profits and funds, and how accounting profits differ from economic profits. Rational resource allocation decisions must be made on a sound economic basis. This statement holds true whether the decision pertains to a short-term investment, such as investment in inventory, or to a long-term investment, such as investment in a new machine with an expected life of 15 years. Both investments consume scarce resources of the company.

A major theme of this book is shown by Illustration 1.1, "How to Go Broke . . . While Making a Profit." Later chapters will make repeated reference to this example since it exemplifies the mismanagement of liquidity that is found in many companies.

Key Concepts

Accounting profit

Economic profit

Funds flow

Goal of wealth maximization

How to go broke while making profit

Liquidity management

Net working capital

Residual income

Solvency

Appendix

Reconciliation of Residual Income and Net Present Value

The net present value (NPV) model is generally accepted as being appropriate for evaluating investment decisions. A general specification of the model is

$$\text{NPV} = -I_0 + \sum_{i=1}^{N} \frac{F_i(1-t)}{(1+k)^i} \geq 0, \tag{A.1}$$

where I_0 is the necessary incremental investment, F_i is the incremental pretax cash flow occurring in period i, t is the marginal corporate tax rate, and k is the appropriate risk-adjusted discount rate. Management is willing to accept projects down to the point where the NPV is zero, for at this point marginal revenue from the project equals its marginal cost.

The NPV model can be readily converted to a cash flow – residual income model by analyzing the solution at $\text{NPV} = 0$. Assume that F_i is constant and N approaches infinity; that is, the life of the project is infinite. Equation (A.1) can be rewritten as

$$\text{NPV} = -I_0 + \frac{F(1-t)}{k} = 0. \tag{A.2}$$

If both sides of the equation are multiplied by k, NPV can be stated as

$$\text{NPV} = F(1-t) - kI_0 = 0. \tag{A.3}$$

This equation is the definition of residual income given in the chapter as Eq. (1.1). The term $F(1-t)$ represents net income, or, rather, after-tax cash flows; k is the opportunity cost of funds; and I_0 is the average investment. Thus management is fulfilling the wealth maximization objective whenever it undertakes investments where $F(1-t) \geq kI_0$.

Questions

1.   Discuss the objective of liquidity management.

2.   How is the objective of liquidity management related to the economist's concept of wealth maximization?

3.   What are the differences between economic profit, accounting profit, and residual income?

4.   What are the differences between funds and profits? Which is the treasurer of the company more concerned with? Why?

5.   What does the following statement mean? "You can't pay your bills with profit." Is it possible for a profitable firm to go broke? Explain.

6.   Describe the difference between *actual solvency* and *technical solvency*. Relate this difference to the "How to Go Broke . . ." example.

7.   Johnson Company has been having problems paying debts as they come due. The company operates on a seasonal cycle, with production and sales at their peaks in the summer months. Inventory must be ordered four months before the beginning of summer to avoid a shortage in supplies. Management cannot understand why the company is experiencing payment difficulties since the income statement has shown profits increasing over the past few years. Analyze and discuss this problem.

Problems

1.   From the following information, determine the amount of residual income for the year. Explain why this figure is more appropriate than the net income amount.

Current assets	$ 220
Current liabilities	$ 185
Fixed assets	$ 400
Net operating income	$1500
Cost of capital	18%

2.   Should management invest $10,000 in a project that has a forecasted net operating income of $2500 and an opportunity cost of capital of 20%? Explain. Assume all numbers are stated after tax (if applicable).

CHAPTER 2 □
Economic Fundamentals for Analysis of Liquidity

The traditional economic functions of business are the production of goods and services and the consequent generation of wealth. Production, production planning, and the sale and distribution of goods and services take time. Managers must acquire stocks of financial assets and commodities in order to offset costs associated with the unsynchronized revenue and expenditure flows caused by time-consuming production and distribution processes.

From the economist's point of view *acquisition of assets takes place until the marginal benefits of holding each asset just equal the marginal costs.* For instance, in the case of money or commodities the marginal benefits can come from lower transaction costs to the firm. For customer loans the benefits may arise because of lower transaction costs to the firm's customers. In either case the underlying unsynchronized cash flows must induce a demand for the financial liabilities and equity capital to finance both the fixed and working capital assets desired by the firm's managers.

Most treatments of economics fail to discuss liquidity management in a manner that allows the reader to relate the topic to the disciplines of accounting and finance. The purpose of this chapter is to relate liquidity management to the economist's profit maximization model. It does so by discussing what economic costs are, by examining a number of constraints that affect managerial decisions, and by relating economic concepts to financial statements.

Economic Costs

To most people, expenditures involve what are called outlay costs. These costs are the moneys expended in order to carry on a particular activity. Some examples of outlay costs to a business are wages and salaries of employees, expenditures on plant and equipment, payments for raw materials, power, transportation, rent, advertising, insurance, and taxes to the government. Such costs are also called explicit costs, historical costs, or accounting costs because they are the tangible expenses that an accountant records in the company's books.

Economists use a more basic concept of cost: *opportunity cost*, defined as the value of the benefit that is forgone by choosing one alternative rather than another. This concept is extremely important because *the real cost of any activity is measured by its opportunity cost, not by its outlay cost.*

The concept of opportunity cost arises whenever the inputs of an activity are scarce and have alternative uses. The real cost or sacrifice is then measured by the value of the forgone alternative. The variable k (the weighted average cost of capital) in the residual income model, discussed in Chapter 1, captures this opportunity cost concept.

Many opportunity costs are the result of *constraints*. That is, certain conditions exist in nature, in law, and in society that limit the actions of management. These constraints arise because of influences of time, production, factor markets, product markets, and funds flow.

The environment within which a business operates is *imperfect* to the extent that the manager does not have complete information (i.e., is constrained by lack of information) about all aspects of the competition. Questions about the number of competitors in the market, how each competitor will react to decisions of other competitors, the financial condition of competitors, and so on, are not known with certainty.

In an imperfect market products are not perceived as being homogeneous. Substitute products exist, which makes it difficult for most producers to know the exact costs involved in competing in this market. Price is a decision variable that affects performance and overall results. Too high a price causes consumers to buy elsewhere. Too low a price results in price competition. Both cases can have an unfavorable influence on profits and cash flows.

If both the level of competition and knowledge are increased (i.e., more buyers and sellers), then the imperfectly competitive conditions move toward perfect markets. In *perfect competition* management's decision variables (e.g., price) are reduced. The objective in a perfect market is production efficiency, or, stated differently, cost minimization, since management cannot influence price or differentiate the product noticeably. A model with imperfect competition and various constraints is used in the following discussion because it is more realistic.

Time Constraints

A feature of the residual income model, discussed in Chapter 1, is the use of an infinite time horizon. This assumption does nothing more than simplify the residual income model, but the use of infinite time raises the question of the model's usefulness, particularly if the user does not understand how different time intervals affect decisions. The decision process confronting management is complex and involves numerous constraints that an infinite time model may not adequately incorporate.

For convenience, we will divide decision making into three different time dimensions: immediate, short run, and long run.

Immediate Time

Immediate time is the here and now. When a customer wishes to buy immediately, either the firm has the goods to sell or it does not. Similarly, when a creditor demands payment, either the firm has sufficient liquidity to honor the request or it does not. Each of these situations influences liquidity management. Can a firm afford to increase working capital investment in inventories to ensure that customers will always be satisfied? Should the firm carry large cash balances to reduce insolvency risk? Later chapters will discuss these and related issues in detail.

Clearly, the importance of the immediate market means that the firm must protect itself from the possibility of numerous influences. However, the protection against insolvency dominates other issues. The protection provided by cash or cash equivalents has virtually no perfect substitute. Insolvency risk is not lessened by high profitability but, rather, by sufficient liquidity. The degree of risk acceptable depends upon the forecasting ability of managers and the risk profile acceptable to them.

The Short Run

The *short-run time* is described as the time needed to change some of the conditions influencing the firm. These changes must occur in tune with certain other conditions. It is in this short-run framework that the concept of matching cash inflows and outflows and analyzing sources and uses of funds gains significant prominence.

The firm makes profits through involvement in production across time, but it survives day to day by having sufficient liquidity to honor ongoing and currently due obligations. Management needs sufficient time to extend accounts receivable, to build inventory, and to negotiate or renegotiate a loan. Time is a necessary but not a sufficient condition for these actions. Unless the firm has liquidity reserves, it will not survive to take the necessary actions.

The Long Run

In the *long-run time* today's decisions commit the firm to a course through time. This time path is interpreted to mean that the physical production conditions have the possibility of being expanded or contracted, along with financial balances. Only in this way may management take advantage of the potential variability of productive factors. Management must recognize the essential difference in the degree of variability in resources, the impact these differences have on possible actions, and the associated risk to the firm.

In summary, time constraints influence all management decisions. Many plans need to be completed in a relatively short period of time. Unfortunately, the current literature of economics and finance tends to ignore the importance of these daily or weekly recurring decisions. The development of good operating policies and the control of short-term operations should not be simply assumed to exist if management expects to achieve a long-run maximization position. Keynes once said, "in the long-run we shall all be dead," implying that short-run decisions take precedence over long-run concerns. Or in the context of this book, liquidity cannot be ignored. Understanding the time dimension, as it constrains the decision process, is essential for good management.

Physical Production Constraints

Even if adequate financial resources exist, technological constraints determine what can be produced and how long it takes to produce it (thus involving the time constraint discussed previously). The analysis of how to employ technology requires an understanding of the firm's production function. Although this analysis belongs properly with production managers, the impact that technology-related decisions have on the financial future of the firm is direct and compelling.

Production efficiency directly influences cost decisions. If the rules that lead to production efficiency are known, then these rules can be employed for cost analysis. The reason for examining this issue is that the concept of maximum production efficiency is frequently associated with maximum profitability in introductory finance and accounting texts and in financial newspapers. This association is a misconception, which is clarified later in this chapter.

Overview

Knowledge of the basic steps in combining factors in the most efficient physical input/output relationships is important to the financial manager. This person is responsible for ensuring efficient resource allocation within the firm. This task requires communicating with nonfinancial personnel to convince them of the merits of making decisions consistent with wealth maximization.

Output capable of satisfying demand is the direct result of combining various productive factors (resources). These productive factors have a relative degree of scarcity, which makes them *economic goods.* This term is used to differentiate them from those factors that have no scarcity and therefore have no economic cost — resources for which there is effectively a zero price.

For purpose of discussion, consider a factory with an assembly line for the production of refrigerators. If one employee is required to manufacture the entire refrigerator, that person must perform each of the numerous activities necessary to construct it. Output from such a combination of labor and capital is going to be quite small.

As additional units of labor are added to this production system — holding constant the amount of fixed inputs (capital) — output expands rapidly. The intensity with which the capital resource is used increases with the additional labor input, and an increasingly efficient input combination results. The improvement in capital utilization resulting from the increased labor employment can mean that the *marginal physical product* (increase in output) of each successive employee actually increases over some range of labor additions. This increasing marginal productivity results from each unit of labor using a more manageable quantity of capital than is possible with less total labor input. Specialization of labor leads to an increasing marginal physical product for labor as successive units are employed. Similarly, specialization in liquidity management results in improved marginal physical product (service) for liquidity management.

Table 2.1 illustrates a situation where the marginal product of an input changes. The inputs are deliberately defined in *generic terms* rather than in the economist's tradition of labor and capital. To relate this discussion to liquidity management, think of the variable input as being liquid resources being added to a fixed-investment base. The first unit of variable input V results in 8 units of output. With 2 units of V, 24 units are produced — the marginal physical product of the second unit of V (16) exceeds that of the first (8). Similarly, addition of another unit of V results in output increasing to 42 units, indicating a marginal physical product of 18 for the third unit of V.

Eventually, enough variable input V is combined with the fixed input that the benefits of further V additions are not as large as the benefits achieved earlier. When this result occurs, the rate of increase in output per additional unit of V (the marginal physical product of V) drops. Although total output continues to increase as added units of V are employed (the marginal physical product of V is positive), the rate of increase in output declines (the marginal product decreases). This diminishing marginal productivity is exhibited by units of input V in excess of 4 units.

Finally, a point is reached where the quantity of V (the variable input factor) is so large that total output actually begins to decline with additional employment of that factor. This situation may occur when the variable input becomes so large that congestion occurs and hinders the process.

TABLE 2.1
Physical Production Data

Units of variable factor V	Total output in units	Average physical product per variable input (APP$_V$)	Average physical product per fixed input (APP$_F$)	Average physical product per total input (APP$_T$)	Marginal physical product per variable input (MPP$_V$)
0	0				
1	8	8	0.8	0.73	8
2	24	12	2.4	2.00	16
3	42	14	4.2	3.23	18
4	64	16	6.4	4.57	22
5	85	17	8.5	5.67	21
6	96	16	9.6	6.00	11
7	105	15	10.5	6.18	9
8	112	14	11.2	6.22	7
9	117	13	11.7	6.16	5
10	120	12	12.0	6.00	3
11	121	11	12.1	5.76	1
12	120	10	12.0	5.45	−1
13	117	9	11.7	5.09	−3
14	98	7	9.8	4.08	−19

Note: APP$_V$ is total output divided by the number of V units; APP$_F$ is total output divided by the unit value of the fixed factors (which is assumed to be 10); APP$_T$ is total output divided by the sum of the fixed- and variable-factor inputs; MPP$_V$ is the change in total output divided by the change in the number of V units.

In Table 2.1 this point is reached when more than 11 units of input V are combined with the fixed factor. The twelfth unit of V results in a 1-unit reduction in total output (its marginal physical product is −1), while units 13 and 14 cause output to fall by 3 and 19 units, respectively. Figure 2.1 graphs the physical relationships of Table 2.1.

Geometry of Total, Average, and Marginal Products

The first thing to notice in Fig. 2.1 is the shape of the total product (TP) curve. Total output changes according to the *law of diminishing returns;* that is, total output at first increases to a maximum amount of total output and then decreases.

As variable input increases from zero, the TP curve goes through three stages — first rising rapidly, then tapering off until it reaches a maximum, and then declining. These stages are labeled stage I (*0AB*), stage II (*BC*), and stage III (*CD*), and they are explained in terms of the relative efficiency of the factors employed. At the beginning of production management commits an amount of fixed factors to the process. In the short

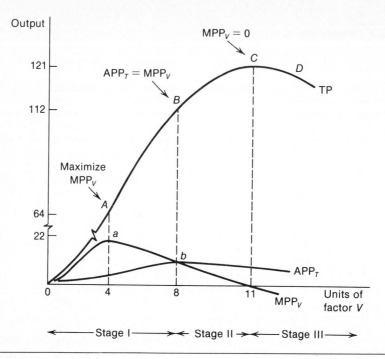

FIGURE 2.1
Graph of Physical Production

run these fixed factors cannot be changed. This investment by itself is not sufficient to cause any production. Management then adds increasing amounts of the variable factor V. Total product starts to increase and changes according to the technical laws of production.

Stage I represents production up to the point of maximum total average physical product (APP_T) (i.e., 8 units of V or 112 units of output in Table 2.1). During this stage both average and marginal physical product of factor V have reached their maximums and have begun to decline (APP_V is not shown in the graph).

The efficiency of inputs of all kinds is measured by their *average physical product*, since this product indicates the amount of output obtained per unit of input. Because APP_T is increasing throughout this range, we say that production efficiency is also increasing. Fixed factors are underutilized in the initial phase of the production process.

Analysis of production efficiency in stage II is not as straightforward. At the beginning of stage II the marginal physical product of the variable factor, MPP_V, and the average total physical product, APP_T, are equal (or approximately so in Table 2.1: APP_T is 6.22 versus an MPP_V of 7). As the process moves further into this stage, the MPP_V is less than the APP_T, and both are decreasing. At the end of this stage (at about 121 units of output), MPP_V is zero, whereas the average product of the fixed factor, APP_F, is maximized (see Table 2.1). This point is also the point where total output is maximized.

Marketing and sales managers want the firm to operate at point C in Fig. 2.1 since the chance of product shortage is reduced. In contrast, production managers are most interested in achieving production efficiency in terms of physical factor use, which occurs at point B, the start of stage II. However, the decision of how much to produce should not be solved simply by consideration of physical efficiency. Shareholder wealth maximization requires the additional consideration of consumer demand and the firm's financial capabilities. These topics are discussed later in this chapter.

Stage III is a particularly interesting area of production. In this range total output falls, and variable marginal physical product is negative; yet average physical product for both the variable and fixed factors, while decreasing, is still positive. The efficiency of all factors falls. The reason for this situation is that there is far too much of the variable factor relative to the fixed factor. To increase efficiency, management should decrease the variable input, which is possible in the short run, or increase the fixed factor, which may only be possible in the long run. Continued operation within stage III is irrational and occurs because of poor management.

Integration of Output and Costs

The discussion of the physical production constraints indicated that *production efficiency occurs whenever APP_T equals MPP_V* (point b in Fig. 2.1). The assignment of costs to the productive factors allows for the connection between average physical product and average cost, and between marginal physical product and marginal cost.

The assumption regarding production was that all factors except factor V were fixed. Therefore *average variable cost* (AVC) equals per-unit cost (c) of the variable factor times the number of units of the variable factor (V) used, divided by the output produced (Q). Since the APP_V is Q/V, by a little algebraic manipulation we obtain

$$AVC = \frac{c}{APP_V}. \tag{2.1}$$

A similar algebraic exercise can be used to show that *marginal cost* (MC) is the cost of the variable factor divided by MPP_V:

$$MC = \frac{c}{MPP_V}. \tag{2.2}$$

Table 2.2 monetizes the unit production information of Table 2.1. Monetization is accomplished by using Eqs. (2.1) and (2.2) and assuming that the fixed-factor cost is \$245 and the variable-factor cost is \$30 per unit.

TABLE 2.2
Production and Cost Data

Units of V	Total output	Fixed costs	Average fixed cost	Variable costs	Average variable cost	Total costs	Average total cost	Marginal cost
0	0	$245				$245		
1	8	245	$30.63	$ 30	$3.75	275	$34.38	$ 3.75
2	24	245	10.21	60	2.50	305	12.71	1.88
3	42	245	5.83	90	2.14	335	7.97	1.67
4	64	245	3.83	120	1.88	365	5.71	1.36
5	85	245	2.88	150	1.77	395	4.65	1.43
6	96	245	2.55	180	1.88	425	4.43	2.73
7	105	245	2.33	210	2.00	455	4.33	3.33
8	112	245	2.19	240	2.14	485	4.33*	4.28
9	117	245	2.09	270	2.31	515	4.40	6.00
10	120	245	2.04	300	2.50	545	4.54	10.00
11	121	245	2.02	330	2.73	575	4.75	30.00
12	120	245	2.04	360	3.00	605	5.04	—
13	117	245	2.09	390	3.33	635	5.43	—
14	98	245	2.50	420	4.29	665	6.79	—

*Minimum: The true minimum lies between 8 and 9 units at the point where average total cost (ATC) equals marginal cost (MC).

Figure 2.2 summarizes Tables 2.1 and 2.2 to show the relationship between physical production and costs. *They are inverted images of each other.* The importance of this finding is that production management generally thinks in terms of physical output. Financial management, in contrast, thinks in monetary terms. Since the most efficient unit production level (i.e., $APP_T = MPP_V$) is also the least cost level, financial managers who understand this concept should be able to communicate better with other managers about why the firm *should not* operate at this level. *Achieving a production optimum is not synonymous with achieving maximum profitability in an economic sense under conditions of imperfect competition.* This result is shown in the next section.

Incorporating the Product Market

Production management defines efficiency as maximizing the unit output per last dollar of expenditure. However, investors and creditors do not directly reward production efficiency; rather, they reward those producers who are most profitable in an economic sense.

The level of production should not rely solely on the production and cost structures unless the firm operates in perfect markets. If such

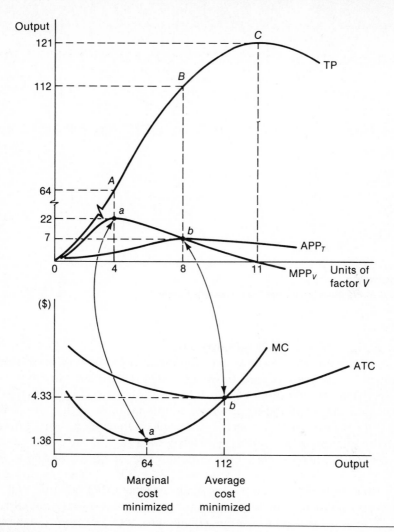

FIGURE 2.2
Graphical Relationship Between Production and Costs

markets exist, then cost minimization for all factor use is an appropriate strategy. This situation occurs when average total cost is minimized. At this point marginal cost (MC) equals average total cost (ATC) as well as average revenue (AR) and marginal revenue (MR). In other words, the firm operates at economic breakeven — it simply earns a normal profit. Figure 2.3 summarizes this situation.

If the firm operates under the more usually encountered imperfectly competitive conditions, *cost minimization is not an appropriate strategy.* In imper-

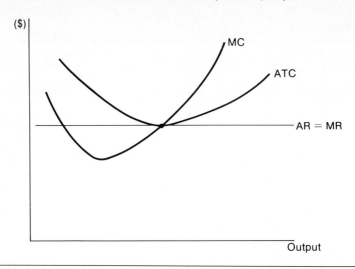

FIGURE 2.3
Profit Maximization in Perfect Product Markets

fect markets the *law of demand* implies that the demand curve — also called the *average revenue* (AR) curve — facing the firm will be downward sloping. Price *(P)* is inversely related to quantity *(Q)* demanded. Any extra units $(Q_2 - Q_1)$ produced cannot be sold at the previous market price (P_1) because consumers are unwilling to purchase additional units at that price. When the price is lowered (P_2) to sell extra units, management must lower the price for all units sold. It cannot just lower the price for the extra customers to whom it wishes to sell. Total revenue (TR) changes from $P_1 \times Q_1$ to $P_2 \times Q_2$. The change in total revenue $(TR_2 - TR_1)$ divided by the change in volume $(Q_2 - Q_1)$ results in *marginal revenue* (MR) per unit. The MR curve also slopes downward to the right and falls faster than the AR curve.

Whenever marginal revenue equals zero, total revenue is maximized. Figure 2.4 depicts the relationships between demand, marginal revenue, and total revenue. However, analysis that concentrates solely on the revenue relationships is as faulty as analysis restricted to examination of cost relationships. *The optimal quantity to produce and sell is neither where costs are minimized nor where revenues are maximized.* This result is illustrated in Table 2.3 and Fig. 2.5.

Several important conclusions can be made. A production efficiency strategy results in minimizing average total cost ($4.33), that is, producing 112 units. If all of these units are sold, profits are about $806. Given a downward-sloping demand curve, total revenue is maximized when marginal revenue equals zero (105 units). It is more profitable for management to produce and sell a lesser quantity (96 units) and at a higher average cost ($4.43), since economic profits ($850.84) are larger than can be realized

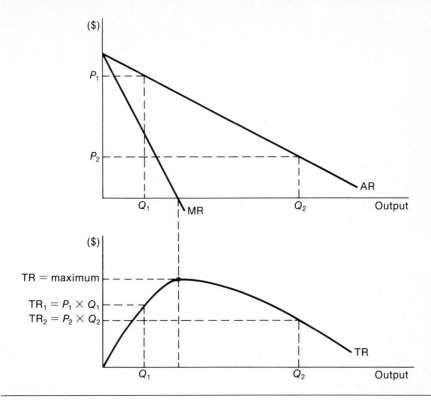

FIGURE 2.4
Demand, Marginal Revenue, and Total Revenue in Imperfect Product Markets

TABLE 2.3
Revenue-Cost-Profit Relationships

Total output	Total revenue	Average revenue	Marginal revenue	Total cost	Average total cost	Marginal cost	Profit
0				$245			−$245.00
8	183.76	22.97	22.97	275	$34.38	$ 3.75	−91.24
24	509.04	21.21	20.33	305	12.71	1.88	204.04
42	807.66	19.23	16.59	335	7.97	1.67	472.66
64	1075.84	16.81	12.19	365	5.71	1.36*	710.84
85	1232.50	14.50	7.46	395	4.65	1.43	837.50
96	1275.84	13.29	3.94	425	4.43	2.73	850.84*
105	1291.50*	12.20	1.74	455	4.33	3.33	836.50
112	1291.36	11.53	−0.02	485	4.33*	4.28	806.36
117	1284.66	10.98	−1.34	515	4.40	6.00	769.66
120	1278.00	10.65	−2.22	545	4.54	10.00	733.00
121	1275.34	10.54	−2.66	575	4.75	30.00	700.34

*A maximum or a minimum. Profit is actually maximized between 96 and 105 units at the point where marginal revenue (MR) equals marginal cost (MC).

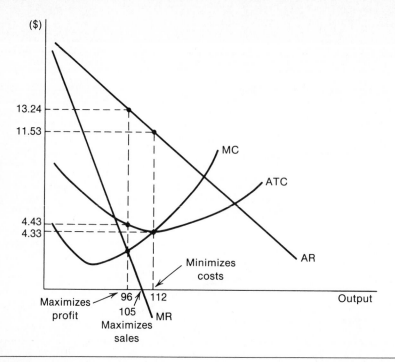

FIGURE 2.5
Profit Maximization

at any other output level. *Whenever marginal revenue equals marginal cost, profits are maximized.*

We emphasize again that the discussion of profits pertains to *economic profits* and not accounting profits. Thus to say that (economic) profits are maximized is to say that *cash flows* are maximized. This statement follows from the definition of economic profits provided in Chapter 1, and it provides the critical linkage between the economist's profit-maximizing model and liquidity management. The next section elaborates on this connection.

Economic Concepts and Financial Statements

The factors of production can be related to sources and uses of funds and cash flows available to the firm. In the firm's financial statements factors of production no longer appear, for instance, as hours of potential service or acres of land but as obligations (liabilities), value potentials (assets), and created value (equity).

Studies by the Boston Consulting Group and others indicate that the most profitable firms generally have the largest market shares. Thus these firms have significant market power in terms of influencing how business is conducted in their markets. Market leaders also have an advantage over their competition in dealing with suppliers, creditors, and investors. These groups feel more secure in transacting with the more profitable leading firms. This advantage, in turn, leads to beneficial effects accruing to the firm in terms of managing liquidity. Trade credit is more readily available, as is long-term debt and equity financing. Suppliers, anxious to have the market leader's business, may give preferential treatment on orders. This treatment may take the form of significant price concessions and/or warehousing materials longer than normal and then shipping them in the most expeditious manner to the leading firm. In this way the leading firm can minimize its inventory investment and liquidity requirements.

Income Statement

The primary recording of cash flow is through the *income statement*. This statement presents the record of product revenues and factor costs. Since most businesses use an *accrual accounting system,* this statement neither reflects economic profit nor shows all the necessary information concerning cash flows. That is, accrual accounting recognizes revenues as goods are sold and as services are rendered, independent of the time when cash is received. Expenses are recognized in the period when the related revenue is recognized, independent of the time when cash is paid out.

Thus one must adjust sales for the change in the accounts receivable balance, adjust cost of sales for changes in inventory and accounts payable balances, and add to net income any noncash expenses, such as depreciation, bad-debt expense, and deferred taxes, in order to convert the income statement to a cash-flow-from-operations statement. By deducting an amount for the opportunity cost of funds, the cash flow statement becomes a statement of residual income that reasonably represents economic profit in a practical sense.

Balance Sheet

The *balance sheet* is often used to identify the funds available and the funds used in the normal cycle of business activity. The sources of funds come about through the use of factors of production that are funded by the owners of these resources to the extent that the owners allow the firm time differences between the use of the factors and the payment for their use. The timing differences are partially recognized on the balance sheet by the segregation of assets and obligations into *current* and *fixed categories.* This division ignores the reality that part of the current assets and part of the current liabilities have a fixed nature. In most firms many current balances seldom drop below a certain amount. This part of the total is as fixed as any of the so-called fixed assets. What it means is that a certain part of the capital of the firm is used to finance the assets, and this investment is expected to continue. If part is fixed, then some part is variable, and these parts have entirely different liquidity demands and, consequently, present different management problems.

The same argument may be made for virtually all the accounts listed on the balance sheet. The balance sheet does not directly or completely indicate the timing nature of accounts nor the time constraint on factors. The liquidity component is virtually ignored in the balance sheet, and what is there is often the poorest of data. Additionally, any account changes need careful analysis.

To illustrate, assume that a bank extends a loan to the firm. The initial changes are to the cash account and to the notes payable account. It is expected that the firm will use these funds to facilitate its production and sales position but at the same time to prepare for the repayment of the loan. Management might use the funds to buy more factors and, one hopes, to increase the efficiency of factor use. In addition, part of the credit might go to fund an expansion in credit sales via an increase in accounts receivable. Both of these increases can be considered permanent investments. Since the change in current liabilities is matched by the change in current assets, it might be concluded that liquidity has not changed.

Economic Constraints

What might be perceived as having changed is the balance presented in the statements. The inventory and receivable changes are permanent, whereas the change in liabilities is not intended to be permanent. The creditor may be concerned with this situation and deem it wise to increase assurity of repayment by imposing a minimum cash balance constraint to be held at the bank. The minimum cash balance has the effect of increasing the cost of the loan and causes both the average and the marginal cost curves in Fig. 2.5 to shift upward. This shift will result in a new optimal output level.

From a liquidity perspective the effect of the cash constraint is to reduce the estimate of cash generation, since the firm has less of the loan to use productively. If noncash charges remain the same, the estimate of net cash generation should still increase relative to the preloan period. The creditors' concerns should be eased as they see that their short-term loan is replaced by cash generated through increased sales. The only remaining *concern of the creditors is whether or not the timing of the new cash flows matches the timing demands for repayment of the loan.*

As another example, suppose that creditors insist that management use the credit extended to the firm to employ a more capital-intensive, and more costly, production method, causing the average total cost curve and the marginal cost curve to shift upward. This request is not an unreasonable one, since the creditors might view the difficulties of securing equipment a greater threat to the firm's success than the difficulty of obtaining labor.

Management may attempt to pass the cost changes on to its customers. This action may be possible if the cost changes are industrywide and not just associated with this firm. If only this firm experiences cost changes, and if this firm is selling in a competitive market, then the probability of shifting costs to the customers is low. If management shifts the additional costs, the consumer price must increase. If the product has competitive substitutes, management simply prices the firm out of the market. The only other solutions available to management are to have the initial constraint removed or to have the equity investors bear the burden of the increased costs.

If management is constrained in this way, *it should still follow the usual rules and expand production and sales until marginal revenue equals marginal cost.* The result would be higher fixed costs and lower profits. A positive influence may be that management now has reduced operating risk. The relatively small profit erosion is the cost for lowering the risk of operations. This decreased risk, at least as perceived by creditors, might be sufficient to encourage them to extend additional credits with no additional constraints. This argument is intended to illustrate that the firm's operations, while constrained by conditions of factor supply, time, and technology, may also be constrained by creditors' perception of risk. It also illustrates that *additional fixed costs may actually reduce operating risk* — a result contrary to general wisdom.

One of the most demanding constraints is the limitation of funding. The flow of resources from the cycle of production and sales and from the change in balance sheet accounts must all work smoothly. Otherwise, the firm is constrained to operate at a lower level of output, efficiency, and profit than that allowed by the market forces.

In the short-run situation the usual assumption is that the cycle of funds is sufficient to generate enough cash at the right time to service debts as they come due. This decision is important and should not be left to chance. Variability of some factor is the assumption of the short run, yet risk is present throughout this period. The risk involves all facets of the business, including the risk of technical insolvency — the risk of not having sufficient liquidity upon demand.

In the long run all costs must be recognized. Thus the demand for factors depends on both the total costs of production and the total revenues of sales, as well as on the resultant cash flows. Any long-term equilibrium depends on the ability of the firm to survive both the immediate and the short-run market conditions.

The firm might attempt to increase its resources by borrowing additional short-term funds or by not paying accounts either within the discount period or as these accounts come due. If borrowing is possible, one impact is to expand the resources available. Another impact is to increase the product cost by the addition of an interest charge or the loss of purchase discounts and to suffer the loss of credit availability through nonpayment of accounts due. In addition, the liquidity and leverage ratios change. Possibly, these changes may violate some constraint, such as an indenture constraint on the leverage ratio. Raising funds in this manner clearly can have other affects, any one of which can cause other constraints.

Summary

This chapter reviewed basic microeconomic concepts as they pertain to production and sale of products in an imperfect market environment. A major theme is the impact of timing of financial matters on the use of factors and the derived goods and services output. The concept of management means the firm is involved in a series of decisions, some immediate, others short term, and still others of a long-term nature. In the immediate time liquidity either exists or does not exist. If it exists, the firm is solvent; otherwise, it is either technically or actually insolvent. The long-term horizon allows management ample time to structure a liquidity strategy that is consistent with the objective of economic profit maximization. The difficulty in managing liquidity falls primarily within the short-term horizon. Cash balances, credit decisions, payable policies, investment decisions, including these pertaining to current assets — all must harmonize in order for the firm to achieve long-run economic profit maximization.

Much discussion is found in the financial press about cost minimization efforts and productivity gains. These reports often leave the impression that cost minimization is the same as profit maximization. This equivalence is only the case under pure competition — a situation not faced by most firms. Management must determine the most profitable level of operations that is consistent with adequate cash flow generation. This level may satisfy neither the desires of marketing and sales personnel, who seek maximum product availability, nor the wishes of production management, who want the lowest per-unit cost the technology is capable of producing. Financial managers need to understand the different viewpoints and be able to convince managers of other functional areas of the relevance of marginal analysis for generating profits and cash flows. As will become apparent in future chapters, the economist's decision rule of continuing to operate until marginal revenue equals marginal cost is the only legitimate criterion for maximizing shareholder wealth.

Key Concepts

Average cost
Average physical product
Average revenue
Constraint
Cost minimization
Economic cost
Economic profit
Factor markets
Immediate time

Imperfect competition
Long-run time
Marginal cost
Marginal physical product
Marginal revenue
Opportunity cost
Perfect competition
Profit maximization
Short-run time

Questions

1.   Contrast the concepts of diminishing returns to scale and diminishing marginal productivity.

2.   What is meant by economic profit? Is profit maximization an appropriate goal for owners? For managers? What tends to happen if owners are themselves managers?

3.   Differentiate between immediate time, short-run time, and long-run time in their components as far as effects on the firm's liquidity strategies are concerned.

4.   What is wrong with the following explanation by the production manager?

> The plant is working at its most efficient output level. However, I could meet an increase in short-run demand by operating the machines a little faster and deferring maintenance. In the short-run my marginal cost is zero.

5.   For what reason(s) should managers not desire to operate the plant at a level where APP_T equals MPP_V? Under what circumstance(s) would it be an appropriate strategy to produce where APP_T equals MPP_V?

6.   Starting from the following total revenue (TR) function, show how the average revenue and marginal revenue functions are derived.

$$TR = 50Q - 0.2\,Q^2$$

7.   In terms of the general relationships among total, average, and marginal quantities, which of the following statements are true and which are false?

(a)   When the average total cost function is rising, the marginal cost function is rising.

(b)   When the total revenue function is rising, the marginal revenue function is positive.

(c)   When the total cost (revenue) function is rising, the marginal cost (revenue) function lies above it.

(d)   When the marginal cost function is rising, the average cost function is also rising.

(e)   When the average revenue (cost) function is falling, the marginal revenue (cost) function lies below it.

(f)   When the marginal cost function is neither rising nor falling, the average cost function is constant.

8.   Why do we assume diminishing marginal returns in operations (whether it be in production, cash management, or whatever)?

9.   Why is it important for the financial manager to argue against the production manager's insistence that the firm operate at a level that maximizes output?

10.   Timing differences are only partially recognized on the balance sheet by the segregation of assets and liabilities into current and fixed (or long-term) categories. Explain why this practice can be misleading for the true timing of accounts.

11. Assume that a banker requires a firm seeking a loan to hold 5% of the loan in a cash account with the bank. Discuss what happens to the revenue and cost curves in Fig. 2.5 of the chapter. Does the profit maximization output level change?

Problems

1.   Fill in the blanks in Table 2.4.

TABLE 2.4
Output and Input

	Units of variable factor	Total output in units	APP per variable input	MPP per variable input	APP per fixed input
(a)	1	6	6	——	0.3
(b)	2	——	10	14	——
(c)	3	48	——	——	2.4
(d)	4	——	——	8	——
(e)	5	40	——	——	——

2.   Complete Table 2.5, a production and cost table, given fixed costs of $35 and variable costs of $15 per unit of V.

TABLE 2.5
Production and Costs

Unit of V	Total output	Average fixed cost	Average variable cost	Average total cost	Marginal cost
0	0				
1	2				
2	4				
3	8				
4	16				
5	32				
6	40				
7	45				
8	48				
9	50				
10	48				

3. Complete Table 2.6, and show how total and marginal revenue curves are derived from the price equation AR = 15 − 0.1Q, where AR is average revenue and Q is the quantity sold. What is the profit-maximizing output level?

TABLE 2.6
Revenues and Costs

Q	TR	AR	MR	TC	AC	MC
0				150		
5				190		
15				230		
35				270		
55				310		
70				350		
80				390		
85				430		

4. The Keem Company operates in a relatively competitive market. It is large enough to influence the product price but not factor prices. The average revenue (AR) curve is approximated by AR = 26 − 0.050, where Q represents the number of units offered for sale. Fixed costs of production are $285, and variable costs are $25 per unit of variable input. The variable inputs can vary between 0 and 11 units, in increments of 1. There are 10 units of the fixed factor. The relation of product output to variable input is as follows:

Input   0   1   2   3   4   5   6   7   8   9   10   11
Output   0   12   36   56   74   90   105   117   128   138   147   145

(a) Calculate the values for total product, variable and total average physical product, and variable marginal physical product. Determine the most efficient output level.

(b) Calculate the average and marginal curves for cost and revenue. Determine the least cost output. Calculate the approximate profit maximization point.

(c) Determine the impact on output, profit, and factor use if the average revenue curve is AR = 24 − 0.1Q, fixed costs are $500, and variable costs are $35 per unit of variable input.

(d) Discuss the implications of your answer to parts (b) and (c) for managing liquidity.

(e) What are the implications for liquidity management, profit management, and production management if the firm has economic power to influence factor prices?

5. Weber Carpet Company sells its products in a highly competitive market. The firm's current conditions are as follows:

Selling price per unit $12.50
Variable costs per unit $5.27

| Fixed costs | $10,395 |
| Units sold | 1500 |

The balance sheet simply consists of cash and net worth, both equal to $8,502.40. The treasurer has arranged a line of credit with the bank for $5,000. If the line is used, the firm must maintain a current ratio of at least 3:1. Cash sales are 20% of total sales. Credit sales have terms of net 60 days. All resources employed must be paid for by the end of the month. Management expects that average total cost of production will be approximately the same for the next production period.

(a) How many units of production can the firm finance in the next period? Round your answer to a whole number. (*Hint:* Equate the funds available for production to the cost of production, which will give you an equation with Q, the production quantity, as the unknown.)

(b) Estimate the end-of-period balance sheet. What will the current ratio be at the end of the next period assuming the firm sold all it could finance?

(c) What adjustments must management make to its production plans in order to not violate the bank constraint?

PART II □
Financial Analysis of Liquidity

CHAPTER 3 □
Traditional Financial Analysis: Some Shortcomings

The complexity, continuity, and joint nature of economic activity creates problems in measuring the effects of these activities and associating them with specific processes, products, and time frames. Measuring the resources and obligations of a firm and measuring the changes in them are two aspects of the same problem. Management attempts to capture and understand these dynamics as they affect the firm through the use of financial statements and analysis of these statements.

Financial statements report where resources come from, where they are invested for the time being, and how often they turn over. These statements have the appearance of completeness, exactness, and finality. However, generally accepted accounting principles permit alternative treatments of many accrual accounting events. Which treatment management chooses will affect the balances and flows reported in the financial statements of the company and thus any subsequent financial analysis.

The analysis of financial statements is meant to result in the presentation of information that will aid decision making by managers, investors, and creditors as well as other groups who are interested in the financial status of the firm. Traditionally, these parties have relied on financial ratios to analyze a firm's performance. Ratios such as the current ratio, debt-equity ratio, and interest coverage ratio have been firmly entrenched in analysts' tool kits for decades. But do these ratios really provide a strong basis for drawing meaningful conclusions about a firm, particularly its liquidity?

The purpose of this chapter is to review limitations of traditional financial ratios used in analyzing corporate liquidity. The discussion purposely concentrates on negative aspects of the measurements since these aspects are generally not discussed in other books. This discussion may stimulate you to think critically when analyzing liquidity.

Throughout this chapter reference will be made to W. T. Grant Company's financial statements (see Appendix B for the financial statements and calculation of financial ratios). W. T. Grant was chosen because prior to declaring bankruptcy in 1975, it was a major retailer in the United States, had a significant presence in Canada through a 50.2 percent wholly owned retail subsidiary called Zeller's Limited, and was looked upon favorably by the capital markets. Although modern finance theory strongly supports the concept of efficient markets (i.e., the market is all-knowing), W. T. Grant appears to have fooled the capital markets. As will be shown in Chapter 6, W. T. Grant had significant liquidity problems as much as nine years before bankruptcy finally occurred.

Quality of Earnings

In an effort to place the discussion of liquidity analysis using financial ratios in proper perspective, this section discusses quality of earnings. *Quality of earnings refers to how closely earnings are correlated with cash flows.* The higher the correlation, the higher the earnings quality is and the lower is the risk associated with liquidity.

Understanding a company's quality of earnings is always a problem for creditors and investors alike. Quality of earnings is as important as the absolute level of earnings. And quality of reported earnings may vary greatly from company to company. A failure to take this reality into account can lead analysts to erroneously conclude that some companies are financially strong. W. T. Grant provides a good example. On March 18, 1974, the accounting firm of Ernst and Ernst gave unqualified certification of W. T. Grant's financial statements for the fiscal year ended January 31, 1974. The stock market had assigned a higher price-earnings multiple to W. T. Grant than to all other variety retail stores in the industry with the exception of Kresge Company. W. T. Grant was also able to sell commercial paper (which is nothing more than an uncollateralized promissory note), thus convincing the debt markets that it had relatively low default risk.

The discussion that follows reviews, through an examination of several sources of low earnings quality, the characteristics of these earnings and how analysts may detect a decline in earnings quality. *Failure to detect low earnings quality makes any form of ratio analysis suspect as a management tool.* Excerpts are taken from W. T. Grant's annual reports and 10-K statements to illustrate points in the discussion.

Fraudulent Actions

Low earnings quality due to fraudulent actions are difficult to detect. As the details of recession-induced bankruptcies seem to indicate, desperate managements sometimes engage in fraudulent activity as they try to stave off their company's approaching bankruptcy. An example is the deliberate misstatement of inventories and cost of sales in order to improve profits.

Above-Average Financial Risk

Earnings quality is influenced by a company's financial condition. Earnings accompanied by an increasing level of financial leverage begin to jeopardize their quality long before the liquidity crisis. Fixed-interest payments build greater volatility into the earnings figure. Analysts should keep track of the changing financial risk due to on – and *off – balance sheet* financial obligations of companies, such as unfunded pension liabilities and leases (explored more fully in Chapter 4).

In the case of W. T. Grant, its 1973 – 1974 commercial paper obligations exceeded the total equity of the company. Maturities ranged from 1 to 270 days and placed a considerable strain on liquidity — particularly since this was a time when the Nixon administration had imposed price controls on the economy in an attempt to slow the rate of inflation.

Less-Than-Conservative Accounting

The principal source of low-quality earnings during periods of waning customer demand and difficult financial times is the use of the following types of accounting practices:

☐ Practices that are less conservative than available alternatives.

☐ Practices that fail to reflect the underlying economic reality of the transactions they represent.

☐ Practices that are based on optimistic assumptions about future events.

Most low-quality accounting practices are within the bounds of so-called *generally accepted accounting principles,* since no public company can afford to have anything less than a clean auditor's opinion if it wants its common stock to trade in the public markets. Consequently, *analysts should not assume that audit certification ensures acceptable earnings quality.* It simply indicates that in the auditor's opinion acceptable accounting standards have been met. In a study of bankrupt firms Ohlson[1] found that the majority of the firms had an unqualified auditor's opinion in the immediate years prior to filing for bankruptcy.

Some hints for detecting accounting-generated low-quality earnings follow:

---

[1] J. A. Ohlson, "Financial Ratios and the Probabilistic Prediction of Bankruptcy," *Journal of Accounting Research* (Spring 1980): pp. 109 – 131.

1. Is there adequate disclosure in the notes to the financial statements? These notes should describe how the company arrived at the dollar figures shown in the statements. As an example, assume a company does not own all the shares of its consolidated subsidiaries. Those shares not owned belong to outsiders, called the minority interest. In the derivation of income to the company's shareholders, the minority interest's share in earnings is subtracted from the earnings of the consolidated group of companies. However, this reduction in income uses no cash or other funds. The notes should provide adequate explanation to determine this fact.

2. What alternative accounting practices might the company have used? Are they considered more or less conservative than those adopted? For example, if W. T. Grant had capitalized all financing leases, its accountants estimated that net earnings for the year ended January 31, 1974, would have been reduced by about $1.6 million, which would have resulted in earnings per share declining 20 percent.

3. What accounting practices does the so-called industry leader follow? Use of less conservative practices by the firm under review may suggest its management is trying to hide a competitive weakness with accounting.

4. What is the earnings process of the company? Low-quality income results when companies recognize income before all of the material uncertainties about whether the company is better off economically from its revenue-producing activities are resolved. For example, W. T. Grant, as of January 31, 1974, was involved in legal proceedings in nine states that involved allegations that the company's finance charges on installment sales exceeded the maximum amounts permissible by law. In two states the court had handed down adverse decisions. Management felt unable to determine the ultimate obligations and had not allowed for any contingency reserves.

5. Are there adequate reserves for future obligations? If the company has obligations to perform future services to customers after income is recognized, determine whether adequate provisions for the costs of these future services have been established. Managements in trouble tend to underestimate their future expenses that relate to income recognized currently.

6. Does the company make dubious claims that certain expenditures should be called assets because they create future benefits? Maybe these expenditures should be called expenses.

7. Has the company changed accounting practices recently? Was a less conservative practice adopted? For example, in 1974 management of W. T. Grant decided to change its accounting principle for finance charges on its customers' installment accounts. This change resulted in increased earnings per share for the financially depressed years 1973 and 1974.

Prior to this period management had seen no need to change when reported net income was relatively good.

8. Has the company changed auditors? The change may have occurred because the previous auditor would not go along with management's decision to adopt a lower-quality accounting practice.

9. Is there a significant difference between tax and book (financial) accounting, as indicated by the size of the deferred tax expense? Tax accounting is typically more conservative than book accounting. The deferred tax expense may be a rough measure of the company's drift from conservatism. For example, W. T. Grant reported profit before taxes of $4.6 million for the year ended January 31, 1974. Yet the provision for *current taxes* claimed a refund of $6.0 million, indicating that tax accounting profits were considerably less than financial accounting profits. Appendix A summarizes the important features of this issue.

10. Is the company picking up liquidity through accounting practices that reflect the influence of the company over the dividend decision of the investee company? For the year ended January 31, 1974, 55 percent of W. T. Grant's earnings per share were contributed by its unconsolidated subsidiaries. Interestingly, during the next fiscal year the chairman of the board of the major subsidiary (Zellers Limited) became chairman of W. T. Grant, indicating that a close relationship existed between investor and investee.

11. Is there a significant difference between the reported and current cost (FASB Statement No. 33) income? If so, reported income may be increased by underdepreciation and phantom inventory profits because of inflation.

12. Are the interim accounting results in line with what would be expected given analysts' knowledge of the industry? Pay particular attention to gross margin percentages, which may be estimated rather than based on actual physical inventory count.

13. Does the company provide minimal data for analysis? If there are not enough data for you to understand the figures, assume low quality.

Reported earnings that are a long way from turning into cash are a common form of low-quality earnings. Analysts can detect this situation by thoroughly analyzing the cash conversion cycle (CCC) and cash flow from operations (CFFO). These techniques are discussed in detail in Chapters 5 and 6, respectively. These approaches indicate how much and how fast cash is generated from the company's cycle of buying goods and services, creating inventories, selling for credit, and collecting payments from customers. Companies that have trouble turning sales into cash often have lengthening ages of receivables, inventories, and payables and declining cash flow from operations. In doing this analysis, analysts should be alert to attempts by the reporting company to improve the impression given by these tests by selling accounts receivables, either to the company's unconsolidated finance subsidiary or to an unrelated outside entity.

If management and analysts had been paying attention to the CCC and CFFO for W. T. Grant, they could have foreseen the company's serious liquidity problems much sooner than they did.

One-Time Transactions

Another frequent source of low-quality earnings is one-time transactions. Analysts should discount these low-quality earnings heavily, since they do not represent recurring income. Common one-time transactions are sales of subsidiaries, of investments in various companies, and of corporate real estate. Debt-restructuring gains are another common source of one-time earnings. These gains generally occur in high – interest rate, low – bond price environments. W. T. Grant participated in this tactic to some extent. They reported a miscellaneous gain of over $2 million for the fiscal year ended January 31, 1974, which is a period when a large tax loss was recorded. Evidently, management was looking for (financial reporting) profits wherever it could find them.

Analysts should have no trouble identifying one-time earnings gains. They are often reported prominently in special income statement categories, such as extraordinary items, and timely disclosure is required by Securities and Exchange Commission regulations.

Borrowing from the Future

Earnings included in current reports that represent deductions in future earnings should be considered low-quality because they are not indicative of future earnings levels. The most frequent practice is to accelerate sales to customers in advance of the normal delivery date. This procedure is usually done during the last weeks of the accounting period. The maneuver is difficult, however, during recessionary periods when customers are unwilling to build inventories and are actually trying to have suppliers hold inventories longer. To convince customers during such periods to accept orders in advance, suppliers tend to provide generous direct or indirect financing at low or no interest cost. Usually, the disclosure of the customer financing arrangement or a substantial buildup of receivables (before the sale of receivables) is a clue that customer shipments are being accelerated.

Reaching into the Past

Profits earned (and stored in the balance sheet) in past periods that are run through the current period's income are considered to be low-quality. Typical ways to include past profits in current income are to reduce bad-debt reserves, warranty reserves, and other contingency type of reserves. In the past the charge to establish these reserves reduced income. The accounting entry in the current period to reverse the reserve improves income. *Cash flow, however, may not be improved.* For example, estimated warranty expense does not qualify as a tax deduction. The cost of providing the warranty service becomes a tax deduction when the actual repair is made.

When analysts encounter reserve reversals, they should determine whether the reversal was justified by a change in circumstances. If it was not, management is manipulating profits, which is a good indication that reported income may include other low-quality earnings. W. T. Grant's change in accounting practices for finance charges on installment sales, discussed earlier, is indicative of adjusting reserves to generate profits.

Riding the Depreciation Curve Down and Other Factors

Current earnings can be a misleading indicator of future earnings potential if management fails to make the technological, marketing, and fixed-asset investments necessary to maintain earnings. In addition, failure to make these investments may result in low-quality boosts to current earnings through reductions in managed costs, such as research and development or advertising expenses, and depreciation charges. This situation most frequently arises when companies run into operating difficulties. To detect this source of lower-quality earnings, analysts should proceed as follows:

1. Compare the level of capital expenditures indicated in the company's funds flow statement (discussed in detail in Chapter 6) with the *current cost* depreciation expense shown in the inflation disclosure notes that accompany the financial statements (discussed in Chapter 5). A ratio of less than one [i.e., (capital expenditures)/(price-level-adjusted depreciation expense) < 1] may indicate that the replacement expenditures for fixed assets needed to compete effectively in the future are not being made and that management is milking the company for cash.

2. Compute the average age of a company's assets. This age can be computed by dividing the reported depreciation expense into the accumulated depreciation reserve [i.e., (accumulated depreciation)/(depreciation expense) = estimated age of assets]. A lengthening of the average age may indicate declining earnings quality due to inadequate replacement investments and a boosting of current earnings from lower depreciation charges relative to sales. This feature is called *riding the depreciation curve down*.

3. Adjust research and development and marketing expenditures for inflation over the previous five years to determine their real trend. Alterna-

tively, the trend in the ratio of these expenditures to sales can be computed. In both cases a downward trend is indicative of lower earnings quality.

The relationship between reinvestment and earnings quality is a critical one. The ability of companies to compete effectively may be determined in large measure by their reinvestment practices. W. T. Grant, for instance, was not riding the depreciation curve down. In fact, its commitment to upgrading retail stores was a source of its liquidity problems, since these investments required large amounts of funding.

In summary, earnings quality is an important issue that must be incorporated into any formal financial analysis. Failure to recognize the quality of earnings can lead to incorrect interpretations of financial ratios both within the company and across the industry.

Standards of Financial Comparison

The previous discussion indicates that financial analysts must practice diligence if they are to understand reported financial statements. Assuming that the quality-of-earnings issue can be resolved by analysts, two types of comparisons can be used to analyze financial data: industry and trend.

Industry Comparisons

Industry comparisons involve comparisons of a particular ratio within the firm with the same ratio for a representative number of other firms in the same industry line. This comparison indicates whether figures on the firm's balance sheet or income statement are out of line with the figures on financial statements of similar companies.

There are no standardized financial statement forms used by all businesses. Furthermore, the classification of some of the statement items varies widely. These variations are frequently a result of the following:

□ Management's intention and the use that is to be made of the statements.

□ Differences of opinion among those who prepare the statements.

□ Differences in the accountants' knowledge, training, and experience.

□ Failure to adopt generally accepted current changes in terminology and classifications.

Standard ratios for various industry lines are available from a number of sources, including trade associations and regulatory agencies. Possibly the best known are the ratios published annually by Dun & Bradstreet, a nationwide credit-reporting firm, by Robert Morris Associations, an organization of bank credit officers, and by the *Almanac of Business and Industrial Financial Ratios* (shown as Table 3.1). The implicit assumption in making industry comparisons is that the consensus of other firms — as expressed in the standard ratio — represents a norm from which any significant deviation on the part of the firm would require explanation.

Great care must be exercised in defining industries since firms are very diverse. For example, if W. T. Grant was still in existence today in the form it was as of 1974, a comparison of it to Sears would be misleading. Although Sears is in the retail business, the majority of its revenues and profits today are from financial services — selling insurance, real estate, and securities.

If standard ratios are to be meaningful and informative, they should be developed for the following types of companies of an industry:

☐ Companies that use a uniform accounting system and accounting procedures, including a uniform classification of accounts and similar depreciation methods.

☐ Companies that follow a uniform accounting period, preferably on a natural business year basis.

☐ Companies that follow similar asset valuation and amortization policies.

☐ Companies that represent a homogeneous product line.

☐ Companies that adopt and maintain somewhat uniform managerial policies.

Because of diversity across firms in their access to product, factor, and financial markets, these points may not hold rigorously. Thus the analyst, when using either inter- or intraindustry comparisons, must constantly be aware of the limitations of the data in drawing meaningful conclusions. Table 3.2 summarizes some of the more obvious differences in financial and operating data of companies.

Trend Analysis

Although intercompany and interindustry financial comparisons are difficult, evaluating the same firm over a period of time is less of a problem. However, even this seemingly simple comparative analysis can prove hazardous.

Trend ratios generally are not computed for all of the items on the financial statements, since the fundamental objective is to make comparisons between items having some logical relationship to one another. This type of presentation can be useful in discerning whether certain segments of a firm's financial picture are deteriorating or improving and what can be expected in the future. Many times, this presentation is accomplished by plotting trend lines of a company's ratios. However, no conclusions can be made about the operations of the firm as a whole by examining only a single measure, such as a trend in the current ratio. These trends, important

TABLE 3.1
Retail Trade: General Merchandise Stores

Item description for accounting period 7/73 through 6/74	A Total	B Under 100	C 100 to 250	D 250 to 500	E 500 to 1000	F 1000 to 5000	G 5000 to 10,000	H 10,000 to 25,000	I 25,000 to 50,000	J 50,000 to 100,000	K 100,000 to 250,000	L 250,000 and over
						Size of Assets in Thousands of Dollars (000 Omitted)						
1. Number of establishments	24,524	11,555	6368	3110	1681	1365	133	134	59	50	24	45
2. Total receipts (in millions of dollars)	138,989.8	1899.7	2847.1	2709.7	2844.1	6543.7	2107.8	4783.0	5231.9	5921.5	6713.4	97,387.3
Selected operating factors in percent of net sales												
3. Cost of operations	63.6	69.0	69.2	68.3	68.9	66.8	69.0	69.0	68.3	66.8	67.1	61.8
4. Compensation of officers	—	4.1	2.7	2.7	1.9	1.7	1.1	0.6	—	—	—	—
5. Repairs	0.5	—	—	—	—	—	—	—	—	—	—	0.5
6. Bad debts	—	—	—	—	—	—	—	—	—	—	—	0.5
7. Rent on business property	2.6	3.9	2.9	2.9	2.1	2.8	2.6	3.3	3.5	2.9	2.2	2.5
8. Taxes (excl. federal tax)	2.5	2.2	1.8	1.7	1.8	2.0	2.1	1.9	2.2	2.2	3.0	2.7
9. Interest	2.2	—	0.5	—	0.5	0.7	0.7	1.0	0.9	1.6	1.4	2.7
10. Deprec./deplet./amortiz.†	1.5	1.1	0.8	0.7	0.8	1.1	1.0	1.1	1.0	1.6	1.7	1.6
11. Advertising	2.7	1.1	2.0	1.7	2.0	2.2	2.3	2.4	2.1	2.5	2.0	2.9
12. Pensions and other benefit plans	0.8	—	0.5	0.6	0.6	0.6	—	—	—	—	0.5	0.9
13. Other expenses	23.1	16.7	17.2	17.9	18.4	20.8	21.5	22.3	21.0	22.9	21.6	24.2
14. Net profit before tax	*	0.7	2.1	2.8	2.4	0.9	*	*	*	*	*	*

Selected financial ratios (number of times ratio is to one)

15. Current ratio	1.6	2.1	2.4	2.8	2.1	2.1	2.1	2.0	2.0	2.0	1.9	1.5
16. Quick ratio	0.8	0.5	0.6	1.0	0.7	0.8	0.9	0.6	0.7	0.7	0.9	0.9
17. Net sales to net working capital	6.0	8.9	5.6	5.2	5.6	5.5	5.1	5.8	6.5	5.0	6.7	6.1
18. Net sales to net worth	3.9	9.6	4.8	3.9	4.5	4.3	3.9	5.0	5.1	3.6	4.2	3.7
19. Inventory turnover	4.7	5.1	4.2	4.2	3.9	4.3	3.8	4.0	5.3	4.2	0.9	—
20. Total liabilities to net worth	1.5	1.6	0.8	0.5	0.9	0.9	0.9	1.2	1.2	1.2	1.2	1.7

Selected financial factors in percentages

21. Current liability to net worth	102.0	94.6	59.4	41.8	68.7	68.5	65.3	79.6	77.8	66.6	66.7	114.1
22. Inventory to current assets	41.5	71.1	69.1	62.7	64.6	56.1	52.8	64.8	56.9	58.6	48.8	36.5
23. Net income to net worth	15.1	48.9	21.4	21.9	23.5	19.8	14.9	24.9	22.5	12.1	11.9	13.8
24. Retained earnings to net income	69.7	96.6	91.3	89.7	87.2	92.8	89.4	93.9	89.0	76.9	72.9	60.9

Source: From the book *Almanac of Business and Industrial Financial Ratios,* 1977 edition, by Leo Troy. © 1977 by Prentice-Hall, Inc., Englewood Cliffs, NJ 07632. Used by permission of the publisher.

Note: Because the *Almanac* deals with *all* returns, those with and without income, a loss before tax in any industry, or asset size within an industry, is shown by an asterisk (*) at number 14. This will explain those instances in which the sum of the operating factors exceeds 100%.

† Depreciation largest factor.

TABLE 3.2
Some Financial and Operating Differences of Companies

1. Wide separation geographically, with different price levels and costs of operations
2. Operation of owned or leased properties or a combination thereof
3. Ownership of large or small amounts of investments in properties that are not used in connection with regular operations
4. Different price levels reflected in noncurrent asset items
5. New rather than old properties
6. Manufacture of one or a large number of products
7. Utilization of a high or low percentage of maximum plant capacity
8. Purchase or production of raw materials or semifinished goods
9. Vertical or horizontal integration
10. Maintenance of large inventories or adoption of an informal policy of purchasing raw materials or merchandise
11. Valuation of inventories on FIFO, LIFO, moving average, or some other basis
12. Sale of merchandise largely on either short- or long-term credit or mainly for cash
13. Sale of entire product to a single purchaser or to a large number of wholesalers, retailers, or consumers
14. Dependence on creditors for financing to a greater extent than owners' equity financing, or vice versa
15. Different systems of accounting and accounting procedures including classification of financial statement items, accounting periods, and depreciation methods

as they may be, will not, for example, answer such questions as the following: How effectively is the firm utilizing its resources? How has its past growth been financed? Where are funds for future growth likely to come from? How well can the firm meet its current obligations? How soon can it collect its receivables? How rapidly can it convert its inventory into cash?

The analyst must keep in mind that ratios are never conclusive in and of themselves. The comparability of trend ratios is adversely affected by the extent to which accounting principles and policies reflected in the accounts have not been followed consistently throughout the periods being studied. Comparability of the data is also adversely affected when the price level has changed materially during the years under review. Some analysts deflate the statement data by dividing the dollar amounts by a related price index, thereby providing figures that will give a rough picture of changes exclusive of price changes. This technique is used in some later chapters.

Even if the analyst identifies an apparently deteriorating trend in some ratio or a significant deviation from published standards, these anomalies are merely circumstantial evidence of a financial defect. They should be taken as warning signals indicating that additional investigation is necessary and not as conclusive evidence of financial strength or weakness. It is in the interpretation and evaluation of these anomalies — and in the recognition of what constitutes an anomaly — that the judgment, skill, and experience of the analyst receives the most severe test.

There are no hard-and-fast rules to guide the analyst in this task of drawing meaningful information about the firm's financial condition from reported data. Instead, the analyst must use her or his accumulated skill and experience to frame conclusions. The numbers on the financial statements are merely representations of states (in the case of the balance sheet) or flows (for the income statement and funds statement) within the financial framework of the firm. With minor exceptions, they take on meaning and significance only in the light of a detailed understanding of the basic considerations used in the financial management of the firm. The analyst should carry this viewpoint into any discussion of financial analysis. There are no rules or shortcuts that will eliminate the need for seasoned judgment.

Traditional Financial Analysis

Financial ratios are usually categorized according to the rapidity with which assets can be turned into cash, the efficient management of assets, the degree of protection for creditors and investors, and the profitability of assets. The result is four categories corresponding to these descriptions: (1) liquidity, (2) activity, (3) coverage, and (4) profitability. Each category can be related (either directly or indirectly) to liquidity management. However, from the perspective of short-term financial management, these categories decline in relative importance as you go from category (1) to category (4). This decline should be apparent from the "How to Go Broke . . ." scenario examined in Chapter 1.

The following discussion of the ratios does not include any calculations. Appendix B at the end of this chapter shows the calculations by using the financial statements of W. T. Grant Company. You are encouraged to refer to this appendix while reading the rest of this chapter.

Liquidity Ratios

Liquidity is defined as the ability to meet demands for cash as they occur. From early in this century to recent years the most widely used measure of the firm's liquidity position has been the *current ratio,* defined as the ratio of current assets to current liabilities:

$$\text{current ratio} = \frac{\text{current assets}}{\text{current liabilities}}. \tag{3.1}$$

The current ratio is thought to be important because all current liabilities (i.e., liabilities that will require cash during the current operating period) are usually paid with funds generated by the liquidation of current assets turned over into cash within the current operating period.

The intent of the current ratio is to provide a measure of the margin of safety in meeting obligations that will mature during the current period. If a firm's current assets are large relative to the value of current liabilities, there is a high probability that the liabilities can be paid as they fall due. This probability is embodied in the widespread acceptance of a current ratio of 2:1 as the standard or norm for adequate liquidity. The standard current ratio should be viewed with some skepticism, for a high current ratio by itself does not guarantee adequate liquidity. A satisfactory current ratio does not disclose the fact that a portion of the current assets may be tied up in slow-moving inventories and prepaid expenses. With inventories, especially raw materials and work in process, there are questions of how long it will take to transform them into finished products and what ultimately will be realized on the sale of the merchandise.

In the absence of cash and near-cash holdings, liquidity depends entirely on the relationship between cash inflows and required cash outflows. What is appropriate liquidity for a firm varies widely, and no general standard can possibly be applicable to all firms under all circumstances. In a detailed study of bankrupt and nonbankrupt firms, Ohlson[2] found that the average current ratio of the failed firms was above the mystical 2:1 standard in all five years preceding the ultimate bankruptcy.

A test considered to be a more rigorous test of a firm's liquidity is the *quick ratio*, sometimes called the *acid test ratio*, which compares with current liabilities only those current assets that could be expected to produce relatively sure cash if the firm were to cease operations. For the quick ratio both inventory and prepaid items are deduced from current assets; prepaid expenses, of course, produce no cash, while the amount of cash that can be realized from inventory if the firm ceases operations is highly uncertain. Thus, the quick ratio is defined as

$$\text{quick ratio} = \frac{\text{cash} + \text{marketable securities} + \text{receivables}}{\text{current liabilities}}. \tag{3.2}$$

The widely held rule of thumb for the quick ratio is 1:1. The quick ratio attempts to emphasize values at liquidation rather than going-concern values — thus eliminating differences in operating requirements. If a liquidation perspective is meaningful to the analysis, the 1:1 rule deserves somewhat more credence than the similar figure attached to the current ratio. However, it must be viewed with skepticism if analyzing a going-concern business.

The current and quick ratios are functions of many variables that

---

[2] *Ibid.*

affect liquidity differently. Recognition of the relevance of cash flow data to liquidity has led a number of analysts to question the traditional significance of the current and quick ratios. Some have explicitly censured the static character of these ratios as their fundamental shortcoming. Although the limitations have long been recognized, the customary directive is to allow for them in interpreting performance, which makes reliable interpretation a truly virtuoso performance.

The *defensive-interval ratio* has been proposed as an alternative to the current ratio. This ratio measures the time span during which a firm can operate on present liquid assets without resorting to revenues from next year's income sources. The defensive-interval ratio is computed as follows:

$$\text{defensive interval} = \frac{\text{defensive assets}}{\text{projected daily cash operating expenses}}. \tag{3.3}$$

Defensive assets consist of the quick assets: cash, marketable securities, and net receivables. Daily cash operating expenditures are computed by dividing annual cost of sales plus selling and administrative expenses and other ordinary cash expenses (may include interest expense) by 360 days. When the ratio is used for *pro forma* analysis, a review of past expenses can be the basis for the projection. The only necessary adjustment to the total cash operating expense figure of the income statement is an adjustment for any known changes in planned operations from previous periods.

Whether this ratio provides a better measure of liquidity than either the current ratio or the quick ratio is difficult to evaluate. It does depart from the strictly static analysis of the current and quick ratios and tries to focus attention directly upon the relationship between liquidity and the need for liquidity. However, the ratio is based on the stock level of defensive assets and not on the inflow of cash. Liquidity needs of the going-concern company are settled with cash and not illiquid receivables or inventory.

Another liquidity measure in popular use is the amount of *net working capital* of the firm. Net working capital is defined as the difference between current assets and current liabilities and should not be confused with *working capital*, which is often used as a substitute for current assets (although accountants usually define the difference between current assets and current liabilities as working capital).

Financial managers look at current assets as funds invested in assets that are closely linked to day-to-day operations. Any item included in current assets can be expected to turn into cash within the firm's operating cycle or one year, whichever is longer. These assets are arranged on the balance sheet in order of their nearness to cash, that is, in descending order of liquidity. In this context the term *liquidity* means flexibility and exchangeability of assets into cash.

Current liabilities are debts due to be paid within the firm's operating cycle or one year, whichever is longer. These debts are bona fide current debts owed outside the business and payable only with cash. Each current debt exposes the business to the risk of insolvency. The distinction between the insolvency risk of individual current liabilities is not as easily defined as the difference between the liquidity risks of individual current assets, and therefore they are not arranged on the balance sheet in terms of insolvency risk.

The interpretation placed on the calculation of net working capital is that if current assets exceed current liabilities, the firm is solvent. This interpretation is not necessarily true, since the *net working capital amount fails to indicate anything about liquidity.* Cash and near-cash assets are truly the only liquid assets. A high positive net working capital amount may arise from extraordinarily high investment in receivables and inventories. Thus one must analyze net working capital in conjunction with receivable and inventory management, which frequently rely on the use of turnover ratios. However, as will be discussed in Chapters 12 and 15, turnover ratios can lead to erroneous conclusions. They must be used with caution.

Net working capital is more informative when defined as

$$\text{net working capital} = (\text{long-term and indeterminate debt}) \\ + (\text{net worth}) - (\text{fixed and other assets}), \qquad (3.4)$$

where *indeterminate debt* is defined as deferred income taxes, pension liabilities, and minority interest claims (which arise from less than 100 percent ownership of subsidiaries). This definition shows net working capital to be permanent capital invested in current assets. Transactions that affect current assets and current liabilities in equal measure never influence the level of net working capital.

The only way that net working capital can change is as a result of a transaction that affects current assets or current liabilities as well as either net worth, debt other than short-term debt, or fixed and other assets. Thus net working capital has three general sources: transactions that increase net worth, transactions that increase long-term and indeterminate debt, and transactions that reduce fixed and other assets. Conversely, there are three competing uses for the sources of net working capital: transactions that reduce net worth, payments or reductions of long-term and indeterminate debt, and increases of fixed and other assets.

An interesting relationship between the current (or quick) ratio and net working capital can be illustrated to indicate the difficulty with using these techniques for evaluating liquidity. If current assets (CA) are $200 and current liabilities (CL) are $100, the current ratio (CR) is 2:1 and net working capital is $100. Now suppose that the firm increases both current assets and current liabilities by $50. This increase causes the current ratio to fall to 1.67:1, indicating a deteriorating liquidity position. The net working capital amount, however, does not change. Table 3.3 summarizes the

TABLE 3.3
Relationship Between Current Ratio and Net Working Capital

Assumption	Current ratio	Net working capital
CR > 1:1		
Increase CA and CL equally	Decreases	No change
Decrease CA and CL equally	Increases	No change
CR < 1:1		
Increase CA and CL equally	Increases	No change
Decrease CA and CL equally	Decreases	No change

relationship between the current ratio and net working capital under other assumed conditions. Obviously, great care must be exercised in interpreting these liquidity measures.

Activity Ratios

The activity ratios — also called turnover ratios — are often cited as indirect measures of cash flow. *Activity ratios attempt to reflect the relative efficiency of funds management* by relating the level of investment in various asset categories to the level of operations.

Figure 3.1 illustrates that the cash flows within a firm begin in a cash reservoir and move to raw materials (if a manufacturer) through purchases. Raw materials are placed into production, and the funds representing finished goods are accumulated through production costs and move on again to finished goods. Finally, as finished goods are sold, the funds return to the cash reservoir directly or via accounts receivable and collections. The funds flowing in this arrangement are expanded by a finished good markup so that an increment of profit is carried along with the flows on their return journey. The flow of funds, in financial statement analysis, usually faces an inspection at two critical points — finished goods and accounts receivable — to ascertain that they are flowing freely.

The commitment of funds to receivables is customarily examined by an *accounts receivable turnover* calculation:

$$\text{accounts receivable turnover} = \frac{\text{sales}}{\text{accounts receivable}}. \tag{3.5}$$

Most analysts use credit sales in the numerator and divide by year-end receivables. However, some analysts prefer to use an average of beginning

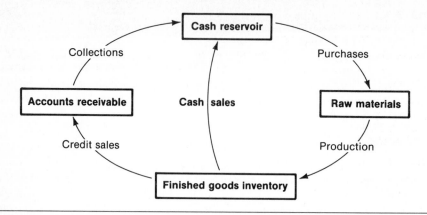

FIGURE 3.1
Flow of Net Working Capital

and closing receivables for the denominator. However, if seasonal factors are significant, the receivable turnover ratio will be distorted. In any case, net receivables (net of the allowance for doubtful accounts), instead of gross receivables, should be used for the computation. Frequently, net sales are substituted for credit sales since credit sales are not available. Net sales can be a poor substitute if cash sales are a significant proportion of total sales.

A closely related ratio is the number of *days sales outstanding* (also called the *average collection period*). It is calculated as

$$\text{days sales outstanding} = \frac{\text{accounts receivable}}{\text{sales}/360}. \tag{3.6}$$

This ratio can be derived directly from the accounts receivable turnover ratio by dividing 360 (which represents the number of days in the year) by the turnover ratio.

Both the receivables turnover and the collection period are rough measures of funds flow. The information they provide supposedly gives some indication of the quality of the receivables and also an idea of how successful the firm is in collecting its outstanding receivables. The general rule credit managers often use is that the time allowed for payment by the selling terms should not be exceeded by more than 10 to 15 days. As will be explained in Chapter 12, these general rules can severely distort accounts receivable management.

An unusually high accounts receivable balance relative to sales may be indicative that the next period's sales have been pulled into the current period. Sales are moved in this way by overloading dealers, distributors, and customers. To hide a growth in receivables, companies can sell receivables, arrange customer financing with third parties to pay for orders shipped earlier than required by the customer, or sell on an operating lease rather than a capital lease basis (leases are examined in Chapter 4). Therefore analysts should check the notes to annual reports to see whether receivables have been sold, contingent liabilities for customer obligations to third parties have been assumed, and the mix of capital and operating leases has shifted toward operating leases so that fewer lease payments receivable have to be shown in the balance sheet.

An unusually low receivable balance can also be bad. It may indicate that credit terms are too restrictive and the company is losing business. Credit terms are examined in Chapter 9.

Another measure of accounts receivable management is the *aging schedule,* which shows the proportion of receivables initiated in each month as a percentage of total sales. Chapter 12 will discuss days sales outstanding, turnover calculations, and aging schedules in some detail and show that they present problems for evaluating accounts receivable management whenever credit sales are not constant from period to period.

The commonly accepted measure of inventory utilization is *inventory turnover.* It attempts to measure how quickly inventory is sold. The accepted view is that the higher the inventory turnover ratio, the better the company is performing. Possibly, however, the firm is incurring high stockout costs because not enough inventory is available.

The inventory turnover ratio is customarily defined as the ratio of cost of goods sold to the average of beginning and ending inventory. The calculation is

$$\text{inventory turnover} = \frac{\text{cost of goods sold}}{\text{average inventory}}. \tag{3.7}$$

As will be discussed in Chapter 14, sales may replace cost of sales in the numerator, and the denominator may be defined as either year-end inventory or a monthly average inventory. Some consider the use of sales a poor substitute since sales include the profit markup, with the result that the turnover is inflated. However, if consistency is maintained over time, this problem is not serious. Knowing the inventory valuation method used is often more important than the problem of inflated turnover. Different valuation methods may affect liquidity analysis more drastically than will the numerator of the inventory turnover ratio being stated by using cost or by using selling price.

Analysis of the efficiency of fixed-asset utilization can provide insights into liquidity management. A *fixed-asset turnover ratio* attempts to measure the intensity of utilization of fixed assets. It does so by relating sales to net fixed assets (i.e., after depreciation):

$$\text{net fixed-asset turnover} = \frac{\text{sales}}{\text{average net fixed assets}}. \tag{3.8}$$

If the turnover ratio is high, the implication is that the company is using its fixed assets effectively to generate sales and, thereby, one hopes, cash flows. If the turnover ratio is low, the implication is that the company either has to use its assets more efficiently or dispose of some of them.

The turnover of net fixed assets can be relatively high for two reasons. A new plant may improve the quality of the product, leading to a high and rising sales volume. In this case the high ratio would be coveted by all. A heavily depreciated plant can also lead to a high turnover ratio, even when the firm's sales are low and falling, a condition that would not be envied. To determine which of these two possibilities is actually the case, one must consider other facts. For example, did the profit margin per item change? What is the trend in sales? What is the firm's depreciation policy?

Analysis of *total asset turnover* provides information of resource management efficiency at an aggregate level. This ratio provides a gross indication of asset utilization and is defined as follows:

$$\text{total asset turnover} = \frac{\text{sales}}{\text{average total assets}}. \tag{3.9}$$

This ratio is meant to be a summary of other turnover ratios, and thus it is an overall indication of productivity of invested funds. As such, it is susceptible to a couple of problems. First, the problems inherent in the individual ratios are embodied in the total turnover ratio. Second, the contribution of each asset to the total asset turnover cannot be measured directly. Chapter 5 will discuss a technique for overcoming this latter problem.

Coverage Ratios

Coverage ratios are computed to help one determine the long-run solvency of the firm. The issue of debt capacity is of critical importance because of its impact on margins of profitability and on solvency. If a firm wishes to reduce the risk of insolvency to a minimum, it would employ only equity capital. However, in so doing, management reduces the opportunity for higher gains (or losses) on equity capital, since it is not taking advantage of the leverage that results from *trading on the equity*. In other words, it is not fully utilizing the relatively cheap source of debt financing to earn project returns in excess of the cost of debt. Conversely, if management wishes to take advantage of leverage, it would increase the amount of debt capital employed in the financing of current assets; in so doing, it must be prepared to accept more risk.

When the work *risk* is applied to debt, it refers to the chance of running out of cash. This risk is inevitably increased by a legal contract requiring the business to pay fixed sums of cash at predetermined dates in the future, regardless of the financial condition at that time. We emphasize that although debt necessarily increases the chance of cash insolvency, this risk exists whether the company has any debt or not. So the debt-equity choice is not between some risk and no risk, but between more and less.

The conventional form for expressing debt capacity rules is in terms of some *debt-to-capital ratio:*

$$\text{debt to capital} = \frac{\text{debt}}{\text{capitalization}}. \tag{3.10}$$

The numerator of the ratio can include all liabilities, all but current liabilities, or only long-term, interest-bearing debt. The analyst must decide whether to include the indeterminate liabilities of deferred taxes, minority interest, and pension liability. The denominator of the ratio is similarly variable. It sometimes includes only owner's equity, sometimes only long-term sources of capital (i.e., long-term debt plus owners' equity), and sometimes all the items on the right-hand side of the balance sheet. A variation of this ratio is often found in debt contracts that limit new long-term borrowings to some percentage of net tangible assets.

Unfortunately, any of these debt-to-capital ratios can seriously mislead unwary analysts. In many cases adjustments for off – balance sheet items (e.g., inventory profits, leases, pensions, deferred taxes, in-substance debt defeasance), which are the subject of Chapter 4, should be made to the ratio.

Debt-paying ability is a dynamic concept and is a function of the profitability of the enterprise, the rate of conversion of assets into cash, and its creditworthiness. *In the short-run a firm's debt capacity is predicated largely upon cash flow* rather than earnings that are reported on the income statement.

Generally, the longer the maturity of the debt, the less risk the firm assumes, since management has adequate opportunity to acquire funds from operations to satisfy the debt, or it will have sufficient opportunity to refinance the obligation. Conversely, the shorter the maturity, the greater the risk is, since the firm will have less time to accumulate sufficient funds to liquidate the debt or have less time to refund the loan.

There are obvious weaknesses of the long-term, debt-to-capital ratio as a way of looking at the chances of running out of cash (other than the fact that many off – balance sheet items exist). First, there is a wide variation in the relation between the principal of the debt and the annual obligation for cash payments under the debt contract. The annual cash outflow associated with $10 million on the balance sheet may, for example, vary from $1,500,000 (interest only at 15%), to $1,523,000 (interest plus principal repayable over 30 years), to $1,992,494 (interest plus principal repayable over 10 years). Second, as loans are repaid by partial annual payments, as is customary, the principal amount declines and the percent-of-capitalization ratio improves, but the annual cash drain for repayments remains the same until maturity is reached. Third, there may be substantial changes in asset values, particularly in connection with inventory valuation and depreciation policies; and as a consequence, there will be changes in the percent-of-capitalization ratio that have no bearing on the capacity to meet fixed cash drains.

An alternative form in which to express the limits of long-term borrowing is in terms of the income statement data. This form is the *fixed-charge coverage ratio* — the ratio of earnings available for servicing debt and other fixed charges to the total amount of these charges. The numerator is earnings before taxes adjusted for such fixed charges as interest and lease obligations (among others). The denominator can include tax-deductible interest, lease payments, and nondeductible dividends and sinking fund payments, both grossed up (by dividing by 1 − tax rate) to show pretax cash amounts that are necessary to service them:

$$\text{fixed-charge coverage} = \frac{\text{adjusted earnings before taxes}}{\text{interest} + \text{leases} + \dfrac{\text{sinking fund charges} + \text{dividends}}{(1 - \text{tax rate})}}. \qquad (3.11)$$

The *simple interest coverage ratio* is derived by defining the numerator as earnings before interest and taxes and the denominator as interest charges. Under a fixed-charge coverage rule no new long-term debt can be contemplated unless income available for servicing debt and other fixed charges is equal to or in excess of some multiple, say 3, of the debt-servicing and fixed charges. The reason for this rule is to allow a company to survive a period of decline in sales and earnings and still have enough earnings to cover the fixed charges.

The fixed-charge (or interest) coverage ratio is influenced by the *earning power* of the assets (i.e., *return on assets,* discussed later in this section), the debt-equity ratio, the fixed charges (e.g., the interest and lease payments), and the proportion of debt repayment each period. Implicit in the coverage ratio is the idea of variability. The greater the variability in earning power of assets, the higher the required ratio is. Conversely, the lower the variability, the lower the required coverage standard must be — in other words, the more debt and other fixed obligations the firm can support.

The fixed-charge (or interest) coverage ratio has limitations as a basis for determination of debt capacity. First, it is a point-in-time measure — that is, it is a static measure and thus cannot adequately measure flows available to meet obligations. Second, the earnings figure found in the income statement is derived under normal accrual accounting procedures and is not the same as net cash inflow — an assumption that is implicit in the coverage ratio. Even when adjustments are made for the noncash items (e.g., depreciation), this equivalence cannot safely be assumed. Ideally, the analysis should be in terms of cash and not accrual accounting information. Third, the ratio fails to reflect the financial position of the firm under adversity when earnings may be down and interest up. Finally, nothing is reported about the state of the capital markets and the fact that financing capacity varies markedly for many firms over the business cycle.

The *degree of financial leverage* is often employed to measure the extent of a firm's borrowings. The higher the degree of financial leverage, the higher is the risk of the firm's not being able to meet financial obligations. Financial leverage refers to the use of fixed-income securities — debt and preferred stock — in an effort to boost earnings per share. The calculation is as follows, where EBIT is earnings before interest and taxes:

degree of financial leverage

$$= \frac{\text{EBIT}}{\text{EBIT} - \text{interest} - \dfrac{\text{preferred dividends}}{(1 - \text{tax rate})}}. \qquad (3.12)$$

Financial leverage is frequently shown in graphical form, as in Fig. 3.2, to highlight the impact of additional debt on earnings per share. Favorable financial leverage results in higher earnings per share (EPS) and is thought to be good. Unfavorable leverage results if the EPS declines as more debt is added. In the first case, management is able to invest the debt funds and earn more on them than they cost. In the second case, it earns less on the funds than they cost.

Unfortunately, the *EPS – EBIT analysis* contributes little to an under-

FIGURE 3.2
Financial Leverage: The Debt-Equity Trade-off

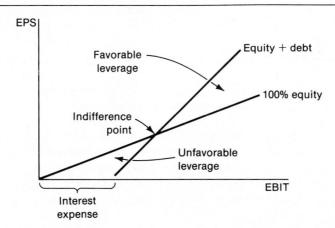

standing of liquidity. Impact on earnings, and not cash flow, is the determining factor in the analysis. The model emphasizes maximization of earnings per share, which is not consistent with maximizing shareholder wealth, as discussed in Chapters 1 and 2. Management can always increase short-term earnings per share, usually at the expense of long-term shareholder value.

Additionally, *earnings per share* is an unreliable standard for measuring economic value for shareholders. There are several important reasons why it is unreliable. First, earnings vary with the use of different accounting methods (e.g., last-in, first-out inventory valuation vs. first-in, first-out inventory valuation). Second, earnings do not reflect differences in business and financial risk faced by various companies. Third, earnings do not account for relative rates of investment in net working capital and fixed capital needed to support sales growth. Finally, reported earnings do not incorporate changes in a company's cost of capital due to either shifts in inflationary expectations or changes in business or financial risk.

A much-used basis for evaluating the net worth and any changes in it from year to year is found in the *book value* or *equity value per share* of stock. Book value per share of stock is the amount each share would receive if the company were liquidated on the basis of amounts reported on the balance sheet. The figure loses much of its relevance since the valuations on the balance sheet (generally) do not approximate fair market value or even the liquidation value of the assets. It is computed by allocating the stockholders' equity items among the various classes of stock and then dividing the total so allocated to each class of stock by the number of shares outstanding:

$$\text{book value per share} = \frac{\text{common shareholders' equity}}{\text{outstanding shares}}. \tag{3.13}$$

A popular, but poorly understood, measure is *cash flow*, or in ratio form, *cash flow per share*. This so-called cash flow figure is computed by adding noncash charges to net income. In the conversion to a ratio the cash flow is divided by the number of shares of common stock outstanding:

$$\text{cash flow per share} = \frac{\text{net income} + \text{noncash adjustments}}{\text{outstanding common shares}}. \tag{3.14}$$

This amount represents neither the flow of cash through the firm nor the residual of the cash received minus the cash disbursed divided by the outstanding shares of stock. It is frequently used to determine approximately the amount of resources generated internally. However, for this purpose changes in accounts receivable, accounts payable, and inventory balances need to be factored into the numerator. These changes will be shown in Chapter 6.

Profitability Ratios

Profitability is frequently used as the ultimate test of management effectiveness in directing the firm and ensuring that its liquidity needs are satisfied. An amazing number of financial ratios are based on the idea that a period's earnings reveal a company's financial strength. However strong the *profit motives* of management may be, they can *never* wisely be permitted to *take precedence over safety*. Safety means solvency — the capacity of the corporation to meet its obligations as they become due. The appropriate levels of liquidity are the result of fundamental decisions concerning the firm's various net working capital investments, the firm's fixed-asset investments, and the maturity composition of its debt. In turn, these decisions are influenced by a trade-off between profitability and risk. The risk of running out of cash can be reduced or even eliminated, of course, by maintaining a high proportion of liquid assets. However, the cost involved is the forgone profit on the investment of these funds in other assets.

Ratios are often used to measure profitability, or effectiveness, at one or both of two levels: that of the fundamental profitability of the firm's operations and the profitability on the owners' investment, which reflects not only operating profitability but also capital structure.

A widely used measure of the basic profitability of the firm is *return on assets*, which is frequently defined as the ratio of net income to total assets. This ratio reflects the ability of management to generate income on a given amount of total assets. Earnings before interest and taxes (EBIT), rather than net income after taxes, can be used in order to eliminate the influence of differential tax treatment and different capital structure decisions on earnings performance. Any nonoperating income and expenses may also be eliminated from EBIT.

If net income after tax is used, some analysts add back the after-tax interest charge [i.e., net income + interest (1 − tax rate)]. This procedure has the effect of eliminating the financing charge from the calculation but not the taxes. The rationale is that interest is a financing charge, not an operating expense, and should be eliminated from any evaluation of earning potential of the investment. On the other hand, taxes are an operating cost and should be included. Another adjustment many analysts make is to use only net operating assets in the denominator. This adjustment eliminates miscellaneous and intangible assets from the calculation.

The return-on-assets concept is particularly useful because it can be broken down into various components to identify reasons for a change in earning power over time. The ratio is usually defined as the product of percentage return on sales (possibly adjusted to eliminate the interest charge) times asset turnover:

$$\text{return on assets} = \underbrace{\frac{\text{net income}}{\text{sales}}}_{\substack{\text{Return on} \\ \text{sales}}} \times \underbrace{\frac{\text{sales}}{\text{total assets}}}_{\substack{\text{Asset} \\ \text{turnover}}} .$$

(3.15)

The usefulness of this construct is that it helps the analyst integrate ratio analysis, because it shows that a change in return on assets may come about through a change in the profitability of sales or through more intensive utilization of the firm's assets by increasing asset turnover.

Breakeven and *margin-of-safety analyses* are often used along with profitability ratios to show management how income and risk varies with changes in sales volumes, costs, or prices. From an examination of the relationship between costs, prices, and income, management attempts to gain insight about the operating risk (and indirectly about the liquidity risk) of the firm.

If a high percentage of a firm's total costs are fixed costs, then the firm is said to have a high degree of operating leverage. This implies that a relatively small increase (decrease) in sales results in a large increase (decrease) in operating income. Other things being held constant, the higher a firm's operating leverage, the higher its operating risk is.

The equation for calculating *breakeven sales dollars* is

$$\text{breakeven sales dollars} = \frac{\text{fixed costs}}{\text{contribution margin percent}} .$$

(3.16)

Fixed costs are sometimes defined to include only operating fixed costs (depreciation may or may not be included) or all fixed costs used in calculating net income, which would include interest payments on debt.

Margin of safety indicates the proportion that sales can decline (or need to increase) before breakeven profit is reached. It is calculated as

$$\text{margin of safety} = \frac{\text{actual sales}}{\text{breakeven sales}} - 1.$$

(3.17)

In terms of liquidity analysis a major concern with traditional breakeven analysis and its associated margin-of-safety concept is that they fail to incorporate cash flows. This problem can be alleviated to some extent, as will be discussed in Chapter 5. Other problems usually associated with breakeven analysis are as follows:

□ The analysis is only appropriate for a single product or a constant mix of products.

□ A distinction between fixed and variable costs is necessary.

☐ The analysis is only appropriate for a relevant range of production.

☐ All costs and prices must be known at each level of output.

☐ Costs are generally assumed to be linear (however, nonlinear costs can be easily introduced).

Another measure of profitability is *return on equity*. It indicates the success of management in generating earnings (*note:* not cash flow) for the firm's owners and is defined as the ratio of earnings available to the common stockholders' equity divided by equity:

$$\text{return on equity} = \frac{\text{earnings available to equityholders}}{\text{total equity}}. \tag{3.18}$$

If there is any preferred stock outstanding, the amount of the preferred stock dividends are deducted from net income after taxes. The par amount of preferred stock outstanding is deducted from net worth to obtain the common stockholders' equity.

This ratio can also be expanded as follows to provide a broader perspective for analyzing profitability:

$$\text{return on equity} = \underbrace{\frac{\text{net income}}{\text{sales}}}_{\substack{\text{return} \\ \text{on sales}}} \times \underbrace{\frac{\text{sales}}{\text{total assets}}}_{\substack{\text{asset} \\ \text{turnover}}} \times \underbrace{\frac{\text{total assets}}{\text{equity}}}_{\text{leverage}} \tag{3.19}$$

The first and third ratios on the right-hand side relate to the income statement and balance sheet, respectively. The middle ratio combines these two statements. If no preferred stock is outstanding, net income equals earnings available to equityholders. The interest deduction paid to debtholders is included in the calculation of net income since return to shareholders is being measured. The return-on-equity ratio encompasses all the problems inherent in the liquidity, activity, and coverage ratios, since these ratios are embedded here.

Summary

The purpose of this chapter was to examine some preconceived notions about financial analysis. The discussion pertained to inherent weaknesses in many of the traditional ratios. The intent was not to have you forgo using these ratios (although a strong argument was made in some cases to do so) but to have you use the ratios more intelligently by understanding their weaknesses.

An important problem of financial analysis is ascertaining the quality of earnings of a firm. Management often stretches the interpretation of accounting principles or, less frequently, commits outright fraud in preparing financial statements. The obvious purpose is to make the financial statements look better than they really are in order to attract capital and to bolster or support the firm's common stock price.

Probably the most-often-heard criticism of financial analysis is the difficult problem of achieving comparability among firms in a given industry or access to sufficient internal information about the firm. Achieving comparability among firms that apply different accounting procedures is difficult and requires that the analyst identify basic differences existing in accounting and adjust the balances to achieve comparability. Even that may not be enough if the analyst relies too heavily on the generally accepted ratios.

Problems associated with the generally accepted ratios of liquidity, activity, coverage, and profitability were discussed in detail. A common theme throughout the discussion was the inability of any of the ratios to truly measure funds flow. This limitation is a serious one. Since the firm is a series of funds flows, analysts must provide a clear picture of past receipts, expenditures, and disbursements to debt and equity suppliers. This information is essential for assessing liquidity risk and prediction of future cash flows and profitability.

Key Concepts

Activity ratios

Coverage ratios

Industry analysis

Liquidity ratios

Profitability ratios

Quality of earnings

Trend analysis

Appendix A
Deferred Income Taxes

Under current accounting regulations deferred income taxes can occur when the accounting methods used for financial reporting purposes differ from those used for tax purposes. For example, in its annual report a corporation might depreciate an asset by the straight-line method over an eight-year life; it may, however, use a five-year life and the ACRS method for its tax purposes. The tax expense shown in the annual report would be based on income calculated with the eight-year, straight-line method, while the taxes actually paid would be based on the five-year ACRS method. The difference between the annual report's tax expense and the actual amount paid to the government is called a *deferred tax*. Over the life of each asset the total depreciation under both methods would be the same, so the timing differences that occur in the early years of an asset's life that result in deferred taxes (and conserved liquidity) would be reversed in its later years.

Although the deferred taxes that arise from each individual asset would eventually be paid, in practice, the total amount in the deferred tax account frequently increases each year. Under normal economic circumstances a going concern may never have to pay the balance on deferred taxes. If this is the case, some practitioners argue that deferred taxes are not a true liability, but rather, they are a form of equity.

Regardless of whether deferred taxes represent debt or equity, in selecting among alternative methods for tax purposes, management tries to minimize the present value of the firm's tax liabilities for a given set of operating results. The principles of income tax management are summarized by the expression "Pay the least amount of tax, as late as possible, within the law."

The major differences between taxable and accounting income can be classified as follows:

☐ Permanent differences arising from special legislative allowances or restrictions permitted or required for economic, political, or administrative reasons not related to the computation of accounting income.

☐ Differences arising from the direct charges or credits to retained earnings of items included in the computation of taxable net income.

☐ Differences in timing of charges and credits to income.

The main controversy regarding tax allocation is centered on timing differences as discussed previously. Some of the ways in which the timing differences can arise are as follows:

□ Depreciation for tax purposes is larger than shown in the financial records because different asset lives or different depreciation patterns, or both, are used for the two purposes. In such cases the company shows the reduction in taxes currently payable on the balance sheet as *deferred income taxes*.

□ Revenues from installment sales are entered in the financial records on the date of sale but are entered in the tax returns for periods when payments are collected.

□ Revenues from long-term construction projects are recognized in financial records on the percentage-of-completion basis but on tax returns under the completed-contract basis.

A basic argument against income tax allocation (i.e., the use of deferred income taxes) is that taxes affect cash flows by the amount of the tax obligation. Therefore the current tax obligation is more meaningful to investors and creditors than some artificially allocated tax expense.

ILLUSTRATION A.1

This illustration highlights some of the differences between financial accounting and tax accounting. It is based on the following assumptions:

□ 200,000 units were sold at a price of $115 each.

□ Selling, general, and administrative expenses, excluding officers' salaries, are $2,250,000.

□ $250,000 was paid as salaries to officers, and options were awarded to purchase common stock in the company. The options have a market value of $120,000 and expire at the end of next year. For financial reporting purposes the option expense is amortized over the exercise period.

□ Depreciation for financial reporting purposes is $500,000; for tax purposes it is $1 million.

□ An investment tax credit (ITC) of $500,000 is to be taken this year for tax purposes but amortized over 10 years for financial reporting purposes.

□ Inventory purchases for the year were as follows: January 1, 80,000 units @ $50/unit; May 1, 90,000 units @ $55/unit; September 1, 100,000 units @ $60/unit. The firm uses LIFO inventory accounting (that is, the last product purchased is the first product sold). Income tax regulations require a company to use LIFO in its financial statements if it uses LIFO for its tax return.

☐ The income tax rate is 40%.

The income statement follows.

	($000)	
	Financial	*Tax*
Sales	$23,000	$23,000
Expenses:		
Cost of sales	11,450	11,450
Depreciation	500	1,000
Officers' compensation:		
Salaries	250	250
Stock options	60	0
Selling, general, administrative	2,250	2,250
Total expenses	$14,510	$14,950
Income before taxes	$ 8,490	$ 8,050
Taxes	3,346	2,720
Net income	$ 5,144	$ 5,330
Computation of tax:		
Income before taxes	$ 8,490	$ 8,050
Income tax on income	$ 3,396	$ 3,220
Less ITC	50	500
Income tax expense	$ 3,346	
Income tax payable		$ 2,720
Deferred income tax	$ 626	
Effective tax rate	39.4%	33.7%

The journal entry follows.

Debit	Income tax expense	$3346	
Credit	Income tax payable		$2720
Credit	Deferred income tax payable		626

The debit appears on the income statement, whereas the credits are shown as liabilities on the balance sheet.   ☐

Ratio Calculations for W. T. Grant Company

The ratios discussed in this chapter have been calculated for W. T. Grant for two years. Table B.3 summarizes results for the years ended January 31, 1973 and 1974. Supporting calculations for the year 1974 follow. The financial statements for W. T. Grant are included as Tables B.1 and B.2.

TABLE B.1
W. T. Grant Company and Consolidated Subsidiaries
Consolidated Income Statement
For the Year Ended January 31
($000)

	1974	1973
Operating section:		
Net sales	$1,849,802	$1,644,747
Less cost of sales (1)	1,163,998	1,023,014
Gross profit	$ 685,804	$ 621,733
Less: Selling, general, and administrative (2)	518,279	442,211
Depreciation and amortization	13,579	12,004
Leasing	105,367	90,243
Net profit from operations	$ 48,579	$ 77,275
Nonoperating section:		
Income from concessions	3,971	3,753
Interest earned on installment sales	1,035	602
Miscellaneous (3)	2,027	586
Earnings before interest and taxes	$ 55,612	$ 82,216
Creditors' section:		
Interest expense	51,047	21,127
Owners' section:		
Earnings before taxes	$ 4,565	$ 61,089
Less taxes: Current	⟨6,020⟩	11,255
Deferred	6,807	17,163
Earnings before unconsolidated subsidiaries	$ 3,778	$ 32,671
Equity in net earnings of unconsolidated subsidiaries (4)	4,651	5,116
Total net earnings	$ 8,429	$ 37,787
Less dividends on preferred stock	293	335
Net earnings available to common stock	$ 8,136	$ 37,452

Notes:
1. 2% of this expense is assumed to include fixed-overhead allocations.
2. 25% of this expense is assumed to be variable.
3. Includes gains of $315,000 and $1,960,000 for the years ending January 31, 1973 and 1974, respectively, for the early extinguishment of long-term debt.
4. Represents the portion of subsidiaries' profits owned by W. T. Grant.

TABLE B.2
W. T. Grant Company and Consolidated Subsidiaries
Balance Sheet
As of January 31
($000)

	1974	1973
Assets		
Current assets:		
Cash and marketable securities	$ 45,951	$ 30,943
Accounts receivable (net) (1)	598,799	542,752
Inventories (lower of cost or market) (2)	450,637	399,533
Prepaid expenses	7,299	6,648
Total current assets	$1,102,686	$ 979,876
Miscellaneous assets:		
Investment in subsidiaries	$ 32,600	$ 29,030
Investment in debentures of unconsolidated subsidiaries	11,651	5,951
Total miscellaneous assets	$ 44,251	$ 34,981
Fixed assets:		
Building and equipment	$ 152,922	$ 138,607
Less accumulated depreciation	52,546	47,926
Net building and equipment	$ 100,376	$ 90,681
Land	608	739
Total fixed assets	$ 100,984	$ 91,420
Other assets:		
Common stock of W. T. Grant held for deferred compensation plan	$ 2,500	$ 2,381
Other	1,200	600
Unamortized debt expenses	1,362	1,440
Total assets	$1,252,983	$1,110,698
Liabilities and equity		
Current liabilities:		
Trade accounts payable	$ 58,192	$ 60,973
Short-term commercial notes payable (3)	453,097	380,034
Bank loans payable	0	10,000
Accrued wages payable	14,678	19,000
Other miscellaneous	31,040	24,443
Federal income taxes payable	0	8,480
Total current liabilities	$ 557,007	$ 502,930
Long-term liabilities	$ 220,336	$ 126,672
Indeterminant liabilities:		
Deferred contingent compensation	$ 2,396	$ 2,394
Deferred income taxes (4)	14,649	11,926
Deferred credits, principally income taxes related to installment sales (5)	133,057	130,137
Other	1,800	2,300
Total indeterminant liabilities	$ 151,902	$ 146,757

TABLE B.2 (Cont.)

Shareholders' equity:		
Cumulative preferred stock—3¾%, $100 par value; authorized 250,000 shares	$ 7,465	$ 8,600
Common stock—22,500,000 shares of $1.25 par value authorized	18,599	18,588
Capital surplus	84,271	84,718
Amounts paid by employees under purchase contracts for common stock	1,638	1,429
Retained earnings (6)	248,461	261,153
Less treasury stock	(36,696)	(40,149)
Total shareholders' equity	$ 323,738	$ 334,339
Total liabilities and equity	$1,252,983	$1,110,698

Notes:

1. Over $2 million of loans to directors and officers were outstanding as of the end of the 1973 and 1974 fiscal years. In the fiscal year ended January 1973, $245,000 of loans to directors/officers were written off as uncollectible. In the following year $301,500 in loans were written off.

2. Inventories, as of January 31, 1974, increased 12.8% over the previous year's level. Since sales increased 12.5% during the same period, management stated in the annual report that the inventory increase was satisfactory. Chapter 14 will examine the fallacy of this conclusion.

3. Maturities ranged from 1 to 270 days from the date of issuance.

4. $30 million more depreciation was taken for tax purposes than for financial reporting purposes in the fiscal year ended January 31, 1974.

5. Revenues from installment sales were entered in the financial records on the date of sale but were entered in the tax returns for periods when payments were collected. This step allowed $133 million in taxes to be deferred for the year ended January 1974.

6. Common dividends of $20,829 were paid in 1974.

You should keep in mind that the ratio can be computed a number of different ways by defining numerators and denominators differently from the definitions shown in our calculations.

The ratio calculations follow.

Liquidity Ratios

$$\text{current ratio} = \frac{1,102,686}{557,007} = 1.98$$

$$\text{quick ratio} = \frac{644,750}{557,007} = 1.16$$

$$\text{defensive interval} = \frac{644,750 \times 360}{(1,163,998 + 518,279 + 105,367 + 51,047)}$$
$$= 126.2 \text{ days}$$

This ratio is sometimes calculated by excluding the interest payment ($51,047) in the denominator.

$$\text{net working capital} = 1,102,686 - 557,007 = 545,679$$

TABLE B.3
W. T. Grant and Company
Financial Ratios

	1974	*1973*	*Traditional interpretation*
Liquidity ratios			
Current ratio	1.98	1.95	It is apparent from these
Quick ratio	1.16	1.14	ratios that liquidity has
Defensive interval (days)	126.2	132.0	not changed materially
Net working capital ($000)	545,679	476,946	
Activity ratios			
Receivables turnover	3.09	3.03	Differences are insignifi-
Days sales in receivables	116.5	118.8	cant
Inventory turnover (cost)	2.58	2.56	
Inventory turnover (sales)	4.10	4.12	
Net fixed-asset turnover	18.32	17.99	
Leverage			
Total debt/equity	2.87	2.32	Greater reliance on long-
Long-term debt/equity	1.15	0.82	term debt, coupled with
Total debt/capital	0.74	0.70	lower operating earn-
Long-term debt/capital	0.30	0.25	ings, has greatly de-
Fixed-charge coverage	1.13	1.14	creased simple
Simple interest coverage	1.09	3.89	interest coverage and
Degree of financial leverage	13.21	1.36	degree of financial le-
Book value per share ($)	21.26	21.91	verage
Cash flow per share ($)	1.48	3.35	
Profitability			
Breakeven sales ($000)	1,518,346	1,217,650	Significant increase in
Margin of safety	0.22	0.35	breakeven sales; prof-
Return-on-operating assets	0.04	0.01	itability down consider-
Return-on-operating assets			ably
adjusted for interest	0.04	0.05	
Return-on-equity	0.01	0.12	

Activity Ratios

$$\text{receivable turnover} = \frac{1,849,802}{598,799} = 3.09 \text{ times}$$

Sometimes, this ratio uses average receivables in the denominator.

$$\text{receivable days sales outstanding} = \frac{598,799}{1,849,802/360} = 116.5 \text{ days}$$

This ratio can also be calculated by using average receivables.

$$\text{inventory turnover} = \frac{1{,}163{,}998}{450{,}637} = 2.58 \text{ times} \qquad \text{(using cost of sales)}$$

$$\text{inventory turnover} = \frac{1{,}849{,}802}{450{,}637} = 4.10 \text{ times} \qquad \text{(using sales)}$$

Average inventory can be used in the denominators.

$$\text{net fixed-asset turnover} = \frac{1{,}849{,}802}{100{,}984} = 18.32 \text{ times}$$

Average net fixed assets could be used in the denominator.

Leverage

$$\left.\begin{array}{l} \text{total debt-equity} = \dfrac{929{,}245}{323{,}738} = 2.87 \\[1.2em] \begin{array}{l}\text{long-term and}\\ \text{indeterminant} = \dfrac{372{,}238}{323{,}738} = 1.15 \\ \text{debt-equity}\end{array} \end{array}\right\}$$ Other debt-equity ratio calculations lie between these extremes

$$\left.\begin{array}{l} \text{total debt-capital} = \dfrac{929{,}245}{1{,}252{,}983} = 0.74 \\[1.2em] \begin{array}{l}\text{long-term and}\\ \text{indeterminate} = \dfrac{372{,}238}{1{,}252{,}983} = 0.30 \\ \text{debt-capital}\end{array} \end{array}\right\}$$ Other calculations lie between these extremes

fixed-charge coverage

$$= \frac{4565 + 51{,}047 + 105{,}367}{51{,}047 + 105{,}367 + \dfrac{293 + 20{,}829}{1 - 0.172}} = 1.13 \text{ times}$$

The numerator is earnings before tax adjusted to eliminate the effect of interest and lease expenses. The denominator is interest ($51,047) and lease payments ($105,367) plus after-tax dividend payments for preferred stock ($293) and common stock ($20,829) adjusted to the cash required before taxes.

$$\text{simple interest coverage} = \frac{55{,}612}{51{,}047} = 1.09 \text{ times}$$

$$\text{degree of financial leverage} = \frac{55{,}612}{55{,}612 - 51{,}047 - \dfrac{293}{1 - 0.172}}$$

$$= 13.21$$

$$\text{book value per share} = \frac{316{,}273}{14{,}879} = \$21.26$$

$$\text{cash flow per share} = \frac{8429 + 13{,}579}{14{,}879} = \$1.48$$

Profitability

$$\text{return on assets} = \frac{48{,}579}{1{,}849{,}802} \times \frac{1{,}849{,}802}{1{,}203{,}670} = 0.040$$

This calculation is based on net profit from operations before taxes and operating assets (i.e., total assets less miscellaneous assets and other assets), rather than as defined in the chapter. The reason for using this calculation basis is that significant nonoperating income/expense exists. Sometimes, current liabilities are subtracted from the operating assets.

$$\text{return on assets} = \frac{[8429 + 51{,}047(1 - 0.172)]}{1{,}849{,}802} \times \frac{1{,}849{,}802}{1{,}203{,}670}$$
$$= 0.042$$

This calculation adjusts net income after taxes for interest expense (i.e., it excludes the interest charge). Sometimes, total assets are used, and current liabilities may be subtracted from these assets.

$$\text{breakeven sales} = \frac{581{,}982}{0.3833} = \$1{,}518{,}346$$

Sometimes, depreciation and amortization and interest payments are excluded from fixed costs for this calculation.

$$\text{margin of safety} = \frac{1{,}849{,}802}{1{,}518{,}346} - 1 = 0.2183$$

$$\text{return on equity} = \frac{8136}{1{,}849{,}802} \times \frac{1{,}849{,}802}{1{,}252{,}983} \times \frac{1{,}252{,}983}{316{,}273} = 0.026$$

The \$8136 amount is net income less preferred dividends, that is, earnings available to common. Sometimes, current liabilities are subtracted from total assets.

Questions

1.   What is the significance of earnings quality to liquidity management? How can low-quality earnings be detected?

2.   What does *riding the depreciation curve down* mean?

3.   "The significance of financial statement data is not in the amount alone." Discuss the meaning of this statement.

4.   Of what significance is the current ratio? If this ratio is too low, what may it signify? Can this ratio be too high? Explain.

5.   What are some limitations of ratio analysis?

6.   Comparative balance sheets and comparative income statements that show a firm's financial history for each of the past 10 years may be misleading. Discuss the factors or conditions that might contribute to misinterpretations. Include a discussion of the additional information and supplementary data that might be included in or provided with the statements to prevent misinterpretations.

7.   The controller of your company has requested you to include in your report certain balance sheet and income statement ratios so that comparisons may be made. Indicate the types or categories of ratios that might be provided, and explain their significance.

8.   The financial statements of a firm are prepared at discrete intervals. Some financial theorists have suggested that a more appropriate period for reporting on a particular project is the life of the project itself. Evaluate the merits and difficulties of this approach.

9.   Why should a firm strive to hold liquid balances, since it can earn a profit by drawing down its liquid balances and investing the funds that it frees?

10.   Might there be a decrease in the amount of net working capital and at the same time an increase in the current ratio? Explain.

11.   On December 31, 1983, the book value per share of the common stock of the Eastern Company was $25. At the same time the price of the shares on the market was quoted at $38. What reasons might there be for this difference? If the market price was $18, what reasons might explain the difference?

12.   What are the benefits and shortcomings of industry analysis?

13.   Is the defensive-interval measure any better than either the current ratio or the quick ratio? Explain.

14.   What is the benefit of the EPS – EBIT analysis to liquidity management? Is breakeven analysis any better or worse? Explain.

Problems

The problems that follow use the financial data shown in Tables 3.4 and 3.5.

TABLE 3.4
Homeland Variety Corporation
Income Statements
For the Years 1983 – 1985
($000)

	1985	1984	1983
Sales	$400	$302	$285
Cost of sales	170	121	108
Gross margin	$230	$181	$177
Expenses:			
Selling and administrative	120	93	82
Rent	20	20	20
Utilities	10	10	10
Earnings before interest and taxes	$ 80	$ 58	$ 65
Interest	18	15	14
Profit before taxes	$ 62	$ 43	$ 51
Taxes	19	13	15
Net income	$ 43	$ 30	36

1. Calculate the liquidity, activity, leverage, and profitability ratios for the years 1983 through 1985.

2. Evaluate the financial performance of the company over the 1983 – 1985 period. Pay particular attention to interpretation of these ratios and overall management of liquidity.

3. From your ratio analysis and financial evaluation in Problems 1 and 2, project Homeland Variety Corporation's financial statements for 1986.

4. Using the industry ratios that follow, project the financial statements for Homeland Variety Corporation for 1986. Use the common stock and paid-in capital of 1985 and estimate the retained earnings for 1986 in order to determine the equity amount for 1986.

Total debt-equity ratio	0.75
Current debt-equity ratio	0.43
Current ratio	1.96
Return-on-equity ratio	12.5%

Return-on-sales ratio   7.0%
Gross margin   58.0%
Days sales outstanding   82 days
Inventory turnover   6.0 based on sales
Fixed-assets/equity   0.91

TABLE 3.5
Homeland Variety Corporation
Balance Sheet
For the Years Ending December 31, 1983 – 1985
($000)

	1985	1984	1983
Assets			
Current assets:			
Cash	$ 10	$ 15	$ 20
Net accounts receivable	90	95	96
Inventory	80	68	60
Total	$180	$178	$176
Net plant and equipment	200	176	172
Total assets	$380	$354	$348
Liabilities and capital			
Current liabilities:			
Accounts payable	$ 45	$ 48	$ 54
Notes payable	75	60	62
Total	$120	$108	$116
Long-term debt	60	50	40
Common stock ($1 par)	40	40	40
Paid-in capital	125	125	125
Retained earnings	35	31	27
Total liabilities and capital	$380	$354	$348

Note: Depreciation is $17, $18, and $20 for years 1983, 1984, and 1985, respectively. It is charged to cost of sales. Notes payable as of 1985 are a $20,000 demand note at 12.5% annual interest rate and a $55,000 line of credit at 13% annual interest rate. Long-term debt as of 1985 is as follows: $60,000 due in 1990 at 14% annual interest rate. Dividends in 1985 are $0.975 per share.

CHAPTER 4 □
Off – Balance Sheet Financing and Financial Analysis

During the 1970s and into the 1980s inflation became a major concern of management. Investors' expectations and concerns regarding inflation were reflected by a substantially reduced interest in the stock market. This reduced interest led to greater difficulty for management to provide funds by selling new equity. Inflation also made it difficult for management to turn to the debt markets because of the undesirability of bonds as a means of raising capital during inflationary periods. This undesirability occurred because the debt portion of the firm's capital structure kept increasing with inflation whenever new debt financing was undertaken while equity remained measured on a historical cost basis. The result was a deterioration in the quality of the firm's debt-to-equity ratio.

In an effort to find a method to keep its capitalization from appearing debt-heavy and unfavorably affecting the balance sheet and liquidity analysis, management sometimes resorted to *off – balance sheet financing*. Off – balance sheet financing is the means by which companies finance the acquisition of assets without presenting the assets and related obligations on the balance sheet. As a result of the exclusion of many liabilities, a balance sheet may not reflect the reality of a firm's financial position and obligations. Therefore potential creditors, financial analysts, and investors all have vested interests in understanding the nature of off – balance sheet financing. Once they understand the type of items that may be excluded from the balance sheet, they are better prepared to make the adjustments needed to arrive at the true economic position of the corporation. An analyst who carefully examines the 10-K and annual reports can usually discover most of the hidden liabilities.

The focus of this chapter is on common types of off – balance sheet financing and on what an analyst can do to overcome distortions caused by balance sheet exclusions. Thus this chapter, in a very particular way, continues the discussion of the previous chapter about the shortcomings of ratio analysis. The emphasis is not on the ratios themselves but, rather, on the discovery of amounts excluded from the analysis. Particular emphasis is placed on off – balance sheet liabilities since they affect the future liquidity condition of the corporation.

Significance of Off – Balance Sheet Financing on Ratios

Obligations of a firm pose future cash outlay requirements that have significant effects on liquidity. If these economic liabilities are excluded from the balance sheet, the ratios are subject to further distortion. The exclusions may preclude the uncritical generation of ratios by computers that only have balance sheet data to use. Off – balance sheet financing gives even more importance to the skills and judgment of an analyst working with financial statements. Certainly, current accounting standards limit the reliance placed on liability ratios.

Table 4.1 provides a summary of why analysts must understand off – balance sheet financing. It shows how the conventional debt-to-capital ratio compares with adjusted ratios for General Motors and J. C. Penney. The adjusted ratio indicates that less unused debt capacity exists than a traditional approach might indicate.

The items included in the adjusted ratio are by no means all off – balance sheet adjustments. However, the table shows that by getting debt off the balance sheet, management improves the character, or quality, of the balance sheet.

The most common types of off – balance sheet financing consist of liabilities that fall into six basic categories: (1) unfunded pension liabilities, (2) leases, (3) sale of receivables, (4) unconsolidated subsidiary debt, (5) in-substance defeasance of debt, and (6) project financing with unconditional commitment arrangements. Each category is examined in the remainder of this chapter.

Unfunded Pension Liabilities

To clarify the off – balance sheet issue with respect to pensions, we must examine two cost concepts: past/prior service costs and current/normal service costs. Prior service costs refer to credit granted to employees for work performed prior to the inception of the pension plan or retroactive changes in a plan. Normal costs refer to pension costs incurred since the inception of the plan.

TABLE 4.1
Conventional and Adjusted Debt-Equity Ratios for 1977 ($ million)

	GM	J. C. Penney
From the balance sheet		
1. Long-term debt	$ 1,091.7	$ 415
2. Current deferred taxes	0	346
3. Long-term deferred taxes	104.6	111
4. Owner's equity	15,766.9	2,167
From notes to the statements		
5. Excess of FIFO value of ending inventory over reported LIFO value	697.3	122
6. Present value of noncapitalized financing leases	0	300
7. Present value of unrecognized pension cost	7,300.0	63
8. Long-term debt of unconsolidated subsidiaries	8,067.7	580
Conventional debt-capital ratio: $(1)/[(1) + (4)]$	6%	16%
Adjusted debt-capital ratio: $$\frac{(1) + (6) + (7) + (8)}{(1) + (2) + (3) + (4) + (5) + (6) + 0.48^*(7) + (8)}$$	56%	33%

Source: Adapted from D. A. Lasman and R. L. Weil, "Adjusting the Debt-Equity Ratio," *Financial Analysts Journal* (September – October 1978): 50.
* Assumes a 48% tax rate.

One should also know that the fund has separate legal and accounting identity for which a set of books is maintained and financial statements are prepared. Thus the *pension fund is not shown as an asset of the firm* on its financial statements.

Recognition of Pension Liabilities and Expenses

The past/prior and current/normal cost categories are important since each one affects funding differently. Accounting principles require all current costs to be recognized as expenses as they are incurred. Prior service costs expense for the year must satisfy some minimum and maximum limits computed according to an acceptable actuarial cost method that is applied consistently from year to year. The only portion of the prior service costs recognized in the financial statements is the portion expensed. However, note that expense recognition is not synonymous with pension funding.

The pension liability that frequently appears on company balance sheets represents an accounting credit that results from an excess of amounts

TABLE 4.2
Largest Unfunded Pension Liabilities in 1982
($ million)

	Deficit	As percent of net worth
General Motors	1915	10
Chrysler	901	91
Bethlehem Steel	830	67
LTV	203	18
Trans World	164	19
Caterpillar	151	4
Westinghouse	102	3
Armco	94	5
Alco	70	2
Allied Corporation	69	2

Source: Data from Standard & Poor's Compustat Services Inc.

expensed over amounts contributed to the pension fund. It does not represent the economic obligations under the plan and usually does not represent the amount legally owed to the pension fund, that is, the unfunded pension liability. For instance, the ordinary pension-related entries are handled first as a debit to pension expense and a credit to pension liability:

Debit   Pension expense $1,000,000
Credit   Pension liability $1,000,000

Then the liability is funded with a debit to pension liability and a credit to cash:

Debit   Pension liability $ 750,000
Credit   Cash $ 750,000

However, as shown, the actual funding need not be equal to the *pension expense* recognized in the period. This condition exists even though the corporation is in full compliance with Accounting Principles Board Opinion Number 8, called "Accounting for the Cost of Pension Plans." Table 4.2 summarizes the unfunded pension obligations of major corporations as of 1982.

Unfunded Pension Liabilities

Unfunded pension liabilities represent future demands upon the resources of the company and arise from cost-conscious management cutting funding and even eliminating contributions for several years in an effort to conserve cash. In 1983 about 60 percent of all major industrial companies cut their pension expenses an average of 3.5 percent.

The manner in which the assets making up the pension fund are valued has a direct effect on the value of the fund. Determination of an appropriate dollar value of the assets is important because it determines whether the firm can meet its pension-funding obligations.

Funding of the pension plan is sensitive to the interest rate assumptions used in determining actuarial present values of benefits. It is estimated that a 0.25 percent change in the interest rate assumption generally affects the annual pension cost by 6 percent. For instance, in 1970 Penn-Dixie Cement Corporation disclosed in a footnote that an increase in the actuarial assumption from 4 percent to 6 percent resulted in a decrease in pension expense for the year of approximately $665,000 and an increase in after-tax net income and cash flow of $338,000.

In the recessionary period of 1980 – 1982 about 90 New York Stock Exchange firms each year raised their assumed pension asset earnings rate. Such an exercise causes profit and cash flow for the year(s) to improve because of this change in assumption. The question remains: Did portfolio return really improve, or did management simply borrow from later periods? This issue is one of quality of earnings, which, as discussed in Chapter 3, has ramifications for determining funds flow.

Analysts must be alert to companies increasing the assumed rate earned on their pension assets. It is a device to increase earnings that successful companies do not need to use.

The unfunded pension liabilities can be determined from the footnotes to the corporation's financial statements. The Financial Accounting Standards Board (FASB) requires that the following information, if not disclosed in the body of the financial statements, should be disclosed in footnotes:

- □ A brief statement that a pension plan exists, identifying the employee groups covered.
- □ A brief statement of the company's accounting and funding policies.
- □ The provision for the pension cost for the period.
- □ The excess, if any, of vested benefits over the amount funded or accrued.
- □ The nature and effect of significant matters affecting comparability for all periods, such as changes in accounting methods, changes in circumstances, or significant amendments.

Effect of Full Funding on Debt Ratios

Proposed accounting rule changes could force companies to add billions of dollars of liabilities to show what will be owed to their employees when they retire. An example serves to show the impact of including unfunded pension liabilities on the balance sheet. For 1981 balance sheet data the debt-equity ratios for Republic Steel and Bethlehem Steel stand at 0.85

and 1.01, respectively. When unfunded pension adjustments are made, the ratios deteriorate to 1.48 and 1.96, respectively. The ratio of Bethlehem Steel looks almost twice as good from balance sheet data than it is in reality.

Critics of any changes to pension accounting suggest that incorporating unfunded liabilities into the balance sheet would be accompanied by adverse effects, such as the renegotiation of loan agreements, reduced credit ratings, and more costly debt. If this is truly the case, then bankers and analysts do not understand the firm's financial condition.

Regardless of whether or not fuller disclosure is required, if the solvency of the firm is in question, government regulations hold the company liable for either the unfunded vested amount or 30 percent of stockholders' equity, whichever is less. This limitation would seem to benefit most the highly leveraged firm whose equity base is small relative to its pension liabilities. A going-concern firm will be responsible for the entire liability.

Circumventing Disclosure

If changes are to be made in pension disclosure, a proposal advanced by FASB would likely be the one adopted. This proposal provides management an opportunity to avoid reporting unfunded pension obligations as a liability. The proposal suggests that *defined-contribution plans need not be reported on the balance sheet.* Thus management could simply replace defined-benefit pension plans with defined-contribution plans.

In a *defined-benefit plan* the employer's cash contributions and pension expense are adjusted in relation to actuarial experience in the eligible employee groups and the investment performance of the pension fund. A *defined-contribution plan* is based on formula or discretion; the employer makes cash contributions to eligible individual employee accounts under the terms of a written plan. Further benefits of defined-contribution plans are that they shift risk from the firm to the employee, and they enable management to have better control over cash flows consumed by the pension plan.

Leasing

From the viewpoint of the lessee a lease offers certain advantages over purchase of the asset. For instance, the lessee may not have sufficient resources or credit to purchase the asset but can lease it. If the firm has low profitability, it might not be able to take advantage of the tax benefits of an investment tax credit and accelerated depreciation associated with owning the asset. A lessor can take advantage of the tax implications and pass some of the savings along to the lessee by lowering the lease payments.

The conventional reasons for leasing are as follows:

□ Leases give firms with limited capital budgets alternative sources of obtaining resources.

□ The period of a lease for equipment is often longer than the repayment period allowed by conventional financing.

□ Leases are frequently tailored to meet the cash budget needs of the lessee.

□ Leasing *may be perceived* as not affecting debt capacity of the company, primarily because of accounting conventions in use today (to be discussed later).

□ The entire lease payment is tax deductible.

□ Leasing avoids underwriting and flotation costs associated with new issues of capital.

The major disadvantage of leasing, as perceived by managers, is that the net present value cost of leasing generally exceeds the net present value of purchasing, since the lessor must earn a profit. Given all the advantages just listed, though, this may be a small price to pay.

The debate among accounting and finance professionals through the mid 1970s concerned a firm's ability to lease (which in fact meant "to acquire") an asset without the initial necessity of substantial cash outlays and without the need to increase the firm's indebtedness on the balance sheet. In reality, a long-term lease gives the firm the benefit of an asset's productive capacity. The firm has all the control benefits of ownership. The corporation also assumes the liability burdens of making payments for the asset over the term of the lease. Especially under long-term leases, the economic effect of the lease is the same as a purchase of an asset on an installment basis. In effect, the lessor is financing the asset for the firm. The lease imposes significant debt and cash outflow requirements on the lessee.

Financial Reporting Requirements

In December 1976 the FASB attempted to remedy the exclusion of leasing liabilities from the balance sheet by issuing FASB Statement No. 13 on lease financing. In summary, it says that if at the date of the lease agreement the lessee is party to a noncancelable lease that meets one or more of the following four criteria, the lessee shall classify and account for the arrangement as a *capital lease*.

1. The lease *transfers ownership* of the property to the lessee by the end of the lease.

2. The lease has a *bargain purchase option*.

3. The *lease term* is equal to 75 percent or more of the estimated economic life of the leased property.

4. The *present value* of the lease payments at the beginning of the lease is equal to or greater than 90 percent of the leased property's original cost.

If a lease does not meet any of these requirements, it is classified as an *operating lease*.

Under the operating lease method the lease is simply treated as an expense. The leased asset does not appear within the body of the balance sheet, but the lessee discloses the minimum future rental payments, in total and for each of the next five years.

Capitalizing the Lease

Under the capital lease method the lessee treats the lease transaction as if an asset were being purchased on time, that is, as a financing transaction in which an asset is acquired and an obligation is created. The lessee records a capital lease as an asset and as a liability at the lower of the following two values:

1. The present value of the minimum lease payments during the lease term.

2. The fair market value of the leased asset at the inception of the lease.

Accounting rules require capitalized leases to be shown on the lessee's income statement. Both depreciation and the interest expense *implicit* in the lease payments are deductions from income. The criterion that causes the lease to be capitalized determines the depreciation method. If a bargain purchase option exists or if the lease transfers ownership, then the firm's normal depreciation policies apply. However, if neither of these criteria are satisfied, but if the lease term is equal to or greater than 75 percent of the leased asset's economic life, or if the present value of the lease payments is equal to or greater than 90 percent of the leased asset's original cost, then the asset is amortized over the life of the lease contract.

ILLUSTRATION 4.1

The terms of a noncancelable lease require payments of $103,762 at the beginning of each year for 5 years. The equipment has a fair value at the inception of the lease of $450,000, an economic life of 5 years, and no residual value. The lessee's borrowing rate is 15% per year. The amount to be capitalized as a leased asset is computed as follows:

$103,762 × (present value of an annuity due for 5 periods
                                    at 15%; see the Appendix)
   = $103,762 × 3.85498 = $400,000

Thus reported assets and liabilities increase $400,000. Annual depreciation expense is $80,000 (assuming straight-line depreciation), and interest is based on an amortization schedule with the first period's expense being $60,000 (i.e., 15% × $400,000). Total charges against pretax income are $140,000. If this lease could be recorded as an operating lease, only $103,762 would be charged to operations.

Thus in management's quest for higher, short-term reported profits, it generally prefers to record leases as operating leases. Because of the "debt" amortization, later periods will result in higher profits for the capitalized lease whenever the imputed interest plus depreciation become less than the operating lease payment.   □

Circumventing Disclosure

Management would rather report leases as operating leases because they are not included on the balance sheet and imputed depreciation and interest expenses can be excluded from the income statement. Apparently, management feels that debt capacity is somehow not impaired if leases are omitted from the balance sheet. Implicit in this statement is the idea that the capital markets can be fooled if leases are not shown as liabilities. Indeed, a study by Abdel-Khalik and colleagues[1] found that credit analysts penalize a firm's debt capacity if it capitalizes leases.

Another reason for attempting to structure leases as operating leases is that management feels that return on equity will be impaired by structuring leases as capital leases. This impairment happens because of depreciation and capitalization requirements of FASB, as shown in Illustration 4.1.

ILLUSTRATION 4.2

The information of Illustration 4.1 is used here to show how management can cause a capital lease to become an operating lease. Equipment with an economic life of 5 years is leased for a period of 3 years and 8 months, which means that requirement 3 is not met. The present value of lease payments can be as much as (90% × $450,000) − $1, which is just below the threshold of requirement 4. The only other requirements are to write

---

[1] A. Abdel-Khalik, R. Thompson, and R. Taylor, "The Impact of Reporting Leases off the Balance Sheet on Bond Risk Premiums: Two Exploratory Studies," Accounting Research Center Working Paper No. 78–2, University of Florida, 1978.

the lease contract so that ownership is not transferred to the lessee by the end of the lease (which satisfies requirement 1) and to ensure that the lease does not have a bargain purchase option (which satisfies requirement 2). These actions result in off – balance sheet financing since the lease does not have to be capitalized.   □

Liquidity Analysis

For purposes of liability analysis all leases should be included in the data that is used to assess liquidity. However, a problem exists in dealing with leases that are not capitalized on the balance sheet. Capital leases are disclosed on the balance sheet at their present value. Operating and capital leases disclosed in the footnotes to the financial statements are at an aggregate value of future payments for each. The year-by-year minimums are shown for five years, and then the remainder is shown as one sum. None of these figures are discounted. Usually, not enough information to present-value the operating leases is given.

A rough approximation technique for calculating the present value of operating leases is shown in Table 4.3. Using this technique, an analyst can get an estimate of the present value of the operating leases so that this figure can be added to the present value of the capital leases (already shown on the balance sheet). Otherwise, the analyst would be adding unlike quantities. The key to the technique is to make the same proportional reduction in the operating leases as is made in the present value of the capitalized leases (as seen by comparing footnote and balance sheet data for the capitalized leases).

The significance of adjusting the liabilities by capitalizing all leases is for ratio and funds flow analysis. The all-inclusive lease capitalization

TABLE 4.3
Estimating the Present Value of Operating Leases

	Capital	Operating
Total minimum lease payments	$518,810*	$634,000†
Present value of minimum lease payments	$400,000	$488,811

Present value of operating leases, developed by applying the following formula:

$$\frac{\text{present value of capital leases}}{\text{total minimum capital lease payments}} \times \text{total minimum operating lease payments}$$

$$\frac{\$400,000}{\$518,810} \times \$634,000 = \$488,811$$

* From Illustration 4.2: $103,762 × 5.
† An assumed number.

method (i.e., capitalizing both financial and operating leases) enhances the comparability of different firms and industries. It also promotes a more accurate picture of the reliance the firm places on debt versus equity.

The importance of being able to keep leases off the balance sheet is that numerous studies have revealed that accounting income figures and ratios are used extensively to evaluate risk. Bond-rating studies show accounting ratios to be highly informative for determining bond risk. Similarly, bankruptcy studies show the predictive behavior of ratios in determining bankruptcy. Thus management's concern about keeping debt off the balance sheet may be legitimate.

Table 4.4 summarizes the effect of the omission of lease obligations

TABLE 4.4
Effect of Leasing on Ratios

	Alternatives	
	Borrowing	Leasing
Balance sheet		
Current assets	$ 2,000	$ 2,000
Net fixed assets	5,000	3,600
Total assets	$ 7,000	$ 5,600
Current liabilities	$ 1,500	$ 1,500
Long-term debt	3,000	1,600
Total debt	$ 4,500	$ 3,100
Equity	2,500	2,500
Total liabilities and equity	$ 7,000	$ 5,600
Income statement		
Sales	$10,000	$10,000
Income before depreciation, interest, and lease payments	$ 3,000	$ 3,000
Depreciation	<1,000>	<800>
Interest on debt (15%)	<450>	<240>
Lease expense	0	<190>
Income before taxes	$ 1,550	$ 1,770
Taxes (40%)	620	708
Income after taxes	$ 930	$ 1,062
Ratios		
Asset turnover (times)	1.4	1.8
Return on assets	13.3%	19.0%
Debt to equity	1.8	1.2
Times interest coverage (before depreciation)	6.7	12.5

Note: This example assumes that management is able to circumvent having to capitalize the lease.

on the financial statements and ratio analysis. The ability to keep the lease off the balance sheet results in significant improvement in ratios. Both profitability and asset management appear to be better, and financial leverage is less. This improvement is an illusion, though, since the lease payments represent a contractual obligation. Note, however, that this obligation is less burdensome on the firm in times of bankruptcy or reorganization than is debt. Although the lessor retains ownership of the asset in bankruptcy, it has a claim on only one year's lease payments. If the firm is in reorganization, the lessor has a claim on three years' lease payments. Further, in cases where the solvency of the firm is called into question, the operating leases are subordinate to the capital leases in their claim status.

Sale of Accounts Receivable with Recourse

When a company sells its receivables, and the buying company retains the right to hold the selling company responsible for paying accounts receivable that turn out to be bad debts, then that sale is *with recourse*. The accounting profession takes the position that the sale of receivables with recourse is, in substance, a financing transaction. The cost of financing should be accounted for as an interest cost over the life of the receivables and a contingent liability should be reported in the balance sheet.

To circumvent the accounting requirements, management will pay the purchasing company a premium so that the transaction is structured to appear as if it were without recourse — and hence does not have to be reported on the balance sheet. The agreement is also written so that the selling company retains physical control of the assigned accounts, collects amounts remitted by customers, and then forwards the proceeds to the company that purchased the receivables.

As the company makes collections and turns them over to the lender, it is really paying off an "unrecorded" note payable. But since the transaction was initially structured as a sale of receivables, with no new debt obligation recorded, management can use the proceeds from the sale to pay existing liabilities. The effect is that some receivables and some recorded liabilities are eliminated from the balance sheet and the new obligation goes unrecorded.

The result of this transaction is to lower leverage and improve the current ratio, assuming it is greater than 1:1 to start with. Thus the company is able to generate cash without having to report the corresponding liability. The debt-equity ratio remains the same at the time of the sale but quickly improves if existing debt is paid off. Liquidity appears improved, but in reality, it is not. The company must pay any moneys collected for the sold receivables to the lender. No accounting transaction is recorded for the collection of accounts by the seller of the receivables since it is merely acting as an intermediary for the buyer. However, if recourse is exercised, then the selling firm will have to make some sort of restitution to the buyer and record an entry on the ledger.

ILLUSTRATION 4.3

Assume that a company sells receivables on a recourse basis to a bank for $76,000, face value $80,000. The following accounting entry might be recorded:

Debit	Cash	$76,000	
Debit	Deferred finance expense	4,000	
Credit	Accounts receivable		$80,000

The deferred financing expense would then be amortized at a constant rate on the declining balance of the company's obligation to repay on these receivables.

The following simplified balance sheets illustrate the significance of treating the sale as one without recourse. It assumes that funds from the sale of receivables are used to pay off existing debt. In actuality, *management is using the receivables as collateral for a loan* (to be discussed in Chapter 17), but it wants to give the impression that a sale of receivables has occurred and not a new debt obligation.

1. Before the Sale

Balance Sheet

Receivables	$ 80,000	Debt	$100,000
Other assets	200,000	Equity	180,000

Debt/equity ratio = 0.56:1

2. At the Time Receivables Are Sold

Debit	Cash	$76,000	
Debit	Loss on sale	4,000	
Credit	Accounts receivable		$80,000

Balance Sheet Reported

Cash	$ 76,000	Debt	$100,000
Other assets	200,000	Equity	176,000

Debt/equity ratio = 0.57:1

3. They Should Report

Debit   Cash $76,000
Debit   Unamortized debt
              discount   4,000
Credit   Debt $80,000

Balance Sheet That Should Be Reported

Cash	$ 76,000	Debt	$180,000
Receivables	80,000	Unamortized discount	<4,000>
Other assets	200,000	Equity	180,000

Debt/equity ratio = 0.98:1

4. Disbursement of Funds from Sale

Balance Sheet Reported

| Other assets | $200,000 | Debt | $ 24,000 |
| | | Equity | 176,000 |

Debt/equity ratio = 0.14:1

Balance Sheet That Should Be Reported

Receivables	$ 80,000	Debt	$104,000
Other assets	200,000	Unamortized discount	<4,000>
		Equity	180,000

Debt/equity ratio = 0.56:1

The improved leverage ratios show why management is willing to pursue this tactic if it thinks it can deceive readers of its financial status. Management is able to significantly increase the firm's *apparent* debt capacity and present the firm as a relatively low-risk firm as measured by the debt/equity ratio.   □

Debt of Unconsolidated Subsidiaries

Debt of unconsolidated subsidiaries is a substantial source of off – balance sheet financing. According to current accounting requirements, a corporation that owns over 50 percent of another company reports its financial statements on a consolidated basis. The exceptions to this rule are finance, insurance, or leasing subsidiaries of companies in an unrelated line of business. Many of these subsidiaries are 100 percent owned by the parent corporation. The parent corporation accounts for these unconsolidated subsidiaries by the *equity method of accounting*.

Under the equity method a substantive economic relationship is acknowledged between the parent company and the subsidiary company. The investment is originally recorded as an asset at the cost of the shares acquired but is subsequently adjusted each period for changes in the net assets of the investee. That is, the investment (asset) carrying amount is periodically increased or decreased by the parent's proportionate share of the profit or loss of the subsidiary and decreased by all dividends received by the parent from the subsidiary:

initial investment (at cost) + proportioned share of subsidiary's profit or
   − proportioned share of subsidiary's loss
   − dividends received from subsidiary
= investment in subsidiary

With the equity method *none of the liabilities of the subsidiary are shown on the parent company's balance sheet.*

   Given the diversified nature of many businesses today, the accounting profession's rationale for excluding the subsidiary's debt from the parent company's financial statements is misguided. From an economic perspective, when an investor buys the stock of the parent, the market value reflects the performance and the financial condition of the entire economic entity controlled by the company.

   By setting up a financial subsidiary and transferring assets and liabilities to the subsidiary, the parent company can considerably improve the appearance of its balance sheet and the presentation of its financial ratios. Yet in most cases the parent company guarantees the obligations of its subsidiary, so its real liabilities are not decreased.

   The parent company may also, in effect, raise additional financing. A financial subsidiary is usually highly leveraged. It may issue new debt at a reasonable rate because the parent company backs the subsidiary's liabilities. The subsidiary may in turn buy the receivables of the parent company. The economic substance of the transaction is that the parent corporation has raised cash through its subsidiary but has not changed its own liabilities on the balance sheet. Many variations in the use of subsidiaries to raise funds are possible.

   Adjustment of the balance sheet data of the parent corporation to reflect the substance of its obligations is relatively easy. So that the same results are obtained as with full consolidation of the financial subsidiary, the assets and the liabilities of a subsidiary company, after elimination of intercompany profits, are included on a line-by-line basis in consolidated financial statement balances. Any minority interest in the subsidiary company appears on the liability side of the consolidated balance sheet.

ILLUSTRATION 4.4

Assume that the parent corporation is constrained by its lenders to not have its debt/equity ratio exceed 1:1. In an effort to circumvent the constraint, management creates a wholly owned finance subsidiary that does not get consolidated with the rest of the corporation. The primary purpose of the subsidiary is to buy the parent's receivables. It does so by raising debt and pledging the receivables as collateral. In addition, the parent corporation stands ready to satisfy the subsidiary's obligations if necessary. The following balance sheets illustrate the procedure.

1. Before the Sale of Receivables

Consolidated Balance Sheet of Parent

Receivables	$2000	Debt	$5500
Investment in subsidiary	1000	Equity	5500
Other assets	8000		

Debt/equity ratio = 1:1

Balance Sheet of Unconsolidated Subsidiary

Cash	$1000	Equity	$1000

Debt/equity ratio = 0:1

2. Parent Sells Receivables to Subsidiary

Consolidated Balance Sheet of Parent

Cash	$2000	Debt	$5500
Investment in subsidiary	1000	Equity	5500
Other assets	8000		

Debt/equity ratio = 1:1

Balance Sheet of Unconsolidated Subsidiary

Cash	$1000	Debt	$2000
Receivables	2000	Equity	1000

Debt/equity ratio = 2:1

3. Combined Balance Sheet After the Sale

"Consolidated" Balance Sheet

Cash	$3000	Debt	$7500
Receivables	2000	Equity	5500
Other assets	8000		

Debt/equity ratio = 1.36:1
(which exceeds the debt
limit imposed by the bank)

Management has been able to raise additional debt capital without violating the debt covenant. This example points to an inefficiency in the capital markets.[2]   □

In-Substance Defeasance of Debt

In November 1983 the Financial Accounting Standards Board (FASB) decided to permit companies to consider their fixed-rate, known maturity debt to be extinguished for financial reporting purposes when the debtors enter into an *in-substance defeasance of debt transaction*. This can be an attractive way for companies with low coupon debt outstanding to boost earnings and improve the debt-to-equity ratio. Indeed, Standard & Poor disregards any debt issue defeased, and its related interest and escrowed assets, when computing financial ratios for debt-rating purposes.

The following types of debt are not eligible for defeasance:

- □ Debt with a floating interest rate.
- □ Debt that is payable on demand.
- □ Convertible debentures.
- □ Any kind of debt that does not permit advance determination of future debt service requirements.
- □ Issuance of new debt and its concurrent extinguishment through an in-substance defeasance.

Arguments in favor of in-substance defeasance are that the reported gain may exceed the amount of any future gain that could be obtained if the debt were retired at a later date when different interest rates might be in effect. If creditors and investors are not aware of the situation, the removal of the debt may be perceived as a favorable development by creditors and investors.

How It Works

The debtor irrevocably segregates assets with a third party (i.e., establishes an irrevocable trust) who invests them in direct obligations of the U.S. government, U.S. government–guaranteed obligations, or securities backed by U.S. government obligations as collateral under which the interest and principal payments on the collateral generally flow immediately to the holder of the security. The Federal National Mortgage Assocation (Fannie Mae) and other government agencies are not adequate since they are not direct or guaranteed obligations of the U.S. government.

---

[2] V. L. Andrews discusses the market inefficiencies in "Captive Finance Companies," *Harvard Business Review* (July – August 1964): 80 – 92.

This investment, and the interest on it, is then used to satisfy scheduled payments of principal and interest on the outstanding debt. The outstanding debt has a lower coupon yield than the segregated assets, so less funds must be set aside to satisfy the outstanding lower coupon debt obligation than would be required if management just retired the debt. If the debtor is virtually assured that no further funds will need to be transferred to the third party, the debtor can account for the transaction as an extinguishment of the outstanding debt. The debtor can then take any difference between the face value of the outstanding debt and the funds set aside as a gain, to be reported in the income statement. Defeased debt must be disclosed through a description of the transaction as long as the debt is outstanding.

Two restrictions apply. First, the timing of cash flows from the securities placed in trust must approximately coincide with the scheduled payments of debt principal and interest. Second, the probability that a company will be required to make any future payments on the debt must be remote.

ILLUSTRATION 4.5

Assume that a company has $10,000,000 of debt outstanding, at book value, which has a fixed coupon rate of 5% and 10 years until maturity. Interest is paid annually. Management decides to segregate assets to defease this debt. It can earn 10% by investing in government securities. Therefore

TABLE 4.5
In-Substance Debt Defeasance

Year	Value of segregated funds at the beginning of the year	Annual payments to debtholders	Value of segregated assets at the end of the year before 10% interest is earned
0	$ 6,927,680		
1	7,620,450	$ 500,000	$7,120,450
2	7,832,490	500,000	7,332,490
3	8,065,740	500,000	7,565,740
4	8,322,320	500,000	7,822,320
5	8,604,550	500,000	8,104,550
6	8,915,000	500,000	8,415,000
7	9,256,500	500,000	8,756,500
8	9,632,150	500,000	9,132,150
9	10,045,370	500,000	9,545,370
10	10,500,000	10,500,000	0

Note: Beginning balances are grossed up to include the interest earned. For example, the balance starting in year 5 is $7,822,320 × 1.1 = $8,604,550.

it must segregate $6,927,680 of government securities in order to retire annual interest payments of $500,000 and the principal repayment in year 10 of $10,000,000:

segregated amount = $500,000(PVIFA 10%, 10)
+ $10,000,000(PVIF 10%, 10)
= $500,000(6.14457) + $10,000,000(0.38554)
= $6,927,680

where (PVIFA 10%, 10) is the present value interest factor of an annuity at 10% for 10 years, and (PVIF 10%, 10) is the present value interest factor at 10% in year 10 (see the Appendix).

Table 4.5 summarizes the annual transactions and confirms that $6,927,680 is needed to retire the $10,000,000 worth of bonds. The difference of $3,072,320 becomes an extraordinary pretax gain to the company in the year the funds are set aside.   □

The effect of defeasance on the company's capital structure can be shown by extending Illustration 4.5.

ILLUSTRATION 4.6

Assume the company has net income of $5,000,000 before defeasance and a tax rate of 40%. The after-tax gain from defeasance is $1,843,390.

1. Before In-Substance Debt Defeasance

Balance Sheet ($000)

Cash	$10,000	Debt	$20,000
Other assets	40,000	Equity	30,000

Debt/equity ratio = 0.67:1
ROE ratio = 0.17

2. After Debt Is Defeased

Balance Sheet ($000)

Cash*	$ 3,072.32	Debt	$10,000.00
Other assets	40,000.00	Deferred taxes	
		on gain	1,228.93
		Equity	31,843.39

Debt/equity ratio = 0.35:1
ROE ratio = 0.21

* Opening balance ($10,000) less amount segregated with a trustee ($6,927.68).

The firm has given up present liquidity to enhance profitability and lower perceived financial risk as measured by the debt-equity ratio. If the deferred taxes payable on the capital gain are eliminated from the leverage calculation, financial risk appears even lower.   □

Pros and Cons

In-substance debt defeasance transactions have both advantages and disadvantages to the corporation over the more traditional ways of retiring debt before maturity.

Advantages

1. The use of defeasance circumvents dealing with individual bond-holders. It avoids paying redemption premiums, and the debt can be effectively retired without driving its price up through open-market, buy-back transactions.

2. Debt defeasance transactions can be attractive to the debtholders. Since the debt is now backed by government securities, rather than the general credit of the issuer company, its quality and price may rise. The establishment of an irrevocable trust may improve the debt rating of the extinguished debt issue since future payments are guaranteed.

3. Debt defeasance results in lower debt-equity and interest coverage ratios in future periods.

4. A current gain can result for accounting purposes, which, if material, may be classified as an extraordinary item in the income statement.

5. Any gain recognized ordinarily does not result in a current tax liability. Since the company is still legally obligated for the debt, no gain is recognized for tax purposes at the time of the transaction. At maturity a capital gain tax will be due on the government securities since they were bought at a discount.

Disadvantages

1. The company is not legally released from being the primary obligor under the debt instrument (e.g., collateral is not released and debt covenants generally still apply).

2. The trust arrangement must be irrevocable. Management does not have access to future trust assets if it needs additional funds.

3. Yields on U.S. government securities typically are less than the returns available on other investments by the firm. Consequently, such investments cost more in relative terms.

4. In some cases the interest costs associated with financing the purchase of government securities may exceed the interest costs of the debt being extinguished.

5. Any income from the irrevocable trust, because there is not a perfect match between the cash flows of the government securities and the debt being defeased, may flow back to the company and be recorded as income from a nonexistent asset. Accounting principles do not allow such income on the company's financial statements. This problem can be avoided by using zero-coupon treasury bonds.

One can argue that in-substance defeasance of debt is a questionable practice on two counts, since liquidity analysis can be distorted.

First, defeasance amounts to balance sheet manipulation (as shown in Illustration 4.6) and a poor use of corporate cash, particularly for the shareholders. Since securities are placed in an irrevocable trust, management gives up current liquidity and is forced to forgo potentially higher yields available on other (riskier) investments that could be disposed of more readily. Debtholders, however, gain a reduction in risk (because the debt is defeased) without a loss in yield.

Second, in-substance debt defeasance may also be an indication that management is struggling to keep its earnings up. In this case the quality of earnings is suspect, which means that cash flow (i.e., liquidity) analysis requires careful study.

Unconditional Commitment Arrangements and Product and Project Financing

Unconditional Agreements

Unconditional commitment arrangements, as a method of off – balance sheet financing, relate mostly to capital-intensive industries such as mining and public utilities. One form is the *take-or-pay contract,* which is an agreement between a buyer and a seller for the buyer to pay specified amounts periodically for products even if the buyer does not take delivery. Another form is the *throughput contract,* which is similar to the take-or-pay contract except that it represents contracts to acquire services rather than goods and requires payment whether or not the service is rendered.

There are many ways a take-or-pay arrangement can be structured. For instance, U.S. Steel financed a $690 million seamless steel plant this way. U.S. Steel proposed to build a seamless-pipe plant since seamless pipe was in great demand by the oil companies. The oil companies, as customers, signed take-or-pay contracts with U.S. Steel. These contracts provided more-than-necessary cash flow to service the financing needed to pay for the plant. U.S. Steel then found an investing group that was willing to accept the purchase agreements as credit support (i.e., acts as a form of collateral) to fund the plant. The plant operates under a sale-leaseback arrangement (which is discussed in Chapter 17) between U.S. Steel and the investment group. The result was that U.S. Steel raised $690 million to build a steel plant. It furnished none of the financing, so its liabilities did not increase on the balance sheet and liquidity was not impaired.

If the lease agreement is structured so that it does not meet any one of the four criteria for treatment as a capital lease, as discussed earlier, the lease can be recorded as an operating lease.

Product Financing

With *product financing* one company sells an asset to another because it needs earnings and as a result improves its liquidity. What is not shown on the books is that the seller made a deal to buy back that asset at some point in the future, that deal being a liability of the firm. So earnings are improved and debt has been kept off the balance sheet. The transaction is treated as a sale rather than as a loan, and no recognition is made in the accounts of the agreement to purchase. Neither the loan nor the promise to buy back is reported in the balance sheet of the borrower.

The Securities and Exchange Commission issued a statement in late 1978 stating that sale of a product with an agreement to repurchase should be recognized as a loan and not as a sale. But frequently, the agreement to buy back the asset is hidden in legal contracts, and off – balance sheet financing prevails.

Project Financing

In *project financing* the project is usually created as a joint venture, which is usually considered a separate legal entity with no one firm owning more than 50 percent of the project (company). The equity accounting method is used, with the result that each company reports only its share of the investment (which incorporates the earnings of the venture) and none of the debt. In other words, consolidated statements are not required. The project is thinly capitalized and highly leveraged, generally with the debt guaranteed by the venturers. Also, no disclosure of the debt guarantee is made on the venturers' balance sheets.

An important benefit of this method of financing is that greater lever-age can be achieved for projects employing these concepts than would be permissible if the projects were carried on the balance sheets of their equity sponsors. Debt leverage of up to 90 percent is not uncommon, depending on the creditworthiness of the backers.

When companies contribute noncash assets to the joint venture, they frequently transfer the assets at a fair market value and recognize the difference between historical cost and fair market value as either a profit (loss) or a deferred profit. If a very close economic relationship exists between the company and the joint venture, the appropriateness of recognizing a gain or loss seems questionable. It is not acceptable accounting to recognize a gain or loss on a contribution of capital to a related party.

Careful financial analysis is required of a firm involved in a joint venture. Before the financial ratios of a company and its joint venture are computed, additional steps and decisions are necessary. The first is to always eliminate the company's investment account in the joint venture with its share of joint-venture equity. If there are no other intercompany transactions, the analyst may simply elect to combine the company's share of joint-venture assets, liabilities, revenue, and expense accounts with the company's own accounts. However, if most of the joint venture's sales are to the company, the combining process would result in dubious figures, since total sales would be overstated in computing certain financial ratios.

As long as joint ventures exist, analysts will need to understand a company's economic relationship with its joint ventures and make the necessary adjustments to the company's financial statements.

Summary

This chapter discussed several ways management can raise debt financing without having to report it in the balance sheet. Exclusion of these economic liabilities diminishes the credibility, completeness, and comparability of the balance sheet. Off-balance sheet financing has the effect of making the liquidity of a firm look better than it really is. Incorporating off-balance sheet information into financial ratios and other methods of assessment can have dramatic effects on the financial picture that the ratios portray. Financial positions are often not what they seem to be. For the average user of financial statements the credibility of the data conveyed will become increasingly poor.

Any prudent user of balance sheet information should become acquainted with the nuances of off-balance sheet methods. A careful and critical analysis of the footnotes to the financial statements must be made in order to correctly assess the economic reality of a firm's financial position. Important adjustments can be made by using footnote data in order to arrive at an accurate picture of the total corporate liabilities. Financing methods are changing so fast that only personal vigilance can protect the analyst from being deceived or uninformed.

Key Concepts

Accounts receivable sale with
  recourse
Capital lease
Debt of unconsolidated subsidiaries
Defined-benefit pension plan
Defined contribution plan
Equity method of accounting
In-substance defeasance of debt

Off – balance sheet financing
Operating lease
Pension expense
Product financing
Project financing
Take-or-pay contract
Throughput contract
Unfunded pension liabilities

Present Value Factors

Present Value Interest Factor of an Annuity Due (PVIFAD) of $1

Period	4%	5%	7%	10%	12%	15%
5	4.62990	4.54595	4.38721	4.16986	4.03735	3.85498
6	5.45182	5.32948	5.10020	4.79079	4.60478	4.35216
7	6.24214	6.07569	5.76654	5.35526	5.11141	4.78448
8	7.00205	6.78637	6.38929	5.86842	5.56376	5.16042
9	7.73274	7.46321	6.97130	6.33493	5.96764	5.48732
10	8.43533	8.10782	7.51523	6.75902	6.32825	5.77158
19	13.65926	12.68957	11.05909	9.20139	8.24970	7.12793
20	14.13394	13.08532	11.33559	9.36492	8.36578	7.19823
30	17.98368	16.14113	13.27763	10.36959	9.02182	7.55090

Present Value Interest Factor of an Annuity (PVIFA) of $1

Period	4%	5%	7%	10%	12%	15%
5	4.45182	4.45182	4.10020	3.79079	3.60478	3.35216
6	5.24214	5.07569	4.76654	4.35526	4.11141	3.78448
7	6.00205	5.78637	5.38929	4.86842	4.56376	4.16042
8	6.73274	6.46321	5.97130	5.33493	4.96764	4.48732
9	7.43533	7.10782	6.51523	5.75902	5.32825	4.77158
10	8.11090	7.72173	7.02358	6.14457	5.65022	5.01877
19	13.13390	12.08530	10.33560	8.36490	7.36580	6.19820
20	13.59033	12.46221	10.59401	8.51356	7.46944	6.25933
30	17.29200	15.37250	12.40900	9.42690	8.05520	6.56600

Present Value Interest Factor (PVIF) of $1

Period	4%	5%	7%	10%	12%	15%
5	0.82193	0.78353	0.71299	0.62092	0.56743	0.49718
6	0.79031	0.74622	0.66634	0.56447	0.50663	0.43233
7	0.75992	0.71068	0.62275	0.51316	0.45235	0.37594
8	0.73069	0.67684	0.58201	0.46651	0.40388	0.32690
9	0.70259	0.64461	0.54393	0.42410	0.36061	0.28426
10	0.67556	0.61391	0.50835	0.38554	0.32197	0.24719
19	0.47460	0.39570	0.27650	0.16350	0.11610	0.07030
20	0.45639	0.37689	0.25842	0.14864	0.10367	0.06110
30	0.30830	0.23140	0.13140	0.05730	0.03340	0.01510

Questions

1. What does the expression *off – balance sheet financing* mean?

2. How do unfunded pension liabilities arise?

3. What is the difference between defined-benefit pension plans and defined-contribution plans? Which plan provides management with more flexibility for financial reporting and liquidity management?

4. Describe the difference between an operating lease and a financial (capital) lease. Which type of lease would management rather report? Why?

5. What is a sale of accounts receivable with recourse?

6. What are the necessary conditions for in-substance debt defeasance? How does debt defeasance work?

7. Describe take-or-pay and throughput contracts.

8. What disclosures should be made by a lessee if the leased assets and the related obligations are not capitalized?

9. A company that owns less than 50% of another company is not required to report its financial statements on a consolidated basis. Which method is usually employed by these companies, and what impact does it have on the financial statements?

Problems

1. Mixel Company's pension fund consists entirely of marketable securities. The current market value of the fund is $7,218,481. According to the pension fund agreement, the discounting factor is 5% and the pension period is 20 years. The accrued benefits are $600,000, and the vested benefits are $400,000.

    (a) Does the firm have an unfunded pension liability or a surplus? How much?

    (b) The firm is contemplating changing the discount rate to 7%. What change would this rate make to the answer in (a)? What would be the effect if the rate was changed to 4%? Discuss in terms of the impact on corporate liquidity.

2. Chandler Ballon, Inc., is expanding its operations and is in the process of selecting the method of financing this program. After careful investigation management determines that it may purchase the needed assets either by using the proceeds received from issuing bonds or by leasing the assets on a long-term basis. Without knowing the comparative costs, answer these questions.

(a) What might be the advantages of leasing the assets instead of owning them?

(b) What might be the disadvantages of leasing the assets instead of owning them?

(c) In what ways will the balance sheet be differently affected by leasing the assets as opposed to issuing bonds and purchasing the assets?

(d) Will liquidity be affected at all? Discuss.

3. The Pacific South Company must install a new machine costing $30,000. The machine has an economic life of 12 years and is not expected to have any residual value. Straight-line depreciation will be used. Management has three options to acquire the machine:

☐ Option 1. It can borrow $30,000 from a local bank at 10%, with principal and interest amortized over the 12 years.

☐ Option 2. It can lease the asset with annual payments of $4438 (prepaid one period) for a 10-year term. The first payment will be strictly for reduction of principal. The asset will be amortized over the life of the lease.

☐ Option 3. It can lease for maximum allowable terms and payments to qualify as an operating lease. All payments will be annual, with a one-period prepayment.

The firm's most recent financial statements are given in Table 4.6.

TABLE 4.6
Pacific South Company, Inc.
Income Statement and Balance Sheet
For the Latest Year

Income statement

Sales		$200,000
Cost of sales		140,000
Gross margin		$ 60,000
Less: Operating expenses	$10,000	
Depreciation	10,000	
Lease expense	0	
Interest expense	15,000	
		35,000
Profit before taxes		$ 25,000
Taxes		10,000
Net income		$ 15,000

Balance sheet

Current assets	$ 30,000	Current liabilities	$ 20,000
Net fixed assets	120,000	Long-term debt	50,000
		Shareholders' equity	80,000
Total	$150,000	Total	$150,000

(a) Assume that as a result of acquiring the new machine, Pacific's sales increase to $280,000, the cost of goods sold increases to $196,000, and operating expenses, excluding interest, depreciation, and lease expense, increase to $12,000. Calculate the net income for each of the first three years after the new machine became available for each financing option.

(b) Assume that depreciation on the old fixed assets is as shown on the income statement and that straight-line depreciation is used on all assets. Develop the balance sheet for the end of the first year after the new machine became available for each of the financing options. Use current assets as the balancing item.

(c) From the income statements and balance sheets generated for the borrowing and leasing options, calculate the following ratios: debt-equity, times interest earned, total asset turnover, return-on-assets, and return-on-equity.

(d) Discuss the effects of the borrowing and leasing options on the firm's financial picture as indicated by the ratios calculated in part (c).

4. Peacock Enterprises' annual report indicates financial leases of $10,000,000. These leases are noncancelable for a period of 10 years. The total minimum payments for these leases amount to $15,802,156, or $1,580,215.60 per year. The following is a schedule, by years, of future minimum rental payments required under noncancelable operating leases:

Next year	$ 2,552,628
2 years from now	2,552,628
3 years from now	2,552,628
4 years from now	2,533,506
5 years from now	2,437,896
Later years	35,090,315

Assume that all lease payments are made at the beginning of the period.

(a) What rate is used to capitalize the financial leases?

(b) What is the approximate present value of operating leases?

(c) What effect would the capitalization of operating leases have on ratio analysis?

5. A corporation has a choice of either purchasing a machine or leasing it. The purchase price is $1,200,000, whereas the annual lease payment is $500,000 for 5 years. If the company leases, can it record the lease as an operational lease if the useful life is 7 years and the purchase price at the end of the lease is $100,000? If the lease were capitalized at a 15% cost of capital, what would be the book value?

6. York Enterprises has $20,000,000 of debt with a coupon rate of 7%. The debt matures in 5 years. The treasurer is considering in-substance debt defeasance as a means of improving this year's profit figure and lowering the debt-equity ratio. If government securities are yielding 10%, how much must the treasurer segregate with a trustee in order to use debt defeasance? How much will the gain be? Is liquidity of the firm improved?

7. Calculate the conventional debt/capital and adjusted debt/capital ratios, using the following data, and discuss your findings.

Long-term debt	$ 1,500,000
Owners' equity	4,000,000
Current deferred taxes	250,000
Long-term deferred taxes	10,375,000
Present value of noncapitalized leases	750,000
Present value of unrecognized pension costs	3,429,000
Tax rate	40%

8. Determine the capitalized value of an operating lease if the lease requires annual payments of $87,492 at the beginning of each year for 7 years. The lessee's borrowing rate is 12%.

9. Determine the annual lease payments of a capitalized asset valued at $447,207.48. Lease payments are made at the end of each year for 7 years, and the borrowing rate is 12%.

10. **(a)** If the lessee in Problems 8 and 9 has a choice of classifying the lease as either a financial lease or as an operating lease, which alternative would he choose? Discuss in terms of the effect on both the income statement and liquidity for the life of the lease by calculating the net cash outflows and charges against operations for each alternative. Assume a tax rate of 40%.

(b) Which alternative causes net income to be lower in year 5, and by how much?

(c) Calculate the internal rate of return between the two alternatives.

CHAPTER 5 □
Indicators of Liquidity: Part I

Ratio analysis is a much-used technique for unraveling a firm's financial performance. Chapters 3 and 4 discussed many of the problems inherent with traditional ratios. The tone of those chapters was largely negative so as to stimulate you to question many of the commonly accepted notions about ratios and be more critical when conducting financial analysis.

Since many of the ratios discussed in Chapter 3 have been used for at least three decades, many managers and analysts often place more credence on them than they deserve. If these people are to discard old habits, one must convince them that superior methods of liquidity analysis exist. It is the intent of this chapter and the next to do so. Implicit in any discussion in these chapters is that off – balance sheeting financing is not used by the firm. This assumption is made to simplify the discussion. Obviously, if off – balance sheet financing exists, one must adjust the ratios to reflect it.

This chapter discusses a number of imperfect liquidity indicators. They are imperfect since they rely on some of the traditional ratios and provide but an overview of liquidity. The analysis that follows indicates important interrelationships between those areas normally considered in liquidity analysis and those areas commonly thought to be outside the realm of managing liquidity. The analysis is based on management by exception — information is sought only if it is thought to provide insight. This viewpoint is in contrast to traditional forms of analysis, where many of the traditional ratios are calculated and the analyst then sifts through them to find evidence of problems. Included in this chapter is analysis of return on equity (ROE); ROE-maximizing debt level; sustainable growth; and the calculation of the cash conversion cycle, cash breakeven sales level, and inflation-adjusted ratios.

Return on Equity

Invariably, when inexperienced analysts are asked to conduct financial ratio analysis, they calculate most of the traditional ratios before conducting any analysis. A more direct and productive approach is to start with a ratio that attempts to capture the shareholders' wealth objectively, namely, the return-on-equity (ROE) ratio.

Maximization of ROE is consistent with maximization of residual income (net present value). A mathematical proof is shown in Appendix A. However, an analyst should not lose sight of the many accounting-based problems associated with ROE, as were discussed in the previous chapter. An analyst must be cautious about unequivocal acceptance of any conclusions drawn using this ratio.

In addition to the proof shown in Appendix A, a theoretical rationale exists for the use of return on equity as a wealth maximization surrogate. Consider the situation where all investments undertaken by management earn a net present value of zero. That is, all investors simply earn their minimum required returns — debtholders earn the market cost of debt, and equityholders earn the market cost of equity. Thus, return on equity equals the cost of equity (k_e), and the market value of the stock equals its book value. Whenever management's investments generate positive net present values, the excess accrues to the equityholders; and in this situation the market value of equity should exceed the book value of equity, and ROE should be greater than k_e. This situation is desirable and is one that management strives for. However, management is confronted with a difficult problem in determining the cost of equity. The academic literature favors the Gordon dividend growth model and the capital asset – pricing model (CAPM) as being appropriate for calculating k_e.[1]

The Gordon model is stated as

$$k_e = D_1/P_o + g, \tag{5.1}$$

where D_1 is expected dividends next period, P_o is the current stock price, and g is the expected perpetual growth rate in dividends. The CAPM is defined as

$$k_e = r_f + (r_m - r_f)\beta, \tag{5.2}$$

where r_f is the risk-free rate, r_m is the expected return on the market portfolio, and β (beta) is the systematic risk of the equity return with returns

---

[1] A detailed discussion of the Gordon model is found in M. J. Gordon, *The Investment, Financing, and Valuation of the Corporation* (Homewood, Ill.: Irwin, 1962). An article by W. F. Sharpe, entitled "Capital Asset Prices: A Theory of Market Equilibrium Under Conditions of Risk," *Journal of Finance* (September 1964): 425 – 442, provides an excellent discussion of the capital asset pricing model.

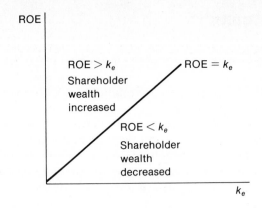

FIGURE 5.1
Relationship Between ROE and k_e

on the market portfolio. Theoretically, the CAPM is more appealing than the Gordon model.

Practitioners have encountered problems with both models. Reliable estimates for equity are influenced by the time period used and the available data. Estimates for beta are the center of much controversy with the CAPM, whereas the forecast for growth is the primary problem with the Gordon model. Assuming these problems are not insurmountable, the maximization of ROE − k_e (or, equivalently, the maximization of $NI − k_e E$) is a useful equivalent to wealth maximization (see Appendix A).

The remaining discussion in this chapter pertains simply to maximizing ROE under the assumption that $ROE/k_e > 1$. If managers find that $ROE/k_e < 1$, even when ROE is maximized, they need to give serious consideration to reallocating resources more profitably. If reallocation is not possible, liquidation may be in the shareholders' best interests. Figure 5.1 summarizes the important relationship between ROE and k_e.

ROE Model

Return on equity can be separated into the following three components:

$$\text{ROE} = \frac{\text{net income}}{\text{sales}} \times \frac{\text{sales}}{\text{total assets}} \times \frac{\text{total assets}}{\text{equity}}. \qquad (5.3)$$

| Return on sales | Asset turnover | Financial leverage |

TABLE 5.1
ROE for W. T. Grant Company
for the Year Ended January 31

Year	ROE	Return on sales	Asset turnover	Financial leverage
1974	0.026	0.004	1.476	3.962
1973	0.115	0.023	1.481	3.410
1972	0.110	0.025	1.455	2.983
1971	0.134	0.031	1.553	2.762
1970	0.148	0.034	1.713	2.531

Note: Multiplication of the components results in a small rounding error for ROE.

Analysis of each of these components against budget and/or prior years' performances (and maybe industry, although it is doubtful how beneficial this analysis will be) may well reveal patterns. If no problem exists with a particular component, there is little need to pursue further analysis of that component. When significant deviations exist, the component can be broken down to pinpoint problems.

Table 5.1 summarizes data for W. T. Grant during the period preceding its liquidity crisis and subsequent bankruptcy. The trend in ROE has been down and, surely as of 1974, is less than any reasonable estimate for the cost of equity. This trend was a signal that severe action was required to return the firm to a profitable and liquid state.

What has contributed to this dismal ROE performance for 1974? Table 5.1 indicates that each of the components should be analyzed to reveal the reasons. Although management of return on sales is the major deficiency, asset turnover is less efficient than in three of the four previous years. The leverage component needs analysis since it indicates that ROE has been supported through an ever-increasing debt component. However, what is not readily apparent is how the increased leverage has affected the other two components. The interactions are examined shortly.

Profitability

The return on sales (ROS) ratio can be further analyzed by using *common-size income statements* (see Table 5.2). These statements reflect each item on the statement as a percentage of net sales. By comparing each category of expense across years (or against budget), analysts can isolate problem areas. Answers to questions such as "What is the reason for the falling gross profit margin?" are revealed by such an analysis.

For example, Table 5.2 indicates that W. T. Grant's gross profit margins have declined steadily for the past four years. Is this decline a result of

TABLE 5.2
W. T. Grant Company
Common-Size Income Statements
For the Year Ended January 31

	1974	1973	1972	1971	1970
Sales	100.0%	100.0%	100.0%	100.0%	100.0%
Cost of sales	62.9	62.2	61.6	61.4	62.4
Period costs: Gross profit	37.1%	37.8%	38.4%	38.6%	37.6%
Selling, general, and administrative	28.0	26.9	27.0	26.1	25.1
Depreciation and amortization	0.7	0.7	0.8	0.8	0.7
Leasing	5.7	5.5	5.4	5.0	4.4
Net profit from operations	2.7%	4.7%	5.2%	6.7%	7.4%
Other income	0.3	0.3	0.4	0.5	0.4
Earnings before interest and taxes	3.0%	5.0%	5.6%	7.2%	7.8%
Interest expense	2.8	1.3	1.2	1.5	1.2
Earnings before taxes	0.2%	3.7%	4.4%	5.7%	6.6%
Taxes: Current	<0.3>	0.7	1.0	1.8	2.3
Deferred	0.3	1.0	1.2	1.1	1.2
Earnings before unconsolidated subsidiaries	0.2%	2.0%	2.3%	2.9%	3.2%
Equity in net earnings of unconsolidated subsidiaries	0.2	0.3	0.3	0.3	0.3
Total net earnings	0.4%	2.3%	2.5%	3.1%	3.4%

higher costs for merchandise, selling price declines, and/or a change in product mix? According to W. T. Grant's annual report, all three reasons contributed to the decline. Increased selling, general and administrative costs, and higher leverage have continued over the period. These higher costs, coupled with lower margins, are the main reason for the decline in total net earnings.

A plot of return-on-sales (ROS) data is shown in Fig. 5.2. For the purpose of discussion, *assume* that management budgeted a −1.0 percent return for the year ended January 1974. Since actual performance was better than that budgeted, management possibly ignored any analysis of the variance. This procedure could be most unfortunate, particularly if the budget was based on a strategy to remove the firm from this declining trend. Possibly the better-than-budgeted performance was achieved by not implementing some strategic decisions. The result of such action may be to perpetuate factors that are detrimental to the long-run survival of the firm.

The list that follows outlines possible reasons for beating a budget. Each reason results in either expense reduction or cash flow conversion, or both, in the current period. These "savings" may imperil future growth and market position since a firm that grows less rapidly than competition

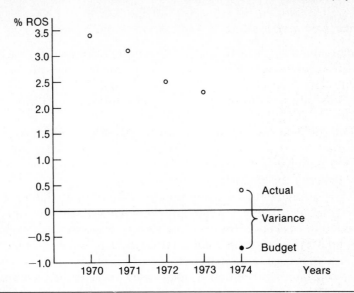

FIGURE 5.2
W. T. Grant Company Trend in Return on Sales

(even though it is on trend) will erode market position and profitability — and eventually liquidity — relative to past performance and to competition.

Possible Reasons for Beating a Budget

□ Advertising and R&D expenses slashed

□ Product planners/engineers laid off in order to cut costs

□ Actuarial assumptions regarding the pension plan changed (discussed in Chapter 4)

□ Selling prices increased, but volume down

□ Extraordinary gain recorded

□ Inventory valuation method changed (discussed in Chapter 13)

□ Marketable securities sold for a profit

□ Debt defeasance used (explained in Chapter 4)

Asset Turnover

When a problem lies with the trend in the sales-to-asset ratio (*asset turnover*), management's attention is directed to the balance sheet. It is seeking to determine the productivity of investments in current assets and fixed assets for supporting sales. The denominator of the ratio can be represented as

$$\text{assets} = \text{current assets} + \text{fixed assets} + \text{other assets.} \qquad (5.4)$$

This denominator allows turnover ratios to be calculated for each component. However, once these calculations are made, they cannot be added to obtain the total asset turnover ratio since no common denominator exists. This result is unfortunate, since the relative contribution of each component cannot be readily assessed.

The problem can be overcome by inverting the individual asset turnover ratios. Since the common denominator is now sales, the turnover ratios are additive and equal to the total (inverted) turnover ratio. Table 5.3 summarizes the problem and the solution.

The traditional turnover statistics for 1974 indicate that total turnover is lower than in three of the four previous years. Each asset category contributed to this decline. However, the relative importance of each category to the total turnover ratio cannot be easily determined. Once the ratios are inverted, it becomes apparent that each asset category has maintained a fairly constant contribution to total asset turnover in each year. W. T.

TABLE 5.3
W. T. Grant Company
Analysis of Asset Turnover
For the Year Ended January 31
($000)

	1974		**1973**		**1972**		**1971**		**1970**	
Sales	$1,849,802		$1,644,747		$1,374,812		$1,254,131		$1,210,918	
Current assets	$1,102,686		$ 979,876		$ 831,229		$ 719,182		$ 628,409	
Fixed assets	100,984		91,420		77,173		61,832		55,311	
Miscellaneous and other assets	49,313		39,402		36,268		26,614		23,075	
Total	$1,252,983		$1,110,698		$ 944,670		$ 807,628		$ 706,795	
Traditional turnover ratios										
Current assets	1.678		1.679		1.654		1.744		1.927	
Fixed assets	18.318		17.991		17.815		20.283		21.893	
Miscellaneous and other assets	37.511		41.743		37.803		47.123		52.477	
Total	1.476		1.481		1.455		1.553		1.713	
Inverted turnover ratios and their contributions										
Current assets	0.596	88%	0.596	88%	0.605	88%	0.574	89%	0.519	89%
Fixed assets	0.054	8	0.055	8	0.056	9	0.049	8	0.046	8
Miscellaneous and other assets	0.027	4	0.024	4	0.026	3	0.021	3	0.019	3
Total	0.677	100%	0.675	100%	0.687	100%	0.644	100%	0.584	100%

Grant's management appears to be following a policy of maintaining a constant mix of current, fixed, and other assets.

Even if the turnover ratios display an upward trend, the analyst must be aware of hidden future problems associated with favorable trends in turnover ratios. The following list outlines some of these problems.

Hidden Problems in Favorable Turnover Ratios

- Equipment is old and nearly fully depreciated.
- Receivables have been sold to a finance subsidiary or with recourse to an independent third party (discussed in Chapter 4).
- Inventories are too low.
- Replacement cost greatly exceeds cost carried on the books.
- LIFO (last-in, first-out) inventory valuation is used instead of FIFO (first-in, first-out) (discussed in Chapter 13).
- Liquidity is dangerously low.
- Fixed assets are misstated — some expenditures are expensed rather than capitalized.
- Contra accounts for receivables and inventories are too large.
- Current liabilities are overstated.

Financial Leverage

The third component of the ROE ratio is the ratio of net assets to equity. This ratio measures *financial leverage*. Whenever the leverage ratio equals 1, the firm has no debt. As debt is added to the firm's capital structure, the ratio increases above 1. Although the absence of debt makes liquidity management easier, it is not in the firm's best interest to forgo debt financing whenever the firm is in a growth pattern. Growing less rapidly than competition erodes market position and profitability relative to competition.

If management chooses not to fully utilize its *debt capacity*, this choice may imply a high and increasing degree of business risk. The properly levered competitor can grow faster than the more conservatively financed company and with a lower required rate of return since its cost of capital will be lower. This argument is simply stating that by judiciously using debt to help compete for growth, management may be able to reduce its weighted average cost of capital relative to competitors. Hence *the ultimate risk of overconservatism (failure to utilize debt more) is increasing business risk if competition is aware.* On the other hand, the use of too much debt leads to higher financial risk and a higher cost of capital. Management must find some trade-off between too much debt and too little.

The conventional debt capacity rule such as that long-term debt should not exceed, say, 50 percent of total capitalization clearly implies that debt in excess of this limit is too risky. Just what this phrase means is not always clear. The obvious inference is that if further additions are made to fixed-debt servicing charges, the time may come when the company does not have enough cash to go around. In the extreme case there may not be enough cash to meet legal commitments, and hence the company may become insolvent. In a less extreme form the drain of debt servicing may prevent management from covering expenditures it desires to preserve. This situation is called *cash inadequacy*.

Hindsight indicates that W. T. Grant was flirting with cash inadequacy as of January 1974. However, as Table 5.4 summarizes, diligent analysis would have revealed the debt problem confronting W. T. Grant prior to this period. Analysis of the leverage component of the ROE equation indicates the major reasons for the increase in financial leverage to be a continuing reliance on short-term debt (i.e., commercial paper) and a significant increase in long-term debt in the last period.

Analysis of Table 5.3 indicates that current assets comprised about 88 percent of total assets. The heavy reliance on short-term debt suggests that W. T. Grant was following a policy of financing short-term assets with short-term debt. On the surface this policy appears appropriate. However, note that most of the current assets are really *permanent*. There was about a 75 percent increase in current assets during the 1970 – 1974 period. W. T. Grant's reliance on short-term debt to finance these current assets meant that it was constantly having to refinance them. That is, cash generated from operations was reinvested in additional current assets.

An even more striking aspect of W. T. Grant's financing policy is revealed by looking at investors' expectations for interest rates over the 1969 – 1974 period. These expectations are captured in yield curves for

TABLE 5.4
W. T. Grant Company
Analysis of Leverage
For the Year Ended January 31

Year	$\dfrac{\text{Assets}}{\text{Equity}} =$	$\dfrac{\text{Current liabilities}}{\text{Equity}} +$	$\dfrac{\text{Long-term liabilities}}{\text{Equity}} +$	$\dfrac{\text{Indeterminate liabilities}}{\text{Equity}} +$	$\dfrac{\text{Preferred stock}}{\text{Equity}} +$	$\dfrac{\text{Equity}}{\text{Equity}}$
1974	3.962	1.761	0.697	0.480	0.024	1.000
1973	3.410	1.544	0.389	0.451	0.026	1.000
1972	2.983	1.145	0.406	0.403	0.029	1.000
1971	2.762	1.246	0.110	0.373	0.033	1.000
1970	2.531	1.025	0.127	0.338	0.041	1.000

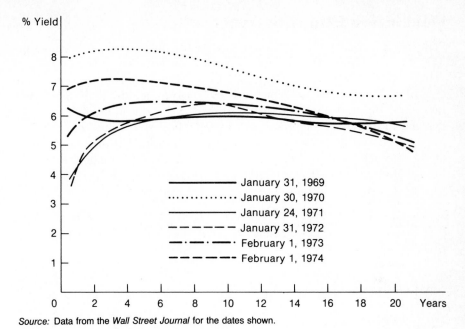

Source: Data from the *Wall Street Journal* for the dates shown.

FIGURE 5.3
Yield Curves for U.S. Treasury Bonds

U.S. government treasury bonds. A yield curve depicts the relationship between the yield on debt securities (of constant default risk) and the maturity of the debt (see Fig. 5.3).

W. T. Grant's heavy reliance on issuing debt in the money market to finance growth suggests that either it did not understand what interest rates were expected to do or else it thought it could forecast interest rates better than the financial markets. For instance, with the exception of the yield curves for January 31, 1969, and January 29, 1971, financing with long-term debt with a maturity of 15 years or more would have resulted in an interest rate that was not very much different than that in the money market. If W. T. Grant had financed with long-term debt around the January 30, 1970, period, interest costs could have been reduced since long rates were more than a point lower than short rates.

Thus either asset expansion in W. T. Grant was not financed with a targeted debt-equity ratio in mind, or else the targeted ratio, in retrospect, was much higher than it should have been. Management did not have a clear understanding of the significance of debt servicing on cash flows.

Maximizing ROE with Debt

Previous discussion in this chapter has shown the relevance of managing ROE for satisfying the shareholder wealth objective and the influence of debt on ROE. The pursuit of shareholder wealth maximization takes advantage of relatively low-cost debt funds to help finance the firm. Since debt can cause liquidity (and survival) problems, the question of how much debt a firm should use needs to be answered. Many researchers have devised elegant theoretical models to answer this question. Unfortunately, most of the models are too difficult to implement in any practical way. The following discussion offers a technique for maximizing ROE by using debt.

An alternative definition of return on equity is[2]

$$\text{ROE} = (1 - \text{tax rate}) \left[\frac{\text{EBIT}}{\text{assets}} + \left(\frac{\text{EBIT}}{\text{assets}} - \text{cost of debt} \right) \frac{\text{debt}}{\text{equity}} \right] \quad (5.5)$$

or

$$\text{ROE} = (1 - t) \left[r + (r - i)\frac{D}{E} \right]. \quad (5.6)$$

Equation (5.6) shows the firm's earning power of assets, as embodied in the earnings before interest and taxes (EBIT) to asset ratio, r, as being important. Whenever r exceeds the cost of debt, ROE is improved by the difference between r and i times the debt-equity ratio. This equation emphasizes the importance of debt for undertaking projects whose before-tax return r exceeds the interest rate i. Even if the corporate bond rating is falling, as long as r exceeds i, ROE increases.

ROE Maximization

The amount of debt for maximizing ROE can be determined by using calculus. The maximum ROE, with respect to the debt-equity ratio, is found at the point where

$$\frac{D}{E} = \frac{r - i + \partial r/\partial(D/E)}{\partial i/\partial(D/E) - \partial r/\partial(D/E)}, \quad (5.7)$$

---

[2] This expression is Modigliani and Miller's (MM) proposition II, stated in terms of return on equity rather than the cost of equity. Its use here, however, is removed from the sterile MM world of perfect markets and constant cost of debt, so the value of the firm can change with the use of leverage. The following two articles by F. Modigliani and M. H. Miller develop and discuss proposition II: "The Cost of Capital, Corporation Finance, and the Theory of Investment," *American Economic Review* (June 1958): 261 – 297; and "Corporate Income Taxes and the Cost of Capital," *American Economic Review* (June 1963): 433 – 443. Appendix B of this chapter contains further discussion.

where $\partial r/\partial(D/E)$ and $\partial i/\partial(D/E)$ represent the change in r and i for a change in the debt-equity ratio, respectively. A formal proof is shown in Appendix B.

To simplify the discussion, assume that the before-tax operating return on assets (r) does not change as the capital structure is changed; that is, $\partial r/\partial(D/E) = 0$. This assumption is reasonable whenever management realigns the capital structure without affecting the composition of the assets or their earning power. Hence ROE is maximized at the point where

$$\frac{D}{E} = \frac{r - i}{\partial i/\partial(D/E)}. \tag{5.8}$$

For example, if the interest schedule confronting management is approximated by the equation $i = a + b(D/E)^2$, then $\partial i/\partial(D/E)$, the change in the interest rate as the debt-equity ratio changes, is $2b(D/E)$. Substituting i and $\partial i/\partial(D/E)$ into Eq. (5.8) and solving for D/E leads to

$$\frac{D}{E} = \left(\frac{r - a}{3b}\right)^{1/2} \tag{5.9}$$

The solution to Eq. (5.9) represents the debt-equity capital structure that maximizes the ROE of the firm (assuming the interest schedule is appropriate).

ILLUSTRATION 5.1

Assume that management has approached a number of lenders and asked them the following questions: If the debt-equity ratio is 0.25, how much would debt cost me? If it is 0.50, how much would debt cost me? And so on. If the interest schedule from this line of questioning is found to be $i = 0.10 + 0.117(D/E)^2$, then the optimal capital structure for maximizing ROE, when $r = 0.487$ and the tax rate is 50%, occurs when the debt-equity ratio is

$$\frac{D}{E} = \left(\frac{0.487 - 0.10}{3(0.117)}\right)^{1/2} = 1.05. \tag{5.10}$$

At this level the interest cost before taxes is

$$i = 0.10 + 0.117\,(1.05)^2 = 0.229, \tag{5.11}$$

and after-tax ROE is

$$\text{ROE} = (1 - 0.5)\,[0.487 + (0.487 - 0.229)(1.05)] = 0.379. \tag{5.12}$$

Deviations from the optimum result in lower ROE, as shown in Fig. 5.4 and in the following illustration. Return on assets occurs where the curve intersects the ROE axis.   □

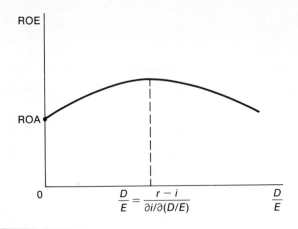

FIGURE 5.4
ROE-Maximizing Leverage

The return-on-equity maximization technique is contrasted with the EPS – EBIT analysis discussed in Chapter 3. Although EPS – EBIT analysis is frequently suggested as being appropriate for determining debt capacity, it is flawed as a wealth-maximizing criteria *whenever premiums paid for share repurchase result in a new equilibrium share price* (which is usually the case).

ILLUSTRATION 5.2

Assume that the *pro forma* statement with all equity financing is EBIT = $9,905,000; assets = $20,340,000; tax rate = 50%; shares outstanding = 2,217,325; present stock price = $12 per share; and EPS = $2.23.

Assume that a minimum of $7 million debt can be issued; flotation costs are too expensive for anything less than this amount. If management replaces some equity with debt (which has no effect on assets or operating earnings), premiums payable for stock repurchases are as follows:

Up to $8 million	20% premium
$8.1 to $10 million	24% premium
Above $10.1 million	30% premium

From the interest rate schedule of Eq. (5.11) EPS is maximized when $8 million of debt is used, as shown in Table 5.5. Note that all proposed debt levels result in an EPS as good as or higher than the firm's projection for an all-equity capital structure of $2.23.

TABLE 5.5
Maximization of EPS ($000)

	Proposed debt levels					
	$7,000	*$8,000*	*$9,000*	*$10,000*	*$10,418*	*$11,000*
EBIT	$9,905	$9,905	$9,905	$9,905	$9,905	$9,905
Interest	926	1,193	1,563	2,094	2,386	2,885
Earnings	$8,979	$8,712	$8,342	$7,811	$7,519	$7,020
Taxes	4,490	4,356	4,171	3,906	3,760	3,510
Net income	$4,489	$4,356	$4,171	$3,905	$3,759	$3,510
Shares	1,731,214	1,661,769	1,612,486	1,545,282	1,549,504	1,512,197
EPS	$2.59	$2.62	$2.59	$2.53	$2.42	$2.32
D/E	0.525	0.648	0.794	0.967	1.050	1.123
ROE	33.7%	35.3%	36.8%	37.8%	37.9%	37.6%

Interest calculations

Debt	Interest schedule		Rate		Expense
$ 7,000	$i = 0.10 + 0.117(7000/13,340)^2$	=	0.132	→	$ 926
8,000	$i = 0.10 + 0.117(8000/12,340)^2$	=	0.149	→	1193
9,000	$i = 0.10 + 0.117(9000/11,340)^2$	=	0.174	→	1563
10,000	$i = 0.10 + 0.117(10,000/10,340)^2$	=	0.209	→	2094
10,418	$i = 0.10 + 0.117(10,418/9922)^2$	=	0.229	→	2386
11,000	$i = 0.10 + 0.117(11,000/9340)^2$	=	0.262	→	2885

Price-per-share calculations

Debt	Current price	×	1 + premium	=	New price		Shares retired
$ 7,000	$12	×	1.20	=	$14.40	→	486,111
8,000	12	×	1.20	=	14.40	→	555,555
9,000	12	×	1.24	=	14.88	→	604,839
10,000	12	×	1.24	=	14.88	→	672,043
10,418	12	×	1.30	=	15.60	→	667,821
11,000	12	×	1.30	=	15.60	→	705,128

The capital structure for ROE maximization is $10,418,000 debt and $9,922,000 equity ($D/E = 1.05$), with 1,549,504 shares outstanding. The EPS at the debt-equity ratio for ROE maximization is 7.6% lower than the EPS maximization debt level of $8 million.   □

The same ROE-maximizing solution found in Table 5.5 can be derived by using Eqs. (5.10) through (5.12). The significance of the ROE model will become clearer later in the chapter when topics are discussed that place it in a better perspective with regard to its relation to liquidity management.

Possible Shortcomings

An apparent shortcoming of this analysis is the implicit assumption that adequate cash flow exists to service the debt. This topic is addressed later in this chapter when sustainable growth is discussed.

Another point of contention is the implicit disregard for bond ratings, as evidenced by the fact that ratings have not been discussed in this analysis. *Ratings should be important to management only to the extent that the ratings do not fall so low that access to credit is wholly precluded.* The interest rate should be of primary importance; ratings are of secondary importance. For example, in Illustration 5.2 the corporation can earn about 49% before taxes on assets. Even by borrowing at about 23% pretax, the firm continues to operate in the region of favorable financial leverage. Thus, to discontinue borrowing because the rate would go from 13% to 23% means that management would prefer to save $10 on a $100 investment pretax than to earn $26 [i.e., $100(49% − 23%)] before taxes on the same investment. In terms of the economic concepts discussed in Chapter 2, management should be willing to borrow until the marginal benefit of the borrowing equals its marginal cost (taking risk into consideration).

Restrictive debt covenants and repayment terms can sharply reduce debt capacity by increasing the annual liquidity problem, either by a rapid repayment schedule or by an inability to refund if ratios drop below agreed levels. The critical element is management's willingness to give in on higher interest rates in favor of more generous terms. Debt management orients more closely to liquidity requirements than the actual cost of money, as long as that cost stays below the corporation's operating earning rate r.

In summary, pragmatic constraints exist in terms of institutional perceptions and self-imposed perceptions or trade-offs. There is no definitive answer for the question of how far a company should go with debt financing. Rather, the answer must be based on an analysis of the stability, financial return, and competitive characteristics of each business the company is in.

Sustainable Growth

At various points in the discussion of ROE the importance of growth has been mentioned. The question is: "How much growth can a firm afford, either real or inflationary?"[3] Operating and financial policies and growth

---

[3] Much of the discussion in this section is based on R. C. Higgin's article, "How Much Growth Can a Firm Afford?" *Financial Management* (Fall 1977):7 – 16.

objectives must be compatible for sustainable growth to exist.

Earlier discussion in this and prior chapters mentioned the change in strategy that management of W. T. Grant was pursuing, namely, making significant investments in new stores so as to become a more dominant firm in its product markets. Ratio analysis indicated that profitability problems developed but failed to reveal any real liquidity problems. However, as investors of W. T. Grant were painfully aware, the growth that the company enjoyed over the 1970 – 1974 period did not enhance shareholder wealth. Growth was not managed in a manner that was consistent with prudent financial policies. In other words, corporate policy did not adequately address how sustainable growth could be achieved.

Definition of Sustainable Growth

Sustainable growth is normally defined as an ongoing annual percentage increase in sales. Under the assumption that the firm does not issue new equity, this rate is also the same sustainable rate of growth in assets, debt, equity, and earnings. *If sales expand at a rate faster than the sustainable growth rate, something in the company's financial objectives has to give — usually to the detriment of financial soundness.* Conversely, if sales grow at a rate less than the sustainable growth rate, a surplus of funds should exist. Management will be able to increase dividends, reduce leverage, or build up liquid assets. When the company's sustainable growth rate is known, management can ascertain whether the firm's growth objectives and financial policies are mutually feasible. If they are not, management must find a more appropriate mix of financial and growth objectives.

Sustainable growth (g_s) can be written as

$$g_s = \frac{\Delta S}{S} = \frac{R(1 - p)(1 + D/E)}{T - R(1 - p)(1 + D/E)}, \tag{5.13}$$

where

$\dfrac{\Delta S}{S}$ = change in sales,

R = profit margin (i.e., return on sales),

$1 - p$ = retention rate; p is dividend payout,

$\dfrac{D}{E}$ = debt-equity ratio,

T = asset-sales ratio (i.e., inverse of turnover ratio).

Appendix C shows the derivation of Eq. (5.13).

If actual sales growth (g_a) is at any rate other than g_s, then R, p, D/E, or T must change. For example, when actual growth exceeds sustainable growth, management must use the firm's assets more efficiently (i.e., R must increase and/or T must decline), or it must adjust its financial policies (i.e., increase $1 - p$ or increase D/E), or it must apply some combination of each.

The "How to Go Broke" scenario presented in Chapter 1 is an excellent example of a company growing too fast for its own good. Actual growth (g_a) far exceeded sustainable growth (g_s). Management failed to realize that rapid growth requires a large amount of cash. The cash needs can be met temporarily by taking advantage of leverage, but whenever the debt capacity is reached, management must turn to some other source of funds for sustaining growth.

Table 5.6 summarizes the liquidity problems of W. T. Grant that were surfacing during the early 1970s because sustainable growth and actual growth were not synchronized. The interpretation of W. T. Grant's sustainable growth is that as of January 31, 1974, growth would decrease at a rate of 3.8 percent annually as long as there was no change in any of the four ratios R, T, $1 - p$, or D/E. In each of the last three years actual growth exceeded sustainable growth. This result indicates that changes needed to be made if the company was to avoid severe growth problems, because *when actual growth exceeds sustainable growth, the company is an absorber of cash. It is a generator of cash when the reverse situation exists,* as was the case for the year ended in 1971.

Unfortunately, significant enough adjustments were not made by W. T. Grant's management in the post-1974 period, with the result that bankruptcy was declared, which lead to subsequent liquidation of the firm. This situation was brought upon by a management decision. The 1973 annual report states:

> The management of your company recognized . . . [the industry] shift from smaller, limited stores to larger, "full line" stores and committed itself to the complete restructuring of the Company.

TABLE 5.6
Sustainable Growth Calculation for W. T. Grant Company for the Year Ended January 31

	1974	1973	1972	1971	1970
Return on sales (R)	0.004	0.023	0.025	0.031	0.034
Inverted asset turnover (T)	0.677	0.675	0.687	0.644	0.584
Retention rate ($1 - p$)	−1.542	0.444	0.402	0.477	0.532
Financial leverage (D/E)	2.962	2.410	1.983	1.762	1.531
Sustainable growth (g_s)	−0.038	0.054	0.046	0.068	0.085
Actual growth (g_a)	0.125	0.196	0.096	0.036	0.096
g_a/g_s	High	3.630	2.087	0.529	1.133

The 10-K report indicates that during the five years ended January 31, 1974, this restructuring had resulted in 369 newer and larger stores opening and 272 smaller stores closing. It is evident from Table 5.6 that management's strategy did not adequately incorporate the sustainable growth formula and its implications for liquidity management.

The following alternatives are often available for management's use whenever actual growth exceeds sustainable growth and this situation is expected to persist:

1. *Sell new equity.* New equity plus the additional borrowing capacity created provides sources of needed cash to finance further growth. In W. T. Grant's case the new equity could have been used to retire debt that was exceedingly high.

2. *Increase leverage.* This alternative utilizes the unused debt capacity and provides funds for further growth. It does not apply to W. T. Grant, as indicated in point 1.

3. *Reduce the payout ratio.* This alternative increases the proportion of earnings available to finance growth opportunities. W. T. Grant's management used this technique in the following year. However, it should have been done much earlier.

4. *Prune product lines.* Firms can sell marginal businesses and commit resources to businesses with stronger market potential. This procedure generates cash and reduces sales growth caused by poor profit/cash flow – generating businesses. W. T. Grant was attempting to use this technique by closing older, smaller, and less profitable stores. Unfortunately, they were investing in larger stores too quickly.

5. *Lease versus buy.* Leases, if they can be structured as operating leases (see Chapter 4), require less investment in assets and thereby improve the asset management ratio. W. T. Grant was following this strategy in that it leased its retail facilities.

6. *Change selling prices.* When actual growth is too high relative to financing capabilities, raising prices will increase the profit margin and may lead to higher sustainable growth. Of course, it may also cause market share to decline. W. T. Grant's management felt it was unable to increase price. The Nixon administration had imposed price controls in an effort to slow the rate of increase in inflation. W. T. Grant's annual report states: "We felt compelled to lower our selling margins during the second half of 1973 in order to comply with government regulation; this involuntary action caused a substantial profit decrease."

7. *Cut operating costs.* Judicious cuts in operating costs should result in a more profitable firm both in the short term and in the long term. W. T. Grant's management was not effectively controlling costs. As shown earlier in Table 5.2, general, selling, and administrative costs increased

from 25.1 percent of sales in 1970 to 28.0 percent in 1974. And during at least a portion of this period management knew that it could not increase selling prices because of government price controls. Much more attention should have been paid to controlling costs.

Growth Maximization

Another specification of the sustainable growth model (and entirely consistent with Eq. 5.13) is the following model:

$$g_s = \frac{(1 - p) \times \text{ROE}}{1 - (1 - p) \times \text{ROE}}, \tag{5.14}$$

where $1 - p$ is the retention rate. This formulation allows the dimension of capital structure (as embodied in ROE) to be explicitly recognized in growth analysis. Growth can be shown to be maximized, with respect to the capital structure, when

$$\frac{\partial(g_s)}{\partial(D/E)} = -\text{ROE}\frac{\partial p}{\partial(D/E)} + (1 - p)\frac{\partial(\text{ROE})}{\partial(D/E)} = 0. \tag{5.15}$$

If the retention rate $(1 - p)$ is fixed, then $\partial p/\partial(D/E) = 0$, and the growth-maximizing capital structure occurs when $\partial(\text{ROE})/\partial(D/E) = 0$. This point is the same point where ROE is maximized with respect to leverage, as shown earlier in Eq. (5.8). *Thus for a constant – dividend payout policy, a management that concentrates its efforts on maximizing sustainable growth will also be meeting the primary objective of ROE maximization* (i.e., shareholder wealth maximization).

Funds, Life Cycle, and Growth

Earlier, we noted that the ROE model says nothing explicitly about funds and cash flow. However, in the long run *sustainable growth implicitly incorporates the idea that adequate funds exist*. By definition, sustainable growth means prolonged growth. Such growth requires a business strategy that incorporates sufficient funds to support it. Thus the sustainable growth model captures the principal components of funds flow management and defines their basic relationships with one another. It defines key points within the financial goals that management must control, namely, return on sales, dividend payout, financial leverage, and the asset-to-sales ratio.

Accumulated evidence demonstrates that a business's competitive position, the growth rates of its markets, and its current strategic decisions have a predictable effect on cash and funds flow. The most significant influences, derived from a study of interrelationships of ROE, cash flow, and market share, can be summarized as follows:

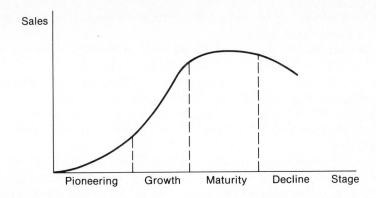

FIGURE 5.5
Life Cycle Curve

□ *Growth drains funds.* Participation in a strong market requires plenty of funds. Even if real market growth is minimal, inflation drains funds.

□ *Funds are generated by a relatively high market share.* And high ROE is associated with high market share. However, building a strong market position consumes large amounts of funds for new-product development, advertising, and promotion.

□ *Sufficient funds can only be ensured through aggressive asset management.* Funds supply is strained by increasing investment-to-sales ratios.

The need for funds is dependent on the firm's position in its *life cycle*. The concept of life cycle is particularly important for financial managers because companies have different needs as they develop. Early recognition of these needs enables the financial manager to make better policy decisions.

The placement of a firm on the life cycle curve (see Fig. 5.5) is a matter of judgment, because no precise method exists for making that determination. Moreover, the phases of the life cycle are functional measures that do not represent time. For example, a firm could remain in the same position on the life cycle curve for many years.

Companies in the *pioneering phase* of the life cycle are heavy consumers of funds. Funds are needed to finance research and development and to market their products. During the growth stage of the cycle a strong demand for funds still exists. They are needed for investment in plant and equipment and working capital in order to increase market share. If management invested in efficient productive capacity in the pioneering stage, the firm may have a competitive advantage during the growth stage because of being a low-cost competitor.

During the *growth phase* of the life cycle prices fall rapidly and profits get squeezed. It follows that firms with low costs can tolerate declining prices better than those with high costs. In fact, the high-volume firm can drive prices down and force high-cost competitors out of the market. Therefore, the offensive strategy is to have sufficient resources to be able to produce and sell a large volume quickly, thereby undercutting competition.

In the *mature stage* growth is minimal, and the demand for funds abates. The firm is established in its markets, and investments are made for product differentiation purposes in order to protect market position. Some products of the firm in this stage are referred to as "cash cows." This term simply means that these products generate more funds than they need to support themselves. Management can use the excess funds to support new growth areas, to pay dividends, and to reduce debt.

In the *decline stage* negative growth exists. Management conserves funds in the sense that no investments are undertaken. The product is truly a "cash cow."

Cash Conversion Cycle

Cash is the net outcome of the activities of a business. When a firm functions efficiently, the operating cycle moves smoothly through its cash-to-inventory-to-receivables-to-cash stages, and final decisions are concerned with the distribution of residual cash. If this *cash conversion cycle* is interrupted or if the flow is distorted, financing problems ensue that may have grave consequences if they are not quickly worked out.

Management should focus its concern on avoiding default situations by emphasizing (1) the firm's ability to cover its obligations with cash flows from an employment of inventory and receivable investments within the normal course of the firm's operations, and (2) the sensitivity of these operating cash flows to changing sales and earnings during periods of economic hardship and growth. Operating cash flow coverage, rather than asset liquidation value, is the crucial element in liquidity analysis. It looks at the problem from the perspective of an ongoing entity.

Incorporating accounts receivable and inventory turnover measures into an operating cycle concept provides a more appropriate view of liquidity management than does reliance on the current or quick ratios as indicators of insolvency. These additional liquidity measures explicitly recognize that the life expectancies of some net working capital components depend upon the extent to which production, sales, and collections are neither instantaneous nor synchronized.

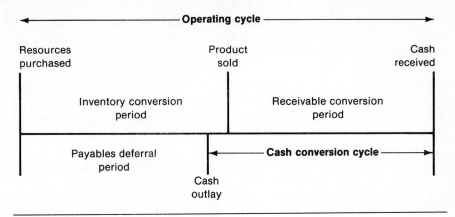

FIGURE 5.6
Operating and Cash Conversion Cycles

Operating Cycle

The cumulative days for turnover of accounts receivable and inventories provides a rough approximation of the length of a firm's *operating cycle*. The operating cycle concept is deficient as a cash flow measure in that it fails to consider the liquidity requirements imposed on a firm by the time dimension of its current liquidity commitments. Integrating the time pattern of cash outflows required to satisfy current liabilities is as important for liquidity analysis as evaluating the time pattern of cash inflows generated by the conversion of its current asset investments. The outflow for current liabilities can be incorporated into the analysis by a payables turnover ratio. This ratio relates operating costs requiring current cash expenditures to the accounts payable and accrued payable liabilities created by the short-term deferral of these operating expenditures.

Definition of Cash Conversion Cycle

A simple extension of the operating cycle concept results in the cash conversion cycle.[4] The cash conversion cycle is defined as the time interval between actual cash expenditures for a firm's purchases of productive resources and the ultimate cash collection from the sale of the product. This integration of cash inflow and outflow patterns provides a fairly complete approach to liquidity analysis.

Figure 5.6 illustrates the cash conversion cycle. This diagram points

---

[4] The cash conversion cycle has been popularized by V. D. Richards and E. J. Laughlin in their article "A Cash Conversion Cycle Approach to Liquidity Analysis," *Financial Management* (Spring 1980):32 – 38.

out that a residual cash flow – financing period (i.e., the cash conversion cycle) is influenced by both expansion and contraction in the three liquidity flow measures: the inventory conversion period, the receivables conversion period, and the payables deferral period. An increase in the length of the operating cycle without a concomitant lengthening of the payables deferral period creates additional liquidity management problems. Management will need to acquire additional *nonspontaneous* (i.e., negotiated) financing.

Mathematically, the cash conversion cycle is defined as follows:

$$\begin{aligned}
\text{cash conversion cycle} &= 360 \left[\frac{\text{inventory}}{\text{cost of sales}} + \frac{\text{receivables}}{\text{sales}} \right. \\
&\quad \left. - \frac{(\text{accounts payable} + \text{other spontaneous current liabilities})}{\text{cash operating expenditures}} \right] \\
&= 360 \left(\frac{1}{\text{inventory turnover}} + \frac{1}{\text{accounts receivable turnover}} \right. \\
&\quad \left. - \frac{1}{\text{accounts payable turnover}} \right).
\end{aligned}$$

(5.16)

Table 5.7 compares traditional ratios with the cash conversion cycle, using W. T. Grant's data. Although overall performance has deteriorated from levels attained in 1970, improvements have been made for the year ended January 31, 1974, relative to the previous year, as measured by the traditional ratios. However, the cash conversion cycle indicates continuing erosion in liquidity. The cash conversion cycle increased again in 1974, as it had in each of the previous years. This increase means that liquidity is worse, even though the traditional ratios signal improvement.

Cash Conversion Cycle Versus Traditional Liquidity Ratios

In general, policies that result in a longer cash conversion cycle produce a larger commitment to cash and noncash current asset investments and a lesser ability to finance these investments with current liabilities. These policies can be expected to produce higher current and quick ratios. This result occurred for W. T. Grant (particularly when commercial paper obligations are excluded from the current and quick ratios). The implication is that higher values for the current and quick ratios are the result of a greater commitment of resources to less liquid forms of working capital. The inclusion of the commercial paper and the bank loans in the calculations

TABLE 5.7
W. T. Grant Company
Cash Conversion Cycle
For the Year Ended January 31
($ millions)

	1974	1973	1972	1971	1970
Sales	$1849	$1645	$1375	$1254	$1211
Cost of sales*	$1164	$1023	$ 846	$ 771	$ 756
Depreciation	13	12	11	10	9
Administration and other*	623	533	446	389	356
Total operating expenses	$1800	$1568	$1303	$1170	$1121
Net operating income	$ 49	$ 77	$ 72	$ 84	$ 90
Cash and marketable securities	$ 46	$ 31	$ 50	$ 34	$ 33
Accounts receivable	599	543	477	420	368
Inventories	451	399	299	260	222
Other	7	7	5	5	5
Total current assets	$1103	$ 980	$ 831	$ 719	$ 628
Accounts payable and accrued expenses	$ 104	$ 104	$ 116	$ 105	$ 95
Taxes	0	8	9	14	10
Commercial paper	453	390	238	246	182
Total current liabilities	$ 557	$ 502	$ 363	$ 365	$ 287
Ratios					
Current ratio	1.98	1.95	2.29	1.97	2.19
Quick ratio	1.16	1.14	1.45	1.24	1.40
Current ratio excluding paper	10.61	8.75	6.64	6.04	5.98
Quick ratio excluding paper	6.20	5.13	4.22	3.82	3.82
Accounts receivable turnover	3.09	3.03	2.88	2.99	3.29
Inventory turnover (on cost)	2.58	2.56	2.83	2.97	3.41
Payables turnover (based on cost of sales and administration)	17.18	13.89	10.34	9.75	10.59
Cash conversion cycle (days)					
Receivables	116.5	118.8	125.0	120.4	109.4
Inventory	139.5	140.6	127.2	127.2	105.6
Operating cycle	256.0	259.4	252.2	247.6	215.0
Less payables	21.0	25.9	34.8	36.9	34.0
Cash conversion cycle	235.0	233.5	217.4	210.7	181.0

* Assumed to be cash operating expenditures.

causes the inverse relationship between the cash conversion cycle and traditional ratios to be blurred. In summary, trade creditors and the debt markets were apparently not aware of W. T. Grant's real and deteriorating liquidity position. Lenders felt secure in providing money to W. T. Grant.

Cash Conversion Cycle, ROE, and Growth

The cash conversion cycle should be inversely related to ROE and sustainable growth, as evidenced by the fact that the cash conversion cycle is a function of turnover ratios. As the turnover ratios for inventory and accounts receivable increase, and that for accounts payable decreases, *assuming all else remains constant,* ROE and sustainable growth increase while the cash conversion cycle decreases.

Thus the point made earlier that ROE management has little to say about funds flow can be relaxed. By optimizing the cash conversion cycle, management can improve ROE and sustainable growth. The better the cash conversion cycle, the greater is the availability of debt and equity capital that can be used to service maturing negotiated debt, to invest in new capacity or cost-saving equipment, and so on.

Cash Breakeven Analysis

Many of the traditional ratio techniques focus on analyzing profits and profitability with little direct concern about solvency. *Cash breakeven analysis* represents a useful first step toward analysis of solvency and is a logical extension to the cash conversion cycle. The cash breakeven point occurs when aggregate cash inflows just equal aggregate cash outflows.

Earning Versus Cash Breakeven

Chapter 3 discussed traditional earnings breakeven. Generally, *earnings breakeven and cash breakeven do not coincide.* Cash breakeven usually requires a higher level of sales. Thus although an accounting profit is realized at the higher sales level, the firm simply breaks even on an aggregate cash flow basis.

ILLUSTRATION 5.3

Since insufficient data is available from W. T. Grant's financial statements to illustrate breakeven, assume a firm's cost and cash flow structure is as follows:

Cash operating fixed costs	$821,180
Depreciation and amortization	69,500
Interest on debt	69,750
Principal repayment on debt	30,000
Dividend to common shareholders	80,000
Variable cost/sales ratio	0.65
Effective tax rate	0.38

Table 5.8 summarizes the sales breakeven levels under two different assumptions about what should be included in fixed costs for traditional breakeven analysis and compares the results to cash breakeven. These breakeven levels have been calculated by starting at the bottom of the columns and working backward to determine sales. The traditional break-even calculation, as discussed in Chapter 3, could have been used to find solutions for cases 1 and 2.

Cash breakeven indicates that sales must be about 6.8% higher than case 2 traditional earnings breakeven. Implicit in the cash breakeven calculation is the assumption of no change in accounts receivable, accounts payable, or inventory balances from the beginning of the period to the end of the period. Additionally, no expenditures for noncurrent assets have been made. If such expenditures were made for either net working capital items or fixed assets, they would be incorporated into the cash breakeven column of Table 5.8 in a manner similar to that used for principal and dividends. For instance, if net working capital investment increased $350,000, break-even sales would need to be $4,543,626, a 55% increase over the $2,930,723 level (verify this result yourself, using Table 5.8's format).

The company may not be able to meet this required cash breakeven sales level without adding additional capacity. For example, assume that another facility, costing $150,000, is required, as is the $350,000 increase

TABLE 5.8
Earnings Versus Cash Breakeven

	Traditional breakeven		Cash breakeven
	Case 1	Case 2	
Sales	$2,544,800	$2,744,086	$2,930,723
Variable costs	1,654,120	1,783,656	1,904,970
Gross margin	$ 890,680	$ 960,430	$1,025,753
Fixed costs	890,680	960,430	960,430
Profit before tax	$ 0	$ 0	$ 65,323
Taxes	0	0	24,823
Net income	$ 0	$ 0	$ 40,500
Plus depreciation			69,500
Equals cash flow from operations			$ 110,000
Minus principal repayment			30,000
Minus dividends			80,000
Equals cash flow			$ 0

Note: In case 1 fixed costs include cash operating costs plus depreciation and amortization of $69,500. In case 2 fixed costs include case 1's fixed costs plus interest on debt.

TABLE 5.9
Cash Breakeven with a New Facility and Additional
Net Working Capital

Sales		$4,842,303
Variable costs		3,147,497
Gross margin		$1,694,806
Fixed costs:		
Before	$960,430	
Additional	27,500	
		987,930
Profit before taxes		$ 706,876
Taxes		268,613
Net income		$ 438,263
Plus depreciation:		
Old	$69,500	
New	15,000	
		84,500
Minus net working capital		350,000
Minus principal:		
Old	$30,000	
New	37,763	
		67,763
Minus dividends		80,000
Minus fixed assets		150,000
Plus long-term financing		125,000
Cash flow		$ 0

Note: Depreciation is included in fixed costs. The additional fixed costs
consist of new interest payments and additional depreciation.

in net working capital. At current costs and prices the additional space
will allow the firm to sell $5 million worth of products. To acquire this
space, management will have to put $25,000 cash down and finance the
balance of $125,000 at 10% with annual payments amortized over 3 years.
The facility will be depreciated straight-line over 10 years.

Table 5.9 shows the new cash breakeven sales level to be $4,842,303.
Additional sales of $1,911,580 are required to support the new facility
and new net working capital investment.   □

Cash Breakeven Formula

Rather than going through the detailed *pro forma* income statement analysis
each time, one can determine the cash breakeven sales level (CBSL) by
using the following equation:

$$\text{CBSL} = \frac{\begin{array}{c}(\text{Total fixed costs})(1 - t) - \text{depreciation} + \text{principal payments} \\ + \text{ dividend payments} + \text{change in fixed assets} \\ + \text{ change in net working capital}\end{array}}{(\text{contribution margin } \%)(1 - t)}. \quad (5.17)$$

Obviously, if fixed assets are sold or net working capital declines, the change in these accounts will be negative and their signs in Eq. (5.17) will change.[5] To illustrate the formula, we use the data from Table 5.9:

$$\text{CBSL} = \frac{987{,}930 \,(1 - 0.38) - 84{,}500 + 67{,}763 + 80{,}000 + 375{,}000}{(1 - 0.65)\,(1 - 0.38)}$$

$$= \$4{,}842{,}303.$$

The last term in the numerator indicates additional total net working capital needed so as to have a \$350,000 increase after all transactions are completed. Since a \$25,000 cash down payment is required, management must initially increase net working capital by \$375,000 in order to have \$350,000 after the transaction.

This expression provides a simple technique for calculating the impact of additional investment, a desired profit or cash flow level, or a change in taxes and margins on cash breakeven levels. For instance, if management desires a cash flow of \$10,000, this amount can be added to the numerator of the equation. Alternatively, simply dividing \$10,000 by $(1 - 0.65)(1 - 0.38)$ (i.e., the denominator) gives the increase in sales (\$46,083) that is required above the current cash breakeven sales level of \$4,842,303 to support the targeted cash flow level.

Cash Breakeven, ROE, and Cash Conversion Cycle

Changes in the cash breakeven level arising from net working capital accounts are directly correlated with the cash conversion cycle. Since return on investment and the cash conversion cycle are inversely related, the cash breakeven level and ROE must also be inversely related. Thus better management of cash and its flow results in improved shareholder wealth maximization.

Keep in mind, however, that useful though the cash breakeven point formula may be, it is not intended to replace cash budgeting. *Cash breakeven analysis indicates the aggregate cash inflows and outflows and not their timing.* Timing is more critical than aggregate inflows and outflows. Only a cash budget can assess the timing risk (this topic is discussed in the next chapter).

---

[5] Total fixed costs in Eq. (5.17) include depreciation expense. When these fixed costs are multiplied by the tax rate, the depreciation expense provides a *tax shield.*

Inflation-Adjusted Financial Analysis

According to economic theory, profit is the amount of money that may be withdrawn from a company and still leave its real capital untouched. Profit as calculated by conventional accounting procedures is more or less in line with this definition *if the quality of earnings are good and the purchasing power of money is stable.*

As Table 5.10 shows, approximately 81% of an American dollar's purchasing power has been eroded by *inflation* since World War II. Whenever there are various lengths between acquisition of inputs and realization of outputs, the time lag between acquisition and realization can cause these transactions to be measured by monetary units of different purchasing power. During a period of inflation price-level adjustments affect reported profit in two opposite directions: (1) Asset revaluation or restatement increases depreciation expenses and the cost of materials used, thereby lowering accounting profits, and (2) asset revaluation or restatement may be greater than equity restatement, depending on financial leverage, thereby raising reported accounting profit above its economic counterpart.

In most companies there are six major parties that lay claim to a share of the profit (and cash flow):

1. Managers through compensation plans.
2. Labor through wage and benefit claims.
3. Suppliers through payment for goods and services.
4. Government through income taxes.
5. Debtholders through amortization and interest.
6. Shareholders through dividends and capital gains.

During a period of inflation the upward bias of reported profit produced by conventional accounting often causes an unjustified withdrawal of resources from the company by the various claimants. For instance, dividends may be declared beyond the real earnings of the company. Income tax may withdraw some of the profit that is in fact only equity maintenance. Managers and labor may demand, and often receive, higher compensation based on illusory profit figures, which may in the long run endanger the company.

For a company to survive in the long run, its sales must at least equal the renewal value (costs) of the inputs used in generating the sales. Therefore only the income that is in excess of replacement requirements is *real profit.* According to this reasoning, in a period of inflation the historical costs of asset inputs should be continually adjusted to replacement values. If this adjustment is made, current sales are matched with real current costs, and the bias of conventional profit calculation is greatly reduced.

TABLE 5.10
Inflation in the United States (Based on the Consumer Price Index)

Year	Consumer price index (1967 = 100)	Purchasing power of the dollar (1979 = $1)	Rate of inflation
1945	53.9	$3.92	2.6%
1946	58.5	3.61	8.6
1947	66.9	3.16	14.2
1948	72.1	2.93	7.8
1949	71.4	2.96	−1.0
1950	72.1	2.93	1.0
1951	77.8	2.72	7.9
1952	79.5	2.66	2.2
1953	80.1	2.64	0.8
1954	80.5	2.62	0.5
1955	80.2	2.63	−0.3
1956	81.4	2.60	1.5
1957	84.3	2.51	3.6
1958	86.6	2.44	2.7
1959	87.3	2.42	0.8
1960	88.7	2.38	1.6
1961	89.6	2.36	1.0
1962	90.6	2.33	1.1
1963	91.7	2.30	1.2
1964	92.9	2.27	1.3
1965	94.5	2.24	1.7
1966	97.2	2.17	2.9
1967	100.0	2.11	2.9
1968	104.2	2.03	4.2
1969	109.8	1.92	5.4
1970	116.3	1.82	5.9
1971	121.3	1.74	3.7
1972	125.3	1.69	3.3
1973	133.1	1.59	6.2
1974	147.4	1.43	10.7
1975	161.2	1.31	9.4
1976	170.5	1.24	5.7
1977	181.5	1.16	6.4
1978	195.4	1.08	7.7
1979	217.4	1.00	11.3
1980	246.8	0.88	13.5
1981	272.4	0.80	10.3
1982	294.2	0.74	8.0

Source: U.S. Department of Labor, Bureau of Labor Statistics.

Appraising the actual replacement cost of a company's existing assets is cumbersome and difficult; indeed, often it is not feasible in practice. A close estimate of replacement cost, which is feasible, can be obtained by using specific price indexes for asset revaluation. Revaluation by a general price level provides poorer estimates because of the divergence of individual price changes from the general one.

Replacement cost represents the cost, in current dollars, of replacing the productive capacity of an existing asset. It does not represent its sale value. Replacement is justified only if the economic value (i.e., the present value of future cash flows) of an asset exceeds its replacement cost. Thus replacement cost should be less than economic value to maintain long-run viability of the firm.

Financial Versus Physical Assets and Capital

Usually, a company holds monetary (i.e., financial) assets and liabilities in addition to nonmonetary (i.e., physical or real) assets and liabilities. The inflationary effect on most monetary assets and liabilities differs from that on nonmonetary assets and liabilities. Whereas the value of most nonmonetary assets and liabilities is, more or less, price level – linked, the value of most monetary assets and liabilities is usually not linked.

An asset or liability is said to be *monetary* if it is denominated in units of currency, and *nonmonetary* if it is not. Cash, marketable securities, and accounts receivable are monetary assets because when the assets mature, the company will receive a specified amount of currency. Inventories, plant and equipment, and land are nonmonetary assets whose ultimate value in units of currency depends, at least in part, on the future inflation rate. Most liabilities are monetary, while net worth (equity) is nonmonetary.

Since monetary assets are not price level – linked, during inflation they do not endow the company with potential gains, as is the case with nonmonetary assets. Thus the larger the share of monetary assets in the balance sheet, the fewer potential gains accrue to the company during a period of inflation.

ILLUSTRATION 5.4

Assume that a company has the following balance sheet at the beginning of the period:

Beginning Balance Sheet

Cash	$100	Equity	$300
Inventory	200		

If the general price level doubles during the year, and no transactions take place, then to be as well-off economically, the firm should have the following balance sheet at the end of the year:

Required Balance Sheet to Be in a Constant Economic Position

Cash	$200	Equity	$300
Inventory	400	Purchasing power gains:	
		Cash	100
		Inventory	200

However, at the end of the period only $100 of cash will exist, and a purchasing power loss from holding a monetary asset will be experienced. Nonmonetary assets (e.g., inventory) do not represent a fixed claim; they retain their purchasing power. Thus the purchasing power – adjusted balance sheet will be as follows:

Balance Sheet Adjusted for Purchasing Power

Cash	$100	Equity	$300
Inventory	400	Purchasing power gain:	
		Inventory	200

□

Use of Inflation-Adjusted Financial Data

The rationale behind working capital ratios is that such current assets as marketable securities, accounts receivable, and inventory can be readily converted to cash in the event of an emergency. In an inflationary environment the historical cost conventions for valuing noncash current assets may not reflect the ability of the firm to raise cash by selling or pledging its current assets. For example, the LIFO method of inventory valuation leaves older, less inflated costs on the balance sheet, and so the book value LIFO inventory may be much lower than the amount of cash the firm could raise through sale.

Current value accounting provides that current assets and liability accounts be adjusted to reflect contemporary values so that they bear a closer relationship to cash-out values. Thus current value working capital ratios communicate more information about the short-run solvency of the firm.

Current value asset values also provide valuable information about the liquidity value of long-term assets. Although the degree of liquidity of these assets typically is less than that of working capital assets, a firm with a cushion of fixed assets is better able to quickly arrange sales, loans, or even leaseback arrangements to meet immediate cash needs.

Calculation of current cost can be complex. Since the purpose is to convey to you an appreciation of the need for understanding the impact of inflation on financial performance, simplifying assumptions have been used in the following discussion without impairing the overall conclusions that can be drawn from the analysis.

Inflation information can be used in conjunction with historical cost information to assess financial performance. The Financial Accounting Standards Board (FASB) requires certain large firms to provide supplementary disclosures of the effects of changing prices. Some firms are required to use current cost accounting (where the attribute measured is changed), while others must use constant-dollar accounting (where the measuring unit is changed). The basic difference between the two approaches is that current cost attempts to measure the effect of inflation in nominal dollars by determining the economic value of assets and liabilities, which conceptually is the present value of future receipts and payments from using the assets and the liabilities. The constant-dollar concept seeks to eliminate

TABLE 5.11
W. T. Grant and Company
Comparative Income Statements
For the Period Ended January 31, 1974
($000)

	Historical cost	Current cost
Sales	$1,849,802	$1,849,802
Cost of sales	$1,163,998	$1,300,000
Depreciation	13,579	17,282
Selling and administrative	518,279	518,279
Leasing expense	105,367	105,367
Total costs	$1,801,223	$1,940,928
Net profit from operations	$ 48,579	$ <91,126>
Other income	7,033	7,033
Earnings before interest and taxes	$ 55,612	$ <84,093>
Interest expense	51,047	51,047
Earnings before taxes	$ 4,565	$<135,140>
Taxes	787	787
Earnings before unconsolidated subsidiaries	$ 3,778	$<135,927>
Equity in net earnings of unconsolidated subsidiaries	4,651	4,651
Net earnings	$ 8,429	
Current cost loss		$<131,927>
Dividends	21,122	21,122
Retained earnings	$ <12,693>	$<152,398>

the effect of inflation by using dollars with uniform purchasing power. Much debate exists about which is the better technique. The following discussion uses a current cost approach since it is more consistent with economic theory.

Illustrative historic and *assumed* current cost income statements and balance sheets for W. T. Grant are summarized in Tables 5.11 and 5.12, respectively. Inflation rates shown in Table 5.10 were used to derive the current cost figures. The FASB did not require price-adjusted data to be reported until 1979 — thus the need to arbitrarily assume price-level effects

TABLE 5.12
W. T. Grant and Company
Comparative Balance Sheets
As of January 31, 1974
($000)

	Historical cost	Current cost
Assets		
Monetary assets:		
Cash and marketable securities	$ 45,951	$ 45,951
Receivables	598,799	598,799
Investment in debentures of unconsolidated subsidiaries	11,651	11,651
Unamortized debt expenses	1,362	1,362
Total monetary assets	$ 657,763	$ 657,763
Nonmonetary assets:		
Inventories	$ 450,637	$ 500,000
Property and equipment	100,984	128,525
Prepaid expenses	7,299	8,116
Stock of W. T. Grant and others	3,700	4,114
Investments in unconsolidated subsidiaries	32,600	36,248
Total nonmonetary assets	$ 595,220	$ 677,003
Total assets	$1,252,983	$1,334,766
Liabilities and equity		
Monetary liabilities:		
Current liabilities	$ 557,007	$ 557,007
Long-term debt	220,336	220,336
Indeterminant liabilities	151,902	151,902
Total liabilities	$ 929,245	$ 929,245
Monetary preferred stock	$ 7,465	$ 7,465
Nonmonetary equity:		
Shareholders' equity	$ 316,273	$ 398,056
Total liabilities and equity	$1,252,983	$1,334,766

for W. T. Grant. Appendix D summarizes the rudiments of current cost accounting and briefly discusses how our approach differs from that used by accountants in meeting FASB reporting requirements. Basically, restatement is as shown in the preceding section: Only nonmonetary assets, liabilities (if they exist), and equity are restated.

ROE Analysis

Since ROE is considered a proxy for measuring wealth-maximizing performance, we may use it in measuring the impact inflation has on financial results:

$$\text{ROE} = \text{ROS} \times \text{asset turnover} \times \text{leverage}$$
$$\text{ROE}_{historical} = 0.004 \times 1.476 \times 3.962 = 0.026 \tag{5.18}$$
$$\text{ROE}_{current} = \langle 0.071 \rangle \times 1.386 \times 3.353 = \langle 0.330 \rangle$$

These results dramatically illustrate the significant impact of inflation. The use of *historical cost ignores the notion of economic asset value,* which is the present value of future receipts generated by assets. The result is that historical cost – based ROE is inflated. The current cost approach attempts to correct this problem by approximating current replacement costs (of the same age and same operating capacity). The following analysis of the ROE components provides insight into the problem.

Return on Sales

Calculation of profitability of sales (ROS) for W. T. Grant is very revealing and indicates serious problems with operations. The accounting (historical) ROS is 0.4%, whereas it is -7.1% for inflation-adjusted costs. Lower current cost net income is expected because costs increase as a result of higher costs of replacing inventories, property, and plant and equipment. Furthermore, W. T. Grant does not value its inventories on a LIFO basis and is thus more seriously affected than if it did, because LIFO acts as a partial surrogate for current cost. Also, firms with substantial physical assets or older physical assets are more affected by inflation than firms with few assets or new assets. Although W. T. Grant's physical assets are relatively new, they account for about 48% of total assets. Thus expenses like depreciation are increased under current cost accounting in order to reflect the cost of replacing the assets.

Another factor contributing to the variation in ROS is the effective income tax rate. This rate is almost always increased by inflation because income taxes are of a monetary nature not affected by inflation. Because income taxes are based on historical costs rather than current costs, the provision for taxes leverages the effect of increased costs on net income.

In effect, inflation represents a tax on capital. For W. T. Grant the effective tax rate based on historical cost is 17.2%, whereas it is in excess of 100% under the current cost approach. W. T. Grant must pay taxes even though it has an inflation-adjusted operating loss.

Investment Turnover

W. T. Grant and other firms with low margins usually try to adopt a strategy of effective asset management to turn their investments over more frequently. Even so, inflation leaves its mark, particularly when physical assets comprise a significant proportion of total assets. The relatively long life of most plant assets means that there is a high probability for their replacement costs to depart substantially from original costs.

For W. T. Grant we estimate that fixed assets are understated from their replacement cost by about 27% (based on estimating the average age of fixed assets by dividing the accumulated depreciation by depreciation expense and then using the consumer price index in Table 5.10 to price-level-adjust them). Since W. T. Grant does not use LIFO inventory accounting, historical inventories closely approximate replacement cost. However, as discussed previously, this practice leads to profits being misstated. Thus management is in a bind when it comes to deciding which technique to use for valuing inventories. With inflation a non-LIFO technique is better for approximating inventory value in the balance sheet, and LIFO is better for showing current cost in the income statement and the ROS calculation. Since consistency is required, whichever technique is used in presenting the balance sheet must also be used in the income statement.

The amount of net assets in the turnover ratio is increased for any unrealized holding gains. These unrealized gains occur on physical assets, such as inventories, property, and plant and equipment, because inflation increases the replacement cost of such assets. While such gains may be "realizable," they are not realized under present generally accepted accounting principles and do not apply to historical costs.

Leverage

An often-heard saying is that it is good to have fixed-rate debt during inflation because the debt is repaid in cheaper dollars in the future. This statement, however, assumes that creditors do not anticipate inflation and thus consistently lose money on their loans. The truth is that creditors attempt to anticipate what inflation will be by incorporating an inflation expectation into the interest rate they charge for the loans or by issuing variable-rate debt. Debtors only gain if creditors underanticipate the rate of inflation. Of course, the opposite is also true, and in such cases the creditors will gain even more than anticipated.

Leverage is measured in the ROE equation as total assets to total equity. The ratio measures the extent to which assets are financed and unrealized holding gains are leveraged by monetary liabilities. A high ratio signifies substantial debt or other monetary liabilities. Calculations based on current costs are always lower than those based on historical costs because holding gains are included in shareholders' equity when current costs are used. Inflation provides an incentive to increase the use of debt to the extent feasible without impairing liquidity in order to maximize the benefits to shareholders from holding physical assets.

Growth

An earlier section demonstrated that growth is positively associated with ROE and earnings retention. Since historical accounting – based ROE exceeds current cost ROE, inflation causes real growth to decline. Inflation also results in an implicit increase in dividend payout, which compounds the problem.

Since dividends represent a monetary flow, the retention ratio may be positive under the historical cost approach and negative under the current cost technique (note that W. T. Grant incurred negative retention under historical accounting techniques in 1974). The negative ratio thus causes negative growth in the current cost analysis. Effectively, the dividends represent liquidating dividends, although they would not be reflected as such under historical cost analysis or accounting techniques. Thus management has a critical role to play in monitoring inflation-adjusted performance and in explaining the problem to the various claimants of the organization.

In summary, current cost statements may give investors and managers an early warning of impending trouble and considerable lead time to take actions to preserve the company's financial integrity. An analyst investigates a large body of information when evaluating a company and projecting earnings, dividends, and cash flows. A substantial part, but not all, of this information is contained in the historical cost financial statements. Through the use of inflation-adjusted statements, the analyst is better able to look for insights that explain both change and change in the rate of change. The adverse cumulative effect of inflation may appear as a need for additional debt, a pressure on dividends to meet cash requirements, a dilution of the common shareholders' interest, or an inability to grow in real terms. Low-inflation-adjusted returns on capital may be a precursor of financial problems.

Summary

This chapter is an extension of traditional financial analysis discussed in Chapter 3. Imperfect indicators of a firm's liquidity have been discussed. They include a return-on-equity model, which is also used to determine debt levels and calculate the rate of sustainable growth. The firm's cash conversion cycle and cash breakeven were examined. Finally, the recasting of historical accounting statements to adjust for the impact of inflation was discussed.

Much interaction exists between these measures. Minimizing the cash conversion cycle and the cash breakeven point should lead to improved management of return on equity, sustainable growth, debt, and, of course, liquidity.

Ideally, analysis incorporates inflation's effects. Ignoring inflation can have a serious impact on both present and future performance. The use of historical accounting principles leads to gross overstatement of ROE during inflationary periods. If management fails to consider the impact of inflation on financial results, policy may be set that is inconsistent with sustainable growth and shareholder wealth maximization.

Key Concepts

Asset turnover
Cash breakeven
Cash conversion cycle
Cash inadequacy
Common-size statements
Debt capacity
Financial leverage
Life cycle cash needs

Maximization of ROE
Monetary versus nonmonetary assets/
    liabilities
Operating cycle
Profitability
Real profit
Significance of inflation
Sustainable growth

Appendix A

Relationship Between Residual Income and Return on Equity

Chapter 1 defined management's objective to be maximization of residual income (RI). This chapter uses return on equity (ROE) as the appropriate objective to maximize. The purpose of this appendix is to show the relationship between RI and ROE.

Residual income is defined as

$$RI = NOI(1 - t) - kI, \tag{A.1}$$

where NOI is net operating income (i.e., EBIT), t is the tax rate, k is the weighted average cost of capital, and I is investment.

This equation can be rewritten as

$$RI = NI + k_dD(1 - t) - kI, \tag{A.2}$$

where NI is after-tax net income and k_dD is the interest payment. The equivalency of $NOI(1 - t)$ to $NI + k_dD(1 - t)$ was mentioned in Chapter 3 when the return-on-asset ratio was discussed.

If both sides of Eq. (A.2) are divided by equity (E), and k is defined as the weighted average costs for debt (after taxes) and equity, the following equation results:

$$\frac{RI}{E} = \frac{NI}{E} + \frac{k_d(1 - t)D}{E} - \left[\frac{k_d(1 - t)D}{I} + \frac{k_eE}{I}\right]\frac{I}{E}, \tag{A.3}$$

where k_e is the cost of equity. Recognizing that NI/E is ROE and simplifying the equation results in

$$\frac{RI}{E} = ROE - k_e \tag{A.4}$$

or

$$RI = NI - k_eE, \tag{A.5}$$

which can also be derived directly from Eq. (A.2) by substituting the debt and equity component cost of capitals for the weighted average cost of capital k.

Thus maximizing the residual income-to-equity ratio is equivalent to maximizing the difference between ROE and cost of equity.

Appendix B

Justification and Calculus for an ROE-Maximizing Capital Structure

Return-on-equity (ROE) models have received much attention as being useful for understanding management's stewardship of the firm. Lerner and Carleton's book *A Theory of Financial Analysis,* published in 1966, relied heavily on ROE to develop an analytical frame of reference for the study of finance. More recently, Fruhan's book *Financial Strategy: Studies in the Creation, Transfer, and Destruction of Shareholder Value* relies on the ratio of ROE to cost of equity for explaining his shareholder value thesis. These authors have greatly influenced us. Modigliani and Miller's seminal work on corporate valuation has also influenced us, as is explained next.[1]

Return on equity is normally defined as

$$\text{ROE} = \frac{\text{profit after taxes}}{\text{equity}} = \frac{(rA - iD)(1 - t)}{E}, \tag{B.1}$$

where

$$r = \frac{\text{EBIT}}{\text{net assets}},$$

A = net assets (i.e., total assets less noninterest-bearing current liabilities),

i = interest rate for debt,

D = interest-bearing debt (both short- and long-term),

t = corporate tax rate,

E = equity.

Since $A = D + E$, the equation can be rewritten as

$$\text{ROE} = \frac{[r(E + D) - iD](1 - t)}{E} = \left[r + (r - i)\frac{D}{E} \right](1 - t), \tag{B.2}$$

which is Eq. (5.6) in the text.

Equation (5.6) requires further discussion to place it in proper perspective. It is equivalent to Modigliani and Miller's (MM) proposition II. Inherent in MM's valuation model are the implicit assumptions that the market values for the firm's debt and equity equal their book values and that the cost of debt is constant. Thus since both debt and equity sell at book

---

[1] See the Selected Readings at the end of the text for the specific references.

values, the total cost of capital and the valuation placed upon the firm will not be affected by changes in the capital structure. However, to get this result, MM assumed that the cost of equity k_e is a rising function of the debt-to-equity ratio D/E: $k_e = r + f(D/E)$. MM then proposed the following specification to describe the way the rate of discount changes as a function of the debt-equity ratio: $f(D/E) = (r - i)D/E$, where, you recall, the cost of debt i is constant. Substituting this expression into the equation for k_e results in MM's proposition II. Note, however, that there is no inherent reason for choosing the precise functional form $f(D/E) = (r - i)D/E$ as a behavioral postulate. We could just as well assume that $f(D/E) > (r - i)D/E$, in which case the price would be less than the book value, or that $f(D/E) < (r - i)D/E$, in which case the price would be higher than its book value. Since Eq. (5.6) was derived as a pure accounting tautology, it follows that MM's proposition II by itself has no behavioral implications.

Relaxation of the unrealistic assumption that the cost of debt is constant as more debt is taken on allows a capital structure to be derived for maximizing return on equity. The proof follows.

The partial differentiation of Eq. (5.6) with respect to the leverage ratio is

$$\frac{\partial \text{ROE}}{\partial(D/E)} = \left\{ \frac{\partial r}{\partial(D/E)} + (r - i) \frac{\partial(D/E)}{\partial(D/E)} \right.$$
$$\left. + \left(\frac{D}{E}\right) \left[\frac{\partial r}{\partial(D/E)} - \frac{\partial i}{\partial(D/E)} \right] \right\} (1 - t). \qquad \text{(B.3)}$$

Setting this equation equal to zero and solving in terms of D/E, in order to find the capital structure that maximizes return on equity, results in Eq. (5.7) of the text:

$$\frac{D}{E} = \frac{(r - i) + \partial r/\partial(D/E)}{\partial i/\partial(D/E) - \partial r/\partial(D/E)}. \qquad \text{(B.4)}$$

Those who are unsure of their skills in calculus should note that the firm's D/E ratio is not given by the solution to the right-hand side of this equation, as is normally the case in solving algebraic problems. *The interpretation of this equation is that when the firm's D/E ratio equals the right-hand side of the equation, then a capital structure exists that maximizes ROE.* Whenever the D/E ratio is not equal to the right-hand side of the equation, ROE is not maximized.

Appendix C
Derivation of the Sustainable Growth Model

A key assumption of the sustainable growth model is that new equity is not raised to support growth. Additional equity is obtained from retained earnings, which are defined as

$$\text{retained earnings} = \text{profits} - \text{dividends}$$
$$= (\text{return on sales}) \times \text{sales} - \text{dividends} \qquad \text{(C.1)}$$
$$= R(S + \Delta S) \times (1 - p)$$

where R is return on sales, $S + \Delta S$ is last period's sales plus the increase in sales this period, and $1 - p$ is the retention ratio.

Because management wants to hold a targeted debt-equity ratio equal to D/E, each dollar of retained earnings allows debt to be increased in the proportion D/E. Thus,

$$\text{new debt} = \text{retained earnings} \times \text{targeted leverage}$$
$$= R(S + \Delta S) \times (1 - p) \times \frac{D}{E}. \qquad \text{(C.2)}$$

The new debt and equity are then used to support growth in assets, which is measured as $\Delta S \times T$, where T is the asset-sales ratio.

Since the uses of funds must equal the sources of funds,

$$\Delta S \times T = R(S + \Delta S) \times (1 - p) + R(S + \Delta S) \times (1 - p) \times \frac{D}{E}. \qquad \text{(C.3)}$$

Solving this equation algebraically results in the sustainable growth model, Eq. (5.13) in the text.

The alternative sustainable growth model (Eq. 5.14) is derived from this model by substituting A/S for T (since T is defined as A/S) and A/E for $(1 + D/E)$ (since $A = D + E$) and then multiplying both the numerator and the denominator by S (where $A = $ assets, $S = $ sales, $E = $ equity). Eliminating common terms and recognizing that $S \times R/E$ is ROE results in Eq. (5.14).

Fundamentals of Current Cost Accounting

Our analysis of price-level effects differs from that of the accountants, as detailed for them in FASB 33. We ignore adjusting the income statement for any holding gains. We do so intentionally to show the impact of inflation on the firm's production operations. Holding gains arise from holding assets, which increase in value with inflation. The objective of most businesses is to produce, sell, and profit from products that satisfy consumer demand. Most firms do not hoard assets to profit from holding gains. The accountant's inclusion of holding gains in the current cost income statement, in our opinion, detracts from the intent of isolating the influence of inflation on operations and management's ability to cope with it.

The following discussion provides a brief summary of the mechanics of current cost accounting. A more in-depth analysis can be found in an intermediate financial accounting book.

Adjustments to the Balance Sheet

Assets and liabilities are monetary if they are to be paid by currency; otherwise, they are physical. The company either receives or pays a specific amount of currency for monetary assets and liabilities, respectively. Thus these assets and liabilities are not restated for price changes. However, for physical assets current cost is the cost of replacing the asset by one of the same age and operating capacity. Current cost is usually approximated by using a specific price index to the book value of the asset.

Most liabilities are monetary, whereas equity is considered physical. Shareholders' equity is computed as the difference between adjusted assets and liabilities (i.e., it is a plug figure).

Adjustments to the Income Statement

Sales are reported at current price levels when sold and therefore receive no adjustment. Cost of sales requires the following adjustment, since materials and labor were purchased in prior periods:

> beginning inventory (at historical cost)
> > \+ purchases (at historical cost)
> > − ending inventory (at historical cost)
> > \+ realized holding gain
> = cost of sales (at current cost).

Realized holding gains (losses) are the difference between the current cost and the historical cost at the time of sale.

Selling and administrative expenses must be reflected at current cost. Unless these expenses are very late in being recorded and paid, current cost and historical cost will be the same.

Depreciation expense is adjusted to current cost as follows:

first cost of depreciable assets (historical cost)
      − accumulated depreciation (historical cost)
      + first cost of depreciable assets (current cost)
= total ÷ 2
= average current cost balance ÷ useful life in years of the assets
= current cost depreciation expense.

Income taxes are reported at historical cost, which equals current cost.

Questions

1. Define the three major components of return on equity (ROE). What is the purpose of defining ROE in this manner?

2. How do common-size statements help an analyst understand a firm's financial condition?

3. Name some of the hidden problems in favorable return-on-sales and turnover ratios.

4. Explain the meaning of Eq. (5.8). What is its significance to liquidity management?

5. What does sustainable growth mean? How can managers manage sustainable growth? Does it affect liquidity?

6. Define the cash conversion cycle. Is it beneficial for managing liquidity? Explain.

7. How does cash breakeven analysis differ from traditional breakeven analysis? How is it useful for liquidity management?

8. What is the relationship among return on equity, sustainable growth, debt capacity, the cash conversion cycle, and the cash breakeven point?

9. How does an understanding of inflation accounting help one to manage liquidity? How does inflation accounting help satisfy the objective of shareholder wealth maximization?

Problems

The financial data in Table 5.13 is to be used in Problems 1 through 7. Make whatever assumptions you feel are necessary to answer the problems.

1. Calculate a common-size income statement and balance sheet. Comment on any significant changes.

2. Calculate return on equity for each year, using Eq. (5.3). Discuss apparent reasons for any change.

3. If the firm is faced with an interest rate schedule of $i = 0.034 + 0.015(D/E)^2$ this year, what is its optimal debt-equity ratio for maximizing return on equity? What is ROE at the derived-debt level?

TABLE 5.13
Financial Data

	Last year	This year
Balance sheet		
Cash and short-term investments	$ 140,690	$ 112,851
Accounts receivable (net)	56,575	66,720
Inventory	17,798	20,848
Other current assets	31,667	33,521
Fixed assets (includes capitalized leases)	2,331,870	2,706,696
Accumulated depreciation	386,933	479,548
Investment and other assets	162,339	182,281
Accounts payable	161,641	123,356
Accrued liabilities	41,201	50,216
Accrued taxes	27,222	57,054
Current portion of long-term debt	44,243	38,756
Long-term debt	875,809	885,714
Capitalized leases	90,314	84,076
Security deposits by franchises	54,633	59,651
Deferred income taxes	106,777	140,423
Common stock	4,515	4,515
Additional paid-in capital	93,508	93,508
Retained earnings	854,143	1,106,100
Income statement		
Sales	$1,937,935	$2,215,463
Expenses:		
Food and paper	602,647	660,869*
Payroll	333,818	384,133*
Rent	18,628	21,758*
Depreciation and amortization	292,240	289,374
Expenses from franchises:		
Rent	23,725	27,791*
Depreciation and amortization	35,276	46,510
General, selling, and administrative	214,501	230,702†
Interest charges	72,592	90,847
Provision for income taxes	155,900	181,700
Earnings per share	$4.68	$6.99
Dividends per share	0.51	0.74
Shares outstanding	40,300	40,300

* Include as cost of sales.
† 30% of these expenses are variable.

4. Calculate the sustainable growth rate for this year, using Eqs. (5.13) and (5.14). What is the actual growth rate? Discuss what management needs to do to ensure sustainable growth.

5. Calculate the cash conversion cycle for both years. Compare your results with calculated current ratios and quick ratios.

6. Calculate both the traditional operating breakeven sales level and the cash breakeven sales level for this year. Discuss the significance of your results.

7. Discuss how inflation affects your answers to Problems 1 through 6. What inflation information would you like to have to do a better analysis of the financial statements?

Problems 8 through 13 use the financial data for Homeland Variety Corporation given in Tables 3.4 and 3.5.

8. Develop common-size balance sheets and income statements for the years 1983 through 1985.

9. Find the debt levels that maximize return on equity for the years 1983, 1984, and 1985. The interest rate is approximated by $i = 0.125 + 0.005(D/E)^2$.

10. Estimate the sustainable growth rate for 1986, and discuss your answer. This problem requires you to do some projections for the year 1986.

11. Find the cash conversion cycle for the years 1983 through 1985, and discuss the results.

12. Find cash breakeven for the years 1984 and 1985, and discuss the results. Assume that no principal payments are made on the negotiated debt. How would your answers change if principal payments were made?

13. Evaluate the results of Homeland Variety, and comment on any differences from the analysis of Chapter 3.

CHAPTER 6 □
Indicators of Liquidity: PART II

The traditional financial statements — balance sheet and income statement — are important for analysis of profitability, but they are not directly useful for analysis of solvency. The income statement is a functional tool used to provide an estimate of revenues and profits for the period. Management uses the results to implement various expense controls, sales programs, and planned future directions. The balance sheet is, of course, but a snapshot of the firm's financial position at a point in time.

If a firm is to continue in profitable operations, it must remain solvent. This criterion would seem to be a matter of obvious interest, and it is too often assumed that a profitable business is a solvent business. Unfortunately, the facts may differ, as highlighted in Chapter 1 by the "How to Go Broke . . ." illustration. In an important sense, solvency and profitability work in opposite directions. At one extreme the most solvent firms would have as assets only cash. They would have no debts and no profit. At the other extreme the most profitable firms would have debts and no cash. Profitable firms risk the possibility of having no cash at the times debts fall due.

The purpose of this chapter is to discuss some techniques for analyzing liquidity that are more refined than those examined in the previous chapter. These techniques include cash budgeting, liquidity indexes, and funds and cash flow statements.

Cash Budget

The liquidity indicators discussed in the previous chapter provide no indication of the pattern of future cash flows or intraperiod cash flows, either past or future. These limitations are serious if management is to understand

157

liquidity needs. Maintenance of liquidity requires that cash outflows be matched by cash inflows (or the difference made up from liquid holdings) on a day-to-day basis. Therefore the *primary instrument of liquidity management is a cash budget.* It attempts to identify the *cash flows* for periods short enough to permit the assurance that embarrassing intraperiod shortages will not be encountered. In the short run a business can operate with an accounting loss. It cannot operate without cash for long.

A cash budget may be described as a detailed estimate for some future period of time of cash inflows from all sources, cash disbursements for all purposes, and the resulting cash balances. As in the construction of most budgets, the usual forecast period for a cash budget is one year. For this period a breakdown is provided in terms of months, weeks, or even days, in some instances.

A cash budget is not like a *pro forma* (projected) income statement. The purpose of a *pro forma* income statement is to account for all sources of income to be tapped and for all classes of expenses to be incurred in a given period, whether or not the income will be realized in cash in the period and whether or not the expenses will be matched by cash payments. The purpose of a cash budget is to account for all expected inflows of cash, whether to be derived from income sources of the period or from those of other periods or from nonincome sources, such as borrowing and stock sales; and to account for all expected outflows of cash, whether payments of expenses accrued in prior periods, those of the forecast period, or those (prepayments) of subsequent periods, or whether payments not immediately related to expenses, such as those for the purchase of fixed assets or for dividend distributions to the stockholders.

How transactions affect cash budgets and *pro forma* income statements in different ways is indicated in Table 6.1. Only a sampling of transactions

TABLE 6.1
Effect of Transactions on Cash Budgets and Income Statements

	Income statement	Cash budget
Collection of receivables of past periods	Excluded	Included
Collection of current sales to customers	Included	Included
Current sales, payments in subsequent periods	Included	Excluded
Payment of current expenses	Included	Included
Depreciation charges	Included	Excluded
Purchase of new fixed assets for cash	Excluded	Included
Prepayment of expenses chargeable to later periods	Excluded	Included
Borrowing from banks	Excluded	Included
Repayment of bank loans	Excluded	Included
Payment of cash dividends to investors	Excluded	Included

is included to show why the results of operations as forecasted for a given period in an income statement may be far different from the projected net change in cash balances expected to result from the cash transactions of the same period.

Preparation of a Cash Budget

For a firm having a complete system of budgeting control, the preparation of a cash budget is a relatively simple matter. Most of the information needed for the cash budget is contained in budgets that precede it in formulation. One need only transfer to the cash budget the details about monthly cash receipts as indicated in sales, accounts receivable, and miscellaneous income budgets; and details about monthly cash expenditures as found in the materials and direct-labor budgets, the various overhead and miscellaneous expense budgets, and the fixed-asset budget. Details about probable borrowing and repayment of loans, sales and retirement of stocks, and payments of cash dividends must be inserted in the cash budget independently of the other budgets.

Much information supporting the cash budget depends on a sales forecast by month in order to establish collections on receivables and to estimate cash costs. Numerous methods of estimating sales exist. It is not our intent here to provide detailed explanations of forecasting methods, but we mention that regression and time series analysis are among the more useful tools employed for this purpose. Sales of refrigerators, for example, may be estimated by a multiple regression model that includes such independent variables as disposal income, rate of household formations, and replacement cycle. These estimates may be modified subjectively by the financial manager for variables not considered in the statistical analysis. Armed with sales estimates, selling credit terms, and experience data on the collection of receivables, the manager can estimate cash receipts.

From the sales predictions and the current level of inventories, the financial manager can help the manufacturing manager plan the production rate. This plan will enable the financial manager to compute cash outlays for materials and labor. The purchases have to be ordered early enough to ensure delivery by the time the material is needed for production. The invoice data can be estimated from previous experience, which, together with purchase credit terms, can be used to determine a payments schedule on accounts payable. In a seasonal business the decision about whether the firm should seek level production with lower unit costs and larger inventories or fluctuating production with small inventories depends upon variables such as inventory carrying costs, costs of obsolescence risk, overtime rates, and employment and discharge costs.

If the analyst were provided with an estimated probability distribution of sales for each month, for example, a distribution of estimated net cash flows could be generated. Realistically, what the financial manager needs to do is forecast a range of net cash flow outcomes, taking into account a set of factors that may cause projections to vary significantly.

ILLUSTRATION 6.1

Management estimates total sales for the period January through July, based on actual sales for the immediate past quarter, to be as provided in Table 6.2.

The following assumptions are made:

1. All prices and costs remain constant.
2. Sales are 75% for credit and 25% for cash.
3. 60% of credit sales are collected one month after the sale, 30% in the second month, and 10% in the third month. Bad-debt losses are insignificant.
4. The company operates with a 20% gross margin and purchases and pays for each month's anticipated sales in the preceding month.
5. Wages and salaries are as follows:

January	$30,000	April	$50,000
February	40,000	May	40,000
March	50,000	June	35,000

6. Rent is $2000 a month.
7. Interest on $500,000 of 16% bonds is due on the calendar quarter.
8. A tax prepayment of $50,000 is due in April.
9. A capital addition of $30,000 is planned in June.
10. The company has a cash balance of $100,000 at December 31, which is the minimum desired level.
11. Excess funds are invested in money market instruments and earn interest at 8% per annum in the month the excess occurs.

TABLE 6.2
Sales: Past and Expected

Historical		Forecast			
October	$300,000	January	$150,000	April	$300,000
November	350,000	February	200,000	May	250,000
December	400,000	March	200,000	June	200,000
				July	300,000

TABLE 6.3
Analysis of Sales ($00)

	Past			Future					
	Oct.	Nov.	Dec.	Jan.	Feb.	Mar.	Apr.	May	June
Cash	750	875	1000	375	500	500	750	625	500
Credit	2250	2625	3000	1125	1500	1500	2250	1875	1500
Total	3000	3500	4000	1500	2000	2000	3000	2500	2000

12. Funds can be borrowed against a line of credit on a monthly basis at 16% per annum. Repayments are assumed to be made at the end of the following month if excess cash or marketable securities exist. Interest is payable on the end of the month in which the borrowing is incurred and is not accrued.

Given this information, a cash budget for the next six months is prepared. The total sales of the company are divided into cash and credit components according to assumption 2. Table 6.3 shows the results.

Since there is a lag in collections, according to assumption 3, the expected cash receipts are as set forth in Table 6.4.

Assumption 4 indicates that purchases are made in the month prior to sale and are paid in full in that month. Other cash outlays are calculated according to assumptions 5 through 9. Table 6.5 summarizes the payment patterns.

The monthly change in the firm's cash position, before any additional borrowing, is found by comparing the total cash receipts with the cash disbursements. Table 6.6 shows the expected change.

Any additional short-term borrowings or repayments depend on the beginning cash position and the net change for the month. Borrowings

TABLE 6.4
Expected Cash Receipts ($00)

	Jan.	Feb.	Mar.	Apr.	May	June
Cash sales	375.0	500.0	500.0	750.0	625.0	500.0
Collections:						
60% prior month	1800.0	675.0	900.0	900.0	1350.0	1125.0
30% 2 months prior	787.5	900.0	337.5	450.0	450.0	675.0
10% 3 months prior	225.0	262.5	300.0	112.5	150.0	150.0
Total collections	3187.5	2337.5	2037.5	2212.5	2575.0	2450.0

TABLE 6.5
Expected Cash Outlays ($00)

	Jan.	Feb.	Mar.	Apr.	May	June
Purchases (80% of sales)	1600	1600	2400	2000	1600	2400
Wages and salaries	300	400	500	500	400	350
Rent	20	20	20	20	20	20
Interest			200			200
Taxes payable				500		
New assets						300
Total	1920	2020	3120	3020	2020	3270

TABLE 6.6
Expected Change in Cash Before Additional Borrowing ($00)

	Jan.	Feb.	Mar.	Apr.	May	June
Cash receipts	3187.5	2337.5	2037.5	2212.5	2575.0	2450.0
Cash outlays	1920.0	2020.0	3120.0	3020.0	2020.0	3270.0
Surplus <shortage>	1267.5	317.5	<1082.5>	<807.5>	555.0	<820.0>

and repayments happen according to assumptions 10 through 12 and are summarized in Table 6.7.   □

Summary

To summarize, preparation of a cash budget requires that the future cash position of the firm be estimated for the time when each disbursement and each collection will be made. From a tabulation of these estimates a forecast of the cash position can be prepared for the next several periods, which readily identifies the cash position. Although Illustration 6.1 shows borrowing from a line of credit, management could possibly postpone payment to some of its suppliers and, in effect, rely more heavily on trade credit. Another option is to try and improve the cash position by accelerating the flow of payments from creditors.

The cash budget is highly dependent on the sales forecast, which is difficult to estimate. An error in this figure will cause many of the other entries, such as collections from receivables, outlays for materials, and so on, to be misstated. One way of minimizing the risk associated with cash budgeting is to prepare several budgets, using different "optimistic" and "pessimistic" estimates for sales, collections and payments. The number of possible combinations of events that can arise, however, is very large.

TABLE 6.7
Expected Borrowings and Repayments ($00)

	Jan.	Feb.	Mar.	Apr.	May	June
Beginning balance	1000.0	1000.0	1000.0	1000.0	1000.0	1000.0
Gain <loss>	1267.5	317.5	<1082.5>	<807.5>	555.0	<820.0>
Total	2267.5	1317.5	<82.5>	192.5	1555.0	180.0
Borrowings* <repayments>				286.2	<286.2>	560.8
Interest†				<3.8>	<3.8>	<7.5>
<Investment> liquidation	<1267.5>	<317.5>	1082.5	525.1	<265.0>	266.7
Ending balance	1000.0	1000.0	1000.0	1000.0	1000.0	1000.0
Investment in securities						
Beginning balance	0	1276.0	1604.1	525.1	0	266.7
Additions <deletions>	1267.5	317.5	<1082.5>	<525.1>	265.0	<266.7>
Cumulative investments	1267.5	1593.5	521.6	0	265.0	0
Interest income	8.5	10.6	3.5	0	1.7	0
Ending balance	1276.0	1604.1	525.1	0	266.7	0

* Short-term loan required = (loss − short-term investments)/(1 − 0.16/12).
† Interest expense = (0.16/12) × (short-term loan).

For example, sales can be high, low, or fair; the receivables collection and payable policies can be fast or slow. Without the use of a computer one can seldom explore many of these combinations.

While the cash budget shows which factors give rise to changes in the firm's cash position, it does not take into account changes in other balance sheet items and overall profitability. For example, is inventory being accumulated too rapidly? Is the ratio of sales to outstanding receivables being maintained at a reasonable level? What is the impact on profits? To answer questions such as these, one can use the changes in ROE that result from changing cash budget scenarios in order to ascertain the effect on shareholder wealth.

Thus it should be apparent that *the cash budget is the most important tool for the financial manager in maintaining liquidity* and in obtaining a reading of liquidity's influence on profitability. Techniques such as those discussed in the previous chapter and those to be discussed next simply raise a suspicion of liquidity problems.

Chapter 8 will extend the discussion of cash budgeting by using a statistical model to estimate daily net cash flows for monthly data. The calculation of daily net cash flows is important since intramonth cash problems can arise that monthly data is not able to highlight.

Liquidity Indexes

Management frequently wants information presented in a summary form rather than in a detailed form. Chapter 3 indicated that there is disagreement about what constitutes a good summary indicator of liquidity. The liquidity indexes discussed next are superior to those measures discussed in Chapter 3 since much of the data used in their calculation is taken directly from the cash budget.

Liquidity Flow Index (LFI)

The cash budget's ratio of operating cash inflows to the required rate of cash outflow for a particular period is termed the *liquidity flow index* (LFI).[1] The operating cash inflows are defined as the total amount of cash available per unit of time to meet required outflows without temporarily drawing on a line of credit or long-term funds or prejudicing future operating efficiency. The required rate of outflow is defined as the amount of obligations falling due for payment per unit of time.

Mathematically, the index is defined as follows:

$$\text{LFI} = \frac{\begin{matrix}\text{opening} & & \text{expected} & & \text{expected} \\ \text{cash} & + & \text{cash} & - & \text{closing} \\ \text{balances} & & \text{receipts} & & \text{cash balances}\end{matrix}}{\text{expected cash payments}} \qquad (6.1)$$

The numerator represents cash inflows from the cash budget; the denominator is the cash budget's outflows.

ILLUSTRATION 6.2

The cash budget discussed in Illustration 6.1 is used to calculate the index. Table 6.8 summarizes the results. Part (a) of the table includes the current month's surplus or deficit as shown in Table 6.6. It ignores any interest earned on surplus balances as well as any monthly incremental changes

---

[1] This measure was developed by K. W. Lemeke in an article titled "The Evaluation of Liquidity: An Analytical Study," *Journal of Accounting Research* (Spring 1970): 47–77.

TABLE 6.8
Calculation of the Liquidity Flow Index ($00)

	Jan.	Feb.	Mar.	Apr.	May	June	Total
(a) Includes current month's surplus/deficit							
Opening cash (Table 6.7)	1000.0	1000.0	1000.0	1000.0	1000.0	1000.0	1000.0
Plus cash receipts (Table 6.6)	3187.5	2337.5	2037.5	2212.5	2575.0	2450.0	14800.0
Minus ending cash (Table 6.7)	1000.0	1000.0	1000.0	1000.0	1000.0	1000.0	1000.0
Equals numerator	3187.5	2337.5	2037.5	2212.5	2575.0	2450.0	14800.0
Divided by cash payments (Table 6.6)	1920.0	2020.0	3120.0	3020.0	2020.0	3270.0	15370.0
Equals index	1.660	1.157	0.653	0.733	1.275	0.749	0.963
(b) Includes adjustments to near-cash balances							
Numerator (as above)	3187.5	2337.5	2037.5	2212.5	2575.0	2450.0	14800.0
Plus near cash (Table 6.7)	8.5	1286.6	1607.6	525.1	1.7	266.7	24.3
Equals adjusted numerator	3196.0	3624.1	3645.1	2737.6	2576.7	2716.7	14824.3
Index	1.665	1.794	1.168	0.907	1.276	0.831	0.965

to the near cash balances. This manipulation provides management with a worst-case scenario. Change in near-cash balances are then incorporated into the index in part (b) to indicate the effect of these balances in helping management satisfy liquidity needs. □

The index embodies a going-concern concept of worst-case, debt-paying ability since lines of credit and use of long-term funds are excluded. Over a period of time (say, 12 months), the LFI should tend to a numerical value of 1.0. An index much in excess of 1.0 suggests inefficient or ultraconservative cash management. An index much below 1.0 indicates cash deficiency problems. Minor variations in the ratio, either above or below the 1.0 level, can be due to seasonal influences, and while they cannot be ignored, generally they only require minor attention, as is apparently the situation in Illustration 6.2.

Although the ratio can be calculated by using data of varying period lengths, if the time is too long (e.g., quarterly or annual periods), two limitations are evident. First, much of the data would be outdated by the time of reporting and may be of little use for projecting cash flows. Second, longer periods smooth out intrayear fluctuations. Thus cash flow problems may not be discovered soon enough.

Relative Liquidity Index (RLI)

The *relative liquidity index*[2] measures the extent to which deviations in net cash flows, during some time period, are covered by cash on hand, unused lines of credit, and cash generated by operations. The index is a component of a complex mathematical process that gives the likelihood that the firm will become temporarily insolvent. This mathematical process provides the index with a strong theoretical base, which is lacking with most liquidity ratios. The index is defined as follows:

$$\text{RLI} = \frac{\begin{array}{c}\text{initial liquid} \\ \text{reserve}\end{array} + \begin{array}{c}\text{total anticipated net cash flow} \\ \text{during the analysis horizon}\end{array}}{\begin{array}{c}\text{uncertainty about net cash flow during the analysis} \\ \text{horizon as measured by the standard deviation}\end{array}} \qquad (6.2)$$

The index is the ratio of cash flow resources to potential cash flow requirements. Low values of the RLI correspond to increased probabilities of technical insolvency. Table 6.9 illustrates the calculation of RLI by using the cash budget data of Illustration 6.1.

TABLE 6.9
Calculation of the Relative Liquidity Index ($00)

Initial liquid reserve

Cash and securities (Table 6.7)	$1000.0
Line of credit (assumed)	4000.0
Total	$5000.0

Net operating cash flows (Table 6.6)

January	$ 1267.5
February	317.5
March	<1082.5>
April	<807.5>
May	555.0
June	<820.0>
Total	<$570.0>
Standard deviation	$ 944.2

$$\text{RLI} = \frac{5000 - 570}{944.2} = 4.692$$

---

[2] This measure was developed by G. W. Emery and K. O. Cogger in an article titled "The Measurement of Liquidity," *Journal of Accounting Research* (Autumn 1982):290 – 303.

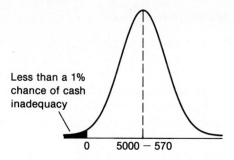

Less than a 1%
chance of cash
inadequacy

0   5000 − 570

FIGURE 6.1
Probability of Cash Inadequacy

The probability of insolvency can be readily computed by treating the index as the number of standard deviations that cash balances are from zero, as shown in Fig. 6.1. According to a table of areas under the normal curve (see the Appendix to this chapter), 4.692 standard deviations indicate less than a 1 percent chance of insolvency. Low initial reserves, low net cash flows, and high variability in the net cash flows attribute to a low RLI. If each of these factors is working against the firm at the same time, insolvency may be the result.

For computing the ratio, the analyst may obtain a value of initial reserves fairly easily by using internal financial reports. The initial liquid reserve is the sum of opening cash and marketable security balances plus the company's short-term borrowing capacity. The net cash flows during the planning period should be adjusted to control for the effect of any large, regularly recurring items. If there are cash inflows (outflows) that are matched with uses for (sources of) funds, then they should be excluded from the data used to estimate net cash flow and variability of net cash flow. Failure to do so injects a systematic bias into the calculation of the index.

Summary

Measurement of liquidity should be done on a going-concern basis, not a liquidation basis (as is embodied in both the current and the quick ratios). Both the LFI and RLI are going-concern measures since they measure cash flows. They also incorporate managements' ability to draw down other current assets or to increase current liabilities, or to utilize credit lines and other sources of financing. All these actions are clearly part of the ability to meet liquidity needs. Thus liquid-asset levels alone are clearly an incomplete characterization of liquidity.

Funds Flow Analysis

A frequently used technique for analyzing liquidity is *funds flow analysis.* Financial annual reports of publicly traded companies endeavor to capture this analysis in a statement called Statement of Changes in Financial Position, or, more commonly, the funds statement. Caution must be exercised when one is using the funds statement, since *funds do not refer to cash,* although, in a sense, funds can be thought of as cash. If a business is operated strictly on a cash basis, it is easy to trace the key commitments and recoveries of cash over a time period. This cash flow pattern presents a picture of economic resource deployment.

The purposes of analyzing funds are to show what buying power has flowed into the firm for the period and to describe resource deployments. For instance, management can grant or obtain credit; and every time it does so, an economic resource is committed. Eventually, such transactions result in cash changing hands, but in the meantime management cannot ignore the fact that a resource commitment has been made. If management grants trade credit to its customers, for example, its funds or resources are in effect used by someone else until the customer pays the account. If a business obtains trade credit from a supplier, the supplier's funds or resources are in effect employed by the company until payment is made.

An imprudent management can overcommit a firm by both taking on and granting too many credit obligations. Although no cash changes hands, it is hard to deny that economic value has been shifted by these transactions.

Definition of Funds

The traditional accounting definition of funds is that they represent net working capital: current assets less current liabilities. In this definition *funds represent the net current resources available to the firm or expected to become available whenever current assets are increased or current liabilities are decreased, when these changes are not offset by changes in other net working capital items.* Funds are decreased, on the other hand, when current assets are decreased or current liabilities are increased without affecting other current accounts.

This definition of funds indicates that they are not a true cash flow concept. Increases in receivables arising from the sale of goods and services are considered a *constructive receipt* of cash. Increases in accounts payable are considered to represent the *constructive payment* for goods and services received. This definition assumes that the collection of receivables and the actual payment of accounts payable simply represent conversions from one (quasi) monetary form into another.

Usefulness of Net Working Capital as Funds

Successfully meeting the production and distribution objectives of an organization requires capable funds management. The availability of funds sets the limits of what an organization can do. Funds management is the control and strategic deployment of the inflow of funds generated by a business and of funds secured from outside sources.

Analysis of changes in net working capital provides a picture of management's handling of *circulating capital*. The funds statement summarizes the results of financial activities of a business for the current period and presents the reasons for the net change in financial position. It gives insight into the financial policy of management by providing answers to the following questions:

- □ What has caused the change in the net working capital position?
- □ How much net working capital was provided by operations, and what disposition was made of it?
- □ What was the amount of funds derived from the sale of capital stock or through long-term borrowing, and what use was made of these funds?
- □ Did the company dispose of any of the noncurrent assets, and if so, what were the proceeds?
- □ What additional noncurrent assets were acquired by using net working capital?
- □ In what ways were the resources derived from operations invested?

Additionally, the funds statement can be useful to management as an important aid in controlling net working capital and in the effective utilization of resources in the future.

Disadvantages of Net Working Capital as Funds

While a funds statement based on the net working capital concept is usually a brief presentation, many significant interfirm transactions are not disclosed. For example, significant additions to inventories financed by short-term notes would not be shown because the two items are offset in the computation of the change in net working capital. Furthermore, transactions not affecting net working capital, such as the acquisition of plant and equipment by the issuance of common stock, may or may not be included in this statement, depending on management preference. Therefore the funds statement will, perhaps, disclose neither structural changes in the financial relationships in the firm nor major changes in policy regarding investments in current assets and short-term financing.

A major disadvantage of the net working capital concept of funds is that nonmonetary assets, such as inventories and prepaid expenses, and a few nonmonetary liabilities, such as advance receipts for services to be performed by the firm in the future, are included as if they were monetary items. The inclusion of inventories and prepaid expenses in the concept of funds is particularly disturbing if the information is to be relevant to investors and creditors in their predictions of future liquidity and funds flows. They are disturbing because the dollars assigned to inventories and prepaid expenses are the result of allocations of cost or other measurement over several periods. An increase in the reported amount of these items, for example, could not be interpreted as an increase in general purchasing power available for other uses.

Preparation of the Funds Flow Statement

Funds flow analysis rests heavily on an understanding of commonly accepted accounting methods, since accounting statements serve as the basis for analysis. A thorough funds flow analysis involves a number of fairly complex adjustments as the effect of accounting conventions is translated into funds movements.

Frequently, two balance sheets are used to reflect the net effect of all funds transactions from the beginning of an accounting interval to its end. The assets side shows the way in which funds have been *used,* and the liabilities and equities side shows the *sources* from which funds have been obtained.

In accordance with the dual-aspect concept, total sources of funds must equal total uses of funds. The following relationship therefore exists:

sources = uses,

or

increases in liabilities and equities + decreases in assets
    = increases in assets + decreases in liabilities and equities.   (6.3)

The accounting relationship of assets = liabilities + equity allows the sources and uses relationship to be written as

sources − uses = net working capital change,   (6.4)

or

change in net working capital
        = change in noncurrent liabilities + change in equity
                − change in noncurrent assets.   (6.5)

This definition indicates that funds flow consists of resources (*permanent capital*) supplied by long-term creditors and by shareholders, including both their original investment and the resources they have supplied by permitting earnings to be retained in the business, and the change in noncurrent assets, such as plant and equipment. Changes in the sources of permanent capital and the uses to which they are put are likely to be of more than ordinary interest both to management and to outsiders since these changes reflect the results of the important financial decisions that have long-run consequences.

Part of the permanent capital is invested in buildings, equipment, and other noncurrent assets, but only a fraction of the current assets have to be financed from permanent capital, since vendors and short-term creditors provide the remainder of necessary financing. The amount that is financed from permanent capital is the difference between the total current assets and the total current liabilities, that is, net working capital.

Table 6.10 summarizes the sources-and-uses approach for W. T. Grant's balance sheets.

TABLE 6.10
W. T. Grant Company
Sources and Uses of Funds
For the Period Ended January 31, 1974
($000)

	1974	1973	Source	Use
Assets				
Current assets:				
Cash and marketable securities	$ 45,951	$ 30,943		$ 15,008
Accounts receivable (net)	598,799	542,752		56,047
Inventories (lower of cost or market)	450,637	399,533		51,104
Prepaid expenses	7,299	6,648		651
Total current assets	$1,102,686	$ 979,876		
Miscellaneous assets:				
Investment in subsidiaries	$ 32,600	$ 29,030		3,570
Investment in debentures of				
unconsolidated subsidiaries	11,651	5,951		5,700
Total miscellaneous assets	$ 44,251	$ 34,981		
Fixed assets:				
Building and equipment	$ 152,922	$ 138,607		14,315
Less accumulated depreciation	52,546	47,926	$ 4,620	
Net building and equipment	$ 100,376	$ 90,681		
Land	608	739	131	
Total fixed assets	$ 100,984	$ 91,420		

(continued)

TABLE 6.10 (Cont.)

	1974	1973	Source	Use
Other assets:				
Common stock of W. T. Grant held for deferred compensation plan	$ 2,500	$ 2,381		119
Other	1,200	600		600
Unamortized debt expenses	1,362	1,440	78	
Total assets	$1,252,983	$1,110,698		
Liabilities and equity				
Current liabilities:				
Trade accounts payable	$ 58,192	$ 60,973		2,781
Short-term commercial notes payable	453,097	380,034	73,063	
Bank loans payable	0	10,000		10,000
Accrued wages payable	14,678	19,000		4,322
Other miscellaneous	31,040	24,443	6,597	
Federal income taxes payable	0	8,480		8,480
Total current liabilities	$ 557,007	$ 502,930		
Long-term liabilities	$ 220,336	$ 126,672	93,664	
Indeterminant liabilities:				
Deferred contingent compensation	$ 2,396	$ 2,394	2	
Deferred income taxes	14,649	11,926	2,723	
Deferred credits, principally income taxes related to installment sales	133,057	130,137	2,920	
Other	1,800	2,300		500
Total indeterminate liabilities	$ 151,902	$ 146,757		
Shareholders' equity:				
Cumulative preferred stock — 3¾%, $100 par value; authorized 250,000 shares	$ 7,465	$ 8,600		1,135
Common stock — 22,500,000 shares of $1.25 par value authorized	18,599	18,588	11	
Capital surplus	84,271	84,718		447
Amounts paid by employees under purchase contracts for common stock	1,638	1,429	209	
Retained earnings	248,461	261,153		12,692
Less treasury stock	<36,696>	<40,149>	3,453	
Total shareholders' equity	$ 323,738	$ 334,339		
Total liabilities and equity	$1,252,983	$1,110,698		
Total sources and uses			$187,471	$187,471

Problems with Analyzing Balance Sheet Changes

A problem with simply finding differences in balance sheet accounts is that they do not provide a complete picture of major funds flow. Three major classes of adjustments are needed:

1. The *change in retained earnings* has two elements of interest. The first is net income or loss from operations, and the second is dividends paid to the various classes of shareholders.
2. Net income contains a number of *accounting entries that do not require funds* (e.g., depreciation).
3. The *change in net fixed assets* is a result of both funds and nonfunds movements. It consists of changes in gross fixed assets, changes in accumulated depreciation, and often the effect of nonrecurring adjustments for retirements of plant and equipment.

Changes in Retained Earnings

Changes in retained earnings can be analyzed by the following equation:

ending retained earnings
$$= \text{beginning retained earnings} + \text{net income for the period}$$
$$- \text{cash dividends declared for the period.} \qquad (6.6)$$

For example, for data for W. T. Grant, as taken from Chapter 3, Appendix B, Tables B.1 and B.2, the equation is

$$\$248,461 = \$261,153 + \$8429 - \$21,122,$$

which balances. However, if one substituted the relevant information into the right-hand side of the equation, and it did not equal ending retained earnings, one would have had to look for clues in the published information accompanying the statements about the adjustments made to retained earnings.

Stock dividends are a frequent reason that the equation does not balance. A stock dividend, which is defined as the distribution of additional shares of capital stock without cash payments to existing shareholders, requires a book adjustment to be made reducing retained earnings and increasing capital stock. Strictly speaking, no economic value has resulted, nor has liquidity been affected. But if the amount is significant enough, the analyst must decide whether to include it in the analysis. Stock dividends are frequently given in lieu of cash dividends as a means of conserving liquidity while still allowing stockholders to feel that they are receiving something of value (although of questionable value).

Another prime candidate to consider if the equation does not balance is a change in a reserve account. For example, a reserve for self-insurance or a contingency for a lawsuit may have been established. It can be argued that such items do not represent a funds movement, since no economic values were committed, and should therefore be excluded from the analysis. To do so, however, may be ignoring extremely relevant information to the long-term success and liquidity of the business.

Changes in Net Income

Net income contains many accounting write-offs and adjustments intended to properly account for the effect of past or anticipated revenue and cost elements in the current period. Since analysis of funds flow is an attempt to recognize the impact of resource commitments, *nonmonetary write-offs* such as depreciation and amortization of past expenditures tend to obscure the picture. The true impact of net income on a company's funds is measured before any such items. Reported net income, however, is stated after write-offs and must therefore be adjusted if considered important enough.

Table 6.11 lists several transactions that affect net income but not net working capital. All the items listed enter into the calculation of net income as revenue, expense, or gain or loss. However, they affect noncurrent accounts rather than net working capital accounts. Since analysis of funds balances to the change in net working capital for the period, these adjustments must be made to reported net income.

Noncurrent deferred income taxes are included in the list in Table 6.11. They deserve special attention since they are often misunderstood.

TABLE 6.11
Adjustments to Net Income for Funds Flow

Additions to net income

Amortization of capital leases, deferred charges, and goodwill
Compensation expense from executive stock option plans
Depletion and depreciation expenses
Increases (decreases) in noncurrent deferred income tax and investment credits (debits)
Investment losses under the equity method
Lease obligations
Losses from the retirement of long-term debt and from the sale of plant and equipment
Minority interests in net income of subsidiaries
Pension expense not funded currently

Deductions from net income

Decreases in deferred investment credits
Gains from the retirement of long-term debts and from the sale of plant and equipment
Increases (decreases) in noncurrent deferred tax debits (credits)
Investment revenue from the use of the equity method

This item appears on W. T. Grant's balance sheet and is sizable in many companies. Deferred income tax is the accumulated difference in net income reported for tax purposes and that reported for prepared financial statements. (Refer to Chapter 3, Appendix A, for a review.) For W. T. Grant these differences are due largely to different accounting procedures for installment sales and depreciation. In the case of depreciation net income reported on the accounting books contains the normal depreciation write-offs, while income taxes paid are based on faster write-offs. The amount of income taxes reported on the income statement, however, is an assumed higher figure than actually paid, with the difference shown as an accumulating reserve on the balance sheet. The reserve is built up against the day when the fast write-offs used for tax purposes run out. It is an attempt to average out the tax effect of fast write-offs. Since most companies continue to invest in fixed assets and thus enjoy fresh accelerated depreciation write-offs, the day of reckoning is postponed almost indefinitely, and deferred taxes continue to grow.

From a funds standpoint the nature of deferred tax needs to be recognized for what it is — an income reserve set aside against potential higher tax payments in the future. In that sense it is a proper source of funds for the period, just as other operating income was, and it can be shown together with operating income among the sources.

Net income is often affected by gains and losses from the sale of capital assets. Since the funds effect is normally tied to a combination of circumstances affecting the components of the net property account, the discussion is taken up next.

Changes in Fixed Assets

Analysis of fixed assets requires comparing the change in accumulated depreciation on the balance sheet against the depreciation expense charged to operations for the period. This comparison is made to determine whether any *sale or retirement of fixed assets* has occurred. If

ending accumulated depreciation
$$= \text{beginning accumulated depreciation} + \text{depreciation expense}, \qquad (6.7)$$

then no sales or retirements of assets have occurred. However, if the calculated accumulated depreciation exceeds the ending balance sheet accumulated depreciation amount, then a fixed asset(s) has been disposed of through a sale or a retirement. For example, the depreciation expense on W. T. Grant's income depreciation for the year ended January 1974 is $13.579 million, and the change in the accumulated depreciation account of the balance sheet is $4.62 million (see Table 6.10). Assets with accumulated depreciation of $8.959 million have been written off.

W. T. Grant's balance sheet, as of January 31, 1974, indicates that total gross fixed assets (including land) increased $14.184 million. Since the retired assets were fully depreciated (as was disclosed in the notes to the financial statements), the amount spent on new capital expenditures for the period is $23.143 million ($14.184 million + $8.959 million). Also, since fully depreciated assets were disposed of, any cash received for them would represent a gain on disposal of assets. Notes to the financial statements reveal that it is company policy to report gains under other income and losses under selling, general, and administrative expenses. Since the notes indicate that $1.960 million of the 1974 gain of $2.027 million was from early retirement of debts, the remaining gain is possibly from the sale of fixed assets. Assuming that it is, the accounting entry is as follows:

Debit	Accumulated depreciation	$8,960,000	
Credit	Fixed asset		$8,960,000
Debit	Cash	67,000	
Credit	Gain		67,000

Funds Flow Statement

As the previous discussion reveals, simply calculating changes in balance sheet items can mean that significant factors that affect liquidity are overlooked. In general, the funds flow statement reflects significant elements of management decisions on investments, operations, and financing. The important questions about the flows refer to the magnitude and the type of commitment in relation to the sources from which they were obtained. Have enough long-term funds been raised to support major investments? Do temporary loans or other short-term movements constitute the bulk of sources for long-term use? What do changes in net working capital suggest relative to the ability of the business to generate funds? Is actual growth outstripping sustainable growth?

In the process of identifying and analyzing funds movements and relating them to each other, the selection of periods is often quite important. It is permissible to choose any time period to analyze flows — one month, one year, two or more years, or a period that analyzes economic swings from the low point to the high point, or vice versa. An understanding of the business helps one to determine how the statement should be structured. Table 6.12 shows the funds statements for W. T. Grant as of January 1973 and 1974.

The funds flow statement for W. T. Grant indicates that net working capital for the year ended January 31, 1974, increased $68.733 million. Net operations contributed funds of $23.583 million. However, dividends ($21.122 million) and expanded facilities ($23.143 million) consumed $44.265 million of funds. Without the new bank debt net working capital would have declined by $31.267 million. Although the uses of funds for

TABLE 6.12
W. T. Grant Company
Funds Flow Statement
For the Period Ended January 31
($000)

	1974	1973
Sources of funds		
From operations:		
Net income	$ 8,429	$ 37,787
Less increase in the undistributed equity in unconsolidated subsidiaries	3,570	3,403
	$ 4,859	$34,384
Plus charges to income not affecting working capital:		
Depreciation and amortization	13,579	12,004
Increase in deferred federal taxes	5,643	19,553
Decrease in other liabilities	<498>	<558>
Funds provided by operations	$ 23,583	$ 65,383
Notes payable to bank	100,000	0
Receipts from employees under stock purchase contracts	2,584	3,491
Common stock issued upon conversion of debentures	259	174
Decrease (increase) in other assets	<600>	2,229
Total sources of funds	$125,826	$ 71,277
Use of funds		
Dividends to stockholders	$ 21,122	$ 21,141
Investment in properties, fixtures, and improvements	23,143	26,250
Investment in unconsolidated subsidiaries	5,700	2,040
Retirement of long-term debt	6,074	1,584
Purchase of preferred stock for cancellation	612	252
Purchase of treasury common stock	133	11,466
Conversion of convertible debentures	262	176
Increase <decrease> in sundry accounts	47	<79>
Total uses of funds	$ 57,093	$ 62,830
Increase of net working capital during the period	$ 68,733	$ 8,477
Increase <decrease> in net working capital		
Current assets:		
Cash and short-term securities	$ 15,008	$<18,908>
Accounts receivable	56,047	65,427
Inventories	51,104	100,857
Other current assets	651	1,271
Total assets	$122,810	$148,647
Current liabilities:		
Short-term commercial notes and bank loans	$ 63,063	$152,293
Accounts payable	<2,781>	<15,147>
Accrued wages payable	<4,322>	3,325
Federal income taxes payable	<8,480>	<997>
Other miscellaneous	6,597	726
Total liabilities	$ 54,077	$140,200
Working capital increase	$ 68,733	$ 8,447

fiscal year ended January 1974 are comparable to the previous year's expenditures, they put a strain on the company's liquidity because profits were down about $29.358 million.

The primary applications of funds is revealed in the bottom part of the table. It shows increased investment in accounts receivable and inventories of $107.151 million. This follows a $166.284 million investment in these accounts in the previous year. Trade accounts payable have been lowered by $17.928 million over the two years. To finance these investments, management relied heavily on the commercial paper market and short-term bank loans. Over $63 million was borrowed in the year ended January 31, 1974. The previous period saw the company utilize $152.293 million of financing from these sources.

Thus the funds statement indicates that the use of debt is the main reason that net working capital has increased over the two years. In year ended January 1973 the ability to defer federal taxes saved $19.553 million. An additional $5.643 million of deferred taxes were generated the next year, along with a $100 million bank borrowing. Within the net working capital accounts short-term debt was heavily relied upon to finance the growth in current assets — over $63 million in 1974 and over $152 million in 1973. Thus the one factor apparent from the funds statement is the reliance on both short-term and long-term debt to finance expansion and to make up for deterioration in ability to generate funds from operations. The severity of the problem can be appreciated even more by extending funds flow analysis to cash flow analysis, which is done in the next section.

Analysis of Cash Flows

Previous discussion indicated that funds flow is not synonymous with cash flow. During the past few years, in an effort to better understand liquidity, management has placed less emphasis on changes in net working capital (i.e., funds flow) and more on the change in the cash (and near-cash) balance. In the final analysis, cash flows into and out of a business are the fundamental events upon which liquidity measurements are based. Cash is significant because it represents generalized purchasing power, which can be transferred readily to satisfy obligations.

Definition of Cash Flow

It is often said that cash flow may be defined as net income plus depreciation and other noncash expenses. This definition is quite incorrect. Even if there were no changes in the other current assets or current'liabilities, it is still incorrect to say that the cash flow consists of net income plus noncash expenses. It should be said that the *cash flow* stream is net income plus the tax shield provided by noncash expenses.

Some might argue that this definition is merely a play on words, since the same figure is obtained regardless of which definition is used. However, the notion that the cash provided by operations consists of net income plus noncash expenses leads to the erroneous conclusion that there are two sources of cash: net income and noncash expenses, a fallacy that pervades much accounting, economics, and finance literature. To consider noncash expenses as a source of cash is contradictory. For example, depreciation is the cost of fixed assets that has been assigned to the period under review — a cost, not a gain.

As a result of this erroneous concept, one sometimes hears statements such as a certain corporation is obtaining sufficient cash from depreciation to finance its expansion plans. If this statement were true, it would follow that cash is obtained from bad debts and fire loss, the amortization of bond discounts and patents, and losses on sale of fixed assets. Obviously, all that is obtained is a tax savings, which indeed can be treated as a cash inflow. But this is distinctly different from saying that the total expense is synonymous with a cash inflow.

Objective of Cash Flow Information

Income statements and balance sheets prepared under accrual accounting concepts are accepted on the basis that they represent useful measurements of firm efficiency and provide relevant information for the prediction of future firm activity. Because of problems created by the use of alternative allocation procedures (e.g., inventory valuation, depreciation approaches) and historical transaction prices, which fail to adjust for price changes, traditional accounting methods may not be adequate for reporting the complex economic activities of the firm. A means of minimizing these problems is to emphasize the reporting of cash flows.

Historically, the use of net income and the change in net working capital (funds flow) were claimed to be indicators of the ability of the firm to pay. The fallacy of this approach was demonstrated by the bankruptcy of W. T. Grant. Grant's inability to generate cash from operations was not revealed by the funds flow prepared under the approach of a change in net working capital. For instance, the current year (1974) in Table 6.12 indicates that funds (net working capital) increased a healthy $68.7 million, and about $23.6 million of this amount was provided by operations. Analysis of earlier periods would show this measure to be reasonably stable, as depicted in Fig. 6.2. However, actual *cash flow provided by operations* (which incorporates the changes in accounts receivable, inventories, and accounts payable) was negative for much of the same period (as revealed by Fig. 6.2). This amount can be calculated from Table 6.12 as follows:

funds provided by operations
   +(−) decreases (increases) in accounts receivable and inventories
   +(−) increase (decrease) in accounts payable and accruals.   (6.8)

An illustrative calculation for the period ended January 31 follows.

	1974 ($000)	1973 ($000)
Funds provided by operations	$ 23,583	$ 65,383
Increase in accounts receivable	<56,047>	<65,427>
Increase in inventories	<51,104>	<100,857>
Decrease in accounts payable	<2,781>	<15,147>
Decrease in accrued wages payable	<4,322>	
Increase in accrued wages payable		3,325
Actual cash flow from operations	$<90,671>	$<112,723>

FIGURE 6.2
W. T. Grant's Financial Trends

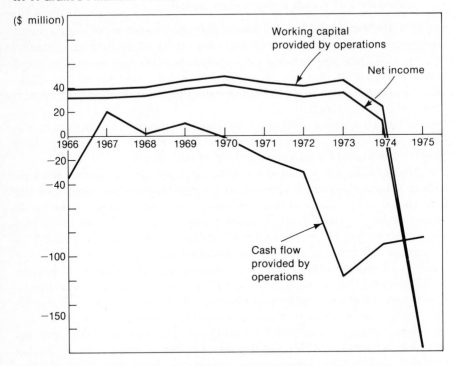

Source: From James Largay and Clyde Stickney, "Cash Flows, Ratio Analysis, and the W. T. Grant Company Bankruptcy," *Financial Analysts Journal* (July–August 1980: 54. Reprinted by permission.

Hence net working capital, or the change in it, is a very poor indicator of the firm's ability to generate cash. For the two years ended January 1974 W. T. Grant's operations consumed over $203 million. The knowledge that net working capital increased about $75.2 million over this same period means little in terms of understanding liquidity. Unfortunately, many were not aware of this discrepancy. A Morgan Guaranty vice⁄president who handled the W. T. Grant loan said, in an interview with *Business Week* magazine (July 19, 1976):

> The *first* [our emphasis added] signs of trouble were apparent to us in the spring of 1974. We agreed to help because they looked sound if they received some bank help. . . . We never knew how bad their internal systems were.

The primary objective of a cash flow statement is to provide information that allows the investor or creditor to forecast the amount of cash likely to be disbursed in the future to satisfy obligations and to evaluate the probable risk. The cash flow statement takes a narrow point of view. Its scope is limited to a summary of the cash transactions during a period, disregarding events that have occurred in prior periods or will occur in future periods but that have a bearing on the operations of the period under review.

Preparation of a Cash Flow Statement

A cash flow statement is superior to a funds flow statement since it shows how the activities reported in the income statement were financed. It also summarizes the financial transactions that caused changes in the assets, the liabilities, and the capital, as shown in the related balance sheet. The cash flow statement summarizes the business transactions involving cash receipts and cash disbursements without considering their relationship to revenue-producing activities and the process of matching revenues and costs.

Instead of lumping all current assets and current liabilities together as net working capital, a cash flow statement considers changes in some or all of these items separately. Except that changes in individual current asset and liability terms are treated separately, the procedures for analyzing transactions are the same as those described earlier for funds flow. Increases in assets and decreases in liabilities and equities indicate uses of cash; decreases in assets and increases in liabilities and equities indicate sources of cash. Transactions that do not involve a flow of cash are eliminated.

The only change required to convert the funds flow statement of W. T. Grant to a cash flow statement is to incorporate the changes in net working capital, excluding cash and near cash, directly into the sources and uses of funds categories. The difference between the revised sources and uses will be the changes in cash and near-cash balances. This approach is shown in Table 6.13.

TABLE 6.13
W. T. Grant Company
Cash Flow Statement
For the Period Ended January 31
($000)

	1974	1973
Funds from operations:		
Net income	$ 8,429	$ 37,787
Less increase in the undistributed equity in unconsolidated subsidiaries	3,570	3,403
	$ 4,859	$ 34,384
Plus charges to income not affecting funds from operations:		
Depreciation and amortization	13,579	12,004
Increase in deferred federal taxes	5,643	19,553
Decrease in other liabilities	<498>	<558>
Funds provided by operations	$ 23,583	$ 65,383
Increase in accounts receivable	<56,047>	<65,427>
Increase in inventories	<51,104>	<100,857>
Decrease in accounts payable	<2,781>	<15,147>
Decrease in accrued wages payable	<4,322>	
Increase in accrued wages payable		3,325
Cash flow from operations	$<90,671>	$<112,723>
Nonoperating sources <uses> of cash:		
Increase in notes payable to bank ·	100,000	0
Increase in receipts from employees under stock purchase contracts	2,584	3,491
Increase in common stock issued upon conversion of debentures	259	174
<Increase> decrease in other assets	<600>	2,229
Dividends paid to stockholders	<21,122>	<21,141>
Increase in investment in properties, fixtures, and improvements	<23,143>	<26,250>
Increase in investment in unconsolidated subsidiaries	<5,700>	<2,040>
Retirement of long-term debt	<6,074>	<1,584>
Purchase of preferred stock for cancellation	<612>	<252>
Purchase of treasury common stock	<133>	<11,466>
Conversion of convertible debentures	<262>	<176>
Sundry accounts	<47>	79
Increase in other current assets	<651>	<1,271>
Increase in short-term commercial notes and bank loans	63,063	152,293
Decrease in federal income taxes payable	<8,480>	<997>
Increase in other miscellaneous liabilities	6,597	726
Increase <decrease> in cash and short-term securities	$ 15,008	$ <18,908>

Summary

This chapter discussed cash budgets, improved liquidity indexes, and funds flow and cash flow analyses as being better indicators of liquidity than the techniques discussed in the previous chapter.

The cash budget is the most important tool for managing liquidity. Failure to perform cash budgeting means lack of serious effort to understand and manage liquidity.

The liquidity indexes discussed capture flows and allow management to meet obligations better than do traditional ratios (as were discussed in Chapter 3). These indexes do not replace cash budgets; rather, they provide summary measures of the cash budget, which management can use to help monitor liquidity performance.

An analysis based on sources and uses of funds provides a gross indication of the flow of funds within the firm. These flows involve the decisions made by management regarding movement of investment into and out of the firm by either creditors or investors. Formal analysis using funds flow statements is required to better understand resource movements.

Cash flow analysis was shown to be an extension of funds flow analysis. Rather than balancing to the change in net working capital, as is done in funds flow analysis, cash flow analysis reconciles the change in the cash (and near-cash) accounts. A full understanding of how cash has been affected by operations and investments requires considerable knowledge of noncash items arising as a result of the use of accrual accounting.

Key Concepts

Cash budget

Cash flow

Cash flow analysis

Cash flow provided by operations

Changes in retained earnings

Funds

Funds as net working capital

Funds flow analysis

Liquidity flow index

Nonmonetary write-offs

Permanent capital

Relative liquidity index

Sale/retirement of fixed assets

Sources and uses of funds

Appendix

Normal Probability Distribution Table

Area of the Normal Distribution That Is Z Standard Deviations to the Left or Right of the Mean

Number of standard deviations from the mean (Z)	Area to the left or right	Number of standard deviations from the mean (Z)	Area to the left or right
0.00	0.5000	1.55	0.0606
0.05	0.4801	1.60	0.0548
0.10	0.4602	1.65	0.0495
0.15	0.4404	1.70	0.0446
0.20	0.4207	1.75	0.0401
0.25	0.4013	1.80	0.0359
0.30	0.3821	1.85	0.0322
0.35	0.3632	1.90	0.0287
0.40	0.3446	1.95	0.0256
0.45	0.3264	2.00	0.0228
0.50	0.3085	2.05	0.0202
0.55	0.2912	2.10	0.0179
0.60	0.2743	2.15	0.0158
0.65	0.2578	2.20	0.0139
0.70	0.2420	2.25	0.0122
0.75	0.2264	2.30	0.0107
0.80	0.2119	2.35	0.0094
0.85	0.1977	2.40	0.0082
0.90	0.1841	2.45	0.0071
0.95	0.1711	2.50	0.0062
1.00	0.1577	2.55	0.0054
1.05	0.1469	2.60	0.0047
1.10	0.1357	2.65	0.0040
1.15	0.1251	2.70	0.0035
1.20	0.1151	2.75	0.0030
1.25	0.1056	2.80	0.0026
1.30	0.0968	2.85	0.0022
1.35	0.0885	2.90	0.0019
1.40	0.0808	2.95	0.0016
1.45	0.0735	3.00	0.0013
1.50	0.0668		

Questions

1. A cash budget cannot tell one what specific course of action to follow to alter the firm's cash flows. What considerations are involved in this direction?

2. What is the difference between a cash budget and a projected income statement or a projected balance sheet?

3. What is the relationship between a cash budget and a sales budget? A production budget? A direct-labor budget?

4. If cash flows are random, of what significance is a cash budget?

5. Define the LFI and RLI models, and explain why they are better measures of liquidity than the current and quick ratios.

6. What is meant by the term *funds*? Is it the same as cash? Why or why not?

7. How is a sources and uses statement calculated? What are the problems with it?

8. Explain how the changes in retained earnings, net income, and fixed assets should be calculated.

9. What is the difference between net working capital provided by operations (i.e., funds flow from operations) and cash flow provided by operations? What are some of the advantages and disadvantages of each definition?

Problems

1. Prepare a cash budget for Barney Associates for the months of June, July, and August. Discuss your results. The necessary data follow.

Forecasted sales	June	$2000
	July	3000
	August	2500
Historical sales	March	$1500
	April	2250
	May	1500

Sales are 75% for credit and 25% for cash. Credit sales are paid 70% in the current month, 15% the following month, and 15% the month following that. Wages and salaries are 10% of sales. Rent is $200 a month. A tax payment of $150 is due in August. Purchases are 80% of sales and are paid one month following the month of sale.

2. The cash manager of Xtra Company gathered the following data related to the company's cash position for the next six months.

Cash balance, January 1	$ 5,000
Estimated monthly payroll	40,000
Payroll accrued at the end of the year as well	4,000
as at the end of each month	
Interest payable in June	500
Taxes payable in March	10,000

Other data are given in Table 6.14. Credit sales are collected 50% in the month sales are made, 45% in the month following, and 5% in the second month. Accounts payable represent unpaid purchases. Prepare a monthly cash budget for the period January through June.

3. The C&W Manufacturing Company had sales of $90,000 last month. It expects sales of $80,000 next month. Sales levels should increase 10% per month for the next five months. Cash sales normally are 30% of total sales, with the remainder collected in the following month. Other cash income is approximately 5% of monthly sales. Payroll costs are constant at $30,000 per month. Rent and utilities are constant at $3500 and $3000, respectively. Other operating expenses have a fixed component of $6000 per month and a variable portion that is 2% of monthly sales. Cost of sales are approximately 45% of sales and are paid in the month of purchase. The firm has $8000 in its bank account and $15,000 in a money market fund. Prepare a monthly cash budget for the next six months.

4. The Siggle Company must pay off a $2000 loan on July 31. Its January 1 cash balance is zero. From the following information, will there be enough funds to repay the loan?

□ Raw materials are purchased at 50% of their final sales price. These purchases are made two months in advance of sales. The company pays its suppliers one month after it receives the goods.

□ 10% of sales are for cash, with 60% of sales collected the following month

TABLE 6.14
Financial Data

	Cash sales	Credit purchases	Accounts payable	Credit sales
November				$60,000
December			$18,000	70,000
January	$15,000	$12,000	14,000	65,000
February	14,000	16,500	30,000	80,000
March	12,000	14,000	25,000	72,000
April	16,000	18,000	30,000	60,000
May	14,500	25,000	24,000	75,000
June	18,000	12,500	30,000	68,000

and another 25% collected the month after that. The remaining 5% are uncollected.

☐ Estimated collections are $1140 in January and $350 in February for its November and December sales. Projected sales for the first nine months of the year are as follows:

Jan.	$600	Apr.	$1600	July	$1500
Feb.	800	May	2000	Aug.	1000
Mar.	900	June	1800	Sept.	900

☐ Other monthly cash expenditures are $200. Taxes of $150 are paid each quarter, beginning in March.

5. Beta Food Services is trying to forecast its cash position as of its fiscal year end. Its opening balance was $50,000. Sales last year were $1 million, evenly spread over the 12 months. All sales are for credit, with collection 50% in the month of sale and 50% in the following month. Purchases are paid for with cash, and products are marked up 100% of purchase cost for sale. Selling prices and purchase costs are expected to be the same as last year. Expenses are $30,000 per month. Funds may be borrowed from the bank at an annual rate of 15%, up to a maximum of $250,000. Assume a 50% tax rate and that taxes are paid monthly. Using a cash budget, find the expected cash balance at the end of the new year.

6. To help management with the preparation of the cash budget and a *pro forma* income statement for the year, you are asked to prepare a table of the following transactions, showing their individual and net effects upon income, cash receipts, and cash disbursements. Total the amounts in each category.

(a) Cash sales for the year: $1,200,000.

(b) Credit sales for the year: $18,000,000.

(c) Collections from this year's credit sales: $16,800,000.

(d) Collections from accounts outstanding at the beginning of the year: $1,800,000.

(e) Returns and allowances: $200,000.

(f) Refunds to customers on account of foregoing returns and allowances: $15,000.

(g) Purchases of raw materials on account: $8,700,000.

(h) Payments to suppliers on foregoing purchases: $7,800,000.

(i) Payments to suppliers for goods bought last year: $650,000.

(j) Total wage and salary charges for the year: $4,300,000.

(k) Total payroll disbursements: $4,175,000.

(l) Purchase of equipment for cash: $875,000.

(m) Purchase of equipment, payment to be made next year: $250,000.

(n) Sale of surplus equipment for cash; book value is $120,000, and tax rate is 40%:$65,000.

(o) Depreciation charges: $450,000.

(p) Cash dividend declared, to be paid next year: $310,000.

(q) Bank loan obtained this year, to be repaid next year: $200,000.

7. Using the financial information of The Six Company given in Tables 6.15 and 6.16, construct a funds flow statement for the year ended December 31, 1985. Explain the changes between the years, particularly as they affect liquidity management.

8. Using the data provided for Problem 7, prepare a cash flow statement for The Six Company for the year 1985. The statement should identify funds from operations and cash flow from operations.

9. The data shown in Table 6.17 have been revealed from an audit of the Sun Devil Company's current year budget and next year forecast. For each period, calculate the liquidity flow index, and compare it with the current ratio. Which measure provides a better indicator of liquidity? Discuss.

TABLE 6.15
The Six Company
Balance Sheets
For the Years Ended December 31, 1984 and 1985
($000)

		1985		*1984*
Assets				
Current assets:				
Cash		$ 14		$ 27
Accounts receivable		149		146
Inventory		188		209
Total current assets		$351		$382
Fixed assets:				
Plant and equipment	$739		$525	
Accumulated depreciation	220		150	
Net plant and equipment		519		375
Intangible assets		50		105
Total assets		$920		$862
Liabilities and capital				
Current liabilities:				
Accounts payable		$117		$ 76
Notes payable		89		146
Total current liabilities		$206		$222
Long-term debt		265		298
Capital:				
Common stock		151		57
Retained earnings		298		285
Total liabilities and capital		$920		$862

TABLE 6.16
The Six Company
Income Statement
For the Period Ended December 31, 1985
($000)

Sales		$506.0
Cost of sales:		
Labor	$105.0	
Material	72.2	
Depreciation	83.0	
Other overhead	70.0	
		330.2
Gross profit		$175.8
General, selling, and administrative expenses (including amortization of intangible assets)		96.9
Income before taxes		$ 78.9
Income tax		35.5
Net income		$ 43.4

Notes:
1. During the year fixed assets were sold for $58,000 (the original price was $71,000).
2. There were no prior-year adjustments.
3. Long-term bonds of $55,000 were refunded by a $22,000 mortgage bond issue, and the remainder converted to common stock.
4. $61,000 of new common were sold.

TABLE 6.17
Sun Devil Company Data

	Budget	Forecast
Cash payments to creditors:		
Purchases	$720	$2820
Cash expenses	170	680
Taxes and dividends	10	40
Cash receipts:		
Cash sales	480	1920
Collection of receivables	450	1800
Cash balances:		
Opening	10	20
Closing	20	40
Current assets	50	120
Current liabilities	20	80

10.   Assume that the Sun Devil Company (Problem 9) had an expected standard deviation of net cash flows of $12 and $72 in the budget and the forecast, respectively.

(a)   Calculate the relative liquidity index for each period, and comment on the results.

(b)   Determine the necessary line of credit to make the forecast index equal to the budget index. Discuss the impact the credit line would have on the firm.

PART III □
Management of Net Working Capital Accounts

CHAPTER 7 □
Overview of Cash Management

Almost every business transaction involves cash, either at the time of the transaction or shortly after. Thus cash must be available to cover all purchases, and it should result from every sale. Having cash available to cover business costs and utilizing it effectively after it is received is of vital importance for fulfilling the shareholder wealth objective.

The objective of cash management is to have enough cash when it is needed but to have as little excess cash as possible. Cash in itself is not a productive asset, because it earns nothing unless it is invested. A good treasurer minimizes the amount of cash on hand but is able to respond quickly to changing supply and demand relationships so that needs are satisfied.

The purpose of this chapter is to provide an overview of the basic principles of cash management. To this end, three topics are examined:

1. Understanding the cash balance.
2. Accelerating cash flows.
3. Selecting and treating banks as an important component of cash management.

Know the Cash Balance

Unless it is effectively controlled, cash has a tendency to accumulate or be deployed into numerous pools. For instance, payments are received at branch offices, bank accounts are established to support outlying plants, warehouses, or offices, and compensating balances are kept in these bank accounts to pay for bank services.

Many managers fail to recognize the potential of their cash system. Often substantial resources lie dormant for at least three reasons:

1. Accounting procedures misstate the cash balances.
2. Management has little understanding of the cash process.
3. Corporate policy hinders imaginative cash management.

Problem with Accounting Procedures

Generally, the amount of funds available to a company in its bank account is different from the cash balances indicated in the company's ledger. This difference is the cumulative result of a series of delays in payment of checks written by the company and the collection of checks received by the company. The difference is referred to as *float*. Checks written by the company result in *disbursement (positive) float,* which is an excess of bank net collected balances over corporate book balances. Conversely, checks received by the company and deposited in the banking system, but not yet shown by the bank, result in *deposit (negative) float* — an excess of book balances over bank net collected balances.

ILLUSTRATION 7.1

The following entries show disbursement and deposit floats.

Balance per bank statement, July 31	$42,165.10	
Balance per ledger, July 31	31,468.27	
Difference	$10,696.83	
Reconciliation:		
Outstanding checks	$15,830.47	(1)
Less: Deposit not recorded by bank	<4,700.00>	(2)
Interest collected by bank on corporate bonds	<400.00>	
Bank charges	<33.64>	
Difference	$10,696.83	

Notes:
1. Disbursement (positive) float.
2. Deposit (negative) float.   □

Types of Float

Figure 7.1 outlines three types of floats found in the payment process. *Mail float* is the time the check is in the postal system. *Processing float* is the amount of time the company receiving the check takes to process it

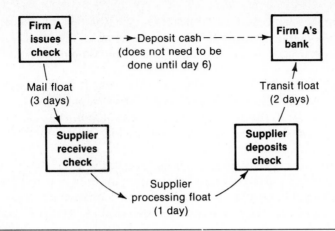

FIGURE 7.1
Deposit and Disbursement Floats

and deposit it in the bank. *Transit float* represents the amount of time it takes the check to clear the banking system and be charged against the company issuing the check. Obviously, a firm wants to maximize the positive float associated with disbursements to its suppliers and minimize the negative float associated with payments from its customers.

Another term for transit float is *Fed float*. The Federal Reserve Bank has established standard times for granting credit for checks deposited with it. These times are based upon the time required to present these checks to the banks on which they are drawn. Some checks are considered one-day items, and others are considered two-day items. Actual times in excess of these standard times are the responsibility of the Federal Reserve Bank. It bears the loss of the use of these funds for any extra time required to clear checks.

Understanding the Check Process

A basic need for the proper understanding of cash management is an understanding of how cash flows through commercial channels and, in particular, through the banking system. Many corporate decision makers have little or no knowledge of how checks are processed. A better understanding of the check-clearing process can aid in more effective use of company cash.

The *check-clearing process* involves several steps. Once a check is deposited into an account, the transaction information on the check is encoded. Since most checks are printed with codes for the bank of issue, the customer's account number, and routing information, it is the dollar amount that is added at this point, in magnetic ink. Machines that read the information sort the checks according to the bank of issue. The combination of encoding and sorting checks is known as processing.

The next step is for the check to be cleared. If it clears, settlement of accounts of the banks involved takes place. Settlement means the crediting and the debiting of funds to and from banks' accounts. After clearing, the check returns to the issuing bank, which debits the customer's accounts. Figure 7.2 summarizes the process.

A check may be sent to a payee in essentially two different ways. It can be mailed (or personally handed) to the payee, or it can be sent to a lockbox (discussed shortly). When checks are sent directly to the payee, the payee credits the payer's account, endorses the check, and deposits it in the bank. When checks are sent to a lockbox, the bank endorses and deposits the check and sends the payment-identifying data to the payee to be used in crediting the payer's account.

An advantage of using a *lockbox* is that it allows checks to be deposited sooner. They are processed by the lockbox bank during the night, or early in the day, so that on the same day the bank can charge them to the payer's account (if drawn on the bank where deposited) or send them to the local clearinghouse, to a correspondent bank, or to the Federal Reserve Bank or the Federal Reserve Regional Check Processing Center (RCPC) (if they are not drawn on the bank where deposited). A RCPC is a facility established in a commercially important city where there is no Federal Reserve Bank or branch. These facilities provide around-the-clock processing for checks and often allow institutions in the areas surrounding major cities the chance to receive same-day credit for their check deposits if certain deadlines are met.

A check does not follow a prescribed route in the collection process. Several alternatives exist at each step, and a check could take a number of different routes. A bank might handle the whole task itself. It processes the checks in-house and sends them directly to the issuing banks for clearing. Banks that follow this approach are usually large banks and use courier services to send checks directly to banks for collection. A bank that does not handle the task itself might use several agents. A local service bureau encodes the checks, a correspondent bank sorts the checks, and a Federal Reserve facility clears the checks. A major reason for using these agents is to clear checks with distant banks. For the clearing of checks with local banks a local clearinghouse may exist that holds daily exchanges of checks among its members.

If a check is drawn on a bank outside the area of the local clearinghouse, the depositor bank has three options for collecting the funds. First, it can send the check directly to the bank on which drawn. This process is used normally when the sending bank has a correspondent relationship with the receiving bank and when it has a large number of checks to present

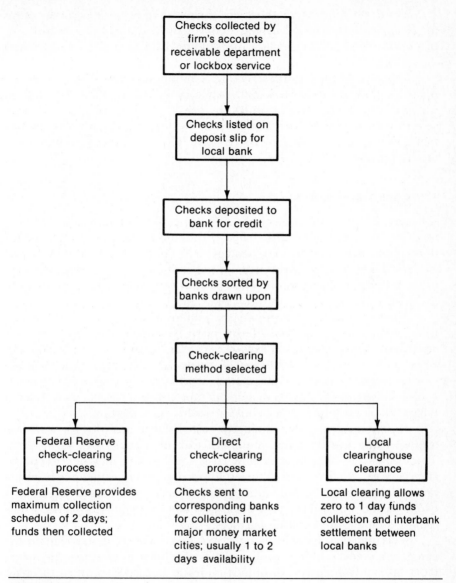

FIGURE 7.2
Check-Clearing Process

to it. The sending bank often uses a courier for this purpose if it has a large dollar volume of checks to present.

Second, the bank can send the check directly to the correspondent. The correspondent, in turn, presents the check to the bank on which it is drawn, either directly or through the local clearinghouse.

Third, the bank sends the check through the Federal Reserve system for clearing. This method usually involves two Federal Reserve banks or processing centers, one serving the sending bank and the other serving the receiving bank.

Most out-of-town checks require a minimum of one day from the time that they are deposited until they can be presented to the bank on which drawn. Some eastern banks, by using a courier plane, have been able to present checks to midwestern or western banks on the same day that they are received by the eastern bank. This technique greatly reduces the transit float.

Corporate Policy

An integral consideration regarding the type of cash management system used by the firm is the idea that a corporation's cash position depends upon all its assets and liability management policies. Cash is the result of all decisions involving investments in noncash assets, borrowing, the payment of dividends, and so on. Thus policies with respect to the minimum and maximum cash balances to maintain must be formulated.

The next chapter will discuss the minimum and maximum balances, using mathematical models. At this point we merely state that *the more control management exercises to maintain minimum balances, the more vulnerable the company is to random fluctuations in receipts and unexpected cash needs that were not forecast accurately.* Obviously, excess balances are nonearning assets and diminish profitability. Management must ascertain a cash management policy that contributes to shareholder wealth maximization.

Most managers set a minimum cash balance and do not want the balance to be less than this minimum except in periods of emergency. The idea is that regardless of how large cash outlays may be, except for emergencies, cash in excess of the established minimum should be available to meet any outlays. Such an attitude encourages the treasurer to maintain excess balances or to have excess standby lines of credit with banks, which require sizable compensating balances.

A second reason for keeping excess cash balances is to maintain the company's credit standing with creditors. As a matter of course, management takes advantage of all opportunities to buy goods and supplies on credit, but suppliers do not, as a matter of course, sell on credit to every company that asks for it. Suppliers sell on credit on the basis of an analysis of the prospective buyer's credit position. They evaluate the buyer to determine whether or not it has, or will have, the capacity to pay within the allowed credit period.

Maintaining good relations with banks from which it borrows is a third reason why management establishes minimum cash balances. Bankers argue that their lending capacity comes chiefly from deposits left with them by customers rather than from capital supplied by stockholders. Firms that wish to borrow should, therefore, contribute to this lending capacity by making it a practice to leave substantial balances with them.

Accelerating Cash Flows

Ever since the initiation of credit, management has sought faster ways to collect outstanding receivables. Because checks are written on banks and deposited with banks, the speed at which they are cleared is partially dependent on the banking system. The past two decades have seen bankers join with management in actively pursuing ways to accelerate processing of receivables in order to make funds available to firms in a shorter period of time. The techniques include concentration banking, zero-balance accounts, lockbox services, preauthorized checks, preauthorized debits, depository transfer checks, wire transfers, and drafts. Each topic will be discussed in turn.

Concentration Banking

The treasurer's objective is to concentrate all available funds into a cash pool for investment or borrowing offset so that no funds ever remain idle overnight. The ability to achieve this goal is affected by the number of bank accounts and their location and the bank services available. Target balance levels should be set for each account, with excess balances invested or offset against borrowings.

There are three major types of balance control systems:

1. Automatic concentration
2. Discretionary concentration
3. Remote control

Automatic concentration can be achieved in one of three ways:

☐ *One operating account.* The cash control merits of this straightforward system are clear. However, a single operating account is probably unrealistic for any sizable company.

☐ *Automatic-transfer systems.* Account balances are transferred under standing instructions on set dates, on a periodic basis (e.g., each Wednesday), on reaching a balance threshold (e.g., $12,000), or on some combination (e.g., each Wednesday, unless balances do not exceed $12,000). Automatic systems are a particularly effective means of managing specific operational accounts or of controlling cash balances where receivables and payables management is decentralized. Although float loss can occur, day-to-day policing is relieved.

□ *Cash concentration/pooling systems.* All balances held with one bank, irrespective of the branch, are consolidated for purposes of interest calculation. Pooling is particularly suited to situations where divisions or manufacturing and salés locations are spread throughout a country with a branch-banking network.

Discretionary concentration can be performed two ways:

□ *Depository transfer checks.* These checks are drawn on remote-control accounts and deposited to the main operating account. They are best used in conjunction with cash forecasts to concentrate cash in anticipation of funds inflows.

□ *Bank transfer.* Balances may be concentrated by instructing banks to transfer funds by telex, telephone, or other transfer mechanisms to the main bank operating account.

Remote control embraces all situations where funds are managed in one or more locations through unrelated operating accounts. The range is from single-location/several-account situations to autonomous accounts managed by division or manufacturing/sales personnel. A system of remote accounts supported by overdraft lines is common where large manufacturing or sales divisions are involved.

Zero-Balance Accounts

A product frequently used with an automatic concentration system is the *zero-balance account* (ZBA). The ZBAs are special disbursement accounts having a zero dollar balance on which checks are written. As checks are drawn against the account, the amount to be funded is accumulated and the company is notified of the total amount needed to bring the account back to a zero balance. Funding can be done internally from a central control account or externally by transferring funds from other banks by wire, depository transfer checks, or other mechanisms.

ZBAs offer the following benefits:

□ Centralized cash control but decentralized disbursements.

□ Elimination of petty cash accounts or balances at outlaying banks, thus freeing funds.

□ Extension of disbursement float, thereby increasing the available cash pool.

From a bank's perspective ZBAs require close attention. At some banks there is a one-day delay in funds collection. This delay occurs because the automated posting systems used by banks post credits to accounts first and then record the daily charges. With a ZBA the transfer of funds to the account is often for yesterday's overdraft. A negative balance is registered until funds are deposited. However, current daily charges are incurred, causing an overdraft for payment the next day. Often banks will require an equivalent day's charges be on balance in the account to reduce the overdrawn status of the account.

The best use of a ZBA for most companies is in conjunction with an automated investment program where funds are transferred automatically to cover presentments, with the balance of the funding account invested each night. An extension of this service is the use of a money fund account with any number of money market funds available; high interest is earned, and checks or drafts are issued against the account. This technique eliminates the need for accurate daily forecasting since any excess funds continue to earn the money market rate.

Lockbox Services

A *lockbox* is a post office box to which the company's (payee's) bank has access. The purpose of the lockbox is to intercept corporate receivables so as to reduce the amount of mail float. The number and the location of lockboxes are very important since these factors affect the mailing time required for mail-in payments to reach the post office. Computer algorithms, using operations research techniques, are frequently employed to determine optimal lockbox locations that minimize mail float and the total cost of the system.

Several times a day the bank collects the lockbox receipts from the post office. The bank opens the receipts and deposits checks directly to the company's account. Details of the transactions are recorded either manually on a sheet of paper or in a machine-usable form such as a magnetic computer tape. Whatever form it takes, the accounts receivable department receives the customer name, the account number, and the amount paid, which it uses to update the accounts receivable ledger.

There are several advantages to a lockbox system. The processing float involved in physically handling receivables and depositing checks for collection is reduced. Collection time is reduced because checks are received at the post office, which reduces mail float time. The availability of funds are often increased by as much as 1 to 4 days over in-house remittance processing. This increase provides a significant infusion of liquid resources to the firm. Receivable-processing costs are often reduced. Reduced costs occur because banks that specialize in high-volume lockbox processing can provide the service for lower-per-item cost than the firm. The company further benefits because its receivable data can be captured in machine-readable form by the bank and made available to update corporate accounts receivable records faster than that of the company using conventional in-house methods. A lockbox system is outlined in Fig. 7.3.

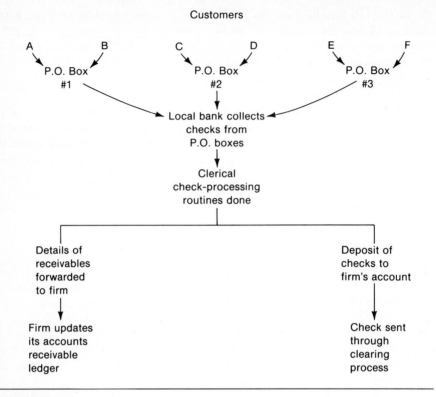

FIGURE 7.3
Lockbox System

ILLUSTRATION 7.2

Federal Equitable Company currently uses a centralized collection system. Customers make all payments to the central location. On the average, customer mail float is 4 days. Processing float is generally 1.5 days. Average daily collections are $500,000.

The bank has recommended a lockbox system, which is expected to reduce the mail float by 2.5 days and processing float by 1 day.

The reduction in cash balances that can be realized by using the lockbox is

3.5 days × $500,000 = $1,750,000.

The opportunity cost of the present system, assuming a rate of 9%, is

9% × $1,750,000 = $157,500.

If the annual cost of the lockbox system is $90,000, then management can realize an incremental saving (which contributes to shareholder wealth maximization) of

$157,500 − $90,000 = $67,500.   □

Preauthorized Checks

A *preauthorized check* (PAC) is a signatureless deposit check used for accelerating the collection of fixed payments. The customer signs an agreement with the corporation allowing the company — or, more usually, the company's bank — to write checks against the customer's account at specified intervals for specified amounts. The company sends to its bank a file of customers and dates when PACs are to be produced. The bank maintains the file and updates it on instructions from the firm. The bank informs the firm by means of a computer tape of the deposit and the availability of funds. This process lowers the uncertainty in income flows and reduces mail float. Figure 7.4 illustrates the flow of a typical preauthorized check system.

Advantages to the cash management function from using PACs are as follows:

□ increased cash flow predictability,

□ elimination of billing costs,

□ elimination of lockbox costs,

□ reduction of mail and processing floats,

□ reduction of corporate collection expenses.

FIGURE 7.4
Preauthorized Check System

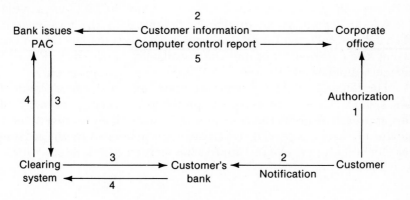

The disadvantages of PACs are the types of business transactions applicable to their use. Generally, PACs are only used with fixed-dollar repetitive types of payment (e.g., mortgage payments, insurance premiums, installment purchases). Another disadvantage, if it can be so classified, is the reluctance of customers to accept the arrangement.

Preauthorized Debits

A system very similar to PACs is the *preauthorized debit* (PAD). PADs are checkless or paperless transactions that require the customer's preauthorization to her or his bank to honor the selling firm's request. By the use of PADs a customer's account is automatically charged for funds due on an agreed-upon date. Funds are electronically wired from the customer's bank to the firm's bank. The system accelerates the flow of cash and eliminates paperwork. Accounting entries to payer's and payee's accounts are made directly.

Although PADs are commonly used by insurance, finance, and utility companies, there is significant consumer resistance to this cash acceleration method. The accelerated payment and clearing process significantly reduces the disbursement float of the firm's customers. PADs eliminate in-transit mail time, late payments, and physical check processing.

Depository Transfer Checks

An inexpensive method of moving funds from one location to another is through the use of *depository transfer checks* (DTCs). A DTC is like a PAC in that it is a signatureless check. It does not require any corporate signature in order to move funds. They are issued by the concentration bank against one of the firm's local collection banks on the basis of deposit information sent from the collection bank to the concentration bank, usually over a data-processing network. The concentration bank receives the deposit data and issues a check the same day for collection. Once the DTCs are presented at the local deposit banks, the checks deposited by the local collection office become collected funds. The bank then sends the information concerning the collected funds and their availability to the firm. Figure 7.5 illustrates the flow and the use of DTCs in a typical application.

The automated DTC system described here is the most commonly used system. Some firms, however, prefer to internally generate DTCs. This approach requires the cash manager to call daily to determine the amount of checks deposited. DTCs are then generated by the treasurer. The chief disadvantage of this approach is increased clerical costs for check production.

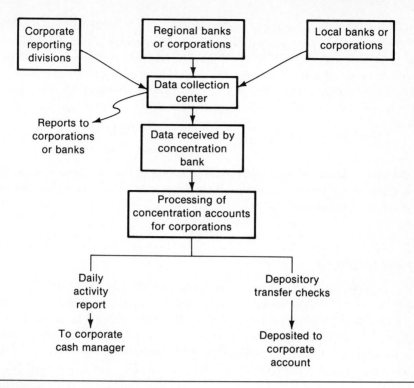

FIGURE 7.5
Depository Transfer Check System

Wire Transfers

Wire transfers are alternatives to depository transfer checks. A criterion for the use of wire transfers is that all funds in excess of a base amount be automatically transferred from a local bank to a concentration bank. Alternatively, transfer may be initiated by the treasurer, who requests movement of funds from one bank to another. The bank where the funds presently reside sends a wire transfer of funds to the bank where management wants the funds to be.

There are two major wire services: the Federal Reserve Wire System, which is operated by the Federal Reserve Bank system, and the Bank Wire System, which is operated by a cooperative of bank members. Wire transfers are more costly than other transfer instruments, such as DTCs. However, same-day availability of funds is usually enough justification to incur the added expense.

Realistically, in determining whether DTCs are better to use than wire transfers, management needs to perform a marginal cost-benefit analysis. Daily depository amounts may be too small to justify DTCs. Transferring funds two or more times a week may be all that is necessary and may make the cost of a wire transfer feasible. The treasurer can calculate the cash balance that makes her or him indifferent between a DTC and a wire transfer by using the following equation:

$$\text{indifference cash balance} = \frac{\text{wire cost} - \text{DTC cost}}{\text{daily opportunity cost of funds}}. \tag{7.1}$$

If the cash balance to be transferred is in excess of the indifference amount, a wire transfer is used. Conversely, if the amount is less than the indifference amount, a DTC is used.

ILLUSTRATION 7.3

The bank charges $7 per wire transfer and $2 per DTC. If a DTC is used, it will be at least one day before the funds are available to the firm since the DTC has to be presented to the field office's local bank. The treasurer can invest funds overnight at an annual rate of 10% (net of transaction costs). The field office has $22,000 to be transferred. The treasurer must decide whether to use a wire or a DTC. The calculation is

$$\text{indifference cash balance} = \frac{\text{wire cost} - \text{DTC cost}}{\text{daily opportunity cost of cash}}$$

$$= \frac{\$7 - \$2}{0.10/360} = \$18,000.$$

A wire transfer should be used since the amount to be transferred exceeds the indifference balance.   □

There have been innovations in the use of wire transfers. Most notable is the ability of the treasurer to initiate a wire transfer from a computer terminal that interfaces either with the bank's computer-controlled wire system or with the data base of a third party that is used by the bank. Often this service is linked with other cash management services, such as programs that forecast a company's cash flows, and produces wire transfers that are less costly and that provide hard-copy verification of funds transferred.

Drafts

Drafts represent an acceleration technique by the fact that they are presented by the seller's (payee's) bank for collection directly to the bank named by the buyer (payer). If the draft is accepted by the buyer, the buyer's bank segregates funds to ensure payment to the seller. Although collection from the buyer's bank is completed through the normal clearing process, knowing that the funds are available to pay the draft speeds up collection since there is no dispute about the goods. Unaccepted drafts are pursued as delinquent open-account items.

Role of Banks

Fed (transit) float reached into the billions of dollars during the 1970s, which meant that the banking system was being financed by the Federal Reserve. In March 1980 Congress passed the Depository Institutions Deregulation and Monetary Control Act (MCA) and dramatically changed the rules in the check-clearing business. The law directed the Federal Reserve to offer its check collection services to all depository institutions, not just to its member banks. It also required the Fed to price those services to cover costs rather than to provide them free. An important aim of Congress in imposing pricing was to promote competition and efficiency in the market for check collection services by removing the subsidy extended to some banks through free Fed services. In other words, it wanted to minimize, or eliminate if possible, the Fed float. This result has been to place greater pressure on banks to charge customers for all services provided.

Banks make their profit by obtaining deposits of money borrowed from customers and relending these same funds at higher rates. Corporations, however, in their pursuit of efficient cash management, desire to minimize idle cash and costs of services provided by the banks. The apparent conflict between the corporation and the bank is the heart of the bank/corporation relationship. Banks are essential to corporations and must be treated as an important part of the corporation's existence. So corporations must provide sufficient deposit business if they expect the bank to help them. A corporation can do so without putting too great a strain on the firm's cash resources. That goal can be accomplished by concentrating as much banking activity as possible at one principal bank. What is a minimum working balance for a company is usually a large and desirable account for a bank.

Working cash balances are significant in and of themselves. Often overlooked in the corporation/bank relationship are such seemingly minor accounts as those set up for dividend payments, payrolls, branch petty cash, and other special purposes. It is a matter of average deposit balances. For example, all paychecks issued on the fifteenth of the month are not cashed that day. Meanwhile, the bank has the use of the funds in the payroll account. Still another collateral benefit to a bank of a payroll account is the tendency of employees to open their personal accounts in the same bank used by the company.

Bank Evaluation

Traditionally, treasurers have evaluated banks when specific needs arose without systematically considering the bank's overall capabilities. This approach usually results in the company using an unnecessarily large group of banks.

Management's fundamental objective should be to develop bank relationships that provide the right mix of quality operational and financial services at a fair price. With respect to operational services the company's type of business, maturity, and size, and the frequency and the character of its cash flows are key factors. Low-volume, high-value firms have different operational needs than do high-volume, low-value cash flow businesses.

A basic rule to use for determining the number of operating banks is "the fewer the better." The use of a large number of operating banks is often rationalized on the basis of the reasoning that it provides competition among the banks, ensures credit availability during tight-money periods, provides specialized operational services, or satisfies some other business relationship. The use of too many banks, however, is counterproductive. Marginally profitable accounts seldom are granted prime terms by the bank. Although availability to credit is important, strong relationships with fewer banks can often yield greater credit availability at better terms.

Management needs to assess its banking needs by using objective criteria of the bank's willingness and ability to extend credit to the firm under difficult circumstances and of the cost-quality of bank services.

Willingness

The most important service of most banks is the provision of credit. Without needed credit the firm may not be able to survive a particular period of economic hardship, take advantage of shareholder wealth-increasing investments, or have financial flexibility to conduct its affairs.

Here are some important factors about credit to consider:

□ The price of the credit relative to the price at other banks.

□ The length of time it takes to be approved for credit.

□ The duration of the credit arrangement — the longer the better.

Senior management of the firm must foster the firm-bank relationship. If top management of the company and the bank have good business (and perhaps personal) relationships, then difficult or rush situations may be resolved to the firm's benefit.

Ability

Management must also determine whether a candidate bank fulfills the company's financial needs. This step requires answers to the following questions: What funding needs will the company have? What form will these funding needs take? Who can best meet the company's funding needs? The amount and the type of financing directly affect the number and the nature of banks. Management can segregate different types of funding into day-to-day needs, medium-term financing, and long-term requirements. It is not unusual to find different types of banks specializing in different kinds of financing.

Obviously, to meet loan commitments to companies, a bank must have an assured source of funds. Strong financial performance over several years should provide these sources. Management can use the expertise of service firms such as Robinson Humphrey/American Express, Inc., and Keefe, Bruyette, & Woods. These companies rate the financial condition and the performance of banks.

Management should be able to identify banks that have limited capabilities to provide large sums to the company owing to legal and/or in-house lending restrictions. The treasurer can simply ask each bank what its maximum lending limit is under favorable conditions. Those banks without sufficient lending capability are discarded from further consideration.

Cost-Effective Operating Services

It is important for the company to have its banks provide high-quality, competitively priced operating services for items such as deposits, lockboxes, paid checks, and account maintenance. Periodically, management requires access to particular expertise and/or operational capability from banks. The first is typically represented by domestic collections and disbursements, tax settlements, and balance-reporting systems. The second includes such elements as foreign exchange and export collections that can be segregated from main current account transactions.

One of the most important services that a bank can provide to a firm is ideas and information. Such services may include new types of financing, improved cash management techniques, developments in foreign exchange markets, credit information on important customers of the firm, and ideas about how to conduct export business.

Summary

This chapter provided an overview of cash management topics pertaining to understanding the cash balance, accelerating cash flows, and evaluating the bank/corporation relationship. Knowing the cash balance requires an understanding of the differences between the bank balance and the ledger balance. Mail, processing, and transit floats, among other things, can cause these balances to differ. If management understands the check-clearing process, it can implement cash systems to make cash management more productive.

The techniques discussed for accelerating cash flows include concentration banking, lockbox services, preauthorized credits and debits, depository transfer checks, wire transfers, and drafts. These techniques have received varying degrees of acceptance by customers, with the result that the most efficient form of cash management cannot always be routinely used by management. A second-best alternative must often be used.

An important aspect of cash management is the selection of banks and the relationship between the corporation and its banking system. Banks play an important intermediary role in the cash management system, and management should treat the banks as important partners. Failure to do so results in a less efficient cash management function of the company. But management cannot select just any banks. Banks used in the corporate cash management system must meet the needs of the company at a reasonable cost and provide the services/expertise needed by management.

Key Concepts

Automatic concentration
Check-clearing process
Deposit float
Depository transfer checks
Disbursement float
Discretionary concentration
Drafts
Lockbox system
Mail float

Preauthorized checks
Preauthorized debts
Processing float
Remote control
Role of banks
Transit (Fed) float
Wire transfers
Zero-balance account

Questions

1. What are the three basic principles of cash management?

2. What are the reasons that excess cash lies dormant?

3. What is the difference between a company's cash ledger balance and the bank's net collected balance?

4. Define and contrast mail float, processing float, and transit float.

5. Briefly describe some ways to accelerate cash inflows.

6. What is the difference between automatic concentration and discretionary concentration?

7. What are the advantages of concentration banking?

8. "Management can maintain too little as well as too much in its cash balances." Is this statement true? Explain.

9. When one firm collects its outstanding accounts faster, another firm loses cash more rapidly. This situation is clearly a zero-sum game for the system as a whole. If there is no gain to business as a whole, why do firms try to streamline their collection system?

10. In the process of check clearing a bank has three options. The checks can be sent directly to the bank on which they were drawn, they can be sent directly to the correspondent bank, or they can be cleared through the Federal Reserve System. Give a brief description of each method.

11. Compare and contrast the advantages of the lockbox system and the preauthorized check method.

Problems

1. Prepare a bank reconciliation statement from the following data.
    □ The bank balance is $200,000.
    □ The bank has charged a service fee of $20 for the month, and it has not been recorded by the company.
    □ The company received but did not deposit $3200.
    □ The company maintains a compensating balance of $1500 with the bank.
    □ The company shows outstanding checks for its payables of $17,775.

2. ABC, Inc., has $100,000 in the bank and issues $10,000 in checks on December 10. On the same day $20,000 in checks were written to the firm by different

companies. How much cash is in ABC's bank account on December 15 under the following conditions?

(a) Disbursements clear in 9 days and incoming checks in 6 days.

(b) Disbursements clear in 6 days and incoming checks in 3 days.

(c) Disbursements clear in 4 days and incoming checks in 8 days.

3. Bruce, Inc., operates through 30 offices covering a ten-state region. Local managers have been mailing checks, totaling an average of $250,000 daily, to the home office in Lafayette. An average of 3 days elapse while checks are in the mail, ½ day while they are being processed in the home office, and 2 days while they are being collected through the banking system. Someone has recommended that each manager instruct the local bank to wire transfer receipts to the home office bank at 2:30 P.M. each day.

(a) How much money is presently tied up in float?

(b) What is the net amount of actual funds freed if each local bank requires a minimum compensating balance of $1500 be maintained at all times?

(c) For wire transfers costing $7 each, calculate the annual cost of this system, assuming 250 transfers per local bank per year. The annual cost of funds is 12% per annum before tax.

(d) Should the company use the wire transfer system?

(e) What other forms of cash acceleration should management look at?

4. Hurd Associates bills its customers and collects all accounts receivable at its home office, located in Buffalo, New York. Credit sales to customers in the Southwest region of the country are $48 million per year. Average mail, processing, deposit, and collection float is 7 days. Valley Bank of Arizona has suggested a lockbox system be used. Valley Bank would collect the checks from the lockboxes and electronically transfer the collections daily to Hurd's main bank in Buffalo. It would also transmit records of collections to Hurd's computers on a daily basis. Valley requires a minimum compensating balance of $36,000 and charges a fee of $3600 per month for this service. Hurd's treasurer estimates that clerical and record-keeping costs at the Buffalo office would be reduced by $1500 per month. Total float time would be reduced to 3 days.

(a) How much funds will be freed by the lockbox system? Use a 360-day year.

(b) How much is the actual annual dollar cost of the lockbox system?

(c) What is the net annual percentage cost of the funds freed?

(d) If the opportunity cost of funds for Hurd is 10% before taxes, should the system be adopted? Explain.

5. ValueDisc Corporation, headquartered in San Francisco, has annual credit sales of $840 million. It has eight regional sales offices. All billings and collections are handled by head office staff. Management is considering a concentration banking system under which collections are made by the regional offices and deposited in their local banks. Funds would then be transmitted to the concentration bank in San Francisco via wire transfers. The average elapsed time between customers' mailing checks and funds becoming available to the concentration bank would be reduced by one day. Compensating balances in the regional banks would be increased by $1,200,000. Annual service charges and regional office expenses would be increased $200,000 greater than the amount of reduction in the San Francisco headquarters.

(a) How much net cash is freed if the concentration banking system is adopted?

(b) What is the net annual cost of the actual funds freed? Ignore the opportunity cost at this point.

(c) If the opportunity cost of funds is 10% before tax, should the concentration banking system be adopted?

6.   The Wilt Company has an inventory turnover of 5 times and a receivables turnover of 11 times. All sales are on credit. It purchases inventory in equal amounts daily and issues checks to vendors 30 days after invoice dates. It experiences an average disbursement float of 9 days. Its clearing float on checks received from customers averages 4 days. Assume a 360-day year to answer the following questions.

(a) What is the elapsed time of the operating cycle? How many days is the cash conversion cycle when adjusted for float?

(b) If daily payments for inventory are $100,000 and daily sales are $130,000, what are the total funds tied up in net working capital at any time according to the company's ledger? How is the ledger balance affected by receivable and disbursement float?

7.   The firm writes checks for $600,000 each day and charges them against its cash balance the same day (i.e., day 1). It takes the firm's bank, on average, three days (i.e., until day 4) to clear the checks. Any deposits made by the firm are credited to the firm's account by the bank on the same day.

(a) Determine the firm's cash balance, per its ledger account and its bank account, if on day 1 the firm deposits $400,000.

(b) If the firm continues to write $600,000 in checks daily, how much must it deposit, and when, in order to maintain a constant bank balance?

(c) Assume that the bank borrowing rate is 12%. Determine whether the firm can profit by using float.

8.   Each business day Ashmore Corporation issues checks for $400,000 and deducts them from its cash ledger balance. Its bank clears the checks, on the average, the sixth business day after issue. Ashmore's $8 million bank line of credit requires a 10% compensating balance. This amount is in excess of any balance needed for precautionary purposes.

(a) If the collected balance (available funds) is $800,000, how much must Ashmore deposit on days 1 through 6 to maintain this balance? Assume that collection patterns are stable and average two days of the checks included in Ashmore's deposits.

(b) How much outgoing float does Ashmore have at all times?

(c) What amount should Ashmore show on its books if the bank is to show a balance of $800,000?

9.   Westmount Mill wishes to determine whether or not it should establish a lockbox system with the local bank. The cost, net of any home office cost savings, would be $22,000 per year. The bank would require a $40,000 minimum balance be maintained. Collection float time would be reduced by four days. The firm's

opportunity cost of funds is 12% before taxes. What is the breakeven credit sales level (i.e., where residual income equals zero)? Assume a 360-day year.

10. The Kitchener Company expects daily credit sales to average $50,000, with a standard deviation of $9500. A local bank has offered the company a lockbox service to accelerate cash receipts to the company. The bank requires a minimum balance of $45,000 be maintained and charges a service fee of $15,000 per year. The service would speed collection of credit sales by four days. Assume a 360-day year.

(a) If the company's opportunity cost of capital is 12%, what is the breakeven credit sales level?

(b) What is the probability of daily sales being below the breakeven sales level?

CHAPTER 8 □
Minimizing Cash Balances

The most important of all the liquidity responsibilities of the financial manager is the managing of cash, both flows and balances. In recent years increasing attention has been devoted to the maintenance of safety and anticipation stocks of liquid assets and marketable securities. Interest has focused on an objective determination of the proper level of such cash reserves and on methods of minimizing idle cash balances and their associated opportunity cost.

Cash has a value apart from its being critical to the operations of a business. This value is the cost of possessing it — the cost of not lending it out for someone else to use, or the saving from not having to borrow it. In effect, cash is a commodity, an inventory. The cost of cash varies from day to day, and it varies significantly over months or years.

Any attempt to maintain a minimum cash balance that is consistent with shareholder wealth maximization requires input about liquidity needs. When a company is plagued with poor cash management, it often ignores its own carelessness with the explanation that it is in a dynamic industry where one cannot be sure of changes from one day to the next, a sink-or-swim market, and so on.

To minimize cash balances, management needs to forecast needs. An annual forecast provides an indication of direction and need. A quarterly or monthly forecast alerts management to needs during the approaching period. These forecasts, however, may not be sufficient. The firm's operating cycle may have weekly or daily needs not revealed by either quarterly or monthly forecasts.

The purpose of this chapter is to examine models for minimizing cash balances. The traditional accounting-based techniques of ratio analysis and adjusted earnings are examined, as are more sophisticated mathematical models that incorporate the cost of money.

Estimating Cash Balances to Service Growth Forecasts

The cash manager's goal should be to provide reasonable estimates of future cash positions that satisfy growth forecasts. Most companies produce a cash plan or a budget as part of their annual budget process. The plan identifies either month- or quarter-end cash positions and may be updated as the year progresses. Several companies supplement this report by short-term forecasts, varying from detailed monthly projections to a comparison of actual against budget.

Cash balance variance to forecast rarely receives the same attention as those of sales or expense goals. It should, since the cause of error is more difficult to identify. A good monitoring system should direct analyses at both operational and financial variances. The former pertains to sales, production, and purchasing, whereas the latter concentrates on receivables control or assumptions used to extrapolate known revenues and expenses. Both operational and financial personnel must share responsibility for providing accurate cash forecasts.

What is a practical method of forecasting cash balances for growth forecasts? Historically, there are four different methods:

1. Balance sheet or ratio projection method.
2. Adjusted-earnings method.
3. Cash receipts and disbursement method (i.e., cash budgeting, examined in Chapter 6).
4. Baumol's economic order quantity model.[1]

The first three methods are interrelated since they depend on the same basic sources of information: the budgeted balance sheet and/or the budgeted income statement. The Baumol model differs in that its solution is based on the trade-off of holding and ordering costs.

Ratio Approach

The *ratio approach* to cash management is couched in terms of ratio analysis. Its guiding principle is that management should keep so many day's worth of payables or a certain percentage of sales in its cash account. The industry average is usually suggested as the standard.

---

[1] William J. Baumol, "The Transactions Demand for Cash: An Inventory Theoretical Approach," *Quarterly Journal of Economics* (November 1952): 545–556.

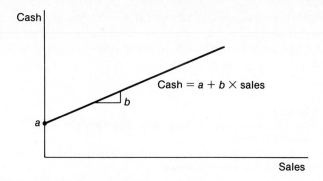

FIGURE 8.1
Ratio Approach to Forecasting the Cash Balance

A ratio approach suffers from the same deficiencies as all ratio analyses. Furthermore, it assumes a fixed-regression slope (see Fig. 8.1), which is usually not the case for most functional relationships in finance. It fails to account for any economies of scale, as shown later when the Baumol model is discussed.

Adjusted-Earnings Method

The *adjusted-earnings method* depends on a sales and profit forecast or what is also called a profit projection report. Naturally, the accuracy of the cash forecast depends directly on the accuracy of the profit projection report. The cash forecast is developed from such a report as follows:

1. Assume that net profit after taxes generates cash.
2. Add to it those costs and expenses that, in fact, do not require an actual cash outlay (e.g., depreciation, bad debts).
3. Add (subtract) to it any foreseeable excess (shortage) of collections over sales.
4. Add (subtract) to it any foreseeable increase (decrease) of payables over purchases.
5. Subtract from it cash outlays that will not affect profit (e.g., acquisition of fixed assets or payment of dividends).

The *pro forma* Change in Cash Position Statement in Table 8.1 illustrates these steps. The analysis is based on projected data for the same six months that were considered in the cash budget example, Illustration 6.1 in Chapter 6, with the additional assumption that depreciation for the half year, after new additions, is $86,000.

Although the result is the same as that calculated by the cash budget in Chapter 6, considerably less detail is available to evaluate cash needs. In particular, the adjusted-earnings method does not pinpoint times during the horizon when cash needs are excessive or when a shortage exists.

TABLE 8.1
Adjusted-Earnings Method for Estimating the June
Cash Position

Pro forma *income statement*

Sales		$1,300,000
Cost of sales:		
Beginning inventory	$ 120,000	
Purchases	1,160,000	
	$1,280,000	
Ending inventory	240,000	
		1,040,000
Gross margin		$ 260,000
Expenses:		
Rent	$ 12,000	
Wages and salaries	245,000	
Depreciation	86,000	
		343,000
Operating earnings		$ <83,000>
Interest: Income	$ 2,430	
Expense	<41,510>	
		<39,080>
Earnings before taxes		$<122,080>
Taxes at 45%		<54,936>
Net income		$ <67,144>

Pro forma *balance sheet*

	January actual	June forecast
Cash and securities	$ 100,000	$ 100,000
Receivables	427,500	247,500
Taxes receivable	0	54,936
Inventory	120,000	240,000
Net fixed assets	686,000	630,000
Total	$1,333,500	$1,272,436
Accounts payable	$ 0	$ 0
Bank loan	0	56,080
Taxes payable	50,000	0
Equity:		
Beginning retained earnings	1,283,500	1,283,500
Net income		<67,144>
Total	$1,333,500	$1,272,436

TABLE 8.1 (Cont.)

Pro forma *change in cash position* statement

Funds provided by operations:	
Net income	$ <67,144>
Depreciation	86,000
Funds from operations	$ 18,856
Change in receivables	180,000
Change in inventory	<120,000>
Change in accounts payable	0
Cash flow from operations	$ 78,856
Plus bank loan	56,080
Total sources	$ 134,936
Less: Capital addition	30,000
Tax payment	50,000
Taxes receivable	54,936
Change in cash and securities	$ 0

Baumol Model

Early research by Baumol on the demand for money used an *economic order quantity* (EOQ) *model* similar to that used in inventory management (which is discussed in Chapter 14). The idea is that cash is simply another commodity. Thus the *Baumol model* incorporates both the cost of holding idle cash balances and the cost of ordering (i.e., securing) cash. It can be used to find an optimal (average) cash balance.

The model incorporates the following features:

1. A known demand for D dollars of cash for the period, which is used at a constant rate.

2. The requirement that all demands for payment from the cash balance be filled immediately.

3. A lump cost of c dollars to transfer from assets into cash.

4. An annual opportunity cost of $v/\$1$, which is equal to the interest forgone on bonds.

Items 3 and 4 can be explained further as follows: If it is necessary to add to or subtract from the inventory of cash by making a transfer to or from a portfolio of securities, there is an order cost involved, partly in the form of internal clerical and decision-making costs and partly in the form of brokerage fees, wire transfer costs, and the like. In the other direction, if the cash manager tries to cut down these in-and-out costs by holding large cash balances, there is a substantial holding cost in the form of the interest loss on the funds tied up in the balance. The decision rule

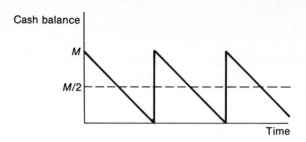

FIGURE 8.2
Baumol Cash Model

requires minimizing total costs with respect to the cash balance M. By the use of calculus, the optimal cash balance M is found to occur whenever

$$M = \left(\frac{2cD}{v}\right)^{1/2}, \tag{8.1}$$

the familiar square-root equation of the EOQ inventory model. The operating rule that leads to Eq. (8.1) generates a cash balance that takes the sawtooth pattern of Fig. 8.2. The average amount of cash is $M/2$.

ILLUSTRATION 8.1

The cash balance is steadily and uniformly drawn down over time. The cost of each transaction to secure cash is $50. Management anticipates $1,500,000 in cash outlays during the next year. The company's annual opportunity cost of funds from investing in marketable securities is 12%. All cash demands are met by selling marketable securities.

The optimal cash replenishment level is

$$M = \left(\frac{2 \times 50 \times 1,500,000}{0.12}\right)^{1/2} = \$35,355.$$

Average cash balances are one-half of M, or $17,678.   □

The Baumol model is an improvement over the ratio approach for estimating a *pro forma* cash balance. The ratio approach assumes a direct relationship between the cash amount and sales. According to the ratio approach, if forecasted sales increase, say 10%, the cash amount in the balance sheet also increases 10%. Such an approach overlooks economies of scale and invests needless amounts of resources in cash. The Baumol model indicates that if sales grow at a rate of 10%, then the cash balance should only increase at a rate of about 4.9%.

ILLUSTRATION 8.2

Cash outlays are anticipated to increase 10% over the $1,500,000 amount used in Illustration 8.1. Ordering costs and opportunity costs are not expected to change.

The optimal cash replenishment level is

$$M = \left(\frac{2 \times 50 \times 1,650,000}{0.12}\right)^{1/2} = \$37,081,$$

or about 4.9% greater than the level of Illustration 8.1 (i.e., $37,081/ $35,355). □

Daily Management of Cash Balances

The techniques discussed in the previous section and in Chapter 6 (i.e., monthly cash budgeting) are not very amenable to managing daily cash balances. They do not allow the cash manager to answer this important question: How large a buffer stock of cash should the company keep on hand to protect itself from adverse cash drains? The cash budgeting techniques examined to this point require the cash manager to prepare a single estimate of certain values. The *receipts and disbursements method* of cash budgeting (in Chapter 6) assumes that the company knows its specific cash inflows from sales and collections of receivables in the months to come, as well as the cash outlays for labor, materials, dividend payments, and so forth. Then by subtracting the total of all monthly outlays from monthly inflows, the cash manager can determine the most likely change in the company's cash position for each month in the future.

In practice, few firms, if any, are able to forecast their inflows and outflows with this precision. Sales forecasts are notoriously unreliable, for actual sales depend in part on factors that lie outside the control of management. Changes in the styling or marketing of competitive products, as well as changes in general economic conditions, can lead to large forecasting errors.

Cash forecasts inevitably focus on period-end positions. However, management should not hesitate to change the focal point of the projection when another date has more meaning. The most meaningful data will usually be captured in weekly or *daily cash forecasts*. More important than the period-end balance is the range of cash positions during the period. Ranges provide far more useful and practical indications of cash resources and needs than do period-end estimates. Two models that can be used by the cash manager to manage daily cash balances are the Miller-Orr model[2] and the Stone model.[3]

Miller-Orr Model

In large firms the cash balance fluctuates irregularly (and to some extent, unpredictably) over time — building up cash balances when receipts exceed expenditures and falling off when the reverse is true. If the buildup is prolonged, the cash manager will decide that cash holdings are excessive and will transfer a quantity of funds for temporary investment in securities or to loan retirement. In the other direction, if a prolonged cash drain persists, a level is reached where securities are liquidated or the treasurer borrows to restore the cash balance to what is regarded as an adequate working level.

A model that incorporates irregular cash patterns is known as the *Miller-Orr model.* This model incorporates these conditions:

□ The cash manager operates in a two-asset environment: One asset is the firm's cash balance, and the other is a separately managed portfolio of liquid assets whose marginal and average yield is v percent per day.

□ Transfers between the two asset accounts can take place at any time at a marginal cost of c dollars per transfer. This cost is independent of the size of the transfer, the direction of the transfer, or the time since the previous transfer.

□ Transfers are regarded as taking place instantaneously.

□ Cash flows are completely stochastic (i.e., random).

□ The treasurer allows the cash balance to wander freely until it reaches either its lower bound, zero, or its upper bound, h, at which times a portfolio transfer is undertaken to restore the balance to a level of R. The policy implies that when the upper bound is hit, there is a lump-sum transfer from cash of $h - R$; and when the lower bound is triggered, a transfer of R is made to cash.

Management's objective is to minimize total costs associated with cash. By the use of stochastic calculus, the optimal return point (R) and average cash balance (ACB) in dollars are

---

[2] Merton H. Miller and Daniel Orr, "A Model of the Demand for Money by Firms," *Quarterly Journal of Economics* (July 1968): 413–435.

[3] Bernell K. Stone, "The Use of Forecasts and Smoothing in Control-Limit Models for Cash Management," *Financial Management* (Spring 1972): 72–84.

$$R = \left(\frac{3c\sigma^2}{4v}\right)^{1/3},$$

(8.2)

$$\text{ACB} = \frac{4R}{3},$$

(8.3)

respectively, where σ^2 is the daily variance of changes in the cash balance. The upper bound is $h = 3R$, and the lower bound is a zero balance.

The optimal return point R is below the midpoint of the range over which the cash balance is allowed to wander. Thus there are more sales of portfolio assets than purchases. Figure 8.3 depicts the model.

The vertical orientation of the model can be changed without affecting the relationship between R and h. If management desires to keep a minimum balance, the lower limit becomes the minimum balance so desired. The Appendix to this chapter discusses an *ad hoc* technique for determining a minimum balance (for use with the Miller-Orr model or any other model/plan requiring a minimum balance).

Illustration 8.3

Management uses the Miller-Orr model to monitor and control cash balances. It has estimated the transaction costs to be $75 per transaction, the annual opportunity cost of funds to be 11%, and the variance of daily cash flows to be $27,000. It is interested in determining the upper limit (h), the optimal return point (R), and the average cash balance. The mini-

FIGURE 8.3
Miller-Orr Model

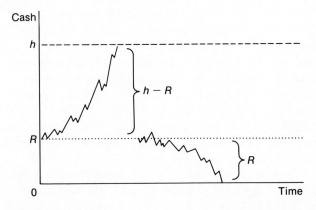

mum cash balance is zero. Assume a 360-day year. The calculations are as follows:

$$R = \left(\frac{3 \times 75 \times 27{,}000}{4 \times 0.11/360}\right)^{1/3} = \$1706,$$

$$h = 3 \times \$1706 = \$5118,$$

$$\text{average balance} = \frac{4R}{3} = \$2275. \qquad \square$$

The Miller-Orr model is a definite improvement over the Baumol model for managing daily cash balances since it does not place the restrictive assumption of constant use on the cash flows. Miller and Orr have shown their model to have practical usefulness. In a study of Union Tank Car Company's cash management practices, the Miller-Orr model was superior to the *ad hoc* procedures utilized by the company's assistant treasurer. The model resulted in fewer transactions while allowing the firm to keep a lower average cash balance. In other words, the model resulted in better cash management, which translates into increased shareholder wealth.

Stone Model

In practice, cash managers attempt to consider not only their present cash position but also their cash position over the next few days. They attempt to minimize unnecessary transactions.

The Miller-Orr model automatically and immediately returns the cash balance to the target level R whenever a control limit is pierced. If cash forecasts, however crude, are available, such a system is generally not optimal. For example, consider a firm with an R of $4 million and control limits of $12 and $0 million. If current balances are $15 million, an automatic-return model such as Miller-Orr requires the purchase of $11 million in marketable securities to restore the balance to $4 million. If additional inflows of $1 million and $2 million are expected over the next two days, the cash manager might want to purchase $14 million so that the balance would be back on target in two days rather than immediately. In another situation, if expected outflows of $1 million and $3 million are expected over the next two days, then the cash manager might prefer to make no purchase (depending on the overnight money rate), since the cash balance will automatically restore itself below the upper limit over the next two days.

The *Stone model* operationalizes such an approach. It uses two sets of control limits and does not depend on stochastic calculus to set the limits, as does the Miller-Orr model. Figure 8.4 depicts the structure. The target

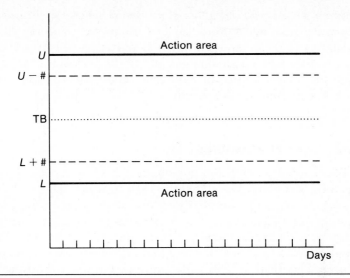

FIGURE 8.4
Stone Model

level of cash balances is denoted by TB. The outside set of control limits, denoted by U and L, are the upper and lower control limits for initiating consideration of a transaction. The inside limits are defined by $U - \#$ and $L + \#$. These inside limits determine whether a transaction will actually be made.

The cash manager takes no action unless the actual current cash balance is outside the outer control limits (i.e., in the action areas). When either U or L is exceeded, then the cash forecast for the next N days (which can be arbitrarily chosen) is used to determine whether a marketable security transaction should be made. A transaction is only made if the expected cash balance in N days exceeds the inner control limits, $U - \#$ or $L + \#$. If a transaction is made, the amount is such that expected balances in N days will be at the target level of cash balances, TB. This procedure is illustrated later.

Both the number of days used in the forecast and the values of the control limits are parameters that the cash manager assigns. Typical values of N are between 3 and 12 days. The limits can be assigned arbitrarily or calculated by using classical statistical techniques, $X \pm Z\sigma$; that is, the upper and lower limits are Z standard deviations from the mean. The value for Z indicates the probability of the measures being within the limits. The Appendix to Chapter 6 is a table of Z values.

The Miller-Orr model could be used to determine the limits. Thus L could be assigned the value of 0, and U could be assigned the value of h.

The important point is that the values of the control limits and the length of the forecast period should not be treated as fixed parameters. The target level of cash balances can be an adjusted target to reflect past history. If balances are either too low or too high for some part of the period, the cash manager can adjust the limits to bring the cash balance into line so that the average balance is as expected for the month.

Daily Cash Forecasting

Daily cash forecasts are needed to implement the Stone model. A technique developed by Stone and Wood[4] can be used in which daily cash forecasts are separated into major items (which are easily identifiable) and many minor receipts and disbursements (which are not readily identifiable). Taxes, dividends, and debt repayment are examples of the first case. Payments for materials, office supplies, and telephone expenses are examples of the second case. The focus of daily cash forecasting is the forecasting of non-major items, with the major items subsequently added to this forecast to get a total daily budget.

With the use of bank statements all major items can be identified and deleted from the analysis to derive the nonmajor flows. This deletion is necessary to minimize statistical bias of the results. The nonmajor flows can be identified for day of the month and day of the week. This identification allows the calculation of the proportion of the monthly cash flow that occurs on work day j as well as the calculation of the proportion of total flows occurring on weekday i.

For example, assume that Table 8.2 summarizes both day-of-the-month and day-of-the-week proportions for the month of March for the past three years, as well as the average values for this period. Furthermore, assume that the major items have been purged from the data.

Since the jth day of the month (a_j in Table 8.2) is not always the same day of the week, one must adjust the day-of-the-month proportion for any day-of-the-week (d_i) proportion. A day-of-the-week effect may arise for the following reasons: Management may schedule payments to out-of-state vendors on a Thursday; payments to other vendors occur on Wednesday; payroll is paid on Friday; and collections are normally larger on Monday than any other day.

The day-of-the-week adjustment is accomplished by calculating a factor d_i^*. It is calculated as follows, where $\bar{d}$ represents the average of the d_i's:

---

[4] Bernell K. Stone and Robert A. Wood, "Daily Cash Forecasting: A Simple Method for Implementing the Distribution Approach," *Financial Management* (Fall 1977): 40–50.

	d_i	$d_i - \bar{d}$	$=$	d_i^*
M	0.264	$0.264 - 0.200$	$=$	0.064
T	0.203	$0.203 - 0.200$	$=$	0.003
W	0.153	$0.153 - 0.200$	$=$	-0.047
T	0.083	$0.083 - 0.200$	$=$	-0.117
F	0.297	$0.297 - 0.200$	$=$	0.097
	1.000			0

TABLE 8.2
Cash Flow Distributions

Workday	Last year	First prior year	Second prior year	Average (a_j)
Day of the month				
1	0.045	0.040	0.042	0.042
2	0.050	0.052	0.048	0.050
3	0.060	0.055	0.058	0.058
4	0.065	0.060	0.067	0.064
5	0.070	0.075	0.069	0.071
6	0.070	0.080	0.072	0.074
7	0.065	0.064	0.066	0.065
8	0.060	0.058	0.062	0.060
9	0.055	0.060	0.058	0.058
10	0.050	0.050	0.048	0.049
11	0.050	0.048	0.052	0.050
12	0.045	0.049	0.046	0.047
13	0.040	0.035	0.039	0.038
14	0.030	0.033	0.041	0.035
15	0.030	0.034	0.033	0.032
16	0.025	0.020	0.024	0.023
17	0.030	0.027	0.025	0.027
18	0.035	0.040	0.033	0.036
19	0.040	0.041	0.037	0.039
20	0.040	0.045	0.039	0.042
21	0.045	0.034	0.041	0.040
	1.000	1.000	1.000	1.000
Day of the week				(d_i)
M	0.250	0.280	0.260	0.264
T	0.200	0.220	0.190	0.203
W	0.150	0.140	0.170	0.153
T	0.100	0.080	0.070	0.083
F	0.300	0.280	0.310	0.297
	1.000	1.000	1.000	1.000

This information, coupled with that in Table 8.2, allows a monthly cash budget for nonmajor items to be distributed over the days of the month.

ILLUSTRATION 8.4

Assume that next March's monthly net cash budget for the minor items is \$75,000, and the first workday of the month is a Friday. Table 8.3 summarizes the daily budget for these minor items. The total $a_j + d_i^*$ sums to more than 1.0 since an extra day, Friday, appears in the month. The normalized column restates the proportions so that they sum to 1.0. The daily budget column is simply each day's normalized factor times \$75,000.

The major cash flow items need to be added to these daily projections. This information can then be used with Stone's control limit cash management model if the budget amount is still appropriate as of the time

TABLE 8.3
Allocation of Monthly Budget by Day

Workday	a_j	d_i^*	$a_j + d_i^*$	Normalized	Daily budget	Cumulative
1	0.042	0.097	0.139	0.1266	\$ 9,493	\$ 9,493
2	0.050	0.064	0.114	0.1033	7,751	17,244
3	0.058	0.003	0.061	0.0555	4,166	21,410
4	0.064	−0.047	0.017	0.0159	1,193	22,603
5	0.071	−0.117	−0.046	−0.0416	−3,121	19,482
6	0.074	0.097	0.171	0.1554	11,655	31,137
7	0.065	0.064	0.129	0.1170	8,776	39,913
8	0.060	0.003	0.063	0.0577	4,325	44,238
9	0.058	−0.047	0.011	0.0101	760	44,998
10	0.049	−0.117	−0.068	−0.0615	−4,611	40,387
11	0.050	0.097	0.147	0.1335	10,016	50,403
12	0.047	0.064	0.111	0.1007	7,555	57,958
13	0.038	0.003	0.041	0.0376	2,823	60,781
14	0.035	−0.047	−0.012	−0.0108	−810	59,971
15	0.032	−0.117	−0.085	−0.0770	−5,773	54,198
16	0.023	0.097	0.120	0.1090	8,172	62,370
17	0.027	0.064	0.091	0.0827	6,203	68,573
18	0.036	0.003	0.039	0.0360	2,697	71,270
19	0.039	−0.047	−0.008	−0.0068	−513	70,757
20	0.042	−0.117	−0.075	−0.0680	−5,102	65,655
21	0.040	0.097	0.137	0.1246	9,345	75,000
	1.000		1.098	1.0000	\$75,000	

Note: Normalized calculation for day 1: 0.139/1.098 = 0.1266, where the numerator is the adjusted day-of-the-month factor and the denominator is the column total.

management must make a cash decision. If it is not, a new forecast must be made.   □

ILLUSTRATION 8.5

Assume that $10,000 and $30,000 are the lower (*L*) and upper (*U*) control limits, respectively. The inner control limits are arbitrarily set at ±$3000 of the outer control limits. Management has a target balance of $20,000, which is the balance on the first workday of March. Table 8.4 details the cash flows and management action based on a four-day moving forecast. This illustration assumes no major flow items for purposes of simplification.

The decision to buy or sell securities is based on the following decision

TABLE 8.4
Cash Management Activites for a Four-Day Moving Forecast

Day	Beginning cash balance	Actual cash flow	Adjusted cash balance	Marketable securities	Ending cash balance	Next 4-day forecast
1	$20,000	$ 8,430	$28,430		$28,430	
2	28,430	6,000	34,430	<$28,323>	6,107	$13,893*
3	6,107	3,905	10,012		10,012	
4	10,012	1,214	11,226		11,226	
5	11,226	−5,000	6,226		6,226	25,516
6	6,226	7,281	13,507		13,507	
7	13,507	6,430	19,937		19,937	
8	19,937	8,700	28,637		28,637	
9	28,637	2,000	30,637	<26,420>	4,217	15,783
10	4,217	−7,308	−3,091		−3,091	19,584
11	−3,091	8,570	5,479	10,727	16,205	3,795
12	16,205	7,500	23,705		23,705	
13	23,705	3,111	26,816		26,816	
14	26,816	0	26,816		26,816	
15	26,816	−4,310	22,506		22,506	
16	22,506	8,325	30,831	<14,117>	16,714	3,286
17	16,714	6,415	23,129		23,129	
18	23,129	2,100	25,229		25,229	
19	25,229	−1,204	24,025		24,025	
20	24,025	−6,111	17,914		17,914	
21	17,914	9,512	27,426		27,426	
		$65,560		<$58,134>		

Average daily ending cash balance = $17,890

Note: A < > represents investment in marketable securities. No < > means a sale of marketable securities.
* This forecast is from Table 8.3, the daily cash budget column, for days 3 through 6.

rule: Whenever an outer limit is pierced, the forecasted cash flows for the next four days are summed to see whether the cash balance will be within the inner control limits by day 4. If it is, no action is taken. If it is not, then cash is transferred to marketable securities if the upper limit is violated, while marketable securities are sold and cash transferred to the cash account if the lower limit is violated. In Table 8.4 there were four transactions actually made, whereas the limits were violated seven times. Thus in three cases the forecasted cash balances during the next four days were expected to bring the system back into control. The transactions for days 2, 9, 11, and 13 are shown in Table 8.5.

Table 8.6 summarizes the situation if a no-forecast policy exists. Marketable securities are bought once the upper limit is violated. They are sold whenever the lower limit is violated. The amount bought or sold restores the cash balance to its target level of $20,000.

A comparison of the next four-day forecast with the no-forecast model reveals two things: The no-forecast policy has a higher investment in marketable securities at the end of the period (which will not happen in all situations), and it has a higher average balance invested in cash for the period (which is likely to be the case in all situations).

The residual income model can be used to evaluate each approach. Table 8.7 summarizes the analysis and indicates that the forecast approach is clearly superior. The results are misstated somewhat since weekend effects are not included in the calculation of income earned from marketable security investments.

Different examples would produce similar results. The ability to forecast a few days' cash flows with a reasonable degree of accuracy gen-

TABLE 8.5
Marketable Security Transactions

Day	Adjusted cash balance	Four-day forecast	Expected cash balance in four days	Target balance	Marketable securities	
2	$34,430	$13,893	$48,323	$20,000	$28,323	Buy
9	30,637	15,783	46,420	20,000	26,420	Buy
11	5,479	3,795	9,273	20,000	10,727	Sell
16	30,831	3,286	34,117	20,000	14,117	Buy

Note: No transaction is undertaken for day 5 even though the adjusted cash balance plus the next four-day forecast exceeds the outer upper control limit. In this example it is management's decision to avoid transactions when the situation goes from violating one limit to violating the opposite limit within the forecast period. Such a policy may not be the most efficient. Computer simulation of this possibility would help determine whether another decision rule would be more profitable.

TABLE 8.6
Cash Management Activities for a No-Forecast Policy

Day	Beginning cash balance	Actual cash flow	Adjusted cash balance	Marketable securities	Ending cash balance
1	$20,000	$ 8,430	$28,430		$28,430
2	28,430	6,000	34,430	<$14,430>	20,000
3	20,000	3,905	23,905		23,905
4	23,905	1,214	25,119		25,119
5	25,119	−5,000	20,119		20,119
6	20,119	7,281	27,400		27,400
7	27,400	6,430	33,830	<13,830>	20,000
8	20,000	8,700	28,700		28,700
9	28,700	2,000	30,700	<10,700>	20,000
10	20,000	−7,308	12,692		12,692
11	12,692	8,570	21,262		21,262
12	21,262	7,500	28,762		28,762
13	28,762	3,111	31,873	<11,873>	20,000
14	20,000	0	20,000		20,000
15	20,000	−4,310	15,690		15,690
16	15,690	8,325	24,015		24,015
17	24,015	6,415	30,430	<10,430>	20,000
18	20,000	2,100	22,100		22,100
19	22,100	−1,204	20,896		20,896
20	20,896	−6,111	14,785		14,785
21	14,785	9,512	24,297		24,297
		$65,560		<$61,263>	

Average daily ending cash balance = $21,818

Note: A < > represents investment in marketable securities.

erally results in lower investment in cash and a higher residual income amount.   □

The results of Illustration 8.5 take on added importance as the size of the cash budget increases. For instance, if the amounts were in millions of dollars rather than thousands, the advantage to forecasting would be $46,680 for this *one month*, or $560,160 when annualized. Thus management could invest a considerable amount of resources (assuming it is done productively) in the cash management area, which would result in increased profits, cash flow, and shareholder wealth.

TABLE 8.7
Residual Income Analysis of Forecasting Versus
Not Forecasting

Investment		Days invested		Daily rate		Interest earned
Four-day forecast						
$28,323	×	7	×	0.1/360	=	$ 55.07
54,743	×	2	×	0.1/360	=	30.41
44,016	×	5	×	0.1/360	=	61.13
58,134	×	5	×	0.1/360	=	80.74
						$227.35
No forecast						
$14,430	×	5	×	0.1/360	=	$ 20.04
28,260	×	2	×	0.1/360	=	15.70
38,960	×	4	×	0.1/360	=	43.29
50,833	×	4	×	0.1/360	=	56.48
61,263	×	4	×	0.1/360	=	68.07
						$203.58

Residual income = cash flow − k(average cash investment)

$$RI_{fcst} = \$227.35 - 21 \times \frac{0.1}{360}(\$17,890) = \$122.99$$

$$RI_{no\ fcst} = \$203.58 - 21 \times \frac{0.1}{360}(\$21,818) = \$76.31$$

Note: The average cash investment amounts are stated in Tables 8.4 and 8.5.

Summary

Efficient cash management requires managers to maintain minimal cash balances, since idle cash balances are nonearning assets (or minimal earning assets). The cash manager must forecast requirements over a period of time. Often this forecast is done on a monthly basis, but this time period has a serious deficiency. Monthly forecasts fail to indicate intramonth cash needs and surpluses, with the result that management may find itself unexpectedly short of cash or with large balances. The minimum requirement is a weekly cash forecast. If the cash manager is able to forecast daily cash flows, it is even better.

This chapter discussed both the traditional techniques and the more recent mathematical models for forecasting cash balances. The traditional models include the ratio approach and the adjusted-earnings method (the cash receipts and disbursements method, i.e., the cash budget, was examined in Chapter 6). The cash budget is the best of these techniques, but it requires relatively more work since more information is needed. Thus this method forces the analyst to think through the process rather than simply use some ratio proportions that are assumed to incorporate complex relationships. The cash budget is the lifeline of the treasury function.

The mathematical models examined were the Baumol model, the Miller-Orr model, and the Stone model. The Baumol model is the simplest model; the Miller-Orr model is the most mathematically complex. The Stone model is probably better than either the Baumol and Miller-Orr models. It is mathematically simple, yet it can incorporate the thought processes of the cash manager with its look-ahead feature.

The chapter also discussed the Stone-Wood model for disaggregating a monthly cash budget into a daily budget. The technique incorporates both day-of-the-month and day-of-the-week effects. This technique was then incorporated into the look-ahead Stone model in order to provide a rigorous model for managing cash balances on a daily basis.

Key Concepts

Adjusted-earnings method

Baumol model

Daily cash forecasting

Economic order quantity model

Miller-Orr model

Ratio approach

Receipts and disbursement method

Stone model

Ad Hoc Procedure for Determining a Minimum Cash Balance

A simple procedure that the treasurer can use to determine what the bank considers to be the minimum cash balance is to reduce the average bank balance, say 5 percent, every other month. When the balance becomes too low, a bank officer will call to find out what the problem is. At that point a working cash level is attained that if not maintained will cause problems with the bank.

This crude procedure can be improved upon with a little understanding of how banks assess required balances. Using cost accounting procedures, banks analyze their accounts to determine the profit or loss on each account. Unfortunately, the general principle they follow is to contact only customers whose accounts run at a loss for them. The basic procedure most banks follow in analyzing profitability is to determine what funds left on deposit are available for investment, assign an assumed rate of earnings to calculate gross revenues from the available funds, and then subtract the costs of all transactions associated with the account.

The bank starts with the average level of funds on deposit in the company's account and then reduces the level by an amount equal to the required reserves the bank must keep at the Federal Reserve Bank. Note that the balance on the company's ledger is not used. This fact is elementary but is often overlooked. The treasurer must analyze the cash account the way a banker does, not the way an accountant does. Because of the various types of float (mentioned in Chapter 7), the bank balance most likely does not equal the company's ledger balance.

An earnings rate is next applied by the bank to the usable funds to determine the gross revenue from the account. This arbitrary earnings figure supposedly gives the gross revenue available to the bank from the customer's account. Wide disagreement exists among banks about the proper rate for computing earnings. The effect of using too low a rate is that the bank will require customers to keep larger deposit balances than necessary. Finally, by subtracting the actual costs of the checks written and deposited, the bank derives either a positive or a negative earnings figure for each account.

The corporate treasurer can use this procedure to estimate necessary minimum balances. Estimates are required since the bank is generally unwilling to disclose certain information about its required-earnings rate.

ILLUSTRATION A.1

The bank is required to keep 20% of the company's deposit on reserve (R) with the Federal Reserve Bank. The cash manager forecasts the bank's earning rate (ER) to be 5% and its profit margin (M) to be 1%. Costs (C) incurred by the bank to maintain the company's account and various requests are estimated to be $5000. From these estimates the cash manager determines that the average deposit (AD) should be $156,250. This amount is calculated by using the following breakeven formula:

$$\text{AD} = \frac{C/(1-R)}{\text{ER}-M} = \frac{\$5000/(1-0.2)}{0.05-0.01} = \$156,250. \tag{A.1}$$

The sensitivity of the estimated average required deposits to changes in any of the variables in the breakeven equation can be readily examined by substituting new values into the equation. For example, if the reserve requirement declines to 15%, the average required deposit is about $147,060, or approximately 6% lower.   □

Questions

1. What is a major deficiency of the ratio approach in estimating the required cash balance?

2. What are the key factors that should be incorporated into a model for determining minimum and maximum cash balances?

3. Are the concepts of inventory theory applicable when cash inflows and cash outflows are variable but completely predictable? Explain.

4. If cash inflows and outflows are random, how can minimum and maximum cash balances be determined?

5. What is the major problem with monthly cash forecasts? How can this problem be overcome?

6. What do h and R refer to in the Miller-Orr model?

7. Contrast the actions management takes when either the upper or the lower control limits are pierced in the Miller-Orr model and in the Stone look-ahead model.

8. How can the adjusted net income method of cash forecasting be used to calculate the effect on funds of a change in inventory policy or receivable policy?

9. How would you judge whether or not a given corporation is maintaining excessive cash balances?

10. Of what significance are daily and monthly cash reports in cash budget control?

11. Explain the difference between a cash budget and a projected income statement.

12. How can the mathematical cash models be used in conjunction with the traditional cash planning models?

Problems

1. In December of last year a distributor of consumer goods was planning his financial needs for one year ahead. As a first indication, he wished to have a *pro forma* balance sheet as of December of the next year to gauge the funds needs at that time. The estimated financial condition as of December 31, last year, is reflected in the balance sheet given in Table 8.8. The operations for the ensuing year were projected with the following assumptions:

TABLE 8.8
Estimated Balance Sheet for Last Year

Cash	$ 217,300	Accounts payable	$ 612,300
Receivables	361,200	Notes payable	425,000
Inventories	912,700	Accrued expenses	63,400
Total current	$1,491,200	Total current	$1,100,700
Net fixed assets	204,200	Term loan	120,000
Other assets	21,700	Equity	496,400
Total assets	$1,717,100	Total financing	$1,717,100

□ Sales were forecasted at $10,450,000, with a gross margin of 8.2%.

□ Purchases were expected to total $9,725,000, with some seasonal upswings in May and August.

□ Accounts receivable would be based on a collection period of 12 days (based on sales), while 24 days' accounts payable would be outstanding (based on purchases).

□ Depreciation was expected to be $31,400 for the year.

□ Term loan repayments were scheduled at $10,000, while the bank notes payable was expected to remain at $425,000.

□ Capital expenditures were scheduled at $57,000.

□ Net profits after taxes were expected at the level of 1.9% of sales.

□ Dividends for the year were scheduled at $12,500.

□ Other assets and accrued expenses were not expected to change.

□ Cash balances were desired at no less than $150,000.

□ The effective income tax rate was forecasted at 50%.

Develop a *pro forma* balance sheet. Verify your *pro forma* cash balance by developing a statement of changes in cash position (see Table 8.1 for an example). Discuss your findings.

2. Beta Food Services is trying to forecast its cash position as of its fiscal year end. Its opening balance was $50,000. Sales last year were $1 million, evenly spread over the 12 months. Sales were expected to grow at an annual rate of 4%. All sales are for credit, with collection 50% in the month of sale and 50% in the following month. Purchases are paid for with cash, and products are marked up 100% for sale. Selling prices and purchase costs are expected to be the same as last year. Expenses are $30,000 per month. Funds may be borrowed from the bank at an annual rate of 15%, up to a maximum of $250,000. What is the cash balance at the end of the new year under the (a) ratio approach and (b) cash budget approach?

3. The Artie Corporation expects $2 million in cash outlays during the next year. The outlays are expected to occur uniformly during the year. Management's opportunity cost of funds is 10% from investments in marketable securities. The cost of each transaction to secure cash is $90, which includes both direct and indirect costs. All cash demands are met by selling marketable securities.

(a) Determine the optimal size of a transfer of funds from marketable securities to cash.

(b) What is the average cash balance?

(c) How many transfers to cash from marketable securities are needed during the year?

(d) What is the total cost associated with the firm's cash requirements?

(e) How are the answers to (a) and (b) affected if transaction costs are $50 per transaction? $125 per transaction?

4. Determine the maximum cash balance, the average cash balance, and the optimal return point, using the Miller-Orr model for each of the following situations:

	Variance of daily cash flows	Transaction cost	Annual interest rate
(a)	$ 5,000	$90	12%
(b)	5,000	90	15
(c)	5,000	45	15
(d)	50,000	45	15
(e)	50,000	45	10
(f)	30,000	55	10

5. Management has determined the extreme lower and upper control limits of the Stone cash management model to be $7000 and $28,000, respectively. The target balance is $17,500. The inner lower and upper limits are $10,000 and $25,000, respectively. Using the daily budget data shown in Table 8.3 and a three-day moving forecast, reconstruct Tables 8.4, 8.5, 8.6, and 8.7. Use the actual cash flows shown in Table 8.4. The opening cash balance is $20,000.

6. At the start of a 90-day planning period, the cash manager estimates cash needs of $27,000. The market rate of interest on government securities is 10% per annum, and the brokerage commission is a constant $50 per buying-and-selling transaction.

(a) Determine the economic order quantity of cash, using the Baumol model.

(b) What is the average cash balance?

(c) If the brokerage cost doubles, how much does the economic order quantity increase?

7. Given average day-of-the-week proportions of

M = 0.246,   T = 0.198,   W = 0.152,   Th = 0.117,   F = 0.287,

calculate day-of-the-week adjustment factors.

8. Given the historical information shown in Table 8.9, determine the allocation of the month's $80,000 budget by day. Assume that day 1 is a Monday.

TABLE 8.9
Historical Proportions

	Day-of-month proportions						Day-of-week proportions	
1	0.040	9	0.060	17	0.029		M	0.244
2	0.052	10	0.047	18	0.034		T	0.196
3	0.056	11	0.052	19	0.041		W	0.090
4	0.066	12	0.045	20	0.040		T	0.271
5	0.069	13	0.040	21	0.044		F	0.199
6	0.072	14	0.033		1.000			1.000
7	0.067	15	0.034					
8	0.058	16	0.021					

9. Use the Stone model and the data that follow. What should XYZ Company's strategy be with regard to marketable securities if a four-day forecast is used?

target balance = $10,000,
upper outer limit = $20,000,
upper inner limit = $15,000,
lower outer limit = $0,
lower inner limit = $5000.

Forecasted cash flow:

Day	2	3	4	5	6
Amount	$1000	$6000	−$10,000	$500	−$5000

The adjusted balance for day 1 is $25,000.

10. A company uses the Stone model for managing cash. The target balance is $15,000, with upper and lower control limits of $25,000 and $5000, respectively. Inner control limits are ±$2000 of the outer limits. On Friday, August 1, the company's cash balance was $12,000. Actual cash flows during August occurred as listed in Table 8.10. The firm's daily cash budget is as shown in Table 8.3 (in the chapter).

TABLE 8.10
Cash Flow

Day	Cash flow	Day	Cash flow	Day	Cash flow
1	$4500	8	$ 3,020	15	$4900
2	2400	9	945	16	4150
3	4210	10	−1,900	17	5970
4	2090	11	11,640	18	9900
5	−2300	12	6,750	19	620
6	9900	13	−9,000	20	1370
7	6980	14	−7,790	21	8250

(a) Set up a table showing the beginning, adjusted, and ending daily cash balances for August. Indicate any investment activity in marketable securities. Do not assume any look-ahead forecast.

(b) Redo part (a) assuming a three-day look-ahead forecast.

(c) Using a 12% cost of money, calculate the residual income for parts (a) and (b). Which method is preferred?

CHAPTER 9 □
Analysis of Credit Terms

The extension of credit by a firm to its customers often involves a trade-off between holding inventory or holding accounts receivable. The credit decision should be taken only after one has made a complete consideration of all aspects of granting credit and how this decision integrates with other decisions and policies of the firm. The decision involves factors such as how much should be invested in credit, what the credit terms should be, who the recipients of credit should be, how the receivables should be monitored, and how the collection process should be structured. These factors must be evaluated in conjunction with other corporate policies. If scarce funds are used for credit extension, then fewer investable funds are available for both long-term purposes (e.g., plant and equipment investment) and short-term investments (e.g., inventory investment). Thus credit decisions can be thought of as determining the level of receivables, on the one hand, and the composition of assets, on the other hand.

The goal of credit decisions should be to maximize shareholder wealth. Unfortunately, all too often the credit decision is a passive one. Many firms extend credit because other firms in the industry do so. Too little consideration is given to the effect of credit on the firm's revenue and cost structures. For instance, W. T. Grant, until 1975, allowed customers 36 months to pay, with a minimum payment of $1 per month. Given the serious cash flow problems W. T. Grant had, this policy was not in the best interests of either investors or creditors — particularly in light of the fact that receivables were sold for about 15 percent of their face value when W. T. Grant was liquidated.

The purpose of this chapter is to analyze the establishment of credit terms that contribute to shareholder wealth. First, we discuss some theoretical underpinnings. Next, we examine how assets, liabilities, and cash flows are affected by changing credit terms. And finally, we present a steady-state model for evaluating credit terms.

Theoretical Foundations

Credit is extended in response to either direct or indirect customer demand for the firm's products or services. This principle implies that sales might not occur without the extension of credit. While that may be true, management cannot afford the luxury of such a micro view of its affairs. Instead of starting with the question "Do customers receive the credit requested?" a firm should establish a policy involving all credit decisions.

The decision to extend credit and the decision about the terms offered can be viewed as similar to a change in the price of the product or service. Price is the result of a great number of market forces, some of which are controllable but most of which are not. Under the assumption that the firm operates within the classic definition of imperfect competition in both the product and the factor markets, then management has some influence over product demand. Although the firm's products or services may be similar to those offered by competitors, sufficient product or service heterogeneity can be created by the firm through customer relations, pre- and postservices, and pricing policies.

The establishment of a market price implies that a quantity of goods are offered and taken in a market exchange setting. This statement does not suggest that all possible demanders are satisfied or that the supply cannot be changed. Rather, it means that a given amount of product is offered and the same amount is purchased at the market price. From the firm's view, does the transaction price allow for a profit? Can profit be enhanced by charging some other price?

Answers to these questions require analysis of marginal revenue and marginal cost relationships. Marginal analysis should also be chosen by management to establish credit terms. Failure to do so results in lower shareholder wealth. Since most firms differ with respect to their production capabilities, their access to the capital markets, the types of customers they serve, and so forth, their credit terms should also differ in the pursuit of shareholder wealth maximization.

Credit and Collection Variables

Investing in accounts receivable requires consideration of several interrelated aspects: investment costs, losses from bad debts, the impact of credit terms on sales, and the related cash flows, for instance, for inventory purchases. The important decision variables can be divided into two groups.

The first group contains three *credit policy variables:* cash discounts, discount period, and credit period. The second group consists of three *collection policy variables* that are associated with late payments and bad debts: the collection expense of the seller as a percentage of overdue accounts, the penalty rate charged on overdue accounts, and the time when accounts are sold to a collection agency.

The credit policy variables directly affect total credit sales and the proportion of early payments and indirectly affect the proportion of overdue payments. Generally, as the discount is increased, more customers take advantage of the discount. Conversely, as the credit period is lengthened, fewer customers take the discount since the implicit cost is reduced.

Value of Cash Discounts

Cash discounts offer substantial financial advantage to buyers. Thus an understanding of the full value of the cash discount is important. Consider a discount package 2/10, *n*/30. That is, a 2% cash discount can be taken if the invoice is paid within 10 days; otherwise, the invoice is due in full in 30 days. Most people would approximate the cost of a missed discount to be equal to 36% per annum: 2% × 360/20 = 36%. There are three errors in this calculation:

1. The length of the payment acceleration assumed (e.g., payment is in 10 days instead of 30 days; therefore payment is accelerated 20 days).
2. The implicit assumption that the transaction will not be repeated.
3. The worth of the discount once taken.

The calculation should reflect the actual acceleration period. Rarely do companies not accepting discounts pay on the due date (i.e., the 30th day). Also, the benefit should be compounded to approximate the ongoing value of the discount to the buyer. Whenever sales are continuous, the *annualized implicit cost* (AIC) of a cash discount may be measured by the formula

$$\text{AIC} = \left(\frac{1}{1-y}\right)^{360/@} - 1, \tag{9.1}$$

where @ is the number of days of actual acceleration and y is the discount rate offered (stated as a decimal number). When a transaction is unlikely to be repeated, a simple interest equivalent is more appropriate:

$$\text{AIC} = \left(\frac{y}{1-y}\right)\left(\frac{360}{@}\right). \tag{9.2}$$

ILLUSTRATION 9.1

Assume that invoices displaying 2/10, n/30 credit terms are normally paid 40 days from the invoice date. The traditional approach assigns a cost of 36%, as shown previously. Actually, the benefit of discount settlement, or the AIC, after 10 days (i.e., @ = 40 − 10 = 30) is equivalent to about 27.4% on a continuous basis,

$$\text{AIC} = \left(\frac{1}{1 - 0.02}\right)^{360/30} - 1 = 0.274,$$

or 24.5% on a single-event basis,

$$\text{AIC} = \left(\frac{0.02}{1 - 0.02}\right)\left(\frac{360}{30}\right) = 0.245.$$

If the invoices were normally paid 30 days from the invoice date, the single-event AIC would be 36.7%, whereas the continuous-event AIC would be 43.8% (prove these figures for yourself).   □

Figure 9.1 graphically depicts annual implicit costs for discount rates of 1, 2, and 3 percent and for payment accelerations up to 60 days. Generally, as either the discount rate or the discount period is increased, more custom-

FIGURE 9.1
Cost of Discounts: Compound Interest Case

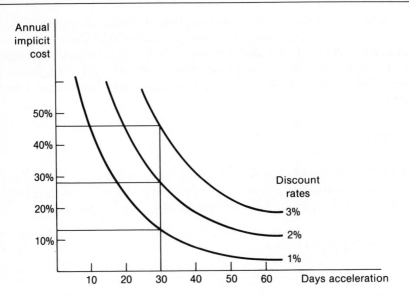

ers should take advantage of them, since forgoing the cash discount increases the implicit cost. Conversely, as the credit period is lengthened, fewer customers will take the discount, since the implicit cost is reduced.

If the discount amount, discount period, or credit period is increased, sales should improve. The firm gains sales from competitors and from new customers to the market since increasing these credit variables effectively lowers the market price. The increased discount amount results in the buyer remitting a smaller amount. Lengthening the discount period and the credit period means that the present value of the amount due is now less.

Graphical Solution

A graphical solution for determining optimal credit terms is provided in Fig. 9.2. Expected sales, shown in Fig. 9.2(a), are a positive function of credit terms. Lengthening the credit period and increasing the cash discount lead to greater sales, since customers view these credit changes as implicit price reductions. The firm loses sales as restrictive credit terms force some customers to buy from competitors. Failure to offer credit terms results in only cash sales (and lower profits).

The level of accounts receivable in Fig. 9.2(b) bears the expected close relationship with sales. Easier credit terms lead to higher sales and higher receivable balances.

Figure 9.2(c) shows expected profit on sales (exclusive of any revenues and costs directly associated with credit) as a function of sales. This function reaches a maximum at the point that marginal revenue from sales equals marginal cost of sales. The intercept of the curve with the expected-sales axis indicates breakeven sales for the firm.

Figure 9.2(d) is used to determine optimal credit policy. The profit-on-sales curve is shown in relation to expected level of accounts receivable and is derived geometrically from the three functions given in Figs. 9.2(a), 9.2(b), and 9.2(c). The dotted lines trace three points in the construction of the curve.

For example, credit policy 1 results in expected sales of A in Fig. 9.2(a), expected receivables of B in Fig. 9.2(b), and expected profit (before credit revenues and costs) of C in Fig. 9.2(c). This policy translates into point D in Fig. 9.2(d). The cost of carrying accounts receivable is an increasing function of accounts receivable. Its position and shape indicate both fixed and variable carrying costs. The revenue curve represents interest charged on overdue accounts. It is an increasing function of accounts receivable balances since large accounts receivable balances are likely to have more overdue accounts, which are assessed interest charges. The total profit curve is derived by adding credit charge income to the profit on sales and subtracting the cost of carrying receivables.

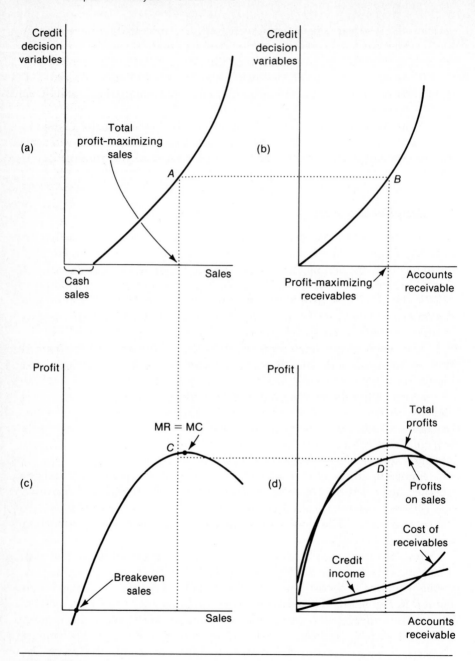

FIGURE 9.2
Graphical Solution for Optimal Credit Terms

The highest point on the total profit curve occurs where total marginal revenue from both product sales and credit charges equals the marginal cost of product sales and carrying receivables. This point determines the profit-maximizing level of receivables in Fig. 9.2(b), the profit-maximizing level of sales in Fig. 9.2(a), and the optimal credit terms (i.e., optimal set of credit and collection policies).

The multifaceted nature of optimal receivable balances is evident from this graphical representation. A changing sales function, cost function, cost of capital function, or receivable investment function affects optimal credit terms and receivable investment. Managers must be cognizant of the interrelationships that exist since it is evident that *full* marginal analysis is required in order to determine a shareholder wealth-enhancing decision. Appendix C of this chapter describes a mathematical approach for implementing this graphical solution.

Asset, Liability, and Cash Flow Considerations

Changes in credit policy, and specifically in the credit terms, can significantly affect asset and liability balances and cash flows. New credit terms can stimulate sales growth, which in turn causes production to increase to meet the higher sales demand. Higher production results in increased inventory requirements, financing, and so on.

In an effort to indicate the dynamics of the problem, assume that the firm is in a relatively stable operating position. The market sets the price of the product, and the firm produces a given quantity for sale at that price. The internal structure of purchasing and using materials and labor in production, creating inventory, and selling takes place on a repetitive basis. The lead times necessary for delivery of raw materials, the manufacturing cycle, and the sales pattern are known. This information allows management to establish an asset-liability structure, establish sources and uses of funds, project profits, and predict the cash cycle of the firm.

No Credit Extended

In the previous market setting the cash flow pattern of a firm that does not extend credit follows a predictable and stable pattern. This pattern means that the firm's liquidity risk is greatly reduced, as indicated in the following illustration.

ILLUSTRATION 9.2

Assume that the firm operates in the type of environment outlined in the preceding paragraph. Relevant data are as follows: market demand

TABLE 9.1
Income Statement for the First Month (No Credit Extended)

Sales		$1000
Costs:		
Variable	$500	
Fixed	150	
Total		650
Profit before taxes		$ 350
Taxes		140
Profit after taxes		$ 210

per month is 100 units; market price per unit is $10; fixed-labor cost per month is $150; variable cost per unit is $5; the corporate tax rate is 40%; and credit available for financing inventory is $500. All sales are made for cash. These data result in profit of $210 for month 1, as shown in Table 9.1.

Assuming that the opening balance sheet for month 1 consists only of inventory and accounts payable (see Table 9.2a), then the closing financial position is represented by Table 9.2(b).

Immediately following the end of month 1 the firm makes payments for accrued wages, outstanding accounts payable, taxes, and dividends, in this order. It then purchases, on credit, new materials to satisfy month 2's sales demand. The new financial position beginning month 2 is the same as that shown in Table 9.2(a). Since market and production conditions in month 2 are similar to those in month 1, month 2's ending financial position is as shown in Table 9.2(b). This process continues month after

TABLE 9.2
Balance Sheet

(a) As of the start of the first month of no credit

Cash	$ 0	Accounts payable	$500
Receivables	0	Accrued wages	0
Inventories	500	Taxes payable	0
		Retained earnings	0
Total	$ 500	Total	$500

(b) As of the end of the first month of no credit

Cash	$1000	Accounts payable	$ 500
Receivables	0	Accrued wages	150
Inventories	0	Taxes payable	140
		Retained earnings	210
Total	$1000	Total	$1000

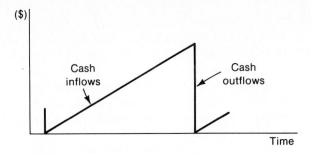

FIGURE 9.3
Cash Flow Patterns: No Credit Offered

month, with the result that cash flows follow the predictable pattern shown in Figure 9.3.

This highly simplified system ignores replacement of fixed assets. They could be included, but they are not necessary to show the effects of credit. Thus the firm achieves a stable and repetitive situation.

It is the nature of this situation that is important. Net working capital reaches a high of $210 (see Table 9.2b) and a low of $0 (see Table 9.2a), and inventory turnover is every 30 days. Cash inflows occur evenly throughout the month, and all cash outflows take place on the last moment of the month. Corporate financing is arranged through suppliers of materials. If these traditional forms of liquidity analysis are used by the firm and its creditors, the conclusion is that although some degree of liquidity risk exists, it is within acceptable limits.　　　　　　　　　　□

Whenever cash flow stability is lacking, creditors and stockholders experience different degrees of risk exposure. They may react to such a situation to the detriment of management. Hence management must satisfy these special-interest groups.

Credit Extended

How might these special-interest groups and the firm be affected by changing credit terms? As the following illustration indicates, the firm enters a *transition period* that takes it from its current steady state to a new steady state. Liquidity management can be subjected to much stress during this transition period.

ILLUSTRATION 9.3

Assume that management decides to change from a policy of cash on delivery (COD) to one in which the terms are 2/10, *n*/30. Management forecasts that these credit terms will encourage new customers to purchase 50 units per month. It is expected that the cash discount will be taken by all the original customers but by none of the new customers. In addition, a credit and collection department will need to be established. It is estimated that costs of this department will have both variable and fixed components: 15% of incremental sales plus $5 fixed costs per month. As a support for the new credit policy additional inventory must be purchased and financing arranged before the time of sale.

Table 9.3 indicates the start of the new credit policy. Inventory and accounts payable have increased by $250 to support the new credit terms.

During the month, production and sales occur in the usual fashion, except that the scale of each has increased. The consolidated income statement, shown in Table 9.4, indicates that the new credit terms result in profit increasing $93.96 to a level of $303.96. Assuming that sales occur at a constant rate, Table 9.5 shows daily receivable balances and collections.

TABLE 9.3
Balance Sheet
As of the Start of the First Month of Credit

Cash	$ 0	Accounts payable	$750
Receivables	0	Accrued wages	0
Inventory	750	Taxes payable	0
		Retained earnings	0
Total	$750	Total	$750

TABLE 9.4
Income Statement
First Month That Credit Is Offered

	Without credit	With credit	Change
Sales	$1000.00	$1500.00	$500.00
Less cash discounts	0	13.40	13.40
Net sales	$1000.00	$1486.60	$486.60
Costs:			
Variable	$ 500.00	$ 825.00	$325.00
Fixed	150.00	155.00	5.00
Total	$ 650.00	$ 980.00	$330.00
Profit before taxes	$ 350.00	$ 506.60	$156.60
Taxes	140.00	202.64	62.64
Profit after taxes	$ 210.00	$ 303.96	$ 93.96

TABLE 9.5
Daily Sales, Receivable Balance, and Cash Inflow

Day	Sales per day		Receivable balance	Cash inflow
	Original	New		
1	$33.33	$16.67	$ 50.00	$ 0
2	33.33	16.67	100.00	0
3	33.33	16.67	150.00	0
4	33.33	16.67	200.00	0
5	33.33	16.67	250.00	0
6	33.33	16.67	300.00	0
7	33.33	16.67	350.00	0
8	33.33	16.67	400.00	0
9	33.33	16.67	450.00	0
10	33.33	16.67	500.00	0
11	33.33	16.67	516.67	32.66*
12	33.33	16.67	533.34	32.66
13	33.33	16.67	550.01	32.66
14	33.33	16.67	566.68	32.66
15	33.33	16.67	583.35	32.66
16	33.33	16.67	600.02	32.66
17	33.33	16.67	616.69	32.66
18	33.33	16.67	633.36	32.66
19	33.33	16.67	650.03	32.66
20	33.33	16.67	666.70	32.66
21	33.33	16.67	683.37	32.66
22	33.33	16.67	700.04	32.66
23	33.33	16.67	716.71	32.66
24	33.33	16.67	733.38	32.66
25	33.33	16.67	750.05	32.66
26	33.33	16.67	766.72	32.66
27	33.33	16.67	783.39	32.66
28	33.33	16.67	800.06	32.66
29	33.33	16.67	816.73	32.66
30	33.33	16.67	833.40	32.66
1	33.33	16.67	833.40	49.33†
2	33.33	16.67	833.40	49.33

* Collection of day 1's sales from customers who take the discount; that is,

$$\$33.33 - \$0.67 \text{ discount} = \$32.66.$$

† Collection of day 1's sales from customers who do not take the discount plus collection of day 21's sales from customers who take the discount; that is,

$$\$16.67 + (\$33.33 - \$0.67) = \$49.33.$$

TABLE 9.6
Financial Position When Credit Is Offered (1)

(a) Balance sheet as of the end of the first month of credit

Cash	$ 653.20	Accounts payable	$ 750.00
Receivables	833.40	Accrued wages	230.00
Inventories	0	Taxes payable	202.64
		Retained earnings	303.96
Total	$1486.60	Total	$1486.60

(b) Balance sheet as of the start of the second month of credit

Cash	$ 0	Accounts payable	$1076.80
Receivables	833.40	Accrued wages	0
Inventories	750.00	Taxes payable	202.64
		Retained earnings	303.96
Total	$1583.40	Total	$1583.40

The end of the first period's and the beginning of the next period's financial positions when credit is extended are reflected by Tables 9.6(a) and 9.6(b), respectively. As a result of selling on credit, cash flow during the first month of the credit transition period is less than before. The initiation of credit results in total cash flow of $653.20 ($32.66 per day times 20 days), as opposed to $1000 in the period before the change. The difference is a result of no cash inflow during the first 10 days of the discount period and amounts deducted for discounts. Increased inventory requirements result in higher accounts payable (under the assumption that the needed financing is available through material suppliers). In addition, sizable accounts receivable are now outstanding.

After the settlement process shown in Table 9.6(b), and including new credit purchases of materials for the second month, the firm is unable to pay suppliers in full for prior purchases. Only $423.20 (i.e., $653.20 cash − $230.00 wages) is available to pay supplier debt of $750, since employees are paid first. Therefore accounts payable increase to $1076.80 to start the second period. It is one thing for suppliers to expand their sales and resultant receivables, but it is an entirely different matter for them to be asked to carry additional obligations to finance buyers. Suppliers, however, are not the only group financing the new credit policy. The lack of sufficient cash flow results in taxes payable remaining outstanding and stockholders receiving no dividends. Therefore both the government and the shareholders are also financing the new credit policy.

Table 9.7 represents the start of the new static phase. Daily collections of $49.33 (see Table 9.5) result in a cash buildup of $1479.90 at the end of the second month. Outstanding receivables are constant at the prior period's level of $833.40. Higher retained earnings reflect the current peri-

TABLE 9.7
Financial Position When Credit Is Offered (2)

(a) Balance sheet as of the end of the second month of credit

Cash	$1479.90	Accounts payable	$1076.80
Receivables	833.40	Accrued wages	230.00
Inventories	0	Taxes payable	402.60
		Retained earnings	603.90
Total	$2313.30	Total	$2313.30

(b) Balance sheet as of the start of the third month of credit

Cash	$ 0	Accounts payable	$ 750.00
Receivables	833.40	Accrued wages	0
Inventories	750.00	Taxes payable	229.50
		Retained earnings	603.90
Total	$1583.40	Total	$1583.40

od's profit after taxes of $299.94. Profit decreases $4.02 from the previous period's level since cash discounts are now taken for the full 30-day period as opposed to 20 days when credit was initiated.

In the settlement for month 2 (see Table 9.7b), wages are paid and accounts payable are restored to a current status. The tax obligation, however, increases over the previous settlement period's balance, and shareholders still do not receive dividends.

Table 9.8 represents the financial positions at the end of month 3 and the start of month 4, respectively. From an analysis of Table 9.8(b)

TABLE 9.8
Financial Position When Credit Is Offered (3)

(a) Balance sheet as of the end of the third month of credit

Cash	$1479.90	Accounts payable	$ 750.00
Receivables	833.40	Accrued wages	230.00
Inventories	0	Taxes payable	429.46
		Retained earnings	903.84
Total	$2313.30	Total	$2313.30

(b) Balance sheet as of the start of the fourth month of credit

Cash	$ 0	Accounts payable	$ 750.00
Receivables	833.40	Accrued wages	0
Inventories	750.00	Taxes payable	0
		Retained earnings	833.40
Total	$1583.40	Total	$1583.40

TABLE 9.9
Financial Position When Credit Is Offered (4)

(a) Balance sheet as of the end of the fourth month of credit

Cash	$1479.90	Accounts payable	$ 750.00
Receivables	833.40	Accrued wages	230.00
Inventories	0	Taxes payable	199.96
		Retained earnings	1133.34
Total	$2313.30	Total	$2313.30

(b) Balance sheet as of the start of the fifth month of credit

Cash	$ 0	Accounts payable	$ 750.00
Receivables	833.40	Accrued wages	0
Inventories	750.00	Taxes payable	0
		Retained earnings	833.40
Total	$1583.40	Total	$1583.40

we see that all liabilities are current, and residual cash flows of $70.44 have been paid as dividends to shareholders. This result is evident from the decrease in the retained-earnings balance.

A fourth month of sales, collections, and payments are necessary to bring the system to full stability. Table 9.9 reflects the closing position for month 4 and the opening position for month 5 now that credit influences have worked their way through the system. Cash flows are regular and predictable, suppliers are paid on a regular basis for the amount of current purchases, and stockholders receive regular dividends of $299.94, which are in excess of the precredit policy period.   □

Important Considerations

The previous illustrations highlight three important considerations. First, credit decisions have a significant influence on cash flows. An unstable transition period may follow the initiation of new credit terms because of insufficient funds. Management must know how the credit policy will be financed. Management needs to project all inflows and outflows since failure to do so can lead to unhappy creditors and shareholders.

Second, suppliers are often required to expand their investment in the firm making a credit change. From the buyer's perspective the higher accounts payable amount is permanent and considered costless, unless, of course, discounts are not taken. However, from the supplier's point of view the commitment is only for a short period of time. Therefore how stable is this "permanent" incremental investment? Should the firm attempt to replace short-term capital with more permanent and stable long-term funds? If the answer is yes, then the new long-term capital has a cost to the firm, either a real cost in the case of debt or an opportunity cost in the case of equity. The firm should look upon this added cost as a form of insurance payment to reduce liquidity risk.

Finally, the posture of the stockholders must be considered. In Illustration 9.3 shareholders lost two dividends and received a smaller than usual one in another period. It was not until a new *steady state* was reached that dividends were greater than before and as stable. However, what if the steady state takes a long time to reach or is never reached? Has management now contributed to stockholder dissatisfaction, with the result that a successful takeover can occur? Also, is the present value of the new dividend stream greater than that of the original stream? If not, the value of stockholders' wealth is diminished.

ILLUSTRATION 9.4

Under the no-credit policy shareholders receive $210 in dividends each period. The new credit policy results in no dividends in periods 1 and 2, $70.44 in period 3, and $299.94 in period 4 and thereafter.

If the new credit policy is expected to stay constant for the foreseeable future, and shareholders can earn 1% per period on their investments for comparable risk, it takes about 9.5 periods before the new policy contributes more to shareholder wealth than does the old policy. This is determined by solving for n, the number of periods, in the following present value equation:

No Credit   Credit

$$\$210(\text{PVIFA } 1\%, n) = \$70.44(\text{PVIF } 1\%, 3)$$
$$+ \$299.94[(\text{PVIFA } 1\%, n) - (\text{PVIFA } 1\%, 3)].$$

Rearranging and solving for the annuity factor (PVIFA 1%, n) results in an answer of 9.0478. This value is approximately equivalent to the annuity discount factor for 1%, 9.5 periods.   □

Steady-State Time Value Approach

The balance sheet approach illustrated in the preceding section is a laborious technique for analyzing proposed credit decisions. The residual income (RI) model (discussed in Chapter 1 and in Appendix A to this chapter) is popular for evaluating marginal credit decisions. *Its results are equivalent to the balance sheet approach as long as a steady state prevails.* If a new credit policy results in investment and financial changes that require time for establishing a new steady state, then the balance sheet approach and the residual income approach are not equivalent.

Under the assumption of no inflation, the RI model is

$$RI = [S_n(1 - V) - w - f](1 - t) - kI_0 \geq 0, \qquad (9.3)$$

where

S_n = new incremental gross sales,

V = incremental variable-cost ratio,

w = incremental amount of cash discounts taken,

f = any incremental fixed costs and bad debts incurred,

t = marginal corporate tax rate,

k = opportunity cost of capital,

I_0 = incremental investment at time 0.

Both academicians and practitioners view this model as a useful decision model. The first expression on the right-hand side is incremental profit. The second expression, kI_0, represents an adjustment for the opportunity cost of funds invested. The decision rule is to undertake the new credit policy whenever RI is greater than or equal to zero.

Explanation of I_0: Changing Credit Terms

It is important to understand how to interpret incremental investment I_0 under *changing credit terms*. If the firm eases credit by lengthening the credit period, sales should be stimulated. Receivable balances, in turn, should increase because present customers will now take longer to pay and new customers will be attracted by more attractive credit terms. Inventory investments will likely increase because of the changing credit policy's stimulus on sales. Increases in spontaneous liabilities, such as accounts payable and accrued wages, will offset some of the asset investments. In this case the incremental investment is

I_0 = (increased investment in receivables associated with
     original sales, stated at cost plus profit — i.e., selling price)   (a)

  + (investment in receivables associated with new
                       sales, stated at cost)   (b)

  + (increased investment in inventories, stated at cost)   (c)

  − (increased spontaneous non-interest-bearing liabilities),   (d)

or

$$I_0 = DSO_o\left(\frac{S_o}{360}\right) + V(DSO_n)\left(\frac{S_n}{360}\right) + H - L.$$
$$\qquad \text{(a)} \qquad\qquad \text{(b)} \qquad\quad \text{(c)} \quad \text{(d)}$$
$$(9.4)$$

Here DSO represents incremental days sales outstanding in receivables; S and V are incremental dollar sales and percent variable costs, respectively; the subscripts o and n refer to old and new customers, respectively; H represents incremental inventory investment; and L represents incremental spontaneous liabilities arising as a result of the credit decision.

The *increased investment in accounts receivable for original sales* [expression (a) of Eq. 9.4] *includes the full dollar amount of those receivables,* that is, both inventory cost and profit.[1] However, *the investment in receivables from new sales* [expression (b) of Eq. 9.4] *excludes all profit margin.* The difference is that only variable costs are invested in new receivables, whereas there is an opportunity cost associated with the existing outstanding receivables. If management does not change the credit period, then the receivables that are stated at cost plus profit (i.e., selling price) will be collected at the normal average collection period. If the *average collection period* for the old accounts changes as a result of changing credit terms, then the profit embedded in the receivable balance will not be collected at the normal time and, therefore, will not be available for reinvestment. Thus an opportunity cost is associated with the profit amount since management implicitly has reinvested it in the outstanding accounts by extending the payment period.

ILLUSTRATION 9.5

Implementation of the RI model is illustrated by using the following data: current annual sales (S_o) are $12,000, variable costs are $6000, and fixed costs are $1800. Presently, all sales are made for cash. Assume that management is considering the introduction of credit sales with terms of 2/10, $n/30$. These terms are expected to increase sales (S_n) by $6000 per year; variable costs by $3900 [resulting in the incremental variable-cost ratio (V) becoming 65%, that is, incremental variable costs divided by incremental sales: $3900/$6000]; fixed costs (f) by $60; and inventory ($H$) by $250. Spontaneous liabilities (L) of accounts payable and accrued wages increase $250 and $80, respectively.

Ninety percent of the old customers are forecasted to take the discount and pay on the 10th day (DSO_o) that their receivables are outstanding. The remaining old customers and all the new customers are not expected to take the discount. They are expected to pay on the 35th day (DSO_n). Discounts taken (w) will be $216. The opportunity cost of funds (k) is 10% after taxes, and the corporate tax rate (t) is 40%. No bad debts are expected.

---

[1] We assume that old customers are affected by the changing credit terms. If they are not, DSO will not change and there will be no incremental investment for old accounts.

Incremental investment is

$$I_0 = \text{DSO}_o\left(\frac{S_o}{360}\right) + V(\text{DSO}_n)\left(\frac{S_n}{360}\right) + H - L$$

$$= \left[\left(0.90 \times 10 \times \frac{\$12,000}{360}\right) + \left(0.10 \times 35 \times \frac{\$12,000}{360}\right)\right]$$

$$+ \left(0.65 \times 35 \times \frac{\$6000}{360}\right) + \$250 - \$330$$

$$= \$795.83 + \$250 - \$330 = \$715.83.$$

Residual income is

$$\text{RI} = [S_n(1 - V) - w - f](1 - t) - kI_0$$
$$= [\$6000(1 - 0.65) - \$216 - \$60](1 - 0.4) - 0.1(\$715.83)$$
$$= \$1094.40 - \$71.58 = \$1022.82.$$

Since RI is positive, the new credit policy should be implemented.   □

Explanation of I_0: Changing Credit Standards

Whenever the credit decision relates to loosening *credit standards,* the incremental investment is redefined to exclude the first expression on the right-hand side of Eq. (9.4), that is, expression (a) of the equation equals zero:

$$I_0 = V(\text{DSO}_n)\left(\frac{S_n}{360}\right) + H - L. \tag{9.5}$$

The revised specification indicates the incremental investment in receivables and inventories, stated at cost, that arises from new customers being granted credit. A *loosening of credit standards has no effect on present credit customers since they already qualify* under the old credit standards.

ILLUSTRATION 9.6

Subsequent to implementation of the credit policy in Illustration 9.5, management decides to loosen credit standards. This policy is expected to attract an additional $5000 in sales ($S_n$) from new customers. The variable-cost ratio (V) is expected to remain at 65%, inventory investment (H) will increase $225, and spontaneous liabilities (L) will increase $200. The new accounts are not expected to pay until 45 days after the sale. The opportunity cost of capital for this type of risky customer is 15% after taxes. Present accounts should not be affected by this change.

Incremental investment is

$$I_0 = V(\text{DSO}_n)\left(\frac{S_n}{360}\right) + H - L$$

$$= 0.65(45)\left(\frac{\$5000}{360}\right) + \$225 - \$200$$

$$= \$406.25 + \$225 - \$200 = \$431.25.$$

Residual income is

$$\text{RI} = [S_n(1 - V) - w - f](1 - t) - kI_0$$
$$= [\$5000(1 - 0.65) - 0 - 0](1 - 0.40) - 0.15(\$431.25)$$
$$= \$1050 - \$64.69 = \$985.31.$$

Since RI is positive, management should loosen credit standards.   □

Whenever credit standards are tightened, some present customers will be affected. In this situation Eq. (9.5) is still appropriate.

ILLUSTRATION 9.7

Management is considering tightening the credit standards, with the expectation of losing \$3000 in sales (S_n). Inventories (H) should decline \$1000, and accounts payable (L) should decrease \$500. The variable-cost ratio (V) is expected to remain at 65%. Average days sales outstanding (DSO_n) for these accounts is 50 days. The tax rate is 40%, and the opportunity cost of funds is 15%.

The incremental investment freed is

$$I_0 = V(\text{DSO}_n)\left(\frac{S_n}{360}\right) + H - L$$

$$= 0.65(50)\left(\frac{-\$3000}{360}\right) + (-\$1000) - (-\$500) = -\$770.83,$$

whereas the residual income generated by this decision is

$$\text{RI} = [S_n(1 - V) - w - f](1 - t) - kI_0$$
$$= [-\$3000(1 - 0.65) - 0 - 0](1 - 0.40) - 0.15(-\$770.83)$$
$$= -\$514.38.$$

Since residual income is negative, management should not institute the proposed change in credit standards.   □

Reconciliation of the RI Model and the Balance Sheet Approach

The RI model requires steady-state conditions. The following example reconciles the simplistic *steady-state RI model* results to the *changing balance sheet approach.* The balance sheet data have been annualized and used in the RI model that follows.

In summary, the data are as follows:

Precredit period:

> current annual sales (S_o) = \$12,000,
>> variable costs = \$6000,
>>> fixed costs = \$1800.

Upon initiation of credit:

> incremental sales (S_n) = \$6000,
>> variable costs = \$3900,
>>> fixed costs (f) = \$60,
>>> inventory (H) = \$250,
> spontaneous liabilities (L) = \$330,
>> discounts taken (w) = \$240.

Old customers take the discount and pay on day 10; new customers do not take the discount and pay on day 30.

> opportunity cost of funds = 10%,
>> tax rate = 40%.

On the basis of this data incremental investment is

$$I_0 = \text{DSO}_o\left(\frac{S_o}{360}\right) + V(\text{DSO}_n)\left(\frac{S_n}{360}\right) + H - L$$

$$= 10\left(\frac{\$12,000}{360}\right) + \left(\frac{\$3900}{\$6000}\right)(30)\left(\frac{\$6000}{360}\right) + \$250 - \$330$$

$$= \underbrace{\$658.33}_{\substack{\text{Receivable}\\\text{investment}}} + \$250 - \$330$$

$$= \$578.33.$$

Residual income is

$$\text{RI} = [S_n(1 - V) - w - f]\,(1 - t) - kI_0$$
$$= [\$6000(1 - 0.65) - \$240 - \$60]\,(1 - 0.4) - 0.1(\$578.33)$$
$$= \underbrace{\$1080}_{\text{Profit}} - \underbrace{\$57.83}_{\text{Cost of capital}}$$

$$= \$1022.17.$$

A quick check of the two approaches reveals that incremental profits are equal — or nearly so; \$1080 for the RI model (see the previous results) versus \$1079.28 for the balance sheet illustration [see Table 9.1 and the discussion following Table 9.8: (\$299.94 − \$210) × 12]. Incremental investments in inventories, accounts payable, and accrued wages are the same for both approaches. An investment difference of about \$175 exists in accounts receivable between the two models (RI model: \$658.33 — see the previous I_0 calculation; balance sheet model: \$833.40 — see Table 9.9).

The investment difference is the profit margin included in receivables in the balance sheet approach. For example, outstanding receivables are calculated as

$$\text{DSO}_o \times \frac{\text{old sales}}{360} + \text{DSO}_n \times \frac{\text{new sales}}{360}$$

$$= 10 \times \frac{\$12,000}{360} + 30 \times \frac{\$6000}{360} = \$833. \qquad (9.6)$$

This result agrees with the balance sheet model in Table 9.9, with the exception of a small rounding difference. If the profit embedded in the new receivables is excluded, for the reasons discussed earlier, the investment in receivables is \$658, the amount used in the calculation of I_0:

$$10 \times \frac{\$12,000}{360} + 0.65 \times 30 \times \frac{\$6000}{360} = \$658,$$

where 0.65 is the variable-cost factor to exclude profit in the new receivables.

Given the assumptions that have been made, it is apparent that *once a steady state is reached, the simple RI model is appropriate for analyzing receivables.* However, if the steady state takes a long time to reach, or if it is never reached, the usefulness of the RI model is uncertain. During the transition from one steady state to another, the cash demands may be too great for the firm to remain solvent. Careful planning is as much a prerequisite in establishing credit policy as it is in other types of investments.

Summary

Credit terms are often used by management to stimulate sales or meet competition without much regard for how they influence other facets of the business. Since management's objective should be to maximize long-term wealth of shareholders, analysis must be conducted in this frame of reference. The models presented in this chapter adhere to the wealth maximization concept.

A balance sheet approach was presented first. This technique is laborious to use and overstates the economic investment in receivables. It does, however, pinpoint potential cash flow problems that management faces before a steady state is attained.

The residual income (discounting) model was discussed next. This model is prevalent in most finance book discussions of receivables. Major shortcomings of the model, as normally stated, are the assumptions of a steady state and no inflation. Appendix B extends the residual income model to incorporate inflation. The only remaining weakness of the residual income model is the necessity of assuming a steady state. This problem can be overcome, however, by using a discrete net present value model that allows conditions (assumptions) to change from period to period.

The appendixes are an integral part of this chapter for those desiring insight into more complex credit models. The application of computers to credit problems can allow management to use more sophisticated models to simultaneously determine the optimal discount amount, discount period, and credit period. Needless to say, these optimums are unique to each firm. If sales, cost, and payment functions are reasonably well specified by management, then there is little reason to match credit terms with competition. Terms considered optimal for one company are very likely not optimal for another firm.

Key Concepts

Annualized implicit cost
Average collection period
Change in credit standards
Change in credit terms
Collection policy variables

Credit policy variables
Investment at cost versus investment at selling price
Steady state
Transition period

Derivation of the Residual Income Credit Model

A generalized formulation of a credit model is

$$\text{NPV} = \frac{-\sum_{T=0}^{M} I_T + \sum_{T=0}^{M} F_T(1 - t)}{(1 + k)^T} \geq 0, \tag{A.1}$$

where

I_T = incremental investment in time period T as a result of credit decision,

F_T = marginal net cash flow occurring at time period T [i.e., $S(1 - V) - w - f$],

t = marginal corporate tax rate,

k = appropriate risk-adjusted discount rate for evaluating decision,

M = number of periods policy is expected to remain in effect.

The decision rule is to accept the credit policy if NPV is greater than or equal to zero. If two mutually exclusive credit policies are compared, the decision is to accept the policy with the higher NPV, assuming it is positive. Since positive NPVs accrue to shareholders, the result is improved shareholder wealth.

Under the often-invoked assumptions that investments are only made at $T = 0$ and that cash flows are constant and exist in perpetuity, Eq. (A.1) becomes

$$\text{NPV} = -I_0 + \frac{F(1 - t)}{k} \geq 0, \tag{A.2}$$

where I_0 is the incremental investment at the start of the new credit policy. Implicit in this formulation are the assumptions of a noninflationary environment and of no additional investments subsequent to the initiation of the new credit policy.

By equating Eq. (A.2) to zero and multiplying both sides by k, we obtain

$$F(1 - t) - kI_0 = 0. \tag{A.3}$$

This result is Eq. (9.3), with $F = S_n(1 - V) - w - f$. The model is similar to models suggested in leading managerial finance textbooks as being appropriate for evaluating credit decisions. It represents the point of profit maximization, that is, where marginal revenue equals marginal cost.

APPENDIX B
Inflation-Adjusted Credit Model

When discussing the RI (NPV) model in Appendix A, we stated that the conversion of the finite NPV model to a perpetuity NPV model assumed a noninflationary environment. Under inflationary conditions the expected cash flows must be adjusted for inflation-induced increases in product, factor, and financial prices.[1] Failure of management to raise product prices to offset increased costs results in reduced cash flow (assuming no possibility of making up the deficiency in increased volume).

The incorporation of inflation adjustments for both cash inflows and cash outflows result in the following NPV model:

$$
\text{NPV} = -I_0\left[1 + \sum_{T=1}^{M} \frac{(1+d)^T - (1+d)^{T-1}}{(1+k)(1+p)^T}\right]
$$
$$
+ \sum_{T=1}^{M} \frac{F(1+u)^T(1-t)}{[(1+k)(1+p)]^T} \geq 0, \tag{B.1}
$$

where

d = rate of increase in net investment per period because of inflation,
u = increase in net cash inflows per period because of inflation,
k = real rate of return required on investment,
p = financial market's perception of inflation.

The expression $I_0[(1+d)^T - (1+d)^{T-1}]$ represents the increase in net investment that is required in period T because of inflation.

For example, the following time line shows the incremental inflation investment required at times 0, 1, and 2:

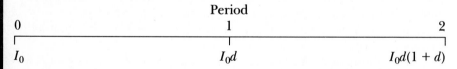

	Period	
0	1	2
I_0	$I_0 d$	$I_0 d(1+d)$

In Eq. (B.1) the expression $F(1+u)^T$ reflects the fact that the net cash inflows are growing over time at a constant rate of inflation of u percent per period. The discount factor $(1+k)(1+p)$ can be restated as

---

[1] This appendix is based on the article by J. A. Halloran and H. P. Lanser, "The Credit Policy Decision in an Inflationary Environment," *Financial Management* (Winter 1981):31–38.

$(1 + i)$, where i is the required rate of return in nominal terms and is usually stated as $i = k + p$. The cross-product term kp is often ignored since it is generally insignificant and k and p are estimates. Rate i is strictly greater than both d and u since it is a market-determined rate that incorporates any inflation premiums.

If cash flows are assumed to exist in perpetuity, then Eq. (B.1) can be simplified to

$$\text{NPV} = \text{RI} = -I_0\left(\frac{i}{i - d}\right) + \frac{F(1 + u)(1 - t)}{(i - u)} \geq 0. \tag{B.2}$$

The most general form of the model is derived from Eq. (B.2) by analyzing it where $\text{RI} = 0$:

$$F(1 - t)(1 + u)(i - d) - i(i - u)I_0 = 0. \tag{B.3}$$

If no inflation exists in the factor, product, or financial markets, then $u = d = p = 0$, with the result that $k = i$. The model then reduces to the simple RI model shown as Eq. (9.3).

ILLUSTRATION B.1

Assume the same facts as in the reconciliation of the residual income model and the balance sheet approach. However, inflation is now expected to cause investment to increase at the rate (d) of 5% per period, cash inflows are expected to increase (u) 6% per period, the real rate of interest (k) is 10%, and the nominal rate (i) is 12%.

Residual income is

$$\begin{aligned}
\text{RI} &= [\$6000(1 - 0.65) - \$240 - \$60](1 - 0.4)(1 + 0.06)(0.12 - 0.05) \\
&\quad - 0.12(0.12 - 0.06)(\$578.33) \\
&= \$80.14 - \$4.16 = \$75.98.
\end{aligned}$$

Since RI is positive, management should initiate the credit change, although it is now considerably less profitable than in the no-inflation situation. Different assumptions about inflation obviously lead to different residual income expectations. ☐

APPENDIX C
Comprehensive Credit Model

A comprehensive credit value maximization model[1] can be constructed that incorporates most of the concepts discussed in the chapter. Since customers have no incentive for making early payments within the discount or credit periods, it is assumed that all payments are made at the end of these time intervals. A realistic picture of payments is depicted in Table C.1. Some proportion q of total credit sales (S), less the cash discount of y percent, is paid at the end of the discount period i, another proportion $(1 - x)(1 - q)$ is paid at the end of the credit period j, and the balance is either paid $[x(1 - q)(1 - b)]$ to the firm or sold $[xb(1 - q)]$ to a collection agency at time m, with z percent of the account amount remitted to the firm. Accounts not paid by the credit period are assessed an interest charge of r percent of the face value of the overdue account.

TABLE C.1
Payment Sequence

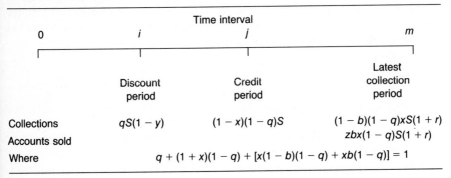

	Time interval		
0	i	j	m
	Discount period	Credit period	Latest collection period
Collections	$qS(1 - y)$	$(1 - x)(1 - q)S$	$(1 - b)(1 - q)xS(1 + r)$
Accounts sold			$zbx(1 - q)S(1 + r)$
Where		$q + (1 + x)(1 - q) + [x(1 - b)(1 - q) + xb(1 - q)] = 1$	

The present value of these cash flows can now be calculated. For payments received at the end of the discount period, the present value, discounted at a risk-adjusted rate k, is

[1] This appendix is based on the following articles: Ned C. Hill and Kenneth D. Riener, "Determining the Cash Discount in the Firm's Credit Policy," *Financial Management* (Spring 1979): 68–73; Zvi Lieber and Yair E. Orgler, "An Integrated Model for Accounts Receivable Management," *Management Science* (October 1975): 202–211.

$$\frac{(1-y)qS}{(1+k)^i}. \tag{C.1}$$

Credit balances paid at the end of the credit period have a present value of

$$\frac{(1-x)(1-q)S}{(1+k)^j}. \tag{C.2}$$

If the proportion of early payments (q) increases, the proportion of overdue accounts (x) may increase. A possible reason is as follows: The proportion of early payments will increase because of the higher implicit cost associated with not taking the discount. Thus some customers who originally planned to pay at time j will now pay at time i and receive the cash discount. Since customers with financial difficulties will be the last ones to pay, a higher proportion of overdue balances will exist among customers who do not take the discount. There will be no change in overdue balances only if the change in early payments does not affect the average risk profile of customers who do not take the discount.

Balances that are not paid within the credit period, $x(1-q)S$, are classified as overdue and are subject to collection efforts by the seller up to time m, that is, within the period $m-j$. For simplicity, assume that any successful collection efforts result in payments being made at time m for the face amount of the invoice plus an interest charge of r percent of invoice value. Unsuccessful efforts result in the overdue balances being sold to a collection agency for z percent of their face value and penalty charge. The NPV of the collections and sale of accounts at time m is

$$\frac{x(1-q)(1+r)(1-b+bz)S}{(1+k)^m}. \tag{C.3}$$

There are two cash outflow streams associated with the revenue streams. The first stream is for normal variable cost incurred in production and sales (e.g., materials and labor). These costs can be represented as

$$\frac{vS}{(1+k)^n}, \tag{C.4}$$

where v is the fraction of sales (S) that represents variable costs paid at time n. Time n is not necessarily equal to times i, j, or m since the firm's payment schedule can differ from its receipts schedule.

The second category of costs is for collection expenses incurred (for simplicity, assumed to be at time m) in the attempt to collect overdue accounts:

$$\frac{cx(1-q)S}{(1+k)^m}, \tag{C.5}$$

where c represents the percentage these costs are of overdue collections.

Profit (P) from accounts receivable is determined by summing all the elements of the model indicated by Eqs. (C.1) through (C.5):

$$P = \frac{(1-y)qS}{(1+k)^i} + \frac{(1-x)(1-q)S}{(1+k)^j}$$

$$+ \frac{x(1-q)(1+r)(1-b+bz)S}{(1+k)^m} - \frac{vS}{(1+k)^n} - \frac{cx(1-q)S}{(1+k)^m}. \tag{C.6}$$

Optimal credit and collection policies can be derived through the use of calculus. The partial derivatives of P with respect to each decision variable — y, i, j, c, r, m — must be taken. This manipulation results in six equations and six unknowns, which are then solved simultaneously. *A straightforward solution is not possible without specifying credit sales (S) and customer payment (q) functions*, since these both depend on the credit terms y, i, and j, that is, y percent in i days, net in j days. Computer methods need to be used to solve this problem quickly.

The model can be simplified to make it easier to use for decision-making purposes by combining all receipts realized after the discount period, that is, by combining the second, third, and fifth terms of Eq. (C.6). The result is

$$P = \frac{(1-y)qS}{(1+k)^i} + \frac{g(1-q)S}{(1+k)^j} - \frac{vS}{(1+k)^n}, \tag{C.7}$$

where

$$g = (1-x) + x\{[1-b(1-z)](1+r) - c\}(1+k)^{j-m}.$$

The second expression in Eq. (C.7) approximates the present value of the net amount collected after time i. Because of bad debts and collection expenditures, g is less than 1. Overall, Eq. (C.7) states that profit from accounts receivable is equal to the present value of payments at time i (the first expression), plus later collections (the second expression), less variable costs (the third expression).

In the situation where management knows values for i, j, and n, the discount rate y is the only remaining decision variable in Eq. (C.7). And since the discount w affects sales (S), customer payments patterns (q), and bad debts and collection expenditures (impounded in g), the simplified model incorporates all important factors associated with the credit decision.

The optimal value of the cash discount is found by equating the derivative of P with respect to y to zero. Since q and S are influenced by w, and g is influenced by q, the derivative is

$$[(1-y)q'S + (1-y)qS' - qS](1+k)^{-i}$$
$$+ [g'q'(1-q)S + g(1-q)S' - gq'S](1+k)^{-j}$$
$$- vS'(1+k)^{-n} = 0, \tag{C.8}$$

where primes denote partial derivatives with respect to the discount rate y. The optimal discount can be calculated when the sales and the payment functions and all parameters are specified.

In the case where the cash discount has no effect on sales ($S' = 0$) and bad debts exist but are constant ($g < 1$ and $g' = 0$), then Eq. (C.8) reduces to

$$y = 1 - g(1 + k)^{i-j} - \frac{q}{q'}. \tag{C.9}$$

Given a further assumption that no bad debts exist ($g = 1$), then Eq. (C.9) becomes

$$y = 1 - (1 + k)^{i-j} - \frac{q}{q'}. \tag{C.10}$$

In either case the cash discount depends on the seller's time value of money and the ratio of customer payment proportions to the change in the proportions as the discount is increased (q/q'). Terms q and q' represent the proportion of earlier payment and change in that proportion, respectively. They are positive values with an increase in the discount rate. If money has no time value, $k = 0$. Thus in Eq. (C.9) the discount depends on whether $1 > g + q/q'$. In Eq. (C.10) no discount should be offered since the right-hand side would be negative; the seller has no incentive to want to receive early payment. Therefore in the absence of time value of money, the risk of not being paid (i.e., $g < 1$) is sufficient incentive to offer a discount to induce payment.

In the situation where the cash discount affects sales ($S' > 0$), and bad debts exist and are constant ($g < 1$ and $g' = 0$), the optimal discount is given by

$$\begin{aligned} y = 1 - g(1 + k)^{i-j} - [qS(1 + k)^{-i} \\ - gS'(1 + k)^{-j} + vS'(1 + k)^{-n}](q'S + qS')(1 + k)^{-i}. \end{aligned} \tag{C.11}$$

A solution for this situation requires specification of the credit sales (S) and customer payment (q) functions. If the discount has no effect on sales ($S' = 0$), Eq. (C.11) reduces to Eq. (C.9). Furthermore, if bad debts are zero ($g = 1$), the equation reduces to Eq. (C.10).

Assume the sales and payments functions are specified as

$$S = -ey^2 + (e + d)y + L, \tag{C.12}$$

$$q = \frac{(J + D)y^u}{(J + Dy^u)}. \tag{C.13}$$

The sales function is quadratic and indicates L dollars of sales are realized when the discount y is zero. The early payment function is S-shaped and is equal to zero whenever no discount is offered. It rises slowly for low values of y and sharply at high values of y. The partial derivatives of these functions, with respect to w, are

$$S' = -2ey + (e + d), \tag{C.14}$$

$$q' = \frac{u(J + D)y^{u-1}}{(J + Dy^u)} - \frac{(J + D)uDy^{2u-1}}{(J + Dy^u)^2}. \tag{C.15}$$

ILLUSTRATION C.1

The optimal cash discount can be found by solving for y in Eq. (C.11), where S, q, S', and q' are specified by Eqs. (C.12) through (C.15), respectively. Assume that empirical values of the parameters in these equations are defined as $e = 275$, $d = 47.95$, $L = 255$, $J = 0.01$, $D = 50$, and $u = 4$. Assuming that the seller's cost of funds before taxes is 12% per annum, that $j = 2$ months, and that $i = 1$ month, then the discount factor from j to i is about 0.99 [i.e., $(1 + 0.12/12)^{-1}$].

Let the average loss from bad debts, $1 - g$, be 1% of credit sales, and let the variable cost v be equal to 69% of sales. Assume that these costs are paid at period $n = i$. Thus the discount factor is 0.99. The optimal discount is found by substituting these functions and parameters into Eq. (C.11) and solving for y. The result is a discount of approximately 2%. □

Questions

1.   Is the credit policy that maximizes expected operating profit the optimal credit policy? Explain.

2.   What probable effects would the following changes have on the level of the company's accounts receivable?

   (a) The company changes credit terms from 4/15, $n/25$ to 2/10, $n/30$.

   (b) Interest rates increase.

   (c) Production costs associated with the firm's product decrease.

   (d) The economy worsens and slips into a mild recession.

3.   Suppose that Williams Company and the local bank are considering extending credit to the same customer. Why might the Williams Company and the bank arrive at different decisions?

4.   Explain why the credit decision and the inventory decision should be analyzed jointly.

5.   What is the difference between a change in credit terms and a change in credit standards?

6.   How would you decide whether or not to loosen credit standards? Describe the decision analysis.

7.   What is the impact of inflation on investment in accounts receivable?

Problems

1.   Calculate the annual implicit cost of interest for terms of purchase of 3/15, $n/45$ and 4/10, $n/30$ when payments are made on days 45 and 30, respectively. Calculate for (a) nonrepeated sales and (b) continuous sales.

2.   The AXE Company estimates that its opportunity cost of funds is 18% annually. Creditor terms offered the AXE Company are 3/15, $n/30$. Should management take the discounts offered if the company usually pays on day (a) 20, (b) 30, (c) 60, (d) 80, or (e) 90? Discuss the implications of your answer. Use the continuous case.

3.   Oasis Company is considering changing its credit standards in order to attract more customers. These customers will generate an estimated $450,000 additional sales. The collection period for these new accounts is expected to be about 55 days. Present accounts are outstanding an average of 35 days. Variable costs are about 60% of sales. If the credit terms are changed, administrative costs are expected to increase $7000 annually. Management estimates the required return (before taxes) to be 20%. Using a 360-day year, decide whether the credit standards should be relaxed.

4. Grignomics Corporation is evaluating whether to change its credit terms from net 15. The sales manager estimates that 75% of the company's $400,000 annual sales, which are all sold on credit, will take advantage of any discount. The company presently finances its accounts receivable at an after-tax interest cost of 14%. Its marginal tax rate is 35% and variable costs are 60% of sales. Assuming that management can expect the annual sales, default costs, and inventory increases shown in Table 9.10 with each set of alternative credit terms, which credit term alternative is the most profitable? It is expected that 75% of new sales will be discounted. Assume 360 days in the year.

5. From the information in Problem 4, calculate the average investment in accounts receivable, the number of days accounts receivable are outstanding, and the turnover ratio for each alternative.

6. Calculate the breakeven sales level where variable costs are 75% of incremental sales and incremental fixed costs are $13,500. The incremental sales will be 80% for credit and will be collected, on average, 60 days after sale. The opportunity cost of capital is 25%.

7. Determine how sensitive the breakeven sales level in Problem 6 is under the following conditions.

(a) The collection period increases to 66 days.

(b) The new administrative costs increase to $14,850.

(c) The variable-cost ratio increases to 82.5% of new sales.

8. Jakobstellel, Inc., is considering the extension of credit terms in expectation that sales will increase. Management believes that sales will increase 100 units if the current terms of $1/10, n/15$ are changed to $3/10, n/20$. Presently, 75% of customers take the discount. With new terms all old customers are expected to take the discount, but only 50% of new customers are expected to do so. Customers who do not take the discount are expected to pay by the net period. No bad debts are expected. Presently, 300 units are sold per month at a price of $15 per unit. Variable costs are $7.50 per unit, and total fixed costs are $1200. The new credit terms are expected to increase monthly sales by 100 units. The per-unit variable cost for these 100 units will be $8. Incremental fixed costs will be $325. The marginal

TABLE 9.10
Credit Term Alternatives

	Default costs	Credit terms	Additional inventory	Sales
(a)	$6000	2/10, n/45	$50,000	$600,000
(b)	4000	2/10, n/30	25,000	500,000
(c)	5000	net 30	40,000	525,000

tax rate is 42%. (Assume 30 days in a month, and round your answer to two decimal places.)

(a) Determine the expected change in monthly profit under the new credit terms.

(b) Calculate the daily accounts receivable balances and cash flows under the new credit policy. Use Table 9.5 as a model. Assume that the old terms started on day 1 (no outstanding sales prior to day 1) and the new terms become effective on day 16. All customers are expected to abide by the sale terms as on the day of their purchase.

9. The Forwell Company wishes to evaluate a change in credit terms by calculating residual income. The current and proposed business conditions are as follows:

Current	Terms of sale	Cash
	Sales	$54,000
	Variable costs	$27,000
	Fixed costs	$ 1,200
Proposed	Terms of sale	2/10, n/30
	Incremental sales	$18,000
	Incremental variable costs	$ 9,600
	Incremental fixed costs	$250
	Incremental inventory	$900

When the new terms are implemented, 90% of the old customers are expected to discount and pay on the 10th day. Only 30% of the new customers are expected to discount. Management does not expect any bad debts. Sales to nondiscounters are expected to be paid on the 40th day after the sale. The after-tax opportunity cost of funds is 12%. The income tax rate is 42%. Should management implement the new credit terms?

10. Management of Forwell Company (Problem 9) is concerned with the downside risk of the proposed change in credit terms.

(a) Calculate the minimum change in sales necessary for the company to break even at zero residual income.

(b) If the expected level of new sales is $7500 with a standard deviation of $2740, what is the probability of the company having negative residual income?

CHAPTER 10 □
Forecasting Accounts Receivable Flows

The objective of extending credit or changing existing credit terms is to influence sales demand in an effort to enhance profitability. This concept was discussed and evaluated in the previous chapter in terms of models to analyze the changes. A question of much concern in the implementation of those models is, What are the appropriate values to choose for receivables paid by the discount date, paid subsequent to this date, or written off as bad debts? It is the purpose of this chapter to discuss a technique called Markov chain analysis (MCA), which can address these questions.[1] An in-depth understanding of MCA depends on an understanding of matrix algebra (refer to Appendix A for an overview of this subject).

Most firms attempt to grow by increasing sales to existing customers and by attracting new customers. However, as the balance sheet illustrations in Chapter 9 showed, accounts receivable investment and cash flow react differently to a given stimulant. Accounts receivable increased faster than cash inflows because of the credit terms offered to and accepted by the various customers. Eventually, the accounts receivable balance leveled off because the cash inflows grew to equal new sales. If no new incremental sales occur, then the level of accounts receivable and cash flows will not increase further. Such is the nature of the *steady state;* that is, a balance is reached between the funds outflows and the funds inflows (i.e., cash collections).

---

[1] The use of MCA for managing receivables was first discussed by R. M. Cyert, H. J. Davidson, and G. L. Thompson in "Estimation of the Allowance for Doubtful Accounts by Markov Chains," *Management Science* (1962): 287 – 303.

Markov Chain Analysis

Differential *payment patterns* of customers can cause management significant concern about whether it will receive payment. However, analysis of payment patterns can provide insight into the impact a change in credit policy may cause. Ideally, management would like to be able to discriminate between customers on the basis of terms of sale and collection procedures because of different default risk. Legally, this discrimination is not an option. Once credit is extended, all customers must be offered equal terms. The rigidity of terms does have a favorable aspect, however, in that it allows cash flows from receivables to be more easily modeled.

The combination of the concept of steady state with that of credit risk can utilize *Markov chain analysis* as the basis for analysis of credit policy. The discussion that follows uses a lengthy illustration that analyzes two scenarios. First, management wishes the firm to expand its sales through the use of some mechanism other than a decrease in the firm's credit standards. Second, a decline in credit standards is allowed, and results are compared with the results of the first strategy.

Illustration: Constant Credit Risk

Assume that the firm is presently at a steady-state condition wherein its current credit sales are equal to the current cash receipts from prior credit sales plus the current period write-off of bad debts. This state results in a stable level of investment in accounts receivable and in a reasonably stable age distribution of outstanding receivables. The steady-state condition is not without risks to the firm since some exogenous factor, such as an economic recession, may occur. Hence the aging of receivables could increase, and consequently, cash inflows might slow down for a period of time.

Table 10.1 presents customer information taken from the company's accounts receivable ledger. The "Ending state" columns in the July and August statements identify each account in the following way:

P = account is paid in full,
B = account is written off as a bad debt,
0 = oldest invoice is a current charge,
1 = oldest invoice is one month beyond date of sale,
2 = oldest invoice is two months beyond date of sale.

The receivable balance for August is determined as follows:

End of July receivables balance	$348	(a)
Plus sales in August	159	(b)
Minus cash collections	142	(c)
Minus bad debts written off	17	(d)
End of August receivables balance	$348	(e)

TABLE 10.1
Accounts Receivable Reports

July report

| Customer | Months outstanding | | | Receivable | Ending |
number	0	1	2	balance	state
100	$ 13			$ 13	0
125	16		$15	31	2
150	8	$ 5		13	1
175	14	20	9	43	2
200	25	20		45	1
225		15	17	32	2
250			17	17	2
275	10			10	0
300	45			45	0
325		18		18	1
350		21		21	1
375			14	14	2
400	25			25	0
425		10	11	21	2
Total	$156	$109	$83	$348	

(a)

August report

| Customer | Cash | Bad | Months outstanding | | | Receivable | Ending |
number	collections	debts	0	1	2	balance	state
100	$ 13						P
125	15		$ 10	$ 16		$ 26	1
150	5			8		8	1
175	9			14	$20	34	2
200			30	25	20	75	2
225	17				15	15	2
250		$17					B
275	10		23			23	0
300	5			40		40	1
325	18		17			17	0
350					21	21	2
375	14		6			6	0
400	25		35			35	0
425	11		38		10	48	2
Total	$142	$17	$159	$103	$86	$348	
	(c)	(d)	(b)	(f)	(g)	(e)	

The August report differs slightly from the July report, particularly in that it also reflects bad debts. The firm has a policy that if any invoice is more than two months past the point of sale, it is classified as a bad debt (e.g., customer 250). Those customers who purchase and pay in full but do not repurchase every month (e.g., customer 100), normally would not be included in the report. Similarly, the bad-debt invoice normally does not appear on the account summary. Why these accounts are included here will become apparent later.

Aging of Accounts

The aging of accounts is shown in Table 10.2. An explanation of how this table is constructed is given next. Note that the format of Table 10.2 would be the same even if the ledger (Table 10.1) contained hundreds of entries.

The following explanation of the entries in Table 10.2 uses the state 0 transactions. Only four customer accounts had ending state 0 at the end of July, and these four accounts changed during the month of August as follows:

☐ Customer 100 paid in full and did not purchase in August.
☐ Customer 275 settled the July balance of $10 and purchased $23 more goods in August.
☐ Customer 300 owed $45 at the end of July and only paid $5 of this debt in August. Thus the remaining balance aged from group 0 to group 1.
☐ Customer 400 paid the outstanding balance of $25 and purchased $35 worth of more goods.

The cash inflows from these customers amounted to $53, while new sales were $58. The August accounts receivable balance for this group

TABLE 10.2
Aging of Accounts Between July and August

Initial state	Ending state					
	P	B	0	1	2	Total
0	$ 53		$ 58	$ 40		$151
1	23		47	33	$41	144
2	66	$17	54	30	45	212
	$142	$17	$159	$103	$86	$507
	(c)	(d)	(b)	(f)	(g)	

TABLE 10.3
Analysis of July's State 0 Accounts

Account number	July balance	August activity					August ending state
		P	B	0	1	2	
100	$13	$13					P
275	10	10		$23			0
300	45	5			$40		1
400	25	25		35			1
		$53	$0	$58	$40	$0	

was $98. There can be no bad debts from this group since they started the month as current charges (i.e., an initial state of 0) and management does not recognize a bad debt until an invoice is more than two months past due. The remaining rows of Table 10.2 are determined in the same fashion. Table 10.3 summarizes this discussion.

Tables 10.2 and 10.3 are value analyses showing the possible changes in economic activity of sales and credit outstanding between two periods. These dollar amounts can be converted to percentages based on the initial state (end of July) and the ending state (end of August) of all the firm's regular customers. This conversion is shown in Table 10.4.

The economic activity of customers whose accounts started out the month classified as current (i.e., initial state 0 accounts) is explained as follows: 35% of the total activity for the month represents payments, 38% represents invoices outstanding as current charges, and 27% represents invoices that are one month past due. No invoices are two months old. The remaining rows of Table 10.4 can be interpreted in a similar manner.

If this pattern is the usual activity pattern of customers' accounts, and if the firm attracts new customers with similar characteristics using the same credit standards, then we would expect that these new customers would, on average, show the same pattern as the old customers. Thus by

TABLE 10.4
Economic Activity of Accounts

Initial state	Ending state					Total
	P	B	0	1	2	
0	0.35	0	0.38	0.27	0	1.00
1	0.16	0	0.33	0.23	0.28	1.00
2	0.31	0.08	0.26	0.14	0.21	1.00

analyzing these payment- and credit-outstanding probabilities, the credit manager is able to forecast various aspects of accounts receivable for increasing sales to current customers or extending credit to new customers of comparable risk.

Absorbing States

The payment (P) and bad debts (B) are referred to as *absorbing states*. If an invoice is paid or declared delinquent, it is removed from the accounts receivable ledger. Nothing further can happen to it in the next month. Therefore the invoice is absorbed.

Nonabsorbing States

States 0, 1, and 2 are *nonabsorbing states,* or *transitional states.* Accounts in these states can change their status during the month. The change, however, is limited by the passage of one month and the bad-debt policy of the firm. It is perfectly possible in the model's framework for a transitional (customer's) account to never become absorbed into either state P or state B. This result does not mean that the individual invoices are never paid or classified as uncollectable. It simply means that at least one invoice is not paid, which causes the account to be classified in one of the nonabsorbing states.

Transition Matrix

Adding the absorbing states P and B to Table 10.4 results in a square *transition matrix* that can be subdivided into different partitions, as shown in Table 10.5. The upper left matrix is a 2-by-2 identity matrix (I) comprised of 1s and 0s to represent the absorbing states. The lower left 3-by-2 matrix (R) indicates the probability of moving from nonabsorbing states (0, 1, 2) to absorbing states (P, B). The upper right matrix is a 2-by-3 null (O)

TABLE 10.5
Transition Matrix

		P	B	0	1	2
$T =$	P	1	0	0	0	0
	B	0	1	0	0	0
	0	0.35	0	0.38	0.27	0
	1	0.16	0	0.33	0.23	0.28
	2	0.31	0.08	0.26	0.14	0.21

$$T = \left[\begin{array}{cc|ccc} 1 & 0 & 0 & 0 & 0 \\ 0 & 1 & 0 & 0 & 0 \\ \hline 0.35 & 0 & 0.38 & 0.27 & 0 \\ 0.16 & 0 & 0.33 & 0.23 & 0.28 \\ 0.31 & 0.08 & 0.26 & 0.14 & 0.21 \end{array}\right] = \left[\begin{array}{c|c} I & O \\ \hline R & Q \end{array}\right]$$

matrix. The lower 3-by-3 matrix (Q) yields the probability that a customer account in a given nonabsorbing state will end in a particular nonabsorbing state. In other words, it is neither paid in full nor declared delinquent. *The Q matrix represents a set of typical payment patterns and is used to find the joint probability of a large number of like experiences.* The sum of each row of the Q matrix is positive but less than one.

Payment Patterns

Of interest is the number of periods it takes nonabsorbing states 0, 1, and 2 to reach absorbing states P and B, that is, how long on average a receivable starting in any particular nonabsorbing state remains outstanding before it is paid or declared delinquent. A relatively simple way to calculate this relationship is to find the value of the inverse of the matrix $[I - Q]$, that is, $N^{-1} = [I - Q]^{-1}$, where I is a 3-by-3 identity matrix (it is not the previously defined 2-by-2 identity matrix).

The N^{-1} matrix is a *fundamental matrix* of the absorbing chain. The elements of N^{-1} indicate the average number of times that a receivable starting in a particular state will continue to be outstanding before it is either paid in full or declared delinquent. Table 10.6 shows the calculations. The values in the N^{-1} matrix are interpreted as follows:

□ A customer account that is *current* at the start will, on the average, pass through the future states of being current, one month old, and two months old for 2.17 times, 0.81 time, and 0.29 time, respectively, before it is absorbed.

TABLE 10.6
Calculation of Payment Patterns

From Table 10.5:

$$Q = \begin{bmatrix} 0.38 & 0.27 & 0 \\ 0.33 & 0.23 & 0.28 \\ 0.26 & 0.14 & 0.21 \end{bmatrix}$$

N^{-1}, the fundamental matrix:

$$N^{-1} = [I - Q]^{-1} = \left[\begin{pmatrix} 1 & 0 & 0 \\ 0 & 1 & 0 \\ 0 & 0 & 1 \end{pmatrix} - \begin{pmatrix} 0.38 & 0.27 & 0 \\ 0.33 & 0.23 & 0.28 \\ 0.26 & 0.14 & 0.21 \end{pmatrix} \right]^{-1}$$

$$= \begin{matrix} & \begin{matrix} 0 & 1 & 2 \end{matrix} \\ \begin{matrix} 0 \\ 1 \\ 2 \end{matrix} & \begin{bmatrix} 2.17 & 0.81 & 0.29 \\ 1.27 & 1.86 & 0.66 \\ 0.94 & 0.60 & 1.48 \end{bmatrix} \end{matrix}$$

TABLE 10.7
Number of Months Outstanding

Current state	Months outstanding from current state	Months outstanding from point of sale*
0	3.27	3.27
1	3.79	4.79
2	3.02	5.02

* All sales occur in state 0.

☐ A customer account that is *one month old* at the start will, on the average, pass through the future states of being current, one month old, and two months old for 1.27 times, 1.86 times, and 0.66 time, respectively, before it is absorbed.

☐ A customer account that is *two months old* at the start will, on the average, pass through the future states of being current, one month old, and two months old for 0.94 time, 0.60 time, and 1.48 times, respectively, before it is absorbed.

A more important interpretation of the N^{-1} matrix is that the sum of each row (i.e., $2.17 + 0.81 + 0.29 = 3.27$) indicates how many months in the future it takes a receivable balance, which is presently in a particular state, to be absorbed in state P (paid in full) or in state B (declared a bad debt). Thus the average number of months customer balances are outstanding is as shown in Table 10.7.

What is the importance of this information? Since the N^{-1} matrix indicates the average number of times that a customer account will be in a particular state, and the R matrix shows the probability of passing from that state to one of the absorbing states, the credit manager can determine the probability that a receivable will either be paid in full or be declared a bad debt by multiplying the N^{-1} and R matrices. This calculation is shown in Table 10.8.

TABLE 10.8
Probability of Payment

$$
N^{-1} \times R = \begin{bmatrix} 2.17 & 0.81 & 0.29 \\ 1.27 & 1.86 & 0.66 \\ 0.94 & 0.60 & 1.48 \end{bmatrix} \begin{bmatrix} 0.35 & 0 \\ 0.16 & 0 \\ 0.31 & 0.08 \end{bmatrix} = \begin{matrix} 0 \\ 1 \\ 2 \end{matrix} \begin{matrix} P & B \\ \begin{bmatrix} 0.979^* & 0.021 \\ 0.947 & 0.053 \\ 0.884 & 0.116 \end{bmatrix} \end{matrix}
$$

* $(2.17 \times 0.35) + (0.81 \times 0.16) + (0.29 \times 0.31) = 0.979$.

The probability that an outstanding receivable that is now current will ultimately be paid is 0.979, and the probability that it will become delinquent is 0.021. An outstanding receivable that is presently one month old has a probability of 0.947 of being collected and a probability of 0.053 of becoming a bad debt. A two-month-old balance, on the average, will be collected with a probability of 0.884 and be classified as uncollectible with a probability of 0.116.

Forecast of Receivable Balances

Suppose management plans to expand sales via a new advertising promotion with the result that more will be sold to old customers and at the same time more customers with the same creditworthiness will be enticed to purchase goods. In effect, new sales are a reflection of past sales. In August (see Table 10.1) the total sales (the sum of column 0) were $159 to seven customers, or $22.71 per customer. If sales are expanded in this fashion, what will be the distribution of receivables at some future date when this impulse in sales has reached a new *steady-state* condition?

Since there are, on average, $22.71 of new sales per customer each period, multiplying the row vector [22.71, 0, 0] by the N^{-1} matrix gives the answer:

$$N^{-1}$$

$$[22.71 \quad 0 \quad 0] \begin{bmatrix} 2.17 & 0.81 & 0.29 \\ 1.27 & 1.86 & 0.66 \\ 0.94 & 0.60 & 1.48 \end{bmatrix} = [49.28 \quad 18.40 \quad 6.59].$$

Subsequently, there is an *outstanding receivable balance per customer* of $74.27 once a new steady state is attained:

$49.28 + $18.40 + $6.59 = $74.27.

This receivable balance is recorded at sales value. Appendix B provides further mathematical explanation about how this new steady state is reached.

The new steady state occurs when sales equal collections plus bad debts, and gross investment is defined as total accounts receivable outstanding at the steady state. The receivable balances, by the ending state, are multiplied by the R matrix to determine the monthly cash flow of collections and the monthly bad debts:

$$\begin{matrix} & P & B \end{matrix}$$

$$[49.28 \quad 18.40 \quad 6.59] \begin{bmatrix} 0.35 & 0 \\ 0.16 & 0 \\ 0.31 & 0.08 \end{bmatrix}$$

expected value of collections (B) = $22.19
expected value of bad debts (P) =   0.52
    total $22.71

(A rounding error or $0.05 exists; the answer for the matrix multiplication is $22.76.) The steady state has occurred since sales are equal to cash inflows plus bad debts.

Illustration: Changing Credit Risk

To this point, the basic assumption has been that the new sales are to customers with the same creditworthiness as that of the regular customers. While this situation is possible, there are other cases that should be discussed. One case that is most common is the expansion of sales by selling on credit to customers with a different (say lower) creditworthy condition. In this case management is lacking direct information about the payment patterns of these potential customers. Information on these new customers may be gathered from a number of sources, such as competitors, Dun & Bradstreet, or Creditel. Whatever the source of the basic information on these new customers, the credit manager is still responsible for making a decision of whether or not to extend credit.

To illustrate the impact that low-creditworthy customers might have on the firm, the transition matrix of Table 10.5 has been arbitrarily adjusted to show a slow down in cash flow (column P), an increase in bad debts (column B), and an increase in receivables aging (columns 1 and 2). These changes are shown in Table 10.9.

With the same procedures as used before, comparative results of these different risk situations are shown in Table 10.10. The results of Table 10.10 indicate that significant changes may occur through the introduction of low-creditworthy customers.

You are cautioned to appreciate that the transition matrix used in Table 10.9 has no basis other than as an example to show that acceptance of less creditworthy customers, or a decrease in the firm's credit standards, can have a significant impact on receivable investment. In the illustration

TABLE 10.9
Revised Transition Matrix

	P	B	0	1	2
P	1	0	0	0	0
B	0	1	0	0	0
0	0.20	0	0.38	0.42	0
1	0.10	0	0.33	0.23	0.34
2	0.20	0.12	0.26	0.14	0.28

Note: The cell (0, P) has decreased from 0.35 to 0.20; the cell (2, B) has increased from 0.08 to 0.12; and cells (0, 1), (1, 2), and (2, 2) have changed from 0.27 to 0.42, 0.28 to 0.34, and 0.21 to 0.28, respectively.

TABLE 10.10
Comparative Results of Transition Matrices of Tables 10.5 and 10.9

Accounts receivable outstanding from point of sale

Initial state	Table 10.5	Table 10.9
0	3.27	5.37
1	4.79	6.55
2	5.02	6.41

Dollar value of receivables balance per customer based on monthly sales of $22.71

	Initial state	Ending state			
		0	1	2	Total
Table 10.5	0	$49.28	$18.40	$ 6.59	$ 74.27
Table 10.9	0	64.92	38.73	18.29	121.71

Cash flow and bad debts per customer per month

	Cash flow	Bad debts	Total
Table 10.5	$22.19	$0.52	$22.71
Table 10.9	20.52	2.19	22.71

Probability of collection and bad debts at a steady state

	Table 10.5		Table 10.9	
Initial state	P	B	P	B
0	0.979	0.021	0.903	0.097
1	0.947	0.053	0.857	0.143
2	0.884	0.116	0.771	0.229

cash inflow decreases about 7.5% ($20.52/$22.19), while at the same time receivable investment increases 64% ($121.71/$74.27) and bad debts increase 321% ($2.19/$0.52). Many other illustrations can be chosen, but they will not change the basic conclusion that if a firm lowers its credit standards, then investment and bad debts will increase, while cash inflows will decrease. Whether the firm should make such a change depends on the profit margin and whether the firm has *sufficient liquidity* to finance this investment demand.

Timing of Liquidity Drain

If the firm changes one or more of its policies governing the allowance of credit, this change affects sales, cash inflows, and receivables. The impact

TABLE 10.11
Timing and Amount of Liquidity Drain

	Period				
	1	2	3	4	5
Beginning accounts receivable	$ 0	$22.71	$37.47	$48.23	$55.87
Plus sales	22.71	22.71	22.71	22.71	22.71
Minus ending accounts receivable	22.71	37.47	48.23	55.87	61.25
Cash inflow	$ 0	$ 7.95	$11.95	$15.07	$17.23
Minus cost of sales*	18.17	18.17	18.17	18.17	18.17
Liquidity drain	$18.17	$10.22	$ 6.22	$ 3.10	$ 0.94

* Paid in the current month.

does not happen instantaneously; often considerable time elapses before the full impact of the policy change is known. (See Table 9.5 for an illustration of the time involved between the initiation of the policy change and the establishment of the new steady state.) During the growth period the firm experiences an incremental liquidity demand to finance changes in inventory, production, and accounts receivable.

The timing and the amount of the liquidity drain for the earlier illustration of no change in credit risk are shown for five periods in Table 10.11. The net liquidity drain is the investment necessary to finance the growth in accounts receivable (similar to the "How to Go Broke" example in Chapter 1). Outflows for cost of sales are assumed to be 80% of sales. Accounts receivable per customer grow from $0 to $61.25. If this series is continued to infinity, accounts receivable will maximize at $74.27. The details supporting these calculations are reported in Appendix A.

Liquidity Needs

The most significant conclusion that can be drawn from the data in Table 10.11 is that *the liquidity drain to finance receivables happens in the early periods, whereas the cash inflow buildup occurs in later periods.* For the firm to benefit from these incremental sales, management must ensure that sufficient liquidity exists to finance the expansion.

The rate of change of cash inflows is not linear and places a great burden on the firm's resources in the early periods. The result of the expansion is that while profits have increased, so have the costs and the level of investment. The necessary funds for expansion may come from existing liquidity resources. Usually, though, part of this expansion is provided from outside sources via an expansion in trade accounts payable. Sometimes, the expansion is financed through long-term sources. This action might be viewed as a mismatch of sources and uses of funds, particularly once the steady state is reached. Expansion can create an imbalance, since it does the firm little good to expand and at the same time to plant the seeds of its own destruction.

Summary

The chapter discussed Markov chain analysis as a technique for analyzing credit balances and for setting credit policy. The objectives of the technique are multifold: (1) to determine the average number of months before an account is settled in some manner, (2) to calculate the probabilities that the account will be paid or declared a bad debt, (3) to estimate the average number of times the account will be classified in some aging category before it is either paid or declared a bad debt, and (4) to forecast the liquidity drain caused by changing some aspect of credit policy.

An in-depth understanding of Markov chain analysis depends on an understanding of matrix algebra. However, on a conceptual level the technique models the flow of receivable balances through an aging process. The dynamics of the flow process model the transition from one steady state to another.

Appendix C to this chapter discusses a joint probability analysis model as an alternative to Markov chain analysis. The model is less demanding in the knowledge of mathematics required.

Key Concepts

Absorbing state

Fundamental matrix

Markov chain analysis

Nonabsorbing state

Payment patterns

Steady state

Transition matrix

Appendix A

Fundamentals of Matrix Algebra

This appendix focuses on matrix methods that are used in this chapter to solve systems of equations for which ordinary elementary algebra is too burdensome. There are a number of ways of understanding a matrix. It can be thought of as a vector of vectors or as a rectangular array of numbers arranged in rows and columns. The following is an example of a matrix:

$$C = \begin{bmatrix} 2 & 4 & 6 \\ 1 & 3 & 5 \end{bmatrix}.$$

For convenience, matrices are frequently represented by a single capital letter. The number of rows and the number of columns of C define the dimensions of C. So C is a 2×3 (2-by-3) matrix.

Matrices may have one or more rows of elements and one or more columns of elements. A matrix that has the same number of rows as columns is a *square matrix*.

Addition and subtraction of matrices are performed as follows: Two matrices, C and D, may be added to or subtracted from each other provided that they have the same number of rows and columns. The resulting sum or difference will be a matrix, call it E, with the same number of rows and columns as the given matrices. For example, let

$$C = \begin{bmatrix} 2 & 4 & 6 \\ 1 & 3 & 5 \end{bmatrix}, \qquad D = \begin{bmatrix} 5 & 4 & 6 \\ 3 & 2 & 7 \end{bmatrix},$$

and $E = C + D$. Then the elements of E are simply the sums of the corresponding positioned elements of C and D:

$$E = \begin{bmatrix} 2+5 & 4+4 & 6+6 \\ 1+3 & 3+2 & 5+7 \end{bmatrix} = \begin{bmatrix} 7 & 8 & 12 \\ 4 & 5 & 12 \end{bmatrix}.$$

Also, if $C + D = E$, then $D + C = E$; and if $E - C = D$, then $E - D = C$. Note that matrix addition or subtraction requires only that the *matrices that are to be added or subtracted have the same number of rows and columns* — the matrices do not need to be square.

Matrix multiplication is more complex. First, *a matrix C can be multiplied by a matrix F if and only if F has the same number of rows as C has columns.* Finding the elements of the product matrix, call it G, involves solving a number of sums of products. For example, let

$$C = \begin{bmatrix} 2 & 4 & 6 \\ 1 & 3 & 5 \end{bmatrix}, \qquad F = \begin{bmatrix} 3 & 1 \\ 0 & 9 \\ 4 & 7 \end{bmatrix}.$$

Then if $G = C \times F$, we obtain

$$G = \begin{bmatrix} (2 \times 3 + 4 \times 0 + 6 \times 4) & (2 \times 1 + 4 \times 9 + 6 \times 7) \\ (1 \times 3 + 3 \times 0 + 5 \times 4) & (1 \times 1 + 3 \times 9 + 5 \times 7) \end{bmatrix}$$
$$= \begin{bmatrix} 30 & 80 \\ 23 & 63 \end{bmatrix}.$$

Note that since C is 2×3 and F is 3×2, the product matrix G is 2×2.

The order of multiplication is important. Even though CF is defined (as G), the product FC may not be (although in this example it is). For instance, if F was 1×3, CF would be defined but FC would not be defined since the single row of F is not equal to the number of columns of C, which is 2.

Also, note that in this example, although the product matrix exists for FC, it is not equal to the product matrix CF. Prove this fact to yourself by premultiplying matrix F by C (i.e., $C \times F$).

Before matrix solutions can be explored, we must define two special matrices: the identity matrix and the inverse matrix.

The *identity matrix* has the special characteristics that it is square, its diagonal elements (those going from the top left-hand corner to the bottom right-hand corner) are all 1, and its nondiagonal elements are all 0. In other words, the identity matrix, always designated I, is defined as

$$I = \begin{bmatrix} 1 & 0 & \cdots & 0 \\ 0 & 1 & \cdots & 0 \\ \vdots & \vdots & \vdots & \vdots \\ 0 & 0 & \cdots & 1 \end{bmatrix},$$

where the number of rows and the number of columns are equal. It is easy to verify that $IC = CI = C$, where C and I are of equal size.

The *inverse matrix* is analogous to the reciprocal of a number; that is, it is defined only in relation to something else. Thus if G is a square matrix, its inverse is designated G^{-1} and is defined as the matrix that will, when properly multiplied by G, result in a product that is the identity matrix I. Thus G^{-1} is the inverse matrix of G if and only if $G^{-1}G = I = GG^{-1}$. The inverse will also be square and have the same number of rows and columns as G and I.

With these simple techniques in mind, we are now prepared to solve some of the matrix problems shown in the chapter.

Solution for Solving N^{-1}

The fundamental matrix N^{-1} is defined as

$$N^{-1} = [I - Q]^{-1} = \left[\begin{pmatrix} 1 & 0 & 0 \\ 0 & 1 & 0 \\ 0 & 0 & 1 \end{pmatrix} - \begin{pmatrix} 0.38 & 0.27 & 0 \\ 0.33 & 0.23 & 0.28 \\ 0.26 & 0.14 & 0.21 \end{pmatrix} \right]^{-1}$$

$$= \begin{bmatrix} 0.62 & -0.27 & 0 \\ -0.33 & 0.77 & -0.28 \\ -0.26 & -0.14 & 0.79 \end{bmatrix}^{-1}.$$

The first step in finding the inverse of N (i.e., N^{-1}) is to recall that $N^{-1}N = I$. Substituting for N and I yields

$$N^{-1} \begin{bmatrix} 0.62 & -0.27 & 0 \\ -0.33 & 0.77 & -0.28 \\ -0.26 & -0.14 & 0.79 \end{bmatrix} = \begin{bmatrix} 1 & 0 & 0 \\ 0 & 1 & 0 \\ 0 & 0 & 1 \end{bmatrix}.$$

Let the elements of N^{-1} be designated by the letters a, b, c, and so on:

$$N^{-1} = \begin{bmatrix} a & b & c \\ d & e & f \\ g & h & i \end{bmatrix}.$$

Then recalling the procedure for multiplication of matrices, we can write the following:

$$\begin{bmatrix} (0.62a - 0.33b - 0.26c) & (-0.27a + 0.77b - 0.14c) & (0a - 0.28b + 0.79c) \\ (0.62d - 0.33e - 0.26f) & (-0.27d + 0.77e - 0.14f) & (0d - 0.28e + 0.79f) \\ (0.62g - 0.33h - 0.26i) & (-0.27g + 0.77h - 0.14i) & (0g - 0.28h + 0.79i) \end{bmatrix}.$$

Equating corresponding elements of $N^{-1}N$ and I gives the following equations:

$$\left. \begin{array}{r} 0.62\,a - 0.33\,b - 0.26\,c = 1 \\ -0.27\,a + 0.77\,b - 0.14\,c = 0 \\ 0\,a - 0.28\,b + 0.79\,c = 0 \end{array} \right\} \quad \text{which can be solved for } a, b, c$$

$$\left. \begin{array}{r} 0.62\,d - 0.33\,e - 0.26\,f = 0 \\ -0.27\,d + 0.77\,e - 0.14\,f = 1 \\ 0\,d - 0.28\,e + 0.79\,f = 0 \end{array} \right\} \quad \text{which can be solved for } d, e, f$$

$$\left. \begin{array}{r} 0.62\,g - 0.33\,h - 0.26\,i = 0 \\ -0.27\,g + 0.77\,h - 0.14\,i = 0 \\ 0\,g - 0.28\,h + 0.79\,i = 1 \end{array} \right\} \quad \text{which can be solved for } g, h, i$$

Solving these nine equations in sets of three for the elements of N^{-1} gives

$$N^{-1} = \begin{bmatrix} 2.17 & 0.81 & 0.29 \\ 1.27 & 1.86 & 0.66 \\ 0.94 & 0.60 & 1.48 \end{bmatrix}.$$

Solution for $N^{-1} \times R$

The solution is straightforward if the rules of multiplication, as discussed earlier, are followed:

$$N^{-1} \times R = \begin{bmatrix} 2.17 \times 0.35 + 0.81 \times 0.16 + 0.29 \times 0.31 \\ 1.27 \times 0.35 + 1.86 \times 0.16 + 0.66 \times 0.31 \\ 0.94 \times 0.35 + 0.60 \times 0.16 + 1.48 \times 0.31 \end{bmatrix}$$

$$\begin{bmatrix} 2.17 \times 0 + 0.81 \times 0 + 0.29 \times 0.08 \\ 1.27 \times 0 + 1.86 \times 0 + 0.66 \times 0.08 \\ 0.94 \times 0 + 0.60 \times 0 + 1.48 \times 0.08 \end{bmatrix}$$

$$= \begin{bmatrix} 0.979 & 0.021 \\ 0.947 & 0.053 \\ 0.884 & 0.116 \end{bmatrix}.$$

Other Matrices in the Chapter

By simply following the rules of matrix multiplication, you can find solutions for any remaining matrix problems discussed in the chapter.

Appendix B

Explanation of the Transition from One Steady State to Another Steady State

This appendix shows the transition from one steady state to another. For the transition matrix of Table 10.5, each customer's average accounts receivable balance at the new steady state is $74.27, based on sales each period of $22.71 and a constant payment pattern. At the new static state funds flows are in equilibrium, and no new investment is required. However, prior to that time the firm faces a net liquidity outflow. To determine this outflow and its estimated timing, we may make further use of the original transition matrix.

The original transition matrix is an estimate of the probability of payment of incremental sales through time to the average customer. The steady state, or equilibrium, is calculated as the sum of the following payment series to infinity:

$$I + T + T^2 + \cdots + T^\infty, \tag{B.1}$$

where I represents the matrix for period 1's transition, T represents the matrix for period 2's transition, T^2 represents the matrix for period 3's transition, and so on. Table B.1 summarizes the transitions for the first 5 periods *for row 0 of the transition matrix*. Only these entries are reported because the concern is with new sales that can only be generated at time 0.

Accounts receivable for each period may be determined by adding each of the transitional values (states 0, 1, 2) of each new sales row in a

TABLE B.1
Row 0 of the Transition Matrices

Period	P	B	0	1	2	Total
$I \rightarrow 1$	0	0	1.0000	0	0	1.0000
$T \rightarrow 2$	0.3500	0	0.3800	0.2700	0	0.6500
$T^2 \rightarrow 3$	0.5262	0	0.2335	0.1647	0.0756	0.4738
$T^3 \rightarrow 4$	0.6577	0.0060	0.1627	0.1115	0.0620	0.3362
$T^4 \rightarrow 5$	0.7517	0.0110	0.1148	0.0783	0.0442	0.2373

Note: I is the identity matrix; T is the T matrix of Table 10.5; T^2 is found by multiplying $T \times T$; T^3 is found by multiplying $T^2 \times T$; and so on.

291

TABLE B.2
Estimated Accounts Receivable Balance

Period	Sum of row values for states 0, 1, 2		Sales	Ending accounts receivables
	Sum	Cumulative		
1	1.0000	1.0000 ×	$22.71 =	$22.71
2	0.6500	1.6500 ×	22.71 =	37.47
3	0.4738	2.1238 ×	22.71 =	48.23
4	0.3362	2.4600 ×	22.71 =	55.87
5	0.2373	2.6973 ×	22.71 =	61.25
⋮	⋮	⋮ ⋮	⋮ ⋮	⋮
∞	—	3.2704 ×	22.71 =	74.27

cumulative fashion (the last column of Table B.1), and multiplying each row's cumulative sum by the sales of that period (assumed constant at $22.71). These manipulations are reflected in the data of Table B.2.

By period 5 accounts receivable have increased from $22.71 to $61.25. As the number of periods approach infinity, the receivable balance will approach $74.27. This sum is calculated from Eq. (B.1) by realizing that

$$I + T + T^2 + \cdots + T^\infty = [I - T]^{-1}.$$

Solving this inverse matrix gives the desired new steady-state result.

Appendix C
Joint Probability Analysis

A less elegant technique than the Markov chain process for analyzing customer payment patterns is *joint probability analysis*. Each customer of a firm who is current with respect to her or his receivables has three options: keep the account current by paying regularly and making additional purchases; pay off the debt completely; or defer payment to another period. Analysis of each customer's (or of similar groups' of customers) payment pattern allows the credit manager to make projections of payment. If the manager assumes that customer categories are independent of each other, then the joint probability of payment can be calculated. For example, suppose the question is, What is the probability that customer category A will take the discount? Then the probability that they do discount plus the probability that they do not must equal one.

ILLUSTRATION C.1

The procedure for determining the joint probability of cash flow, as of a specific point in time (e.g., the discount period, the credit period, or the default period), is as follows: Assume that management changes its sales policy from cash to credit terms of 2/10, *n*/30. Customer groups A and B are expected to increase purchases by $200 and $300, respectively. If discounts are taken, group A will remit $196 and group B will pay $294. Their expected payment patterns are shown in Table C.1.

TABLE C.1
Payment Patterns

| | Probability of | | | |
| | Paying by the | | | |
Category	Discount period	Credit period	Defaulting	Total
A	0.40	0.40	0.20	1.00
B	0.35	0.35	0.30	1.00

TABLE C.2
Joint Probabilities of Cash Flows: A Two-Group Case

Customer group A				Customer group B		
	Probability	($)	Probability ($)	Pay by discount period	Pay by credit period	Default
				0.35 $294	0.35 $300	0.30 $0
Pay by discount period	0.40	$196		0.14 $490	0.14 $496	0.12 $196
Pay by credit period	0.40	$200		0.14 $494	0.14 $500	0.12 $200
Default	0.20	$0		0.07 $294	0.07 $300	0.06 $0

TABLE C.3
Joint Probabilities of Expected Cash Flows: A Three-Group Case

Customer groups A and B*	Probability	($)	Customer group C					
			Pay by discount period		Pay by credit period		Default	
			Probability 0.55	($) $98	Probability 0.25	($) $100	Probability 0.20	($) $0
$A_d; B_d$	0.14	$490	0.077	$588	0.035	$590	0.028	$490
$A_d; B_c$	0.14	$496	0.077	$594	0.035	$596	0.028	$496
$A_d; B_B$	0.12	$196	0.066	$294	0.030	$296	0.024	$196
$A_c; B_d$	0.14	$494	0.077	$592	0.035	$594	0.028	$494
$A_c; B_c$	0.14	$500	0.077	$598	0.035	$600	0.028	$500
$A_c; B_B$	0.12	$200	0.066	$298	0.030	$300	0.024	$200
$A_B; B_d$	0.07	$294	0.0385	$392	0.0175	$394	0.014	$294
$A_B; B_c$	0.07	$300	0.0385	$398	0.0175	$400	0.014	$300
$A_B; B_B$	0.06	$0	0.033	$98	0.015	$100	0.012	$0

* From Table C.2. Subscripts mean d = pay by discount period; c = pay by credit period; B = defaults.

295

The joint probability matrix of incremental cash flows is shown in Table C.2. The cell entries consist of a joint probability and the dollar payment amount if each category pays according to the row and the column headings. The joint probabilities are calculated by multiplying the row and the column probabilities. For instance, the joint probability of both categories taking the discount is $0.4 \times 0.35 = 0.14$. If they both take the discount, they remit $490 — $196 from group A and $294 from group B.

The total expected cash flow of $366.30 is calculated by multiplying the dollar amount in each cell by its associated joint probability and summing the values. Although expected cash inflows of $366.30 may be adequate to meet expected cash outflows, a 44% chance exists that the cash flow may be $300 or less and a 6% joint probability exists for nonpayment by both categories. Can the firm sustain itself if either of these conditions prevails? This question can only be answered through detailed analysis of variation in sales demand and required expenditures.

The addition of a third group of customers with different payment propensities may result in an improved cash flow and risk position. For example, assume that new customer category C purchases $100 of merchandise and historically discounts invoices 55% of the time, pays by the end of the credit period 25% of the time, and does not pay 20% of the time. Table C.3 shows the revised joint probabilities and cash flows for each cell for the three – customer group case. The expected cash flow is $464.60 with a probability of zero cash flow of 6% and a probability of cash flow being $300 or less of 32.8%.

Rather than introduce a third type of customer group, management

TABLE C.4
Alternative Credit Strategies

Sales scenario	Expected cash flow	Probability of zero cash flow	Probability of cash flow less than $300
A = $200 B = 300	$366.30	6.0%	44.0%
A = $200 B = 400	$435.60	6.0%	44.0%
A = $300 B = 300	$445.50	6.0%	44.0%
A = $200 B = 300 C = 100	$464.60	1.2%	32.8%

could increase sales to either of its present groups. Assuming that additional sales of $100 could be generated by selling to either group A or group B, expected cash flow calculations can be revised. Table C.4 summarizes the results. The results indicate that the inclusion of customer group C increases cash flows and reduces liquidity risk more than the alternatives — a most desirable diversification effect. Thus management needs a well-thought-out policy of how credit terms affect expected cash flows.

As additional customer categories are included and/or expected payment patterns change, this analysis must be redone.   □

Questions

Note: Questions 1 through 4 pertain to Markov chain analysis.

1.   Discuss the meaning of the new steady-state accounts receivable balance, given a constant sales stimulus.

2.   What type of information is shown in the transition matrix? What does the fundamental matrix reveal?

3.   How are the probabilities of payment and bad debts determined?

4.   How can a new steady-state receivables balance be determined?

5.   Discuss the sources of the information used in developing the joint probability matrix of Table C.2 (see Appendix C). How useful is this information?

Problems

1.   Company policy is to write off delinquent accounts if the accounts are of age three months. The transition probabilities are given next.

	P	B	0	1	2
P	1	0	0	0	0
B	0	1	0	0	0
0	0.5	0	0.4	0.1	0
1	0.4	0	0.3	0.2	0.1
2	0.3	0.2	0.1	0.1	0.3

It is expected that 100 new accounts will be created each month. The average dollar value of accounts in states 0, 1, and 2 is estimated to be $20, $30, and $40, respectively. Cash costs are 70% of sales.

(a) Compute the fundamental matrix N^{-1} and explain what it means.

(b) What is the expected number of months before an account, initially in a nonabsorbing state, is absorbed?

(c) Calculate the probability that an account that is initially in a nonabsorbing state will be written off.

(d) What is the expected number of accounts in each nonabsorbing state? What is the expected dollar value of receivables in each nonabsorbing state?

(e) What is the expected dollar value of monthly cash flow and accounts written off?

2.   Tables 10.12 and 10.13 give the accounts receivable reports of the Grub Company for the months of October and November, respectively. New accounts

TABLE 10.12
Accounts Receivable Report for October

Customer number	Balance outstanding	Period outstanding		
		0	1	2
50	$ 350	$ 212		$ 138
57	280	95	$ 105	80
62	260	260		
63	100	100		
64	245		245	
71	95	95		
72	525	229	296	
74	479	40	380	59
80	385		385	
82	272			272
83	50	50		
84	170			170
86	427	125	302	
90	281		200	81
91	197	150	47	
95	318			318
97	85	85		
98	414	250	164	
99	302	100	202	
	$5235	$1791	$2326	$1118

Bad debts are zero this month

are defined as those that were not on the receivable ledger in the prior month but that appear in the current month. Bad debts are identified at the bottom of each monthly statement. Variable costs of sales are estimated to be 75% of sales.

(a) Prepare a transition matrix for the month.

(b) Assuming that new sales will continue as in November, determine the incremental investment necessary to support the new level of sales when the new steady state is reached.

(c) Determine the monthly cash flow and bad debts at the new steady state.

(d) Discuss the problems in implementing this type of analysis.

3. The Wright Company expects to increase monthly sales to its present customers by $150 monthly. From past experience the credit manager has determined that the transition matrix for these customers is as shown in Table 10.9 in the chapter. Variable production cash costs are estimated to be 72% of sales and are paid monthly as incurred. What will the firm's incremental investment in accounts receivable be after four months and at the new steady state?

4. Using the transition matrix shown in Table 10.9 of the chapter and a sales stimulus of $22.71 per period, calculate the following:

TABLE 10.13
Accounts Receivable Report for November

Customer number	Balance outstanding	Period outstanding 0	Period outstanding 1	Period outstanding 2
50	$ 260	$ 165	$ 95	
54	87	87		
57	95	95	95	
58	330	330		
62	289	29	260	
69	140	140		
72	525		229	$ 296
74	480	100		380
80	195	195		
81	370	370		
83	60	60		
84	190	190		
86	427		125	302
87	280	280		
90	512	312		200
91	230	80	150	
94	319	319		
98	332	82	250	
99	200		100	100
110	480	480		
	$5801	$3219	$1304	$1278

Bad debts: Customer 82, $272

(a) The number of periods that accounts receivable are outstanding from the point of sale.

(b) The probability of collections and bad debts for each state, once the steady state is reached.

(c) The dollar aging of accounts receivable.

(d) The monthly cash flow and bad debts associated with receivables.

The answers to this problem are shown in Table 10.10 of the chapter.

5.   Management is attempting to evaluate two different credit policies. The transition matrix for each policy is shown next.

	A	B	0	1
A	1	0	0	0
B	0	1	0	0
0	0.3	0	0.4	0.3
1	0.2	0.2	0.5	0.1

	A	B	0	1	2
A	1	0	0	0	0
B	0	1	0	0	0
0	0.5	0	0.3	0.2	0
1	0.3	0	0.3	0.3	0.1
2	0.2	0.2	0.2	0.2	0.2

(a) Briefly discuss how these matrices are determined. What are the major differences between them in terms of credit flows?

(b) Compute the fundamental matrix N^{-1} for each policy. Explain the economic meaning of each fundamental matrix calculated.

6. From the matrix information of Problem 5, calculate the probability of collection and bad debts for each state for each policy. Plot and discuss your findings.

Appendix A Problems

1. Add the following matrices:

$$\begin{bmatrix} 6 & 8 \\ 7 & 2 \end{bmatrix} \quad \begin{bmatrix} 14 & 10 \\ 7 & 5 \end{bmatrix} \quad \begin{bmatrix} 3 & 6 \\ 4 & 8 \end{bmatrix}.$$

2. Multiply the following matrices:

$$\begin{bmatrix} 23 & 24 \\ 18 & 15 \end{bmatrix} \quad \begin{bmatrix} 4 & 7 \\ 2 & 6 \end{bmatrix}.$$

3. Find the inverse of each of the following matrices:

$$\begin{bmatrix} 4 & 6 \\ 3 & 3 \end{bmatrix} \quad \begin{bmatrix} 2 & 8 \\ 5 & 2 \end{bmatrix}.$$

Appendix C Problems

1. Our company deals with two types of customers, classified as A and B. On average, these classes purchase $1000 and $500, respectively, per period. We offer credit terms of 3/10, n/30. The collection experience is given in Table 10.14.

(a) What is the probability of both groups taking the cash discount? How much will be remitted if they do?

TABLE 10.14
Collection Experience

| | Payment by | | |
Customer	Discount period	Credit period	Defaulting
A	0.60	0.35	0.05
B	0.30	0.50	0.20

TABLE 10.15
Collection Experience

| Customer | Payment by | | Defaulting | Sales |
	Discount period	Credit period		
A	0.65	0.30	0.05	$1500
B	0.70	0.25	0.05	2000

(b) How much is the total expected cash flow?

(c) What is the probability that expected cash flow will be less than $1200? Less than $1000? Less than $800? Less than $500? Less than $200? Zero?

2.   Management is considering changing credit terms from 2/10, $n/30$ to 3/30, $n/60$. It believes that these new terms will increase sales by 25%. Currently, the firm sells to two major groups, with the collection experience as shown in Table 10.15. The collection experience is not expected to change with the increase in sales.

(a) Prepare the joint probability matrix of cash flows for these customer groups before and after the policy change.

(b) What is the expected cash flow for each policy? What is the probability of having the cash flow between $1600 and $2000 for each policy?

(c) Under the old credit terms, what is the joint probability that both groups will pay by the tenth day? What is the joint probability that neither group pays by the tenth day? How do your answers change under the new credit terms?

CHAPTER 11 □
Credit Selection Models

The credit sale relationship between customer and supplier is a trust based on mutual needs. The customer selects the supplier on the basis of its reputation as a source of a quality good at an acceptable price. The supplier accepts the order and extends the necessary credit to facilitate the sale if it believes the customer will honor the contract by paying the invoice according to the agreed-upon terms. Usually, this procedure is completed without complications. Both parties agree to a contract and are expected to live up to its terms. While much is written about poor suppliers and late-paying customers, it is sometimes forgotten that the bulk of all transactions go through the system in a normal way. If they did not, business transactions in modern society would not take place and the entire commercial system would come to a halt.

The system works because both parties to every transaction do the necessary pretransaction investigation and are prepared to contract. The quality of the seller's product is evaluated by the buyer following those criteria which he or she deems important. This information can usually be gathered through discussions with other buyers and trade associations. In the same way, credit managers gather information about customers.

Credit managers may use different techniques for evaluating credit applicants. At one extreme is the approach used by W. T. Grant, as reported by a former W. T. Grant financial executive to *Business Week* magazine (July 19, 1976):

> We gave credit to every deadbeat who breathed. The stores were told to push credit and had certain quotas to fill.

This chapter discusses more meaningful approaches that provide better control over credit risks. The models discussed range from the simplistic five C's to a reasonably complex sequential decision system.

Five C's of Credit

Through the process of investigation, credit decision making, and risk reduction, the credit manager seeks to grant more good and fewer bad loans than would be possible in her or his absence. The traditional standard of investigation has been the *five C's of credit:* character, capacity, capital, collateral, and conditions. Each of these factors are evaluated in terms of the firm's position as a supplier (i.e., seller) and not according to some prescribed format.

Character

The *character* of a credit applicant refers to the probability that the applicant will make every effort to honor the contract, that is, pay for the purchase. The issue is a moral one that many credit managers consider to be the most important. Possibly the best information concerning this attribute is obtained from other suppliers. Many metropolitan areas have credit manager associations for the sharing of credit information. This arrangement, while common, is not without the possibility of error. Every credit manager must be constantly on guard to protect the reputation of a credit applicant. A credit manager who refuses a credit applicant must have legitimate reasons for refusal, since it is contestable in the courts under the laws of discrimination.

Character of the buyer may be preserved if in difficult times all dealings between the buyer and the supplier are aboveboard. This condition implies that the applicant keep the supplier aware of any difficulties that might hinder the successful completion of the contract. If the applicant experiences some problems in paying the contract on time, these problems should be made known to the supplier as soon as possible so that other arrangements may be made. It is to the benefit of both parties that difficulties be shared. This approach is reasonable since a good customer is of value, even in times of trouble.

Capacity

The *capacity* of an applicant is the subjective evaluation made by the credit manager about the customer's ability to pay. Were perfect information available, then this problem would not exist. While it may be trite to recall that debts are usually settled by a cash flow, it is still one of the most important criteria considered by the credit manager. The question is: Does the customer have a sufficient cash flow to settle the debt? Traditional forms of ratio analysis (see Chapter 3) are often used to provide information, but they do not always provide the best evidence of the cash flow of the business. (See Chapters 4, 5, and 6 for better methods.)

Cash flow is frequently defined as profits after tax plus noncash charges. As discussed in Chapter 6, this evaluation demands the assumption that the relative asset and liability positions do not change. Even if we allow for this assumption, we see that financial statements made after the fact means that the needs of the credit manager are not being correctly met. Better information comes from a cash budget, which is a before-the-fact financial statement presenting the cash flow *plans* of the business. Unfortunately, it may be based on a set of unrealistic assumptions. Even if it is not, the best plans do not always work as perceived.

The credit manager may be able to consider the trade credit as a type of self-financing credit. This system implies that any cash provided from the sale of the goods is used to repay the credit (e.g., floor planning as used in the auto industry). Usually, the credit manager cannot identify cash flow this clearly and, as a result, is forced to seek other means. It is usually at this point that the credit manager asks for information about the customer from other trade creditors.

In examining capacity, a credit manager should consider whether he or she is willing to become a *quasi-permanent* investor in the applicant's firm. This investment comes about in a normal way as management hopes that customers are a source of repeat sales. In the same way, the customer expects the firm to supply goods on a continual basis. The resale nature of business can mean that the supplier sells additional goods before the earlier orders are paid. Ultimately, this resale condition has the effect of making the supplier a quasi-permanent investor in the customer's business.

Capital

The *capital* of an applicant is presented in the balance sheet provided to the credit manager. Assets less liabilities equal capital, which in some sense suggests a surplus available to settle claims. The problem of capital is at least twofold. First, the most recent balance sheet is by definition a historical position. It shows the financial position as of a particular date. Second, and more importantly, the balance sheet provides very little indication about the liquidity of the applicant's assets.

It might be better to consider the issue of capital more as an answer to this question: Does the applicant have enough capital to support her or his level of operations? Generally, most credit managers seem to rely on a few standard financial ratios to decide the question of the applicant's capital. The ratios used typically concern the ability of the applicant to manage debt. If the ratios indicate a relatively stable relationship, then the credit manager takes the position that sufficient liquid capital exists. If the credit manager is concerned with the possibility of potential bankruptcy or nonpayment by the applicant, then the correct decision may be to not extend credit.

Collateral

The supplier of trade credit normally extends credit without the protection of collateral. *Collateral* speaks of a fallback position in times of great difficulty and is generally only involved in asset-based loans (see Chapter 17). From a trade credit perspective, the value of an applicant's collateral is in general terms. It represents the estimated market value of the assets of the firm and should exclude all assets that have liens against them.

The liabilities of the applicant are usually well documented. Thus the credit manager can get some idea of the value of the free assets. These free assets may be used in two ways. First, they are salable in distress conditions, and second, they represent a potential borrowing base for the applicant. The applicant may, under certain circumstances, be technically insolvent; yet by a lengthening of debt maturity, based on the free collateral, the solvency question may be resolved. The free assets may be used as security against a longer-term loan. Remember that these assets do not provide cash flow to service and/or to settle the outstanding obligations. While it is not in the best interests of the supplier to have customers insolvent, these situations do arise on occasion. Thus a reasonable free balance of highly marketable assets is a desired condition.

Conditions

The last of the five C's is *conditions,* which refer to the current and expected general economic situations as they affect a supplier/customer contract. The phase of the business cycle must be interpreted as specific to the individual customer.

The credit manager is concerned with the financial strength of the applicant relative to the severity of an adverse movement in business conditions. The applicant may have significant collateral yet lack liquidity. In adversity this applicant might fail and experience forced sale to secure liquidity. Thus the impact of adverse economic conditions on a firm may result in a departure from the norm. The strength of a firm depends not only upon its financial structure but also upon the relationship of its structure to the particular phase of the business cycle. A firm may be secure under one set of circumstances; but if these conditions change, the firm may be insecure. As in other cases, the issue is one of financial balance under conditions of risk.

Ad Hoc Scoring Model

The importance of the five C's is that they cause the credit manager to consider the overall financial and operational circumstances of both her or his firm and of the applicant. It is not unusual for the credit manager

TABLE 11.1
Credit Application Summary

Assign points in the range of 0 to 15. The higher the points assigned, the more favorable is your evaluation.

				Points
Character				
Average past payment		On time		
		Up to 30 days late		_____
		Up to 60 days late		
Capacity				
Profit margin	0% – 5%	6% – 12%	13% – 20%	_____
Quick ratio	<1.0	1 – 2	>2.0	_____
Cash flow	Low	Average	High	_____
Capital				
Current ratio	<2.0	2 – 3	>3.0	_____
Debt to equity	<1.0	1 – 2	>2.0	_____
Interest earned	<2×	2× – 3×	>3×	_____
Collateral				
Net worth	Low	Average	High	_____
Percent assets free	Low	Average	High	_____
Market value of net worth	Low	Average	High	_____
Conditions				
	Recession	Average	Prosperity	_____
			Total points	_____

to design an *ad hoc scoring model* to encompass the five C's. Table 11.1 provides an example.

In each of the items in Table 11.1, a high degree of subjective judgment is required. As an example, the credit manager must make a subjective decision concerning whether or not a quick ratio of 1:1 differs substantially from a ratio of 1.1:1. Many of the items are divided among low-average-high. Who, or what, distinguishes among these categories? If in the illustration point values can range from a low of 0 to a high of 15, then the total score can range from 0 to 165 points. The next problem becomes, What constitutes an acceptable score for credit extension?

Evaluation

This system creates almost as many problems as it attempts to solve. Why did the managers only include 11 items? How did they decide on the various steps in each category? Where do they get their information? Does an applicant have to receive a minimum value in each group to be acceptable? Does a forecast of recession change any of the values in the other items, and conversely, does a forecast of prosperity outweigh a negative value of another item? The answers to these questions are critical to the success of the firm and deserve substantial debate before resolution.

Each firm has its own criteria in the establishment of this system. The credit manager subjectively determines which of the items are relatively more important variables and to what degree. Each variable is assigned a threshold value for acceptable performance, and the applicant's credentials are measured against this list. The applicant's total points are determined and then compared with a predetermined, overall, minimum acceptable value. If the credit manager prepares the system carefully and has properly evaluated the data supplied by the applicant, then the decision should have a reasonable expectation of success.

Window Dressing

While a good system is critical, its results are influenced by the data input. The following example is offered to call attention to problems that might arise in interpreting the data supplied by the applicant. Assume that a point method is used that relies strictly on the current ratio of the applicant. Also, assume that the minimum acceptable ratio is 6:1. The balance sheets in Table 11.2 indicate that applicant A is denied credit whereas applicant B receives it.

The two balance sheets shown in Table 11.2 could be of the same applicant at virtually the same time. In this case the difference for B is that this applicant knew of the firm's standards and simply adjusted the figures in balance sheet A to produce the desired ratio. This operation is referred to as *window dressing* since $28 is taken from the cash account

TABLE 11.2
Analysis of Credit Applicants

Applicant A's balance sheet

Cash	$100	Payables	$200
Receivables	960	Equity	860

Current ratio: 5.3

Applicant B's balance sheet

Cash	$ 72	Payables	$172
Receivables	960	Equity	860

Current ratio: 6

---

and is used to reduce payables to produce a current ratio of 6:1. Is there any real change between A and B? This operation reduced cash and payables an equal amount, and net working capital has not changed. Liquidity, however, may be lower. Although payables are lower, the balance sheet fails to indicate *off – balance sheet* liabilities and all future known liabilities that will be paid after this date. Also, the reduction in cash could possibly threaten any minimum cash position requirements imposed by creditors.

There are other ways the applicant could produce the desired result, but they all indicate that if the credit manager establishes an evaluation system of the type just suggested, then he or she must be aware of the possible bias within the system because of poor design. In addition, the credit manager must investigate and carefully consider the information offered by potential customers.

Credit managers who use simple point scoring systems usually recognize the difficulties inherent in them. They believe, and rightly so, that these systems are better than nothing at all. They allow organization of the applicant's information within the parameters of what management believes to be important. The following sections discuss more complex models for capturing information.

Simple Probability Model

The acceptance or rejection of a specific credit request must be made by the credit manager with care and with reason. While the past payment record of the applicant may be the single most important item, the credit manager must question the future financial viability of the applicant. This task is made easier if the applicant is considered from the perspective of expected cash flow contributions to the supplier's firm. A decision rule can be established that indicates that the firm should extend credit or should carry an existing customer as long as the probability of the customer paying is equal to or greater than some predetermined level.

For example, let us assume that

probability of collection = P,
probability of noncollection = $1 - P$,
sales = S,

and cost of sales is as follows:

variable production costs = vS,
finance charge per month = fS,
collection charge per month on overdue accounts = c,

where v and f are decimal proportions. Breakeven for this problem implies that the expected profit of a successful sale equals the expected cost of an uncollectible sale:

$$P(S - vS - fS - c) = (1 - P)(vS + fS + c).$$

Expected profit   Expected cost   (11.1)

Solving in terms of P yields

$$P = \frac{vS + fS + c}{S}.$$ (11.2)

The breakeven probability (P) is the total cost – to – sales ratio (which is less than or equal to one). This relationship may be used to solve for the probability of collection for any number of months into the future.[1]

ILLUSTRATION 11.1

Assume that $S = \$22.71$, $v = 0.7$, $f = 0.01$ per month, and $c = \$2$ per month for each month that the bill is overdue. Terms are net one month. The breakeven probabilities of sales collections, using Eq. (11.2), are as follows:

$$\text{by the due date} = \frac{0.7 \times \$22.71 + 0.00 \times \$22.71 + \$0}{\$22.71} = 70.0\%,$$

$$\text{one month late} = \frac{0.7 \times \$22.71 + 0.01 \times \$22.71 + \$2}{\$22.71} = 79.8\%,$$

$$\text{two months late} = \frac{0.7 \times \$22.71 + 0.02 \times \$22.71 + \$4}{\$22.71} = 89.6\%.$$

The breakeven point changes over time because of the impact of assessed collection and finance charges. Other cost variables could be included and the flows discounted (as was done in Appendix C in Chapter 9) to better reflect the costs of credit. The results here are conventional in that they indicate that the firm needs a higher degree of assurity of payment as the account ages.   □

In Chapter 10 Markov chain analysis was used to determine the probabilities of payment and bad debts, given that accounts were aged by initial state. This information is used in conjunction with the breakeven data just developed to determine how long uncollected accounts should remain

---

[1] This analysis is consistent with acceptance cost/rejection cost analysis, which in turn is equivalent to the discounted cash flow approach. Some people recommend that the profit be eliminated from sales before the finance charge is applied. If this approach is followed, the term fS in Eq. (11.2) would change to vfS. We do not use this approach since finance charges are usually based on the sales amount, not the cost amount.

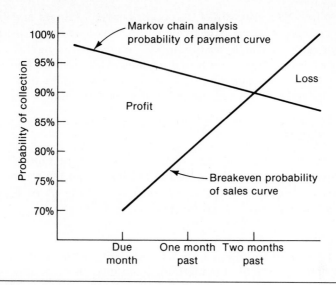

FIGURE 11.1
Breakeven Analysis of Accounts Receivable

on the books before they are deemed uncollectible. Figure 11.1 depicts the results.

The decreasing curve in Fig. 11.1 depicts the probability of accounts being paid when they are current, when they are one month past due, and when they are two months past due. The increasing curve indicates the probability of payment that is necessary for the firm to break even. *Wherever the probability of payment curve exceeds the breakeven probability curve, a profitable sale is expected to result.* Conversely, wherever the probability of payment curve is less than the breakeven probability of collection curve, a loss is expected from the sale. Thus the analysis indicates that if management intends to expand through incremental sales to customers with payment problems of the type shown in Table 10.4, and does so with the costs described previously, then it should not extend credit for any longer than three months (two months past due). At this point in time the probability of collecting an outstanding account is reduced to 88 percent, and the expected-value profit/cost indifference is 91 percent.

Linear Discriminant Model

Linear discriminant models have been used in credit selection decisions for several years. These models attempt to discriminate among customers on the basis of a profile of several variables. The linear discriminant function is expressed as a score based on the linear relationship between variables.

This score indicates an indifference point between success and failure of customers relative to some objective relationship of similar customers. The basis of the score is usually past financial data and, consequently, is biased by this procedure. The basic strength of linear discriminant models is that they do relate, in an objective fashion, several variables that the credit manager deems important to the evaluation of customers.

The Model

Assume that the credit manager feels that the current ratio (R) and the debt-to-equity ratio (L) of the applicant are important for assessing credit risk — they are not contaminated by window dressing. A multiple linear discriminant model would then be specified as follows:

$$Z = b_0(R) + b_1(L), \tag{11.3}$$

where Z is the *score* and the b_i's are the *coefficients* of the ratios.

The mathematics of this method is outlined in Appendix A of this chapter. In summary, the theory of discriminant analysis implies that if the credit manager can compare the past financial data of customers with the individual success or failure of these customers over time, then like applicants in the future should behave in a similar fashion. This assumption is not unreasonable since its basis is the data of success or failure of these customers over time relative to their behavior of honoring their credit contract. In the past the credit manager extended credit to these customers to determine which ones would prove to be good customers and which would not. However, discriminant models can be sensitive to changing economic conditions. A prudent procedure is for the credit manager to periodically evaluate the model to ensure that it has not significantly changed with the passage of time.

The criterion of success is the absence of financial difficulty in paying the outstanding receivable. If the Z score is to discriminate between good and bad applicants, then the score should be significantly different for each type of customer. Thus the credit manager should be able to determine an *indifference* or *cutoff point* between the different risk categories such that new applicants can be evaluated by using the discriminant model.

A new applicant's score can be calculated by multiplying the current ratio by b_0 and the leverage ratio by b_1. If the applicant's score is in the rejection region, this result is viewed as strong evidence for not extending credit. Credit will be extended if, in the opinion of the credit manager, this applicant has other significant attributes such as never having been delinquent or alway paying, albeit late. The point is that this system offers a better approach to credit evaluation than does the simple five C's point system. It still does not, however, replace the intelligence of a well-trained credit manager or analyst; it supplements her or his knowledge.

ILLUSTRATION 11.2

Assume that in the past year the majority of the firm's customers fulfilled their credit contracts, yet a few were delinquent. The credit manager requests that all credit applicants submit audited financial statements. In this way the credit manager has the current ratio and the leverage ratio of each customer prior to the extension of credit. At a later period management conducts an analysis of credit customers to determine the result of extending credit. The customers are divided into successful or delinquent groups, depending upon the outcome of the credit extension. The ratios and Z scores of each customer are shown in Table 11.3.

The Z scores range from a low of -1.53 (for customer 14) to a high of 2.96 (for customer 10), with no scores between -0.82 and 1.07. Any credit applicant with a score of 1.08 (the lowest successful score) or greater is offered credit, whereas any applicant with a score of -0.83 (the highest delinquent score) or less is denied credit. Any applicant whose score falls between -0.82 and 1.07 is investigated further before credit is granted or denied.   □

TABLE 11.3
Classification of Credit Customers

Customers	Current ratio	Leverage ratio	Z score
Successful			
1	3.0	0.6	1.08
2	3.3	0.2	1.92
3	3.9	0.3	2.17
4	4.0	0.4	2.07
5	2.9	0.5	1.17
6	2.7	0.3	1.35
7	3.0	0.2	1.72
8	3.1	0.6	1.14
9	4.2	0.7	1.73
10	4.6	0.1	2.96
Delinquent			
11	1.0	1.0	−0.92
12	0.9	0.9	−0.83
13	1.1	1.2	−1.17
14	0.8	1.3	−1.53
	$Z = 0.6782(R) - 1.5969(L)$		

Note: See Appendix A for the calculations.

Concerns

This system seems to offer the credit manager a relatively simple method for evaluating credit applicants. As with any statistical technique, though, there are a number of possible problems. For example, are the ratios employed in the model the best ratios, or are they even usable as an indication of future success of credit customers? Throughout this text many warnings have been given about the possibility of firms' using creative accounting methods. It is folly to suggest that customers, as a general rule, establish accounting procedures to defraud. However, manipulation of accounting data is done frequently in order to allow the firm to gain some advantage. Thus the credit manager has no guarantee that the ratios selected are the best indicators of creditworthiness.

The Z scores in Table 11.3 were designed to give clear signals of successful and delinquent customers. Generally, there is an overlap of the groups. In this case the credit manager must decide what is desirable, what is not desirable, and where the "maybe" range is. Also, if two variables are good, possibly three or more are even better. The question of how many variables to include can only be determined through analysis and testing of the model. In reality, how many variables end up in the final model is a subjective decision.

Sequential Decision System

Collection of information is costly and time-consuming. It is to the firm's benefit to expedite the decision process as much as possible. In this context the standard rule of marginal analysis is applied: Continue the process until marginal cost equals marginal revenue. The essence of the rule is that some applicants are better than others and therefore need less evaluation. While the credit manager is concerned with all credit accounts, he or she should be more concerned with the marginal accounts and leave the clear-cut applications to be handled in a routine fashion. This technique is the very nature of the *sequential decision approach*.[2]

This system is based on several principles. First, information gathering is costly and time-consuming, as mentioned above. Second, some information is virtually impossible to gather, while other information is useless. Third, past experience with the applicant is meaningful and may be used as a predictor of the future.

The intention in using this system is to facilitate the granting of credit. In this regard there are three possible outcomes for each application: grant

---

[2] A more comprehensive exposition of the approach is given in an article by Dileep Mehta, "The Formulation of Credit Policy Models," *Management Science* (October 1968): B30 – B50.

the credit, refuse the credit, or postpone the decision. Each of these decisions has its own associated cost.

If the credit is granted, then the firm may experience the costs of nonpayment. These costs include the following:

☐ The variable costs of the goods sold.

☐ The opportunity cost of the investment in the accounts receivable.

☐ The average collection cost.

If the credit is not granted, the cost includes the opportunity cost of the lost contribution margin. If the decision is postponed in order to investigate the applicant further, then the incremental cost is the cost of further investigation. These incremental costs must be included in the costs of the subsequent rejection or approval decision.

TABLE 11.4
Accounts Receivable Payment and Cost Data

	Initial state		
	0	1	2
From Table 10.6			
Probability of an account that starts in state *i* and ends in state *j*: Initial state:*			
0	0.664	0.248	0.088
1	0.335	0.491	0.174
2	0.311	0.199	0.490
From Table 10.8			
Probability of:			
Payment	0.979	0.947	0.884
Bad debt	0.021	0.053	0.116
From this chapter			
Sales per customer	$22.71		
Variable costs	15.90		
Margin	$ 6.81		
Other costs:			
Finance charge	$0.01 × sales × months overdue		
Collection charge	$2 per month on overdue accounts		
Credit terms	Net 30 days		

* These proportions are calculated from Table 10.6 as follows: 2.17/(2.17 + 0.81 + 0.29) = 0.664, and so on.

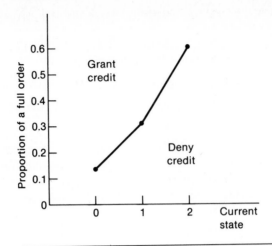

FIGURE 11.2
Indifference Curve for Granting or Refusing Credit, Based on Accounts in State 0

In Chapter 10 we noted that management could make predictions on the basis of past experience of customers at the static state with initial-state accounts receivables. This data also provided the average size of a sale. Earlier, this chapter provided a breakeven cost/benefit analysis of accounts receivable. Both data groups can be used in the sequential decision process. Table 11.4 summarizes information needed for this analysis.

If these customers request credit, the opportunity cost of granting credit becomes the cost of nonpayment of the debt, or in order words, the cost the firm incurs by making a wrong decision. In the same sense, if the firm refuses to grant credit, the opportunity cost is the margin forgone when the correct decision was to allow credit, that is, the cost incurred by making a wrong decision. Using the data of Table 11.4 and testing according to the states 0, 1, and 2, we can determine the opportunity costs. These calculations are shown in Appendix B, Part 1. Figure 11.2 summarizes the results. Conceptually, the calculations are made by *equating the incremental costs incurred in extending credit to nonpaying customers to the incremental profits lost by not extending credit to customers who would pay.*

An analysis of Fig. 11.2 indicates the following three points:

1. For accounts presently in state 0 the opportunity cost of refusing to extend credit for new orders is greater than the opportunity cost of granting credit whenever more than 0.136 of a full order is placed.

2. For accounts presently in state 1 the opportunity cost of refusing

credit for new orders is greater than the opportunity cost of granting credit whenever more than 0.310 of a full order is placed.

3. For accounts presently in state 2 the opportunity cost of refusing credit for new orders is greater than the opportunity cost of granting credit whenever more than 0.603 of an order is placed.

The conclusion is that the credit manager should not arbitrarily grant new credit to any account. The granting of credit (and profitability) depends on the size of the potential new order. It may not be in the firm's best interest to immediately refuse credit for quantities less than the indifference values. Additional information might prove the orders to be worthwhile.

Additional information may be supplied by a *point evaluation system*. This system is expensive and time-consuming, but it can be useful. Assume that customers presently in state 1 can be divided into three subgroups having the characteristics shown in Table 11.5. The collection period information has been upgraded by investigation. That is, the information of the N^{-1} matrix (of Chapter 10) has been replaced by new estimates.

The opportunity costs of granting or refusing credit to group 1 is determined by combining the payment and cost data in Table 11.4 with that of Table 11.5. The calculations are shown in Appendix B, Part 2. Figure 11.3 summarizes the new decision rules.

The original data for state 1 (Fig. 11.2) indicated that for orders of less than 0.310 unit credit should be refused. Further investigation (Fig. 11.3) by the credit manager indicates that credit should be extended if the applicant is classified as having a good credit rating and orders at least 0.076 of a full order; otherwise, credit should be refused. If the applicant has an average credit rating, then credit should be extended if at least 0.334 order is placed. Credit should only be extended to customers in the poor-rating category if they order at least 1.23 units. Similar analyses can be conducted on customers initially denied credit who are in states 0 and 2.

TABLE 11.5
Subgrouping Data for State 1 Accounts

Rating	Probability of payment	Probability of bad debts	Probability of collection in period			Per-period marginal collection costs
			0	1	2	
Good	0.99	0.01	0.40	0.55	0.05	$0.75
Average	0.96	0.04	0.35	0.35	0.30	2.00
Poor	0.89	0.11	0.25	0.10	0.65	3.50

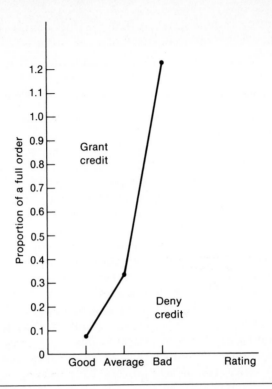

FIGURE 11.3
Indifference Curve for Granting or Refusing Credit, Using the Point Evaluation System

The information derived from the point evaluation system is useful in structuring a cost function for the linear discriminant model examined earlier. From the information of Table 11.3 the credit manager believes that customers who default on credit usually have a Z score of -0.83 or less, and customers who usually pay their outstanding credit have a score

TABLE 11.6
Summary of Credit Information

Z score	Probability of payment	Probability of bad debt	Probability of collection in period			Marginal collection costs
			0	1	2	
≤−0.83	0.10	0.90	0.20	0.10	0.70	$3.50
≥1.08	0.95	0.05	0.30	0.60	0.10	0.75

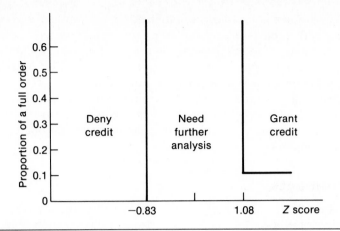

FIGURE 11.4
Indifference Curve for Granting or Refusing Credit, Using the Linear Discriminant Model

of 1.08 or more. Experience may indicate that these two groups have the characteristics shown in Table 11.6.

The data of Table 11.6 can be combined with the opportunity costs of granting and refusing credit to determine a new opportunity cost schedule for credit by using the discriminant model. The calculations are shown in Appendix B, Part 3. Figure 11.4 summarizes the results.

From the figure the credit manager would conclude that applicants with a linear discriminant Z score of -0.83 or less should always be denied credit. If the score is 1.08 or more, credit should be granted if at least 0.109 order is placed. For orders less than 0.109, the cost of granting credit exceeds the cost of refusing credit. Applicants in this situation, and applicants whose scores fall between -0.83 and 1.08, need to be evaluated in a different way. The best method is to conduct a thorough credit analysis of the applicant.

With the use of additional investigation the credit manager has better information for making the credit decision. A reasonable conclusion is that this approach results in improved probability of collection of accounts and better overall profitability of the company. This conclusion is reasonable since the analyses are based on equating marginal benefits to marginal costs.

Summary

This chapter examined a number of techniques for determining who should receive credit. A simplistic approach is to use a point estimation model based on the five C's of credit. Such a model has two basic problems:

The categorization of applicants into high, low, average, and so on, is subjective; and credit evaluation costs are generally ignored.

The remaining models discussed in this chapter are based on statistical probability concepts and incorporate cost functions. The Markov chain analysis of Chapter 10 is incorporated into the decision process in order to determine marginal revenues and marginal costs. Since economic profits are maximized whenever marginal revenue equals marginal cost, credit managers can use these models to help attain the shareholder wealth – maximizing objective.

Key Concepts

Five C's of credit
Indifference value of X
Linear discriminant model
Marginal breakeven point

Opportunity cost of credit
Sequential decision making
Window dressing

Appendix A
Fundamentals of Discriminant Analysis

Discriminant analysis begins with the wish to statistically categorize two or more groups of cases, such as good and bad credit risks or solvent and insolvent companies. To distinguish between the groups, the analyst selects a collection of discriminating variables that measure characteristics on which the groups are expected to differ. The mathematical objective of discriminant analysis is to weigh and linearly combine the discriminating variables in some fashion so that the groups are forced to be as statistically distinct as possible. In other words, the analyst wants to be able to discriminate between the groups in the sense of being able to tell them apart.

Discriminant analysis attempts to form one or more linear combinations of the discriminating variables. These discriminant functions are of the form

$$Z_i = b_{i1}X_1 + \cdots + b_{ip}X_p,$$

where Z_i is the score on the discriminant function i, the b's are weighting coefficients, and the X's are the standardized values of the p discriminating variables used in the analysis. The maximum number of functions that can be derived is equal to one less than either the number of groups or the number of discriminating variables, whichever is less. The functions are formed in such a way as to maximize the separation of the groups.

An example based on two groups and two variables follows. The variables used to discriminate are simply called R and L. Group 1 has 10 observations, and group 2 has 4 observations. Table A.1 shows the calculation of the discriminant function.

The b_i coefficients can be interpreted much as they are in regression analysis. They serve to identify the variables that contribute most to differentiating the function.

The discriminant function for this two-variable model is

$$Z = 0.6782R - 1.5969L.$$

This model can be used to classify observations. Assuming that variables R and L provide satisfactory discrimination for cases with known group membership, a set of classification functions can be derived that will permit the classification of new cases with unknown memberships.

TABLE A.1
Two-Variable Discriminant Function

Observation	R	L	$(R - \bar{R})$	$(R - \bar{R})^2$	$(L - \bar{L})$	$(L - \bar{L})^2$	$(R - \bar{R})(L - \bar{L})$
Group 1							
1	3.0	0.6	−0.47	0.2209	0.21	0.0441	−0.0987
2	3.3	0.2	−0.17	0.0289	−0.19	0.0361	0.0323
3	3.9	0.3	0.43	0.1849	−0.09	0.0081	−0.0387
4	4.0	0.4	0.53	0.2809	0.01	0.0001	0.0053
5	2.9	0.5	−0.57	0.3249	0.11	0.0121	−0.0627
6	2.7	0.3	−0.77	0.5929	−0.09	0.0081	0.0693
7	3.0	0.2	−0.47	0.2209	−0.19	0.0361	0.0893
8	3.1	0.6	−0.37	0.1369	0.21	0.0441	−0.0777
9	4.2	0.7	0.73	0.5329	0.31	0.0961	0.2263
10	4.6	0.1	1.13	1.2769	−0.29	0.0841	−0.0290
Sum	34.7	3.9		3.8010		0.3690	0.0674
Average	3.47	.39					
	(a)	(b)		(c)		(d)	(e)
Group 2							
1	1.0	1.0	0.05	0.0025	−0.10	0.0100	−0.0050
2	0.9	0.9	−0.05	0.0025	−0.20	0.0400	0.0100
3	1.1	1.2	0.15	0.0225	0.10	0.0100	0.0150
4	0.8	1.3	−0.15	0.0225	0.20	0.0400	−0.0300
Sum	3.8	4.4		0.0500		0.1000	−0.0100
Average	0.95	1.1					
	(f)	(g)		(h)		(i)	(j)

$$b_1 = \frac{(a - f)(d + i) - (b - g)(e + j)}{(c + h)(d + i) - (e + j)^2} = 0.6782$$

$$b_2 = \frac{(b - g)(c + h) - (a - f)(e + j)}{(c + h)(d + i) - (e + j)^2} = -1.5969$$

Appendix B
Calculation of Indifference Values

The calculations shown in the three parts of this appendix are more detailed than necessary. The details have been provided for the convenience of those readers who have difficulty understanding the relevant costs. The calculations are simply identification of incremental costs and benefits incurred by either granting or refusing credit. The following discussion uses the state 0 results to explain the input to the equations.

The number 0.021 represents the probability of a customer who is granted credit who will not pay. The number 15.90 is the dollar sales margin associated with a sale before any financing or collection costs are incurred. Thus if a sale is uncollectible, this amount will be lost. The next series of decimal numbers — 0.664, 0.248, and 0.088 — are the probabilities that an account, presently in state 0, will end in state 0, state 1, and state 2, respectively. These numbers are calculated from Table 11.4 as follows: $2.17/3.27 = 0.664$, $0.81/3.27 = 0.248$, and $0.29/3.27 = 0.088$. The numbers within the brackets are as follows, reading from left to right: (the finance charge of 1%) × (state i) × (the sale value per unit × units sold — which is an unknown called X) + (collection charge) × (state i), where $i = 0, 1, 2$. The unknown X represents the number of orders, with $X = 1$ being a full order for $22.71.

Part 1: Opportunity Cost of Granting or Refusing Credit, Based on the Current State

The current state is 0; credit is granted. The opportunity cost is

$$(0.021)\{15.90X$$
$$+ 0.664[0.01(0)(22.71X) + 2(0)]$$
$$+ 0.248[0.01(1)(22.71X) + 2(1)]$$
$$+ 0.088[0.01(2)(22.71X) + 2(2)]\}$$
$$= 0.336X + 0.018.$$

The current state is 0; credit is refused. The opportunity cost is

$$(0.979)\{6.81X$$
$$- 0.664[0.01(0)(22.71X) + 2(0)]$$
$$- 0.248[0.01(1)(22.71X) + 2(1)]$$
$$- 0.088[0.01(2)(22.71X) + 2(2)]\}$$
$$= 6.573X - 0.830.$$

Also,

indifference value for $X = 0.136$.

The current state is 1; credit is granted. The opportunity cost is

$(0.053)\{15.90X$
$\quad + 0.335[0.01(0)(22.71X) + 2(0)]$
$\quad + 0.491[0.01(1)(22.71X) + 2(1)]$
$\quad + 0.174[0.01(2)(22.71X) + 2(2)]\}$
$\quad = 0.853X + 0.089.$

The current state is 1; credit is refused. The opportunity cost is

$(0.947)\{6.81X$
$\quad - 0.335[0.01(0)(22.71X) + 2(0)]$
$\quad - 0.491[0.01(1)(22.71X) + 2(1)]$
$\quad - 0.174[0.01(2)(22.71X) + 2(2)]\}$
$\quad = 6.269X - 1.589.$

Also,

indifference value for $X = 0.310$.

The current state is 2; credit is granted. The opportunity cost is

$(0.116)\{15.90X$
$\quad + 0.311[0.01(0)(22.71X) + 2(0)]$
$\quad + 0.199[0.01(1)(22.71X) + 2(1)]$
$\quad + 0.490[0.01(2)(22.71X) + 2(2)]\}$
$\quad = 1.875X + 0.274.$

The current state is 2; credit is refused. The opportunity cost is

$(0.884)\{6.81X$
$\quad - 0.311[0.01(0)(22.71X) + 2(0)]$
$\quad - 0.199[0.01(1)(22.71X) + 2(1)]$
$\quad - 0.490[0.01(2)(22.71X) + 2(2)]\}$
$\quad = 5.783X - 2.084.$

Also,

indifference value for $X = 0.603$.

Part 2: Opportunity Costs of Credit to State 1, Using the Point Evaluation System

The credit rating is good; credit is granted. The opportunity cost is

$0.01\{15.90X$
$\quad + 0.40[0.01(0)(22.71X) + 0.75(0)]$
$\quad + 0.55[0.01(1)(22.71X) + 0.75(1)]$

$$+ 0.05[0.01(2)(22.71X) + 0.75(2)]\}$$
$$= 0.160X + 0.005.$$

The credit rating is good; credit is refused. The opportunity cost is

$$0.99\{6.81X$$
$$- 0.40[0.01(0)(22.71X) + 0.75(0)]$$
$$- 0.55[0.01(1)(22.71X) + 0.75(1)]$$
$$- 0.05[0.01(2)(22.71X) + 0.75(2)]\}$$
$$= 6.596X - 0.483.$$

Also,

indifference value for $X = 0.076$.

The credit rating is average; credit is granted. The opportunity cost is

$$0.04\{15.90X$$
$$+ 0.35[0.01(0)(22.71X) + 2(0)]$$
$$+ 0.35[0.01(1)(22.71X) + 2(1)]$$
$$+ 0.30[0.01(2)(22.71X) + 2(2)]\}$$
$$= 0.645X + 0.076.$$

The credit rating is average; credit is refused. The opportunity cost is

$$0.96\{6.81X$$
$$- 0.35[0.01(0)(22.71X) + 2(0)]$$
$$- 0.35[0.01(1)(22.71X) + 2(1)]$$
$$- 0.30[0.01(2)(22.71X) + 2(2)]\}$$
$$= 6.330X - 1.824.$$

Also,

indifference value for $X = 0.334$.

The credit rating is poor; credit is granted. The opportunity cost is

$$0.11\{15.90X$$
$$+ 0.25[0.01(0)(22.71X) + 2(0)]$$
$$+ 0.10[0.01(1)(22.71X) + 2(1)]$$
$$+ 0.65[0.01(2)(22.71X) + 2(2)]\}$$
$$= 1.784X + 0.539.$$

The credit rating is poor; credit is refused. The opportunity cost is

$$0.89\{6.81X$$
$$- 0.25[0.01(0)(22.71X) + 2(0)]$$
$$- 0.10[0.01(1)(22.71X) + 2(1)]$$
$$- 0.65[0.01(2)(22.71X) + 2(2)]\}$$
$$= 5.778X - 4.361.$$

Also,

indifference value for $X = 1.227$.

Part 3: Opportunity Costs of Granting or Refusing Credit, Based on the Linear Discriminant Model

The Z score is less than or equal to -0.83; credit is granted. The opportunity cost is

$$0.9\{15.90X$$
$$+ 0.20[0.01(0)(22.71X) + 3.5(0)]$$
$$+ 0.10[0.01(1)(22.71X) + 3.5(1)]$$
$$+ 0.70[0.01(2)(22.71X) + 3.5(2)]\}$$
$$= 14.617X + 4.725.$$

The Z score is less than or equal to -0.83; credit is refused. The opportunity cost is

$$0.1\{6.81X$$
$$- 0.20[0.01(0)(22.71X) + 3.5(0)]$$
$$- 0.10[0.01(1)(22.71X) + 3.5(1)]$$
$$- 0.70[0.01(2)(22.71X) + 3.5(2)]\}$$
$$= 0.647X - 5.25.$$

Also,

indifference value for $X = -0.376$.

The Z score is greater than or equal to 1.08; credit is granted. The opportunity cost is

$$0.05\{15.90X$$
$$+ 0.30[0.01(0)(22.71X) + 0.75(0)]$$
$$+ 0.60[0.01(1)(22.71X) + 0.75(1)]$$
$$+ 0.10[0.01(2)(22.71X) + 0.75(2)]\}$$
$$= 0.804X + 0.030.$$

The Z score is greater than or equal to 1.08; credit is refused. The opportunity cost is

$$0.95\{6.81X$$
$$- 0.30[0.01(0)(22.71X) + 0.75(0)]$$
$$- 0.60[0.01(1)(22.71X) + 0.75(1)]$$
$$- 0.10[0.01(2)(22.71X) + 0.75(2)]\}$$
$$= 6.297X - 0.570.$$

Also,

indifference value for $X = 0.109$.

Questions

1. Indicate the sources of credit information. Which are the most expensive? Which provide the best information?

2. Credit managers generally give more weight to character than to any of the other five C's. Explain.

3. What is meant by the term *window dressing?* Explain whether or not you think it an honorable practice.

4. What is the advantage of an *ad hoc* point-scoring model? What are the disadvantages?

5. Discuss the advantages and disadvantages of using a linear discriminant analysis model for evaluating credit risk.

6. Describe an approach for handling numerous small accounts when making credit decisions. Will your system differ for large accounts?

7. When management chooses credit customers, what should its attitude be toward bad-debt losses?

Problems

1. The Wellington Fabricating Company has a large number of customers. Credit losses are about normal for the industry, yet customer turnover seems relatively high. No formalized, consistent credit analysis is performed on credit applicants. Management wants this practice changed and has given you the responsibility of developing a point system. The information shown in Table 11.7 has been gathered from the credit files.

(a) If you assign 15 points to each classification, what will be your good, average, and bad customer scores?

(b) Discuss the relative value of each piece of information to the total.

(c) Should each type of information be weighted the same? If not, how would a different weighting system influence the results?

(d) Discuss what other information might be included.

(e) How might the credit manager apply this information to new customers?

TABLE 11.7
Credit Application Survey Information on Customers' Characteristics

Customer	1	2	3	4	5	6	7	8	9	10
Past 10 payments										
On time	4	5	10	4	7	6	9	4	0	2
30 days late	4	2	0	5	3	0	0	5	8	2
60 days late	2	3	0	1	0	4	1	1	2	6
Profit margin										
5% or less				X	X	X				
6% to 12%	X	X						X	X	X
13% or more			X							X
Quick ratio										
< 2	X			X	X					X
2 to 3		X					X	X	X	
> 3			X						X	
Inventory turnover										
< 4	X			X	X	X		X		
4 to 7		X					X			
> 7			X						X	X
Debt/equity										
< 1	X			X				X	X	
1 to 2		X	X			X	X			
> 2					X					X
Times interest earned										
< 2			X	X					X	X
2 to 3		X					X	X		
> 3	X				X	X				
Net worth										
Low										
Average	X	X	X	X	X	X	X	X	X	X
High										
Percent free assets										
Low		X		X		X				
Average	X		X				X	X	X	X
High					X					

2.   Change the probabilities of payment and bad debts in Table 11.4 to those shown in the following table:

	Initial state		
	0	*1*	*2*
Payment	0.95	0.90	0.80
Bad debt	0.05	0.10	0.20

Leave all other information as it is, and determine the opportunity cost of granting or refusing credit based on the initial state. Refer to Appendix B for an example. Discuss your conclusions.

3.   Quigley Containers experiences the following financial conditions: The average sale (S) value is $85, with variable production costs of 0.65S. Monthly finance and collection charges on overdue accounts are 0.015S and $2.50, respectively. Terms of sale are net 30 days.

(a) Determine the breakeven probability of sales collection by (i) the due month, (ii) one month late, (iii) two months late.

(b) Determine how the following situations influence the breakeven probability of sales collection. Evaluate each change independently: (i) Variable cost of sale increases to 0.7S; (ii) average sales value doubles; (iii) finance charge doubles; (iv) collection charge doubles.

(c) Discuss the cause of the results found in (b) as compared to those in (a).

4.   The Albright Company uses Markov chain analysis for credit policy decisions. Recent use of this analysis resulted in the following relationships between the probability of payment (P) and the probability of bad debts (B) by initial states 0, 1, and 2:

	P	B
0	0.90	0.10
1	0.75	0.25
2	0.65	0.35

Average sales values range between a low of $30 and a high of $285, with an expected value of $85. Incremental variable costs are 65% of sales. Monthly finance and collection charges on overdue accounts are 1.5% and $2.50, respectively, of sales. Prepare a graph similar to Fig. 11.1, and discuss the interpretation of the results.

5.   The 13 – 5 Company has been in business since the turn of the century and is now recognized as the leader in its markets. Over these many years the 13 – 5 Company's credit policy has been the model used by the competition. Because of the company's dominance in the markets, management has been able to be relatively selective in who it extends credit to. Recently, the company experienced a substantial increase in delinquent accounts. In an attempt to correct this problem, the credit manager decided to develop a linear discriminant model to evaluate potential credit customers. After sampling past records of customers, the credit manager decided to develop a model that used cash flow as a percentage of sales (C) and inventory turnover (T) as the discriminating variables. Table 11.8 identifies successful and delinquent customers based on these two ratios.

(a) Determine the linear discriminant function from the data.

(b) Apply the function in (a) to the customers, and evaluate the results.

(c) Discuss the application of this procedure in this situation.

TABLE 11.8
Customer Analysis

	Successful			Delinquent	
Customer	C	T	Customer	C	T
1	0.27	15.4	1	0.10	2.7
2	0.19	9.6	2	0.12	5.1
3	0.34	12.9	3	0.30	4.0
4	0.42	10.4	4	0.06	3.7
5	0.20	21.2			
6	0.36	14.7			
7	0.14	8.4			

6. Credit terms are net 30 days. Average sales value is $150, and variable cost is 70% of sales (i.e., $0.7S$).

(a) Determine the maximum carrying charges (i.e., financial and collection charges) the firm could accept in order to simply break even.

(b) If the finance and collection charges per month are $0.05S$ and $7 per account, respectively, and management expects the probability of collection of credit sales to average 90%, how many months can credit accounts be outstanding and still allow a profit?

(c) How many months should the company carry these credit accounts?

7. Assume that sales revenue will be $50, $90, or $145. Variable costs are 65% of the sales level, and the finance charge is 5% of sales per month overdue. A collection charge of $5 per month is incurred on overdue accounts. Markov chain analysis indicates that current accounts are collected 65% of the time, accounts one month old are collected 50% of the time, and accounts two months old are collected 35% of the time.

(a) How long should an account be carried for each sales scenario? Usual terms of sale are net 30 days.

(b) Management has the opportunity to purchase a superior credit investigation system. Experience with this system indicates that the probability of collecting current accounts is 92%, the probability of collecting accounts one month old is 75%, and the probability of collecting accounts two months old is 65%. How much should management pay for the system?

8. Kinderspiel A. G. (KAG) of West Germany is just starting to sell in North America. The firm has successfully used a discriminant analysis model in West Germany to analyze credit risks. The model is

$$Z = 1.6X - 0.5Y,$$

where X is the cash conversion cycle as a percentage of business days per month and Y is the total debt-to-equity ratio.

(a) Given the following information for North American customers, how should KAG rank the prospective clients?

Customer	1	2	3	4	5	6
X	0.6	0.4	0.8	0.2	0.5	0.3
Y	1.4	0.8	2.0	1.6	1.0	1.0

(b) Table 11.9 shows the credit experience KAG has in West Germany. Determine the ranking of customers in part (a), and discuss your results.

TABLE 11.9
Customer Analysis

Customer	Successful		Customer	Delinquent	
	X	Y		X	Y
1	0.6	1.2	9	0.3	2.0
2	0.9	0.8	10	0.9	1.7
3	1.0	1.1	11	0.3	0.9
4	0.4	0.6	12	0.7	1.8
5	0.7	0.0	13	0.8	2.8
6	1.1	0.4			
7	0.9	1.4			
8	0.6	2.5			

Monitoring Accounts Receivable

Monitoring accounts receivable includes an evaluation of the quantity and the quality of outstanding credit accounts as well as the planning and the execution of a collections policy should some of these accounts default. The monitoring of accounts receivable involves at least two aspects: preparation of aggregate information for senior management and analysis at the customer level by the credit manager.

The aggregate information is an overall summary of the results of credit extended and a forecast of credit yet to be extended. Management needs to know, in the opinion of the credit manager, whether economic conditions have shifted significantly to warrant a change in credit policy. In particular, management needs to know how customers have managed the credit extended. Have there been significant changes in payment patterns, and if so, are these changes to be expected in the future? The cash inflows of the firm are directly affected by the pattern of payments; thus any change must be seriously considered.

Traditionally, credit managers use turnover ratios (or their complement, days sales outstanding) and aging schedules to analyze receivables. This chapter reviews these approaches and shows their shortcomings. Techniques that offer better insight into credit management are discussed. Before these better techniques are examined, however, analysis of information and collection procedures are reviewed.

Changes in Payment Habits

A sale facilitated by credit is worthwhile to the firm only if the receivable is eventually collected. The credit manager's functions include the evaluation and the extension of credit to specific customers and the enforcement of the contract. As discussed in the previous chapter, certain information is available to the credit manager concerning each customer before credit is actually extended. Once credit is extended, the manager should be concerned if the customer deviates substantially from her or his expected *payment pattern norm.*

As an example, if an old and well-known company fails to take a discount when it has regularly done so in the past, this behavior may be a signal that the customer is experiencing financial difficulty. The cost of lost discounts is usually high enough to be of major concern.

Change in the customer's payment habits may be the result of any of the following three conditions:

1. Internal change in the customer's firm.
2. A change in the mix of purchases by the customer.
3. Some exogenous change in economic conditions.

In all three cases the credit-extending firm experiences a decrease in its cash inflows and an increase in the probability of default by the customer.

Internal Change

An *internal change* may be caused by one of the following problems:

☐ The payment procedure of the customer faults through some administrative error.

☐ The customer experiences cash flow problems.

☐ The opportunity cost of discounts lost is less than the opportunity cost of funds invested in the customer's firm.

If the problem is the result of an administrative error, then the corrective action can be made quickly, with the result that the customer returns to her or his earlier payment pattern. If the change is a result of cash flow problems, then the possibility of potential insolvency exists. If the opportunity cost of lost discounts is irrelevant to the customer, then the seller's discount policy is apparently meaningless (at least to this customer). It does not facilitate rapid payment of credit sales, since the decrease in the cost of goods is less than the earning power of funds held to the net credit period in the customer's firm.

Each of these conditions stems from a fundamentally different set of circumstances. The credit manager must have some information concerning these conditions so that he or she can properly monitor the account and make appropriate recommendations to senior management.

Change in Product Mix

A *change in the product mix* the customer purchases may cause her or his payment payments to change. As an example, for highly seasonal and high-style products there is a long production and marketing lead time. The high-style product is usually produced and sold long in advance of the consumer market period. Terms of credit for this product may be as long as six to nine months. These terms are frequently referred to as *seasonal-dating terms*. If the firm produces this type of product as well as the more usual shorter – lead time products, with sales to the same customer, then the collection pattern of this customer reflects the type of products purchased.

The usual practice in industrial credit is that all bills are paid by invoice. Thus the credit manager must be informed not only of the amount of credit outstanding but also of the type of product for which credit has not been paid in order to keep collection difficulties to a minimum.

Economic Conditions

Economic conditions have an important influence on the actions of creditors. Economic slowdowns cause creditors to decrease their purchases, to delay their payments, and possibly to deteriorate in terms of credit quality. The overall result is that cash flows and subsequent profits of the credit-granting firms are adversely affected.

Later Payments

The situations just described, while of concern to the credit manager, differ considerably if the customer is *in default*. The term *default* has both a legal meaning and an operating meaning. Legally, default means that the customer has not paid the invoice by the end of the credit period. In an extremely loose operating context, default means that a customer has not paid by her or his usual payment time. Delayed payment can give cause for concern, of course; but unless the customer goes beyond the credit period, the credit manager certainly has no recourse against the customer.

It is not unusual for large firms to miss the discount date of payment yet still take the discount when payment is made. Also, some large firms do not pay by the net credit period. They are financially sound and not considered to be bad debts, even though they are technically in default. There are two possible reasons for this behavior:

1. A cycle payment procedure is used that ignores the seller's discount date.
2. The firm buys on its own terms and not on the terms of the seller.

Both reasons can be summarized by the statement that the large firm simply uses its competitive powers to its own advantage. This situation presents the credit manager with a problem. The manager must decide whether to grant this account special consideration or to enforce the contract and probably lose future sales. This decision is not an easy one, since the profit margin on these accounts is generally assured relative to smaller and less financially strong firms. Usually, management concedes to the larger firm.

However, the majority of sales are made to relatively small firms. These firms have common conditions in that individually they buy only a small percentage of the seller's output and they have relatively limited financial resources. Collectively, these small firms constitute a large proportion of the seller's total sales and take up the majority of the administrative time of the credit department. Owing to the size and the financial similarities of small customers, the credit manager knows that adverse economic conditions will probably affect most of the small firms in a similar fashion. As the country's gross national product decreases and/or interest rates increase, the credit manager expects that sales to and collections from these firms will decrease. Thus the credit manager must monitor these accounts daily and be aware of changing environmental conditions.

The corrective action of the smaller firm's account differs from that of the large firm. The credit manager might attempt to determine the cause of any payment behavior change by direct contact with the customer or by making inquiries to other credit managers who sell to the same customer. If the best information is that the customer is experiencing cash flow problems, then the credit manager might request additional information regarding the ability of the buyer to pay, should an additional order be placed. A warning flag may be put on the account so that the customer will be notified promptly when the account is overdue, which may minimize any possible loss to the seller. If the situation deteriorates further, then immediate action to collect is warranted.

Default Versus Bad Debt

The question of what to do with an account in default is not easily answered. All accounts that are overdue are not bad debts. Most firms with overdue accounts pay, given some additional time. The dividing line between default accounts and bad debts is one that gives credit managers much concern.

When is an account a *bad debt*? Some situations lend themselves to a simple definition: the probability of collection is low, and the probability of future sales or the willingness of the seller to engage in further credit sales to this customer is also low. In this case there is every reason to label this account a bad debt and to attempt full collection by whatever means possible.

The usual situation is that a particular invoice is significantly overdue, yet the customer continues to purchase and pay for additional goods. Is this account a bad debt? Most likely it is not. Although the default invoice can be classified as a bad debt, to do so risks the loss of a customer who apparently has a good payment record in all but this one invoice.

A better practice is to substitute an interim condition so that the credit spectrum becomes good account — disputed account — bad-debt account. Before payment of an invoice is made, all aspects of the invoice (i.e., product quality and quantity, price, sales taxes, and contract conditions) must be correct.

Usually, goods are shipped with transportation documents and a bill of lading, and the invoice is mailed separately. The bill of lading is used by the buyer's receiver to justify the goods being received. The invoice is received by the accounting office and sent to purchasing for approval. This approval amounts to justifying both the physical character of the goods, by matching the invoice with the bill of lading, and the costs, by matching the invoice with the purchase order. A dispute occurs when there is a discrepancy between the documentation and the merchandise received. Generally, these disputes are resolved with relative ease, and the invoice does not linger outstanding as a bad debt.

If disputes are not solved fairly and amicably, they could cost the seller far more through the loss of future sales than through a significant number of bad-debt customers. It is not surprising, then, that many firms have a policy of accepting any returns without question and of satisfying any dispute to the customer's satisfaction.

Corrective action to collect overdue accounts must recognize two possibilities:

1. There exists some chance (however small) that the account can be saved to become a continuing good account.

2. There exists a concern that not only will the firm fail to realize any margin on the sales but the entire sale value will not be collected; that is, cost of sale *plus* profit margin is lost.

Margin Erosion

In both cases just described, the probability of payment decreases as the time from the point of sale increases. This feature was discussed in the two previous chapters. In addition, the costs associated with delinquent accounts increase because of the monthly administrative and financial charges. Thus the expected margin and the sales value decrease over time. Table 12.1 provides an example.

The expected margin from this sale decreases quickly from a planned 25% to a very large loss in five months. In the same sense, the expected value of the collection decreases from $1000 to $50 within the same period. Clearly, the seller has virtually no margin and very little expected value proceeds once the invoice goes unpaid beyond month 1.

TABLE 12.1
Expected Margin and Sales Proceeds

(a) Current period

Sales	$1000
Product costs	750
Margin	$ 250

Overdue accounts incur a $20-per-period cost.

(b) Expected results

Period	Probability of collection	Expected collection	Expected margin*
0	1.00	$1000	$250.00
1	0.90	900	130.00
2	0.75	750	<40.00>
3	0.50	500	<400.00>
4	0.20	200	<630.00>
5	0.05	50	<800.00>

* Determined by probability × sales − [production costs + (period of collection × $20)]. For example, 0.05 × $1000 − [$750 + (5 × $20)] = <$800>.

Assume that the credit manager recognizes that a serious problem of collections exists with any account that is more than two months outstanding from the point of sale. If at that time a collection procedure is initiated, the credit manager can determine an indifference value of the incremental collection procedure. As long as incremental collection charges do not exceed the incremental margin improvements, the firm will gain some margin from the sale.

One result (using the Table 12.1 example) of employing this collection process is that the financial result is substantially improved if the process is implemented in period 1 rather than in later periods. A secondary consideration is that the number of accounts overdue one or two periods is considerably larger than those that would be overdue five periods. The issue becomes how to distinguish a good account from a bad account in earlier periods. The discriminant analysis model discussed in the previous chapter could be used. Current data about the accounts could be put into the model and new Z scores calculated. The accounts would be classified as good or bad on the basis of their new scores. Most likely what is required is a thorough analysis of the accounts, done by a credit analyst. If the accounts' payment patterns are substantially changed, the credit manager must be concerned with the cause of this change.

The remainder of this chapter discusses techniques that can be used to evaluate accounts receivable.

Traditional Analysis

The monitoring of accounts receivable can be complex. Most credit managers attempt to ascertain the overall status of receivables by analyzing the aggregate balance outstanding. Many factors influence this balance, with the result that a number of the factors may offset each other. Nevertheless, credit managers continue to employ aggregate models because of the ease of calculating performance indexes. The traditional models used are days sales outstanding and aging schedules.

Days Sales Outstanding

When managers monitor total accounts receivable, the most prevalent method they use is the *days sales outstanding* (DSO) *procedure*. This method attempts to express accounts receivable as a number of equivalent days of credit sales:

$$DSO = \frac{\text{accounts receivable}}{\text{sales/number of days in the period}}.$$

For example, on an annual basis, if daily credit sales equal $10 and accounts receivable equal $30, then it is expected that current credit sales will not be collected for 3 days [i.e., $30/($3600/360)].

However, this conclusion may not be sensible. The numerator and the denominator are both historical numbers, whereas the interpretation of the ratio is a projection. It is often argued that the DSO is not intended to be used in this fashion but, rather, as a comparative measure of one period with another. The measure is only used to report a general trend between periods so that management has an index of comparison. If the intention of the analyst is to study the collection of a specific day's sales, then some other analytical method must be used.

A change in any of the conditions that govern the accounts receivable balance makes the interpretation of the DSO index difficult. If the DSO index does not change, but the firm adds new credit customers and/or prices change, then the meaning of the DSO index is obscure. The DSO measure simply will not answer questions concerning the impact on cash flow and the firm's investment in receivables from credit sales.[1]

---

[1] Much of the material in this and the next section is attributed to Wilber G. Lewellen and Robert W. Johnson, "Better Way to Monitor Accounts Receivable," *Harvard Business Review* (May – June 1972): 101 – 109; and Bernell K. Stone, "The Payments-Pattern Approach to the Forecasting and Control of Accounts Receivable," *Financial Management* (Autumn 1976): 65 – 82.

ILLUSTRATION 12.1

Table 12.2 can be used to illustrate some of the problems with the DSO index. Keep in mind that credit sales are the result of two forces:

1. The general economic climate and how it applies to the firm's products.
2. The general efficiency of the selling firm's sales, production, and shipping functions, and its credit-granting policy.

A change in one or more of these forces affects current and future sales (both cash and credit sales). In the same way, the accounts receivable balance is affected by the credit payment pattern of all customers.

The data of Table 12.2 indicate that the sales have a large seasonal effect, with the high sales period occurring in the fifth month. The collection pattern is the same for each month; that is, collections of the month are comprised of 20% current sales, 40% from last month's sales, and 40% from sales of two months ago. Accounts receivable, thus, are comprised of 80% of current sales and 40% of last month's sales. No bad debts exist. Total collections increase from $100 in month 1 to a maximum of $185 in month 6, and then they fall back to $100 in month 11. Accounts receivable increase from $120 in month 1 to a maximum of $230 in month 5. They decrease to $120 in month 10.

TABLE 12.2
Sales, Collections, and Accounts Receivable ($000)

Month	Sales	Collections				Receivables			
		T	T − 1	T − 2	Total	T	T − 1	T − 2	Total
11	100	20				80			
12	100	20	40			80	40		
1	100	20	40	40	100	80	40	0	120
2	125	25	40	40	105	100	40	0	140
3	150	30	50	40	120	120	50	0	170
4	175	35	60	50	145	140	60	0	200
5	200	40	70	60	170	160	70	0	230
6	175	35	80	70	185	140	80	0	220
7	150	30	70	80	180	120	70	0	190
8	125	25	60	70	155	100	60	0	160
9	100	20	50	60	130	80	50	0	130
10	100	20	40	50	110	80	40	0	120
11	100	20	40	40	100	80	40	0	120
12	100	20	40	40	100	80	40	0	120

TABLE 12.3
Days Sales Outstanding

	For the last 30 days		For the last 60 days		For the last 90 days	
Month	Sales per day	DSO	Sales per day	DSO	Sales per day	DSO
1	3.33 (1)	36.0 (2)	3.33	36.0	3.33	36.0
2	4.17	33.6	3.75 (3)	37.3 (4)	3.61	38.8
3	5.00	34.0	4.58	37.1	4.17 (5)	40.8 (6)
4	5.83	34.3	5.42	36.9	5.00	40.0
5	6.67	34.5	6.25	36.8	5.83	39.5
6	5.83	37.7	6.25	35.2	6.11	36.0
7	5.00	38.0	5.42	35.1	5.83	32.6
8	4.17	38.4	4.58	34.9	5.00	32.0
9	3.33	39.0	3.75	34.7	4.17	31.2
10	3.33	36.0	3.33	36.0	3.33	33.2
11	3.33	36.0	3.33	36.0	3.33	36.0
12	3.33	36.0	3.33	36.0	3.33	36.0

Notes:
1. $100/30 = $3.33
2. $120/$3.33 = 36.0
3. ($100 + $125)/60 = $3.75
4. $140/$3.75 = 37.3
5. ($100 + $125 + $150)/90 = $4.17
6. $170/$4.17 = 40.8

Various DSO calculations for these sales are listed in Table 12.3. The reason for showing different DSO calculations is that credit managers use different historical sales periods for the calculation. It is possible to reflect the DSO calculation in a favorable light simply by choosing a different historical sales period.

The interpretation of these DSO calculations is difficult. On the basis of sales per day for the past 30 days (column 2), the DSOs (column 3) for months 2 through 5 are less than the DSO for the first month. This result occurs because sales are increasing during this period. As sales decrease in months 6 through 9, the DSO begins to increase and reaches a maximum in month 9, when the sales level returns to its preseasonal level.

On the basis of sales per day for the past 60 days (column 4), DSO (column 5) jumps from the preseasonal level of month 1 to a maximum in month 2 but then declines each month during months 3 through 9, when sales are either increasing or decreasing. The DSO index of 36.0 is the same for months 1, 10, 11, and 12 for calculations based on both 30 and 60 days sales. This result occurs because sales are level at $100 per month for these months.

On the basis of sales per day for the past 90 days (column 6), the DSO (column 7) reaches a maximum in month 3, which is greater than the high under either of the previous two cases. The low for both the 60-day and the 90-day methods occurs in the same month in which the high occurs for the 30-day method. The 90-day DSO index increases similarly to the sales increase for months 2 through 5 but falls below the preseasonal level as sales start to decrease to the preseasonal level in months 7 through 10.   □

Which of the indexes in Illustration 12.1 is correct? Actually, none of them are. A DSO index confounds sales effects and collection efficiency and allows the credit manager to select a sales base that reflects the so-called collection effort in the best possible light. *The basic difficulty of the DSO index is that it is sensitive to both changing sales patterns and changing collection patterns.* These patterns can cause the DSO index to signal the need for corrective action when none is needed or to overlook the need for action when it is needed. This difficulty is evident in Illustration 12.1. Note, again, an assumption of this illustration: Customers' payment patterns are identical, and they pay for 20% of their purchases in the current month, 40% in the next month, and 40% in the month after that. Thus *it is possible for customer payment patterns to be constant even though the DSO index is not.*

Aging Accounts Receivable

The *aging of accounts receivable* is another of the traditional methods used to analyze these balances. It attempts to show the proportions of the current outstanding balance that originates from sales of the previous periods. It is believed that if these proportions change, then something of significance has happened to accounts receivable.

Illustration 12.1 assumed that the payment patterns associated with each month's sales were constant. This assumption was made to show the fallacy of DSO calculations. Constant payment patterns are unreasonable to expect in practice. Assume that the *new* monthly payment patterns are represented by the data in Table 12.4. Here the credit manager recognizes bad debts once an account is more than three months old.

The cumulative payment patterns of Table 12.4 allow end-of-month accounts receivable balances to be calculated. These results are shown in Table 12.5. The origination of these balances is identified with the month in which the sale occurred. Sales for months $T - 3$, $T - 2$, and $T - 1$ are assumed to be $100 each. The payment patterns for these months are the same as those for months 10, 11, and 12, respectively. All amounts are rounded to the nearest dollar.

The conventional way to age the outstanding accounts receivable balances is to classify these accounts on the basis of time from point of sale.

TABLE 12.4
Payment Patterns

Period	Sales ($000)	Cumulative payment pattern				Accounts delayed
		T	T + 1	T + 2	T + 3	
1	$100	20.0%	60.0%	90.0%	99.0%	1.0%
2	115	19.7	61.3	89.7	98.4	1.6
3	122	19.8	58.7	91.6	99.4	0.6
4	140	20.1	59.2	87.5	98.6	1.4
5	158	18.5	58.0	90.3	98.5	1.5
6	175	19.2	59.5	91.4	99.1	0.9
7	164	20.2	60.1	90.7	99.3	0.7
8	125	20.1	60.2	89.4	99.4	0.6
9	119	19.7	60.1	88.6	99.6	0.4
10	104	19.5	60.7	91.2	98.7	1.3
11	102	20.2	59.4	90.4	99.1	0.9
12	100	20.6	59.2	90.1	98.9	1.1
Mean		19.8	59.7	90.1	99.0	1.0

TABLE 12.5
End-of-Month Accounts Receivable Balance ($000)

Month	Sales	Month											
		1	2	3	4	5	6	7	8	9	10	11	12
T − 3	100	1											
T − 2	100	10	1										
T − 1	100	41	10	1									
1	100	80	40	10	1								
2	115		92	45	12	2							
3	122			98	50	10	1						
4	140				112	57	18	2					
5	158					129	66	15	2				
6	175						141	71	15	2			
7	164							131	65	15	1		
8	125								100	50	13	1	
9	119									96	47	14	0
10	104										84	41	9
11	102											81	41
12	100												79
Total		132	143	154	175	198	226	219	182	163	145	137	129

These groups are then presented as a percentage of the total outstanding balance. Generally, it is desirable to have the largest and fastest-growing percentage originating from the most recent sales. The rationale is that as an account ages, the probability of collection decreases. Table 12.6 summarizes the aging of accounts shown in Table 12.5.

From Table 12.6 we see that the age of receivables is predominantly current, ranging from a low of 55% in month 8 to a high of 65.2% in month 5. It is interesting to note that the cumulative payment patterns for month 8 (in Table 12.4) indicate above-average cumulative collection performance for months T and $T + 1$, whereas month 5 indicates below-average collection performance for these same months. These results are contrary to the aging schedule interpretations. The problem is that the aging schedule is wrong. It is wrong because the *aging percentages are directly affected by the sales trend, which can cause significant distortion in the aging.* This characteristic is examined in more detail later in this chapter.

Use of Balance Proportions

Rather than review accounts receivable data in conventional ways, a manager should review the payment patterns of customers relative to how they pay for each sale. That is, he or she should analyze the proportion of the

TABLE 12.6
Traditional Accounts Receivable Aging Schedule

					Distribution by months							
Month	1	2	3	4	5	6	7	8	9	10	11	12
$T - 3$	0.008											
$T - 2$	0.076	0.007										
$T - 1$	0.305	0.070	0.006									
1	0.611	0.280	0.065	0.006								
2		0.643	0.293	0.069	0.010							
3			0.636	0.285	0.050	0.004						
4				0.640	0.288	0.080	0.009					
5					0.652	0.292	0.069	0.011				
6						0.624	0.324	0.082	0.012			
7							0.598	0.357	0.092	0.007		
8								0.550	0.307	0.090	0.007	
9									0.589	0.324	0.102	0.000
10										0.579	0.300	0.070
11											0.591	0.318
12												0.612

Note: These entries represent Table 12.5's column amounts expressed as a proportion of their respective column total.

TABLE 12.7
Accounts Receivable Outstanding as a Proportion of Original Sales

Month	Sale ($000)	Proportion by month											
		1	2	3	4	5	6	7	8	9	10	11	12
$T-3$	100	0.01											
$T-2$	100	0.10	0.01										
$T-1$	100	0.41	0.10	0.01									
1	100	0.80	0.40	0.10	0.01								
2	115		0.80	0.39	0.10	0.02							
3	122			0.80	0.41	0.08	0.01						
4	140				0.80	0.41	0.12	0.01					
5	158					0.82	0.42	0.10	0.01				
6	175						0.81	0.40	0.09	0.01			
7	164							0.80	0.40	0.09	0.01		
8	125								0.80	0.40	0.11	0.01	
9	119									0.80	0.40	0.11	0.00
10	104										0.80	0.39	0.09
11	102											0.80	0.41
12	100												0.79

Note: These balance proportions can be derived from either Table 12.4 or 12.5.

sale of month T that is still outstanding in months $T, T + 1, \ldots, T + n$. Table 12.7 summarizes these *balance proportions* (rounded to two decimal places).

Interpretation of Balance Proportions

The interpretation of Table 12.7 is clear and simple. For instance, the row for month 5 indicates that 82% of month 5's sales are outstanding at the end of month 5, 42% are still outstanding at the end of the next month, 10% are still outstanding 2 months after the initial sale, and 1% are still outstanding 3 months after the initial sale. The accounts receivable balance for month 5 (the column for month 5) consists of 82% of month 5's sales, 41% of month 4's sales, 8% of month 3's sales, and 2% of month 2's sales. This column's set of numbers provides a distinctly different view of balances than that provided by the aging schedule. Overall, the use of balance fractions allows the credit manager to readily see whether any shifts are taking place in customer payment patterns, since the analysis is related directly to the sale initiating the account receivable. The conventional methods shown in Tables 12.5 and 12.6 do not allow such interpretation.

Criticism of DSO and the Aging Schedule

Considerable controversy surrounds the DSO and aging procedures as acceptable methods for monitoring accounts receivable. While these methods are still used often, their results may be misleading and are capable of frequent error. The difficulty with using DSO and aging schedules is that an upward trend in sales produces an impression of improved customer payment behavior when, in fact, behavior may be just the opposite or have changed very little. A comparison of month 5 of the aging schedule (Table 12.6) with month 5 of the balance fraction schedule (Table 12.7) highlights this fact. The aging schedule indicates that receivables are more current than normal, as shown by the 65.2% current month outstanding figure. The other "current" months range from a low of 55% in month 8 to a high of 64% in month 4. The balance fractions, however, indicate the true state of the receivables. A smaller proportion of current month's sales have been paid in month 5 than in any of the other months, contrary to implicit conclusions of the traditional aging method.

The criticism of DSO and aging schedules centers on the sensitivity of the calculations to the sales pattern and the sales averaging period selected (e.g., see Table 12.3). If sales are falling, both monitoring techniques give the appearance of receivables being less current than they really are. This is the case even though total sales may be the same for both the upward and downward trend patterns. It is only when the sales pattern is flat that misleading signals are not emitted by DSO and aging schedules. Most analysts recognize the sales pattern influence and attribute it to a seasonal factor. They attempt to eliminate, or at least minimize its effect, by comparing calculated DSO ratios and aging schedules against comparable historical periods. This approach is not satisfactory, though, since history seldom repeats itself exactly. Also, it may be hard to find data with which relevant comparisons can be made, especially when one is comparing companies of different sizes and types.

Variance Analysis Model

Another technique that can be used to overcome the problems associated with traditional techniques of DSO and aging schedules is to use a *weighted-DSO scheme*. This technique allows the DSO calculation to be independent of both the sales averaging period and the sales pattern. Also, it provides a comparison with a standard (such as budget or last year's results) and gives information that an aging schedule attempts to provide.

Relevant information for discussing the *variance analysis model* is summarized in Table 12.8. The actual receivables and sales data are taken from Table 12.5; the budget data for receivables and sales is new. Noticeable in this table is that actual receivables exceed the budget even though total

TABLE 12.8
Sales and Receivables Information ($000)

Sales and receivables

| | Receivables | | | Sales | | |
| | Actual | Budget | Difference | Actual | Budget | |
Month	Actual	Budget	Difference	Actual	Budget	Days*
January	$ 1	$ 0	$ 1	$100	$120	30
February	12	12	0	115	120	30
March	50	36	14	122	120	30
April	112	54	58	140	120	30
Total	$175	$102	$73	$477	$480	120

Days sales outstanding

Actual $120 \times \dfrac{\$175}{\$477} = 44.0$ days

Budget $120 \times \dfrac{\$102}{\$480} = 25.5$ days

Aging schedule

Month	Actual	Budget
January	0.6%	0%
February	6.9	11.8
March	28.5	35.3
April	64.0	52.9
Total	100.0%	100.0%

* 30 days are used for ease of later computations.

sales are only marginally lower than the budget. The conventional DSO measure indicates that actual receivables are outstanding longer than expected. However, the traditional aging schedule reveals a higher proportion of receivables to be current than expected. These traditional measures are in conflict with each other.

Table 12.9 allocates the $73,000 receivable balance variance shown in Table 12.8. The variance is unfavorable since the actual receivable investment exceeds the budget. The credit manager's responsibility is to understand the factors contributing to this variance. A first level of analysis can partition the variance into two components:[2]

[2] An article by James A. Gentry and Jesus De La Garza ["Monitoring Accounts Receivable: Revisited," *Financial Management* (Winter 1985): 28–38] recommends that a joint variance be calculated so as to make the collection effect and sales pattern variances "pure." A forthcoming article by George W. Gallinger and A. James Ifflander ("Monitoring Accounts Receivable Using Variance Analysis," *Financial Management*) discusses in a footnote some reasons for not calculating the joint variance.

TABLE 12.9
Variance Analysis of Accounts Receivable Balances ($000)

Month	Actual sales per day × actual DSO	Actual sales per day × budget DSO	Sales per day restated in budget proportions × budget DSO	Budget sales per day × budget DSO
Jan.	$ 1	$ 0	$ 0	$ 0
Feb.	12	11.50	11.93	12
Mar.	50	36.58	35.78	36
Apr.	112	63.00	53.66	54
	$175	$111.08	$101.37	$102

Collection experience variance $63.92; unfavorable

Sales pattern mix variance $9.71; unfavorable

Sales quantity variance $0.63; favorable

Sales pattern variance $9.08; unfavorable

1. A collection experience variance.
2. A sales pattern variance.

If greater understanding of the sales pattern variance is sought, a second level of analysis partitions this variance into two parts:

1. A sales pattern mix variance.
2. A sales quantity variance.

The calculation of these variances is shown in the Appendix. Discussion of each variance is given in the sections that follow.

Collection Experience Variance

The *collection experience variance* (CEV) is a direct measure of collection efficiency. This variance is free of any influence of changing sales pattern, which hampers the traditional measures of DSO and aging schedules. This freedom exists because *a new budget for receivables is derived on the basis of the sales level actually achieved. This new budget recognizes that outstanding receivables should increase or decrease directly with changes in sales.*

Analysis of the CEV indicates that actual receivables are $63,920 higher than expected on the basis of the new budget's expected collection efficiency. The most pronounced problem is with the latest month's collections. Days sales outstanding for April are about 78% higher than the new budget indicates they should be. This figure translates into excess receivables of $49,000, or approximately 77% of the total CEV variance. The variance for March's outstanding receivables is the other major component of the variance; it represents 21% of the total CEV variance.

The credit manager needs to ascertain the following:

1. Whether collection efficiency really has deteroriated.
2. Whether customers are experiencing cash flow problems.
3. Whether credit terms have changed from those used in the budget.

The third point is relatively easy to determine, since the credit manager generally is part of the decision-making process for establishing credit terms. The first two points require more analysis. For the first point the manager should consider questions such as the following: How effective is the company's lockbox collection system? Is transit float being minimized? How long is processing float? Are there an inordinate number of invoices in dispute? For the second point analysis of payment patterns of individual accounts and follow-up conversations with customers, where deemed necessary, can provide insight into customer cash flow problems.

Sales Pattern Variance

The *sales pattern variance* (SPV) is the other major component of the receivables variance. This variance indicates the effect that changing sales pattern has on receivable balances. One might argue that credit managers cannot be held accountable for the sales pattern variance. Although this is generally true, circumstances can exist that negate this claim. For example, one of the credit manager's duties is to determine whether credit should be extended to customers. A too lenient credit-granting policy, as a result of inadequate analysis of credit applications, results in higher sales and in higher receivable balances that are outstanding longer. In this case the credit manager is responsible for at least a portion of the sales pattern variance. The credit manager should be aware of her or his responsibilities here, since a company officer may raise questions about the trend of accounts receivable and about management's effectiveness with regard to investment in productive assets. Selling goods to poor credit risks is generally not a good use of scarce investment dollars.

Regardless of who is responsible for the sales pattern variance, an understanding of this variance is important in analyzing resource allocations. However, the sales pattern variance can be difficult to interpret. For example, in Table 12.8 the fact that total actual sales are practically equal to total budgeted sales may lead management to conclude that sales are not the cause of any receivable variance, when in fact they contribute $9080 to the higher receivable level (see Table 12.9). This result occurs because sales in April are $20,000 higher than budgeted.

The real significance of any sales pattern on receivables can be discovered by separating the sales pattern variance into a sales pattern mix variance and a sales quantity variance.

Sales Pattern Mix Variance

Although total sales are practically as budgeted, the proportion of each month's sales to total sales differs from the budget proportions. These different proportions give rise to the *sales pattern mix variance*.

Analysis of this variance provides insights that an aging schedule attempts to reveal. The mix variance indicates that $430 (i.e., $11,500 − $11,930) less receivables are outstanding for February than expected, $800 (i.e., $36,580 − $35,780) more receivables are outstanding for March than expected, and $9340 (i.e., $63,000 − $53,660) more receivables are outstanding for April than expected. The aging schedule in Table 12.8, however, provides contrary information when it is interpreted in the usual manner. It shows a much larger proportion of receivables to be current versus the budget (64% vs. 52.9%) and smaller proportions to be one and two months old versus the budget. The interpretation is that accounts receivable are more current than budgeted. It is the higher April sales that are causing this conclusion to be drawn. Thus a simple aging schedule is unable to effectively identify aging (i.e., sales mix) problems.

Sales Quantity Variance

The remaining component of the sales pattern variance is the *sales quantity variance*. This variance represents the true volume influence of sales on receivables and is not influenced by collection efficiency or change in sales pattern.

Since total sales are marginally lower than budget, sales volume has a minimal effect on receivable balances. The $3000 lower sales result in receivables being lower by $630 — this is the true effect of sales volume on receivables.

Overall Analysis

An overall analysis of Table 12.9 indicates that the total receivable variance of $73,000, as of April, is largely attributable to the collection experience variance, which may indicate serious collection problems. The imbalance in sales, as compared with budget, contributes a lesser amount to the total variance, but it is by no means insignificant. If sales continue to deviate from budget, and if collection effort continues to lag, cash flows may be significantly reduced. As a result of such reduced liquidity, management may have to delay both required and discretionary investments and/or revise plans if the cash flow problem cannot be corrected.

Neither the DSO calculations nor aging schedules provide the same insights. For instance, conventional DSO calculations in Table 12.8 indicate that actual performance (44 days) has deteriorated from budget expectations (25.5 days) but fails to provide a reason why. The aging schedule leads to similar misleading conclusions (as discussed earlier).

Although our discussion and illustration have pertained to an analysis of total outstanding receivables, the proposed variance techniques can effectively be used to analyze receivables at the customer level. Such analysis simply requires budget figures for individual accounts, which can be compared with actual receivable balances. Analysis at this level will provide credit managers with information about the effectiveness of credit-granting procedures, about the impact of changing credit policies (e.g., payment terms) on individual accounts, about the influence of changing credit standards (e.g., loosening credit) on receivable balances, and about customer purchase patterns and volumes that may be overlooked by management in its effort to keep abreast of various other facets of the business.

Summary

This chapter examined explanations for changing payment behavior and techniques for monitoring accounts receivable balances. Changes in customer payment habits can occur because of internal changes within the customer's business, changes in accounts receivable balances owing to changes in the product mix purchased, and changes in the economic environment. The question of what constitutes a default payment was examined and found to be largely a subjective decision by management. Analysis showed expected profitability of sales to diminish quickly as an account ages. Thus management needs to determine the point at which an account is no longer classified as slow in being paid but, rather, as uncollectible.

The major part of this chapter was devoted to analysis of techniques for evaluating receivable balances. The traditional measures of DSO and aging schedules have serious shortcomings. They are influenced by changing sales patterns and fail to correctly identify changing collection patterns. Balance fractions, payment proportions, and variance analysis offer superior evaluation techniques. Each method associates the receivables outstanding with the sale that generated it. These methods overcome the aggregation problems inherent in the DSO and aging approaches.

The variance model allows superior analysis since it forces reconciliation of differences between budget expectations and actual performance.

This reconciliation provides the credit manager with better information for evaluating receivables. He or she can then determine the influence of changing collection efficiency in isolation from changing volume and sales mix efforts.

Key Concepts

Aging schedule

Bad debt

Balance fractions

Collection experience variance

Days sales outstanding

Default

Payment patterns

Sales pattern mix variance

Sales pattern variance

Sales quantity variance

Appendix

Mechanics of Variance Analysis

The calculation of accounts receivable variances requires information pertaining to each month that is represented in the accounts receivable balance. The information needed includes actual and budget sales per day for each month, actual and budget days sales outstanding for each month's sales, and actual sales per day for each month, restated as a proportion of each month's budget sales per day to the total budget sales per day for the entire period. The computations in the following subsections outline the steps for calculating the variances, using the data presented in the chapter. These data are repeated in Table A.1.

TABLE A.1
Data for Variance Calculations

Sales per day by month

Month	Actual	Budget	Proportion
January	$100/30 = $ 3.333	$120/30 = $ 4.00	0.25
February	115/30 = 3.833	120/30 = 4.00	0.25
March	122/30 = 4.067	120/30 = 4.00	0.25
April	140/30 = 4.667	120/30 = 4.00	0.25
	$15.900	$16.00	1.00

Days sales outstanding by month

Month	Actual	Budget
January	30 × $1/$100 = 0.30	30 × $0/$120 = 0
February	30 × $12/$115 = 3.13	30 × $12/$120 = 3.00
March	30 × $50/$122 = 12.30	30 × $36/$120 = 9.00
April	30 × $112/$140 = 24.00	30 × $54/$120 = 13.50

Restatement of actual sales per day in budget proportions

January	$15.90 × 0.25 = $ 3.975	
February	15.90 × 0.25 = 3.975	
March	15.90 × 0.25 = 3.975	
April	15.90 × 0.25 = 3.975	
	$15.90	

Collection Experience Variance

The collection experience variance is calculated as

$$\sum_i \{(\text{actual sales per day})_i \times [(\text{actual DSO})_i - (\text{budget DSO})_i]\},$$

where $i = 1, 2, 3, 4$, which correspond to January, February, March, and April, respectively.

The actual variance is as follows:

$$
\begin{array}{ll}
\$3.333(0.30 - 0) = & \$\ \ 1.00 \\
\$3.833(3.13 - 3.00) = & 0.50 \\
\$4.065(12.30 - 9.00) = & 13.42 \\
\$4.667(24.00 - 13.50) = & \underline{49.00} \\
& \underline{\$63.92}
\end{array}
$$

Sales Pattern Variance

The sales pattern variance is calculated as

$$\sum_i \{(\text{budget DSO})_i \times [(\text{actual sales per day})_i - (\text{budget sales per day})_i]\}.$$

The actual calculation is as follows:

$$
\begin{array}{ll}
0(\$3.333 - \$4.000) = & \$\ \ \ \ 0 \\
3.00(\$3.833 - \$4.000) = & -0.50 \\
9.00(\$4.065 - \$4.000) = & 0.58 \\
13.50(\$4.667 - \$4.000) = & \underline{9.00} \\
& \underline{\$9.08}
\end{array}
$$

Sales Quantity Variance

The sales quantity variance is calculated as

$$\sum_i \{(\text{budget DSO})_i \times [(\text{actual sales per day in budget proportions})_i$$
$$- (\text{budget sales per day})_i]\}.$$

The actual variance is as follows:

$$
\begin{array}{ll}
0(\$3.975 - \$4.000) = & \$\ \ \ \ 0 \\
3.0(\$3.975 - \$4.000) = & -0.07 \\
9.0(\$3.975 - \$4.000) = & -0.22 \\
13.5(\$3.975 - \$4.000) = & \underline{-0.34} \\
& \underline{\$-0.63}
\end{array}
$$

Sales Pattern Mix Variance

The mix variance is the difference between the sales pattern variance and the sales quantity variance:

$$\sum_i \left[(\text{sales pattern variance})_i - (\text{sales quantity variance})_i\right].$$

The actual calculation is as follows:

$$
\begin{array}{rcl}
\$0 - \$0 & = & \$\quad 0 \\
\$-0.50 + \$0.07 & = & -0.43 \\
\$0.58 + \$0.22 & = & \quad 0.80 \\
\$9.00 + \$0.34 & = & \underline{\quad 9.34} \\
& & \underline{\$9.71}
\end{array}
$$

Questions

1. What are some causes of changing customer payment patterns? Discuss.

2. The average collection period for ABC Company is 46 days, whereas the XYZ Company collects its accounts in 35 days. As the financial manager of ABC, react to this observation.

3. In an evaluation of how well a company's receivables are managed, what advantage does the aging schedule have over the days sales outstanding and accounts receivable turnover ratios?

4. What is meant by *payment proportions* and *balance fractions*? How are they calculated? What advantage does each have?

5. How is the collection experience variance calculated? What does it measure?

6. What is the usefulness of the sales pattern mix variance? How is it calculated?

7. Which technique is best for evaluating accounts receivable? Why?

Problems

1. Approximately 20% of sales are paid in cash, with the remaining 80% sold to established credit customers on a 30-day charge account. Historically, 70% of the charge accounts are paid in the month following sale, with the remaining 30% being paid the second month following sale. Bad-debt losses are insignificant. Accounts receivable at the end of April 1984 amounted to $4200. Credit sales for the year were as follows:

January	$2000	May	$10,000	September	$21,000
February	2000	June	9,000	October	15,000
March	4000	July	8,000	November	13,000
April	3000	August	14,000	December	18,000

Starting with April, calculate the following:

(a) End-of-month accounts receivable balances for each month.

(b) End-of-month aging schedule for each month.

(c) Days sales outstanding for each month, using 30-, 60-, and 90-day intervals. Assume 30 days in each month.

Compare your results, and draw conclusions about why differences exist among them. Which approach is best for analyzing accounts receivable balances?

2. Iffinger Corporation's budget for credit sales and accounts receivable is as follows:

Month	Sales	Receivables
July	$ 5,000	$ 7,000
August	11,000	14,000
September	22,000	19,000

The September receivable balance consists of $15,000 from September sales, $3000 from August sales, and $1000 from July sales. Using the actual credit sales and receivables balances for these months as determined in Problem 1, calculate the collection experience variance, the sales pattern variance, the sales pattern mix variance, and the sales quantity variance. Assume each month has 30 days. What conclusions do you draw from the analysis to present to senior management?

3.   Sales per month are $950, with variable costs 68% of sales. Financial and administrative costs on overdue accounts are $25.50 per period overdue. Sales terms are net 30 days.

   (a) Determine the planned margin on sales.

   (b) The probability of collection of accounts follows. Calculate the expected collection and the expected margin on sales for each period that the account is outstanding.

Period	0	1	2	3	4	5	6
Probability	100%	95%	90%	80%	60%	30%	20%

4.   Alpha, Inc., had the following sales over the past 20 months:

Month	−1	0	1	2	3	4	5	6	7	8
Sales	100	100	100	120	140	225	400	500	450	380

Month	9	10	11	12	13	14	15	16	17	18
Sales	350	200	180	120	120	142	168	270	480	580

Collections for each month are comprised of 25% of current sales, 40% of last month's sales, and 35% of sales made two months ago. Assume each month has 30 days.

   (a) Calculate the monthly cash flow from collections and the monthly accounts receivable balances for months 1 through 18.

   (b) Calculate the days sales outstanding for months 1 through 18 based on sales of the last 30 days and of the last 90 days.

   (c) Discuss the days sales outstanding patterns in part (b) in relation to the sales pattern.

5.   Home Bakery Company has sales and cumulative payment patterns for receivables as shown in Table 12.10. Assume payments for months −1, −2, and −3 are the same as for months 12, 11, and 10, respectively.

   (a) Calculate the end-of-month accounts receivable balances (round to zero decimal places).

   (b) Calculate the traditional accounts receivable aging schedule and the balance proportions of accounts receivable outstanding (to three decimals, e.g., 0.001 instead of 0.1%).

   (c) Discuss the results of the two methods used in part (b).

TABLE 12.10
Sales and Payment Patterns

Period	Sales ($000)	Cumulative payment pattern				
		T	T + 1	T + 2	T + 3	Later
−3	185					
−2	210					
−1	225					
1	250	20.0%	45.6%	84.8%	98.0%	2.0%
2	350	18.6	46.9	86.9	98.9	1.1
3	375	21.1	44.8	85.9	98.4	1.6
4	400	19.8	44.8	84.8	98.0	2.0
5	380	22.4	46.1	86.1	99.2	0.8
6	600	21.5	45.8	85.2	98.8	1.2
7	550	22.0	44.9	84.7	99.3	0.7
8	425	22.1	44.9	85.6	98.8	1.2
9	375	21.6	44.5	85.3	98.4	1.6
10	250	22.0	45.2	84.8	98.9	1.1
11	190	20.5	46.8	87.1	99.0	0.8
12	200	21.0	44.8	84.4	98.2	1.8

6.   Suppose sales of the Home Bakery Company in Problem 5 increase by 20% next year. How may accounts receivable balances change? Consider real and inflationary increases, as well as a change in credit quality of customers.

7.   Table 12.11 shows the sales and receivable balances as of the end of September for the Maloof Manufacturing Company. Management wishes to know the contribution of the collection experience and sales pattern variances to the total variance. Assume that each month has 30 days.

TABLE 12.11
Sales and Receivables

Month	Receivables		Sales	
	Actual	Budget	Actual	Budget
June	$ 10	$ 15	$110	$100
July	25	35	95	100
August	90	106	121	110
September	107	110	130	120
Total	$232	$266	$456	$430

CHAPTER 13 □

Inventory Accounting and Cash Flow Effects

The financial executive is charged with safeguarding company assets and ensuring that they are properly managed. This responsibility applies equally well to inventories. The changing and renewable nature of inventory demands constant attention. The accounting for inventories is an important part of this attention since one must determine the proper assignment of costs to periods.

From an accounting perspective the total cost of goods available for sale or use during a period must be allocated between the current period's use (cost of items sold or used) and the amounts carried forward to future periods (the end-of-period inventory). This allocation affects cash flow through the amount of profits reported and the taxes paid on these profits.

Inventory valuation problems arise because there are two unknown quantities in the basic inventory equation:

ending inventory = beginning inventory + purchases − withdrawals.

The values of beginning inventory and purchases are known, but unknown are the values of withdrawals or ending inventory. The question is whether to value the ending inventory by using the most recent costs, the oldest costs, the average cost, or some other alternative. Of course, the question could have been put in terms of valuing the withdrawals, because once the value of one is determined, the inventory equation automatically values the other. The relation between the two unknowns in the inventory equation is such that the higher the value given to one of them, the lower must be the value given to the other.

There are no historical cost-based accounting methods for valuing inventories and, inversely, withdrawals *that allow the accountant to show current values on both the income statement and the balance sheet.* If current, higher costs are to be shown on the income statement, then older, lower costs must be shown on the balance sheet, and vice versa. The accountant can present current values in one place but not in both. Of course, combinations of current and out-of-date information can be shown in both places. It is this problem that leads to cash flow considerations when one is selecting an inventory accounting technique.

Therefore, if the financial manager is to have significant input in inventory decisions, the manager must have a basic understanding of inventory accounting and its effect on cash flows. This understanding, in turn, requires knowledge of inventoriable costs, valuation bases, and flow assumptions. Each of these topics is examined in this chapter.

As a means of emphasizing the importance of this material, one needs only to read published reports about W. T. Grant. For instance, buyers relied on vendors to keep them posted on inventory needs; significant delays existed between the time the goods were received and accounting entries were made; and inventory was understated about $70 million when the firm declared bankruptcy. In summary, no controls existed, which meant that management was never sure of inventory's effect on liquidity.

Inventoriable Costs

What costs are to be included in inventories? Of course, costs not included in inventory become an expense of the period. Thus *the true cash flow consideration arises at the time of the transaction* in the factor (material and labor) markets. *Inventoriable costs* are simply costs deferred until the eventual time of sale as far as recognition of income is concerned. But income is not cash flow, and depending on tax implications, these costs can affect cash flow.

Definition of Inventoriable Costs

In defining cost as it applies to inventories, one must define inventoriable costs (product costs), that is, those costs that are said to attach to the inventory and are considered to be part of the inventory valuation. Charges directly connected with bringing goods to the place of business of the buyer and converting such goods to a salable condition are accepted as proper inventoriable costs. Such charges include freight and hauling charges on goods purchased, other direct costs of acquisition, and labor and other production costs incurred in processing the goods up to the time of sale.

Under this definition it would seem proper to allocate to inventories a share of any buying costs or expenses of a purchasing department, storage costs, and other costs incurred in storing or handling the goods before they are sold. Because of the practical difficulties involved in allocating such costs and expenses, however, these items are not ordinarily included in valuing inventories; instead, they are charged as an expense in the period incurred (thus matching the expense with the cash outflow). Inventoriable costs are therefore manufacturing costs. Ideally, to increase cash flow, management should immediately expense as much cost associated with inventory as possible. Since material, labor, and overhead cash outflows are incurred in the production of the product, regardless of the accounting procedures adopted, the ability to expense as much cost as possible leads to lower taxes and improved cash flow.

Variable Versus Absorption Costing

Two concepts are involved in costing inventory. These concepts are variable (direct) costing and absorption (full) costing. In a *variable-costing system* all costs must be classified as variable or fixed. Only those costs that vary directly with the volume of production are charged to products and subsequently appear either in the balance sheet as inventory or in the income statement as cost of goods sold. Fixed inventoriable costs are considered period costs; that is, they are charged as expenses to the current period.

Under *absorption costing* all manufacturing costs, variable and fixed, direct and indirect, incurred in the factory or in the production process attach to the product and are included in the cost of inventory. When the firm uses absorption costing, it will have higher inventory amounts and lower cumulative expense totals. When the firm uses variable costing, it will have lower inventory amounts and higher cumulative expense totals. *From a cash flow perspective variable costing results in a closer matching of costs and cash outflows.* This result is shown in Table 13.1, which also shows the impact of inventory costing on ratio analysis.

Absorption costing causes a false impression of liquidity and costs incurred. Both the current ratio and the net working capital are higher in using absorption costing, whereas total costs are lower. The $30,000 lower cost for absorption accounting results because this amount has been deferred to the balance sheet as part of ending inventory. The reality of the situation is that the differences exist solely because of accounting methodology — not because of cash flow management.

Insofar as the firm must choose between absorption costing and variable costing, the choice made will affect the trade-off between inventory costs and period expenses. For tax purposes most firms should choose to accelerate expense recognition in order to defer recognition of taxable income; thus they should prefer variable costing. In practice, firms are not allowed much choice. Variable costing is not acceptable for income tax purposes or for use in published external financial reports because it is claimed that it understates inventories as a reasonable representation

TABLE 13.1
Variable Versus Absorption Costing

Assumptions

1. No beginning inventory; ending inventory of 25,000 units
2. Total production costs of $200,000 are split between variable and fixed costs as $80,000 and $120,000, respectively; 100,000 units produced
3. All production costs are paid before the end of the year
4. Current assets, excluding inventory, are $100,000. Current liabilities (excluding production expenditures) are $75,000.

Data

	Absorption	Variable
Beginning inventory	$ 0	$ 0
Plus production costs	200,000	80,000
Minus ending inventory	50,000	20,000
Equals cost of sales	$150,000	$ 60,000
Plus period costs	0	120,000
Equals total costs	$150,000	$180,000
Cash outflow	$200,000	$200,000
Minus total costs	150,000	180,000
Equals ending inventory	$ 50,000	$ 20,000
Current ratio	2.0	1.6
Net working capital	$ 75,000	$ 45,000

of a firm's investment in this asset. Both the accounting profession and the Internal Revenue Service (IRS) treat the significance of cash flow as being of secondary importance, at best. The position of the accountants is questionable. Their concern about the understatement of inventory investment could be handled by reporting, in a footnote, the amount of fixed costs associated with inventory. Readers of the financial statements would then have a better grasp of the cash flow implications of inventory accounting.

Bases of Inventory Valuation

The valuation method used to price inventories affects periodic income, cash flow, and any ratios that reflect inventories. Currently, there are at least four bases of valuation in use: (1) original cost, (2) lower of cost or market (also referred to as original cost or replacement cost), (3) standard cost, and (4) selling price. The first two methods are the most prevalent.

Original-Cost Basis

Conceptually, the simplest of all inventory policies is the specific-invoice method, which requires that the cost of each item sold or inventoried be known. With this *original-cost technique* the gains on items sold are simply the difference between their selling prices and their costs, and the value of inventory is the sum of items in stock. There is a complete correspondence between the flow of goods and the reported flow of costs. The inventory amount shown in the balance sheet, however, is usually out of date, depending on how prices have changed.

Cost includes the invoice price of merchandise and supplies plus the cost of transportation, less trade and cash discounts. Other costs such as purchasing, receiving, handling, and storage can be included; however, such costs are usually expensed in the period of their occurrence. If the business is a manufacturing enterprise, this definition of cost applies to its raw materials and supplies; for its other inventories cost includes all of the manufacturing costs that may have been incurred in producing the goods in process or the finished products (i.e., value added). Thus manufacturing expenses (i.e., overhead) are assigned to the items by using some reasonable expense allocation basis.

When *perpetual-inventory* records are kept, valuation by the original-cost method is usually easiest, since original-cost figures are commonly used in such records. For *periodic inventories* replacement cost is often easier to determine since recent prices are usually more accessible than prices at various dates in the past.

If materials or goods have become damaged, shopworn, or obsolete, they should be written down to a figure below cost, such as *net realizable value*. Original cost applies only to goods that are undamaged and can be used effectively in current operations.

Lower of Cost or Market

The *lower-of-cost-or-market* (original cost or replacement cost, whichever is lower) *valuation basis* is not always feasible in practice, particularly in a manufacturing firm. However, it is the generally accepted accounting rule when no other procedures have been adopted.

Use of the lower-of-cost-or-market basis involves the determination of both cost and market information for each item in the inventory. A problem immediately arises in defining *market*. Basically, three different types of market valuation must be determined: replacement cost, net realizable value, and net realizable value less a normal markup. The use of the lower-of-cost-or-market rule requires the accountant to follow the decision process shown in Fig. 13.1.

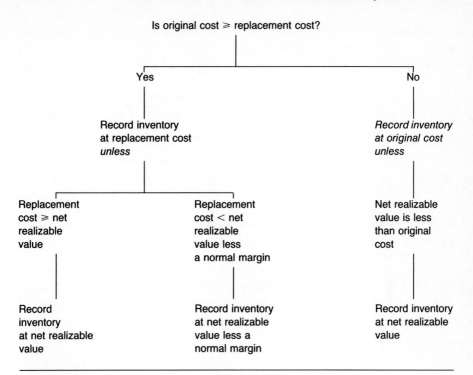

FIGURE 13.1
Lower-of-Cost-or-Market Decision Rule

Realization value is, of course, a paraphrase of "what you can get for it." Replacement cost, on the other hand, is something quite different, and, indeed, one may question why it needs to be considered at all in the determination of market. To this question accountants have two answers, conservatism and expediency. The extreme of conservatism is to consider market as the lower of realization value or replacement cost. Even when there is no conscious effort at such conservatism, to determine replacement cost and to demonstrate that it is below realization value is often easier than to determine an exact or even an approximate realization value.

The difficulty in determining realization value is that additional costs must be incurred to realize on any item in the inventories. And such costs must be deducted from the selling price of the item to determine the true net amount that can be realized from its sale.

The difficulty of gathering the necessary market information for each of the hundreds or thousands of items in an inventory — to say nothing of the difficulty of calculating the cost of work in process and finished goods on the basis of present material prices, present labor costs, and present prices for each of the other costs of production operations — certainly leads to the conclusion that the method has limited application. Its use is frequently restricted to the case where valuable raw materials and other items have had significant price declines.

As mentioned earlier, the lower-of-cost-or-market basis for inventory valuation is justified as being a conservative policy. The approach, however, is questionable and, as will be discussed later, cannot be used with the inventory flow assumption of last-in, first-out (LIFO). The effect of the rule is to take a loss when the market price has declined but not to take a gain when it has risen. Such losses are paper losses, which are only realized when the items are sold. That an unrealized loss is recognized while any unrealized gain is not does not conform entirely with logical reasoning. But the accounting profession defends its position on the conservatism principle, an attitude characterized by fearing to overstate profits but not fearing to understate them.

For any one unit of goods there is only one income or loss figure — the difference between the original cost and the selling price. The valuation rule merely determines how this figure of income or loss is to be spread over the accounting periods, with total disregard for how the cash flows were incurred. When the lower-of-cost-or-market price is used, the net income of the present period may be lower than if the original cost basis were used, but the net income of the period when the unit is sold will then be higher. *It is the timing of reported profit that affects tax liabilities and cash flows.*

Standard Costs

One of the most convenient methods of assigning costs to an inventory is to use predetermined *standard costs* for the items in it. A standard cost reflects what an item should cost to produce under assumed conditions for prices, technology, and operational efficiency. It is generally based on studies of past cost data and planned production methods. This method is probably more widely used than any other in valuing the labor and overhead elements of inventories. It is particularly convenient where goods pass through a number of processes or are manufactured on mass production lines.

There is always a danger that when standard costs are used to value inventories, they may not reflect current conditions unless they are revised frequently. Of course, if the revisions are too frequent, inventories are effectively priced at current replacement costs, which may violate the accountant's conservatism principle of lower of cost or market. The use of standard costs, however, can greatly aid management in quickly evaluating various inventory investment, profit, and cash flow scenarios.

Selling Price

Selling price is occasionally used in inventory valuation. This approach indicates the value of the goods to the firm. Agricultural products and by-products of manufacturing operations, on hand at the close of an accounting period, are often valued at selling price less costs of marketing, so *the income is recognized in the period of production rather than in the period of sale. The tax liability, however, is not incurred until the product is actually sold. Cash flow is realized at the time of a cash sale or whenever the receivable is collected.*

The influence of the accounting valuation methods on financial analysis should be obvious. Ratios that use cost of sales and/or inventory balances (i.e., current ratio, inventory turnover ratio, all profitability ratios, and the calculation of net working capital and cash flow) will be directly affected. It is critical that the analyst make adjustments for significant inventory valuation differences (if possible) when comparing one firm with another or a firm's present performance against its historical performance. Failure to do so makes financial comparisons less meaningful.

Flow Assumptions

If individual units can be identified, ascertaining original cost does not present a special problem. The cost can be marked on the unit or on its container, or the item can be traced back to its purchase invoice or cost record. The accounting profession and the IRS have long recognized that even small businesses find it difficult to keep track of the cost of each specific item in inventory. In most cases new items are mixed with old on shelves, in bins, or in other ways, and physical identification is impossible or impractical. If more than one purchase of the same item at differing prices is made, then some assumption must be made about the flow of costs in order to estimate the original cost applicable to the inventory.

Therefore several inventory accounting procedures have been developed that break the direct link between flow of goods and flow of costs. The discussion that follows concentrates on two such methods — first-in, first-out (FIFO) and last-in, first-out (LIFO) — because of their importance and because they generally represent the extremes in the range of choices faced by management. Of several other inventory accounting methods, two relatively common ones are the average cost method and the retail cost method. A complete discussion of the mechanics of the various techniques can be found in most intermediate accounting textbooks. Keep in mind that these different flow assumptions can affect financial analysis similar to the way that different inventory valuation methods do.

First In, First Out (FIFO)

Under the *FIFO inventory method* the cost of goods sold is computed as if these items were the oldest in inventory. As this is probably not an unreasonable flow-of-goods assumption, the resulting costs (and, therefore, profits) that are reported in the firm's income statement are probably not dissimilar from those that would result from using the specific-invoice method. The remaining inventory, which is entered in the balance sheet, is valued at the cost of the most recently acquired or produced items and therefore approximates market value or replacement cost of the inventoried stock.

Last In, First Out (LIFO)

The logic of the *LIFO method* is the opposite of that of the FIFO method. With this technique the cost of goods sold is taken as the cost of the items most recently produced or added to inventory. This cost approximates the expense of replacing the item in inventory, whereas FIFO values the sold good at close to its original cost. Generally, LIFO cannot be physically justified since it assumes current operations and sales are carried on with the use of items purchased most recently. No attempt is made to link the actual flow of goods and flow of costs: Nobody would seriously recommend a policy of shipping the most recently produced goods and holding the oldest output in stock. The advocates of LIFO explain that it does not matter which of any identifiable goods are taken out of stock first, since *it is the flow of costs and not the flow of goods that is to be considered.*

Since LIFO charges the most recently produced or inventoried items against goods sold, the stocks carried forward and reflected on the balance sheet are treated as if they were the earliest acquired or produced. In times of inflation this practice can seriously understate the value of inventory relative to current or replacement value on the balance sheet of firms that have produced or acquired at least as many items as they sold for several years. This drawback is partially overcome since most LIFO firms report the cumulative balance sheet difference between LIFO and FIFO. Also, *since the tax liability is reduced under LIFO (during a period of increasing prices), more cash is available. And in an economic sense the firm is better able to replace inventory under LIFO than under FIFO.*

Comparison of Methods

In an environment of permanently stable prices, LIFO and FIFO policies yield identical income statements and balance sheets. However, in a world with relative and absolute price changes, the two methods yield significantly different results.

Prior to the early 1970s inflation was reasonably low. So most firms used FIFO inventory accounting. However, as inflation grew to double-digit levels during the 1970s and into the 1980s, many firms switched to LIFO. The rationale for switching is straightforward. Under FIFO the inventory amount in the balance sheet reflects costs relatively close to current costs, because the latest purchases dominate the inventory valuation. In the income statement, however, the cost of goods sold reflects older purchase prices, because FIFO assumes earlier purchases are sold first. During inflationary periods FIFO leads to the highest reported net income of the two methods, and it leads to the smallest net income when prices are falling. When FIFO is used, both perpetual- and periodic-inventory methods provide the same cost-of-goods-sold figure and the same ending inventory amount.

LIFO provides opposite results. LIFO results in balance sheet figures that may be far removed from present costs and a cost-of-goods-sold amount that is close to current costs. The cost-of-goods-sold figure under LIFO is the largest of the two methods when prices are rising and the smallest when prices are falling. LIFO ordinarily results in the least fluctuation in reported income, because selling prices tend to change as current prices of inventory items change.

ILLUSTRATION 13.1

The difference between LIFO and FIFO can be shown further by examining the income statement and inventory balance sheets of a very simple hypothetical firm. This company may be viewed as acquiring and selling the same product. At any time the acquisition and selling prices are the same, so the only type of profit possible for this firm is that due to the appreciation of inventoried goods, that is, inventory profits. Table 13.2 lists the activities, income, and inventory valuation for this firm for 14 periods.

In period 0 the firm simply acquires a stock of 10 items. Periods 1 through 4 are characterized by a steady increase in price and by sales that just match acquisitions. Thus ending inventory remains constant at 10 units. Although selling price equals the latest purchase price, FIFO accounting reports profits of $54 during the first four periods; LIFO profits are zero. The value of inventory under FIFO accounting approximates market value, whereas LIFO accounting, relative to FIFO, greatly understates it.

Both sales and inventories grow in periods 5 through 7. This growth changes the situation very little with FIFO, since profits are still reported as the increase in value of each period's initial stock of inventories. There are no LIFO profits as long as acquisitions at least match sales.

Prices stabilize in period 8 and decline in periods 9 and 10. Sales just match acquisitions, so inventories remain stable at 13 units. While

TABLE 13.2
FIFO Versus LIFO Inventory Accounting

Period	Price ($)	Units Purchased	Units Sold	Revenues ($)	Unit inventory Initial	Unit inventory Final	Cost of sales ($) FIFO	Cost of sales ($) LIFO	Value of ending inventory ($) FIFO	Value of ending inventory ($) LIFO	Profits ($) FIFO	Profits ($) LIFO
0	8	10	0	0	0	10	0	0	80	80	0	0
1	8	7	7	56	10	10	56	56	80	80	0	0
2	10	7	7	70	10	10	56	70	94	80	14	0
3	12	7	7	84	10	10	64	84	114	80	20	0
4	14	7	7	98	10	10	78	98	134	80	20	0
5	16	8	7	112	10	11	92	112	170	96	20	0
6	18	9	8	144	11	12	122	144	210	114	22	0
7	20	10	9	180	12	13	156	180	254	134	24	0
8	20	10	10	200	13	13	194	200	260	134	6	0
9	18	10	10	180	13	13	200	180	240	134	<20>	0
10	16	10	10	160	13	13	186	160	214	134	<26>	0
11	16	8	10	160	13	11	166	166	176	96	<6>	<6>
12	16	6	10	160	11	7	160	136	112	56	0	24
13	16	0	7	112	7	0	112	56	0	0	0	56
All periods		109	109	1716			1642	1642	0	0	74	74

Note: Acquisition prices = selling prices in each period.

LIFO profits remain zero, FIFO accounting results in a loss (and, hence, tax savings or credit) for these periods.

Prices are stable in periods 11 through 13, but the firm gradually liquidates inventories. The FIFO method now reports zero profits, while the LIFO method reports large profits as inventoried items (some still valued at the acquisition cost of period 0) are sold.

As the last row of the table shows, the firm has a cumulative pretax profit of $74 under either system (because all inventory is sold), but the time patterns of income differ. Under the FIFO system income is reported as the value of inventory increase, but under LIFO it is recorded only when the inventory is liquidated. The source of the $74 LIFO profit is clear when one tabulates net acquisitions as 10 units at $8 (period 0), 1 unit at $16 (period 5), 1 unit at $18 (period 6), and 1 unit at $20 (period 7), for a total cost of $134. These 13 units were sold in periods 11 through 13 at $16 apiece for a total revenue of $208. ☐

There is some logic behind both sets of numbers. Table 13.3 attempts to capture it. For instance, in periods 1 through 4 the firm has generated

TABLE 13.3
Cash Flow Analysis

	FIFO			LIFO		
	After tax		Cumulative net cash	After tax		Cumulative net cash
Period	Profits	Sum	flow	Profits	Sum	flow
0	0	0	<80.0>	0	0	<80.0>
1	0	0	<80.0>	0	0	<80.0>
2	8.4	8.4	<85.6>	0	0	<80.0>
3	12.0	20.4	<93.6>	0	0	<80.0>
4	12.0	32.4	<101.6>	0	0	<80.0>
5	12.0	44.4	<125.6>	0	0	<96.0>
6	13.2	57.6	<152.4>	0	0	<114.0>
7	14.4	72.0	<182.0>	0	0	<134.0>
8	3.6	75.6	<184.4>	0	0	<134.0>
9	<12.0>	63.6	<176.4>	0	0	<134.0>
10	<15.6>	48.0	<166.0>	0	0	<134.0>
11	<3.6>	44.4	<131.6>	<3.6>	<3.6>	<99.6>
12	0	44.4	<67.6>	14.4	10.8	<45.2>
13	0	44.4	44.4	33.6	44.4	44.4
Total	44.4			44.4		

Note: Tax rate = 40%. Total numbers of units sold are the same for both methods. All inventory is sold. Total cumulative cash flow is the same for both methods because of items 2 and 3.

no cash inflow since each item is replaced as it is sold (see Table 13.2). This fact is reported under LIFO (the cumulative cash flow has stayed constant at $-\$80$, indicating no additional cash inflow or outflow since period 0). But the stock on hand has appreciated in nominal value, as reflected by cumulative FIFO earnings of \$32.40.

LIFO does not record any profit or loss until periods 11 through 13, because unit purchases have either exceeded or equaled unit sales for periods 1 through 10. Thus *any inventory profits stay hidden in the balance sheet*. However, when unit sales exceed unit purchases, these inventory profits emerge. They emerge because lower cost inventory layers are released from the balance sheet.

In the absence of the corporate income tax cash flows for FIFO and LIFO are the same in our example. This result can be easily verified by calculating the cash flow for any period in Table 13.2 as net income plus or minus the change in inventory. An increase in inventory is subtracted from income and vice versa. For example, in period 7,

FIFO cash flow = (income before taxes of \$24)
       − (\$44 increase in inventories) = $-\$20$,

LIFO cash flow = (income before taxes of \$0)
       − (\$20 increase in inventories) = $-\$20$.

However, in the presence of taxes cash flows vary by period and by method. For example, in period 7 FIFO has an after-tax cash flow of $-\$29.60$ (i.e., <\$182.0> − <152.4>, as shown under the column for cumulative net cash flow for periods 7 and 6, respectively). But LIFO has an after-tax cash flow of $-\$20$ (i.e., <\$134.0> − <114.0>). The \$9.60 difference in favor of LIFO is the tax paid on the FIFO profits (\$24 × 0.40 = \$9.60); see Table 13.2.

Advantages of LIFO

As long as purchased units exceed or equal sales units, LIFO results in lower tax liability, higher quality of earnings, and higher cash flow during periods of rising prices. *LIFO is consistent with an economic perspective that includes only realized gains*, whereas *FIFO reflects accounting profits and losses as they accrue.*

It is the economic perspective and not the accounting viewpoint that is important to shareholder wealth maximization. In terms of financial analysis Tables 13.2 and 13.3 implicitly indicate how profitability ratios, the inventory turnover ratio, and the current ratio are influenced by the inventory flow assumption. However, these ratios should be of secondary importance. *Cash flow is the most significant factor in the management of firm liquidity, and it should be emphasized in any analysis.*

There is no doubt that during inflationary times LIFO results in a higher after-tax cash flow to shareholders. The economic income of a firm before taxes may not be easily identifiable, but it is certainly not affected by management's arbitrary decision to use FIFO versus LIFO. On a pretax basis the selection of LIFO or FIFO simply affects the level of reported profits — it can have no impact on pretax economic income. Yet since the government bases taxes due to it on reported taxable income, actual taxes are lower under LIFO. Thus after-tax economic profit and cash flows are higher under LIFO. Besides reducing (but not eliminating) taxes on inventory profits, LIFO has the additional advantage of stating reported income closer to real economic income than does FIFO. Economic profits are best estimated by using replacement costs of inventory, and LIFO is a closer estimate of such replacement costs than FIFO.

Recognizing the difference as that between realizations and accruals should make it clear that the tax savings arising from choosing LIFO in an inflationary period may actually amount to the deferral of taxes. Should prices drop to their original level or should the firm liquidate its inventory, LIFO inventory profit and taxes would exceed those under FIFO. The gains would be completely eliminated or "repaid," although no interest would have been charged on the "loan."

For maximum tax benefits the optimal time to adopt LIFO may be when inventories are relatively low. With proper management the difference between tax savings and tax deferral may be virtually eliminated; the postponement may be made sufficiently long to permit virtual escape of taxes under the realization (LIFO) system. Furthermore, even if taxes avoided in one year must be made up in a subsequent year, financial managers are generally pleased with the deferment. Cash saved from current tax payments can be used temporarily for expanded operations, and expanded operations may be expected to increase the corporation's capacity to pay taxes in future years. For a variety of reasons managers are inclined to think that improvements in future years will be less burdensome than they would be at the moment. And there is always the hope that tax rates in the future will be lower than they are at present.

Another reason for the choice of inventory valuation methods that result in the lowest possible profit figures is the avoidance of pressures on corporate directors to raise the rate of cash dividends to be paid to the stockholders. In ordinary circumstances the higher a company's profits, the greater are the stockholders' expectations for generous dividends. If the directors prefer to use available cash for expansion rather than for increases in cash dividend rates, they will hold down, by whatever means possible, the amount of profits to be reported — which includes a careful choice among inventory valuation methods. Also, lower reported earnings might be attractive to regulated firms or to firms that face negotiations with powerful labor unions.

Disadvantages of LIFO

Lowering reported earnings may, however, impose difficulties on the corporation and its management. Often a firm is constrained in its dividend and borrowing policies by the terms of its existing bonds and bank credit. These constraints often depend on such figures as reported net income and the firm's ratio of liabilities to either assets or net worth, both of which will be lower under LIFO in an inflationary economy. Furthermore, most profit-sharing and executive bonus plans are tied directly to reported earnings. Altering these programs to compensate for the switch from FIFO to LIFO may be difficult.

Further reasons for not switching to LIFO can be extracted from the examples given in Tables 13.2 and 13.3. The first is the expectation of falling prices, which may be important in a few industries (for example, semiconductors). The second reason is that companies whose inventories are frequently liquidated — perhaps involuntarily — owing to strikes, bad weather, or particularly volatile demand or supply conditions experience little benefit from LIFO because of the frequent realization of the gains on the value of their inventories. In other words, falling prices and the need to sell inventory carried at a relatively low cost result in higher profit and tax obligations.

When the LIFO flow assumption is elected for tax returns, the Securities and Exchange Commission requires that it also be used for reports to stockholders. Furthermore, all firms must request permission from the Internal Revenue Service to use the LIFO flow assumption. Once a firm has chosen to adopt the LIFO flow assumption, it must request permission to change back to FIFO and may incur a tax liability if it does so. In recent years many firms that earlier adopted LIFO so that income taxes would be lower (at the cost of reporting lower net income in the financial statements) have switched back to FIFO so that reported earnings per share will be higher (at the cost of paying larger current income taxes).

The emphasis on earnings per share is a questionable practice. A corporation using LIFO may indicate, by footnote in the annual financial statements, the effect on earnings if FIFO were used in the year of change. Also, there is some question about whether the reduction in earnings as a result of switching to LIFO affects the price of the corporation's stock. The sophisticated investor realizes that in a period of rising prices inflated inventory values artificially inflate profits. As the investing public becomes more sophisticated, the emphasis will increasingly be on the quality of profits rather than on the quantity. Accordingly, LIFO should continue to be the more popular inventory valuation method.

The Internal Revenue Service requires that if the lower-of-cost-or-market valuation basis is used, it may not be coupled with a LIFO flow assumption. Consider the effect of allowing both LIFO and lower-of-cost-or-market techniques. When prices are rising, the LIFO flow assumption results in a lower closing inventory amount and lower reported income than does FIFO. When prices are falling, the lower-of-cost-or-market basis with LIFO leads to a closing inventory amount equal to that of FIFO coupled with a lower-of-cost-or-market basis. The Internal Revenue Service is unwilling to allow a flow assumption that results in lower taxable income when prices are rising and no higher taxable income when prices are falling. LIFO coupled with a lower-of-cost-or-market basis, were it allowed, would result in a guarantee of no worse position (falling prices) and the hope of a better position (rising prices), as compared with FIFO plus a lower-of-cost-or-market basis.

Summary

This chapter discussed inventory accounting and the effect of taxes on financial ratio analysis and cash flows. Inventory measurements affect both the cost-of-goods-sold expense on the income statement for the period and the amount shown for the asset inventory on the balance sheet at the end of the period. The sum of the two must be equal to the beginning inventory plus the cost of purchases.

The allocation between expense and asset depends on three factors: (1) the types of manufacturing costs included in inventory, (2) the valuation basis used, and (3) the flow assumption. The first factor involves a choice between absorption costing and variable costing. The second factor involves a choice between the cost basis and the lower-of-cost-or-market basis. The third factor involves a choice among FIFO, LIFO, or some other (e.g., average cost) flow assumption. The allocation decision directly affects the firm's cash flow via the tax calculation and the analysis of various ratios that incorporate cost of sales and/or inventory balances.

The tax code is the common element running through these three factors. Without taxes the argument of which inventory accounting alternatives to use becomes moot. *If there were no taxes, the different inventory techniques would have no effect on cash flow.* A number of different financial ratios would still be affected by the different accounting alternatives. However, as discussed elsewhere in this book, it is the analyst's responsibility to interpret ratios with caution. This chapter has identified the reasons for exercising caution in analysis of inventory.

Key Concepts

Absorption costing
Direct (variable) costing
FIFO
Inventoriable costs
LIFO
Lower-of-cost-or-market basis

Original-cost basis
Periodic inventory
Perpetual inventory
Selling price
Standard costs

Inventory Methods: Periodic Versus Perpetual

There are two types of inventory procedures used to arrive at the quantity and the amount of an inventory: the periodic-inventory method and the perpetual-inventory method. The perpetual method offers more advantages for planning and controlling the investment in inventories and in periodically calculating cash flow from operations.

Periodic Inventories

The *periodic-inventory procedure* consists of making a physical count of all articles in stock at least once a year at the end of the accounting period. At all other times during the year there is no complete information available on the amount of the inventory of goods or the cost of goods sold. The main benefit of this inventory system is its simplicity.

It is seldom possible to prepare operating (and cash flow) statements more frequently than once a year when the inventory figures are obtained only from periodic counts. An assumption of the periodic approach is that all goods not accounted for by the physical count of inventory have been sold or used. Any shrinkages or losses from such causes as theft, evaporation, and waste are hidden in the cost of goods sold or the cost of materials used.

The periodic-inventory method determines the ending inventory figure of units by physical count multiplied by cost per unit and uses the inventory equation to determine the withdrawals. A problem arises when a change in the replacement price has taken place since certain items were acquired. Accordingly, the question arises about whether the units will be priced at the cost price or at the current market price. The answer to this question is discussed in more detail later, but it is based on the generally accepted rule that the items in inventory be priced at cost or at market, whichever is lower.

Perpetual Inventories

Under the *perpetual-* (or continuous) *inventory method* the system of records is designed so that the cost of merchandise sold or the cost of material used is recorded at the time these assets are sold or consumed. The perpetual method determines the withdrawals by physical observation (e.g., material withdrawal requisitions) and uses the inventory equation to determine (what should be in) the ending inventory. This method allows operating (and cash flow) statements to be prepared without a physical count and allows for greater analysis of inventory investment and its impact on liquidity.

When a perpetual-inventory system is used, there is a constant record of goods in stock. Nevertheless, the book inventory must periodically be verified by a physical count because goods become lost, are stolen, or deteriorate. The dollar amount of any missing goods is treated as a loss, contrary to what is done in the periodic method. Analysis of the loss account should thus result in more efficient operations and better control. All items should be counted at least once a year, and certain items may be checked more frequently, either because of their high value or because of a high probability of errors in recording their withdrawals.

Appendix B
Inventory Accounting Errors

If inventory items are incorrectly (maybe, purposefully) included or excluded for inventory purposes, there will be errors in the financial statements and analysis. To illustrate, suppose that certain goods that the firm owns are either not recorded as a purchase or not counted in ending inventory. To disregard such purchases results in an understatement of inventories and accounts payable in the balance sheet and an understatement of purchases and ending inventories in the income statement. The net income for the period is not affected by the omission of such purchases, since purchases and ending inventories are both understated by the same amount, with the error offsetting itself in cost of goods sold. Total working capital is unchanged, but the current ratio, assuming it is greater than 1 before the omission, is higher because of the omission of equal amounts from current assets and current liabilities. (The use of the current ratio in this example is done for expediency.)

To illustrate the effect of errors, assume the following balances are reported at the end of the period:

Current assets	$120,000	Cost of sales	$100,000
Current liabilities	$40,000	Ending inventory	$25,000
Current ratio	3:1	Inventory turnover	4.0

If $40,000 for goods in transit should have been included in ending inventory, then the following balances would be presented:

Current assets	$160,000	Cost of sales	$100,000
Current liabilities	$80,000	Ending inventory	$65,000
Current ratio	2:1	Inventory turnover	1.5

The correct current ratio is 2:1 instead of 3:1, and the turnover ratio should be 1.5 times instead of 4 times. In other words, the missing inventory should be reported in purchases, ending inventory, and accounts payable.

What would happen if the beginning inventory and the goods purchased are recorded correctly, but some items on hand are not included in ending inventory? In this situation ending inventory, net income, current ratio, and net working capital are all understated, and inventory turnover is overstated. Net income is understated because cost of goods sold is larger than it should be; the current ratio and the net working capital are understated because a portion of ending inventory is omitted; the inventory turnover ratio is overstated because cost of goods sold are overstated while ending inventory is understated.

To illustrate the effect on funds flow, assume that the ending inventory is understated and that all other items are correctly stated. The effect of this error will be to decrease net income and funds from operations in the current period and to increase net income and funds from operations in the following period. The error will be offset in the next period, because the beginning inventory will be understated and net income and funds flow will be overstated. In other words, both net income and funds flow are misstated, but the total for the two periods is correct.

If a purchase is not recorded but is included in ending inventory, the reverse result occurs. Net income, the current ratio, and net working capital are all overstated, and inventory turnover is understated. The effect on net income and funds flow will be offset in the subsequent period (assuming purchases are recorded in the next period), but both periods' financial statements will be misstated.

These illustrations indicate that an accurate computation of purchases and inventory is needed to ensure that proper income, assets and liabilities, and funds flow figures are presented for analysis.

Questions

1. What is the basic conceptual difference between a standard cost system and an historical cost system? Which system is more appropriate for helping one to manage cash flows?

2. In a period of falling prices, is it better for a firm to value its inventory by FIFO or by LIFO? Why?

3. Ignoring income taxes, what affect does a change from FIFO to LIFO have on net earnings, working capital, and cash flow during a period of rising prices? During a period of falling prices?

4. Two retailers have identical stock of goods on hand, but their inventory balances, as stated in their respective balance sheets, differ. Explain.

5. "Original cost for inventory valuation is reasonable from the standpoint of the income statement but misleading for balance sheet purposes." Comment.

6. Why would a financial manager select an inventory valuation method that would result in lower reported profits? Does not this choice directly clash with the oft-stated doctrine that corporations seek always to maximize their profit? Explain.

7. Why is it claimed that the LIFO valuation method gives a "truer" picture of operating results than do other methods of inventory valuation?

8. What is the distinction between an inventoriable cost and a period cost? How does absorption costing differ from variable costing? What is the significance of each of these approaches for cash flow management?

9. Chapter 6 discussed the importance of the cash conversion cycle in planning liquidity needs. The cash cycle was defined as the number of days of inventory outstanding plus days sales outstanding in receivables less trade credit days outstanding. How does the choice of an inventory valuation method affect the cash cycle?

10. Distinguish between a periodic-inventory method and a perpetual-inventory method. Which one is more appropriate for providing information about inventory cash flows? (*Note:* This question requires you to be familiar with the material in Appendix A.)

Problems

1.   The inventory records of a company show the following picture for the last fiscal year:

On hand, at start of year	500 units @ $5.00 = $ 2,500	
Purchases during the year:		
February 1	500 units @ $6.00 =	3,000
May 1	1000 units @ $6.50 =	6,500
August 1	3000 units @ $6.50 =	19,500
November 1	2000 units @ $7.00 =	14,000
On hand, at end of year	800 units	

A periodic-inventory record approach is kept in amounts as well as quantities. Calculate the cost of sales under both FIFO and LIFO. What is the value of ending inventory under each method? Which method results in larger cash flows, assuming the tax rate is 40%? How are the current ratios and inventory turnover ratios affected by each method?

2.   Calculate the inventory of Department K at the original cost, the present market cost, and the lower of cost or market from the data in Table 13.4. Apply the method on an item-by-item basis. How does this accounting procedure affect cash flow? Does it affect either the current ratio or the inventory turnover ratio? Explain.

3.   The Manhatton Publishing Company had in its inventory on July 1 three units of item K, all purchased on the same date at a price of $60 per unit. Information relative to item K is given in Table 13.5. Compute the cost of goods sold and the ending inventory in accordance with the following valuation methods: specific identification of units sold, FIFO, LIFO. Assume that a perpetual-record approach is followed for both quantities and dollar amounts. What affect does each method have on profits, on balance sheet investment, and on cash flow?

4.   For the data in Table 13.6, compute the gross margin on sales for each year (a) under the cost basis and (b) under the lower-of-cost-or-market basis in valuing inventories. Assume that the beginning inventory is zero. Discuss whether the

TABLE 13.4
Data for Department K

Item	Quantity	Original unit cost	Present unit cost
P	50	$15	$14
Q	70	18	20
R	20	25	25
S	100	27	28

TABLE 13.5
Data for Item K

Date	Explanation	Units	Unit cost	Tag number
July 1	Inventory	3	$60	k – 515,516,517
3	Purchase	2	65	k – 518,519
12	Sale	3		k – 515,518,519
19	Purchase	2	70	k – 520,521
25	Sale	1		k – 516

TABLE 13.6
Sales and Inventory Data

	Year 1	Year 2	Year 3
Sales	$300,000	$330,000	$450,000
Purchases	280,000	260,000	350,000
Inventory:			
At cost	80,000	95,000	95,000
At market	75,000	80,000	100,000

lower-of-cost-or-market basis is conservative in terms of cash flows, inventory turnover, and the current ratio. (*Hint:* If inventory is written down to lower of cost or market, the journal entry is a debit to a loss account and a credit to inventory.)

5.   The Stelz Corporation started business three years ago on January 1. It purchased inventory costing $100,000 in the first year, $125,000 in the second year, and $135,000 in the third year. Information about Stelz's inventory, as it would appear on the balance sheet under different valuation methods and flow assumptions, is shown in Table 13.7.

(a) Did prices go up or down in the first year?

(b) Did prices go up or down in the third year?

TABLE 13.7
Data for Stelz Corporation

Year	LIFO	FIFO	Lower of (FIFO) cost or market
1	$40,800	$40,000	$37,000
2	36,400	36,000	34,000
3	41,200	44,000	44,000

(c) Which inventory basis would show the highest income in the first year? The second year? All three years combined?

(d) For the third year, how much higher or lower would income be on the FIFO cost basis than it would be on the lower-of-cost-or-market basis?

(e) Why can't LIFO be used with a lower-of-cost-or-market basis?

6. At the start of the year Anchor Company had $3000 invested in inventory, which represented 1500 units. During the year management purchased the following quantities:

June 15	1700 units @ $2.50
August 15	2190 units @ $2.75
November 15	1400 units @ $3.10
February 15	2100 units @ $3.45

Inventory on hand at the end of the year was 2700 units. Freight-in costs averaged $0.50 per unit. The purchasing department's direct and allocated overhead costs for the year were $10,450 and $3200, respectively. Selling price averaged $7.50 per unit, and the corporate income tax rate was 30%. As of February 28, current assets were $125,000, and current liabilities were $92,500. Use a weighted average flow assumption.

(a) Determine the value of ending inventory, first by using a variable-costing approach and then by using an absorption-costing approach.

(b) Determine the difference in after-tax profit for the year between the two methods in part (a).

(c) For each method, determine the cash flow for the year and the net working capital at the end of the year. Assume all sales and purchases are on a cash basis.

7. The Ajax Manufacturing Company uses a standard cost system for internal control of inventory. The opening inventory was 750 units, valued at a standard cost of $3 per unit. The following entry was made to record this inventory:

Debit	Raw materials	$2250	
Debit	Price variance	375	
Credit	Cash		$2625

During the next year, three inventory purchases were made:

(a) 300 units at $4.00 per unit

(b) 400 units at $4.25 per unit

(c) 500 units at $2.75 per unit

Determine the cost of goods available for sale after each of the new purchases, using the standard cost system. Discuss how a standard cost system influences cash flows and profits.

8. The firm produces a product that is sold through a government marketing board that values inventory at selling price. Using the data in Table 13.8, determine the profit after taxes and cash flow for years 1 and 2. The tax rate is 40%. Discuss your answers, and compare them with the more usual cost basis of inventory valuation.

9. The management of Fluke, Inc., wishes to have a better understanding of the differences that occur to (a) ending inventory, (b) cost of sales, and (c) profit

TABLE 13.8
Sales and Cost Data

	Year 1	Year 2
Sales	$ 0	$12,000
Beginning inventory:		
Cost	0	9,000
Selling price		12,000
Purchases at cost	9,000	0
Ending inventory:		
Cost	9,000	0
Selling price	12,000	0
Operating expenses	1,000	1,000

before tax when goods are valued by using FIFO and LIFO. Use Table 13.9 to prepare a table showing the ending inventory values under each approach. Assume that there is no beginning inventory.

TABLE 13.9
Data for Fluke, Inc.

Period	Purchase price per unit	Units Purchased	Units Sold	Selling price per unit
1	$10	40	30	$15
2	11	44	28	14
3	9	35	55	15
4	8	36	35	14
5	10	40	30	13
6	12	35	35	14

Appendix B Problems

1. The income statement of the Furniture Centre for the year ended December 31 is as follows:

Sales		$244,700
Cost of sales:		
Opening inventory	$ 40,900	
Purchases	156,000	
Total	$197,000	
Ending inventory	35,900	
		161,200
Gross margin		$ 83,500
Operating expenses		74,800
Profit before taxes		$ 8,700

After this statement was prepared, the following errors were discovered:

☐ Opening inventory was overstated by $3400.

☐ A $4200 invoice has not been recorded, although the goods have been received and counted in ending inventory.

☐ A $3000 invoice, terms FOB shipping point, was recorded in December, but since the goods have not arrived, they are not included in the ending inventory's physical count.

Revise the income statement for these errors and omissions. How will liquidity be affected? What is the impact on net working capital? If the corrections are not made, will current year net income be overstated or understated? How is cash flow affected?

2. On December 31 of last year inventory amounting to $750 was received and included in the December 31 inventory. The invoice was not received until January 4 of this year, at which time the acquisition was recorded. Indicate the effect (overstatement, understatement, none) on each of the following amounts:

	Last year	*This year*
Inventory, December 31		
Cost of sales		
Net income		
Accounts payable		
Retained earnings		
Net working capital		
Cash flow		

Assume that the error was not discovered by the firm when the invoice was received.

CHAPTER 14 □
Inventory Investment: How Much?

Inventories represent a capital investment and must, therefore, compete with other assets for the firm's limited capital funds. As a consequence, total investment in inventories must be related to some optimal investment level that contributes to the overall wealth objective of the shareholders. This optimal level can be determined (at least theoretically) through the use of sophisticated operations research models. To expect finance managers to have an in-depth knowledge of these techniques is unrealistic. However, they should be able to ask probing questions, since the proper management of inventory has a significant influence on profitability. Excessively large inventories, on the one hand, penalize profits through costs that are higher than necessary. On the other hand, keeping inventories too low handicaps sales, thus lowering potential profits.

The managerial objective must be the avoidance of overinvestment and underinvestment in inventories — a proposition that appears to indicate that there must be some "right amount" of inventory investment. But while indicating the harmfulness of overinvestment or underinvestment is easy, recognizing these situations is often most difficult. Thus asking managers to set an inventory volume that is exactly the right amount is unrealistic.

For most firms the investment in inventories is a very significant dollar amount and percentage of assets. The 1982 U.S. Bureau of the Census reports that in the aggregate nonfinancial U.S. corporations have a larger percentage of their resources invested in inventory than in any other current asset. Indeed, many firms in the wholesaling and retailing sectors have in excess of 40 percent of total assets invested in inventory.

The purpose of this chapter is to provide financial managers with a fundamental understanding of inventory management. Most inventory decisions are made by specialists within the production or purchasing departments. However, since inventories consume scarce resources, financial managers should have a conceptual understanding of inventory management if they are to effectively supervise resource allocations and manage liquidity.

Need for Inventories

If production and delivery of goods are instantaneous, there is no need for inventories except as a hedge against price changes. However, uncertainties exist between the production and delivery phases. In many respects inventories are more sensitive to general business fluctuations than are other assets.

In periods of prosperity when sales are high, merchandise can be disposed of readily, and quantities on hand may not appear excessive. But when even a slight downward trend in the business cycle occurs, many lines of merchandise begin to move slowly, stock piles up, and obsolescence becomes a real possibility. Because of the heavy costs of carrying surplus inventories, an intense effort must be made by management to liquidate them. Prices will fall until either consumption increases or production falls off sufficiently.

These problems are compounded by the fact that there are at least four conflicting views about the appropriate inventory investment:

1. The *marketing manager* has a natural desire to have plenty of finished goods inventory on hand so that no customer is ever turned away or forced to wait because of lack of stock.

2. The *production manager* likes to have large quantities of both raw materials and work-in-process inventories available to ensure that he can concentrate on continuous production runs. In this way he can spread setup, changeover, spoilage, and learning costs over longer production runs.

3. The *purchasing agent* often prefers to buy in large quantities in order to take advantage of quantity discounts and lower freight costs. Sometimes, the purchasing agent likes to try and outguess changing market prices and either postpone or accelerate purchases accordingly.

4. The *finance manager's* responsibility is to pry loose as much inventory investment as is feasible so that it may be channeled into more profitable opportunities.

Because of these conflicting functional objectives, any inventory policy must be carefully drawn if it is to benefit the business as a whole. Such a policy must address raw materials, work-in-process, and finished-goods

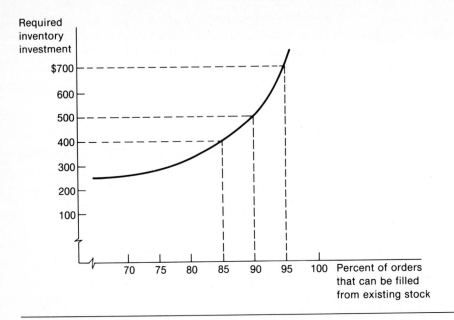

FIGURE 14.1
Trade-off Between Inventory Investment and Level of Customer Service

inventories separately, since each of these fulfill a different need in the firm.

The actual level of investment in raw materials inventory depends on the time it takes to receive orders, the frequency of use, and the cost per part, among other factors. The factors that affect the level of investment in work-in-process inventory are the complexity and the length of the production process and the availability of materials and labor to complete the job. The level of finished goods is largely determined by forecast sales, the availability of storage facilities, and the frequency of product changes. Various inventory specialists are responsible for each of these different inventories.

Inventory Overinvestment

It is unrealistic for a company to carry the amount of stock that would virtually guarantee no stockouts. Inventory investment increases at an increasing rate as the customer service standard approaches 100%. A typical cost relationship is illustrated in Fig. 14.1. For example, in order to be able to fill 85% of the total received orders from existing stock, the company has to carry an inventory valued at $400,000. To raise the customer service standard by 5 percentage points, to 90%, the inventory investment must be increased by $100,000. To raise the customer service standard another 5 percentage points, to 95%, inventory investment must now be increased by $200,000.

This acceleration of investment does not mean, however, that increases in customer service are never warranted. Obviously, increases in service spell increases in patronage and sales. But how much do sales, profits, and cash flow increase with product availability? This is the crucial question. The graph does not indicate whether sales, profits, and cash flow will increase enough to justify the higher investment in inventories. This issue requires careful analysis of expected demand and acceptable stockout rates.

The obvious evils that result from overinvestment in inventories are as follows:

1. *Liquidity problems.* The erring management is likely to find itself short of cash for other purposes, as for the payment of maturing liabilities, the carrying of accounts receivable, and the expansion of fixed assets. Instead of generating its own funds for these purposes, as might be possible with a better-designed inventory program, management is likely to find it necessary to increase its borrowings, thereby adding to the overhead expenses by way of interest costs, and increasing the risk of insolvency.

2. *Misuse of facilities.* Facilities that could be better used for other purposes may have to be used for storage, or indeed, additional facilities may have to be bought, erected, or rented. Costs of handling, inspection, and accounting are also increased, as are insurance charges and personal property taxes, since they are based upon the value of property.

3. *Inventory losses.* Losses through shrinkage, spoilage, theft and obsolescence may increase substantially.

4. *Competitiveness problems.* Management may find itself with a high-cost inventory at a time when its competitors are carrying on their operations with goods purchased more recently at lower prices.

Inventory Underinvestment

A management that is unduly niggardly in its inventory investment policy also faces problems. Here are some of them:

1. *Loss of customers.* For example, customers of a retail firm in this position may go elsewhere because they cannot find a sufficient variety of goods of a given line to make a reasonable selection or because they are precluded from one-stop shopping since the firm does not carry a sufficient variety of lines. Customers of a manufacturing firm, similarly situated, may turn away because of what they consider unreasonable delays in the delivery of goods ordered.

2. *Unnecessary costs of operations.* Shortages of raw materials may bring

temporary shutdowns, with many kinds of overhead expenses continuing to accumulate during the periods of idleness. Labor costs, too, tend to mount, perhaps as a result of slowdowns whereby workers try to stretch out the limited supplies of raw materials to make them last as long as possible or perhaps through labor turnover as dissatisfied workers quit their jobs to seek employment elsewhere.

3. *Being at the mercy of rising prices.* Lack of foresight in the accumulation of inventories, at a time of plentiful supplies and relatively low prices, may result in substantial increases in costs of goods manufactured or in costs of goods sold.

Finding a Compromise

The solution to the appropriate amount of inventory involves making compromises between two or more sets of conflicting cost factors. The objective is to maintain adequate inventory levels at minimum inventory cost. Classical inventory analysis identifies four major cost components. Depending on the structure of the inventory environment, some or all of the following components may be included in the analysis.

1. *Purchase/production costs.* These costs may be constant for all replenishment quantities or may vary with quantity purchase discounts. Similarly, unit costs may decrease as larger production runs are made, owing to economies of scale.

2. *Order/setup costs.* These costs are incurred whenever an inventory is replenished and are independent of the quantity replenished. Ordering cost is primarily clerical and administrative in nature. Typical ordering cost elements are the costs associated with processing and expediting the purchase order, follow-up, transportation, receipt, inspection, location of the items, and payment for the order. Setup cost includes the same types of clerical and administrative costs, plus the costs of labor and materials used in setting up machinery for the production run.

3. *Carrying/holding costs.* These costs are proportional to the amount of inventory and the time over which it is held. They essentially represent the explicit and implicit cost of maintaining and owning the inventory. A significant component of carrying cost is the opportunity cost associated with owning the inventory. The opportunity cost often reflects the rate of return the company might expect to earn on the money invested in inventory. Out-of-pocket costs that are normally accounted for include the cost of storage space (rent or cost of ownership), handling costs (including warehouse personnel, forklift trucks, and other equipment), insurance and taxes, allowances for depreciation, quality deterioration, obsolescence, and costs of administering inventory and maintaining records.

4. *Stockout costs.* These shortage costs are computed differently depending upon whether or not back-ordering is possible. When back-ordering is permitted, explicit costs are included for overtime, special clerical and administrative efforts, expediting, special transportation, and possibly customer goodwill. When back-ordering is not permitted, the primary costs reflect immediate and future lost sales or, in the case of raw materials inventory, the cost of idle facilities, disrupted schedules, and lost sales.

Precise cost data is not always critical in developing useful results from inventory models. In many instances the optimal solution varies slightly with rather substantial changes in one or more cost factors in the total cost equation. The analyst needs to determine which variables in the model significantly affect the solution, since it may be possible to simply use reasonable estimates for most of the variables.

Economic Order Quantity (EOQ) Model

Within limits set by the economics of the firm or the firm's industry, there exist many appropriate inventory control models that incorporate the costs just outlined. Although many of the techniques are far too diverse and complicated for in-depth treatment in this book, the financial manager should be prepared to use the contributions of specialists who have developed effective procedures for minimizing inventory investment.

A model commonly cited in business books for determining the optimal order quantity for an item is the classic deterministic *economic order quantity* (EOQ) *model*. It is the simplest of the inventory models and is based on the concept of cost trade-offs. As shown in Appendix A, EOQ is consistent with maximizing residual income — our surrogate for shareholder wealth maximization.

Assumptions of the EOQ Model

The EOQ represents the size of inventory investment that results in minimum total annual cost of the item in question. The basic EOQ model makes the following nine assumptions:

1. Annual (or period) demand (D) is known with certainty and is at a constant (linear) rate.
2. Lead time (t_L) is known with certainty and equals zero.
3. Stockouts are not permissible.
4. Replenishment is instantaneous (i.e., the entire order is received in one batch).
5. Order quantities (Q) are always the same size and are not restricted to being discrete.

6. The unit cost for items is constant (no discounts).
7. Single-item inventories are used.
8. An infinite planning horizon is used.
9. Demand, lead time, and costs are stationary (i.e., remain fixed over time).

These assumptions lead to inventories being replenished in the amount of the EOQ and depleted at a uniform rate over time until exhausted. Then inventories are restored and the pattern continues. Figure 14.2 depicts the assumptions. Note that *deterministic demand* and deterministic *lead time* allow for the placement of orders in such a way that the new supply arrives at the instant the old stock is used up. Each sawtooth portion of Fig. 14.2 represents the behavior of inventory during an inventory cycle, which requires time t_C.

This scenario is unlikely to happen in real life. That is, none of the EOQ assumptions describe the real situation. For instance, although average demand may be for 2500 units per year, daily demand (assuming 250 workdays) may not be very well represented by $2500/250 = 10$ units per day. There may be no orders today, then orders for 100 tomorrow, then none for the next week, and then on three successive days orders for 20, 50, and 5, respectively.

Thus neither are inventories drawn down to zero nor are lags between order and delivery dates stable. Customer demand controls the use rate.

FIGURE 14.2
Behavior of the Classic EOQ Model

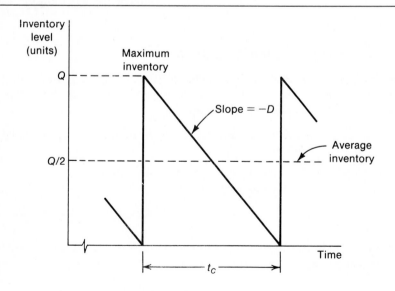

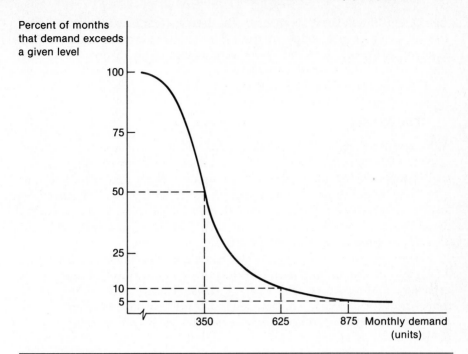

FIGURE 14.3
Distribution Showing the Percentage of Months That Demand Exceeds a Given Level

Similarly, supply lines are not constant. It could take longer than usual for the supplier to fill the order because he is out of stock owing to equipment breakdowns, labor troubles, or a host of other delays. The shipment time from the supplier is also subject to variability. If the use rate and/or the lead time exhibits variability (i.e., assumptions 1 through 3 are violated), then a higher order point is necessary to avoid stockouts. These levels act as safety stocks to accommodate uncertainty about the behavior and the rate of inventory replenishment.

Safety Stock

The determination of *safety stock* is based on a knowledge of the demand distribution during lead time together with a decision regarding the risk of stockout that management is willing to accept. This determination can be made from the distribution of demand in Fig. 14.3. Approximate average monthly use is 350 units (corresponding to 50% in Fig. 14.3). If normal lead time is a month for the item, and management wishes to be 90% sure of not running out of stock, it must have 625 units on hand when the replenishment order is placed. The safety stock is then $625 - 350 = 275$ units. From the shape of the demand curve we see that for high levels of assurance the safety stock required goes up disproportionately, and therefore the cost of providing this protection goes up. (Note the similarity between Figs. 14.3 and 14.1).

The Model

Although the EOQ model has been surpassed by more sophisticated computer models for controlling inventories, it does provide an excellent conceptual framework for analyzing more complex models and considerations. The EOQ model shows that as a firm increases its inventory, an inventory level is reached where the additional costs of carrying inventory equal the additional costs of obtaining inventory. This inventory position represents the optimum for minimizing costs.

The criterion to be minimized is the total cost associated with inventory. This cost consists of purchase (production) costs, ordering (setup) costs, carrying (holding) costs, and shortage costs. However, in the basic EOQ model no shortage cost will be incurred. And *since unit purchase costs are assumed constant, the pertinent variable costs per period are ordering cost plus carrying cost.*

Since one order is placed per cycle, the ordering cost per cycle is C_o. Annual ordering costs (W) can consist of many cycles; that is,

$$\text{annual ordering cost} = \frac{\text{units of item demanded annually}}{\text{units of item per order}} \times \text{order cost per order,}$$

or

$$W = \left(\frac{D}{Q}\right) C_o. \tag{14.1}$$

Annual carrying cost (H) is computed as (average number of units in inventory) × (annual holding cost per unit of item). Observation of Fig. 14.3 indicates that the average number of units in inventory during any inventory cycle equals $Q/2$. The annual holding cost per unit is C_h. Thus annual carrying costs are

$$H = \left(\frac{Q}{2}\right) C_h. \tag{14.2}$$

Total annual cost (T) is defined as the summation of ordering and carrying costs:

$$T = W + H = \left(\frac{D}{Q}\right) C_o + \left(\frac{Q}{2}\right) C_h. \tag{14.3}$$

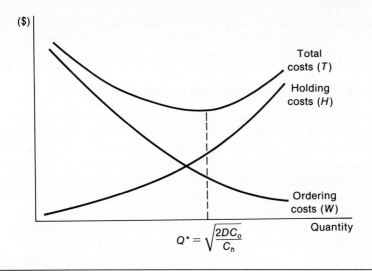

FIGURE 14.4
Inventory Costs in the EOQ Model

Figure 14.4 indicates the behavior of ordering costs, carrying costs, and their sum as a function of Q. The order quantity Q^* that minimizes total cost is determined by differentiating T with respect to Q, setting the result equal to zero, and solving for Q^*. This manipulation yields the classic EOQ formula:

$$Q^* = \left(\frac{2DC_o}{C_h}\right)^{1/2}. \tag{14.4}$$

ILLUSTRATION 14.1

Assume annual demand for an item is 600,000 units, ordering cost per order is $100, and carrying cost per unit is $0.25. The EOQ is

$$Q^* = \left(\frac{2 \times 100 \times 600,000}{0.25}\right)^{1/2} = 21,909.$$

This value results in an average number of units of 10,955 being carried in inventory. The total number of orders placed for the year is 27 ($=D/Q^*$). ☐

The unrealistic assumptions of the EOQ model can be relaxed to allow more practical applications of the model. Appendix B examines some of these situations. The conceptual nature of the model remains intact, however. Thus the basic EOQ model is still useful for financial managers to use in evaluating inventory levels and asking intelligent questions of production and purchasing personnel.

Just-in-Time Inventory System

Corporate management historically believed that it needed high inventory levels to keep assembly lines flowing. Material resource planning (commonly called MRP) systems had to be created to schedule, order, and maintain large amounts of inventory on hand. Elaborate computers were bought or leased, and salary payrolls bulged with the addition of systems analysts, programmers, data-processing operators, inventory managers, and cycle checkers. This conventional wisdom revolves around EOQ types of models and buffer stocks that are aimed at avoiding running out of stock.

Over the past few years management has come to realize that *inventory is really an expense*, not an asset — regardless of how the bookkeeping is done. Inventory is the most costly liability of any manufacturing company. Inventory drains cash for reasons that range from interest costs incurred in the financing of inventory to expenditures incurred to support large handling staffs.

An entirely different approach from MRP is the *just-in-time* (JIT) *system* developed in Japan and slowly being adopted elsewhere in the world. Reduced to its simplest terms, JIT is an approach to manufacturing that is designed to cut waste and thereby improve profits and cash flow. The JIT approach calls for slashing production, purchase lot sizes, and buffer stocks — but a little at a time, month after month, year after year. Less inventory means less storage, which means less obsolescence and spoilage and smaller buildings. That, in turn, implies lower inventory and real estate taxes and lower building and maintenance costs. Reduced material handling means less manpower and fewer conveyors, racks, and so on. These direct savings in inventory carrying costs can be substantial.

The greater benefits of JIT, however, accrue from enforced problem solving. Without extra inventory small ripples in the rate of production or delivery at one stage of manufacturing appear as large waves. The idea is to induce parts starvation deliberately in order to get the underlying problems resolved. Solving the problems cuts down the safety stock requirements, improves efficiency, and shifts inventory holding costs onto the suppliers and carriers.

If a JIT system is to function effectively, top quality is demanded of suppliers. Close and continuous checks are necessary to ensure that this quality is maintained throughout the production process. The system also requires timely, reliable deliveries. If suppliers and carriers cannot, or will not, work closely together, the right number of parts or goods does not get delivered when it should. The end result is a JIT system that works only on paper.

Internally, the success of JIT systems, as practiced in Japan, are dependent upon a virtually frozen master production schedule, highly skilled and disciplined cross-trained workers, and a high degree of job automation. The result is relatively standardized machine processes and setup times with little variation. These characteristics that contribute to the success of the JIT system in Japan are not frequently found in non-Oriental countries. So still uncertain is how successfully Japanese JIT systems can be utilized in other parts of the world.

A large computer simulation study conducted by American researchers indicates that a Japanese-style JIT process cannot automatically be applied to North American production systems with the same results as achieved in Japan, especially during a transition period. The transition period would likely be lengthy because of the many differences between American and Japanese production systems.

A large portion of the transition period would be devoted exclusively to preparation of the production environment for implementing JIT. A substantial amount of worker training and cross-training would be expected in order to standardize machine processing time and setup times. Thus significant worker-related costs would accrue to the firm, which must be considered prior to adoption of a JIT system. The firm's workers would also have to become long-term, loyal employees, as they are in Japan.

For companies that experience substantial variability in their demand schedule or that cannot expect to freeze their master production schedule, a JIT system will probably never be cost effective, regardless of the firm's commitment to worker training. Companies that most closely resemble Japanese companies in terms of size, resources, and market share (such as the large automobile manufacturers, electronics firms, and appliance manufacturers) will have the best chance of successfully implementing a JIT system. Smaller companies with diverse product lines and variable demand can expect less success. Nevertheless, these smaller firms may find it beneficial to analyze JIT systems for the purpose of embracing some of the principles and components without adopting a JIT system in its entirety.

Target Inventory Balances

Sometimes, comprehending the enormous number of items that some companies keep in stock is difficult. An effective physical inventory control system, whether it be an EOQ or a JIT system, will not have all items in inventory treated in the same manner under the same control technique. The inventory classification method discussed next provides a solution to the broadest range of physical inventory control desired. Later in this chapter turnover ratios and an EOQ analytical technique for monitoring inventories are examined.

A – B – C Method

Many managers find it difficult to divide materials, parts, supplies, and finished goods into subclassifications for purpose of stock control. For example, Table 14.1 shows inventory items that are subclassified in step-by-step fashion by (1) itemizing total annual volume of each item needed and (2) grouping in decreasing order of annual costs. This technique is often called the $A – B – C$ method. This approach allows for management by emphasis, where emphasis is placed on the few items that bring about the most results.

The final $A – B – C$ classification in Table 14.1 demonstrates that only 7% of the items represent 82% of the total cost. The standard relationship normally cited in $A – B – C$ analysis is that 20% of the items handled will contribute 80% of the annual sales dollars. However, the selection of A, B, and C items is mostly subjective. It should be dependent on whether different types of control are planned for each group and on what resources (such as control system, people, computer assistance) are available for controlling inventory activities.

TABLE 14.1
A – B – C Inventory Classification

Step 1: Calculate total sales volume and costs

Item	Unit sales	%	Unit price	Costs	%
1	10,000	7.0	$10.00	$100,000	81.8
2	1,000	0.8	0.05	50	0.0
3	10,000	7.0	0.02	200	0.2
4	11,000	7.7	1.00	11,000	9.0
5	110,000	77.5	0.10	11,000	9.0
	142,000	100.0		$122,250	100.0

Step 2: Group items in descending order of total cost

Item	Classification
1	A
4	B
5	B
3	C
2	C

The A – B – C analysis allows priorities to be established for control of replenishment ordering, with top control on A items and less control on B and C items. Class A items should be under continuous review. A JIT system works well with type A items. In contrast, an EOQ system does not work well with these items because of its periodic-review concept.

With A items the situation is reviewed after each transaction, and an order can be placed at any time. The order must be placed early enough to provide adequate assurance that the replenishment will arrive before the supply is exhausted. This type of control means frequent ordering, low safety stocks, and a willingness to incur expediting costs on A items, because the costs of placing and following up on orders are relatively low in comparison with costs of carrying excess inventories.

Class B items represent much of the company's inventory. These items can be controlled well with a JIT system if it can be properly implemented. Otherwise, the EOQ model of normal periodic review, based on order point forecasts, is appropriate.

Both type A and type B items are ordered according to budget schedules prepared by a production-planning department. Essentially, sales forecasts are the cornerstone for production scheduling. In turn, these production schedules are *exploded* (a commonly used term for giving detailed breakdowns of data) into the various direct material, parts, and supply components. These explosions result in purchase schedules for major items. The purchase schedules are adjusted for lead times, planning changes in inventories, and normal waste and spoilage. Purchases are made accordingly, and follow-ups are instituted by the purchasing department as needed.

Class C items are not critical — from an investment viewpoint — so an arbitrary fixed-time supply (e.g., a six-month supply) order quantity could be permitted. A two-bin system is often established by management to control C items. When the first bin is depleted, an order is placed to replenish the inventory consumed. The C items result in less frequent ordering, higher safety stocks, and less paperwork.

Inventory Turnover Ratios

The computation of an *inventory turnover ratio* is frequently relied upon by management to get an idea of whether inventory investments are appropriate. This method was used by W. T. Grant. It was corporate policy to have a constant turnover ratio — inventories were to increase by the same percentage change that sales increased. This technique is, at best, a very rough method of testing for the reasonableness of inventory investment. Very serious errors can result if turnover figures are accorded greater weight in arriving at judgments than they deserve. Many complex circumstances bear upon policy formulation in the individual firm, and these factors can influence inventory investment. Thus turnover ratios cannot be used routinely or mechanically in judging inventory investment policies; they must be used in conjunction with an analysis of underlying economic and financial factors.

The inventory turnover for a given period of time can be computed by the solution of either of the following two formulas:

$$\text{turnover} = \frac{\text{cost of goods sold}}{\text{average inventory}} \qquad (14.5)$$

or

$$\text{turnover} = \frac{\text{sales}}{\text{average inventory}}. \qquad (14.6)$$

Equation (14.5) is often advocated as being the correct formula. Some analysts, however, find the use of Eq. (14.6) more convenient; department stores, for example, customarily value their inventories at selling prices, using the so-called retail method for this purpose. As long as consistency is maintained, which equation is used is generally immaterial.

For greatest accuracy in the computation of inventory turnover, monthly inventories should ordinarily be used, especially if the size of inventories fluctuates substantially in the course of the year. Average inventory for a year, then, is the sum of the opening inventory and the inventory at the end of every month, this total to be divided by 13. Many firms operate on a fiscal year other than the calendar year, for the very reason that they want their yearly operations to conclude at a time when inventories are at or near their lowest level. This arrangement makes possible appreciable economies in the work of inventory taking and valuation. However, as Table 14.2 shows, for a firm in this position a turnover ratio computed on the basis of the average of opening and closing inventories would be

TABLE 14.2
Monthly Inventory Balance and Turnover Ratios

January 1 balance	$ 55,000	July	$160,000
January	70,000	August	175,000
February	85,000	September	190,000
March	100,000	October	145,000
April	115,000	November	100,000
May	130,000	December	55,000
June	145,000		

Assume cost of goods sold = $420,000

	Average inventory	Turnover
Based on monthly balances	$117,308	3.6
Based on opening and closing balances	55,000	7.6

much higher than one computed on the basis of an average of monthly inventories; accordingly, it would be quite misleading.

An inventory turnover ratio, standing by itself, generally means absolutely nothing. To state that the turnover of a particular firm is, say, 3.6 times indicates nothing about the wisdom of its inventory management policies. To give meaning to a turnover ratio, management often compares it with the firm's historical turnover ratio, with a budgeted value, or with those of other firms operating in the same area of business activity, that is, with the ratios of one's competitors. It is very difficult, however, to gain access to competitors' figures that would prove useful.

Should a firm's turnover ratio be decreasing over time, some evidence of growing deficiencies in inventory management is brought out — not conclusive evidence, by any means, but likely sufficient to warrant a thorough analysis of the situation. Likewise, should a firm's turnover ratio be lower than those of competitors, an investigation of the causes of what appears to be a record of poor performance might be in order.

A comparison of turnover ratios can easily lead to unsound conclusions. Comparative ratios, standing alone, can never wisely be taken as proof that inventory management has been good or bad. When ratios are found to be out of line, praise or blame to the makers of policy must be withheld until the reasons for the out-of-line result have been sought and found.

Inventory ratios vary according to the methods of inventory valuation that are used (e.g., LIFO versus FIFO), especially if the methods of valuation are changed. For example, a relatively low ratio may result from the heavy stocking of inventory in anticipation of price increases; should price increases actually come about, the managers would surely be deserving of praise rather than of blame. Or it may result from a stabilization of production, that is, the spreading out of productive operations over the year, as by a manufacturing firm whose sales are heavily concentrated in a few months.

On the other hand, a relatively high turnover ratio may not really be an indicator of favorable results and prospects. It may indicate a serious underinvestment in inventories. Surely there would be strong evidence of underinvestment should sales be falling off while the turnover figure is rising or should a firm's sales be expanding at a slower rate than those of other firms while its turnover ratio is rising. A loss of customers because of an inability to show them complete lines or to make prompt deliveries could hardly be regarded as a favorable development.

EOQ-Based Turnover Ratio

The question that arises from the previous discussion is what to compare the turnover ratio with. Ideally, management wants inventories to contribute to the wealth maximization objectives of the company. However, what ratio is consistent with this objective? The EOQ model can be tied to the turnover calculation to help answer this question. Of course, the answer is dependent on accepting the assumptions and usefulness of the EOQ model. The following illustration demonstrates this approach.

ILLUSTRATION 14.2

W. T. Grant's policy was to maintain a fixed relationship between inventory and sales. For the year ended January 31, 1974, sales of $1,644,747,000 were supported by year-end inventory of $399,533,000. Thus inventory was 24.3% of sales and turnover (based on sales) was 4.12 times. The following year, sales were $1,849,802,000 and inventory was on target at $450,637,000.

This approach is inconsistent with the EOQ wealth maximization approach. The percentage-of-sales technique overstates inventory balances relative to the EOQ model. The EOQ model shows inventory to be a function of sales demand, holding costs, and ordering costs. If the ratio of holding costs to ordering costs does not change, W. T. Grant's inventory ending January 1974 should be $423,707,000, or $26.9 million less than what it actually was.

This amount is calculated as follows: *Assume* that last year's inventory was optimal. Therefore with the EOQ formula (stated in thousands of dollars and not in units), the ordering cost-to-holding cost ratio, C_o/C_h, is as follows:

$$\$Q^* = \left(\frac{2DC_o}{C_h}\right)^{1/2},$$

$$\$399,533 = \left(\frac{2 \times \$1,644,747 \times C_o}{C_h}\right)^{1/2}.$$

Solving for the ordering cost-to-holding cost ratio gives

$$\frac{C_o}{C_h} = 48,526.$$

When this ratio is held constant, the January 1974 inventory balance should be

$$\$Q^* = (2 \times \$1,849,802 \times 48,526)(\tfrac{1}{2}) = \$423,707.$$

An alternative method of calculating the forecast balance is as follows:

$$\text{(last period's inventory)} \times (1 + \text{expected growth in sales})^{1/2}. \quad (14.7)$$

For W. T. Grant the calculation is

$$\$399,533 \times \left(\frac{\$1,849,802}{\$1,644,747}\right)^{1/2} = \$423,707.$$

At the (assumed) efficient inventory level of \$423,707,000, turnover increases from 4.12 times to about 4.37 times; the inventory-to-sales percentage decreases from 24.3% to about 22.9%. Thus *the traditional percent-of-sales method allows \$26.9 million excess inventory.* If 1971 is used as the base period (sales = \$1,254,131,000, inventory = \$260,492,000), \$134 million excess inventory exists as of January 31, 1974; that is,

$$\underbrace{\$450,637}_{\substack{1974 \\ \text{actual} \\ \text{inventory}}} - \$260,492 \times \left(\frac{\$1,849,802}{\$1,254,131}\right)^{1/2}.$$

Since management frequently thinks of inventory in terms of turnover (and percentages simply being the inverse of the turnover ratio), the targeted turnover ratio that incorporates the wealth-maximizing objective of the EOQ model is

$$\text{turnover} = \frac{\text{forecast sales}}{\text{EOQ forecast inventory}}$$

$$= \left[\frac{(\text{forecast sales})(\text{last year's sales})}{(\text{last year's inventory})^2}\right]^{1/2}. \tag{14.8}$$

Substituting numbers from this example into the revised turnover equation results in a turnover of 4.37 times:

$$\text{turnover} = \left[\frac{\$1,849,802 \times \$1,644,747}{(\$399,533)^2}\right]^{1/2} = 4.37.$$

The targeted percentage of sales is the inverse of this figure, or 22.9%.
□

The major advantage of the turnover ratio is its simplicity. Unfortunately, this is also its major disadvantage. *The inventory turnover ratio is not able to measure the efficiency of inventory management.* The mere relationship of cost of sales (or sales) to inventory fails to tell much of anything about efficiency. Adjusting it to incorporate EOQ concepts does lead to more efficient inventory balances. However, there is still no indication of how any change in price, product mix, or quantity affect efficiency. These factors are examined in the next chapter.

Summary

Many firms have a substantial proportion of their total assets invested in various kinds of inventories, and pressures to increase inventories are substantial. So effort must be made to keep inventories within reasonable limits. However, inventory management is usually not under the direct responsibility of the financial manager. He or she must rely on many nonfinancial specialists in an effort to determine the "proper" inventory investment level.

This chapter examined inventory costs and models that provide the financial manager with a conceptual basis for overseeing inventory investments. The traditional cost categories used in analyzing inventories are carrying (holding) costs and ordering (setup) costs. The trade-off between these two costs leads to a cost minimization solution for the economic order quantity (EOQ) model. The model is consistent with shareholder wealth maximization as embodied in the residual income model (discussed in Chapter 1).

Another model, which has gained acceptance in Japan and is finding acceptance with some large companies in other parts of the world, is the just-in-time (JIT) technique. This technique is an improvement over the EOQ system in that if properly implemented, product quality improves, management attains a better understanding of the production process, and lower inventory investment results. Unfortunately, the characteristics that make the system so successful in Japan are not easily transferred to Western cultures.

The next topic discussed in the chapter was monitoring inventory balances. The A – B – C system of physical inventory control was discussed first. This system can be implemented with either an EOQ or JIT system. It is based on the premise that a small fraction of the items generate a large fraction of the total revenues of the business. These items require a different type of control than items that contribute little to the revenues of the business.

Financial techniques for monitoring inventories were discussed next. Traditional turnover ratios are fraught with problems. An EOQ turnover ratio provides more efficient inventory targets since it implicitly incorporates the inventory costs of holding and carrying, which are instrumental to a cost minimization strategy.

Even though the complexity of inventory management is enormous, proper inventory management is important to the short-run liquidity and the long-run profitability of the firm. Lack of control over inventories can be ruinous to a business.

Key Concepts

A – B – C method	Lead time
Carrying cost	Safety stock
Deterministic demand	Setup cost
Economic order quantity (EOQ) model	Turnover ratio

Appendix A
EOQ As a Wealth Maximization Model

The EOQ formula is based on a cost minimization criterion that assumes separation among production, investment, and financing (a common assumption of finance theory). Under these conditions it is compatible with management's value maximization objective, where value maximization is defined as maximizing residual income (RI). The Appendix to Chapter 1 shows that it is valid to maximize RI.

In terms of inventory analysis, the RI model assesses the incremental contribution of inventory to profits less a deduction for the opportunity cost of funds invested in average inventory. Hence

RI = revenue − (cost of goods sold) − (ordering costs)
     − (out of pocket holding costs) − (opportunity holding costs),

or

$$RI = VD - PD - C_o \left(\frac{D}{Q}\right) - i_1 \left(\frac{PQ}{2}\right) - i_2 \left(\frac{PQ}{2}\right), \tag{A.1}$$

where

V = selling price per unit,
D = unit demand rate per period,
P = cost price per unit,
C_o = order cost per order,
Q = units of item per order,
i_1 = carrying cost, expressed as a percentage of P, exclusive of the opportunity cost of funds tied up in inventory,
i_2 = opportunity cost of funds tied up in inventory, as a percentage of P,
$(i_1 + i_2)P = C_h$ = total holding cost per unit of item per time period.

Taking the first derivative of Eq. (A.1) with respect of Q, setting the result equal to zero, and solving for Q leads to the RI-maximizing order quantity:

$$Q^*_{RI} = \left[\frac{2DC_o}{(i_1 + i_2)P}\right]^{1/2}. \tag{A.2}$$

This equation is identical to the traditional EOQ formula. The following discussion shows that maximizing accounting return on investment (ROI) or profit (Z) does not lead to the same conclusion.

If management's objective is to maximize accounting ROI, Eq. (A.1) becomes

$$\text{ROI} = \frac{VD - PD - C_o(D/Q) - i_1 P(Q/2)}{P(Q/2)} \,, \tag{A.3}$$

where the numerator represents profits and the denominator is average inventory investment. Differentiating with respect to Q, setting the result equal to zero, and solving for Q results in

$$Q^*_{\text{ROI}} = \frac{2C_o}{V - P} \,. \tag{A.4}$$

This maximum is distinctly different from the EOQ (and RI) maximum.

Where management's objective is to maximize accounting profits, the numerator of Eq. (A.3) is differentiated with respect to Q, set equal to zero, and solved in terms of Q. The maximizing order quantity is

$$Q^*_Z = \left(\frac{2DC_o}{i_1 P}\right)^{1/2} \,. \tag{A.5}$$

Although this result is similar to the EOQ (and RI) result, it differs in the denominator. The profit-maximizing approach results in higher inventory order quantities since the opportunity cost of funds (i_2) is ignored.

Appendix B
Extensions of the Classic EOQ Vendor Model

Nonzero Lead Times

One of the assumptions of the classic EOQ model is zero lead time. Consider the case where lead time is greater than zero. As before, assume that lead time is deterministic and stationary, as opposed to being stochastic.

Figure B.1 illustrates situations where the number of days of lead time is either less than the optimal cycle time ($t_L < t_C$) or greater than the optimal cycle time ($t_L > t_C$). Note the following:

□ The optimal reorder quantity Q^* is unaffected by the magnitude of the lead time, which means that the EOQ model is still relevant.

□ The optimal reorder point R^* must be determined such that replenishment arrives exactly at the beginning of a new cycle.

□ Time t_C equals the economic order quantity divided by the use per day: $Q^* \times 360/D$.

First, consider the case when $t_L < t_C$. Demand during the lead time is $t_L \times D/360$, which is less than Q^* because $Q^* = t_C \times D/360$ and $t_L < t_C$. Thus one simply places an order when inventory level drops to $R^* = t_L \times D/360$, thereby guaranteeing that replenishment arrives exactly at the end of the current cycle.

Next, consider the case where $t_L > t_C$. Lead time demand is still $t_L \times D/360$; however, this demand is now greater than Q^*. In this case it is not possible to reorder at an inventory level that will exactly absorb lead time demand.

Therefore lead time demand must be satisfied both by the amount of inventory on hand when an order is launched (i.e., by R^*) and by replenishments (from previous orders) that arrive during the lead time under consideration. Thus

$$R^* = \left(t_L \times \frac{D}{360} \right) - \left[\frac{t_L}{t_C} \right] Q^*, \tag{B.1}$$

where $[t_L/t_C]$ represents the integer part of the quotient t_L/t_C, that is, the number of complete cycles during a lead time. Note that $[t_L/t_C] = 0$ when $t_L < t_C$, in which case Eq. (B.1) is simply the result for Fig. B.1(a).

(a)   Lead time less than cycle time

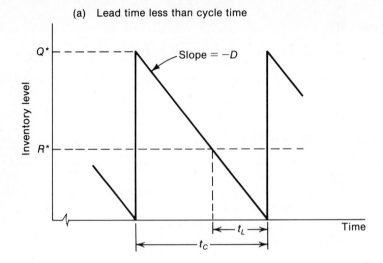

(b)   Lead time greater than cycle time

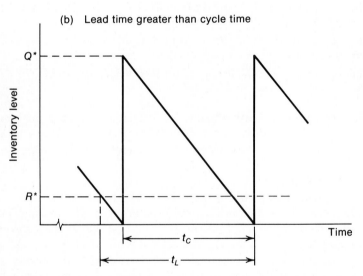

FIGURE B.1
Reorder Points for Lead Times Greater Than Zero

ILLUSTRATION B.1

If the inventory cycle t_C is 18 days and the lead time is 7.2 days, then from Eq. (B.1) the economic order quantity Q^* of 250 items, with an annual demand D of 5000 units, should be placed whenever inventory drops to

$$R^* = 7.2 \times \frac{5000}{360} - \left[\frac{7.2}{18}\right] 250$$

$$= 100 - 0 = 100 \text{ items.}$$

If the lead time is 28.8 days, then

$$R^* = 28.8 \times \frac{5000}{360} - \left[\frac{28.8}{18}\right] 250$$

$$= 400 - [1]250 = 150 \text{ items.} \qquad \square$$

Shortages Allowed

This extension to the model allows shortages to be back-ordered. As before, all demands must be met ultimately; hence at the moment of replenishment all back orders are satisfied prior to meeting new demands. These back orders, however, incur a shortage cost. When back orders are allowed, the assumption of unaffected demand requires that all demand be met. If purchases are delayed, however, part of each incoming order is immediately allocated to back-order demand. Consequently, fewer orders may be made, resulting in lower ordering costs; and average inventory levels

FIGURE B.2
EOQ Behavior with Back Orders

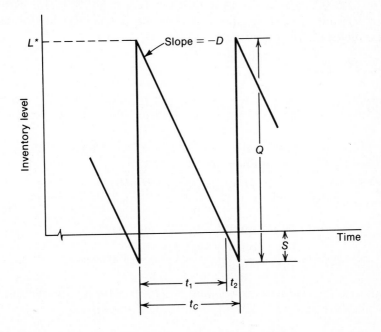

may be lower, resulting in reduced carrying costs. This trade-off between ordering and carrying costs, on the one hand, and back-ordering costs, on the other hand, can be exploited, as shown next.

Figure B.2 portrays the inventory behavior for this model. New variables are defined as follows:

S = maximum number of units short,
C_s = shortage cost per unit per time period,
t_1 = time within a cycle during which inventory is held,
t_2 = time within a cycle during which a shortage exists.

Appendix C shows the derivation of the EOQ back-order model. The optimal order quantity is

$$Q* = \left(\frac{2DC_o}{C_h} \times \frac{C_h + C_s}{C_s}\right)^{1/2},$$

(B.2)

and the maximum shortage quantity is

$$S* = \left[\frac{2DC_o/C_h}{(C_hC_s + C_s^2)}\right]^{1/2}.$$

(B.3)

ILLUSTRATION B.2

Assume annual demand for an item is 600,000 units, ordering cost per order is $100, carrying cost per unit per year is $0.25, and back-ordering cost per unit is $2. Ignoring back-ordering possibilities for the moment, the EOQ is calculated, using Eq. (14.4), as

$$Q* = \left(2 \times 100 \times \frac{600,000}{0.25}\right)^{1/2} = 21,909 \text{ units.}$$

This EOQ results in an average number of units of 10,955 being carried in inventory. The total number of orders placed for the year is 27 (= $D/Q*$).

Compare these results with the case where back ordering is allowed. From Eq. (B.2) the optimal order quantity is

$$Q* = \left[\left(2 \times 100 \times \frac{600,000}{0.25}\right)\left(\frac{0.25 + 2}{2}\right)\right]^{1/2} = 23,238 \text{ units.}$$

From Eq. (B.3) the maximum shortage quantity is

$$S* = \left[\frac{2 \times 100 \times 600,000 \times 0.25}{(0.25 \times 2 + 2^2)}\right]^{1/2} = 2582 \text{ units.}$$

The average inventory on hand is [$Q* - S*$]/2 = 10,328 units, and the total number of orders placed during the year is $D/Q* = 26$. This example shows that being able to back-order product can result in lower inventory investment.   □

Quantity Discounts Offered

Frequently, suppliers offer discounts if buyers purchase in large quantities. The motivation for doing so is straightforward. In vendor models the supplier moves more inventory forward in the distribution channel and lowers carrying costs if buyers purchase in larger quantities. By purchasing a large lot size, the buyer is trading off lowered purchasing and ordering costs (fewer orders) with higher carrying costs.

If a company is offered a single quantity discount, then one approach is to compare the total cost for the best inventory policy without the discount with the total cost if the discount is accepted. Total annual cost (T_d) is defined as the sum of annual ordering cost, annual carrying cost, annual shortage cost, and annual purchasing cost, or

$$T_d = T_s + D \times P \tag{B.4}$$

for the back-order model, and

$$T_d = T + D \times P \tag{B.5}$$

for the no-shortage model. Cost T_s is defined by Eq. (C.6) in Appendix C, T is defined by Eq. (14.3), D is annual demand, P is purchase cost per unit of item, and $D \times P$ represents the annual purchasing cost.

Often suppliers offer a progression of discrete discounts to buyers, each discount corresponding to a larger minimum purchase quantity. To simplify presentation, assume no shortages, and assume ordering costs and carrying costs per unit per period are constant. Since these costs are not functions of price, the purchase price is not a factor in the determination of Q^*. It follows, therefore, that decreases in the purchase price of items do nothing but lower the vertical orientation of the total cost function. In other words, total inventory cost for any order quantity Q is less when the unit purchase cost is lower.

Assume in Fig. B.3 that a supplier will sell at price P_1, unless the buyer agrees to purchase in quantities of Q_1 or more units, in which case P_2 is the selling price. Similarly, if the buyer agrees to buy in quantities of Q_2 or more units, the lower price P_3 applies. If the objective is to minimize the total inventory cost per time period, then this objective is achieved when the order size is Q_2 units and the price is P_3. This action results in a total cost of \$$D$. The buyer will not purchase any more than Q_2 units since total cost will increase. Note that Q^*, the economic order quantity, is not permissible at price P_3 since $Q^* < Q_2$.

The result in this example cannot be generalized; that is, the lowest inventory cost will not always be associated with the policy of purchasing

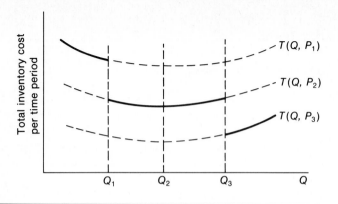

FIGURE B.3
Total Inventory Costs When Two Price Breaks Are Present

the minimum allowable quantity at the lowest price offered. In general, the minimum cost solution is found by first computing Q^*. (Remember that Q^* is independent of purchase price, provided that ordering cost and unit carrying cost remain the same.) Next, compute the total inventory cost for Q^* and the appropriate unit purchasing price for that order size, $T_d(Q^*, P^*)$. The only way in which total cost might be lower is if the buyer purchases the minimum quantity corresponding to a unit purchase price that is lower than P^*. Total costs under these lower-price alternatives must be compared with $T_d(Q^*, P^*)$ to determine the best policy.

ILLUSTRATION B.3

Consider a steel casing that has an annual demand of 2000 units. The cost per order is $90, and the annual inventory carrying rate is $1 per unit. The vendor of this part offers a quantity discount schedule as follows:

0 to 500 units	$18 per unit
501 to 700 units	16 per unit
701 to 1000 units	14 per unit
1001 and more units	13 per unit

There are three price breaks occurring at quantities of 500, 700, and 1000 units, respectively. The EOQ (ignoring unit purchase price) is 600 units — this is left for you to verify.

The total cost incurred at the EOQ level is $32,600:

$$\text{holding costs} \quad = \frac{600}{2} \times \$1 \quad = \quad \$ \quad 300.00$$

$$\text{ordering costs} = \frac{2000}{600} \times \$90 = \quad 300.00$$

$$\text{purchase costs} = 2000 \times \$16 = \quad \underline{32{,}000.00}$$

$$\text{total cost} \qquad \underline{\$32{,}600.00}$$

Next, compute total cost at the $14-per-unit price level, and compare it with the EOQ level total cost:

$$\text{holding costs} \quad = \frac{701}{2} \times \$1 \quad = \quad \$ \quad 350.50$$

$$\text{ordering costs} = \frac{2000}{701} \times \$90 = \quad 256.78$$

$$\text{purchase costs} = 2000 \times \$14 = \quad \underline{28{,}000.00}$$

$$\text{total cost} \qquad \underline{\$28{,}607.28}$$

Since total cost declines if 701 units are purchased, this purchase volume dominates the EOQ level. We must see whether costs can be lowered further; we do so by checking the next price break level:

$$\text{holding costs} \quad = \frac{1001}{2} \times \$1 \quad = \quad \$ \quad 500.50$$

$$\text{ordering costs} = \frac{2000}{1001} \times \$90 = \quad 179.82$$

$$\text{purchase costs} = 2000 \times \$13 = \quad \underline{26{,}000.00}$$

$$\text{total cost} \qquad \underline{\$26{,}680.32}$$

Buying 1001 units results in the lowest total cost. This is the amount that should be purchased.   □

Appendix C
Derivation of the EOQ Back-Order Model

In the back-order model the decision variables are Q, the order quantity, and S, the maximum shortage. The order cost component is the same as in the classical EOQ model:

$$W_s = \left(\frac{D}{Q}\right) C_o. \tag{C.1}$$

Carrying cost per cycle is determined as in the classic model. It can be stated as

$$(Q - S)^2 \frac{C_h}{2D}. \tag{C.2}$$

When carrying cost is annualized (by multiplying by the number of cycles per period, D/Q), total annual carrying cost (H_s) becomes

$$H_s = (Q - S)^2 \frac{C_h}{2Q}. \tag{C.3}$$

The final component is the shortage cost, which is determined in a manner similar to that used for carrying cost. Shortage cost per cycle is given by (average number of units short) $\times$ (time short per cycle) $\times$ (shortage cost per unit per time period). It is stated as

$$\frac{S^2 C_s}{2D}. \tag{C.4}$$

Multiplying by the number of cycles, D/Q, gives the annual shortage cost C_s:

$$C_s = \frac{S^2 C_s}{2Q}. \tag{C.5}$$

Combining the three cost components, we can express the total variable cost T_s for this model as

$$T_s = C_o \left(\frac{D}{Q}\right) + (Q - S)^2 \frac{C_h}{2Q} + \frac{S^2 C_s}{2Q}. \tag{C.6}$$

Taking partial derivatives of Eq. (C.6), with respect to Q and S, and solving for the stationary point gives the optimal order and shortage quantities, Eqs. (B.2) and (B.3) of Appendix B, respectively.

Questions

1.   What is the primary function of inventory?

2.   How do various inventory carrying or ordering costs affect decisions concerning the size of inventory to be carried?

3.   In a graph of cost-quantity inventory relationships, why is the total cost curve high at both low and high quantities and lower between them?

4.   What are some limitations of the economic order quantity approach to the analysis of inventory problems?

5.   What is the A – B – C method?

6.   How is proper inventory management linked to the short-run liquidity of the firm? How is it linked to the long-run profitability of the firm?

7.   What is the purpose of safety stock? Will the size of the safety stock be influenced by the firm's attitude toward risk? Why? How will a JIT system affect safety stock?

8.   Discuss some of the problems of determining the variables that enter into the determination of the EOQ.

9.   What costs are associated with procurement of materials and with carrying inventories?

10.   What are the evils of carrying inventories that are excessive in relation to current sales?

11.   What is the significance of inventory turnover ratios in testing the soundness of inventory investment policies?

12.   In calculation of the turnover ratio, when might the use of an average of beginning and ending inventories lead to an inaccurate result?

13.   Does the choice of an inventory valuation method affect the turnover ratio? Explain, using examples.

14.   Describe the disadvantage of underinvestment in inventories.

15.   How do quantity discounts affect the analysis of quantities to purchase with use of the economic order quantity formulas?

Problems

1. The Brutus Manufacturing Company carries a wide assortment of items for its customers. One item is particularly popular. Wishing to keep its inventory under control, management selects this item to initiate its new problem of ordering only the optimal economic order quantity each time. From the following information, help them solve the problem.

Annual demand	160,000 units
Price per unit	$2.00
Carrying costs	$0.10 per unit, or 5% of value
Cost per order	$5.00

Fill in the missing amounts:

Number of orders	1	10	20	40	80	100
Size of order						
Average inventory						
Carrying costs						
Order costs						
Total costs						

Determine the optimal EOQ by inspection and by the use of the formula in Eq. (14.4).

2. Vanessa's Bridal Shop stocks rolls of flowered ribbon. The annual demand reaches 2000 for these rolls. Each roll costs $10, and the order cost is $40 per order. Carrying costs are 10% of purchase price. The Bridal Shop is currently ordering on an optimal basis. The wholesaler, in an effort to shift some of its inventory to the Bridal Shop, points to the high ordering cost of $40 and suggests that orders be placed only once a year. As an inducement, the wholesaler offers Vanessa a 3% discount if the annual ordering policy is adopted. Evaluate this offer, and make a reasonable recommendation to accept or reject it. Show your calculations. If you reject the offer, what reasonable counteroffer might you make?

3. The Cormick Industries Group had the following inventory balances during the year:

January 1	$25,000	July	$ 90,000
January	45,000	August	75,000
February	25,000	September	25,000
March	15,000	October	101,000
April	80,000	November	60,000
May	60,000	December	35,000
June	45,000		

Cost of goods sold = $360,000

Determine average inventory and inventory turnover based on beginning and closing balances, and compare the answer with a calculation based on a 13-point average. Explain the differences.

4. Last year's sales of $15,000 were supported by an average inventory of $5000. The forecast for the coming year estimates sales of $25,000. Using the EOQ dollar approach, calculate the following:

   (a) The implied ordering cost – to – holding cost ratio.

   (b) The EOQ dollar amount.

   (c) The average inventory investment.

5. Last year's sales were $800,000, and the average inventory balance was $200,000. This year sales are expected to be $1,000,000.

   (a) What should the average inventory balance be, using the EOQ model?

   (b) What should it be by using the percent-of-sales approach?

   (c) Which method is best? Explain.

6. GHI Company forecasts sales for the period to be $200,000. Last period's sales were $150,000, and the beginning inventory balance was $25,000.

   (a) What is the targeted turnover ratio if the beginning inventory balance for this period is $35,000?

   (b) What is the targeted percentage of sales? Use the EOQ turnover equation to work this problem.

7. Using the following data, determine and discuss the sensitivity of EOQ, total inventory policy costs, and average investment to changes in cost and usage. Carrying cost is 5% of purchase price.

	Annual demand	Ordering costs	Price per unit
(a)	100,000	$5.00	$10.00
(b)	150,000	5.00	10.00
(c)	100,000	5.00	15.00
(d)	100,000	7.50	10.00

8. A company purchases a part that is a component of one of the assemblies it manufactures. This component is used at a uniform rate throughout the year, and the supplier delivers the entire lot at one time. The manufacturer finds it necessary to take the following factors into consideration when ascertaining the economic lot size:

   consumption rate per year = 25,000 units,
   cost of placing and receiving an order = $10,
   cost of carrying 1 unit of inventory for 1 year = 20% of price,
   price per unit = $\begin{cases} \$1 \text{ for lot sizes of 1 to 1999 units,} \\ \$0.50 \text{ for lot sizes of 2000 to 4999 units,} \\ \$0.30 \text{ for lot sizes of 5000 or more units.} \end{cases}$

   (a) What is the economic order size at each of these prices?

   (b) In what order quantity should the manufacturer purchase the part? What annual cost will this order quantity generate?

Note: Problems 9 and 10 require familiarity with the material in Appendix B.

9. Compute the reorder points, given the following information:

	(a)	*(b)*	*(c)*
Lead time	15 days	25 days	25 days
Cycle time	25 days	15 days	25 days
EOQ	694 units	417 units	694 units
Annual demand	10,000 units	10,000 units	10,000 units

Assume 360 days in the year.

10. Stevenson Corporation sells a single product that has an annual demand of 75,000 units. As best can be determined, carrying costs per unit of this product amount to $0.01, and ordering costs are $60. Back-ordering cost per unit is estimated at $10 per unit. Price per unit is $100.

(a) What is the EOQ in units and in dollars?

(b) What is the maximum shortage quantity in units and dollars?

(c) How many orders are placed per year if optimal inventories are maintained?

(d) What is the average investment in inventory in dollars?

CHAPTER 15 □
Monitoring Inventory Balances

The predominant aim of inventory management is to keep inventory investments in line with targets (or budgets) so that resources are allocated efficiently and profit targets are realized. The previous chapter discussed the use of turnover ratios for measuring performance. This technique has serious deficiencies, for it is not able to answer the following questions: How do actual reported inventories compare with budgeted inventories? What factors have caused variations? Who or what is responsible for favorable or unfavorable variances? Is the product mix appropriate? The factors upon which answers to these questions may be based will be considered in this chapter through analysis of sales and cost of sales in the income statement, and of inventory levels in the balance sheet.

The importance of monitoring inventories is vividly indicated in the following excerpts about W. T. Grant, which were published in *Business Week* magazine (July 19, 1976):

> Grant was unable to keep track of its inventory. The company was reluctant to reduce inventories by taking markdowns because that reduced gross selling margins. . . . Headquarters did not know what was going on in the field. . . . It was easy for managers to manipulate their inventory. They would order goods and delay passing the invoice to [headquarters for payment]. This increased their ordering budget and understated the cost of sales.

> Further complicating the inventory problem was Grant's lack of a sales classification system to indicate what specific items were selling.

> Procedures were so lax that I am not sure how any reasonable estimate of inventory, accounts receivable or profit could be obtained.

The specific means of testing the reasonableness of inventory investment in this chapter is the computation of inventory variances. *Variance*

417

analysis models offer a significant improvement over turnover ratios in evaluating inventory performance. Since the primary function of inventory is to decouple sales and production, it is beneficial to conduct the evaluation in terms of analysis of the components of gross profit — sales and cost of sales — and then translate this analysis into analysis of cash flow from operations.

The purpose of this chapter is to examine monitoring of inventories by using variance analysis. The discussion starts with a simple one-way variance analysis; next, it separates the single variance into components representing price and volume. Finally, it breaks the volume variance into a mix variance and a quantity variance. These analyses take as given whatever accrual accounting policy that management follows with respect to inventories. For simplicity, analysis of these variances focuses on changes in gross profit. A subsequent section incorporates *cash flows* directly into the variance analysis model. The final section reveals the superiority of variance techniques over inventory turnover ratios.

One-Way Variance Analysis

Comparative analysis of inventory levels in the balance sheet and of cost-of-goods-sold amounts in the income statement are often used as a means of inventory analysis. The procedure is simple and sometimes provides satisfactory results. However, it can often be more misleading than informative. Percentages have significance only when the base remains stable and provides truly comparative data. Very often, a change in the base obscures facts that should be brought to light. The data given in Table 15.1 illustrates the point.

The cost percentages appear to be entirely unfavorable. A 20% increase in volume required a 44% increase in cost, and unit cost increased 20%. The analyst cannot conclude that all costs increased. Because some of the costs are fixed, the increase in volume could cause a decrease in fixed unit costs. Therefore the analyst must determine what part of the change

TABLE 15.1
Analysis of Cost of Sales

	Budget	Actual	Change Amount	Change %
Cost of goods sold	$200,000	$288,000	$88,000	44
Units	$20,000	$24,000	$4,000	20
Cost per unit	$10.00	$12.00	$2.00	20

TABLE 15.2
Analysis of Fixed and Variable Cost of Sales

	Budget		Actual	
	Total	Per unit	Total	Per unit
Cost of sales:				
Variable	$ 80,000	$ 4.00	$158,000	$ 6.58
Fixed	120,000	6.00	130,000	5.42
Total	$200,000	$10.00	$288,000	$12.00

in unit cost is attributable to volume and what part, if any, is the result of cost reduction. If the variable and fixed inventory costs are identified, the analyst may find that some costs have increased, as shown in Table 15.2.

According to the data in the table, a favorable *volume variance* has partially offset an increase in per-unit variable costs. This conclusion is apparent from looking at the $0.58-per-unit decrease in fixed costs.

A more reliable comparative analysis of inventories is gained by examining gross profit variances, which are shown in Table 15.3. Since gross profit equals the difference between sales and cost of sales, this *one-way analysis of variance* results in a fuller understanding of how inventories affect profits and cash flows.

A cursory glance at the figures in Table 15.3 indicates deteriorating

TABLE 15.3
One-Way Variance Analysis of Gross Profit

	Budget		Actual		Variance	
	Amount	%	Amount	%	Amount	%
Sales	$400,000	100.0	$403,200	100.0	$ 3,200	0.8
Cost of sales:						
Beginning inventory	$194,250	48.5	$337,000	83.6	$142,750	73.5
Purchases	117,500	29.4	159,750	39.6	42,250	36.0
Ending inventory	<111,750>	27.9	<208,750>	51.8	<97,000>	86.8
Total	$200,000	50.0	$288,000	71.4	$88,000	44.0
Gross profit	$200,000	50.0	$115,200	28.6	<$84,800>	<42.4>

performance relative to budget. It appears that sales volume is up marginally, while costs are up significantly. If the increase in sales revenue is
caused by higher selling prices, this result is less desirable than an increase
arising from greater volume of sales. The market forces that have allowed
an increase in selling price can react to drive the price down, resulting in
excess inventories. Similarly (although not apparent in the data), cost decreases that result from increased sales volume are not as desirable as
those achieved through more efficient use of labor, materials, and equipment. The former type of decrease may be temporary, and the latter type
is more likely to be permanent.

Cost-of-sales analysis indicates that opening inventory has released
$142,750 additional cost, relative to budget, from the balance sheet to
the income statement. Since ending inventory exceeds budget by $97,000,
this amount of additional cost has been *deferred* to the balance sheet, to
be released next period. A large and unfavorable purchase variance represents the remaining variance in cost of sales. Do these cost-of-sales variances
lead to the conclusion that the manager of inventory deserves criticism?
This comparative analysis is unable to provide the answer.

The change in gross profit is the result of change in sales revenue
and change in cost of sales. If a single product is sold, each of these sources
is affected by two factors: price and volume. When, as usual, more than
one product is sold, gross profit is also influenced by the product mix
(discussed later in this chapter) because all products do not normally bear
the same profit margins.

Usually, the net change in gross profit results from an interplay of
several factors, some causing increases and some causing decreases. An
increase in selling price may be accompanied by an increase in volume,
thereby causing a substantial increase in sales revenue. However, consistent
with the downward-sloping demand curve facing most firms, an increase
in selling price is often accompanied by a decrease in volume, with the
result that sales revenue and gross profits may increase only a small amount
or perhaps even decline. Knowledge of the elasticity of the demand curve
is important for understanding the price-volume relationship.

Responsibility for gross profit changes varies. For example, whereas
a sales manager may not be able to claim credit for sales revenue generated
by price increases, he or she is more likely to be responsible for increases
generated by volume. A production manager cannot be held responsible
for cost increases and higher inventory caused by a drop in production
due to lack of sales, but he or she can be charged with increases traceable
to inefficiencies in production or excessive spending. Ideally, answers need
to address how these variances affect operating cash flows. For simplicity,
much of the discussion that follows in this chapter focuses on analysis of
changes in gross profit. *Cash flows will be directly incorporated into the analysis
in a later section.*

Two-Way Variance Analysis

The analysis of changes in gross profit can be better understood by examining changes in sales revenues and cost of sales such that the various influencing factors are isolated separately. As indicated earlier, three factors can affect sales and cost of sales: *price, volume,* and *mix.* For the present the complexities of mix are deferred, and it is assumed here that a single product is manufactured and sold.

If price and volume factors are to be separated,[1] two basic principles must be adhered to:

1. The volume factor must be held constant when one is determining the effect of a price change.

2. The price factor must be held constant when one is determining the effect of a change in volume.

Application and explanation of these principles is given in the following illustration, which uses the information in Table 15.3.

ILLUSTRATION 15.1

(a) Analysis of Change in Sales Revenue

Assume that budgeted sales for a given year were 20,000 units at a $20 selling price, or a total of $400,000. Actual sales for the year of $403,200 were obtained by selling 24,000 units at a price of $16.80 each. Under a horizontal form of analysis sales revenue variances can be calculated as shown in Table 15.4.

Two-way variance analysis provides obvious benefits over the one-way model. Interpretation is as follows, going from right to left in Table 15.4: Column (c) represents the budget, or 20,000 units to be sold at $20 each. Column (b) represents a *flexible* sales budget. It shows what sales dollars should be given actual sales volume and no change in the budgeted price. When compared with column (c), the $80,000 favorable variance is a result of selling 4000 more units than budgeted. Column (a) is total actual sales. The variance between columns (a) and (b) represents the effect of changing

---

[1] Some people argue that price and volume factors are contaminated by a joint variance and that it is necessary to separately identify the joint effect. Although all cost accountants recognize the existence of the joint variance, most accountants disregard it because assigning responsibility for it and interpreting it are difficult. As will become clear shortly, variances are generally labeled as favorable or unfavorable. Whenever a joint variance is calculated, it is possible to have favorable pure price and pure volume variances and an unfavorable joint variance. Under such circumstances it is difficult to have much enthusiasm for the joint variance.

TABLE 15.4
Two-Way Variance Analysis of Revenues

(a) **Actual volume** × **actual price**	(b) **Actual volume** × **budget price**	(c) **Budgeted volume** × **budget price**
24,000 × $16.80 = $403,200	24,000 × $20,000 = $480,000	20,000 × $20.00 = $400,000

Sales price variance $76,800; unfavorable	Sales volume variance $80,000; favorable

Total sales variance $3200; favorable

prices, relative to budget. Total sales variance, relative to budget, is the difference between columns (a) and (c). The favorable total sales variance is a result of lower selling prices stimulating sales volume. Has this pricing strategy resulted in more profits? Analysis of cost of sales provides some insight.

(b) Analysis of Change in Cost of Sales

The same principles of analysis used in relation to change in sales revenue are also applicable to analysis of change in cost of sales. Here, assume that the budgeted cost of sales is 20,000 units at a unit cost of $10, or a total of $200,000. The actual cost of sales for 24,000 units sold is $288,000, or $12.00 per unit. Analysis of the $88,000 difference between actual and budget requires examination of purchases (or production) and the change between opening and closing inventory balances. Assume that quantities and unit costs for opening and closing inventories are as shown in Table 15.5.

The analysis reveals that the cost-of-sales variance is relatively complex and requires careful interpretation. The change in inventory level contributes a net unfavorable variance of $45,750 — consisting of a net balance of $17,090 nonbudgeted price increases and $28,660 nonbudgeted volume changes released from the balance sheet (thus increasing the cost of sales). Purchases (or production) for the period were $42,250 more than budgeted, resulting in an additional cost-of-sales increase. Higher prices contribute $30,500 to the total purchase variance; the balance is due to a volume effect. The total unfavorable variance of $88,000 consists of $47,590 in price increases and $40,410 in volume changes.

Care must be exercised in interpreting opening and closing inventory

TABLE 15.5
Two-Way Variance Analysis of Cost of Sales

Actual volume × actual price	Actual volume × budget price	Budgeted volume × budget price
Opening inventory		
23,000 × $14.652 = $337,000	23,000 × $9.25 = $212,750	21,000 × $9.25 = $194,250
Price variance $124,250; unfavorable	Volume variance $18,500; unfavorable	
Closing inventory		
10,000 × $20.875 = $208,750	10,000 × $10.159 = $101,590	11,000 × $10.159 = $111,750
Price variance $107,160; favorable	Volume variance $10,160; unfavorable	
Net inventory change		
Price variance $17,090; unfavorable	Volume variance $28,660; unfavorable	
Purchases		
11,000 × $14.523 = $159,750	11,000 × $11.75 = $129,250	10,000 × $11.75 = $117,500
Price variance $30,500; unfavorable	Volume variance $11,750; unfavorable	
Total		
Price variance $47,590; unfavorable	Volume variance $40,410; unfavorable	

Total cost-of-sales variance $88,000; unfavorable

variances. For example, with the price variance, whenever actual inventory exceeds (actual volume) × (budgeted price), an unfavorable variance results for opening inventory and a favorable variance results for closing inventory. The reason is as follows: The opening inventory represents costs deferred to the balance sheet in the previous period under the generally accepted accounting principles of accrual accounting. All these costs are released to the income statement in the present period. *Thus the higher prices incurred in the earlier period are now realized (in terms of profit determination — not cash flow) in the present period.*

The reverse situation occurs with closing inventories. The higher prices (relative to budget) embedded in ending inventory are not realized in the current period for calculating profits — but they can have a significant influence on cash flows if some or all of the purchases are paid for in the current period. Instead, these higher prices are deferred to the balance sheet and will be released to operations next period. Hence the favorable price variance for ending inventory will become an unfavorable price variance for opening inventory next period. Similar analysis applies to the volume variance.

(c) Analysis of Change in Gross Profit

When the sales analysis in Table 15.4 is combined with the cost analysis in Table 15.5, the influence of inventories and purchases on gross profit can be explained, as shown in Table 15.6.

A comparison of this summary with the one-way variance analysis of Table 15.3 reveals the two-way variance model to be more informative. The gross profit deficit from budget of $84,800 is caused by lower selling prices and higher (net) inventory and purchase prices. Higher-than-expected sales and purchase (production) volume offsets some of the unfavorable price effects. The change in inventory investment from its opening to closing balance has contributed about 52% [i.e., ($142,750 − $97,000)/ $88,000] of the total unfavorable cost of sales variance. This result simply means that more costs were released from the balance sheet's opening inventory than were deferred to it through ending inventory.

The overall results could be due to management lowering selling prices in an attempt to obtain larger market share, to protect current market

TABLE 15.6
Summary of the Two-Way Variance Analysis

	Price	Volume	Total
Sales	$ 76,800 U	$80,000 F	$ 3,200 F
Cost of sales:			
Opening inventories	$124,250 U	$18,500 U	$142,750 U
Purchases	30,500 U	11,750 U	42,250 U
Closing inventories	107,160 F	10,160 U	97,000 F
Total	$ 47,590 U	$40,410 U	$ 88,000 U
Gross profit	$124,390 U	$39,590 F	$ 84,800 U

Note: F represents favorable variance; U represents unfavorable variance.

position, or to liquidate some inventories because of expected business slowdown. Whatever the underlying reason, the two-way analysis of variance allows managers to evaluate the impact of inventory and pricing decisions on performance (and cash flow, once the payment patterns for accounts receivable and accounts payable are known) better than they can with the one-way model.   □

Three-Way Variance Analysis

Most firms purchase (or produce) and sell more than one finished product and budget some given normal or standard combination of each to be sold. Because all products do not have the same profit margins, gross profit varies with a change in the proportion of each item produced and/ or sold, that is, with the mix. One must then determine the influence of change in mix on the gross profit — and subsequently on cash flows.

If selling prices and costs remain constant, a shift in volume from less profitable to more profitable products increases the average gross profit per unit on all units sold and thereby improves profit. Conversely, shifts from more profitable to less profitable products lower the average gross profit per unit and cause profits to drop. Therefore the mix element must be brought into the analysis.

Building on the illustration in Table 15.6, assume that actual and budget product line information for revenues and costs is as given in Table 15.7. Also, assume that a periodic FIFO inventory procedure is used. It is noted from the budget that the average gross profit is $10 per unit and, as a percentage, is 50% of sales. As long as the unit sales of products X and Y remain in the ratio 1:1 (10,000:10,000), the average gross profit per unit (and as a percentage of sales) will remain the same. In this case none of the change in gross profit is caused by a *mix variance*. It is attributable entirely to a *quantity variance*. In Table 15.7, since the actual average gross profit of $4.80 is not equal to budgeted gross profit, a mix variance exists. Appendix B summarizes the mix and quantity variance calculations.

Table 15.8 details the calculation of the sales price, mix, and quantity variances for products X and Y. *Three-way analysis* of these variances provides valuable insight into the influence of sales on cost of sales and inventory — and thus on the change in *operating cash flows*.

These variances (relative to budget) reveal that the 25% price reduction in product X stimulated its sales volume by 50%. A 9% price increase for product Y reduced its volume by 10%. The result of these pricing decisions was a shift in sales mix from product Y to product X, resulting in a net $72,000 unfavorable mix variance. The favorable quantity variance of $80,000 is the result of selling 4000 units more than budgeted times the weighted average budgeted price of $20 per unit.

The influence of the sales effort on cost of sales requires analysis of

TABLE 15.7
Product Line Information

	Product X		Product Y		Total	
	Price	Amount	Price	Amount	Price	Amount
Actual						
Sales	$6.00	$90,000	$34.80	$313,200	$16.80	$403,200
Cost of sales	5.10	76,500	23.50	211,500	12.00	288,000
Gross profit	$0.90	$13,500	$11.30	$101,700	$ 4.80	$115,200
%	15.00		32.47		28.57	
Units		15,000		9000		24,000
Budget						
Sales	$8.00	$80,000	$32.00	$320,000	$20.00	$400,000
Cost of sales	5.50	55,000	14.50	145,000	10.00	200,000
Gross profit	$2.50	$25,000	$17.50	$175,000	$10.00	$200,000
%	31.25		54.69		50.00	
Units		10,000		10,000		20,000

Cost-of-sales data

	Product X			
	Actual		Budget	
	Units	Price	Units	Price
Opening inventory	11,000	$5.00	12,000	$5.50
Plus purchases	6,000	5.375	5,000	6.75
Minus closing inventory	2,000	5.375	7,000	6.393
Equals cost of sales	15,000	$5.10	10,000	$5.50

	Product Y			
	Actual		Budget	
	Units	Price	Units	Price
Opening inventory	12,000	$23.50	9,000	$14.25
Plus purchases	5,000	25.50	5,000	16.75
Minus closing inventory	8,000	24.75	4,000	16.75
Equals cost of sales	9,000	$23.50	10,000	$14.50

TABLE 15.8
Three-Way Variance Analysis of Sales

Actual volume × actual price	Actual volume × budget price	Actual volume in budget % × budget price	Budget volume × budget price
Product X			
15,000 × $6 = $90,000	15,000 × $8 = $120,000	24,000 × 0.5 × $8 = $96,000	10,000 × $8 = $80,000
	Price variance $30,000 U	Mix variance $24,000 F	Quantity variance $16,000 F
Product Y			
9000 × $34.80 = $313,200	9000 × $32 = $288,000	24,000 × 0.5 × $32 = $384,000	10,000 × $32 = $320,000
	Price variance $25,200 F	Mix variance $96,000 U	Quantity variance $64,000 F
Total			
$403,200	$408,000	$480,000	$400,000
	Price variance $4,800 U	Mix variance $72,000 U	Quantity variance $80,000 F
	Total sales variance $3200 F		

Note: F represents favorable variance; U represents unfavorable variance.

opening and closing inventory positions and purchases. These items are shown in Table 15.9; the analysis uses a three-way analysis of variance.

The analysis indicates that the $88,000 unfavorable cost-of-sales variance is largely caused by unit price variations from budget. The release of the prior period's price increases from the balance sheet to the income statement, through the opening inventory, contributes $105,500 additional cost in this period's cost of sales. On the other hand, higher ending inventories have deferred some of this period's higher purchase costs to the balance sheet. These costs will be released to the income statement next period, since this period's closing inventories become opening inventories next period.

Similar reasoning applies to the mix and quantity variances. Not only are total opening inventories larger than budget, but the actual proportion of each product to its budgeted proportion is out of line with the budget.

TABLE 15.9
Three-Way Variance Analysis of Cost of Sales

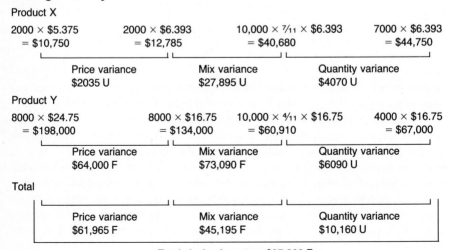

Actual volume × actual price	Actual volume × budget price	Actual volume in budget % × budget price	Budget volume × budget price
Opening inventory			
Product X			
11,000 × $5 = $55,000	11,000 × $5.50 = $60,500	23,000 × $^{12}/_{21}$ × $5.50 = $72,285	12,000 × $5.50 = $66,000
	Price variance $5500 F	Mix variance $11,785 F	Quantity variance $6285 U
Product Y			
12,000 × $23.50 = $282,000	12,000 × $14.25 = $171,000	23,000 × $^{9}/_{21}$ × $14.25 = $140,465	9000 × $14.25 = $128,250
	Price variance $111,000 U	Mix variance $30,535 U	Quantity variance $12,215 U
Total			
	Price variance $105,500 U	Mix variance $18,750 U	Quantity variance $18,500 U

Total opening inventory $142,750 U

Actual volume × actual price	Actual volume × budget price	Actual volume in budget % × budget price	Budget volume × budget price
Closing inventory			
Product X			
2000 × $5.375 = $10,750	2000 × $6.393 = $12,785	10,000 × $^{7}/_{11}$ × $6.393 = $40,680	7000 × $6.393 = $44,750
	Price variance $2035 U	Mix variance $27,895 U	Quantity variance $4070 U
Product Y			
8000 × $24.75 = $198,000	8000 × $16.75 = $134,000	10,000 × $^{4}/_{11}$ × $16.75 = $60,910	4000 × $16.75 = $67,000
	Price variance $64,000 F	Mix variance $73,090 F	Quantity variance $6090 U
Total			
	Price variance $61,965 F	Mix variance $45,195 F	Quantity variance $10,160 U

Total closing inventory $97,000 F

TABLE 15.9 (Cont.)

Actual volume × actual price	Actual volume × budget price	Actual volume in budget % × budget price	Budget volume × budget price
Purchases			
Product X			
6000 × $5.375 = $32,250	6000 × $6.75 = $40,500	11,000 × 5/10 × $6.75 = $37,125	5000 × $6.75 = $33,750
Price variance $8250 F		Mix variance $3375 U	Quantity variance $8375 U
Product Y			
5000 × $25.50 = $127,500	5000 × $16.75 = $83,750	11,000 × 5/10 × $16.75 = $92,125	5000 × $16.75 = $83,750
Price variance $43,750 U		Mix variance $8375 F	Quantity variance $8375 U
Total			
Price variance $35,500 U		Mix variance $5000 F	Quantity variance $11,750 U

Total purchases $42,250 U

Summary

Product	Price variance	Mix variance	Quantity variance
X	$11,715 F	$19,485 U	$13,730 U
Y	90,750 U	50,930 F	26,680 U
Total	$79,035 U	$31,445 F	$40,410 U

Total cost of sales variance: $88,000 U

Note: F is favorable variance; U is unfavorable variance.

The more expensive product Y represents about 52% of opening units, whereas it was budgeted to represent only 43%. Thus a disproportionate amount of cost is released to the income statement through the opening inventory than was expected. This cost is represented by the unfavorable mix variance for opening inventories. And since opening inventories are larger than budgeted, in terms of total units, an unfavorable quantity variance exists.

Similar analyses of purchases and closing inventories lead to the overall conclusion that although both products have contributed to the unfavorable

TABLE 15.10
Three-Way Variance Analysis of Gross Profit by Product Line

	Price	Mix	Quantity	Total
Sales	$ 4,800 U	$72,000 U	$80,000 F	$ 3,200 F
Opening inventory	$105,500 U	$18,750 U	$18,500 U	$142,750 U
Purchases	35,500 U	5,000 F	11,750 U	42,250 U
Closing inventory	61,965 F	45,195 F	10,160 U	97,000 F
Total	$ 79,035 U	$31,445 F	$40,410 U	$ 88,000 U
Gross margin	$ 83,835 U	$40,555 U	$39,590 F	$ 84,800 U

Note: F is favorable variance; U is unfavorable variance.

cost of sales variance, product Y has contributed about three times as much as has product X. The most significant problem area concerns the acquisition cost of product Y. If it can be brought into line, gross profit should quickly improve. Of almost equal importance is the physical quantity of inventory for product Y. The sales strategy (either explicitly or implicitly) appears to be to move the sales emphasis from product Y to product X. The closing inventory is heavily weighted in favor of product Y. Close attention needs to be paid to this product. A cutback in purchases is required to bring product Y back into line.

The overall impact of inventory management on gross profit can be determined by netting the sales variances against the component-cost-of-sales variances, as shown in Table 15.10. A comparison of this three-way product line analysis with the two-way aggregate analysis summarized in Table 15.6 reveals significant differences in the variances. Although the total variance is the same, the allocation of variances differs. This difference is caused by the manner in which actual volume × budget price variances are calculated in each case. The three-way model ensures correct allocations since it uses disaggregated data (i.e., product line data). The two-way analysis is not concerned with the influence of product mix on inventory investment, sales, or profits, with the result that it combines price and mix variances. This result is undesirable from an analysis-and-control perspective since different people are responsible for each of these variances.

The interpretation of results in Table 15.10 is that total beginning inventories exceed their budget levels by $142,750. Since beginning inventories are released to cost of sales at the start of the period, cost of sales is increased by this amount over budget. In the case of total closing inventories, the amount is greater than budget by $97,000. Thus $97,000 more cost, relative to budget, is deferred to the balance sheet. This manipulation has a short-term favorable impact since all this cost will be released to the income statement at the start of the next period. The unfavorable purchase variance of $42,250 arises primarily from the fact that more of product X was purchased than budgeted and the purchase price of product Y increased in excess of 52% of the budget price (see Table 15.9).

Table 15.10 highlights unfavorable performance relative to budget. The problem is attributable mainly to nonbudgeted cost increases, since total mix and quantity variances largely offset each other. Management has been unable to offset these cost increases with selling price increases.

Incorporating Cash Flows

The significance of variance analysis is that it directly focuses attention on problem areas. The previous examples have concentrated analysis on gross profit variances by analyzing sales and cost of sales. The analysis indicates that one must analyze opening and closing inventories and purchases to understand the impact of inventory management on profits. Ending inventories are shown to simply represent *deferred expenses* (in an accrual accounting framework). This feature should come as no surprise, since it has been discussed in previous chapters. *Cash outflows are incurred for inventory investment when accounts payable are paid, and until the inventory is sold and collections of accounts receivable are made, there is no cash inflow.* Management,

TABLE 15.11
Cash Flow Analysis of Gross Margin

(a) Receivables and payables data (assumed)

	Actual	Budget
Opening receivables	$44,800	$50,000
Closing receivables	60,600	55,000
Opening payables	34,500	35,000
Closing payables	42,800	45,000

(b) Variance analysis

	Change in		
	Actual	Budget	Variance
Accounts receivable	$15,800 U	$ 5,000 U	$ 10,800 U
Accounts payable	8,300 F	10,000 F	1,700 U
Inventory change (Table 15.9)*			45,750 F
			$ 33,250 F
Gross margin (Table 15.10)			84,800 U
Gross margin cash flow variance			$ 51,550 U

Note: U is unfavorable variance; F is favorable variance.
* [Opening inventory variances plus closing inventory variances.] X(−1)

therefore, needs to finance this excess investment by managing the cash conversion cycle, as discussed in Chapter 5. This financing is accomplished by stretching accounts payable, using existing lines of credit, or negotiating a new loan.

The gross profit variance analysis can be converted to a cash flow analysis simply by identifying changes in accounts receivable and accounts payable balances, relative to budget. As discussed in Chapter 6, cash flow from operations is defined as (net income) + (depreciation) ± (changes in accounts receivable, accounts payable, and inventories). Table 15.11 (p. 431) converts Table 15.10 from an accrual accounting gross income variance analysis to a cash flow analysis of gross margin variance.

Given the assumptions for changes in accounts receivable and accounts payable, analysis of *cash flow gross margin* indicates that problems are less severe than revealed by the accrual accounting analysis. The variances arising from receivable and payable balances should be analyzed by using the variance models discussed in Chapters 12 and 16, respectively. This analysis will allow management to understand how its various net working capital decisions and actions have affected resource allocations, profitability, and liquidity.

Importance of Variance Analysis Relative to Turnover Ratios

Analysis of the *inventory turnover ratio* by using a variance analysis framework reveals the weakness of the turnover ratio. The three-way variance analysis example illustrated in Table 15.10 shows an $88,000 unfavorable variance between actual and budgeted cost of sales, and ending inventories are $97,000 higher than the budget. Average inventories (using opening and closing balances) are $119,875 higher than budgeted.

Computation of *average* inventory turnover, shown in Table 15.12, is based on the cost-of-sales data from Table 15.9. Total turnover shows a decrease from the budgeted level of 1.31 times to an actual figure of 1.06 times — indicating poor performance. This result translates into excess average inventory of $53,028, assuming that the budget turnover figure is appropriate. This figure is calculated as follows: (actual average inventory) − (what actual average inventory should be so that turnover is 1.31), or ($272,875 − $288,000/1.31). The causes of the declining turnover ratio can be pinpointed by casting the turnover ratio into a three-way variance analysis format. The numerators in these calculations represent cost of sales; the denominators represent average inventory amounts.

Interpretation of Table 15.12 is as follows: Increased sales quantities favorably influenced inventory turnover, both in total and at the product level. However, the sales shift from the more expensive product Y to the less expensive product X has caused actual turnover performance to fall

TABLE 15.12
Variance Analysis of Turnover Ratios

	Actual turnover	Actual turnover restated in budget prices	Actual quantities in budgeted % × budget prices	Budget turnover
Total				
	$\dfrac{\$288,000}{\$272,875} = 1.06$	$\dfrac{\$208,965}{\$189,143} = 1.10$	$\dfrac{\$240,411}{\$157,170} = 1.53$	$\dfrac{\$200,000}{\$153,000} = 1.31$

Price variance 0.04 U	Mix variance 0.43 U	Quantity variance 0.22 F

Total variance 0.25 U

	Actual turnover	Actual turnover restated in budget prices	Actual quantities in budgeted % × budget prices	Budget turnover
Product X				
	$\dfrac{\$76,500}{\$32,875} = 2.33$	$\dfrac{\$88,215}{\$36,643} = 2.41$	$\dfrac{\$68,730}{\$56,483} = 1.22$	$\dfrac{\$55,000}{\$55,375} = 0.99$

Price variance 0.08 U	Mix variance 1.19 F	Quantity variance 0.23 F

Total variance 1.34 F

	Actual turnover	Actual turnover restated in budget prices	Actual quantities in budgeted % × budget prices	Budget turnover
Product Y				
	$\dfrac{\$211,500}{\$240,000} = 0.88$	$\dfrac{\$120,750}{\$152,500} = 0.79$	$\dfrac{\$171,680}{\$100,688} = 1.71$	$\dfrac{\$145,000}{\$97,625} = 1.49$

Price variance 0.09 F	Mix variance 0.92 U	Quantity variance 0.22 F

Total variance 0.61 U

Note: Numerators are cost of sales; denominators are average inventory. Also, F is favorable variance; U is unfavorable variance.

considerably short of budget expectations for product Y and in total (see the mix variances). Price changes have resulted in a decrease in the turnover ratio in total and for product X. The turnover ratio indicates favorable price performance is associated with product Y. (Previous analysis indicates otherwise, which makes the turnover ratio a suspect technique.)

The relationship between these turnover calculations and the cost-of-sales dollar variances summarized in Table 15.10 is shown in Table 15.13. In terms of overall analysis the data summarized in Table 15.13 shows that although the price variance is the most significant variance in dollar terms, it has a minimal effect on total inventory turnover. At the product line level price (cost) increases have contributed to improved turn-

TABLE 15.13
Joint Variance – Turnover Analysis of Inventories

	Total		Product X		Product Y	
	$	T/O*	$	T/O*	$	T/O*
Budgeted cost of sales	$200,000	1.31	$55,000	0.99	$145,000	1.49
Price variance	79,035 U	0.04 U	11,715 F	0.08 U	90,750 U	0.09 F
Mix variance	31,445 F	0.43 U	19,484 U	1.19 F	50,930 F	0.92 U
Quantity variance	40,410 U	0.22 F	13,731 U	0.23 F	26,680 U	0.22 F
Actual cost of sales	$288,000	1.06	$76,500	2.33	$211,500	0.88

Note: F is favorable variance; U is unfavorable variance. Add unfavorable variances and subtract favorable variances.
* T/O means turnover.

over performance for product Y (see Table 15.12), and price (cost) decreases have caused deteriorating turnover performance for product X (see Table 15.12).

These relationships are perverse. At the aggregate level an unfavorable turnover variance accompanies an unfavorable price variance, as one would expect. As mentioned earlier, the mix variance is the primary factor influencing the turnover ratio, contributing negatively to product Y and total inventories and favorably to product X. The shift in sales mix from the expensive product Y to the cheaper product X has resulted in significantly increased investment in product Y and lower investment in product X relative to budget. Unfortunately, increased sales quantities were not sufficient to overcome the unfavorable product mix influence on the turnover calculation.

An important benefit of this comparison should be apparent. Although turnover ratios are easy to compute, they provide relatively little useful information, other than at a gross level for planning aggregate inventory, as discussed in the previous chapter. For example, price variance is the most significant factor contributing to the difference between budgeted cost of sales and actual sales in Table 15.13. However, price variance plays an insignificant role in explaining the turnover variance. An unfavorable contribution of 0.04 to the turnover ratio is insignificant and does not warrant management's attention. The $79,035 unfavorable price variance, representing 90% of the difference between actual and budgeted cost of sales, most certainly requires management's attention.

Two other bothersome observations of the turnover ratio, as shown in Table 15.13, are that (1) unfavorable dollar variances are generally aligned with favorable turnover variances and vice versa (the only exception is the total price variance), and (2) the reconciliation of change in the turnover ratio (i.e., identifying the impact of price, mix, and quantity on the ratio) fails to identify the most significant dollar variance. The problems identified with the turnover ratio should be sufficient to cause management serious concerns about its use.

Summary

This chapter extends the analysis of inventory begun in the previous chapter. The extension analyzes variances to budget, starting with the simple one-way variance analysis model and progressing to a more complex, but also more informative, three-way variance model.

One-way variance analysis offers little information for management to use. It compares actual performance with budget without being able to provide much direction about the cause of differences.

Two-way variance analysis separates the total variance into price and volume components. This analysis allows management to begin to assess the impact of changing product and factor market environments, relative to budget, on performance. A problem with this model is that a changing product mix is not identified. In fact, it is hidden in the so-called price variance.

Three-way variance analysis overcomes this problem. This model identifies the true price, mix, and quantity variances and allows management to assign responsibility where it belongs.

The chapter concludes with a discussion of the inadequacy of the much-used inventory turnover ratio. Turnover ratios fail to adequately pinpoint problem areas, as is shown by a comparison of the dollar variance model with an inventory turnover variance model. Variance analysis of dollar amounts shows the areas where management needs to direct its attention.

Key Concepts

Inventory turnover ratio
Mix variance
One-way variance analysis
Price variance

Quantity variance
Three-way variance analysis
Two-way variance analysis
Volume variance

Appendix A
Analysis of Variance Using Prior Year's Data

In many cases analysis is made of a given year's sales or cost of sales with their counterparts in the prior year rather than with their budgeted amounts for the year in question. The analysis is essentially the same as the one conducted in this chapter. All that needs to be done is to substitute the prior year's volume and price for the budget data.

Sometimes, the required analysis is made slightly more complicated when the prior year's figures are used as the basis of comparison because one does not have information concerning unit prices or the number of units sold for either of the years in question. For example, assume that the sales data are as follows:

1st year	$400,000
2nd year	403,200
Change	3,200

The required analysis can still be made if either the percentage of change in the selling price or the percentage of change in the sales volume can be determined.

Assume, first, that during year 2 the selling price was 1.18% lower than in year 1. With this information the sales revenue of year 2 can be converted into year 1 selling prices as follows:

$$\frac{\text{Year 2 sales at year 2 Prices}}{1 + \text{decimal change in price}} = \frac{\$403,200}{0.9882} = \$408,000.$$

This calculation eliminates the effect of the 1.18% decrease in selling price. It is now known that if the price had not decreased, sales revenue in year 2 would have been $408,000. With this figure one can determine the effect of the price change and the volume change, as shown in Table A.1.

Next, assume that the price decrease of 1.18% is unknown but that the volume of sales increased by 2% in year 2. The effect of any price change must be eliminated by converting the sales revenue of year 2 into year 1 selling prices. Since the volume in year 2 was 2% greater than in year 1, the sales revenue in year 2 would have been 2% higher than the sales revenue in year 1 if the price had not changed. The year 2 sales volume at year 1 selling price would have been $408,000, computed as follows:

(year 1 sales at year 1 prices) × (1 + decimal change in volume)
   = $400,000 × 1.02 = $408,000.

TABLE A.1
Two-Way Variance Analysis

Year 2 sales × year 2 prices	Year 2 sales × year 1 prices	Year 1 sales × year 1 prices
$403,200	$408,000	$400,000

Price volume $4800; unfavorable   Volume variance $8000; favorable

With year 2 sales converted to year 1 selling prices, the revenue changes from price and volume factors can be determined as before.

This model can also be used to assess the influences of inflation on the firm. By separating price effects from volume effects, management is able to determine whether any real growth has occurred.

Appendix B

Explanation of Mix and Quantity Variances

An explanation of the mix and quantity variances can best be described by using the sales data of Table 15.7. Assume that actual and budgeted quantities are as given in Table B.1.

A two-way variance analysis model calculates the volume variance as the sum of the differences between actual and budget units times the budget price for each product. For example, the total volume variance for this example is $8000. It is found as follows:

$$\$8(15,000 - 10,000) + \$32(9000 - 10,000) = \$8000.$$

The separation of the volume variance into its mix and quantity components requires that the total actual number of units be allocated over the product lines in their budget proportions, as in Table B.2. The comparison of columns (1) and (2) by product line allows a mix variance to be calculated. A quantity variance results from analysis of columns (2) and (3) (either by product line or in total, it does not matter).

The original budget, column (3), forecasts 20,000 total units. Since 24,000 units were actually sold, column (2) effectively restates the budget in terms of actual units sold by maintaining the same proportional quantity of each product to the total quantity. Thus the quantity variance is as follows:

X	$ 8(12,000 − 10,000)
Y	32(12,000 − 10,000)
Total	$80,000 favorable

Another way to look at this variance is to multiply the 4000 difference in units sold versus budget by the weighted average selling price of $20, that is, $4000 [(0.5 × \$8) + (0.5 × \$32)] = \$80,000$.

TABLE B.1
Sales Data

Product	Actual	%	Budget	%	Budgeted sales price
X	15,000	62.5	10,000	50	$ 8.00
Y	9,000	37.5	10,000	50	32.00
Total	24,000	100.0	20,000	100	$20.00

TABLE B.2
Actual and Budgeted Quantities

Product	(1) Actual units	(2) Actual total units in budgeted proportions	(3) Budget units
X	15,000	12,000	10,000
Y	9,000	12,000	10,000
Total	24,000	24,000	20,000

The mix variance abstracts from any change in total units. It is concerned with the actual proportion of each product to total units, compared with actual total units allocated to each product in budget proportions. The different proportions between actual and budget represent the change in product mix:

X	$ 8(15,000 − 12,000)
Y	32(9,000 − 12,000)
Total	$72,000 unfavorable

Although this explanation has used but two products, three or more products can readily be incorporated. The logic used to compute the variances is the same.

Questions

1. What does a one-way variance analysis show?
2. How are price and volume variances calculated?
3. What is meant by the term *mix*? How does it affect inventory analysis?
4. Explain the difference between a quantity variance and a mix variance.
5. What is meant by the expression "unfavorable price variance" for (a) sales, (b) closing inventory, and (c) purchases?
6. Cost of sales has a price variance of $10,000 above the revised budget amount. Is this variance favorable or unfavorable? Why?
7. When should the three-way variance analysis be employed in preference to the two-way analysis?
8. What is the usefulness of a three-way variance analysis technique for analyzing inventory turnover?

Problems

1. Given the budgeted and actual sales information in Table 15.14, calculate and discuss the gross profit variance, using a one-way variance analysis.

TABLE 15.14
Sales Data

	Budget		*Actual*	
Sales	$250,000	100%	$185,000	100%
Beginning inventory		32%		28%
Purchases		27%		32%
Ending inventory		40%		35%

2. Assume that budgeted sales for the year were 10,000 units at a price of $10 per unit. Actual sales turned out to be 12,000 units at $8.50 per unit. Calculate the total sales variance, sales price variance, and sales volume variance.

3. Perform a two-way variance analysis of cost of sales for the information given in Table 15.15. Management values inventory with LIFO.

TABLE 15.15
Cost of Sales

	Actual	Budget
Sales volume	20,000 units	18,000 units
Purchases	15,000 units	13,500 units
Closing inventory	14,000 units	15,000 units
Purchase price per unit	$11.50	$11.25
Opening inventory price per unit	$12.00	$11.00

4. The actual and budgeted ending inventory amounts for products X and Y are as follows:

Actual X	$22,000 and 18,000 units
Budgeted X	$20,000 and 16,000 units
Actual Y	$14,000 and 15,000 units
Budgeted Y	$15,000 and 16,000 units

Determine the price variance, mix variance, quantity variance, and total variance for the ending inventory.

5. The unit sales price for widgets was $10 actual and $12 budget; for gadgets it was $5 actual and $5 budget. Actual sales of widgets was 10,000 units, whereas 9500 units were budgeted. Gadgets had actual sales of 12,000 units, whereas they had a budget of 9500 units. Compute the price, mix, quantity, and volume variances for widgets and gadgets.

6. The data in Table 15.16 (p. 442) has been taken from the company's records. Management uses FIFO inventory accounting procedures.

(a) Calculate a two-way variance report, showing revenues, cost of sales, and gross margin.

(b) Calculate a cash flow analysis of gross margin (see Table 15.11 for an example).

TABLE 15.16
Data from Company Records

	Budget	*Actual*
Sales	100 units	90 units
Price per unit	$10	$15
Beginning inventory	70 units	80 units
Price per unit	$8	$12
Ending inventory	60 units	75 units
Price per unit	$?	$?
Purchases	90 units	85 units
Price per unit	$7.50	$12.50
Accounts receivable:		
Beginning	$500	$550
Ending	$700	$600
Accounts payable:		
Beginning	$400	$500
Ending	$350	$510

CHAPTER 16 □
Accounts Payable Management

Accounts payable represent the largest single conduit for cash outflow in most firms. It has become a major and growing source of finance in all sectors of the economy since World War II. Its volume and widespread use has not been matched by any other kind of business financing. Yet accounts payable, like other components of net working capital, has received little attention in accounting and finance books. One reason for this neglect is that trade credit is buried in the distribution activity of the firm. Accounts payable arise typically from the extension of credit from a seller to a buyer both as a sales incentive and to allow the buyer some flexibility in conveniently paying for the delivery of goods and services.

Most companies exercise far greater control over disbursements than over collections. The extent of control is the key difference between these two elements in the cash cycle. In collections management's goal is to prompt cash payments by others. The seller is responsible for timely and accurate invoice dispatch and subsequent enforcement of credit terms. By contrast, the purchaser's concerns are control of and response to credit terms and payment requests. In most circumstances companies possess flexibility in both purchase negotiations and subsequent timing and method of payment.

Accounts payable management has long been viewed as a "poor man's" method of dealing with cash flow problems. But there is a difference between those companies that are poor payees and those that utilize an accounts payable management program. An accounts payable management system should use policies and techniques that benefit the firm while not jeopardizing vendor relations. A system that improves cash flow but destroys vendor relations must be avoided.

The proliferation of electronic technology has affected accounts payable management. However, instruments such as PACs, PADs, drafts, wire transfers, ZBAs, and so on, were discussed in Chapter 7 as payment and cash management mechanisms and will not be examined here. Instead, this chapter focuses on four topics: (1) the objective of disbursement management; (2) the decision of whether or not to take the cash discount; (3) the usefulness of remote and controlled disbursement as means of conserving cash; and (4) monitoring techniques for analyzing accounts payable management.

Importance of the Accounts Payable Function

Accounts payable management has traditionally been treated as a strictly clerical area, with the emphasis on functionality and expediency. The development of cash management as a discipline over the past decade has changed this view by directing attention to all sources and uses of cash within a firm. As a major component of the cash cycle, accounts payable has become another tool for management to use in maximizing the use of its resources.

Trade credit should be used with prudence and with a careful eye toward the firm's ability to meet future commitments. Careful attention should be paid to the cash budget in determining whether accounts payable can be paid according to stated terms or whether the liability is better settled at a different time. Conversely, management should investigate how much and for how long interest-free trade credit can be used to bridge the cash conversion cycle gap.

Management should evaluate trade credit and vendors with the same scrutiny it uses with other sources of credit. For instance, are current vendors offering competitive discount terms for early payment? Can more generous terms be negotiated? As a general rule, the larger the buyer is relative to the seller's customer base, the greater is the buyer's bargaining position. But equally as important as credit terms are the stability and the general business practices of suppliers. A supplier's willingness to work with the firm, both to meet the firm's production schedule and to help it should it fall into a period of financial hardship, may be more important than its terms.

Cash Discount: Take It or Not?

Trade credit is extended to facilitate the purchase and payment for resources that will be used in final goods production. As discussed in Chapter 9, it is common practice for sellers to extend credit and at the same time allow a discount for early payment. The traditional belief was that should a firm not take the discount, then it was on the first step of bankruptcy.

A more realistic view is that these funds are no different than other funds employed in the firm, except for their cost. The normal procedure for testing the desirability of using funds is to net the costs and revenues of the sources and the uses of funds. The rule is that funds should be employed to the point of cost/revenue indifference. This topic is discussed shortly in this chapter.

The major decisions associated with accounts payable are whether or not to take the discount and/or whether to delay payment beyond the due date. If payables are not delayed, management should pay the invoice on the last date of the discount or the last day of the credit period. If management can earn interest (or reduced costs) from its demand deposits at the bank or can invest the funds in a money market account, it should never pay before the last day of the discount period or before the final credit period day. The business community has traditionally used the postmark date on the envelope in which the check is received to determine the date of payment receipt.

Missing the Discount

Omitting the discount is comparable to borrowing the after-discount amount of the invoice on the last day of the discount period and repaying the before-discount amount on the final day of the credit period. The formula for calculating the *annualized implicit cost* (AIC) of this borrowing was shown in Chapter 9. It is reproduced here as Eq. (16.1) for the compound interest case and as Eq. (16.2) for the discrete case:

$$\text{AIC} = \left(\frac{1}{1-y}\right)^{360/@} - 1, \tag{16.1}$$

$$\text{AIC} = \left(\frac{y}{1-y}\right)\left(\frac{360}{@}\right), \tag{16.2}$$

where y is the discount rate and @ represents the number of days of payment acceleration.

ILLUSTRATION 16.1

Consider terms of 1/10, n/60. The benefit of discount settlement (AIC) on day 10 (i.e., @ = 60 − 10 = 50) is

$$\text{AIC} = \left(\frac{1}{1-0.01}\right)^{360/50} - 1 = 0.075$$

on a compound interest basis. It is

$$\text{AIC} = \left(\frac{0.01}{1-0.01}\right)\left(\frac{360}{50}\right) = 0.0727$$

on a single-event basis.

Failure to take the discount is equivalent to borrowing the amount of the payable for 50 days at an annual implicit cost (AIC) of 7.5% on a compound interest basis and 7.27% on a single-event basis. Alternatively, taking the discount is comparable to not taking a loan for 50 days at the costs shown.   □

Stretching Payables

The delaying of payment beyond the credit period, simply for the reason of deferring payment, is defined as *stretching payables*. If stretching of payables is practiced by management, the effective cost of the discount is reduced. The critical questions management must ask are these:

□ Should payables be stretched?

□ If payables are stretched, for how long should they be?

The factors to consider are the loss of credit standing and reputation against the value of using the stretched funds. These considerations require quantification of loss of credit standing and reputation, which is obviously a difficult task. Stretching for a short period of time is less damaging to the firm than stretching for a long period. The cost of stretching is also affected by the firm the payable is owed to. Factors such as the seller's size and relative financial strength, goodwill between the two companies, and alternative sources of supply influence the credit and reputation loss function.

ILLUSTRATION 16.2

The AIC associated with stretching can be calculated by using Eqs. (16.1) and (16.2). Assume that payment terms are 1/10, *n*/60, but management normally pays 80 days from the invoice date. The AIC is

$$AIC = \left(\frac{1}{1 - 0.01}\right)^{360/70} - 1 = 0.0531$$

on a compound interest basis. It is

$$AIC = \left(\frac{0.01}{1 - 0.01}\right)\left(\frac{360}{70}\right) = 0.0520$$

on a single-event basis.

The interpretation of these results is that the *effective annualized borrowing cost* resulting from not taking the discount and stretching payables 20 days beyond the credit period is a little over 5.2%. If this cost is less than any alternative forms of borrowing that might be available to the firm, management should consider stretching payables.   □

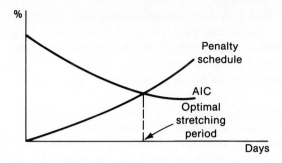

FIGURE 16.1
Optimal Stretching Period

Comparison of the stretching example with the example of paying on the last day of the credit period (Illustration 16.1) shows that deferral of the payment date results in a lower annualized implicit cost (AIC) to payables. For a given discount rate stretching effectively reduces the cost of trade credit financing.

Management must also hypothesize a penalty schedule that incorporates the credit and reputation costs incurred from stretching. The intersection of this penalty schedule with a schedule of AICs determines the optimal stretching period, as depicted in Fig. 16.1.

Management should not stretch if the cost of doing so exceeds the short-term borrowing rate. If the short-term borrowing rate is greater than the cost of stretching, management should only stretch until the cost of doing so equals the estimated cost of credit and reputation loss (which, at best, can only be roughly estimated).

Remote and Controlled Disbursements

Chapter 7 discussed different types of float that exist in the cash management system: mail float, processing float, and transit float. It is transit float that any disbursement system attempts to maximize. This float refers to the amount of time required for intermediating banks to transfer funds between the seller's and the buyer's accounts. The object of *playing the float* is to decelerate cash outflows to provide funds for other needs. This objective is accomplished by tracking disbursements through central bank accounts and not through company books, while maintaining balances sufficient only to cover bank services and daily transactions.

Remote Disbursement

A once-popular technique for improving disbursement float was to use a process known as *remote disbursement*. In this practice the treasurer draws a check on a bank that is not readily accessible to the seller. Usually, the remote bank is located at some distance from the seller in a town where there is no Federal Reserve Bank or check-clearing center. Although the stated maximum Federal Reserve clearing time is two days, in reality it often takes longer for the physical check to be presented against the issuing bank.

The Monetary Control Act of 1980 explicitly discourages remote disbursement. The act mandated that the Federal Reserve charge for Fed float at the Federal Funds rate and pass these charges on to the banking industry, which was expected to subsequently charge the remote-disbursing payor.

When remote disbursement is used, a company may draw its checks on several banks. And for any particular disbursement it chooses the bank that is the most removed from the seller in terms of float time. Some companies use computer programs to select from among their banks the one that maximizes transit float with regard to a particular vendor. Other companies simply draw checks on banks located in cities where they have an office or other facility so that their suppliers may not realize that they are deliberately disbursing from a remote location. Other companies regularly rotate the banks on which they draw checks to pay a particular supplier. This rotation method makes it difficult for the supplier to set up a lockbox system close to the bank on which checks to him are written.

If the seller does not use a lockbox system or some form of electronic transfer, the buyer (payor) often realizes another day of float, since the seller must process the check and do the associated paperwork.

Controlled Disbursements

A technique that has gained widespread utilization now that remote disbursing has fallen out of favor is *controlled disbursement*. The concept of controlled disbursement is to provide early-morning clearance information about the specific dollar amount clearing a disbursement account of the firm. This information enables the treasurer to wire funds to the paying bank on a same-day basis, thereby eliminating unnecessary balances in disbursement accounts.

Controlled-disbursement services are offered by a number of large banks through wholly owned subsidiaries or through branches that are located in less accessible areas such that check clearing is somewhat delayed. The key to effective controlled-disbursement services is the bank's ability to provide a *separate transit-routing number and to domicile all corporate accounts within that subsidiary or branch.* It is desirable that this subsidiary/branch receive only one cash letter from the Federal Reserve daily so that it can compute the dollar amount of clearances early each day and notify the corporate treasurer of the dollar amount required to cover disbursements.

More frequent notifications make it difficult for the cash manager to know how much excess funds exist that can be invested.

A variety of bank-controlled disbursing services exist to help the cash manager. These services include notifying the company of the total amount of checks clearing on a particular day prior to the close of the securities market; funding the company's account for items presented after funds have been invested; forecasting the amount of checks clearing in a day so that excess funds can be invested; offering investment alternatives after the close of the securities market; and providing special information services.

Traditional Techniques for Analyzing Accounts Payable

The control of trade accounts payable usually follows procedures similar to those used in controlling and monitoring accounts receivable. The accounts payable – to – purchases ratio, days purchases outstanding, and aging of accounts payable are traditional monitoring techniques. Each technique is discussed next under the assumption that purchase credit terms are 2/10, *n*/30.

Accounts Payable – to – Purchases Ratio

Table 16.1 summarizes monthly purchases and month-end outstanding balances for a 15-month period. The accounts payable balance is the result

TABLE 16.1
Purchases and Accounts Payable Balances ($000)

Month	Purchases	Accounts payable	Ratio
October	$3600	$2970	0.825
November	4000	3360	0.840
December	5000	4375	0.875
January	2500	2320	0.928
February	2800	1750	0.625
March	3000	1838	0.613
April	3500	2386	0.682
May	4000	3100	0.775
June	4100	3358	0.840
July	3000	2360	0.787
August	3500	2416	0.690
September	4000	3210	0.803
October	4500	3710	0.824
November	5000	4210	0.842
December	5100	4457	0.874
Average			0.788

of purchases in the current month and payments for some proportion of the current month and past months' purchases.

The relationship between payables and purchases averages around 79 percent, with September through January being above average. This relationship is conventional for a firm with its greatest production (and possibly sales) in the last half of the year.

Management often relies on the *accounts payable – to – purchases ratio* to measure whether payables are in line with past performance. Should a significant change occur, management reads it as a signal that further analysis is necessary. The problem with this technique is that some changes go unrecognized. Furthermore, it fails to reveal the proportion of accounts not being discounted. For example, about 21 percent of the accounts in Table 16.1 appear to be discounted (i.e., $1 - 0.788$) on the average. But such a conclusion is erroneous, as is shown shortly.

Days Purchases Outstanding

Another technique often used is *days purchases outstanding* (DPO). It is an extension of the payables-to-purchases ratio in that the ratio is multiplied by the number of days in the period to get the DPO. Table 16.2 summarizes

TABLE 16.2
Days Purchases Outstanding ($000)

		Last 30 days		Last 60 days		Last 90 days	
Month	Pay-ables	Purchases	DPO	Purchases	DPO	Purchases	DPO
Jan.	$2320	$2500	27.8 (1)	$7,500	18.6 (2)	$11,500	18.2 (3)
Feb.	1750	2800	18.8	5,300	19.8	10,300	15.3
Mar.	1838	3000	18.4	5,800	19.0	8,300	19.9
Apr.	2386	3500	20.4	6,500	22.0	9,300	23.1
May	3100	4000	23.3	7,500	24.8	10,500	26.6
June	3358	4100	24.6	8,100	24.9	11,600	26.1
July	2360	3000	23.6	7,100	19.9	11,100	19.1
Aug.	2416	3500	20.7	6,500	22.3	10,600	20.5
Sept.	3210	4000	24.1	7,500	25.7	10,500	27.5
Oct.	3710	4500	24.7	8,500	26.2	12,000	27.8
Nov.	4210	5000	25.3	9,500	26.6	13,500	28.1
Dec.	4457	5100	30.0	10,100	26.5	14,600	27.5

Notes:
1. $2320/($2500/30) = 27.8.
2. $2320/($7500/60) = 18.6.
3. $2320/($11,500/90) = 18.2.

the DPO, using the information in Table 16.1 and assuming that purchases for the last 30, 60, and 90 days are used in the calculation.

Much variation exists in the days purchases outstanding figures. The data for this example indicate that the DPO never goes beyond the net period of the credit extended (i.e., 30 days). This result is incorrect, as will be shown later. The problem with the DPO is the same as the problem inherent in the days sales outstanding calculation for accounts receivable (discussed in Chapter 12) — namely, *a changing purchasing pattern distorts the true underlying payment pattern.* Whenever the trend in credit purchases is not flat, distortions exist in the ratio.

Aging Schedule

A more revealing technique than the DPO is to age the accounts payable according to how many days they are outstanding. Table 16.3 shows such a *payable aging schedule.*

This schedule shows that current payables range from 51.7 to 83.2 percent of total payables; accounts 60 days old range from 14.3 to 43.1 percent of total payables; and accounts 90 days old range from 0 to 6.6 percent of total payables. These proportions seem to indicate that a sizable percentage of purchases are not being discounted, particularly since all purchases are made on terms of 2/10, *n*/30. Although this interpretation is basically correct, it misstates the true picture, as is shown in the next section.

TABLE 16.3
Accounts Payable Aging Schedule ($000)

Month	30 days	%	60 days	%	90 days	%	Total
			Days outstanding				
Jan.	$1200	0.517	$1000	0.431	$120	0.052	$2320
Feb.	1400	0.800	250	0.143	100	0.057	1750
Mar.	1530	0.832	308	0.168	0	0.000	1838
Apr.	1820	0.763	510	0.214	56	0.023	2386
May	2280	0.735	700	0.226	120	0.039	3100
June	2378	0.708	840	0.250	140	0.042	3358
July	1500	0.636	820	0.347	40	0.017	2360
Aug.	1925	0.797	450	0.186	41	0.017	2416
Sept.	2440	0.760	560	0.174	210	0.066	3210
Oct.	2790	0.752	920	0.248	0	0.000	3710
Nov.	3000	0.713	1170	0.278	40	0.009	4210
Dec.	3162	0.709	1250	0.281	45	0.010	4457

Analysis of Payment Patterns

Payment patterns reveal the true nature of outstanding payables. By relating payments to the original purchases, an analyst can show the true payment behavior of the firm. Analysis of the month's purchases (see in Table 16.1) reveals the true dollar amount of payables paid by the discount date. These amounts are summarized in Table 16.4.

A comparison of Tables 16.3 and 16.4 reveals the discrepancy of the aging schedule technique. For Table 16.3 one minus the proportion of accounts that are current (i.e., 30 days old) *implies* the proportion of accounts that are discounted. In Table 16.5 these calculations are compared with the actual proportion of each month's purchases discounted.

Apparently, implying discounts from the aging schedule leads to significant errors about whether or not discounts are being taken. Although management is discounting more than the aging schedule indicates, a significant proportion of invoices are not discounted. Management must discern the reasons for such behavior. Is it because stretching results in a lower AIC? If so, what are the penalty costs? Is this stretching strategy optimal? Management should conduct an analysis as summarized in Fig. 16.1 if it is to understand the benefits/costs of its present disbursement policy.

The aging schedule of Table 16.3 can be used to determine the total payment patterns in a fashion similar to that used to obtain the amount of invoices paid by the discount date. Table 16.6 summarizes outstanding

TABLE 16.4
Amount of Purchases Discounted ($000)

Month	Purchases	30 days old	Purchases discounted	
			Dollars	%
January	$2500	$1200	$1300	0.520
February	2800	1400	1400	0.500
March	3000	1530	1470	0.490
April	3500	1820	1680	0.480
May	4000	2280	1720	0.430
June	4100	2378	1722	0.420
July	3000	1500	1500	0.500
August	3500	1925	1575	0.450
September	4000	2440	1560	0.390
October	4500	2790	1710	0.380
November	5000	3000	2000	0.400
December	5100	3162	1938	0.380

Note: Purchases less 30-day-old invoices equal discounted purchases.

TABLE 16.5
Implied Versus Actual Payables Discounted

| Month | Proportion discounted | | |
	Implied*	Actual†	Error‡
January	0.483	0.520	0.034
February	0.200	0.500	0.600
March	0.168	0.490	0.657
April	0.237	0.480	0.506
May	0.265	0.430	0.384
June	0.292	0.420	0.305
July	0.364	0.500	0.272
August	0.203	0.450	0.489
September	0.240	0.390	0.385
October	0.248	0.380	0.347
November	0.287	0.400	0.283
December	0.291	0.380	0.234

* Implied = (1 − % invoices current) in Table 16.3.
† Actual = the last column of Table 16.4.
‡ The error is calculated as (1 − implied/actual).

TABLE 16.6
Outstanding Payables by Month of Purchase ($000)

Month	1	2	3	4	5	6	7	8	9	10	11	12
Nov.	120											
Dec.	1000	100										
Jan.	1200	250	0									
Feb.		1400	308	56								
Mar.			1530	510	120							
Apr.				1820	700	140						
May					2280	840	40					
June						2378	820	41				
July							1500	450	210			
Aug.								1925	560	0		
Sept.									2440	920	40	
Oct.										2790	1170	45
Nov.											3000	1250
Dec.												3162
Sum	2320	1750	1838	2386	3100	3358	2360	2416	3210	3710	4210	4457

TABLE 16.7
Balance Fractions Based on the Month of Purchase

Month	Purchases	Proportion of balances still outstanding		
		After the discount date*	After day 30	After day 60
January	$2500	0.480	0.100	0.000
February	2800	0.500	0.110	0.020
March	3000	0.510	0.170	0.040
April	3500	0.520	0.200	0.040
May	4000	0.570	0.210	0.010
June	4100	0.580	0.200	0.010
July	3000	0.500	0.150	0.070
August	3500	0.550	0.160	0.000
September	4000	0.610	0.230	0.010
October	4500	0.620	0.260	0.010
November	5000	0.600	0.250	?
December	5100	0.620	?	?

* This column must equal (1 − proportion of invoices discounted) as shown in Table 16.5.

payables based on the month of purchase. For example, the January balance of $2320 consists of $1200 for purchases made in January, $1000 for purchases made in December, and $120 for purchases made in November.

Table 16.6 is similar to the aging schedule in Table 16.3 when each amount is stated as a proportion of its column total. However, when the row amounts are analyzed, *balance fractions* based on the month of purchase are revealed. For example, at the end of January $1200 of January's purchases were still outstanding; at the end of February $250 of January's purchases were still not paid for; at the end of March all payments for purchases in January had been made. Table 16.7 summarizes the analysis in terms of balance fractions. A comparison of these balance fractions with the DPO amounts in Table 16.2 and with the aging schedule figures in Table 16.3 reveals inconsistencies among the various monitoring techniques. However, as was discussed in Chapter 12, balance fractions are superior to days outstanding and aging calculations.

Management needs to analyze the annual implicit cost (AIC) of not taking discounts and stretching payables. Whether this payment pattern is to the liking of the company's suppliers is a matter that can best be answered by looking at the relations, over time, between the firm and its vendors. Suppliers may view the buyer's payment path, while not optimal, as better than an erratic payment path. It is recognized by buyers and suppliers that trade credit should be self-financing, and to this extent, payments beyond the net period may be explained by the product and production time of the buyer. While this argument is not made to condone lateness in payment, lateness is nonetheless understandable; and a customer who buys and pays regularly is generally of greater value to the supplier than the customer who pays infrequently or irregularly.

Variance Analysis of Payables

The criticism of the DPO calculation is that it is sensitive to both the purchases averaging period and the purchasing pattern. However, the use of a variance analysis calculation overcomes both of these problems. When actual disbursements are compared with budgeted disbursements, management can readily distinguish the impact of changes in accounts payable management from changes in volume of services and goods purchased on account. And when the variance analysis for payables is evaluated along with that for inventory (discussed in Chapter 15), management can gain much insight into the joint impact that inventory and payables have on liquidity.

Table 16.8 summarizes the relevant information for analyzing payables. The actual payables and purchases data are taken from Table 16.6. The budget data is new.

The traditional measures of days purchases outstanding and the aging schedule for the data shown in Table 16.8 are listed in Table 16.9 (and closely parallel those of Chapter 12). They provide benchmarks for measuring the variance analyses. Both measures indicate that payables are older than anticipated by the budget.

Table 16.10 shows the allocation of the $786,000 variance between actual payables outstanding and the budget balance, as of the end of April. The appendix summarizes the calculations necessary for determining the variances. The variance is unfavorable since the actual payables balance exceeds the budget balance. The allocation of the total variance into its various components helps management better understand disbursement

TABLE 16.8
Payables and Purchases Data as of the End of April ($000)

Month	Payables			Purchases		
	Actual	Budget	Difference	Actual	Budget	Days
February	$ 56	$ 0	$ 56	$2800	$3000	30
March	510	200	310	3000	2900	30
April	1820	1400	420	3500	2700	30
Total	$2386	$1600	$786	$9300	$8600	90

TABLE 16.9
Traditional Measures of Payables Performance

Days purchases outstanding
Actual   90 × $2386/$9300 = 23.1 days
Budget   90 × $1600/$8600 = 16.7 days

Aging schedule

Month	Actual	Budget
February	2.3%	0%
March	21.4	12.5
April	76.3	87.5
Total	100.0	100.0

TABLE 16.10
Variance Analysis of Accounts Payable Balances ($000)

Month	Actual purchases per day × actual DPO	Actual purchases per day × budget DPO	Purchases per day restated in budget proportions × budget DPO	Budget purchases per day × budget DPO
Feb.	$ 56	$ 0	$ 0	$ 0
Mar.	510	207	216	200
Apr.	1820	1815	1515	1400
	$2386	$2022	$1731	$1600

Payment experience variance $364; unfavorable

Purchase mix variance $291; unfavorable

Purchase quantity variance $131; unfavorable

Purchase pattern variance $422; unfavorable

behavior. Each of these variance components is discussed in the sections that follow.

Payment Experience Variance

The *payment experience variance* (PEV) is a direct measure of disbursement efficiency. It is free of any contamination from changing purchasing patterns that influence the traditional measures of DPO and aging schedules. Actual payables are $364,000 greater than the revised budget (the second column in Table 16.10), which reflects what the budget payable balance should be given the actual volume for the period.

The variance arises from purchases in February and March, which are outstanding longer than the revised budget indicates they should be. Are these invoices in dispute, or is management simply stretching payables longer than anticipated in the budget formulation in order to take pressure off immediate liquidity needs? Are discounts being missed for no apparent reason? Analysis of the invoices supporting the February and March outstanding balances would allow a quick determination of the reason(s).

Purchase Pattern Variance

The unfavorable *purchase pattern variance* (PPV) of $422,000 indicates that accounts payable are higher by this amount because of purchases being higher than budgeted. This variance is not the responsibility of the disbursement manager. It results from purchases for the February-to-April period being $700,000 higher than budgeted (see Table 16.8). Is this variance an indication that inventories are being mismanaged? If so, liquidity could be seriously impaired in the near future when management discovers that it has too much (or obsolete) inventory.

This purchase pattern variance consists of two variances, a mix variance and a quantity variance; both contribute to the overall unfavorable performance. Each type is examined in the following sections.

Purchase Mix Variance

The unfavorable *purchase mix variance* of $291,000 indicates that payables are higher than they should be because of a changing purchase pattern, relative to budget. The budget shows a declining trend in purchases during the February-to-April period, whereas actual purchases were steadily increasing each month. Thus there has been a shift in the actual proportions of purchases in each month versus the budget, leading to the mix variance and a potential liquidity crisis.

Purchase Quantity Variance

The unfavorable *purchase quantity variance* of $131,000 shows the impact of larger purchases on accounts payable balances. It is free of any contamination from payment efficiency or change in purchase patterns and provides insight about inventory accumulations as they affect payables.

Overall Variance Analysis

The variance analysis indicates that the higher payables balance is basically the result of deteriorating payment performance versus budget (i.e., the unfavorable payment experience variance) and the production department's change in purchasing pattern as revealed in the purchase pattern mix variance. Increased total purchases, as shown by the quantity variance, have also contributed to the accounts payable discrepancy with budget.

These variances are a signal that production is out of line with budget expectations. If inventory purchases represent the majority of payables, then these variances indicate that an imbalance exists in inventories, particularly if the sales budget is still representative of what management expects to sell. The unfavorable payment experience variance requires analysis to determine whether discounts are being missed and, if so, why and what the effective cost is. If this cost exceeds short-term borrowing rates, then management should attempt to borrow to pay its invoices by the discount date. Failure to do otherwise will result in lower firm value unless payables can be stretched long enough to lower the AIC without affecting the firm's credit rating.

Summary

This chapter examined four aspects of accounts payable management. The first part discussed the importance of disbursements management; which is an integral part of any successful cash management system.

The second part analyzed the effective cost of trade credit discounts and how it is reduced by stretching payables. The decision to stretch must be evaluated in terms of cost trade-offs. On the one hand, stretching reduces the opportunity cost associated with not taking a cash discount when it is offered. If the payment is stretched long enough, the cost may be lower than that associated with short-term borrowing. On the other hand, stretching may lead to deteriorating business relations between the firm and its suppliers. Costs associated with slower payment patterns are difficult to quantify. However, if management decides to stretch payables, it must make an attempt to quantify the costs so as to determine the maximum stretching period consistent with value maximization.

Remote and controlled disbursement were discussed next. They are means of delaying payment so as to maximize the use of corporate funds. Remote disbursing fell out of favor after the Monetary Control Act was passed by Congress in 1980. Controlled disbursement has largely replaced remote disbursement. It, however, operates within the act so as to allow corporations as much time as possible before they are required to provide funds to their banks to pay checks presented for payment.

The fourth part of the chapter examined techniques for evaluating accounts payable management. Both traditional and new techniques were discussed. Traditional measures include the accounts payable – to – purchases ratio, the number of days purchases outstanding in payables, and the aging schedule. These approaches are flawed because they are influenced by changing purchasing patterns and are unable to indicate the impact these changing patterns have on payables management.

The new measures examined were payment pattern analysis and variance analysis. Payment patterns relate outstanding payables to the source of the obligation. This technique allows management to determine whether payment behavior has shifted. If it has, corrective action can be taken to restore payments to an acceptable pattern. The technique of variance analysis is the most informative of the evaluation techniques. It allows management to identify problem areas by segregating any discrepancy between actual and budgeted balances into a payment experience variance, a purchase mix component, and a purchase quantity component. The payment experience variance indicates the performance of disbursements against a revised flexible budget that incorporates any changes in overall purchase quantities. It thus separates payment performance from changing production decisions. The mix and quantity variances are generally the responsibility of the production or purchasing departments. Any changes in production/purchase plans, relative to budget, are shown by these variances. They indicate the impact of changing plans on accounts payable balances.

Key Concepts

Accounts payable – to – purchases
  ratio
Annualized implicit cost
Controlled disbursement
Days purchases outstanding
Payable aging schedule
Payment experience variance

Payment patterns
Purchase mix variance
Purchase pattern variance
Purchase quantity variance
Remote disbursement
Stretching payables

Appendix
Calculation of Variances

The calculation of the accounts payable variances is similar to the calculation of the accounts receivable variances shown in Chapter 12. One must break purchases down to a per-day figure for both actual and budget. One must also calculate days purchases outstanding for both actual and budget performance. Finally, one must restate actual purchases per day in the budget proportion. This manipulation allows the purchase pattern variance to be broken into its mix and quantity components. These three tasks are done in Table A.1. The sections that follow show the variance calculations.

TABLE A.1
Data for Variance Calculations

Purchases per day by month

Month	Actual	Budget	Proportion
February	$2800/30 = $ 93.33	$3000/30 = $100.00	0.349
March	3000/30 = 100.00	2900/30 = 96.67	0.337
April	3500/30 = 116.67	2700/30 = 90.00	0.314
	$310.00	$286.67	1.000

Days purchases outstanding by month

Month	Actual	Budget
February	30 × $56/$2800 = 0.60	30 × $0/$3000 = 0
March	30 × $510/$3000 = 5.10	30 × $200/$2900 = 2.07
April	30 × $1820/$3500 = 15.60	30 × $1400/$2700 = 15.56

Restatement of actual purchases per day in budget proportions

February	$310.00 × 0.349 = $108.19
March	310.00 × 0.337 = 104.47
April	310.00 × 0.314 = 97.34
	$310.00

Payment Experience Variance

The payment experience variance is calculated as

$$\sum_i \{(\text{actual purchases per day})_i \times [(\text{actual DPO})_i - (\text{budget DPO})_i]\},$$

where $i = 1, 2, 3$, which correspond to February, March, and April, respectively. The actual variance is as follows:

$$
\begin{array}{rl}
\$\ 93.33(0.60 - 0) = & \$\ 56.00 \\
\$100.00(5.10 - 2.07) = & 303.00 \\
\$116.67(15.60 - 15.56) = & \underline{4.67} \\
& \underline{\$363.67} \quad \text{or \$364 rounded}
\end{array}
$$

Purchase Pattern Variance

The purchase pattern variance is calculated as

$$\sum_i \{(\text{budget DPO})_i \times$$

$$[(\text{actual purchases per day})_i - (\text{budget purchases per day})_i]\}.$$

The actual calculation is as follows:

$$
\begin{array}{rl}
0(\$93.33 - \$100.00) = & \$0 \\
2.07(\$100.00 - \$96.67) = & 6.89 \\
15.56(\$116.67 - \$90.00) = & \underline{414.99} \\
& \underline{\$421.88} \quad \text{or \$422 rounded}
\end{array}
$$

Purchase Quantity Variance

The purchase quantity variance is calculated as

$$\sum_i \{(\text{budget DPO})_i \times [(\text{actual purchases per day in budget proportions})_i$$

$$- (\text{budget purchases per day})_i]\}.$$

The actual variance is as follows:

$$
\begin{array}{rl}
0(\$108.19 - \$100.00) = & \$0 \\
2.07(\$104.47 - \$96.67) = & 16.15 \\
15.56(\$97.34 - \$90.00) = & \underline{114.21} \\
& \underline{\$130.36} \quad \text{or \$130 rounded}
\end{array}
$$

Purchase Mix Variance

The purchase mix variance is the difference between the purchase pattern variance and the purchase quantity variance:

$$\sum_i [(\text{purchase pattern variance})_i - (\text{purchase quantity variance})_i].$$

The actual calculation is as follows:

$$
\begin{aligned}
\$0 - 0 &= \$0 \\
\$6.89 - \$16.15 &= -9.26 \\
\$414.99 - \$114.21 &= \underline{300.78} \\
&\ \ \underline{\$291.52} \quad \text{or } \$292 \text{ rounded}
\end{aligned}
$$

Questions

1. Accounts payable are said to be spontaneous financing. Explain. Your answer should include a discussion of the cash conversion cycle.

2. "A firm that misses a trade discount has taken the first step to ruin." Discuss.

3. The stretching of trade accounts payable is another example of indifference analysis. Discuss the conflicting forces of such an analysis.

4. The use of days purchases outstanding as a control measure for accounts payable contains a basic flaw. Discuss.

5. Discuss the application of variance analysis to accounts payable. Your answer should identify the assumptions included in the analysis.

Problems

1. The 16 – 1 Company has been offered a change in trade credit terms by its supplier. The present terms are 2/10, n/45. Proposed terms are 1.5/20, n/36 or 2.5/cash, n/54. Determine and discuss the probable reaction of management to these proposed terms. The company usually forgoes the discount and pays on day 50. Use the compound interest equation to calculate the annualized implicit cost. Assume 360 days in the year.

2. The Berry Company purchases materials from a number of suppliers. Purchase discounts range between 1% and 4% (in 1% increments), with the discount period either 10 or 15 days. The net period is always 30 days. Management wishes to develop a cost profile of stretching trade payables. Prepare a profile that allows the acceleration period to vary between 20 and 90 days, in 10-day increments. Use the continuous-compounding formula, and assume 360 days in the year.

3. A firm purchases $80 of goods monthly on credit terms of 2/10, n/50. Assume 360 days in the year.

    (a) Calculate the annual implicit cost of credit in percentage and dollar terms if the firm usually pays on the net date.

    (b) Calculate the annual implicit cost of credit in percentage and dollar terms if the firm usually pays 40 days after the invoice date.

    (c) Discuss the implications of these two payment arrangements.

4. The Hazel Company purchases $750,600 of goods annually at a constant monthly rate. Its suppliers offer terms of 2/10, n/50. Management has investigated the relationship between credit rating and time of payment of credit purchases and found it to be

$$0.02P + 0.0001(\text{number of days after discount date}) \left(\frac{P}{30}\right)^2,$$

where P is the average monthly purchases. Construct a graph similar to Fig. 16.1, and discuss your findings. Assume 360 days in the year.

5.   The Karlin Corporation wishes to analyze its accounts payable record for the year ending December. Management decides to evaluate payables by calculating the payment ratio and days payables outstanding, using 30, 60, and 90 days purchases for the latter calculation. Complete this analysis by using the data in Table 16.11.

TABLE 16.11
Purchase Data

Month	Purchases	Payables
Last year		
November	$4250	$2750
December	5170	4010
This year		
January	3200	3000
February	1800	1000
March	1250	1000
April	1450	1300
May	2700	2240
June	3240	2587
July	4950	3094
August	6500	5700
September	7100	6250
October	8400	6570
November	8950	7040
December	9400	7190

6.   During the year the Karlin Corporation (Problem 5) had the accounts payable aging schedule shown in Table 16.12.

(a) Discuss the firm's payment behavior, using the aging schedule.

(b) Determine the dollar amount of purchases discounted. Assume all purchases allow a discount.

TABLE 16.12
Accounts Payable Aging Schedule

Month	30 days	%	60 days	%	90 days	%	Total
Jan.	$1956	0.652	$ 912	0.304	$132	0.044	$3000
Feb.	586	0.586	364	0.364	50	0.050	1000
Mar.	429	0.429	503	0.503	68	0.068	1000
Apr.	781	0.601	490	0.377	29	0.022	1300
May	1577	0.704	634	0.283	29	0.013	2240
June	1485	0.574	999	0.386	103	0.040	2587
July	2033	0.657	987	0.319	74	0.024	3094
Aug.	3944	0.692	1693	0.297	63	0.011	5700
Sept.	3463	0.554	2575	0.412	212	0.034	6250
Oct.	3705	0.564	2792	0.425	73	0.011	6570
Nov.	4231	0.601	2703	0.384	106	0.015	7040
Dec.	3983	0.554	3063	0.426	144	0.020	7190

7. The Hartley Corporation uses a budget control system. Actual and budgeted data for the last three months is given in Table 16.13. Use this data to perform a three-way variance analysis. Assume each month has 30 days.

TABLE 16.13
Actual and Budget Data

	Payables		Purchases	
Month	Actual	Budget	Actual	Budget
October	$ 6,570	$ 6,200	$ 8,400	$ 8,500
November	7,040	6,800	8,950	8,750
December	7,190	7,000	9,400	9,000
Total	$20,800	$20,000	$26,750	$26,250

8. Management of Edmonds Emporium wishes to investigate how much of the trade payables are being discounted. The firm buys on credit terms of 2/10, $n/30$. The data given in Table 16.14 relate purchases to accounts payable balances.

   (a) Determine the traditional aging of accounts payable.
   (b) Determine the percentage of each month's purchases that are discounted.

TABLE 16.14
Monthly Purchases and Outstanding Accounts Payable ($000)

Month	1	2	3	4	5	6	7	8	9	10	11	12
−2	400											
−1	1500	100										
1	3000	600	50									
2		3250	780	130								
3			3713	1185	395							
4				5200	900	100						
5					5800	1200	240					
6						4320	1080	270				
7							4080	800	80			
8								3975	825	0		
9									2450	700	100	
10										2160	540	135
11											2000	360
12												2346
Sum	4900	3950	4543	6515	7175	5620	5400	5045	3355	2860	2640	2841
Purchases	5800	6500	7900	10,000	12,000	9000	8000	7500	5000	4500	4000	4600

9. Management of the Edmonds Emporium (Problem 8) is concerned that its trade accounts payable practice is costing the firm a significant amount of lost discounts. Determine the dollar amount of discounts offered and taken on a monthly and annual basis. Comment on the apparent payable policy that the firm is following.

10. Actual purchases for the months of May through July were substantially larger than budgeted. Management wants a three-way analysis of variance performed to explain what has happened. Payables and purchases are summarized in Table 16.15. Discuss your results.

TABLE 16.15
Payables and Purchases

Month	Payables Actual	Payables Budget	Purchases Actual	Purchases Budget	Days
May	$ 270	$ 116	$ 7,000	$ 3,500	31
June	1420	612	6,250	3,600	30
July	3185	1372	5,000	3,400	31
	$4875	$2100	$18,250	$10,500	

CHAPTER 17 □
Asset-Based Financing

In recent years relatively rapid business growth, general inflation, broader economic uncertainties, and unique financing situations have frequently resulted in inadequate liquidity levels. As a result, fewer firms have been able to raise required cash and working capital through short-term unsecured loans. To facilitate the borrowing needs of these companies, an alternative source of financing is proving highly beneficial. Referred to as *asset-based financing,* this alternative has gained increasing popularity and creditability in recent years. Asset-based financing uses such assets as accounts receivables, inventories, plant and equipment, and real estate as collateral for loans.

The subject of asset-based financial services is a total balance sheet concern and, therefore, is of importance to both businesses and creditors alike. The purpose of this chapter is to (1) examine some of the reasons for the importance of asset-based financing and its recent growth, (2) examine characteristics of borrowers, and (3) discuss the various forms of collateral used to improve the firm's liquidity.

Conditions Conducive to Asset-Based Financing

The asset-based financial services industry has matured rapidly in recent years. Historically, the industry was characterized as "lenders of last resort," mainly because of a lack of public understanding and negative attitudes often associated with secured financing. As the number of businesses unable to satisfy borrower requirements increased, the need for asset-based financial services also increased; and the industry inevitably gained credibility.

Commercial finance companies were the primary lenders in the industry's early periods. These companies secured loans on inventory, receivables, and fixed assets. Banks rarely involved themselves in asset-based activities because of the perceived additional risks of lending money to a firm that did not have the creditworthiness to obtain a conventional unsecured bank loan. Banks preferred to make loans on an unsecured basis and extend credit on the strength of a borrower's financial condition and profit performance, without complicating the transaction with collateral requirements. Secured lending was generally recognized as being different in principle and application from conventional banking because of the complex legal issues involved in perfecting loans and the need for daily collateral administration. Many banks remained averse to a secured type of lending arrangement, and until the mid 1960s receivable and inventory financing were still considered nonbanking activities.

By the late 1960s most states had adopted the Uniform Commercial Code (UCC), which standardized and simplified the procedure for establishing loan security. The heart of the UCC is the security agreement, a standardized document or form on which one stated the specific pledged assets. The assets stated were to be of equipment, accounts receivable, or inventories.

The adoption of the UCC was a major force behind the banking community's late expansion into this lending area. The new Bankruptcy Code in 1979 provided close legal supervision of asset-based financiers, which, in turn, ushered in greater acceptability of asset-based financing. A new breed of aggressive bankers recognized the growth potential offered by asset-based lending. Because of the additional risks, the added administrative costs, and the lower degree of elasticity in demand, banks and other firms have realized they can demand a higher rate of interest for these loans and thus increase the return on assets.

While asset-based loans may stem from a variety of transactions, the loan itself tends to follow a set pattern. Structured around a revolving accounts receivable and inventory line, the loan often includes advances against fixed assets as well. The borrowers are generally manufacturers or distributors, or both, with a recognized, stable product. High-tech companies are not attractive to asset-based lenders because these companies are long on ideas and short on capital assets. Conversely, service organizations are able to secure asset-based loans because they often have a very reliable flow of funds from their receivables.

Asset-based financing is selected by the borrower for a variety of reasons. Some of these reasons include marginal creditworthiness, above-average growth, business seasonality, industry cyclicality, turnaround financing for a troubled firm, and acquisition financing. Each of these reasons are examined next.

Marginal Creditworthiness

During the 1970s corporate debt increased faster than either the book value or the market value of equity. The capitalization ratios of many corporations became so low that lenders feared liquidity of borrowers would be impaired by major capital expenditures unless all layers of capitalization were expanded. High interest rates on debt and low market values of equity made conventional methods of raising capital less attractive.

Thus if a borrower's credit risk is suspect and the firm is characterized by high leverage, poor earnings trends, or weak financial ratios, management may rely on secured financing to provide cash or working capital. In this situation the lender prefers the asset-based loan to an unsecured loan. However, both borrower and lender should determine why the poor financial situation exists before relying on asset-based financing.

Business Growth

Firms experiencing above-average growth may require external funds to provide an appropriate level of net working capital to finance the cash conversion cycle — the difference between the period of conversion of inventories and accounts receivable into cash, and the length of time creditors are willing to wait for payment. Cash or borrowing capacity must be available to sustain the sales growth rate. Asset-based financing can be used to supply the needed additional net working capital and at the same time allow a company to reserve its debt capacity, which leaves bank lines open for future needs.

Business Seasonality

A firm may need to carry higher receivables or inventories owing to the seasonality of its business. Management may borrow from external sources if not enough cash is generated internally to carry temporarily higher levels of receivables or inventories. This situation is particularly well-suited for asset-based financing because such borrowing can be tied directly to asset account balances in an effort to maintain an appropriate loan – to – asset value ratio and an appropriate level of net working capital. In effect, as the inventory levels increase, so does the borrowing capacity. Thus the borrower gains access to a revolving line of credit based on the liquid value of the collateralized assets.

Industry Cyclicality

Highly cyclical businesses such as steel and automotive plants require large amounts of permanent net working capital. If internal cash generation is insufficient to maintain a minimum level of net working capital, meet capital expenditures, service debt, pay reasonable dividends, or maintain some borrowing level throughout the economic cycle, asset-based financing may be used to avoid periodic cash shortfalls.

Even though profitability may decrease during an economic recession for a cyclical firm, an asset-based lender may still be willing to provide the firm with needed funds. The lender will do so because the collateral gives the lender additional protection against risk (if the collateral is properly valued and monitored).

Financial Turnarounds

Sometimes, financially troubled firms seek new cash to alleviate creditor pressure or avoid bankruptcy. Loans collateralized by receivables can provide funds that may not otherwise be available to these firms since the loan is self-liquidating. As cash is received on outstanding receivables, it is applied to the loan in full or in some proportion.

Acquisition Financing

Asset-based financing has become popular in leveraged buyouts. In its simplest terms a leveraged buyout (LBO) is the purchase of a company or the subsidiary of a company by an investor group, largely with borrowed funds. In a typical deal an investment banker or other deal organizer assembles a group of investors, almost always including the management of the organization to be bought and usually one or more financial institutions. These investors acquire the stock or assets of the company by contributing a relatively small amount of equity and arranging a relatively large amount of debt financing. The investment banker packaging the buyout purchases an interest in the equity along with the management on the assumption that the leveraging will net the investors as much as $25 for every dollar risked.

The amount of debt financing is based on that company's existing assets. Thus the borrower is able to raise significantly greater amounts of funds than would otherwise have been possible.

These highly levered transactions entail collateral monitoring and detailed negotiations. Because equipment and inventory are often undervalued on the balance sheets of many mid-sized privately held companies, asset-based lenders have been able to apply higher lending ratios in delivering required funds. The *lending formulas used are often based on the company's assets rather than on cash flow predictions, as in conventional borrowing.*

Asset-based – lending packages for these leveraged buyouts may combine a nonamortizing loan with one tied to a repayment schedule. The term loan is based on a quick liquidation value of the acquired company's fixed assets. The nonamortized portion of the financing is provided through a revolving loan against receivables and inventories. The lending formulas typically advance a percentage against the liquid value of eligible receivables, inventory, and the liquidation value of fixed assets.

Acquisitions by purchase of corporate shares are also handled by the asset-based financing industry, although not as frequently as purchase of assets. Acquisition of shares would be indicated if the acquiring firm were interested in utilizing the target company's tax loss. Other possibilities might be that the target corporation has an advantageous lease franchise or other contract.

In summary, *the main advantage to the borrower of an asset-based loan is that the firm can maximize leverage and maintain an appropriate level of liquidity.* An asset-based loan gives management the ability to borrow additional funds beyond monies obtained from more conventional financing. Indeed, many times management cannot take advantage of market opportunities because of the unavailability of conventional unsecured bank financing.

Asset-based financing also gives the firm the opportunity to grow and become more profitable by taking advantage of the leveraging power provided by the collateralized assets. Since an asset-based loan does not require an annual cleanup, this type of financing is particularly helpful to those companies experiencing rapid growth. Additionally, the company borrows only what it needs at the time needed. Borrowings can be kept at a minimum, and the cost of borrowed funds can be reduced.

An unfavorable feature of asset-based financing is that it increases the cost of unsecured debt. That is, asset-based transactions are invariably levered beyond the limits of normal unsecured bank loans. Hence unsecured lenders are exposed to more risk; there are fewer assets available to repay the loan whenever a liquidity crisis occurs.

Evaluation of Borrowers

The evaluation of borrowers is perhaps the most important part of the asset-based financing decision to lenders. This evaluation determines whether or not the lending institution makes an appropriate return on equity. The factors that receive primary consideration in the credit evaluation are cash flow and analysis of collateral.

Cash Flow Analysis

The preliminary evaluation of an asset-based borrower differs from that of a conventional unsecured borrower. In the conventional approach to lending, the lender's protection is primarily in the cash flow of the entity that is being financed. Loans are tied to the expected cash flow of the borrowing firm or of the entity guaranteeing the loan. In this situation the lender must have a history of stable cash flow, and the loan will represent a conservative multiple of that proven cash flow.

In asset-based lending the lender has a different orientation. Although cash flow analysis is used to determine whether the firm generates sufficient cash flow from operations, protection is based primarily on the assets and secondarily on the cash flow of the borrowing firm. Therefore, rather than tie the loan amounts to the cash flow, the leverage, or the amortization ability of the borrower, the asset-based lender ties the loan to the liquid value of the borrowing firm's assets offered as collateral. This is not to say that credit analysis is ignored. The lender must remember that collateral is not a substitute for performing a thorough credit analysis of the borrower. Lenders do not often make money in liquidations, and the presence of collateral does not make a difference in whether or not there will be a liquidation. Collateral only assures a lender that if liquidation does occur, the lender will have the right to negotiate for the proceeds of the borrower's collateral.

Analysis of Collateral

Collateral of superior quality can partially offset poor credit quality. However, collateral analysis should be separated from credit analysis. *Collateral analysis should address the worst case.* In the event that liquidation is necessary, the lender should be able to obtain maximum recovery. Collateral only assures a lender the right to negotiate for the proceeds of liquidation.

Two factors that influence acceptable collateral are the life of the collateral and the suitability and liquidity of the collateral.

1. *Life of the collateral.* Lenders of secured short-term funds prefer collateral that has a life closely related to the term of the loan. In this way lenders are assured that the collateral is sufficiently liquid to satisfy the loan in the event of a default. For short-term loans, collaterals are a firm's short-term (current) assets — accounts receivable, inventories, and marketable securities.

2. *Suitability and liquidity of the collateral.* Although virtually any asset may be pledged to insure payment, not all assets are equally desirable. The suitability of various assets is determined largely by the borrower's line of business. Elements for consideration when one is analyzing the suitability of collateral include standardization of grading, durability, marketability, and stability of demand. The lender of short-term secured funds is more apt than not to find only liquid current assets acceptable as collateral. The *liquidability of an asset refers to the asset's ability to be converted into cash.* The quality of the ability is measured in terms of speed of conversion

and value of exchange. Accounts receivable or inventories having an average age of 180 days are questionable candidates as security for a 90-day note.

Almost any of the firm's assets can be used as collateral, as discussed in the next section. The lender determines the desirable percentage advance to make against certain collateral. This percentage advance is normally between 30 and 90 percent of the book value of the collateral. It varies according to both the type of collateral and the type of security interest being taken. It is low if the collateral is not very liquid and high if the collateral is highly liquid. Several kinds of collateral can be employed. The following sections examine several forms.

Marketable Securities

Marketable securities make excellent collateral because of their highly liquid status. Despite this positive attribute, marketable securities do not play a dominant role as loan collateral. When businesses operate in tight credit environments, large security portfolios are uncommon.

Accounts Receivable

Some businesses find it advantageous to borrow money through the pledging (assignment) of receivables or the factoring (selling) of receivables. With the pledging of accounts receivable as security for a loan, a business will usually apply to a commercial credit company rather than a commercial bank. The former institution has special facilities for investigating and supervising this type of loan.

The factoring of accounts receivable has been traditionally associated with the textiles, apparel, and furniture industries. Until recently, most financial managers prescribed factoring as a last resort to satisfy their client's credit needs. Today many of those same managers highly recommend the services of a factor. This form of financing has gained increased popularity in industries as diverse as automotive parts, consumer electronics, paint, and watch manufacturing.

Pledging Accounts Receivable

Financing through *pledging of accounts receivable* is typically a continuing arrangement rather than a one-time transaction. If a financial agreement exists between the borrower and the lender covering a year, or perhaps covering an unspecified time period, the agreement would normally provide for the assignment of accounts receivable on a selective basis. The lender analyzes the past payment record of the firm's accounts to determine which accounts represent acceptable loan collateral. The lender agrees to advance funds up to a specified percentage of the accounts pledged. This percentage incorporates an amount for any sales returns and allowances. The borrower draws against this amount only as funds are needed. Effectively, a pure line of credit is established. As sales increase (and as do acceptable customers), the line increases.

An evaluation of payment proportions or balance fractions (discussed in Chapter 12) is the logical place to start when one is evaluating accounts receivable collateral and setting an advance rate. Frequently, the lender uses aging schedules and historical turnover ratios, which can lead to questionable conclusions (also discussed in Chapter 12).

The lender must know the client's method of record keeping, who its debtors are, and the nature of the industry. The lender must also know the nature of the agreement between the buyer and the seller so that matters such as time of delivery, overbilling, and so forth, are taken into account. The lender must be familiar with the dilution factor, including returns, allowances, discounts, or bad-debt losses. For example, short-term receivables may possibly be reduced first by a 5% dilution factor and additionally by 10% for a margin of error, resulting in an 85% advance rate.

The borrower's billing and collections should also be scrutinized to determine whether invoices represent goods that have actually been shipped. Whether invoices are being updated to improve aging of accounts receivable, whether payments are prompt, and whether the borrower is trying to "manufacture" collateral through other means. In essence, the lender needs to scrutinize procedures carefully and evaluate the collateral on a liquidation basis rather than on a going-concern basis.

The results of the accounts receivable evaluation will not only determine whether or not the loan is made but also determine the advance rate and the criteria for making the loan. There are many ways to set up the terms of a loan based on accounts receivable, as the following paragraphs indicate.

Accounts receivable may be financed on a notification or a nonnotification basis. Under a *notification plan* the receivables are pledged and payment is made directly to the lender, but the borrower remains responsible for the payment. The lender notifies the borrower's customers that their accounts have been assigned and directs them to make payments directly to the lender. The lender receives power of attorney to endorse notes and checks in the assignor's name.

Under the more satisfactory and more commonly used *nonnotification arrangement,* the borrower collects as agent for the lender. This method is preferable because the relationship between the borrower and its customers is not disturbed and the financing arrangement remains confidential. For pledging of receivables the borrower's new accounts receivable, subject to approval of the lender, qualify as collateral on which advances may be made. This plan creates a revolving and self-liquidating loan that eliminates the necessity for periodic reviews, renewals, and cleanups.

Collections are credited to the account on a daily basis. Interest is charged against the net daily debt and not the full amount available. Generally, the interest rate ranges between 2 and 5 percent over the prime rate, although it is negotiable. The agreed-upon interest rate will depend on the quality of the receivables and the general financial condition of the company.

With either the notification or nonnotification plan, receivables are not sold to the lender but merely pledged as security for the loan. Responsibility for collection, as well as for any losses incurred, rests with the borrower. Frequently, the lender will require the submission of audited financial statements during the term of the agreement.

The advantages to a company borrowing through the pledging of accounts receivable are several:

□ Receivables financing is sometimes effectively used to offset delays in receivables collection time and to finance an increase in receivables.

□ An increased investment in receivables presents an opportunity to increase leverage and thereby improve the firm's return-on-equity.

□ Income tax deductibility of interest paid on new receivables loans significantly subsidizes the cost of carrying additional receivables, especially during times of high interest rates.

□ An increase in receivables financed by external sources produces a swift conversion of receivables to cash (i.e., decreases the cash conversion cycle) and creates reinvestment opportunities or the ability to deploy funds on a timely basis to other areas of the business where the return may be higher.

The chief disadvantages of pledging receivables are also several:

□ The lender probably will be willing to lend only some portion of the face value.

□ The extra burdens of complying with the lender's requirements fall upon the bookkeeping department, which is less likely than the credit department to be under direct control of the treasurer.

□ The lender may insist that all accounts be pledged, even though the amount to be borrowed is much less in amount and the loan is not continuous.

□ The lender may insist on notification to customers and require them to make payments on account directly to the lender.

Factoring Accounts Receivable

Although similar in nature to pledging, *factoring of accounts receivable* differs from a pledging arrangement and is not a form of secured financing. In this arrangement a factor *buys* a client's accounts receivable for cash on an open account. The factor assumes the client's credit and collection functions and its bookkeeping; the factor guarantees or purchases its receivables as they arise, either with or without recourse concerning credit losses. This guarantee is subject to the condition that clients must obtain the factor's approval before shipping any goods, and the merchandise must be received and accepted by their customers without dispute. The straightforward credit and collection service is referred to as maturity factoring or as factored nonborrowing. Old-line factoring or factored borrowing pertains to clients who wish to have funds advanced on uncollected receivables. Such advances are *unsecured* financing. With a sale guarantee the factor assumes all credit risks.

It is often difficult to determine when a firm should utilize factoring services among an array of financing alternatives. The most common reason a company seeks the services of a factor is a sudden difficulty with the firm's operating line of credit. Although most companies have some operating or loan limit with the bank, sometimes the bank cannot or will not renew or extend existing credit lines. Continued high interest rates and a slow commercial paper market have reduced the availability of funds for many companies, making factoring a good financing alternative.

Factoring has been found to be particularly well suited for medium-to large-sized businesses. Although the reasons for borrowing are varied, characteristics common to the many firms seeking a factor can be cited. These companies are often characterized by highly levered capital structures. Seasonal fluctuations in production and sales are often prevalent, as they attempt to operate with unbalanced cash flows or find themselves burdened by a slow receivable turnover. In addition, these firms often lack the capital capacity to form a well-developed internal system for the collection of receivables.

Factoring is a highly personal business that requires close interaction between clients, customers, and the marketplace. Because a factor can become a valuable business advisor, the business seeking the service must be sure to find a factor experienced in its particular field. The factor should have the backing necessary to meet the client's financing needs, in addition to knowledgeable account executives and credit officers on the staff.

A factoring arrangement is accomplished through a written contract established between the factor and the client. This agreement is an important consideration that must be scrutinized and understood thoroughly. The agreement contains provisions permitting either party to terminate the arrangement, usually on 60 days prior written notice. The contract uses informal language in the form of a letter of exchange that confirms the agreement. Basically, the agreement between the seller and the factor is made to specify legal obligations and procedural arrangements.

As orders are obtained, a credit approval slip is written and immediately sent to the factoring company for credit approval. If the factor does not approve the sale, the seller generally refuses to fill the order. This procedure informs the seller, prior to the sale, about the buyer's creditworthiness and acceptability to the factor.

Once a sale is approved and shipment is made, the invoice is stamped to notify the buyer to make payment directly to the factoring company. The client submits, on a daily or weekly basis, invoices for particular goods that have been sold. The factor then pays the client the value of the invoice less a fee (usually in the 3 to 4 percent range). Often the factor will deduct a further 10 to 15 percent of the invoice value, which is held in retention immediately pending satisfactory payment of the invoice value, rather than waiting up to 90 days for payment.

In addition to providing funding arrangements, the factor is equipped to provide a range of other services. Common secondary reasons for companies' involvement with factors are the credit collection and bookkeeping services offered (each factor has a unique variety of services). Services offered may include maintenance of a client's debtor ledger, rendering of month-end statements, collection of accounts, and attention to inquiries. To enable the client to remain fully conversant with the status of its customers, the factor also provides regular management reports to the client.

The benefits of factoring are the following:

□ The rate of cash flow and the flexibility afforded are greatly increased. To companies exposed to the cyclical hazards of seasonal sales, factoring can facilitate the smoothing out of cash flows by drawing advances against expected sales for needed material purchases.

□ The greater availability of working capital to fund production and sales leads to higher utilization of fixed assets and greater profits.

□ Cost savings can result in the purchase of stock and new materials, because with the improved liquidity from factoring a client can obtain discounts from suppliers for prompt payment on bulk purchases.

□ Budgeting becomes easier with an assured cash flow geared to sales and not dependent on debtor payments.

□ Unlike other forms of financing, factoring imposes no requirement to set aside funds for loan repayment, since the factoring debt is repaid by the client's customers.

□ The rapidity of cash flows aids the firm in avoiding the dilution of ownership equity by enabling it to acquire additional net working capital without seeking new investors.

□ The predictability of future cash flows is enhanced through the elimination of uncertainty and risk by fixing the percentage of credit sales receipts that will be absorbed by credit and collection expenses (including bad-debt losses). This percentage will be the commission on credit sales the firm agrees to pay the factor.

□ The services of a factor eliminate the salaries and wages for credit and collection personnel. Also, office costs such as invoice mailing, long-distance telephone calls, and telex costs are reduced. These cost savings make the actual costs of factoring lower than explicitly stated.

□ Factoring also gives management time to concentrate efforts on other business concerns such as production and marketing.

□ Factors help define and organize customer profiles while providing useful business information to allow a business to take on certain credit risks that would have otherwise been unacceptable. Risk reduction is clearly advantageous to firms considering a potential buyer whose credit loss could jeopardize the financial security of the business.

Factoring is not for everyone, though, and there are disadvantages to be considered:

□ When invoices are numerous and relatively small in dollar amount, the administrative costs involved may render this method of financing inconvenient and expensive. A prospective client must decide whether the benefits outweigh the costs.

□ A nonborrowing client must compare the factoring charge with the cost savings of not maintaining a credit and collection department.

□ Qualitative elements must be considered, such as the quality of service, one's ability to work with the account executives, and the ability to turn over receivables.

□ In some circumstances the firm will have reached its maximum credit extension with the bank, so the main consideration will be the cost to owners in terms of dilution of majority ownership or the cost of venture capital.

□ For a long time accounts receivable financing was frowned on by most trade creditors; it was regarded as a confession of a firm's unsound financial position. It is still regarded as such by some people, although many sound firms engage in either receivables pledging or factoring. Still, the traditional attitude causes some trade creditors to refuse to grant credit to a firm involved in this method of financing on the ground that this practice removes one of the firm's most liquid assets.

ILLUSTRATION 17.1

Management is considering an offer by a local bank to factor the company's receivables. Management expects to need an average monthly balance of $150,000 for the months of July through October, with a peak cash need of $200,000 during this period. The terms of the factor agreement are:

□ The bank will hold 20% of the face value of the receivables in reserve.

□ A 1.5% commission will be assessed each month on the basis of the face value of the receivables.

□ The annual interest charge on borrowed funds will be 12%, calculated on a discounted basis.

□ Factoring will be on a nonrecourse and notification basis.

The company's credit terms are net 30 days. Customers remit their payments an average of 30 days after sale. Bad-debt expense is generally 0.75% of sales. Monthly clerical and credit-checking costs during the period of the loan average about $2125 each month. Management forecasts monthly sales of $350,000 during the period the loan is needed.

The maximum amount of loan available to the company is calculated as follows:

Accounts receivable balance (outstanding one month)	$350,000.00
Less:	
Reserve ($350,000 × 20%)	<70,000.00>
Commission ($350,000 × 1.5%)	<5,250.00>
Maximum loan amount	$274,750.00
Interest ($274,750 × 12%/12)	2,747.50
Cash proceeds realized from loan	$272,002.50

If the receivables are factored and an average loan balance of $150,000 exists, the effective annual cost of the factoring arrangement is 16.16%, as is shown next. The net cash proceeds are as follows:

Commission ($350,000 × 1.5%)	$ 5,250
Interest ($150,000 × 12%/12)	1,500
Gross cost	$ 6,750
Less savings:	
Bad debts ($350,000 × .75%)	<2,625>
Clerical and credit checking	<2,125>
Net monthly cost	$ 2,000
Average loan balance	$150,000
Interest ($150,000 × 12%/12)	1,500
Cash proceeds	$148,500

The effective annual cost is $= \dfrac{\$2,000}{\$148,500} \times 12 = 0.1616.$ □

Remember that many companies using factors are doing so for their credit, collection, and bookkeeping services. Companies that are factor borrowing are generally healthy enterprises that have found liquidity tight because of a high investment in current assets. On this same point, we stress that not every company requiring factoring will receive it. Potential clients must meet a number of criteria, including good management, favorable product acceptability, a desired financing package, and, for a new company, imminent profit forecasts supported by orders on hand.

Inventory

Inventory management considerations are not unlike those associated with receivables. Often pressure on net working capital results from the need to carry higher inventories in anticipation of larger sales volume, seasonal stock buildups, or cyclical production patterns. Seasonally patterned inventories accumulate, peak, then fall rapidly as sales grow. Without the ability to invest larger dollars in inventory, the firm may lose out on sales or market share. Therefore, as with investment in accounts receivable, the firm is faced with deciding on how to finance the greater investment in inventories.

A large volume of credit is secured by business inventories. Inventory is a useful form of collateral because it is physical — it can be seen and counted. Businesses that use inventory loans generally are typified by one or more of the following characteristics:

□ Their manufacturing and/or distribution pattern is such that there is an extended period between receipt of raw materials and the sale of finished goods.

□ Inventory is a major current asset.

□ Alternative sources of finance are inadequate for current needs.

□ Major increases in inventory occur sporadically in the normal course of business owing to special purchase opportunities or variances in deliveries, production, or sales.

□ The business is highly seasonal, requiring large purchases or accumulation of finished goods that do not result in sales until a specific time of year.

□ The company anticipates rapid growth in sales that requires an even larger anticipatory buildup of inventory.

Physical possession of the inventory is specified as part of the collateral arrangement. In some cases the borrower retains the pledged inventory and pays the lender when that inventory is sold or used. This procedure typically is used for consumer durables, such as appliances and automobiles, where the presence of a serial number on each inventory item is an easy way to keep track of the collateral. It is not as easy to keep track of parts, materials, and nondurable goods, and the pledged inventory may be entrusted to a third party for safeguarding.

If pledged inventory is kept off the premises of the borrowing firm, it is held in a *public warehouse* by a bonded company that provides warehousing services as part of collateral arrangements. If, instead, the inventory is kept on the premises of the borrower but under the control of a bonded warehouse operator, the arrangement is referred to as a *field warehouse*.

The lender decides the worth (on the basis of cost or market value) of particular items of inventory and then agrees to advance some prescribed percentage of the value as a loan to the firm. The lender will set the advance rate at less than 100 percent and usually less than the advance rate for receivables. Otherwise, full-cost recovery would not be realized should liquidation become necessary. The inventory valuation method used by the borrower can affect the amount of borrowings. The first-in, first-out (FIFO) method of inventory (discussed fully in Chapter 13) reflects the maximum inventory valuation during a period of increasing prices, thus permitting maximum borrowings. Consistency and accuracy in whatever method of inventory valuation is adopted is paramount.

The nature of a particular inventory and its relative stage in the production process affects its estimated value as collateral. Perishability is one property that may cause the inventory to be unacceptable collateral. Specialized items may not be acceptable if the market for them is small. Another characteristic to be considered is the physical size of the inventory. Very large items may not be desirable because of the expense associated with their transportation and storage.

All types of inventories may be offered as collateral, but typically only raw materials and finished goods are considered acceptable. Raw material can often be resold in the market for close to market value. Important considerations regarding finished goods are the spread between manufacturer's cost and the wholesale price, and the marketability of the product. The wider the spread and the stronger the demand for the goods, the higher the advance rate is. Work-in-process inventory is seldom used as collateral. The partially completed goods will not realize a return near either market value or cost in a liquidation. Therefore advance rates are low, if they are made at all.

Types of Collateral

There are three types of collateral in inventory financing: floating inventory liens, trust receipt inventory liens, and warehouse receipt loans. *Floating inventory liens* represent a general claim on a group of inventory. When a firm has a stable level of inventory that consists of a diversified group of merchandise, and no single item has an excessively high dollar value, the lender will generally advance less than 50 percent of the book value of the average inventory, and the interest charge is usually 3 to 5 percent above the prime rate.

A *trust receipt inventory loan* is a loan made against specific collateral that remains in the possession of the borrower, and the borrower physically holds the inventories (collateral) as the lender's trustee. These loans against inventory are available not only from the captive finance subsidiaries of manufacturers but also from commercial banks and commercial finance companies. Loans against collateral are relatively expensive. The legal and control pitfalls of this form of loan security are well recognized. This technique is usually limited to use as a supplemental protection on loans to firms that generally qualify for unsecured credit.

Warehouse receipt loans allow the lender to maintain control over the collateral, which is placed in either a terminal or a field warehouse chosen by the lender. The borrower cannot sell any of the collateral without the lender's written permission. Warehouse receipt loans provide the lender with the best position with respect to collateral — the lender has direct control over its disposition. This type of loan involves greater clerical costs than the floating lien; this increased cost is carried by the borrower. The interest rate is 3 to 5 percent above the prime rate plus a 1 to 3 percent warehouse fee.

Advantages and Disadvantages

Major benefits of inventory financing are twofold. First, cash can be freed up earlier in the inventory-sale-receivable-cash cycle (i.e., the cash conversion cycle is reduced). As raw materials are acquired, the firm may use increased borrowing power, assuming the lender will lend on a secured basis tied to the value of inventories. Cash freed from inventory via secured borrowing can be reinvested or used to satisfy other liabilities such as salaries, taxes, or other maturing debts.

Second, by resorting to asset-based financing, the firm effectively mortgages out its assets. By doing so, the firm earns the tax benefit of interest expense deductibility. This feature lowers the firm's effective carrying rate. In short, the firm alters the cost of capital by leveraging more assets at the secured borrowing rate. At the same time, it improves the velocity of cash flows.

The major disadvantages of inventory loans can be briefly summarized as follows:

□ Financing costs are typically 3 to 5 percent above the prime rate.

□ Not all forms of inventory are equally acceptable.

□ Inventory may be physically removed from the borrower's premises and placed in a bonded warehouse, which may cause production or sales disruptions.

□ A lower proportion of financing is given for inventories.

ILLUSTRATION 17.2

A bank is willing to lend $150,000 on a two-year note to a customer. Interest would be charged at 20% annually and require the loan to be secured by a warehouse receipt. The costs to the customer to maintain a field warehouse arrangement would be $2400 annually. The loan would enable the customer to pay for purchases within the discount period.

The *monthly* cost of the warehouse receipt loan is as follows:

Field warehouse arrangement	$ 200
Interest ($150,000 × 20%/12)	2500
Monthly cost	$2700

The effective interest rate is $2700/$150,000 = 1.8% monthly, or 21.6% annually.   □

Fixed Assets

Management is becoming increasingly aware of the underutilized value of its real property interests and the implied opportunities this value represents with regard to the basic business. A company does not need to own the buildings it uses in order to conduct a profitable business. It does need cash to conduct its business. Thus the question becomes, "How can a company's real assets be utilized to raise cash in the most cost-efficient manner, cash that will be used to support the company's primary business operations?"

There are a number of alternatives that management can use singularly or in combination with one another to address this question. The objective is to make more effective use of assets in order to meet liquidity needs. The alternatives to be discussed in the following subsections are as follows:

1. Disposing of excess properties.
2. Pledging plant and equipment.
3. Mortgaging real estate.
4. Utilizing sale and leaseback agreements.
5. Arranging a tax exchange.
6. Selling an ownership interest.

Sale of Excess Property

Management must identify those real assets that are integral to the company's operations and those assets that are, or will be in the near future, excess. The excess assets could be sold, leased, offered for joint-venture development, or exchanged for other properties. Net present value analysis that incorporates abandonment value is the ideal technique to use to identify properties for potential sale.

Pledging Plant and Equipment

Plant and equipment can be used in asset-based financing by pledging the asset as collateral. The liquidating appraisal value should be used for secured loans made against plant and equipment. A fair market value appraisal, a replacement value appraisal, and an insurance value appraisal are inadequate since they do not tell the lender what the collateral will bring in a distress sale. Background information on the plant and equipment (including their past use) is necessary. If the plant and equipment are highly specialized, their relative liquidity is reduced.

The plant and equipment user assumes the risks and benefits of ownership and operates under a lien until the debt is repaid. The advantage of a loan secured by plant and equipment is that the income generated by the equipment helps offset the cost of its financing. In addition, the cost of acquiring equipment is fixed, providing stability during a time of volatile interest rates.

Mortgages on Real Estate

Mortgages on real estate may be taken as security for a loan, but they are used infrequently and usually as a last resort. Transactions involved in securing loans on real estate are usually heavily detailed in tax and title searches, valuation procedures, and execution of instruments. Should the borrower fail in repayment, the carrying cost of the real estate can quickly dissipate the value of the initial arrangement.

Sale-and-Leaseback Agreement

In a *sale-leaseback agreement* the owner of the asset sells the asset to a second party. The second party then leases the asset to the seller. Sale-leaseback agreements often arise because historical accrual accounting is unable to reflect the impacts of inflation. Any long-term assets that have appreciated in value are understated on the balance sheet. This understatement, in turn, can affect the firm's ability to raise needed capital.

Through a sale-leaseback the selling firm realizes a large, positive initial cash flow and retains the benefits of using the asset. The firm should be able to obtain funds at a reasonable rate because the sale-leaseback is, in effect, the ultimate in a secured loan; the lender obtains title to the collateral at the inception of the loan. In addition to raising needed funds, a sale-leaseback can result in a better-looking financial statement.

ILLUSTRATION 17.3

The sale of assets for $55 million, which have a book value of $47 million, results in a gain reported in the income statement of $8 million and an increase in liquid assets — the old, undervalued assets are replaced on the balance sheet with the higher amount of cash (or notes) received for the assets. Earnings may increase because the reduction of interest expense on corporate borrowings and annual depreciation on the disposed asset may exceed the newly created rent expense. However, annual cash flow from operations may not improve by this decision. For cash flow to improve, the following condition must hold:

$$\text{new rental expense} < (\text{interest savings}) + (\text{depreciation}) \left(\frac{t}{1-t} \right),$$

where t is the marginal corporate tax rate. Thus the cash flow benefit of the sale-leaseback usually comes from the large infusion of cash at the time of the transaction. Subsequent periods' cash flows are usually negative.   □

   The most favorable influence on financial statements results if the lease can be structured as an operating lease (as discussed in Chapter 4). Under this arrangement the firm will show no additional debt on its books even though it has an obligation to make periodic payments. If the asset sold had a book value lower than the selling price, the total reported assets will be increased by the amount of gain on the sale. The result is that the firm's debt-equity ratio decreases, net assets increase, and the current and quick ratios increase (due to cash received). Even if the lease is capitalized and debt is recorded, when book value of the asset is less than the selling price, a gain is recognized under certain conditions. If the gain is recognized, ratios are affected in the same manner as with an operating lease, except that the debt-equity ratio may increase or decrease depending on the ratio prior to the sale-leaseback (assets will increase, but so will debt).
   Although sale-leasebacks are normally associated with capital equipment, creative financial managers can use this method to raise cash by utilizing other assets. For instance, IU International sold macadamia nut orchards to investors but retained a 99-year right to manage the orchards

and market the nuts. This technique allowed the company to *monetize* $10 million of *assets* being carried on the books at ridiculously low values. It was more profitable for the firm to utilize the assets than to own them.

Tax Arrangement Exchange

Whenever excess assets that have a low book value and a high market value are sold, the difference is taxed as a capital gain, with the company netting considerably less in cash. If an exchange of properties can be accomplished, the tax savings may be substantial.

ILLUSTRATION 17.4

Assume that the company finds that its corporate offices are inadequate. The building has a market value of $35 million, a book value of $3 million, and initially cost $10 million. The marginal tax rate is 36%, and the capital gains rate is one-half this rate. A new office complex would cost $20 million to construct. Sale of the old property would result in $7.02 million taxes: 36% × ($10 million − $3 million) + 18% × ($35 million − $10 million). Therefore the firm would net $27.98 million ($35 million − $7.02 million) from the sale but would pay $20 million for the new facilities.

Suppose this property could be exchanged for $18 million cash plus property valued at $15 million. The $2 million difference between the market price ($35 million) of the desired building and the total value of the exchange ($15 million + $18 million) is considered equity to the purchaser for buying the inadequate property. The company will be taxed only on the $18 million cash portion of the sales price. Therefore only $3.96 million in taxes will be paid: 36% × ($10 million − $3 million) + 18% × ($18 million − $10 million). The company will net $14.04 million in cash from this transaction, as opposed to netting only $7.98 million from the sale and new purchase.   □

The advantages of this transaction are obvious. The company has more *liquidity,* higher profits from the gain on the sale, and newer facilities that fit into its operating plan.

Sale of an Ownership Interest

Rather than sell an asset outright, a firm may choose to sell an ownership interest in an asset. Ownership interests can take many forms, including an equity participation by a lender, a loan-and-option agreement, a convertible mortgage, and a right to future income streams from an asset.

Lenders looking for an inflation hedge may find *equity participation* in projects involving appreciating assets to be an attractive alternative to conventional loans. The lender puts up a portion of the cost of the asset from its own funds and lends the borrower the remaining funds at a lower-than-normal rate. The borrower gives up some of the advantages of total ownership but gains liquidity benefits from not having to commit 100 percent of the required funds and obtains funds at below-normal rates.

A *loan and option agreement* gives lenders the option to purchase an asset (or a portion thereof) that the lender has been financing. The option is usually not exercisable until several years after the loan is made. In return for this option the lender supplies funds at a below-market rate.

ILLUSTRATION 17.5

General Motors obtained needed liquidity by obtaining a loan on its former New York headquarters building. The Aa bond rating for General Motors at the time was 15%, while the loan rate was 10%. The lender had the option of buying the building in ten years for $500 million — the principal amount of the loan. If the option was not exercised, General Motors was required to repay the loan. General Motors was effectively paid $25 million a year for the option (the 5% rate difference times the $500 million principal). □

A *convertible mortgage* allows the lender to convert a mortgage debt into an equity interest.

ILLUSTRATION 17.6

Cadillac-Fairview secured a $37.7 million mortgage at well below market rates, thus lessening interest expense and alleviating liquidity needs. In return for the rate concession the lender obtained the right, after ten years, to convert the mortgage to a 50% ownership interest. Otherwise, Cadillac-Fairview has a 30-year mortgage at below-market rates. Unlike General Motors in its loan-and-option agreement, Cadillac-Fairview faces no balloon payment of principal if the option is not exercised. □

Selling the rights to future income derived from an asset allows a firm to obtain cash immediately for assets that are not currently productive.

ILLUSTRATION 17.7

Tucson Electric Power Company and Public Service of New Mexico put a portion of their coal reserves into a trust. Shares in the trust were sold for $60 million. The investors obtained the rights to a 23-year stream of royalty income from the mining of the coal. The royalties were indexed to inflation, 3% above the GNP deflator. The utilities estimated that they would have had to pay 6% above the GNP deflator for conventional floating rate financing. If coal reserves are greater than expected, the investors will earn a higher-than-minimum return. If the reserves are depleted before 23 years pass, the investors get their money sooner. The utilities have given up future, uncertain income for current, low-rate money, which helps corporate liquidity management.   □

Pensions

Chapter 4 discussed unfunded pension obligations as an off-balance sheet item. The present discussion examines pensions as an asset-based – financing source. Many companies have vast amounts of available capital in surplus pension funds that they can recapture. These surpluses have arisen as a result of the following conditions:

1. Minimum-funding standards. The Pension Benefit Guaranty Corporation (PBGC) prescribes how to compute payments per employee per year. These formulas result in overfunding for a young worker and underfunding as he or she ages. The funding is expected to come out even when the employee retires. A company with a new pension plan or a young work force is likely to be overfunded.

2. The stock market. Pension fund assets are invested about 40 percent in stocks. Whenever a bull market occurs, increased equity values boost the value of pension fund assets.

3. The recession. Economic downturns result in employee layoffs and job eliminations. The same pension fund assets therefore cover fewer workers.

4. High interest rates. Many companies have purchased high-yielding annuities to cover their pension promises. The higher the stated yield, the lower the purchase price is for a bundle of pension benefits. Also, the more the annuity rate exceeds the assumed earnings rate of the pension fund, the greater is the paper surplus created.

Table 17.1 lists the 25 most overfunded pension plans as of 1983.

TABLE 17.1
Pension Plan Versus Equity as of 1983
($ million)

Company	Pension surplus	Surplus as % of equity
Martin Marietta	429.30	133.51
A&P	317.18	96.30
Interlake	133.60	41.33
Firestone	373.00	28.63
Celanese	280.00	26.87
United Technologies	744.25	26.73
Du Pont	2,768.00	26.08
Hercules	230.70	21.38
Briggs & Stratton	52.17	20.68
Harcourt Brace	31.65	19.12
AT&T (old)	11,541.00	18.64
AMF	77.46	18.28
Cincinnati Milacron	57.00	17.41
Rohm & Haas	140.30	17.37
Cummins Engine	63.00	16.92
Boeing	469.00	16.67
J. P. Stevens	75.45	15.49
General Dynamics	181.40	15.44
McDonnell Douglas	274.90	15.11
Times Mirror	145.92	14.77
Mohasco	25.40	13.31
Safeway	148.22	13.04
Brunswick	46.70	12.82
Mead	93.70	12.58
TRW	182.61	12.04

Source: Oppenheimer & Co.

Plan Termination as a Source of Capital

Even though pension funds are managed separately from other corporate assets and for the benefit of employees, a *company that terminates a defined-benefit plan can take back any assets left over after accrued benefits are paid.*

The basic procedure for plan termination is simple. The company must notify the PBGC of its intention to terminate the plan at least 10 days in advance of the proposed termination date. If the PBGC finds that the plan is overfunded, it issues a notice of sufficiency within 90 days of the original notification, and the termination proceeds as scheduled.

There is, however, more than one way to terminate a defined-benefit plan:

1. Terminate and replace with a *defined-contribution plan.* This method is the most common and is indisputably legal. The company simply ends its plan and pays off all the accumulated benefits of both retirees and active workers — nonvested as well as vested — usually with annuities or a lump sum. Starting from scratch, it then creates a defined-contribution plan for the active employees.

2. Terminate and replace with a new defined-benefit plan. The new plan that is set up is usually a slight improvement on the original. The legal issue is whether or not a real termination has occurred. If it has not, the excess funds in the plan should not go to the corporation but, rather, to the employees.

3. Spin off the retired workers. The old plan is divided into two parts: one for active and one for retired workers. The first group continues with its defined-benefit plan. After allocating enough assets to cover those benefits, the company places the remaining assets into the retirees' plan. That plan is then terminated, with the company buying annuities for the participants and the company taking whatever surplus cash is left over. ERISA has attacked this plan as not being a true termination.

Many critics of these practices exist. Corporate managers offer the logical explanation that they are still offering retirement benefits at the same time that they are strengthening the company that issues the employees' paychecks.

Indirect Sources of Capital

Many companies are viewing pension assets as a source of capital in a more indirect way. They hold on to the cash they would normally contribute to their retirement plans — thus avoiding the need to tap the capital markets as heavily — and, instead, send along their own corporate bonds (e.g., LTV Corporation), common and preferred stock (e.g., Eastman Kodak, Reynolds Metals, American Airlines), real estate (e.g., Exxon Corporation), and even gas well royalty interest (e.g., Diamond Shamrock). Other companies have been raising capital through the sale and leaseback of corporate property with their own pension funds as the buyer (e.g., United Technologies, Burroughs Corporation).

Summary

Asset-based financing has been a rapidly expanding market in recent years. Inflation has been a significant reason for this growth. Many businesses have doubled their sales because of inflation alone. Thus firms have become more leveraged, making it more difficult for them to finance growth and operations with conventional unsecured loans.

Asset-based financing is playing an extremely important role in the management of net working capital. In general, the advantages for the borrower of asset-based financing include improved liquidity and working capital and the ability to increase leverage when additional borrowing would not otherwise be available.

From the lender's perspective, the lender must evaluate risk-reward trade-offs on asset-based loans by using two types of criteria — one for evaluating the prospective borrower's general creditworthiness and one for evaluating the quality of collateral used to support the loan. After the lender has thoroughly evaluated the collateral, a written document should be prepared setting forth the price and terms of the loan. All terms should be thoroughly documented to protect both parties and prevent misunderstandings. Once the loan is made, the lender should monitor the collateral to determine whether any problems are developing.

The assets involved in asset-based loans can be of any type and can be either pledged as collateral or sold outright. The only criterion that can be advanced for any asset to be included is that it is presently owned and unpledged by the borrower and the lender considers it to have sufficient value to collateralize the loan. The assets discussed in this chapter include marketable securities, accounts receivable, inventory, fixed assets, and pensions. The discussion of accounts receivable examined both pledging and factoring arrangements. The discussion of fixed assets examined sale of excess assets, pledging agreements, mortgages, sale-leaseback arrangements, tax exchanges, and sale of an ownership interest.

Key Concepts

Asset-based financing
Collateral analysis
Convertible mortgage
Equity participation
Factoring of accounts receivable
Floating inventory lien
Defined-benefit pension plan
Defined-contribution pension plan
Loan-and-option agreement

Monetize assets
Notification versus nonnotification
  basis
Pledging of accounts receivable
Sale-leaseback agreement
Selling the rights to future income
Trust receipt inventory loan
Warehouse receipt loan

Questions

1. Name the conditions conducive to asset-based financing. Briefly discuss each condition.

2. Discuss the costs involved in secured loan financing.

3. What are the factors influencing acceptable collateral?

4. How might the use of assets as specific loan collateral influence existing and future nonsecured loan arrangements?

5. How does pledging of accounts receivable differ from factoring of accounts receivable? Discuss the advantages and disadvantages of each.

6. How does a sales-leaseback transaction impact on the demand and supply of liquidity of the selling firm?

7. What factors lead to firms using the employees' pension fund as an asset-based financing vehicle?

8. Discuss the factors that will influence the percentage of face value that will be loaned against (a) accounts receivable and (b) inventories.

9. Which of the following would be most suitable as collateral for a 90-day note from the company's lender? Discuss.

    (a) Units of electric switches premounted on circuit boards.

    (b) Accounts receivable due within 30 days.

    (c) Share of stock of IBM.

    (d) Stock options on American Can stock to buy at $45 per share; the current price is $48.25, and the expiration date is in 6 months.

    (e) Vacant land adjacent to the plant.

    (f) Government marketable securities.

    (g) Ninety-day commercial paper from Xerox.

    (h) Life insurance on the company's president paid for by the company.

10. What are the characteristics of firms that use inventory as loan collateral?

11. Distinguish between floating inventory liens, trust receipt inventory liens, and warehouse receipt loans.

12. What are the advantages and disadvantages of inventory loans?

13. What is a loan and option transaction?

Problems

1.   Hunt Corporation faces a need for seasonal working capital over the next 90 days. The required funds will average $250,000 over the period. However, the peak requirement is estimated at $300,000. The alternatives available to management are as follows:

(a) The corporation will obtain an inventory loan under a field warehousing arrangement. The initial setup cost of the loan is $1000 and warehousing charges of 1% of the goods warehoused. Credit will be extended up to 75% of the value of inventory at a cost of 15%.

(b) Management will use factoring of accounts receivable at a cost of 0.75% of all accounts factored plus 12% on the amount of any cash advances against the receivables. Cash advances will be limited to 60% of accounts factored.

(c) Second National Bank will make the necessary loan for 90 days at an annual interest rate of 13%, secured by a pledge of the company's inventory. The bank requires a minimum compensating balance of 10%, and a 1% prepayment penalty will apply.

Evaluate the dollar cost of meeting the firm's seasonal needs under each of the alternatives.

2.   The XYZ Corporation wishes to decrease its cash conversion cycle by pledging its accounts receivable. After the firm is analyzed by ABC Credit Company, an agreement is reached. XYZ can pledge its short-term receivables to ABC, who will lend to XYZ at $\frac{1}{20}$ of 1% against net daily debt and a service fee of $\frac{1}{100}$ of 1% against net daily pledge. ABC reduces the short-term receivables by a 5% dilution factor and an additional 10% margin-of-error factor. Management can earn 8% per annum on surplus funds. The marginal tax rate for the company is 40%.

(a) What is ABC's advance rate to XYZ Corporation?

(b) How much must XYZ pledge if it needs $50,000 for 30 days?

(c) What is the cost of pledging for 30 days?

(d) If ABC advances $50,000 to XYZ and then collects receivables to pay off the loan, as indicated in the accompanying schedule, how much will XYZ owe in interest and service costs at the end of 30 days? Assume collections are at the end of the day.

Day	4	7	14	18	21	25	29
Collect ($000)	$9	$5	$10	$8	$12	$9	$6

(e) Suppose the XYZ Corporation has the choice of repaying ABC by following either (c) or (d). Discuss which method it should choose. Use the residual income model discussed in earlier chapters (e.g., Chapter 1) to make the decision. The marginal tax rate is 40%.

3.   Five years ago the Thames Company purchased land and a building for $250,000 and $3,500,000, respectively. This purchase was financed by a long-term loan at a 10% interest rate. The loan was to be amortized over the estimated 30-year life of the building. The building was to be depreciated on a straight-line basis. The company has reached the maximum limit of its debt-equity ratio. Since inflation is expected to continue its 5-year annual rate of 7.5%, it was not considered prudent by the Thames management to sell additional equity. To secure additional financing, management is considering a sale-leaseback of the land and building. It is expected that the sale can be made at the inflation-adjusted value of the assets less any accumulated depreciation. Management desires to have the maximum operating lease start immediately (refer to Chapter 4 for a discussion of leases). The company's before-tax cost of debt is 10%. Presently, the firm has current assets of $2.9 million, current liabilities of $1.525 million, net fixed assets of $10 million, long-term debt of $8 million, and equity of $3.375 million. The firm's marginal tax rate is 40%. The capital gain rate is 20%.

(a) If the sale-leaseback is arranged, what changes would occur in the current balance sheet?

(b) Determine the changes to the current and debt-equity ratios before and after the sale-leaseback.

(c) Determine the after-tax operating cash flows with and without the sale-leaseback.

4.   The Diamond D Company needs an additional $325,000 to satisfy the payment of seasonal purchases. It will need this financing for one month. Management is negotiating with its local bank to factor the company's accounts receivable. The bank's interest rate is 12.5% annually, and in addition, the bank charges a commission of 1.25% on the loan amount. The bank will accept 90% of the new credit sales.

(a) How much will the company have to factor?

(b) What will be the total new accounts receivable level?

(c) What will be the total cost of this method of financing?

5.   The Diamond D Company (Problem 4) could pledge its accounts receivable to achieve the required $325,000 cash demand. The bank's policy is to charge interest at prime plus two (which is currently 13.75%) on average daily receivables pledged.

(a) Determine the dollar interest cost of pledging.

(b) Determine the effective annual percentage cost.

(c) Determine the amount of receivables pledged if the advance rate is 85%.

6.   Management wishes to increase its liquidity balance by negotiating a 90-day inventory loan with a local bank. Relations between the company and the bank are good and expected to continue so in the future. The company's inventory, as stated on its ledger, is as follows:

Raw materials	$ 375,268.00
Work in process	3,450,847.82
Finished goods	785,490.90
	$4,611,606.72

The bank charges interest at 1.75% per month, based on acceptable inventory pledged.

(a) What is the maximum loan amount the bank will be willing to allow if raw materials and finished goods are discounted between 5% and 10% and work in process is discounted between 20% and 50%? (Do the calculations for the extreme values.)

(b) What is the range of the dollar interest cost?

Discuss the impact of a change in assumptions about the amount and cost of the loan.

7. The Joy Company has determined that it could field-warehouse $3 million of its inventory for 90 days under a trustee arrangement with the ABC Finance Company. Interest charges would be 1.5% per month (30 days). Warehouse setup costs would be $6250 annually, plus ⅙ of the warehouse manager's annual salary of $30,000. Determine the total cost and the effective interest rate of the arrangement.

8. The Mountain Apple Company (MAC) owns a cold-storage facility. The building was recently constructed at a cost of $6,000,000 and has an estimated life of 12 years. The total cost amount is being financed and amortized as an annuity due over 10 years at 12%. Management is negotiating a sale-leaseback agreement for the facilities. The sale value would be $5,676,724, and the lease would be for 10 years. Annual lease payments would be $882,254.26 and be paid at the beginning of each year. The capital gains tax rate is 25%, and the marginal corporate tax rate is 42%. MAC plans to invest the sale proceeds in a 10% (before-tax) low-risk investment. The cost of debt funds is 12% before taxes.

(a) Determine whether the lease qualifies as an operating lease.

(b) Compare the after-tax profits and cash flows of the sale-leaseback arrangement versus owning the facility. Use straight-line depreciation if the lease is capitalized. What should MAC do?

9. The Charles Company has assets of $250,000, debt of $175,000, and equity of $75,000. Management needs the use of $150,000 of assets next year. This expansion can be financed by a term loan at 12% for 5 years or by a lease agreement at the same terms. Management has assurance that the lease qualifies as an operating lease. Determine the firm's financial leverage at the end of next year under each of these possible financing arrangements.

CHAPTER 18 □
Hedging with Futures and Options

Most executives have identified the corporate mission for their firms. It may be explicitly articulated in a statement of objectives and supporting strategies or loosely defined in management's mind. Whichever the case, the mission normally states the firm's desire to meet the needs of a specific market with a good or service, priced reasonably so as to adequately compensate its investors and to ensure the continued existence of the firm. Seldom does the mission statement expressly define the mission as speculation or gambling in high-risk situations. Very few, if any, corporate charters for industrial concerns mention the firm's anticipated involvement in speculative or gaming activities.

Nearly all managers, however, implicitly speculate with their interest-sensitive assets. For example, speculation occurs whenever cash is held for temporary investment or borrowed on a floating rate basis. The speculation is implicit since management speculates about the higher yield of cash holdings or the lower cost of cash borrowings. Considerable market fluctuations in interest rates increase the uncertainty involved in cash management.

In recent years corporate life has been significantly affected by changing interest rates. For instance, in the 1974–1976 period the prime rate ranged from a low of 6% to a high of 12%. It reached just about 16% in 1979 and was at 21% by December 1980. It then changed 29 times during 1981. Change was less frequent in 1982 and 1983, but when it happened, it was generally to lower the rate. In July 1986 the prime was at 8.5%.

Until late 1975 there was no effective and inexpensive way for financial managers to reduce the risk associated with rising or falling interest rates. However, in October 1975 the Chicago Board of Trade introduced the first interest rate futures market in Government National Mortgage Association (GNMAs) pass-through certificates, and in January 1976 the International Monetary Market of Chicago Mercantile Exchange provided a market for futures trading in three-month treasury bills. Today, nine interest rate future contracts are actively traded on three exchanges in the United States, with additional contracts traded in London and Singapore. Financial futures markets exist for treasury bonds, treasury notes, bank certificates of deposit, and foreign exchange, in addition to GNMAs and treasury bills.

Other instruments that have emerged to help the treasurer manage interest rate risk are options and options on financial futures. In the same set of circumstances futures and options (or options on futures) have different payoff results.

The purpose of this chapter is to examine how the treasurer can use futures, options, and options on futures to protect liquidity and shareholder wealth.

Hedging with Futures

The use of futures to reduce risk is done through a process called *hedging*. Hedging enables corporate cash managers to shift risks to persons (speculators) willing to assume those risks. Many managers do not use the futures market (see Table 18.1) because of the risk image created by speculators who buy and sell contracts at the most volatile ends of the marketplace.

Futures have an image that is difficult to sell to top management. Hedging entails winning most of the time and losing sometimes. It often

TABLE 18.1
Survey of Use of Financial Futures

Industry	Total respondents	Have used	Have considered	Have no interest
Mining	13	1	10	2
Construction	6	0	4	2
Manufacturing	225	2	150	73
Transportation and communication	28	1	19	8
Wholesale trade	12	0	6	6
Retail trade	10	0	5	5
Financial services	80	11	56	13
Other services	20	0	6	14
Total	394	15	256	123
Percentages		3.8%	64.9%	31.3%

Source: J. Miller et al. (Arthur Anderson & Co.), *Interest Rate Futures: The Corporate Decision* (Financial Executives Research Foundation, New York, 1982). Used by permission.

happens that winning in the futures market means losing in the cash market and vice versa. Many executives view hedging as instances where money was ventured and lost. They have difficulty understanding that unhedged investments — stocks and bonds, for example — stand to suffer greater losses during market swings than do hedged investments.

Contrary to this risky image, however, hedging allows the participant to mitigate most or all risks of ownership by balancing a cash position against a roughly equivalent opposite stance in a futures market. Taking a position in the cash market means trading in actual financial vehicles like shares of stock, certificates of deposit, or treasury bills, notes, or bonds. In contrast, the futures market allows traders to control large blocks of these items with a small amount of cash and without purchasing the actual financial vehicles.

Rate-Sensitive Assets and Liabilities

Because volatile fluctuations in commodities are possible, corporate planners and financial executives must anticipate the worst condition when preparing operating budgets and strategic plans and, most importantly, when determining competitive prices for their products. Corporate funding activities involve working with cash budgets and understanding potential borrowing needs.

Corporate borrowings have continued to grow in recent years as the result of increased working capital requirements of most firms. Companies have had to borrow because of reduced operating margins and their inability to generate sufficient cash flow from operations. When funding needs arise, the response is to borrow funds from prearranged lines of credit. When needs diminish, lines are paid back to minimize interest expense.

In this respect the treasurer merely reacts to production requirements. Under this structure the treasurer is generally not being judged on how much interest is paid. In an environment in which interest cost can fluctuate by several hundred basis points (1 basis point equals 0.01 percent) over a few months, this kind of relative measurement can be grossly inadequate. First, it has no relationship to expense budget projections; and second, while it may show that overall interest averaged below the prime rate, it can hide the fact that interest cost is still very high.

Net interest expenses as a percentage of net sales and as a percentage of earnings before interest and taxes have continued to grow in recent years for industrial companies. The reason interest cost has become so significant lies not only in the rate itself but also in the volume of credit. Equity market limitations in the last decade have promoted corporate growth funding in the debt market. This funding has caused debt-to-equity ratios to balloon well above old benchmarks. Furthermore, high interest rates and weakness in long-term markets have resulted in borrowers staying in the short-term end of the market and floating with the market. High interest expense and resulting perceived deterioration in financial strength of the company should provide the impetus for financial managers to carefully examine ways of identifying and reducing this cost in their business.

Many firms have both short-term investments and borrowed funds. Consequently, their managements apparently are speculating between the amount and yield/cost of the interest-sensitive assets (ISAs) and the interest-sensitive liabilities (ISLs).

ISAs are those corporate assets that have their yield determined by short-term money market conditions. Normally, ISAs include cash equivalents and temporary investments tied to short-term rates or floating rates. They also include any noncurrent assets that have returns tied to a floating or variable rate.

ISLs are borrowings that are tied to money market rates of interest. These liabilities include short-term borrowings in commercial paper markets or institutional borrowings at a floating prime rate. Also included are long-term debts and mortgages that feature a variable or floating rate of interest.

Rate-sensitive equilibrium for the firm exists only if the total dollar amount of its ISAs equal its total ISLs for the same maturing period. In such a situation if the firm's cost of borrowings increases, and a perfect correlation exists between borrowing costs and investment yields, then the firm's investment income directly offsets the increased borrowing costs. There is no additional cost to the firm. Such a situation is highly improbable since it presumes that the interest rates and maturities of both ISAs and ISLs are equal. Seasonal needs, changing markets, and new opportunities make it difficult to maintain a rate-sensitive equilibrium. The following illustration shows the impact of interest changes on the firm's financial statements.

ILLUSTRATION 18.1

For simplicity, assume a one-year planning horizon for the firm and a flat interest yield curve. Management expects to collect $1000 of receivables at the end of this one year. It is able to earn 10% return on investments (i.e., the opportunity cost of capital is 10%) and borrow at 8% for 90 days with the right to refund any borrowings at the then-prevailing interest rate. The present value of receivables is $904.84 (i.e., $1000e^{-0.10}$, where $e^{-0.10}$ represents the continuous discounting factor). This amount is financed with debt.

In three months $923.12 (i.e., $904.84e^{0.08(0.25)}$, where $e^{0.08(0.25)}$ represents the continuous compounding factor) will be paid and a new loan taken out for the amount of the payment (assuming interest rates are still at 8%). The loan will continue to be rolled over every 90 days at the same interest rate. Thus in 180 and 270 days the firm will pay (and receive

TABLE 18.2
Cash Flow Analysis: Stable Interest Rates

	Day				
	0	*90*	*180*	*270*	*360*
Investment	<904.84>				
Borrow	904.84	923.12	941.77	960.79	
Refund/pay debt		<923.12>	<941.77>	<960.79>	<980.20>
Collection					1000.00
Net Flow	0	0	0	0	19.80
Equity	17.92	←	— Present value —		⌐
			$19.80e^{-0.10}$		

Present value balance sheet (using 10%)

Receivables (1)	$904.84	Debt (2)	$886.92
		Equity	17.92

Notes:
1. $1000e^{-0.10} = \$904.84$.
2. $980.20e^{-0.10} = \$886.92$.

a new loan) for $941.77 and $960.79, respectively; in 360 days it will pay off the loan in the amount of $980.20.

If interest rates stay stable, the cash flows of this transaction are as shown in Table 18.2. The balance sheet is exposed to interest rate risk because the 10% earning rate of the receivables is fixed, whereas borrowings must be refunded every 90 days. The asset's longer duration implies that a given change in interest rates will change the present value of the receivable more than it will affect the present value of the liability. This change, of course, will change the value of the firm's equity.

Suppose that immediately after the firm obtains the September loan, interest rates increase 200 basis points (i.e., 2%). The increase raises the anticipated refunding costs and the opportunity cost of funds to the firm. For example, the new loan at day 90, of $923.12, will have an interest cost of 10%. Thus $946.49 (i.e., $923.12e^{0.10(0.25)}$) is the amount that will be refunded at day 180. As a result, the amount the firm expects to pay at year end increases to $995.02. Net cash flow falls to $4.98, and its present value is $4.42. Table 18.3 summarizes the impact of increased interest rates.

The increase in interest rates has caused owners' equity to decline $13.50, or about 75%. In contrast, if interest rates had fallen, the present value of the equity would have increased. (Problem 1 at the end of the chapter asks you to solve the case of falling interest rates.) □

TABLE 18.3
Cash Flow Analysis: Increasing Interest Rates

	Day				
	0	*90*	*180*	*270*	*360*
Investment	<904.84>				
Borrow	904.84	923.12	946.49	970.45	
Refund/pay debt		<923.12>	<946.49>	<970.45>	<995.02>
Collection					1000.00
Net flow	0	0	0	0	4.98
Equity	4.42	←	Present value		⌐
			$4.98e^{-0.12}$		

Present value balance sheet just before debt repayment on day 360 (using 12%)

Receivables (1)	$886.92	Debt (2)	$882.50
		Equity	4.42

Notes:
1. $1000e^{-0.12} = 886.92.
2. $995.02e^{-0.12} = 882.50.

As the illustration shows, if the firm is in disequilibrium, its management is speculating that rates or prices will always move in the firm's favor. A company that has a surplus of short-term investments assumes that rates will continually increase so that their yields continue to increase as time goes on. But when the firm is a borrower of funds, its management hopes that interest rates will decline and that its cost of borrowing will be lower in the future. In either case, as a net seller or a net borrower of cash, management is clearly speculating about the future yield or the future cost of the quantity of cash it has placed.

In industries with high seasonal liquidity, such as the commercial and residential construction industry, yields from short-term investments may have a significant impact on the overall performance of the firms in that industry. In other industries short-term, floating rate borrowed funds play an important role in corporate funding and performance. In these instances interest rate movements can predictably determine the profitability of the firms that rely heavily on short-term, rate-sensitive borrowings.

The futures market can assist the treasurer in attempting to put its ISAs and ISLs in equilibrium through the purchase and sale of an appropriate financial futures instrument. Hedging with financial futures provides the means to essentially fix the cost of floating rate borrowings at acceptably lower rates, despite the fact that the firm will be paying a much higher interest rate on a floating rate basis. This conclusion should become evident as hedging concepts are developed in this chapter.

Hedging Fundamentals

To develop any hedging strategy, a corporate treasurer must be familiar with both the cash and the futures markets. These markets are sophisticated and volatile and should be monitored constantly. It is not the purpose of this section to describe all the characteristics or nuances of either of these markets. Rather, the purpose of this section is to provide you with a basic understanding of the concepts, terminology, and mechanics of hedging.

The *basic concept behind hedging is to trade commodities and futures contracts that parallel an equivalent position in a cash or hard goods market* [i.e., sell (buy) a futures contract if you intend to sell (buy) securities in the cash market in the future]. The stance taken in commodities trading is generally 180 degrees opposite the cash position. A hedge is undertaken with the objective of controlling or eliminating risk; there is little expectation of making an overall profit in the futures transaction. The expectation is that the futures gains or losses offset the price fluctuations in the cash market.

Astute managers can expect to do better than to break even when involved in cash and futures. While it may take $100,000 to purchase a certificate of deposit for that amount in the cash market, it may require only $2000 to purchase the rights to buy or sell that $100,000 futures market contract at a given date. This leverage, which allows a manager to control large sums of money with only a small amount of risk capital, enables the manager to retain futures contracts to increase gains or, conversely, to quickly dispose of them to minimize losses.

Cash Market

There are two different kinds of *cash markets,* the spot market and the forward market. In the spot market transactions are made for current sale at current prices. Delivery is to occur within normal commercial periods, that is, the amount of time it would take to deliver the instrument/commodity. The forward cash market, called the forward market, is a direct placement market where the purchase and sale of instruments/commodities is for future delivery. Prices are determined at the time of contract.

The attributes of the cash markets are the following: A legal contract is made between two parties. Physical delivery is expected and must be performed. Price is negotiated between the two parties and is specified in the contract. In this sense there is no standard cash contract. Moreover, cash market contracts are not generally regulated by government agencies. Most importantly, they are not cancelable unless mutually agreed upon.

Payment is not standardized and depends on the trade terms that exist between the parties.

Futures Market

The economic functions of *futures markets* are to provide a competitive market price discovery mechanism, a hedging mechanism for price risk, and a means to improve market efficiency. The price of a futures contract for a financial instrument/commodity represents the expectations of a large number of buyers and sellers concerning the current and prospective effect of all market influences. As events shape the current situation, the expected changes are reflected in the form of changing prices for futures contracts.

In short, futures markets provide a current consensus of knowledgeable opinions about future prices. Futures markets improve market efficiency by providing a central marketplace where price offers are known and compared. This free flow of information defuses attempted monopoly positions. Futures markets enhance competition by allowing the free flow of information relative to prices, volume, and market expectations. Thus futures markets help eliminate market imperfections and contribute to more efficient economic activity.

Futures contracts, simply stated, are a promise between two persons to exchange a commodity at a specified time and place in the future for a stated price. As a commitment between a buyer and a seller, a futures contract specifies precisely the commodity being traded and the terms of delivery. The clearinghouse of the commodity exchange, made up of exchange members, guarantees contract performance by both parties. Individual traders cease to deal with each other and instead become obligated to the clearinghouse, which becomes the guarantor of performance of all futures contracts traded on a particular exchange. At the close of every trading day the clearinghouse matches buy-and-sell contracts for the day and informs every exchange member of its net settlement status.

Mechanics of Interest Rate Futures

Interest rate futures are based on long- and short-term, fixed-income financial debt instruments with prices that vary inversely to their interest rates. For example, treasury bills are sold on a discount basis and then redeemed at maturity at face value. The difference between the face value and the discounted selling price equals the amount of interest earned. Similarly, the price of a futures contract is inversely related to the interest rate of the underlying debt instrument.

Participants in futures markets can take one of two positions in the market: a long position or a short position. A buyer of a futures contract takes a *long position* in the market. A *long hedge* is the purchase of futures contracts as temporary substitutes for a purchase of an actual instrument in the future. The most common reason to place a long hedge is the desire to lock in a high yield on a future investment, coupled with a fear that yields will fall before an actual investment is made. By using a long hedge, the treasurer can attempt to ensure that an attractive return will be earned on funds that will be investable at a later time but that presently are not available. The long position is offset at the time the cash commodity is purchased.

To profit from a long position, the treasurer must sell the contract at a higher price than the purchase price. For an interest rate futures contract, a long position profits from a decline in interest rates. A lower interest rate means a higher contract price, since interest rates (or yields) are inversely related. An increase in interest rates produces a loss in a long position.

A seller of a futures contract takes a *short position* in the market. That is, the seller sells a contract that is a promise to deliver, on a specified date, a commodity or financial asset even though he or she may not currently own that asset. The *short hedge* is used by management as a temporary substitute for the sale of the actual commodity in the cash market at a later date. It is used to protect the price at which the manager wishes to eventually sell the commodity. The short position is offset at the time the cash commodity is sold.

To profit from a short position, the treasurer must purchase the contract at a lower price than the selling price. In financial instruments a short position profits from an increase in interest rates, because the contract price then declines, allowing the contract to be bought at a profit. Conversely, a decline in interest rates produces a loss in a short position.

The process of hedging is temporary. The futures contract is typically made with the intent to offset the futures position prior to the expiration of the contract. The sale (purchase) of futures contracts can be offset by the purchase (sale) of an equal number of identical futures contracts at a later date — as long as it is done before the contract matures. *Offset* is the most frequently used method of settling a futures market position. Offset is extremely important from a risk management viewpoint. Though some cash market participants use futures contracts as delivery vehicles, only a small percentage of futures transactions result in delivery.

By turning over the risk to the market, management forgoes some profit potential. One case where hedging reduces profit potential is when a cash market increases, resulting in a lower-valued futures market. If, on the other hand, management accurately predicts a decline in the cash market, it does not have to accept a diminished return or reduced value in that market. *By purchasing a futures contract that exhibits a high amount of correlation with the cash market asset, the manager can minimize much of the risk of loss of value.*

Managers wishing to hedge in futures should make sure that the hedging vehicle they choose has sufficient trading volume. A healthy futures offering should have a minimum of 5000 open-interest contracts. Open interest is the number of contracts not yet balanced by trade or closing. At least 2000 contracts for the particular commodity being traded each day gives a strong indication that the futures market is liquid. A liquid market offers assurance to the manager that purchases and sales can be done freely. Liquidity is important because it enables traders to minimize losses if the market declines.

Receivables Example Revisited

Illustration 18.1 involving accounts receivable showed the effect that mismatched maturity of assets and liabilities can have on the firm's equity. Futures contracts can be used to hedge the interest rate risk caused by the mismatch.

Confusion exists about the appropriate hedging objective of management and how the hedge should be constructed. One strategy is to protect the present value of the equity of the firm from interest rate fluctuations. Another strategy is to minimize discrepancies in cash flows over time. From a wealth maximization vantage point protecting wealth (i.e., protecting the present value of the equity) is more meaningful. As the following illustration shows, meeting the second objective of reducing cash flow mismatches to zero does not minimize the exposure of shareholders' wealth to interest rate changes.

ILLUSTRATION 18.2

Suppose that on September 15 management undertakes the receivable transaction and its associated financing as shown earlier in Table 18.2. Uncertainty prevails about what will happen to future interest rates. To protect its equity of $19.80 (nondiscounted amount), management sells a treasury bill futures contract yielding 10%. Since the loan is renewable every 90 days at the then-prevailing interest rate, contracts are sold now for maturity in 90 days, 180 days, and 270 days (December, March, and June, respectively). Since the interest yield curve is flat, these contracts are sold for $975.31, $951.23, and $927.74, respectively (using the continuous discounting model).

Shortly after management sells these contracts, interest rates increase 200 basis points. It now costs the firm 10% to finance operations; futures contracts are priced to yield 12%. In terms of refinancing the maturing 90-day debt, the costs are as shown earlier in Table 18.3. As that analysis indicates, equity shrinks from $19.80 to $4.98 because of the higher refunding costs.

However, since management has sold futures contracts short, it is cheaper to buy contracts to close the open positions. If the yield curve stays flat at the 12% level, the higher interest rates translate into futures prices of $970.45, $941.76, and $913.93, for the December, March, and June contracts, respectively (using continuous discounting at 12%). Thus the $28.14 difference between the selling prices and the buying prices represents profit earned on the futures contracts. The balance sheet, just before collection of the receivables and payment of the outstanding debt but after the closing of all open futures positions, is as shown in Table 18.4.

TABLE 18.4
Futures-Protected Balance Sheet (Not Discounted)

Cash (1)	$ 28.14	Debt (3)	$995.02
Receivables (2)	1000.00		
		Equity:	
		Futures (4)	$ 28.14
		Receivables (5)	4.98
			$ 33.12

Note: (1) and (4) are the profit on the future contracts. (2), (3) and (5) are taken from the top part of Table 18.3.

Management has been able to not only protect its equity by using future contracts but actually add to it. The higher borrowing costs have been more than offset. Table 18.4 can be made directly comparable to Table 18.2 by discounting cash flows at 12%, as will be shown later in Table 18.5.   □

We stated earlier that some disagreement exists about whether the hedging strategy should attempt to minimize discrepancies between cash flows over time or to minimize the loss of equity. Quite clearly from Table 18.5 (as shown by the cash flow line, minimizing discrepancies in the cash flows can lead to significant loss of equity. To contribute to the shareholder wealth maximization strategy, one must attempt to maintain (or add to) equity value during periods of uncertainty about interest rates. This objective is accomplished by allowing net cash receipts to vary.

The present value of the firm's balance sheet just before collection of the receivable and payment of the debt is given in Table 18.6.

TABLE 18.5
Total Cash Flow with a Hedged Position

	Day				
	0	90	180	270	360
Investment	<904.84>				
Borrow	904.84	923.12	946.49	970.45	
Refund/pay debt		<923.12>	<946.49>	<970.45>	<995.02>
Collection					1000.00
Cash flow	0	0	0	0	4.98
Futures:					
Sell December (1)		975.31			
Sell March (1)			951.23		
Sell June (1)				927.74	
Buy December (2)		<970.45>			
Buy March (3)			<941.76>		
Buy June (4)				<913.93>	
Net flows	0	4.86	9.47	13.81	4.98

$$e^{-0.12(0.25)}$$

$$e^{-0.12(0.50)}$$

$$e^{-0.12(0.75)}$$

$$e^{-0.12(1)}$$

Equity	30.68	←———— Present value ————————

Notes:
1. Transaction date is September 15, 1986.
2. Transaction date is December 14, 1986.
3. Transaction date is March 14, 1987.
4. Transaction date is June 14, 1987.

TABLE 18.6
Present Value Balance Sheet (Discounted at 12%)

Cash	$ 26.26	Debt	$882.50
Receivables	886.92		
		Equity:	
		Futures	$ 26.26
		Receivables	4.42
			$ 30.68

The variability of these cash flows should not be a serious problem for liquidity management since the hedged position should only be maintained when interest rates are increasing. If interest rates are falling, refinancing costs will be less, with the result that equity will increase. If management enters a hedge, and interest rates subsequently decline, the appropriate strategy is to close the position as soon as possible and take the small loss. Maintaining the hedge throughout the period will not cause the equity to decline from the prehedged balance. It will simply not allow lower refinancing costs to contribute to shareholder wealth.

Basis Risk

While futures provide opportunities to reduce risk exposure, they have pitfalls as well. Their use can actually increase risk under certain circumstances and can result in lower income. In an extreme case the use of futures can jeopardize solvency. Generally, hedging in the futures market replaces the risk of price fluctuation in the cash market with the risk of a change in the relationship between the cash price and the futures price of an instrument. This relationship is called the *basis*. Basis is both stable and predictable because of the tendency of the cash and futures prices of a financial instrument to move together.

Three market forces operate to ensure similar price movements in the cash and futures markets:

1. Changes in economic and financial market conditions influence cash and futures prices simultaneously.
2. The possible delivery of the cash instrument forces cash and futures prices to converge as the delivery date approaches.
3. Arbitrage between the cash and futures markets helps remove distortions in the basis.

Arbitrage is the simultaneous purchase of one commodity against the sale of the same commodity in order to profit from distortions from usual price relationships. For example, if carrying costs and expectations are thought to be at a certain level and the actual cash/futures basis is at another level, there is a distortion; the futures price is either too low or too high relative to the cash price. Thus it benefits the market participant to buy futures and sell in the cash market, or vice versa. As a result, the futures price remains relatively close to the asset's cash price; movements in the cash market are reflected by similar movements in the futures market.

The basis can be positive or negative, depending on whether the futures price is under or over the cash price:

$$\text{basis} = \text{cash price} - \text{futures price.} \tag{18.1}$$

The greater (wider) the basis (i.e., more positive), the greater is its strength; the smaller (narrower) the basis (i.e., more negative), the weaker it is. Basis weakness or strength reflects the relative yields on the underlying instrument vis-à-vis the financing cost.

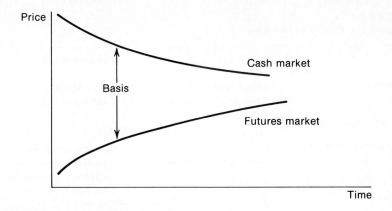

FIGURE 18.1
Behavior of the Basis for Financial Contracts

Futures prices are normally higher than cash prices, reflecting the financing costs or short-term interest rates relative to the yield on the cash commodity. However, *the normal configuration for long-term interest rate futures is for the futures price to lie below the cash price,* reflecting a positively sloped yield curve. This behavior is shown in Fig. 18.1. Note that in Fig. 18.1 if the *Y*-axis was yield, the top curve would be the futures market and the bottom curve would be the cash market.

Though cash and futures prices do not always fluctuate equally, their movements in response to changing market conditions are generally in the same direction. It is this common directional movement that makes the basis more predictable and, therefore, less risky at a given time than the movement of either the cash prices or the futures prices.

Through basis management the manager can seek to profit from changes in the basis given her or his expectations, cash position, and willingness and ability to absorb risk. Vital for hedging in any commodity is consideration of the direction of the market.

Table 18.7 is a summarization of the accounts receivable example illustrated in Tables 18.2, 18.3, and 18.4, with the basis calculated for both the opening and the closing transactions. Since the basis has strengthened (i.e., become less negative), a small net economic gain has resulted—the realized gain exceeds the opportunity loss. Whenever a gain or a loss occurs from the hedge, the hedge ratio is not perfect. Calculation of the hedge ratio will be shown shortly.

A change in equity, relative to anticipations, can occur because the basis may not be the same at the time a futures position is offset as it was when the position first was taken, as is the case in Table 18.7. Only if a

TABLE 18.7
Hedging the Equity of the Firm

Date	Cash market	Futures market
September 15, 1985	Management wants to protect the unrealized equity of $19.80	Sells December, March, and June treasury bill futures for $2854.28
	Basis = −$2834.48	
September 14, 1986	Receivable is collected; actual equity is $4.98	By this date the open futures contracts have been closed; they were bought for $2826.14
	Basis = −$2821.16	
	Opportunity loss $14.82	Realized gain $28.14

hedge is perfect (i.e., the basis does not change) is the opportunity loss in the cash market offset exactly by the gain in the futures market. Usually, a gain or loss in the cash market is not offset exactly. *Depending on the size and the direction of the change in basis, profit rises or falls.*

Certain relationships exist between the basis and profitability. They are summarized in Table 18.8. When the dollar basis weakens (narrows), a short hedge results in a net loss and a long hedge results in a net gain. When the dollar basis strengthens (widens), the short hedge results in a

TABLE 18.8
Hedging Strategies and Outcomes

	Expectations for interest rates (prices)	
	Increase (decrease)	*Decrease (increase)*
Hedging strategy	Short hedge	Long hedge
(a) Dollar basis		
Narrows	Loss realized	Profit made
No change	Zero profit	Zero profit
Widens	Profit made	Loss realized
(b) Percent basis		
Narrows	Profit made	Loss realized
No change	Zero profit	Zero profit
Widens	Loss realized	Profit made

Note: If the basis narrows, it becomes more negative or less positive; if it widens, it becomes more positive or less negative. Also, net dollar profit or loss from the hedge is (dollar basis)$_{buy}$ − (dollar basis)$_{sell}$, where buy and sell are based on transactions in the futures market.

net gain and the long hedge results in a net loss. If the basis remains unchanged from the initial futures transaction (putting on the hedge) to the offsetting transaction (lifting the hedge), there is no net gain or loss on either a long or a short hedge other than the costs of the commission and of providing the margin deposit.

Although the discussion of the basis has been in terms of dollar amounts, the basis is frequently measured by yield spreads. Table 18.8 (b) also shows results when the basis is calculated by using interest rates. Not surprisingly, the results are exactly opposite to dollar-denominated basis results, since increasing interest rates mean declining prices and vice versa.

A necessary requirement for any successful hedge is to monitor the hedge. Once a futures position is undertaken, it has to be watched in much the same way that investment managers monitor cash investments. Of primary concern are movements in the basis and changes in expectations for future interest rates. In short, *the manager must manage basis risk.* While unnecessary placing and lifting of futures positions can amount to *speculation,* placing a hedge and forgetting it in the face of fundamental changes in the basis can amount to imprudent hedging.

For the profit-maximizing firm hedging contains a paradox. If management decides to hedge only part of its overall interest rate risk, it should not be surprised to find its hedging program reporting losses. The reason is that by hedging only part of the risk, management accepts some cash market risk and effectively endorses an interest rate forecast. If this forecast for the cash market is correct, net interest margin will be positive. But by definition, profits in the cash market position mean losses in the futures market. Thus losses in the futures market when only part of the risk is hedged probably mean that the business plan embodied in the cash position was the correct one.

Appendix A contains several other examples of hedging and basis calculations. Since an understanding of this material may be difficult, you may wish to spend time working through the examples in Appendix A.

Establishing the Hedge

Once the interest rate risk is assessed and the hedge vehicle selected, the proper amount for the hedge transaction must be determined. This process has four steps:

1. Determine the dollar amount to be hedged.
2. Determine the face value of the futures contract.
3. Determine the maturity of the asset or liability in question.
4. Determine the correlation between cash and futures prices.

If all securities fluctuate by equal yield and dollar amounts (i.e., are perfectly correlated), one could always use a hedge ratio of one unit of the hedge vehicle security per one unit of the target security, or a 1:1 ratio. Obviously, securities fluctuate by different dollar amounts even if there are identical yield changes, so the interest rate sensitivity of the hedge vehicle must be compared with the dollar impact of the risk. However, if the risk is associated with yield changes on a security or market that exhibits different yield moves than does the hedging vehicle, this difference must also be taken into account.

A number of techniques are used to calculate the hedge ratio. The following discussion describes the computation used extensively by Salomon Brothers, Inc. Through the use of a regression model and elasticity measures, Salomon's approach considers both the dollar impact of the risk and the different yield movements for the cash and futures market securities. Three steps are involved in calculating the hedge ratio:

1. Determine the yield volatility of the asset to be hedged relative to that of the futures contract. The slope coefficient β (Greek beta) in the regression,

$$\text{spot} = a + \beta \times \text{futures} + e, \tag{18.2}$$

is used to measure the yield volatility. The spot (i.e., cash market) and futures variables are measured as percentage price changes. For instance, if an 11-basis-point change in the security to be hedged is associated with a 10-basis-point change in the futures security, the relative yield volatility, β, is $^{11}/_{10}$, or 1.1.

2. Determine the percentage dollar price change (i.e., elasticity) of both the cash market security and the futures market security for a 1-basis-point change in yield.

3. Calculate the *hedge ratio* by using the following equation:

$$\text{hedge ratio} = \beta \times \frac{\text{elasticity of the corporate bond}}{\text{elasticity of the treasury bond}}. \tag{18.3}$$

ILLUSTRATION 18.3

Assume that the treasurer holds an XYZ Corporation 11% bond due September 1, 2002, currently valued at a price of 85 (for a yield of 13.139%). The treasurer determines that a 1-basis-point change will cause the price of the bond to change by 6.1%. He also expects that the yield will fluctuate 1.1 times as much as the treasury bond he will use in the hedge. This result has been estimated by using regression analysis on past data. The

14% treasury bond of February 15, 2002, has a price value per basis point of 7.9% (at its price of 112).

The hedge ratio is

$$\frac{0.061}{0.079} \times 1.1 = 0.85 \text{ futures.}$$

The logic behind the calculation of the hedge ratio is straightforward. If treasury yields move by 1 basis point, the XYZ bond is expected to change by 1.1 basis points. Since each basis point move causes a change of 6.1% for the XYZ bond, 1.1 basis points would cause a change of 6.71%. Now to counteract the risk of one security being likely to move 6.71% per 1-basis-point change in treasuries with another that will move 7.9%, management needs 0.0671/0.079, or 0.85, of the treasury (i.e., the futures security) per XYZ bond held.   □

Two books by Robert W. Kolb (see the Selected Readings) discuss both portfolio and price sensitivity approaches to calculating hedge ratios. Unfortunately, it is almost impossible to determine a perfect hedge with the known hedge ratios. Thus to some extent, every hedge remains a speculation of the basis.

Options

A drawback of hedging with futures contracts is that if interest rates move favorably in the cash market, profits will be forgone: Increased profits in the cash market are negated by losses in the futures market. One way of capturing these potential profits is through options on futures contracts.

Differences Between Futures and Options

Futures and options are distinctly different, and options are a safer vehicle for the manager to hedge with than are futures. By purchasing a futures contract, the manager makes a commitment. Having bought the contract, the hedger is subject to the full obligations of it, including margin calls and market price fluctuations that can make the contract worth more or less than its original purchase price. (See Appendix C for an explanation of margin and the impact of price fluctuations on a futures position.)

By acquiring an *option on a futures contract,* however, the manager has the opportunity to purchase a contract within a given period of time but is not obligated to do so. The option on futures allows the treasurer to monitor the market. If the market appears to be moving in the direction predicted by the treasurer, then the treasurer can purchase the contract. If trends move in an opposite direction, the manager can forgo the option to buy. Options are never subject to *margin calls,* no matter how incorrect expectations might turn out to be.

In this sense an option is more like a form of price insurance in which a premium is paid to insure against the possibility of a particular event occurring. If that event — specifically, a large change in price — does not occur, the purchaser of the option loses only the premium he or she paid for the price insurance. In comparison, losses on short futures positions essentially are unlimited; losses on long futures positions are limited to the price of the contract.

The limited-risk advantage of options can translate into a second important advantage: staying power, or the ability to maintain a market position that has initially moved against the option buyer in the hope that it will eventually become profitable.

Types of Options

There are two types of options: *call options* and *put options.* Options that represent claims to buy are referred to as call options. In this case the underlying asset upon which the option is written can be "called" from the owner of the asset (writer of the option) at a predetermined price until the expiration of the option. That is, exercising a call results in the purchase of the asset from the writer. Options that represent claims to sell are put options. Exercising a put results in the sale of the underlying asset to the writer at a predetermined price until the expiration of the option.

Value of an Option

The price of an option, whether or not it is explicitly traded as a separate security, depends on expectations of future economic conditions as they affect the value of the underlying security. In the abstract, the prospective and the contingent natures of options appear to make evaluation of an option extremely difficult, because future conditions are never known with certainty. Nonetheless, financial economists have devised methods of evaluating such contingent claims.

The analytical breakthrough in the area came in 1973 with the work of Black and Scholes.[1] They reasoned that an option could be valued by inference from the value of portfolios that contained the option. Specifically, they used the idea of a riskless hedge — a portfolio consisting of the option and its underlying security constructed to yield the riskless return. The

---

[1] Fischer Black and Myron Scholes, "The Pricing of Options and Corporate Liabilities," *Journal of Political Economy* (June 1973): 637 – 654.

price that an investor is willing to pay for the options necessary to construct a riskless version of such a hedge depends on the riskless return available elsewhere as well as the anticipated scenario of the stock price movements.

Although the underlying security value may take on a wide range of values, Black and Scholes derived an analytical formula for the price of an option on corporate stock by relying on very general assumptions about the stochastic nature of stock price movements, the current price of the stock, and an assumed riskless real rate of return. Although the user of this formula must provide the estimates of the variability of the stock's future price movements, the implications of the Black-Scholes work is that the price of the option is otherwise unambiguous.

The Black-Scholes formula applies only to European options on corporate stock. But the notion of inferring option values of the underlying security has enabled other researchers to apply the idea to the valuation of options on debt securities as well.

Fundamentals of Options

To make options as versatile an investment vehicle as possible, the Chicago Board of Trade conducts simultaneous trading in options with a number of different *exercise prices* and a number of different expiration months. There are exercise prices both below and above the current futures price, and as future prices increase or decrease, additional options with higher or lower exercise prices may be introduced. At any given time, for instance, government treasury bonds could be trading in call and put options with exercise prices of 60, 62, and 64 (equivalent to $60,000, $62,000, and $64,000 based on the face value of bonds of $100,000). Or there could be trading in options with an even wider range of exercise prices.

A particular option is identified by the delivery month of the underlying futures contract, by its exercise price, and by whether it is a call or a put. For example, an option to purchase a June treasury bond futures contract at an exercise price of 62 would be a June 62 call.

Since options differ in their exercise price, in the underlying futures contract, and in whether they are calls or puts, it follows that the premiums will also differ. Table 18.9 illustrates what the premiums for various options might be on, say, January 2 if futures prices were those indicated immediately below the month (e.g., June 62 – 07). The price and option premiums are quoted in $\frac{1}{64}$ of a point, each point is $1000, and each 64th is $15.63.

While the premium reduces the potential for financial gain, the option provides protection from an unfavorable market swing. Options covering long periods of time tend to have greater premium prices. Premiums are determined daily on exchange trading floors and are the only component of the options agreement that fluctuates during the life of the option. The owner of the option can check the profit or loss of the option contract

TABLE 18.9
Option Prices

Exercise price	March 62 – 00		June 62 – 07*		September 62 – 19	
60 call	2 – 49	($2766)	3 – 44	($3687)	4 – 26	($4406)
60 put	0 – 52	($812)	1 – 38	($1594)	2 – 05	($2078)
62 call	1 – 42	($1656)†	2 – 44	($2687)	3 – 29	($3453)
62 put	1 – 42	($1656)	2 – 30	($2469)	2 – 58	($2906)
64 call	0 – 54	($844)	1 – 54	($1844)	2 – 40	($2625)
64 put	2 – 52	($2812)	3 – 33	($3515)	3 – 58	($3906)

Note: Premium is given in parentheses.
* 62 – 07 = $62,000 + $15.63 × 7 = $62,109.
† 1 – 42 = $1000 + $15.63 × 42 = $1656.

by comparing it with the initial purchase. If because of market movement, the option contract becomes more desirable and worth more, the treasurer may decide to sell the contract back to the market for a profit.

Option premiums are related directly to an option's intrinsic value and its time value. *Intrinsic value* is the difference between an option's *strike price* — the amount at which the option's call holder may buy or its put holder may sell the underlying security — and its present futures price. If the strike price is 60 and the September futures price is $62^{19}/_{64}$ (see Table 18.9), this option has an intrinsic value of $2^{19}/_{64}$. Intuitively, intrinsic value exists if a profit can be made by exercising the rights of the option.

In the example for Table 18.9 the option is valued at $4^{26}/_{64}$. The intrinsic value is only $2^{19}/_{64}$, leaving a difference of $2^{7}/_{64}$. One reason premiums exceed intrinsic value is their time value, the second source of value in an option contract. Because the future is uncertain, there is always the possibility that unexpected events will significantly affect prices. And because this possibility exists, some market participants are willing to buy or sell an option on the chance that one such event will occur. This explains, for example, why an *out-of-the-money option* (the underlying security price is less than the exercise price) still will be traded at a positive premium. That is, some buyers are willing to take the chance that some event will change futures prices enough to make this option a profitable one. Similarly, premiums may be greater than intrinsic value because buyers are willing to pay for the chance that further changes in the futures price may make a profitable option even more profitable before it expires.

An option's expiration date is the key factor in determining its *time value*. As the length of time until expiration decreases, there is less time for the futures price — and, therefore, the option's profitability — to change markedly. Conversely, an option of long duration has more time value

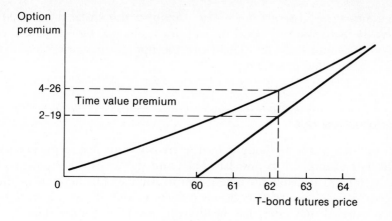

(a)   Call option

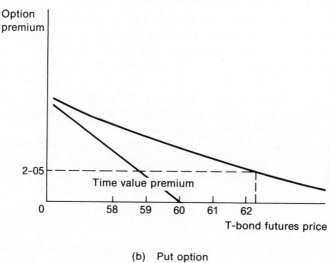

(b)   Put option

FIGURE 18.2
Value of Options

because the probability of an unexpected event changing its profitability is greater.

Figure 18.2 summarizes the value of options. In Fig. 18.2(a), for example, if the strike price is 60 – 00 when the September treasury bond (T-bond) futures are trading at 62 – 19 and the call option premium is 4 – 26 ($4406.38), the option's intrinsic value is 2 – 19, and its time value premium is $2 - 7$. Similarly, in Fig. 18.2(b) if the strike price is $60 - 00$ when the September T-bond futures are trading at $62 - 19$ and the put option premium is $2 - 05$ (\$2078.15), the option's intrinsic value is zero, and its time value premium is $2 - 05$.

ILLUSTRATION 18.4

Call options might be bought by the treasurer to insure an investment yield. For example, it is now late May, and the treasurer expects to have about \$60,000 available for investment in August. The September futures price of $56 - 00$ for treasury bonds reflects a yield of just under 15%, but she is worried that rates may be sharply lower by August. This risk can be reduced by buying a call option. If interest rates decline and bond prices increase, the higher cost of buying a bond in August should be roughly offset by the profit realized when the option is sold.

Assume that in May a September 56 call (reflecting roughly a 15% interest rate) can be bought at a premium of $1 - 32$ (\$1500). And assume that by August the going interest rate of treasury bonds has declined to 13%. This decline should increase the September futures price to about 65, enabling the treasurer to sell the September 56 call option for at least its intrinsic value of \$9000. The net gain is \$7500. The bond price increase from \$56,000 in May to \$65,000 in August is largely covered by the profit from the option. In this way the option has served its purpose of providing insurance against a decline in interest rates.

A major advantage of this strategy is that it establishes an interest rate floor but not an interest rate ceiling. If interest rates were to increase instead of decrease from May to August, the \$60,000 could then be invested at the higher interest rate. The option premium would have been the cost of having protection against a possible decline in interest rates.   □

In summary, options can be used by management to help fulfill the same objectives sought when it uses futures: to protect an investment, to insure an investment yield, to protect the value of an investment, and to establish the cost of borrowing money. The appropriate strategies to use for hedging with options are as follows:

□ If interest rates are expected to increase (prices are expected to fall), then buy puts.

□ If interest rates are expected to fall (prices are expected to increase), then buy calls.

Another alternative is to combine the use of options and futures. This strategy provides even greater flexibility in managing interest rate risk. In Illustration 18.2, where management hedged the duration gap by selling futures contracts, it could have preserved its potential cash market profits (if interest rates were to decline) by buying a call option contract when it placed the short hedge. Then when interest rates declined, management could have exercised its option, offset its futures position without loss, and thereby preserved its cash market profit. Alternatively, it could have sold a put option on the hedged financial instruments.

Summary

The volatile interest rate environment of the 1980s has led many financial executives to obtain a better understanding of interest rate risk and how to manage it so as to protect or improve corporate liquidity. The popularization of commodity and option markets by speculators has made hedging a means of managing price/interest rate risk affecting both assets and liabilities.

The purpose of hedging is to reduce the variance of shareholders' wealth. A hedge is constructed because in the presence of an uncertain future, wealth is greater if management forgoes a cash flow stream that is higher, on average, if it goes unhedged in exchange for a cash flow stream that is lower, on average, from the hedging operation but is more certain.

A financial disaster can occur, though, from the use of futures contracts to hedge interest rate risk if management does not understand the nature of the hedging function. Trading futures for hedging is not intended to generate profits from the trading itself. Rather, its purpose is to establish futures' positions so that corporate liquidity is protected and the owners' wealth is held constant. This purpose will be achieved if the increase (decrease) in value of the firm's holdings of assets and liabilities is offset exactly by the loss (gain) in the futures market.

Through the use of options the treasurer can lower corporate risk exposure more than he can if futures are the hedging instrument. The judicious use of options, in combination with futures, allows management to minimize downside profit risk but to realize any upside profit potential.

Although the fundamentals of hedging are fairly straightforward, much expertise is required in managing a hedging department. This chapter has merely touched on hedging concepts, using futures and options. There are many books dealing solely with this topic that give in-depth discussions of hedging, futures, and options (see the Selected Readings).

Key Concepts

Basis	**Hedge ratio**	**Rate-sensitive equilibrium**
Basis risk	**Hedging**	**Short position**
Cash market	**Long position**	**Speculation**
Exercise price	**Options**	**Strike price**
Futures market		

Appendix A

Further Illustrations of Futures Hedging

This appendix illustrates four additional uses of futures for hedging purposes. Two books by Robert W. Kolb, *Interest Rate Futures: A Comprehensive Introduction* and *Understanding Futures Markets* (see the Selected Readings), are highly recommended if you want a better understanding of futures.

Case 1

A treasurer undertakes a futures market hedge expecting to lock in a level of earnings from a particular investment strategy. Table A.1 summarizes the transactions. Table A.2 indicates the change in the profitability of the hedge resulting from changes in the basis.

Managers need not be completely in the dark about how a change in the basis will affect their earnings. As the delivery date of a futures contract approaches, the price of that contract and the cash market price of the underlying securities should move toward equality. Thus the basis should be approximately zero by the last trading day of a futures contract,

TABLE A.1
Lock in a Level of Earnings (Long Hedge)

Date	Cash market	Futures market
April 1	Proceeds of $1 million from maturing investment expected June 1. Treasurer wishes to lock in current yield of 13%. Cost of $1 million in 3-month T-bills at 13% is $967,500. The discount is $32,500: $1 million × 0.13 × 90/360	Purchases $1 million, June, 3-month T-bills for $967,000. Yield is 13.20%, and the discount is $33,000: $1 million × 0.132 × 90/360
	Basis = − 0.20%, or $500	
June 1	Buys $1 million of 3-month T-bills for $968,625. Yield is 12.55%, and the discount is $31,375: $1 million × 0.1255 × 90/360	Sells $1 million, June, 3-month T-bills for $968,125. Yield is 12.75%, and the discount is $31,875: $1 million × 0.1275 × 90/360
	Basis = − 0.20%, or $500	
	Opportunity loss $1125	Real gain $1125

520

TABLE A.2
Basis Risk and Profitability

	Cash market	Futures market	Basis	Profit
April 1				
Amount	$967,500	$967,000	$500	
Yield	13.00%	13.20%	− 0.20%	
June 1				
Rates fall, dollar (percent) basis unchanged (unchanged)				
Amount	$968,750	$968,250	$500	
Yield	12.50%	12.70%	− 0.20%	
Gain <loss>	<$1,250>	$1,250		$0
Rates fall, dollar (percent) basis decreases (increases)				
Amount	$968,750	$968,875	− $125	
Yield	12.50%	12.45%	+ 0.05%	
Gain <loss>	<$1,250>	$1,875		$625
Rates fall, dollar (percent) basis increases (decreases)				
Amount	$968,750	$967,625	$1125	
Yield	12.50%	12.95%	− 0.45%	
Gain <loss>	<$1,250>	$625		<$625>
Rates rise, dollar (percent) basis unchanged (unchanged)				
Amount	$966,250	$965,750	$500	
Yield	13.50%	13.70%	− 0.20%	
Gain <loss>	$1,250	<$1,250>		$0
Rates rise, dollar (percent) basis decreases (increases)				
Amount	$966,250	$966,375	− $125	
Yield	13.50%	13.45%	+ 0.05%	
Gain <loss>	$1,250	<$625>		$625
Rates rise, dollar (percent) basis increases (decreases)				
Amount	$966,250	$965,125	$1125	
Yield	13.50%	13.95%	− 0.45%	
Gain <loss>	$1,250	<$1,875>		<$625>

and this characteristic can be used to get some idea of how the basis might change.

If the basis for a June delivery contract is −0.20 on April 1, for example, a reasonably good guess is that from April 1 to the last trading day around the third week in June, the change in the basis would be +0.20. An increase in the basis would add to the earnings from a long hedge and reduce those from a short hedge.

Case 2

As shown in Table A.3, the treasurer plans to borrow funds for 60 days one month hence. Since economists expect interest rates to rise, the treasurer locks in April 30 borrowing costs on April 1 by selling seven certificate of deposit (CD) futures contracts. If interest rates increase, prices of futures will decline and the profit from the futures position will help offset the higher rate paid when the commercial paper is issued. Should rates unexpectedly decline and futures prices rise, the futures position loss is offset by the decreased cost of issuing the commercial paper.

Without the hedge the treasurer would have incurred an increased interest expense of $15,000. The futures transaction not only offset this opportunity loss but also generated a net gain of $2500 per contract. This gain allowed the treasurer to achieve an effective borrowing rate of 12.45% on the 60-day paper, 15 basis points less than the April 1 rate:

$$\frac{\$210,000 - \$2500}{60/360 \times \$10,000,000} = 0.1245.$$

TABLE A.3
Borrowing for Seasonal Needs

Date	Cash market	Futures market
April 1	Determine need to issue $10 million in 60-day commercial paper. Current 60-day rate is 12.6%. Projected interest expense is $210,000: $10 million × 0.126 × 60/360	Sells 7* June CD futures contracts at 86.80. Yield is 13.2%, and the discount is $231,000: $7 million × 0.132 × 90/360
	Basis = −0.6%, or $3,021,000	
April 30	Issues $10 million in 60-day commercial paper at prevailing rate of 13.5%. Actual interest expense is $225,000: $10 million × 0.135 × 60/360	Buys 7 June CD futures contracts at 85.80. Yield is 14.2%, and the discount is $248,500: $7 million × 0.142 × 90/360
	Basis = −0.7%, or $3,023,500	
	Opportunity loss $15,000	Realized gain $17,500

* The face value of a CD futures contract is $1 million, so it would be logical to assume that 10 CD futures would be used to hedge $10 million in commercial paper. However, in this case 60-day paper is being hedged with 90-day CD futures. Therefore the hedge is "weighted" by reducing the number of CD futures contracts used by approximately one-third.

Case 3

Table A.4 shows that on June 1 the treasurer expects a seasonal inflow of $10 million one month hence. To protect the present yield of 16.5% on CDs, he buys ten September CD futures contracts. After 30 days, when the cash is received and invested, the hedge is offset by selling the ten contracts back into the futures market. The 1.25% decline in interest rates over the 30-day period in the cash market created an opportunity loss for the company of $31,250. The hedge, however, offset the loss with a $32,500 gain. When the net gain of $1250 on the hedge is added to the income stream for the next 90 days, the treasurer achieves an effective yield on his CD investment of 16.55% — an improvement of 5 basis points over the rate prevailing on June 1:

$$\frac{\$412,500 + (\$32,500 - \$31,250)}{60/360 \times \$10,000,000} = 0.1655.$$

TABLE A.4
Investing Excess Seasonal Needs

Date	Cash market	Futures market
June 1	Anticipates $10 million cash inflow in 30 days. Current 90-day CD rate is 16.5%. Projected return is $412,500: $10 million × 0.165 × 90/360	Buys 10 September CD futures contracts at 83.75. Yield is 16.25%, and the discount is $406,250: $10 million × 0.1625 × 90/360
	Basis = +0.25%, or −$6250	
July 1	Receives $10 million and invests in 90-day CDs at a rate of 15.25%. Actual return is $381,250: $10 million × 0.1525 × 90/360	Sells 10 September CD futures contracts at 85.05. Yield is 14.95%, and the discount is $373,750: $10 million × 0.1495 × 90/360
	Basis = +0.30%, or −$7500	
	Opportunity loss $31,250	Realized gain $32,500

Case 4

This last example hedges foreign exchange risk. In foreign exchange the basis primarily reflects the interest rate differential among countries and expectations.

The procedure is summarized in Table A.5. On June 1 the importer contracts to buy 100,000 West German widgets to be delivered on December 1 at a price of DM500,000. What will be the exchange rate when she takes delivery? She can lock in the cost of those deutsche marks now by purchasing futures contracts for delivery of DM500,000 in that month. On June 1 the deutsche mark is selling for $0.37 on the spot (cash) market and $0.3726 for future delivery in the month of December. The importer hedges her exchange risk in the futures market.

When purchasing the December contracts in deutsche marks, the importer knows that the price quoted is for delivery on December 15 (the third Wednesday of the month). The importer will be lifting her hedge on December 1, when she will offset her futures contracts and purchase spot deutsche marks to pay for the widgets. Since futures and spot prices roughly coincide only on the last trading day, the importer would expect the basis to have narrowed from the June 1 basis but not to have disappeared.

The importer can interpolate between the cash price for deutsche marks on June 1 and the futures price for delivery on December 15. The number she derives from this interpolation is her estimated basis for December 1, six months from now. The arithmetic is as follows: December 1 is $12/13$ of the way between June 1 and December 15. The basis of June 1 is $0.0026. By December 1 that basis should have progressed $12/13$ of the way from 26 points to zero, or down to 2 points. In other words, on December 1 the same futures contracts should be above cash by $0.0002. Since the futures price is known, the importer can compute the cash estimate for that day to be $0.3724. This figure is used by the importer when she makes her bid for the widgets.

The actual cash price on December 1 for deutsche marks ($0.3741) is quite a bit higher than the estimate of $0.3724. The December 1 basis is $0.0003 higher than anticipated. This results in a small profit on the entire hedge transaction. The small profit on this hedge could just as easily have been a small loss if the importer had overestimated the basis.

TABLE A.5
Hedging Foreign Exchange Risk

Date	Cash market	Futures market
June 1	Bid for widgets contract on the estimated price of December 1 spot DM at $0.3724/DM	Buy 4 DM futures contracts (500,000 DM) for December delivery at $0.3726/DM
	Basis = −0.0002	
December 1	Buy spot DM to pay for widgets at $0.3741/DM	Sell 4 DM futures contracts for December at $0.3746/DM
	Basis = −0.0005	
	Opportunity loss $0.0017/DM	Realized gain $0.0020/DM

This forward-pricing example utilizes basis estimation as an alternative for actual spot price forecasting. Because of the relationship between the cash and futures prices, basis estimation is much more reliable than cash price forecasting.

The preceding example may be applied to a variety of actual situations. The following are just a few categories in which futures hedging can be used:

☐ Companies building plants abroad.

☐ Companies financing subsidiaries abroad.

☐ Manufacturers importing raw materials and exporting finished goods.

☐ Exporters taking payment in foreign currencies.

☐ Companies abroad financing operations in Eurocurrencies.

☐ Firms involved in the purchase or sale of foreign securities.

The possibilities are limitless. Virtually everyone who deals in or with foreign countries has a need for this hedge mechanism to avoid major loss due to exchange rate fluctuations.

Appendix B
Futures and Options Marketplaces

For every transaction in a cash market there is a buyer and a seller. Similarly, everytime somebody enters into a sale contract for deferred delivery of an asset in either a futures or an options market, there must be somebody else agreeing to accept delivery on that contract. Investors who have agreed to buy, or have an option to buy, an asset sometime in the future are said to be long a futures or options contract. Investors who have agreed to sell an asset in the future are short a futures or options contract. Since there must be a buyer for every seller, the net long and short positions of all investors in a given futures or options contract must be zero.

Organized futures and option exchanges standardize the reliability of purchasers and sellers by requiring that a well-capitalized clearing corporation, usually owned by the members of the exchange, participate on the other side of every contract. When a buyer and a seller enter into a contract, they do not agree to a bilateral transaction. Instead, the seller agrees to deliver the stated assets to a clearing corporation on the settlement date in return for the agreed-upon settlement price. The buyer agrees to pay the clearing corporation the same amount on the settlement date in return for delivery of the same assets. The buyer and the seller have the clearing corporation as the other party to their contract rather than each other.

The use of a clearing corporation in matching buyers and sellers means that every market participant faces the same transactor (the clearing corporation) on the other side of every contract. The use of a clearing corporation makes contracts homogeneous across participants and simplifies the execution of transactions. An investor who has decided to go long in a contract can ask a broker to contract for the deferred purchase without having to pass on the acceptability or reliability of the seller who is going short in the contract.

The clearing corporations for the exchanges run a balanced book of long and short positions. For every contract on which it is obligated to deliver an asset, it will have a matching contract to receive that same asset. The aggregate amount of contracts on which it is obligated to deliver (or receive) an asset on a given settlement date is called the open interest in that contract.

The existence of clearing corporations also make it possible for market participants to liquidate their positions with offsetting transactions before a settlement date. This endows contracts with a kind of negotiability, in the sense that buyers and sellers can avoid settlement by transferring their contractual rights and obligations to another party. An investor who is long either a futures or an options contract for June delivery of three-month treasury bills and who in April decides he does not want to take actual delivery of those bills can enter into an offsetting contract for sale of bills in June. Since his long and short positions are with the same clearing corporation, his net position is zero.

A major difference between a futures contract and an options contract is that the options contract is a *wasting asset*. If an option is not offset, and it is not worthwhile to exercise at the time of expiration, it becomes worthless, and the holder loses the entire amount paid for the option. In contrast, if the holder of a futures contract does not offset his position, then he is obligated to take delivery of the commodity (if long the contract) or deliver the commodity (if short the contract).

Appendix C

Mark to Market for Futures Contracts

The operation of the futures market is best illustrated by an example. Assume a trader wishes to buy one treasury bill futures contract that calls for the delivery of $1 million face value of treasury bills upon the maturity of the futures contract. The trader's broker may require an initial margin of $1500. The $1500 is deposited and the purchase is consummated. Assume the price moves against the trader so that he suffers paper losses of $600. The value of the margin account will now be $900, which is below the maintenance margin of $1000. This maintenance margin is the minimum value of the margin account that the trader can have without having to post more margin. The broker then requires the trader to make another margin deposit to restore the margin account to the origin level of $1500.

This process of monitoring the market proceeds through the technique of daily settlement, or *marking to the market*. It consists principally of realizing the gains or losses sustained on a futures position each day. When the losses bring the value of the margin account below the maintenance margin level, it triggers a margin call. But when one gains on the futures contract, one can withdraw funds in excess of the $1500 initial margin amount.

Mathematical Determination of the Hedge Radio

An objective of hedging is to minimize the risk of unanticipated changes in the value of cash market positions over some period of time t. In the context of differential calculus the hedging model can be written as

$$X_c \frac{dP^c}{dt} = -\left(P^h \frac{dX_h}{dt} + X_h \frac{dP^h}{dt} \right),$$
(D.1)

where X_c and X_h are the number of units in the cash and hedge positions, respectively, and P^c and P^h are the cash and hedge market prices per unit, respectively. The model shows that the change in the value of the cash position is opposite to the change in the value of the hedge position.

A *static hedge* exists when the size of the hedge position X_h is constant over the hedge period. In this case the hedge condition is

$$X_c \frac{dP^c}{dt} = -X_h \frac{dP^h}{dt}.$$
(D.2)

This relationship implies that the optimal (static) hedge ratio is

$$\frac{X_c}{X_h} = -\frac{dP^h}{dP^c}.$$
(D.3)

A regression model is frequently used to determine this hedge ratio.

There are a number of potential problems involved in hedging. The most important are the differences associated with risk and the term to maturity of the assets. To find a hedge asset that has the same risk as the cash market asset to be hedged is often difficult. And even if a hedge asset is found that has comparable risk, finding one that has the same time to maturity as the cash market asset may be difficult. While no sure methods exist to remedy these problems, the following approaches are suggested as being useful.

Nonmatching Maturities

If the term to maturity for the cash asset is less than the term to maturity for the hedge asset, then the hedge ratio (HR) can be written as

$$\text{HR} = -\frac{\text{COV}(c, h)}{\sigma_c^2} = -\frac{r\sigma_h}{\sigma_c},$$
(D.4)

where $\text{COV}(c, h)$ is the covariance between the cash and hedged assets, σ_c and σ_h are the standard deviations for the cash and hedge assets, respectively, and r is the correlation between the cash and hedge assets.

Duration

Duration D is a measure of the maturity horizon of an asset. It may be written as an elasticity measure:

$$D = \frac{dP/P}{dR/R}, \tag{D.5}$$

where the numerator is the rate of change in price and the denominator is the rate of change in return. With the use of Eq. (D.3) the hedge ratio can be written in terms of duration as

$$\text{HR} = -\left(\frac{P^h}{P^c}\right)\left(\frac{D^h}{D^c}\right)\left(\frac{R^c\, dR^h}{R^h\, dR^c}\right). \tag{D.6}$$

This formulation indicates the contribution of price effects, relative changes in the elasticity of discount rates in the cash and hedge markets, and the ratio of the cash and hedge market durations.

Questions

1. What is meant by *hedging an asset*? How does a hedger differ from a speculator?

2. What is a futures contract? What is the spot market? What is the difference between the cash forward market and the futures market?

3. What does *rate-sensitive equilibrium* mean?

4. Define *basis*. What happens to the basis as the futures contract approaches maturity? Why does this happen?

5. Why are options safer hedge vehicles than futures?

6. What is meant by the term *selling hedge*? How is it different from a *buying hedge*?

7. What is the purpose of the hedging ratio?

8. Who are the parties to the sale of put and call options, and what function is performed by each party?

9. Explain the difference between put and call options.

10. What are the main factors determining put and call premiums?

Problems

1. Rework Tables 18.3, 18.4, 18.5, and 18.6 under the assumption that interest rates fall 200 basis points immediately after the firm receives the September loan. Discuss your results in terms of the appropriate hedging strategy to follow.

2. XYZ Company wants to insure a price that it can sell its product for three months from now. The basis differential between the cash and the future markets is −$0.15.

(a) What does management expect is going to happen to selling prices, and how can it hedge its position?

(b) What will happen in the cash and futures markets if the basis declines to −$0.10? What happens if the basis becomes −$0.20?

3. The treasurer has a portfolio of high-grade corporate bonds with a face value of $5 million (an average price of 73 − 15 per bond), an average coupon of 8%, an average maturity of 20 years, and a current market value of $3,674,000 on January 2. She wants to protect the value of the portfolio from a possible increase in interest rates. There is no corporate bond futures market in which to hedge this risk, so she sells 50 June treasury bond futures at 81 − 20 in the treasury bond futures market. By March 15 interest rates have risen, and the treasurer decides to sell the corporate bonds. She sells them for 64 – 13 per bond. The futures are trading at 69 – 20. Compute the gains/losses in the cash and futures markets. Discuss your results in terms of a change in the basis. (*Note:* The bonds are priced in 32nds.)

4. On March 15 the treasurer of Apex Corporation was worried about the price the company would have to pay to buy gold for use in the company's fabrication process. The present inventory of gold would be depleted in two months. Recent reports have suggested that gold will increase from its present level of $310 an ounce, as quoted in the spot market. On the basis of this news, the treasurer called a broker to hedge the company's position. He is told that two-month gold is selling for $330 an ounce. Assume that in early May gold is purchased for production. Also, assume that brokerage commissions are zero. What are the gains/losses in the cash market and in the futures market if gold has the following prices?

(a) $320 an ounce in the spot (cash) market and $322 in the futures market.

(b) $350 in the cash market and $355 in the futures market.

5. Quik Kamera uses silver in its film-manufacturing process. In early April it will have to purchase more silver to replenish supplies.

(a) If prices are expected to increase during the next couple of months, what strategy should Quik use to protect against higher prices?

(b) If the cash price of silver in February is $5 per ounce and the present futures price is $5.25 per ounce, what is the basis?

(c) Two months later, on April 1, these silver futures contracts are trading at $6 per ounce and the cash price is $5.50 per ounce. What is the new basis? Has the basis strengthened or weakened?

(d) Assume that Quik hedged silver prices on February 1 and offset its position on April 1. Did Quik earn a profit on its hedging activities? Discuss the results.

6. Determine the appropriate hedge ratio to provide a perfect hedge in this scenario: A corporate treasurer holds a 12% corporate bond that is expected to move 4.9% in price for every 1-basis-point change. If a 14% treasury bond were used to hedge the current position, expectations are that the yield on the corporate bond would move 1.3 times as much as the yield on the treasury bond. The treasury bond has a price movement of 5.9% per 1 basis point.

7. The portfolio manager of Hurt Company holds a Smith Corporation 10% bond due October 1, 2010. The yield on the bond is 14.12%. Some calculations indicate that a 1-basis-point change causes the Smith Corporation bond to change by 7.3%. The portfolio manager wants to hedge the position by using treasury bonds. She expects the yield of the Smith bond to fluctuate 1.33 times as much as the treasury bond. The 15% treasury bond of November 1, 2010, has a price per basis point of 10.7%. To hedge her position, how many treasury bonds per Smith Corporation bond does she have to buy?

8. Rogo Company has an overseas plant in Japan that makes pogos. On June 1 Rogo bids for a part used in the manufacture of pogos. On that day the yen is valued at 0.35 American dollars in the spot market. October futures contracts are valued at 0.37 yen to the dollar. If on October 1 the yen is valued at 0.40 American dollars and the futures contract can be sold for 0.45, what is the gain or loss?

9. Verbex Company is expecting $200,000 worth of investments to mature in three months. Management would like to reinvest the money in some risk-free government bonds currently selling at 88 and yielding 11.9%. It feels that interest rates will decline before the money is available for investment.

(a) What futures strategy can it follow?

(b) What options strategy can it follow?

(c) Can management use a strategy that combines both futures and options? Explain.

10. A call option for a treasury bond has a strike price of 65 – 00, and its premium is 4 – 00. The treasury bond futures are trading at 68 – 00.

(a) What is the intrinsic value of this option?

(b) What is the option's time value premium?

11. A call option to purchase a treasury bond futures contract has a strike price of 62 – 00. Given the accompanying information, calculate each option's intrinsic value and time value in dollars.

	March	*June*	*September*
Futures price	62 – 05	62 – 14	62 – 23
Options premium	1 – 38	2 – 61	3 – 42

PART IV □
Related Issues

CHAPTER 19

Corporate Distress: Signals, Reorganization, and Liquidation

The magnitude of corporate bankruptcy and reorganization in the United States has never been as great as it has been within the past 15 years. As proven by Penn Central in 1970, W. T. Grant in 1975, and Wickes and Braniff in 1982, just to name a few, corporate failure is no longer limited to the small undercapitalized firms. It is also affecting large industrial and financial corporations. In fact, between 1972 and 1979, from 29,500 to 35,200 firms a year petitioned the courts to liquidate or to reorganize under the protection of the nation's bankruptcy laws. Since 1979 bankruptcy levels have increased steadily and by 1983 had reached levels exceeding that of the 1922 depression. These facts exemplify the significance of corporate cash problems in the economy today.

Dun & Bradstreet periodically studies the causes of corporate failure. It reports that *managerial incompetence is the primary reason for bankruptcy occurring.* This conclusion can be interpreted to mean management's inability to understand its markets and plan for liquidity needs.

Corporate liquidations and/or reorganizations influence the economy in both positive and negative ways. Because of the snowballing effect that used to be associated with insolvent firms, past views of liquidation and reorganization were much different from today's views. Only negative statements could be made regarding bankruptcy during the Great Depression and for years after, because as companies collapsed, purchasing power was taken away from the unemployed consumer. Eventually, the cash flow of other firms was thereby reduced. Many people claim that the main cause of this collapse was the Federal Reserve Board. When the banking system began to tumble in 1932, the board simply stood back and observed.

Today the Federal Reserve Board is very active in helping American businesses. An example of the board's participation is revealed by the failure of Continental Illinois Bank. In this case Paul Volcker, chairman of the board, was an architect of a plan that resulted in the Federal Deposit Insurance Corporation (FDIC) taking over Continental. This action headed off any panic by effectively nationalizing Continental Illinois and preventing a psychological backlash (i.e., loss of confidence in the banking system) that might have affected many regional banks and numerous depositors and investors. Because of this type of involvement, the general consensus is that the Federal Reserve has substantially diminished the potential for snowballing of corporate failure of all types.

Corporate distress still exists, of course. The purpose of this chapter is to examine three primary areas of the problem: warning signals of insolvency, corporate reorganization, and liquidation through the bankruptcy courts. The first topic is related to the discussion in Chapters 3 through 6. The next two topics provide closure to the discussion throughout this book. If management fails to watch for the signals of pending liquidity problems, it may well find a need to understand reorganization and/or liquidation.

Warning Signals

History has proven that prevention of corporate failure requires constant attention to the firm's operations. *Insolvency* occurs when management cannot pay the firm's debts as they fall due or when the net assets are of negative value. However, some firms are able to pay debts as they come due while being considered insolvent. For this reason a thorough examination is necessary. A firm must remember that insolvency and liquidation are the endpoints of the process of failure. Management must continually review how the company is operating to prevent any movement toward corporate collapse. The techniques discussed in previous chapters in this book can be used in the review.

A model of the business failure succession is presented in Fig. 19.1. There are many causes/symptoms of corporate collapse. A short list of reasons includes lack of understanding of profitability and cash flows, accounting techniques employed, unsustainable growth, and top management problems. These factors are considered next.

Profitability

A topic that frequently surfaces in discussions of corporate reorganizations and liquidity management is that of profit maximization. There also exists, however, a problem in the reliability of profits, as discussed in earlier chapters. *Management tends to stress accrual accounting profits when, in reality, the emphasis should be on economic profits and cash flows.* A firm may be making

Business Failure Events

Minor/temporary ————→ Major/permanent

Alternatives available to the failing firm	Operating results below expectations	Nonpayment of dividends	Net loss and negative cash flow trends	Lowered bond rating	Deteriorating operation results year after year	Debt accommodation	Loan default	Bankruptcy	Liquidation
						Troubled debt restructuring		Bankruptcy petition	Cease operations
					Major reorganization				
		Discontinued operations							
			Merger with solvent corporation						
	Policy changes/ operating reorganizations								

Alternatives available to creditors									
	Careful analysis of financial performance of failing firm								
						Receipt of cash under judicial provisions			
					Debt accommodation/ exchange of debt for equity position				

Source: Gary Giroux and Casper E. Wiggins, Jr., "Chapter XI and Corporate Resuscitation," *Financial Executive* (December 1983), Table 2. Reprinted by permission from *Financial Executive*, December 1983, copyright 1983 by Financial Executives Institute.

accounting profits while mismanaging cash flows. Eventually, collapse may result.

Another signal of insolvency is the erosion of margins. To increase inventory and other asset turnovers, a company will sometimes quote a lower profit margin in order to gain additional business. When the word circulates about its new margin, the company can lose much of its original business. The firm must then replace this loss with business at the new lower margin. The result is increased activity, meaning an increased need for net working capital, with reduced profits available to meet these demands.

Cash Flow Analysis

The absence of cash flow statements and cash budgets is a signal of potential insolvency. Cash flow statements and cash budgets are the only way to compare forecasted cash needs with actual cash inflows and outflows. Cash budgets should be prepared for the short term as well as for the next year and beyond for the firm's cash needs. They describe to management the future effects of its present policies and give early warning to unsustainable growth.

Trade credit flows are also a signal of cash management strength/weakness. When insolvency starts to threaten a business, payments to creditors and collections from debtors become unsystematic. Problems with collections are hard for an outside analyst to detect unless a definite pattern of collection can be observed. Even inside a firm, these problems sometimes go undetected. During a period of insolvency the debts that are easy to collect will be attended to, while other receivables may be forgotten. A collection problem is a symptom that appears late in the insolvency cycle but must be considered as a danger signal.

The pattern of corporate borrowing is also revealing. Since insolvency is a shortage of cash, either temporary or permanent, it is vital for a company to attempt to predict the types of cash flows that are required. Management must be able to match its cash inflows with its outflows. A long-term payable may not pose an immediate problem, but at some time in the future it will become a short-term payable. If the cash is not available to service the debt, insolvency problems will appear.

Accountants' Opinions

Accountants' reports appear to have little, if any, value in the forewarning of solvency problems. In a bankruptcy study conducted by Ohlson,[1] none

---

[1] J. A. Ohlson, "Financial Ratios and the Probabilistic Prediction of Bankruptcy," *Journal of Accounting Research* (Spring 1980): 109 – 131.

of the eventual bankrupt firms had a going-concern qualification or disclaimer of opinion. Ohlson, in a review of the opinions, found that most companies had completely clean opinions, and those that did not had relatively minor uncertainty exceptions. Some of the firms even paid dividends in the year prior to bankruptcy.

Unsustainable Growth

A common cause of insolvency is expanding beyond sustainable growth levels. If actual growth exceeds sustainable growth levels for an extended period, management has not planned where the cash is going to come from. If the problem is not corrected, it can lead to insolvency.

Top Management

An examination of the board of directors can reveal whether all fundamental parts of the business are represented. Ideally, the broader the representation, the more efficiently projects will be analyzed. Obviously, a group with one specialty, say accounting, would not be effective in examining most manufacturing issues. Problems like these do in fact exist in major corporations.

Related to this problem is one of a sole-proprietorship – oriented chief executive officer (CEO). If the CEO tries to run the organization alone, there will be problems; there is a limit to the amount that any individual can do. The board that does not involve itself with collective decision making or does not have a sense of collective responsibility, will not have the necessary powers to avoid insolvency when it threatens. Also, if a firm lacks good middle managers, decisions made by the board will not be implemented properly. Signs of poor management include too many layers of management, rapid personnel turnover, more competition directed internally than directed toward outside competitors, and incongruency among forecasted and actual corporate funds.

Quantification of Warning Signals

Prior to the development of quantitative measures of performance, agencies were established to supply qualitative information — much as discussed in the previous section — to assess the creditworthiness of particular firms. From this information studies were developed that revealed that failing companies exhibited different financial performance than nonfailing companies. As a result of these studies, financial ratios eventually became widely used in predicting business failure.

Univariate Models

A study by Beaver[2] of failed and nonfailed firms found that an analyst, by comparing a number of seemingly independent ratios that measure profitability, liquidity, and solvency, could discriminate between the two types of firms for periods up to five years prior to failure. Figure 19.2 is a profile analysis of mean values for failed and nonfailed types of firms. Although Beaver's results are impressive, this type of study, where emphasis is placed on individual signals of impending problems, is often questionable since the variables' interactions are not revealed. Ratio analysis presented in this manner is susceptible to faulty interpretation, as has been shown in earlier chapters.

Multivariate Models

More meaningful predictive models have been developed that operate in a multivariate prediction framework. A model that has received much exposure is Altman's Z score model. The Z score model uses multiple discriminant analysis (MDA), which is discussed in Appendix A in Chapter 11. Basically, MDA is used to classify an observation into one of several groupings dependent upon the observation's individual characteristics.

Altman's Z score model is a method of linear analysis in that five measures are objectively weighted and summed to arrive at an overall score that then becomes the basis for classification of firms into one of two groupings: bankrupt or nonbankrupt. The five measures used are as follows:

1. X_1 = working capital/total assets. This ratio supposedly indicates what the net liquid assets of a company are relative to its total capitalization.

2. X_2 = retained earnings/total assets. This ratio attempts to measure long-term profitability.

3. X_3 = earnings before interest and taxes/total assets. This ratio is meant to measure the real productivity of the assets.

4. X_4 = market value of equity/book value of total liabilities. This ratio tries to measure how much a company's assets can shrink before they are exceeded by liabilities.

5. X_5 = sales/total assets. This ratio attempts to measure how much revenue the company's assets can bring in.

The discriminant model selects the appropriate weights to use with these measures. The purpose of the weights is to separate, as much as

---

[2] W. H. Beaver, "Financial Ratios as Predictors of Failure," *Empirical Research in Accounting: Selected Studies,* supplement to *Journal of Accounting Research* (1966): 77 – 111.

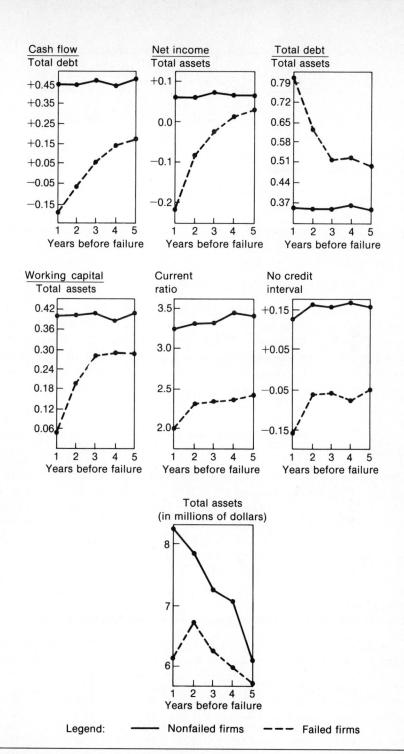

FIGURE 19.2
Profile Analysis of Failed and Nonfailed Firms

Source: William H. Beaver, "Financial Ratios as Predictors of Failure," Fig. 1. Reprinted by permission from the *Journal of Accounting Research* (Supplement 1966).

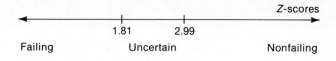

FIGURE 19.3
Altman's Z Score Cutoffs

possible, the average values of each group while at the same time to minimize the statistical distance of each observation and its own group mean. Altman's discriminate function was estimated as

$$Z = 1.2X_1 + 1.4X_2 + 3.3X_3 + 0.6X_4 + 1.0X_5. \tag{19.1}$$

He found (in order of importance) that variables X_3, X_5, and X_4 contributed most to differentiating between firms with liquidity problems and solvent firms. Altman's model classified firms with a discriminant Z score of greater than 2.99 as nonfailing and firms with a score of less than 1.81 as failing (see Fig. 19.3). The range 1.81 to 2.99 was considered a gray area or zone of ignorance where it was difficult to effectively discriminate.

ILLUSTRATION 19.1

The results of applying Altman's model to W. T. Grant for the period January 31, 1971, to January 31, 1975, are summarized in Table 19.1. Prior to the January 31, 1974, results, W. T. Grant was consistently classified as a nonfailing firm (although its Z score was steadily declining). Performance ending January 31, 1974, resulted in the model classifying W. T. Grant in the uncertain range. It was not until January 31, 1975, that

TABLE 19.1
Classification of W. T. Grant, Using the Altman Model (Year Ended January 31)

Year	X_1	X_2	X_3	X_4	X_5	Z score*	Classification
1971	0.44	0.29	0.11	1.10	1.55	3.51	Nonfailing
1972	0.50	0.26	0.08	1.26	1.46	3.44	Nonfailing
1973	0.43	0.24	0.08	0.75	1.48	3.05	Nonfailing
1974	0.44	0.20	0.05	0.38	1.48	2.68	Uncertain
1975	0.16	0.03	<0.07>	0.09	1.63	1.69	Failing

* Z scores were calculated by using Eq. (19.1).

W. T. Grant was clearly labeled a failing firm by the model. On October 2, 1975, W. T. Grant filed for bankruptcy protection under Chapter XI of the Bankruptcy Code.   □

Little satisfaction is derived from the fact that the model was able to predict W. T. Grant's demise. As discussed in Chapters 5 and 6, W. T. Grant had serious sustainable growth problems and was unable to generate a positive cash flow from operations in the six years prior to filing for bankruptcy in October 1975.

Although the Z score model is a useful technique for summarizing complex interrelationships among variables, *it must be reviewed periodically to ensure that the weights for the parameters (X_i's) have not changed or that different parameters might not be more appropriate for predicting problem firms.* Indeed, Altman, Haldeman, and Narayanan[3] have constructed a more comprehensive discriminant model (called the ZETA model). However, for proprietary reasons they have not revealed the discriminant function Z.

Corporate Bankruptcy and the Courts

In the United States the procedure of bankruptcy is a sophisticated legal process of fair treatment to both creditors and debtors, used as a last resort in cases of corporate insolvencies. All bankruptcy cases are heard in federal court.

The Constitution gave Congress the right to enact federal laws governing both personal and corporate bankruptcy procedure. Not until 1898, however, did Congress enact a comprehensive bankruptcy act. The 1898 Nelson Act, although amended some fifty times in the twentieth century, stood for 80 years. The Chandler Act of 1938 was the only significant revision of the Nelson Act during those years. By the 1970s a major reform of the bankruptcy law was long overdue. That came with the Bankruptcy Reform Act of 1978. The new Bankruptcy Code became effective on October 1, 1979, after 9 years in the making.

One big difference between the acts is the role of the bankruptcy judge. Under the old law the judge acted as both judge and administrator. Now these roles are separated. The new act also introduced a new federal bankruptcy court system, effective April 1, 1984, consisting of 95 judicial districts.

The Bankruptcy Code is made up of several odd-numbered chapters:

□ *Chapter I* defines several of the rules and procedures and describes who is a debtor.

---

[3] E. I. Altman, R. G. Haldeman, and P. Narayanan, "Zeta Analysis: A New Model to Identify Bankruptcy Risk of Corporations," *Journal of Banking and Finance* (June 1977): 29–54.

□ *Chapter III* describes how a bankruptcy case is initiated for both voluntary and involuntary cases and defines the role of trustees in the proceedings.

□ *Chapter V* covers the duties and obligations of both creditors and debtors.

□ *Chapter VII* applies to cases where liquidation of corporate assets (straight bankruptcy) is sought by the party that petitioned the proceedings.

□ *Chapter IX* deals with debt adjustments of municipalities.

□ *Chapter XI* is a synthesis of old Chapters VIII (railroad reorganizations), X (other corporate reorganizations), XI (arrangements), and XII (real estate arrangements). The new Chapter XI deals with any corporate reorganizaton: The company continues to operate under the protection of the court while it attempts to work out a plan for paying its creditors.

For a firm with insolvency problems *Chapter XI allows the firm protection from creditors while it attempts to reorganize and survive as a going concern.* Management must decide whether reorganization is the proper course to follow or whether the interests of the firm's owners might not be better served by merger with another company or by liquidation.

Reorganization is an attempt to keep a company in continued operations by correcting and modifying its present financial structure. This strategy should be pursued whenever the firm's future prospects are projected to be profitable. *Liquidation* should occur when the assets of a business are worth more when sold than when used in the continuing business. Liquidation involves the sale of a firm's assets and the application of the proceeds to the satisfaction of all creditors according to their relative priorities; the payment of any residual goes to the stockholders in the form of a (generally) nontaxable liquidating dividend.

Reorganization in Bankruptcy

Reorganizations may be voluntary or involuntary, judicial or nonjudicial. Voluntary reorganizations are those pursued by management on its own initiative, while involuntary reorganizations are imposed on the firm by creditors. Judicial reorganizations are those occurring through the courts, as in bankruptcy proceedings, while nonjudicial reorganizations involve a settlement with creditors outside the courtroom.

Voluntary Reorganizations

Voluntary reorganizations may occur as the firm takes it on itself to find alternatives to its financial difficulties. Such alternatives include the following:

□ *Partial liquidation.* A partial sale of a firm's assets or divestiture of product segments to generate cash.

□ *Dissolution.* A voluntary closing followed in the belief that more can be realized by a piecemeal sale of assets by the existing management than by the sale of the entire business as a unit.

□ *Extension.* A voluntary agreement by one or more of the firm's creditors to delay the date of payment of their claims.

□ *Composition.* The voluntary agreement of all the creditors to accept partial payment in full satisfaction of their debts.

□ *Combination settlements.* A combination of extension and composition.

□ *Sale and merger.* A sale of the business or a merger with a more financially secure firm before problems become too severe.

□ *Refinance/readjustment.* A change in a firm's capital structure to bring debt and other fixed payment charges and terms into line.

Even if these voluntary methods are successful, the firm may still be without current funds to purchase inventory, meet payroll, finance receivables, and meet other liquidity needs.

Whenever a company is insolvent and its creditors are demanding payment, management will generally seek protection in the bankruptcy courts under the protection of Chapter XI of the Bankruptcy Code.

Tool for Restructuring Debt

A business in financial distress has a wide array of tools available for restructuring its debt under Chapter XI:

1. *The automatic stay.* The most powerful weapon available to a business that seeks the protection of the bankruptcy court under Chapter XI is the automatic-stay provision. It provides that as long as the debtor is under protection of the bankruptcy court, a creditor cannot take any action to collect its debt without the permission of the bankruptcy court. The stay prevents creditors from commencing or continuing any litigation against the debtor, enforcing any judgment against the debtor, attempting to obtain possession of any property of the debtor, attempting to enforce any lien against the debtor, and attempting to collect any debts against the debtor, including the set off of any debt by any creditor. The automatic-stay provision gives breathing room to the debtor to allow management to propose a plan of reorganization.

2. *Utility turnoffs.* The code prevents a utility from discontinuing service to the debtor solely on the basis of bills that had accumulated prior to the filing of the Chapter XI proceeding, provided that the debtor, within

20 days of filing, furnishes adequate assurance of payment for current bills.

3. *Strong-arm provisions.* The code allows a debtor in possession to set aside several kinds of prefiling actions such as preferential payments to creditors, the granting of liens or security interests, and transfers of property.

4. *Executory contracts.* A debtor in possession, subject to the court's approval, may assume or reject any executory contract or unexpired lease. An executory contract is one that has not yet been fully performed. Therefore the debtor (management) can pick and choose among contracts he will perform and reject those that are onerous. Included in this category have been labor union contracts. As can be seen from the controversy that erupted over the Continental Airlines Chapter XI filing, a debtor in possession may, with court approval, reject a collective bargaining agreement with a labor union.

5. *Cessation of interest on unsecured debt.* Under the Bankruptcy Code interest will cease on unsecured debt as of the date of the filing.

6. *Orderly liquidation.* A debtor can use Chapter XI to liquidate the business in an orderly manner so that one group of creditors is not preferred over another.

7. *The plan.* Under a plan of reorganization both secured and unsecured debt can be restructured in any way acceptable to the debtor and the requisite majority of creditors. For example, secured creditors might receive a lower interest rate on loans in return for more collateral; unsecured creditors might receive a percentage of their debt immediately or payments on a debt over time; or stockholders may consent that creditors be given a portion of their equity. The main point is that the plan can be tailored to the needs of the parties. Acceptance of a plan requires the vote of two-thirds of the creditors in amount in each class of creditors and more than one-half in number of allowed claims. If a class of creditors is not impaired, it has no vote.

8. *Impairment of classes of claims.* Section 1124 of the code defines an unimpaired claim as one that will not be extended, modified or lessened in duration or amount. Once claimants are classified, each member of a particular class must be treated the same. In preparing a plan, a debtor has almost unlimited leeway in impairing claims of the creditors. For example, interest rates might be lowered on a class of claims, another class might take less than 100 cents on the dollar, and so forth.

9. *Cram down.* Although the code requires two-thirds in amount and more than one-half in number of each class of claims to accept the plan before confirmation, if one or more classes of claims have not accepted

the plan, the court may confirm the plan over their objections, that is, the plan can be "crammed down" on them.

Procedure

A Chapter XI case is commenced by filing a petition with the United States Bankruptcy Court. The petition contains schedules of all assets and liabilities. Liabilities are categorized generally into priority, secured, and unsecured creditors. Upon filing a Chapter XI proceeding, management (the debtor) continues to operate the business as a "debtor in possession" unless the judge orders otherwise. A trustee will be appointed only for cause or if the appointment is in the interest of creditors or equityholders of the business.

Management has 120 days from the filing of the petition to submit a plan of reorganization to the court and the creditors. If management does not file within this time, any party in interest may file a plan. The plan designates the correction of any managerial defects, reduction of fixed charges, reduction of floating debt, and provision of new capital. The plan includes an identification of problem areas and proposals for realistically revising a firm's financial condition in a manner that is both fair to the firm's creditors and shareholders and feasible from the firm's view toward continued operations.

Once a plan has been submitted to the court and the creditors, a hearing is held to confirm or reject the plan. If the plan is confirmed, it will go into effect and will be overseen by the bankruptcy court. If the plan is rejected, then the *debtor in possession* must come up with an alternative plan, or any interested party may submit a plan for approval.

The feasibility of the plan depends on the extent to which the trustee or receiver can utilize various financial expedients in efforts to minimize the initial cost and cash drain to the firm as it tries to improve its ability to continue operations on its own without additional outside support. If the problems cannot be corrected, or if a fair and feasible plan of reorganization does not exist, the matter proceeds to liquidation and dissolution of the corporation.

The troubled firm and its attorneys attempt to convince the creditors that it is in their best interests to keep the company alive for one or more of the following reasons:

1. Creditors will receive little or no money if they ultimately force the troubled firm into liquidation.
2. If they allow the firm to survive, they can continue doing business with the firm.

3. The troubled firm will pay for new supplies, materials, or services on a COD basis while it is in Chapter XI.

4. The plan will allow each creditor to end up with more money than it is likely to receive if it plunges the troubled firm into liquidation.

Reorganization Process

The reorganization process passes through three phases of financial correction:

1. Operating trusteeship or receivership.
2. Revaluation of assets and reallocations of claims.
3. Provision of essential new capital.

Trusteeship/Receivership

The trusteeship or receivership phase consists of actions designed to improve the company's short-run financial position and to correct any managerial defects that may exist. These actions may include the suspension of interest payments and dividends to improve cash flow, the sale of unnecessary assets, and other borrowing — all designed to provide temporary funds for continued operations while awaiting final reorganization.

Revaluation of Assets and Reallocation of Claims

The second phase, after the company has made its most immediate changes, is the revaluation of assets and reallocation of claims. At this stage the trustee determines the worth of a potential reorganization, scales down existing priorities as to principal and income preferences, extends maturities as much as possible, and substitutes contingent interest for dividend preference. These approaches seek to assess the firm's continued ability to sustain operations and to reduce the impact that existing claims will have on the initial phase of reorganization operations.

The company focuses primarily on reducing fixed charges and deferring close maturities at this point. To reduce fixed charges, management may pursue the following actions:

□ Exchange noncumulative preferred or common stock for debt issues.

□ Exchange debt issues with a contingent interest payment for those with a fixed charge.

□ Retire bonds by means of proceeds from a sale of nonessential assets only.

□ Lower the interest rate on bonds issued in the reorganization.

To defer close maturities, the company may pursue these actions:

- □ Extend the maturity dates.
- □ Refund maturing obligations.
- □ Grant bondholders liberal conversion privileges.
- □ Eliminate the bond issues in reorganization entirely by exchanging them for equity securities.

Provision of New Capital

The final phase is the provision of essential new capital. It attempts to properly capitalize the firm so that management will be able to fund continued operations. This phase deals with the company's need to raise immediate cash for net working capital requirements and with its ability to facilitate sound future financing. To raise cash, the company may pursue the following courses of action:

- □ Sell new securities or warrants.
- □ Obtain term loans.
- □ Sell unneeded assets.
- □ Assess existing stockholders.

Pros and Cons of Chapter XI

The overwhelming advantage of a Chapter XI proceeding is that the creditors of the business can be held off for a minimum of four months while a plan is proposed to satisfy their obligations. A reorganization plan can extend the maturity of the various obligations, reduce them to a certain extent, and provide for adjustment of interest rates.

There are serious disadvantages to filing a Chapter XI, though, such as adverse reaction by the public, stockholders, suppliers, employees, and customers. The bankruptcy court is not likely to tolerate, for an extended period, a business with a negative cash flow after filing, and operating capital must be available to avoid cash losses. There are serious time and legal cost constraints involved in filing, and if fraud or serious mismanagement is found, a trustee may be appointed to run the business.

Liquidation

If a reorganization cannot be effected, *liquidation* of the firm occurs. The trustee and the creditors' committee act to convert all assets into cash. Appraisers are appointed by the court to set a value on the property. The property cannot be sold at less than 75 percent of the value set by the appraisers unless the court consents.

The creditors receive distributions of the estate according to a list of *priority of claims* established by the law. The priorities for unsecured creditors are as follows:

1. The trustee's costs for administering the liquidation.
2. Unsecured claims in an involuntary case arising from the ordinary course of business after the bankruptcy proceedings began but prior to the appointment of a trustee.
3. Unsecured wages, salaries, or commissions of up to $2000 per employee earned within 90 days of the filing of the bankruptcy petition. Claims in excess of $2000 are treated as general unsecured claims.
4. Unsecured contributions of up to $2000 per employee for employee benefit plans for services rendered within 180 days prior to the petition for bankruptcy.
5. Unsecured claims of up to $900 for money deposited with the bankrupt company for services and property that were not delivered.
6. Taxes due within three years prior to the bankruptcy petition filing.
7. General creditors' claims.

After all these priorities have been satisfied, any remaining general unsecured creditors participate pro rata in any remaining realization proceeds. The final distribution to unsecured creditors is termed a dividend and is generally expressed in terms of the percentage of the total unsecured claims that will be paid.

A senior priority exists for creditors whose collateral is depleted and for whom the trustee cannot provide adequate protection. In such circumstances the secured creditor has a priority over selected other claims.

The preferred stockholders participate if there is anything left after the unsecured and secured creditors' claims are satisfied. The common shareholders represent the residual claimants. They get the remaining assets, if any still exist.

The liquidation process can take years to complete and is constantly in a state of change as the trustee attempts to value the assets, identify all claims, and liquidate the firm piecewise. The following illustration reveals some of the circumstances in W. T. Grant's liquidation. An hypothesized liquidation, which shows the allocation of the firm to the various claimants, is shown in the Appendix to this chapter.

ILLUSTRATION 19.2

As of January 29, 1976, while W. T. Grant was under the protection of Chapter XI of the Bankruptcy Code, it was reported to have total assets of $512.1 million, including $45 million of inventories when valued at cost (which were subsequently discovered to be undervalued by $70 million). Its total liabilities were $1.11 billion, of which $200 million were established to be claims of landlords. Trade creditors were owed $110 million, which included $82 million in secured liens against inventories, $26 million of bank subordination, and $2 million for unsecured creditors. Secured-debenture holders were owed $24 million, and debtor-in-possession certificates amounted to $90 million. General creditors, administrative costs, and legal fees made up the difference.

Consultants hired during the bankruptcy period cautioned creditors that it would take six to eight years to determine whether W. T. Grant would survive. Because $320 million cash had been accumulated from closing stores and liquidating inventory, bankers on the Committee of Secured Creditors favored liquidation. Representatives of trade creditors on this committee were against liquidation since they were fully secured and were still doing business with W. T. Grant. However, the bankers eventually won out.

Liquidation resulted in claims of $15 million for severance pay to employees, which was not a priority item. The Internal Revenue Service claimed W. T. Grant owed $67 million, an amount later reduced to $29 million. Administrative fees were expected to be about $30 million. Legal fees were expected to have priority status and be in the millions of dollars. It was doubtful that unsecured creditors would receive anything.

Liquidation resulted in the accounts receivable being sold for about 15% of face value plus 5% of the first year's profit earned on them by the purchaser. Secured creditors were offered two alternatives: 90% payment in full satisfaction or a 75% payment with reservation of the right to sue for additional money. The controlling interest in Zeller's was sold for $32.7 million. It had been carried on the books for about $30 million.

In other developments Ernst & Whinney, the CPA firm, paid the W. T. Grant estate $2 million plus interest to settle a suit out of court. The suit stemmed from charges that Ernst & Whinney's auditing of W. T. Grant's accounts, inventory, and internal controls before its collapse in 1975 were inadequate. Morgan Guaranty paid $2.8 million to settle a class action suit by shareholders that accused the bank of concealing the retailer's financial condition and of selling substantial holding of W. T. Grant's stock on inside information.   □

Summary

This chapter provided a broad overview of corporate distress. More probing analysis is required if the financial analyst is to enhance her or his understanding of bankruptcy proceedings and statistical techniques used for monitoring liquidity problems. An understanding of techniques discussed in previous chapters will certainly aid the analyst in uncovering distress signals.

The use of early warning systems and evaluation of management skills can help management analyze and monitor the probability of impending insolvency. Most warning systems are mathematical and require analytical skills that most managers do not possess. However, behavioral and managerial factors are also important.

Although bankruptcy proceedings are predominantly legal proceedings, financial personnel are actively involved whenever bankruptcy occurs. Financial analysts prepare numerous facts and figures pertaining to creditors' claims and restructuring of the company's debt so that the firm can become a viable entity.

Key Concepts

Chapter XI of the Bankruptcy Code   Priority of claims
Insolvency   Reorganization
Liquidation

Appendix

Allocation to Claimants from Liquidation

As an illustration of the liquidation process, assume that the Lang Company had the balance sheet shown in Table A.1 on the date it filed for a voluntary bankruptcy petition.

TABLE A.1
Lang Company
Balance Sheet As of March 30, 1984

Assets		Liabilities and equity	
Cash	$ 8,200	Bank note payable	$ 32,000
Notes receivable	24,000	Accounts payable	195,000
Accounts receivable	47,000	Accrued wages	13,500
Inventories:		Accrued interest:	
Finished goods	56,000	Bank notes	1,100
Work in process	24,000	Mortgage	8,500
Raw materials	39,000	Mortgage note	200,000
Prepaid expenses	1,200	Capital stock	250,000
Investment in Gale	26,500	Retained earnings	<141,200>
Land	42,000		
Buildings (net)	198,000		
Equipment	93,000		
Total assets	$558,900	Total liabilities	$558,900

Additional information concerning estimated realizable values and other balance sheet relationships follow.

☐ The notes receivable are expected to be fully realized, and they have been pledged as collateral on a bank note in the principal amount of $20,000 plus accrued interest of $600.

☐ Accounts receivable have an estimated collectible value of $28,000.

☐ Finished-goods inventory can be sold at a markup of 20% over cost, with selling expenses estimated at 10% of selling price. Work in process has no value unless completed. The estimated cost to complete this work totals $12,000, of which $5000 represents the costs of raw materials. The estimated selling price of the work-in-process inventory (after allowing for selling expenses) is $25,000. The remaining raw materials inventory has an estimated selling price of 70% of its cost.

□ The recovery value of prepaid expense is $600.

□ The Gale Company stock has a current market value of $30 per share and is pledged as collateral on a bank note payable in the principal amount of $12,000 plus accrued interest of $500.

□ Land and buildings have appraised values of $60,000 and $120,000, respectively, and serve as collateral on the mortgage note payable.

□ Much of the equipment is special-purpose equipment having an estimated disposal value of $28,000.

TABLE A.2
Position of Creditors

	Book value			Realizable value
Assets pledged with fully secured creditors				
Notes receivable	$ 24,000		$ 24,000	
Bank note payable		$ 20,000		
Accrued interest		600	20,600	$ 3,400
Investment in Gale	26,500		$ 30,000	
Bank note payable		$ 12,000		
Accrued interest		500	12,500	17,500
Assets pledged with partially secured creditors				
Land	42,000	$ 60,000		
Buildings	198,000	120,000	$180,000	
Mortgage note payable		$200,000		
Accrued interest		8,500	208,500	
Free assets				
Cash	8,200			8,200
Accounts receivable	47,000			28,000
Prepaid expenses	1,200			600
Inventories:				
Finished	56,000			60,480
Work in process	24,000			18,000
Raw materials	39,000			23,800
Equipment	93,000			38,000
Total net realizable value				$197,980
Liabilities having priority:				
Accrued wages				13,500
Net free assets				$184,480
Estimated deficiency to unsecured creditors				39,020
Total	$558,900			$223,500

TABLE A.2 (*Cont.*)

Liabilities having priority			
Accrued wages	$ 13,500	$ 13,500	
Fully secured creditors			
Notes payable	32,000	$ 32,000	
Accrued interest	1,100	1,100	
Partially secured creditors			
Mortgage note payable	200,000	$200,000	
Accrued interest	8,500	8,500	
Total		$208,500	
Land and buildings		180,000	$28,500
Unsecured creditors			
Accounts payable	195,000		195,000
Stockholders' equity			
Capital stock	250,000		
Retained earnings	<141,200>		
Total	$558,900		$223,500

Tables A.2 and A.3 incorporate this information to show the position of creditors and the deficiency report, respectively.

Several features should be noted:

☐ Assets pledged with fully secured creditors have realizable values in excess of the secured debt in an amount of $20,900 (see Table A.2: $3400 + $17,000), which becomes available for distribution to unsecured creditors.

TABLE A.3
Lang Company
Deficiency Account March 31, 1984

Estimated losses		Estimated gains	
Accounts receivable	$19,000	Investment in Gale	$ 3,500
Inventory	16,720	Land	18,000
Prepaid expenses	600	Capital stock	250,000
Buildings	78,000	Retained earnings	<141,200>
Equipment	55,000	Deficiency to unsecured creditors	39,020
Total	$169,300	Total	$169,300

□ Assets pledged with partially secured creditors have a realizable value that is $28,500 less than the total related debt (see Table A.2: $180,000 − $208,000). Thus mortgage holders have a $28,500 remaining debt that ranks as an unsecured one.

□ Free assets are those that have not been pledged with specific liabilities and are available to satisfy general unsecured creditors. Note that the free assets include the excess of the realizable value of pledged assets over the related debts of fully secured creditors.

□ In the deficiency account (see Table A.3) the capital stock and retained earnings are included in the estimated gains column only to indicate the extent to which total potential deficiency is covered by stockholders' equity.

□ The final settlement with the unsecured creditors can be computed by dividing the net free assets by the estimated deficiency to unsecured creditors (see Table A.2):

$$\frac{\$184,480}{\$223,500} = 0.825.$$

Thus each unsecured creditor will receive approximately 82.5% of the amount due under the claim.

Questions

1.   Distinguish between solvency in an accounting sense and in a legal sense.

2.   Distinguish between fully secured, partially secured, and unsecured creditors.

3.   Discuss the importance of financial statements in warning of financial problems.

4.   Name five signals of potential insolvency.

5.   What is a major problem with models like Altman's Z score model?

6.   Discuss some of the tools available under Chapter XI of the Bankruptcy Code that the firm can use to restructure its debt.

7.   Distinguish between *reorganization* and *liquidation.*

8.   What is the reasoning behind the court's attempt to conserve the firm as an ongoing entity rather than liquidate it?

Problems

1.   WLU Company provides the following data:

Working capital	$ 250,000
Total assets	900,000
Total liabilities	300,000
Retained earnings	200,000
Sales	1,000,000
Operating income	150,000
Common stock:	
Book value	210,000
Market value	300,000
Preferred stock:	
Book value	100,000
Market value	160,000

Determine the Z score, using Altman's model. Discuss whether or not the firm is near insolvency.

Appendix Problems

1. The following data are taken from the trustee's records:

Assets pledged with fully secured creditors (realizable value $100,000)	$125,000
Assets pledged with partially secured creditors (realizable value $45,000)	70,000
Free assets (realizable value $60,000)	90,000
Fully secured creditor claims	55,000
Partially secured creditor claims	65,000
Unsecured creditor claims with priority	15,000
General unsecured creditor claims	150,000

Determine the amount that will be paid to each class of creditor.

2. Toronto Cabinets is facing bankruptcy proceedings. Its most current balance sheet is as follows:

Cash	$ 4,000	Accounts payable	$ 80,000
Receivables	35,000	Accrued wages	35,000
Inventories	40,000	Notes payable	45,000
Fixed assets	115,000	Common stock	75,000
		Retained earnings	<41,000>
Total	$194,000	Total	$194,000

Estimated realizable values of the assets are receivables, $15,000; inventories, $20,000; fixed assets, $70,000. Receivables and inventories are both pledged as collateral on the notes payable in the amounts of $20,000 and $25,000, respectively. Prepare a Position of Creditors Statement, and determine the estimated settlement per dollar for general unsecured creditors. Assume that accrued wages are a priority item.

University of Newcastle
Robinson Library
CheckOut Receipt

11/11/2004
09:39 am

em:Liquidity analysis and management / by George W.
allinger, P. Basil Healey.
em ID: M1087055408
Due Date: 20041209

Please keep this receipt as it has details of the date(s)
by which your item(s) should be returned.

To renew your books use the Library Catalogue
either via the web or in the Library.

CHAPTER 20 □
A Summary

Management of liquidity is usually viewed as a series of interesting and vital assets and/or liability groupings and analyses. Clear-cut objectives are usually missing. The reason for this shortcoming is that the linkages are fully understood neither by practitioners nor theorists. Most studies of this problem have relied on some variation of a constrained mathematical model. Much work still needs to be done to derive a meaningful valuation model that explicitly incorporates liquidity objectives.

The purpose of this chapter is to briefly summarize the discussion of economic foundations, techniques of liquidity analysis, and management of various assets and liabilities that influence corporate liquidity. These three areas represent the essential ingredients in determining a cohesive strategy for managing liquidity that is consistent with creating value for shareholders.

Economic Foundations

The theory of finance states that the objective of the firm is to maximize shareholders' wealth. Such a statement assumes that risk can be quantified and (possibly) expressed as the effective rate to discount returns over time as in the residual income (net present value) model. The usual assumption employed with this model is that resources flow freely between firms so as to maximize returns for the entire economic system. In other words, the theory assumes perfect market conditions.

In the real world of the competitive firm the classical perfect-market assumptions do not prevail. Resources used by the firm are classified as fixed or variable, depending on the time frame. For instance, liquidity in the immediate time is fixed, whereas it is variable in the short-run or the long-run time dimensions. It is the immediate and short-run dimensions that are important for liquidity. Management must recognize the existence of conditions that limit its ability to reach a desired wealth-maximizing state because of liquidity needs.

Both the desired state and the liquidity level are affected by the firm's imperfect input and output markets. Market participants have the ability to directly influence the pricing of outputs and/or inputs and thereby influence market demand and/or supply. Management must use whatever information is available to make decisions that attempt to enhance the firm's value. This objective requires managers to combine various factor inputs so that output is salable at an economic profit maximizing quantity and price — that is, to operate where marginal revenue equals marginal cost.

In an operational sense this maximizing output level must be prepared in a cost-benefit framework that explicitly incorporates the timing of cash flows. If management simply assumes that sufficient liquidity exists and is being properly managed, then the analysis most likely will be faulty, and actual results will not be as intended. Each expenditure, whether it be for factor inputs or capital requirements, represents an investment of funds and must be evaluated in terms of its contribution to satisfying the liquidity-constrained shareholder wealth maximization objective — or, in the economist's terms, maximization of economic profit.

Economic profit is defined as the difference between investment and expected future cash flows generated by that investment that is discounted at the opportunity cost of funds. As shown in Fig. 20.1, economic profit is the difference between the discounted terminal value I_n and the initial investment value I_o, where k is the appropriate opportunity cost of capital rate.

Obviously, for an economic profit to exist, the discounted terminal value of investment must exceed the initial investment. Whenever the reverse situation occurs (i.e., an *economic loss* exists), it may simply be a matter of time before periodic *accounting profit* changes from profit to loss and eventual failure of the firm because of the lack of availability of liquid resources from the financial markets. The element of time is crucial to

FIGURE 20.1
Investment and Profit Through Time

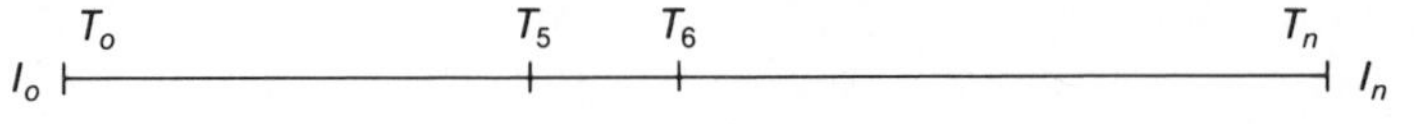

$$\text{Economic profit } (P) = \frac{I_n - I_o}{(1 + k)^{T_n}}$$

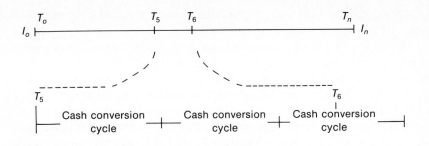

FIGURE 20.2
Cash Conversion Cycle Versus Accounting Cycle

overall corporate objectives and managing the trade-off between liquidity and profitability. Management simply cannot wait for the termination of the project to measure economic profit.

The time interval from T_5 to T_6 in Fig. 20.1 can be thought of as the usual annual accounting period. This period is chosen for estimating performance and satisfying reporting requirements both internally and externally. The time dimension has little relationship to the production-sales pattern (i.e., operating and cash conversion cycles) of the firm. The relationship between the cash conversion cycle and the annual accounting reporting period is stylized in Fig. 20.2.

Annual accounting profit can only estimate the resultant profit from approximately two and one-half cash conversion cycles, as shown in Fig. 20.2. Since accounting profit is determined by following generally accepted accounting principles, these profits do not fully account for all opportunity costs. If anything, these accounting profits overstate true economic profits, since adjustments are not made for either inflation or increase in value because of other market conditions.

Note that operations during any cycle are highly dependent on (1) the composition of the investments and (2) the time dimension. Some of these investments are variable and may be easily withdrawn from the process, while other investments are completely fixed or locked into the production-sales process and only become available for alternative use at the end of the process. The appropriate mixture of fixed and variable investments is determined by the technological rules of the production-sales process. If management finds it necessary to disrupt the process, operating efficiency can be severely damaged, with the result that the recovery values of many of the investments (e.g., receivables, inventories) may become but a small fraction of their original value. If management has time to change some of its constraining conditions, then liquidity is of lesser concern and profit is the more demanding objective. However, while profits can be viewed as an accumulation over time, liquidity must be viewed as some minimum amount of liquid resources at each moment in time.

The lack of liquidity supply, relative to liquidity demand, is the most common reason for disrupting the cycle. Each cycle involves a certain amount of time, and within this time parameter management invests most of its funds into fixed or quasi-fixed investments. Unfortunately, the obligations of the firm do not always match its revenue-deriving operations. The firm's suppliers demand payment according to the terms of the purchase contract. Should these demands exceed the existing supply at the current time, the firm runs the risk of insolvency and eventual bankruptcy.

If the demands at the present time can be temporarily satisfied, management has a number of options to resolve liquidity problems. Additional time provides management with flexibility to adjust the firm's financial position and scale of operations so as to reduce the risk of liquidity shortfall. In other words, within a confined operating structure there exist some variable inputs that, when combined in various proportions with fixed inputs, result in different levels of output and sustainable growth. Understanding the relationship between sale of this output and sustainable growth is crucial. Thus management must make every effort to understand both the endogenous factors (e.g., asset and employee capabilities, debt capacity) and the exogenous factors (e.g., product demand conditions) that affect shareholder wealth – maximizing decisions.

Where time is not a restriction (i.e., in the long run), management can vary any of the factors involved in production and sales. In this way attention can be diverted from the liquidity objective to the economic profit objective.

Liquidity Analysis

The traditional historical accounting – based balance sheet and income statement are used to summarize the economic activity of the firm during the immediate and short-run time dimensions. Many ratios purporting to explain the economic activity are derived from these financial statements and are subsequently used to help management plan future direction. However, the balance sheet and income statement presentations of information are questionable with regard to their usefulness for understanding liquidity. It is not that the information is incorrect; rather, it is that the information presented in these financial statements is often inappropriate for analyzing many management problems.

The importance of managing cash and funds flow is apparent from Chapter 1's illustration "How to Go Broke" and by the frequent references throughout this book to management practices of W. T. Grant Company. The generation of accounting profits is not a guarantee of corporate solvency. Indeed, profits can generally be improved by adopting some alternative and generally accepted accounting principle. The quality of these earnings, however, is suspect. *Solvency and value depend on cash flow*, not some artificially created accounting profit figure that causes economic profits to lag further behind accounting profits.

Sustainability of the firm requires well thought-out strategic decisions pertaining to investments in both short-term and long-term assets, dividend policy, and the firm's capital structure. Often this objective means that conventional financing sources cannot be relied on. Inflation and increased economic instability may mean that some financing sources cannot be used — often at critical times when the firm needs them the most. As a result, managers must be more creative in their financing arrangements without causing perceptible changes in the risk of the firm. Hence they have used creative *asset-based financing* and *off-balance sheet financing* as a means of raising needed capital funds. These financing alternatives cause assets that are important to the production-sales process to also become as important to the financing and liquidity needs of the company.

Management of Liquidity

Interactions between various assets and liability accounts are real and complex. Unfortunately, they are not very well understood from the perspective of their effects on the firm's value and on shareholder wealth maximization. Financial analysts use traditional ratios (e.g., current ratio and return on investment) calculated from the financial statements to reveal the complexities. The emphasis of the analysis is frequently on the firm's financial coverage in case of disaster. Under most conditions where disaster is imminent, such information is often useless because it is too late for management to use the information in an effort to avert bankruptcy.

In a world of certainty management has no need for liquidity balances since all cash inflows and outflows are known. However, managerial decisions are usually made with imperfect information. Thus some level of liquid balances is required to reduce risk. A computer simulation study[1] indicates that an optimal liquidity level does exist and that this level contributes to increasing shareholder wealth. Thus in a practical operational sense management must try to find the optimal liquidity level.

What is needed is information that truly signals, with a sufficient lead time, whether the firm is likely to continue without serious disruptions. Consequently, emphasis must be placed on the firm's cash and funds flows, management's ability to manage inflation and sustain growth, and the creation of shareholder wealth.

---

[1] A. K. Bhattacharya, "The Influence of Liquidity on Corporate Valuation," (Ph.D. dissertation, Arizona State University, 1984).

The most critical asset in the liquidity portfolio is *cash*. Its function is to bridge the gap between cash receipts and cash disbursements. Thus forecasts must be made of expected requirements, and action points must be identified for investing surplus balances or securing additional funds to ensure uninterrupted operations. Understanding the float associated with cash payments and receipts can increase the productivity of cash. This point is important, since cash per se is a nonearning asset and must be carefully monitored so that it does not accumulate unnecessarily in nonproductive balances.

Various cash management models can be used to increase the productivity of cash. Regardless of the model chosen, though, improvement in cash management is likely to result, because the models, in one way or another, analyze the trade-off between holding costs (the opportunity costs associated with having too much cash on hand) and ordering costs (the transaction costs incurred to buy or sell cash). Theoretically, this result is consistent with the economist's profit maximization argument.

The investment in *accounts receivable* depends on the credit and collection policy of the firm. Management uses credit terms as a pricing variable in the hope of influencing the demand curve so as to increase sales and profitability. However, profitability is of low quality if the sales are slow in being collected. The credit decision must be part of an integrative decision based on marginal analysis that addresses changing sales, production, and inventory requirements, as well as spontaneous financing that may result.

Needless to say, if the credit decision results in too many resources being invested in accounts receivable, then less are available for allocation to other productive areas, such as expanding capacity or meeting liquidity needs. A number of credit evaluation models are available for the credit manager to use.

Monitoring of accounts receivable balances has come under increased scrutiny in recent years. The traditional techniques of receivables turnover, days sales outstanding, and aging schedules can provide incorrect conclusions about the status of receivable balances. If sales are not constant from one period to another, these techniques usually give incorrect indicators of the status of receivables. Techniques such as balance fractions, payment proportions, and variance analysis have emerged in recent years as superior monitoring tools.

Inventory is the largest single asset in many firms. It is held in different forms to accomplish a number of objectives. As raw material, inventory provides for uninterrupted production; as work in process and finished goods, inventory recognizes the production constraint that the product cannot be produced instantaneously.

A critical question concerns the necessary level of inventory investment. From the marketing manager's view no customer should be lost owing to the firm's inability to fill an order. From the production manager's view inventory should facilitate production efficiency, (i.e., allow production at the least costly level). From the accounting and financial view inventory represents a consumption of scarce resources and must be analyzed with marginal analysis. Clearly, compromises are made by the different factions within the firm, but if the scarce-resource allocation argument is ignored, the firm may be headed for serious financial difficulties.

It is the finance manager's job to convince other managers that investment in inventory must be consistent with the shareholder wealth objective. The economic order quantity (EOQ) model is a useful tool to help convey this message. Although EOQ is questionable as an operating tool — because of its restrictive assumptions and the existence of better models (e.g., just-in-time systems) — it does provide a useful conceptual approach for explaining the trade-offs involved in minimizing inventory investment while satisfying the shareholder wealth objective.

Management of inventory from a financial perspective also requires analysis of price changes and knowledge of whether *cash flow* savings can result from using a particular valuation approach (e.g., FIFO or LIFO inventory accounting). Depending on the direction of price changes, the valuation method, and the inventory balance, cash flow (i.e., economic profit) may be improved at the expense of accounting profit. Managers in other functional areas must be educated in the validity of this procedure. The discussion in Chapter 2, on the relationship between physical and monetary flows, is useful for explaining this process.

A critical role needs to be assumed by financial management in monitoring inventories. As many firms have discovered, too much inventory can result in significant disruptions within the company — employee layoffs, plant shutdowns, price competition, and so on — which may eventually result in liquidity problems too severe to overcome. The traditional techniques for monitoring inventories are the inventory turnover ratio or days sales in inventories. However, these techniques can provide faulty information. Analysis of variances between actual and budget inventory levels allows management to isolate problems and take corrective actions.

Management of *liabilities* plays an important role in the shareholder wealth maximization objective. As discussed earlier, that sufficient funds be available to meet obligations as they become due is critical. Failure to have sufficient funds can result in a wide range of responses from creditors. At one extreme, they may simply be annoyed that payment is not made on time. At the other extreme, they may bring court action that could result in the firm having to file bankruptcy, with eventual liquidation a possibility.

In recent years the importance of asset-based financing has emerged as a means of obtaining much needed funds. This form of financing is highly dependent on the form of collateral offered to secure the loan. In many cases asset-based financing allows more debt to be raised than does conventional unsecured financing, because the book values of the assets are carried at values much below market values. Thus management is able to monetize unrealized gains it is carrying on the balance sheet.

The wealth objective will also be affected by the cost of financing. Trade accounts payable are frequently viewed as being a costless source of capital. However, if discounts offered by suppliers are not taken, the annualized cost of these missed discounts can be higher than most types of financing. As a result, the opportunity cost of funds is high, and economic profit is decreased.

The cost of other forms of financing is also important. The financial leverage of the firm affects not only value but also liquidity. In recent years management has realized the advantages associated with commodity/financial futures and options as a means of minimizing the financing costs and removing some of the uncertainty so as to improve the liquidity position of the firm.

In Conclusion

When management needs to better understand the firm's liquidity status, it must shed many of the traditional or preconceived notions about how to measure liquidity. Current and quick ratios, accounts receivable and inventory turnover ratios, as well as many other ratios, must be recognized as providing relatively little information. The fact that they have been used for decades and are easy to calculate should not allow them to take precedence over more insightful measures that are newer and usually more tedious to calculate. Cash breakeven analysis, inflation-adjusted ROE, cash and funds flow statements, cash budgeting, and variance analysis models, to name but a few of the techniques, provide management with a better understanding of the firm's financial status than the traditional measures.

Management of liquidity can be described as the daily operating decisions of financial personnel so as to keep the firm solvent while directing policy and operating actions toward maximizing shareholder wealth. This type of management requires an understanding of marginal analysis, since it is the basis for maximizing economic profits. In an operational sense the unifying models for achieving this objective are the maximization of residual income (RI) and return on equity (ROE). Appendices in Chapters 1 and 5 indicate the compatibility of net present value, RI, and ROE. Management of ROE is better from a practical standpoint since it incorporates the profitability of sales and production, the utilization of assets, and the use of both debt and equity to finance the company. Also, maximization of ROE is consistent with maximizing sustainable growth. The importance of managing sustainable growth is underscored by its implicit definition: Sustainable growth means operating within the firm's limits so as to perpetuate growth at a level that avoids liquidity problems. If management does not understand the firm's liquidity, the reason it does not is that it has abdicated the responsibility — usually to the detriment of employees, customers, and investors.

Selected Readings

Chapter 1
Introduction to Liquidity Management

Abd El-Motaal, M. H. B. "Working Capital — Its Role in the Short-Run Liquidity Policy of Industrial Concerns." *Accounting Research* (1958): 258 – 275.

Anthony R. W. "The Trouble with Profit Maximization." *Harvard Business Review* (November – December 1960): 126 – 134.

Bean, V. L., and R. Griffith. "Risk and Return in Working Capital Management." *Mississippi Valley Journal of Business* (Fall 1966): 28 – 48.

Bodenhorn, D. "A Cash-Flow Concept of Profit." *Journal of Finance* (March 1964): 16 – 31.

Branch, B. "Corporate Objectives and Market Performance." *Financial Management* (Summer 1973): 24 – 28.

Cohn, R. A., and J. J. Pringle. "Steps Toward an Integration of Corporate Financial Theory." In *Readings on the Management of Working Capital*, ed. K. V. Smith, 35 – 41. St. Paul, Minn.: West, 1980.

Cossaboom, R. A. "Let's Reassess the Profitability-Liquidity Trade-Off." *Financial Executive* (May 1971): 46 – 51.

Donaldson, G. "Financial Goals: Management Versus Stockholders." *Harvard Business Review* (May – June 1963): 116 – 129.

Drucker, P. F. "The Delusion of 'Profits,'" *Wall Street Journal* (February 5, 1975): 10.

Findlay, M. C., III, and G. A. Whitmore. "Beyond Shareholder Wealth Maximization." *Financial Management* (Winter 1974): 25 – 35.

Glautier, M. W. E. "Towards a Reformulation of the Theory of Working Capital." *Journal of Business Finance* (Spring 1971): 37 – 42.

Knight, W. D. "Working Capital Management: Satisficing Versus Optimization." *Financial Management* (Spring 1972): 33 – 40.

Levin, R. *Buy Low, Sell High, Collect Early and Pay Late: The Manager's Guide to Financial Survival.* Englewood Cliffs, N.J.: Prentice-Hall, 1983.

Levy, H., and M. Sarnat. "A Pedagogic Note on Alternative Formulations of the Goal of the Firm." *Journal of Business* (October 1977): 526 – 528.

Mehta, D. R. *Working Capital Management.* Englewood Cliffs, N.J.: Prentice-Hall, 1974.

Miller, J. W. "Working Capital Theory Revisited." *Journal of Commercial Bank Lending* (May 1979): 15 – 31.

Nunn, K. P., Jr. "The Strategic Determinants of Working Capital: A Product-Line Perspective." *Journal of Financial Research* (Fall 1981): 207 – 219.

Perry, J. E. "Cash Flow — The Most Critical Issue of the 1980s." *Journal of Commercial Bank Lending* (September 1982): 20 – 29.

Seitz, N. "Shareholders' Goals, Firm Goals and Firm Financing Decisions." *Financial Management* (Autumn 1982): 20 – 26.

Smith, K. V. "State of the Art of Working Capital Management." *Financial Management* (Autumn 1973): 50 – 55.

———. *Guide to Working Capital Management.* New York: McGraw-Hill, 1979.

———, ed. *Readings in the Management of Working Capital.* 2nd ed. St. Paul, Minn.: West, 1980.

Solomon, E. *The Theory of Financial Management.* New York: Columbia University Press, 1963.

Walker, E. W. "Towards a Theory of Working Capital." *Engineering Economist* (January – February 1964): 21 – 35.

Chapter 2
Economic Fundamentals for Analysis of Liquidity

Black, F. "The Magic in Earnings: Economic Earnings Versus Accounting Earnings." *Financial Analysts Journal* (November – December 1980): 19 – 24.

Chambers, R. J. *Accounting, Evaluation and Economic Behavior.* Englewood Cliffs, N.J.: Prentice-Hall, 1966.

Gonedes, N. J., and N. Dopuch. "Economic Analyses and Accounting Techniques: Perspective and Proposals." *Journal of Accounting Research* (Autumn 1979): 384 – 410.

Ross, S. A. "Accounting and Economics." *Accounting Review* (April 1983): 375 – 380.

Thompson, A. A., Jr. *Economics of the Firm: Theory and Practice.* Englewood Cliffs, N.J.: Prentice-Hall, 1981.

Chapter 3
Traditional Financial Analysis: Some Shortcomings

Backer, M., and M. L. Gosman. "The Use of Financial Ratios in Credit Downgrade Decisions." *Financial Management* (Spring 1980): 53 – 56.

Bernstein, L. A. *The Analysis of Financial Statements.* Homewood, Ill.: Dow Jones – Irwin, 1978.

Bernstein, L. A., and J. G. Siegel. "The Concept of Earnings Quality." *Financial Analysts Journal* (July – August 1979): 72 – 75.

Briloff, A. J. *Unaccountable Accounting*. New York: Harper & Row, 1972.

———. *More Debits Than Credits: The Burnt Investor's Guide to Financial Statements.* New York: Harper & Row, 1976.

Chen, K. H., and T. A. Shimerda. "An Empirical Analysis of Useful Financial Ratios." *Financial Management* (Spring 1981): 51 – 60.

Davidson, S., G. H. Sorter, and H. Kalle. "Measuring the Defensive Position of a Firm." *Financial Analysts Journal* (January – February 1964): 23 – 29.

Findlay, M. C., III, and E. E. Williams. "Toward More Adequate Debt Service Coverage Ratios." *Financial Analysts Journal* (November – December 1975): 58 – 61.

Heath, L. C. "Is Working Capital Really Working?" *Journal of Accountancy* (August 1980): 55 – 62.

Helfert, E. A. *Techniques of Financial Analysis*. 3rd ed. Homewood, Ill.: Irwin, 1972.

Horrigan, J. C. "A Short History of Financial Ratio Analysis." *Accounting Review* (April 1968): 284 – 294.

———. "The Determination of Long-Term Credit Standing with Financial Ratios." *Empirical Research in Accounting: Selected Studies in Journal of Accounting Research* (1966): 44 – 62.

Hylton, D. P. "Should We Dismantle the Balance Sheet?" *Financial Executive* (August 1977): 16 – 19.

Jarrett, J. E. "An Approach to Cost-Volume-Profit Analysis Under Uncertainty." *Decision Sciences* (July 1973): 405 – 420.

Kennedy, H. A. "A Behavioral Study of the Usefulness of Four Financial Ratios." *Journal of Accounting Research* (Spring 1975): 97 – 116.

Laurent, C. R. "Improving the Efficiency and Effectiveness of Financial Ratio Analysis." *Journal of Business, Finance and Accounting* (Autumn 1979): 401 – 413.

Ohlson, J. A. "Financial Ratios and the Probablistic Prediction of Bankruptcy." *Journal of Accounting Research* (Spring 1980): 109 – 131.

Petty, J. W., and D. F. Scott, Jr. "The Analysis of Corporate Liquidity." *Journal of Economics and Business* (Spring – Summer 1980): 206 – 218.

Pohlman, R. A., and R. D. Hollinger. "Information Redundancy in Sets of Financial Ratios." *Journal of Business Finance and Accounting* (Winter 1981): 511 – 528.

Rappaport, A. "Let's Give Shareholders the Figures They Need." *Wall Street Journal* (March 2, 1982).

Raun, D. L. "The Limitations of Profit Graphs, Breakeven Analysis, and Budgets." *Accounting Review* (October 1964): 927 – 945.

Reiling, H. B., and J. C. Burton. "Financial Statements: Signposts as well as Milestones." *Harvard Business Review* (November – December 1972): 45 – 54.

Scott, D. F., and J. D. Martin. "Industry Influence on Financial Structure." *Financial Management* (Spring 1975): 67 – 73.

Siegel, J. G. "Quality of Earnings Concept — A Survey." *Financial Analysts Journal* (March – April 1982): 60 – 68.

Sorter, G. H., and G. Benston. "Appraising the Defensive Position of a Firm: The Interval Measure." *Accounting Review* (October 1960): 633 – 640.

Wright, F. K. "An Examination of the Working Capital Ratio." *The Australian Accountant* (March 1956): 101 – 107.

Chapter 4
Off – Balance Sheet Financing and Financial Analysis

Abdel-Khalik, A., R. Thompson, and R. Taylor. "The Impact of Reporting Leases Off the Balance Sheet on Bond Risk Premiums: Two Exploratory Studies." Accounting Research Center Working Paper No. 78 – 2, University of Florida, February 1978.

Andrews, V. L. "Captive Finance Companies." *Harvard Business Review* (July – August 1964): 80 – 92.

Beechy, T. H. "Quasi-Debt Analysis of Financial Leases." *Accounting Review* (April 1969): 375 – 381.

Bohan, M. P. "Balance Sheet Financing — On or Off." *Journal of Accounting, Auditing and Finance* (Summer 1981): 360 – 364.

Bower, R. S. "Issues in Lease Financing." *Financial Management* (Winter 1973): 25 – 34.

Bowman, R. "The Debt Equivalence of Leases: An Empirical Investigation." *Accounting Review* (April 1980): 237 – 253.

Comiskey, E. E., and C. A. Trirschler. "On or Off the Balance Sheet — Some Guidelines for Credit Analysis." *Journal of Commercial Bank Lending* (October 1980): 23 – 26.

Crawford, P. J., C. P. Harper, and J. J. McConnell. "Further Evidence on the Terms of Financial Leases." *Financial Management* (Autumn 1981): 31 – 44.

Dieter, R., and A. R. Wyatt. "Get It Off the Balance Sheet!" *Financial Executive* (January 1980): 42 – 48.

Elam, R. "The Effect of Lease Data on the Predictive Ability of Financial Ratios." *Accounting Review* (January 1975): 25 – 43.

Franks, J., and S. Hodges. "Valuation of Financial Lease Contracts: A Note." *Journal of Finance* (May 1978): 647 – 669.

Gant, D. R. "Illusion in Lease Financing." *Harvard Business Review* (March – April 1959): 121 – 142.

Green, R. "How to Owe Money Without Seeming To." *Forbes* (May 26, 1980): 54 – 56.

Gritta, R. D. "The Impact of Lease Capitalization." *Financial Analysts Journal* (March – April 1974): 47 – 52.

Gup, B. E., and M. S. Newman. "Defeasance: What Is Its Effect on Your Firm?" *Financial Executive* (December 1984): 34 – 37.

Hershman, A. "The Ceative New Look in Corporate Finance." *Dun's Review* (July 1981): 28 – 32.

Ingberman, M., J. Rosen, and G. H. Sorter. "How Lease Capitalization Under FASB Statement No. 13 Will Affect Financial Ratios." *Financial Analysts Journal* (January – February 1979): 28 – 31.

Kalata, J. J., D. G. Campbell, and I. K. Shumaker. "Lease Financing Reporting." *Financial Executive* (March 1977): 34 – 40.

Lasman, D. A., and R. L. Weil. "Adjusting the Debt-Equity Ratio." *Financial Analysts Journal* (September – October 1978): 49 – 58.

Levy, H., and M. Sarnat. "Leasing, Borrowing and Financial Risk." *Financial Management* (Winter 1979): 47 – 54.

Lewellen, W. G. "Finance Subsidiaries and Corporate Borrowing Capacity." *Financial Management* (Spring 1972): 21 – 32.

Myers, S. C., D. A. Dill, and J. A. Bautista. "Valuation of Financial Lease Contracts." *Journal of Finance* (June 1976): 799 – 820.

Nelson, A. T. "Capitalizing Leases — The Effect on Financial Ratios." *Journal of Accountancy* (July 1963): 49 – 58.

Norby, W. "Disclosure of Off Balance Sheet Financing." *Financial Analysts Journal* (July – August 1980): 79 – 80.

Pell, P. R., J. E. Steward, and B. S. Neuhausen. "The 1981 Tax Act: Accounting for Leases." *Financial Executive* (January 1982): 16 – 26; (March 1982): 24.

"Pension Liabilities — Now You See Them, Now You Don't." *Industry Week* (November 16, 1981): 72 – 78.

Peterson, P., D. Peterson, and J. Ang. "The Extinguishment of Debt Through In-Substance Defeasance." *Financial Management* (Spring 1985): 59 – 67.

Ro, B. "The Disclosure of Capitalized Lease Information and Stock Prices." *Journal of Accounting Research* (Autumn 1978): 315 – 340.

Roberts, G. S., and J. A. Viscione. "Captive Finance Subsidiaries: The Manager's View." *Financial Management* (Spring 1981): 36 – 42.

Roenfeldt, R. L., and J. S. Osteryoung. "Analysis of Financial Leases." *Financial Management* (Spring 1973): 34 – 40.

Schachner, L. "The New Accounting for Leases." *Financial Executive* (February 1978): 40 – 47.

Tepper, I., and A. R. P. Affleck. "Pension Plan Liabilities and Corporate Financial Strategies." *Journal of Finance* (December 1974): 1549 – 1564.

Chapter 5
Indicators of Liquidity: Part I

Belt, B. "The Cash Breakeven Point as a Tool for Small Business Analysis." *Journal of Small Business Management* (April 1978): 27 – 34.

Bierman, H., Jr. "Measuring Financial Liquidity." *Accounting Review* (October 1960): 628 – 632.

Bierman, H., K. Chopra, and L. J. Thomas. "Ruin Considerations: Optimal Working Capital and Capital Structure." *Journal of Financial and Quantitative Analysis* (March 1975): 119 – 128.

Brinkman, D. R., and P. H. Prentiss. "Replacement Cost and Current-Value Measurement: How to Do It." *Financial Executive* (October 1975): 20 – 26.

Donaldson, G. "New Framework for Corporate Debt Capacity." *Harvard Business Review* (March – April 1962): 117 – 131.

———. *Strategy for Financial Mobility.* Boston: Graduate School of Business Administration, Harvard University, 1969.

Financial Accounting Standards Board. *Illustrations of Financial Reporting and Changing Prices: Statement of Financial Accounting Standards No. 33.* Stamford, Conn.: 1979.

Fruhan, W. E., Jr. *Financial Strategy: Studies on the Creation, Transfer, and Destruction of Shareholder Value.* Homewood, Ill.: Irwin, 1979.

Gordon, M. J. *The Investment, Financing, and Valuation of the Corporation.* Homewood, Ill.: Irwin, 1962.

Grove, M. A. "A Model of the Maturity Profile of the Balance Sheet." *Metroeconomica* (January – April 1966): 40 – 55.

———. "On 'Duration' and the Optimal Maturity Structure of the Balance Sheet." *Bell Journal of Economics and Management Science* (Autumn 1974): 696 – 709.

Higgins, R. C. "How Much Growth Can a Firm Afford?" *Financial Management* (Fall 1977): 7 – 16.

———. "Sustainable Growth Under Inflation." *Financial Management* (Autumn 1981): 36 – 40.

Lambrix, R. J., and S. S. Singhvi. "Managing the Working Capital Cycle." *Financial Executive* (June 1979): 32 – 41.

Lee, C. F., and J. C. Junkus. "Financial Analysis and Planning: An Overview." *Journal of Economics and Business* (August 1983): 259 – 283.

Lerner, E. M., and W. T. Carleton. *A Theory of Financial Analysis.* New York: Harcourt, Brace & World, 1966.

Modigliani, F., and M. Miller. "The Cost of Capital, Corporate Finance, and the Theory of Investment." *American Economic Review* (June 1958): 261 – 297.

———. "Corporation Income Taxes and the Cost of Capital: A Correction." *American Economic Review* (June 1963): 433 – 443.

Richards, V. D., and E. J. Laughlin. "A Cash Conversion Cycle Approach to Liquidity Analysis." *Financial Management* (Spring 1980): 32 – 38.

Runser, R. J. "Opinion: The Conceptual Framework and Inflation Accounting." *Financial Executive* (April 1979): 30 – 40.

Sharpe, W. F. "Capital Asset Prices: A Theory of Market Equilibrium Under Conditions of Risk." *Journal of Finance* (September 1964): 425 – 442.

Shoven, J. B., and J. I. Bulow. *Inflation Accounting and Nonfinancial Corporate Profits: Financial Assets and Liabilities.* Brookings Papers on Economic Activity. Washington, D.C.: Brookings Institute, 1976.

Smith, R. E., and F. K. Reilly. "Price-Level Accounting and Financial Analysis." *Financial Management* (Summer 1975): 21 – 26.

Soldofsky, R. M. "Accountant's Versus Economist's Concepts of Breakeven Analysis." *N.A.A. Bulletin* (December 1959): 5 – 18.

Von Furstenberg, G. M., and B. G. Malkiel. "Financial Analysis in an Inflationary Environment." *Journal of Finance* (May 1977): 575 – 587.

Weston, F. T. "Adjust Your Accounting for Inflation." *Harvard Business Review* (January – February 1975): 22 – 29, 146.

Zakon, A. J. "Capital Structure Optimization." In *The Treasurer's Handbook,* ed. J. F. Weston and M. B. Goudzwaard, 641 – 668. Homewood, Ill.: Dow Jones – Irwin, 1976.

Chapter 6
Indicators of Liquidity: Part II

Anton, H. R., and R. K. Jaedicke. "Financial Statements — Statement of Funds and Cash Flows." In *Handbook of Modern Accounting,* ed. S. Davidson, Chapter 4. New York: McGraw-Hill, 1970.

Emery, G. W. "Measuring Short-Term Liquidity." *Journal of Cash Management* (July – August 1984): 25 – 32.

Emery, G. W., and K. O. Cogger. "The Measurement of Liquidity." *Journal of Accounting Research* (Autumn 1982): 290 – 303.

Gale, B. T., and B. Branch. "Cash Flow Analysis: More Important Than Ever." *Harvard Business Review* (July – August 1981): 131 – 136.

Hawkins, D. F. "Toward the New Balance Sheet." *Harvard Business Review* (November – December 1984): 153 – 163.

Heath, L. C. "Let's Scrap the Funds Statement." *Journal of Accounting* (October 1978): 94 – 103.

Hunt, P. "Funds Position: Keystone in Financial Planning." *Harvard Business Review* (May – June 1975): 106 – 115.

Jaedicke, R. K., and R. T. Sprouse. *Accounting Flows: Income, Funds, and Cash.* Englewood Cliffs, N.J.: Prentice-Hall, 1965.

Johnson, G. L. "Funds Flow Equations." *Accounting Review* (July 1966): 510 – 517.

Largay, J. A., III., and C. P. Stickney. "Cash Flows, Ratio Analysis and the W. T. Grant Company Bankruptcy." *Financial Analysts Journal* (July – August 1980): 51 – 54.

Lemeke, K. W. "The Evaluation of Liquidity: An Analytical Study." *Journal of Accounting Research* (Spring 1970): 47 – 77.

Lerner, E. M. "Simulating a Cash Budget." *California Management Review* (Winter 1968): 79 – 86.

Rogers, D. E. "An Approach to Analyzing Cash Flow for Term Loan Purposes." *Bulletin of the Robert Morris Associates* (October 1965): 79 – 85.

Sorter, G. H. "Emphasis on Cash and Its Impact on the Funds Statement — Sense and Nonsense." *Journal of Accounting, Auditing and Finance* (Spring 1982): 188 – 194.

Staubus, G. T. "Alternative Asset Flow Concepts." *Accounting Review* (July 1966): 397 – 412.

Van Horne, J. C. "A Risk-Return Analysis of a Firm's Working Capital Position." *Engineering Economist* (Winter 1969): 71 – 89.

Chapter 7
Overview of Cash Managment

Agemian, C. A. "Maintaining an Effective Bank Relationship." *Financial Executive* (January 1964): 24 – 28.

Andrews, V. L. "Cash Management: An Overview for the Corporate Treasurer." *Cash Management Forum* (January 1975).

Beehler, P. J. *Contemporary Cash Management.* New York: Wiley, 1983.

Bonocore, J. J. "Getting a Picture of Cash Management." *Financial Executive* (May 1980): 30 – 33.

Connelly, J. "Is Aggressive Cash Management a Myth?" *Institutional Investor* (May 1978): 45 – 50.

De Salvo, A. "Cash Management Converts Dollars into Working Capital." *Harvard Business Review* (May 1972): 92 – 100.

Fielitz, B. D., and D. L. White. "An Evaluation and Linking of Alternative Solution Procedures for the Lock Box Location Problem." *Journal of Banking Research* (Spring 1982): 17 – 27.

Fisher, D. I. *Cash Management in the Moderate-Sized Company.* New York: The Conference Board, 1972.

Frost, P. A. "Banking Services, Minimum Cash Balances and the Firm's Demand for Money." *Journal of Finance* (December 1970): 1029 – 1039.

Giannotti, J. B., and R. W. Smith. *Treasury Management: A Practitioner's Handbook.* New York: Wiley, 1981.

Gitman, L. J., E. A. Moses, and I. T. White. "An Assessment of Corporate Cash Management Practices." *Financial Management* (Spring 1979): 32 – 41.

Hamilton, F. W. "Evaluating a Cash Manager's Performance." *Cashflow* (November 1982): 38, 40 – 41.

Hoel, A. "A Primer on Federal Reserve Float." In *Federal Reserve Bank of New York.* New York: Federal Reserve Bank, undated publication.

Hunt, A. L. *Corporate Cash Management.* New York: American Management Associations, 1978.

Johnson, T. O., and J. M. French. "Electronic Payment Systems." *Journal of Cash Management* (October 1981): 26 – 34.

Jones, R. H. "Face to Face with Cash Management: How One Company Does It." *Financial Executive* (September 1969): 37 – 39.

King, A. M. *Increasing the Productivity of Company Cash.* Englewood Cliffs, N.J.: Prentice-Hall, 1969.

Krieger, G. R., and E. C. Kramer. "How to Reduce the Bureaucratic Float." *Cashflow* (October 1981).

Lordan, J. F. "A Profile of Corporate Cash Management: The Role of the Bank." *Bank Administration* (April 1972): 15 – 19.

Mao, J. C. T., and C. E. Sarndel. "Cash Management: Theory and Practice." *Journal of Business Finance and Accounting* (Autumn 1978): 329 – 338.

Moyer, J. M. "Implementing a Preauthorized ACH Payment System." *Journal of Cash Management* (October 1981): 55 – 57.

Napoli, M. J., Jr. "Float Reduction Along the Cash Flow Timeline." *Journal of Cash Management* (July – August 1984): 44 – 47.

Nouss, R. M., and R. E. Markland. "Solving Lock-Box Location Problems." *Financial Management* (Spring 1979): 21 – 31.

Pogue, G. A., R. B. Faucett, and R. N. Bussard. "Cash Management: A Systems Approach." *Industrial Management Review* (Winter 1970): 55 – 76.

Reed, W. L., Jr. "Profits from Better Cash Management." *Financial Executive* (May 1982): 40 – 56.

Searby, F. W. "Use Your Hidden Cash Resources." *Harvard Business Review* (March – April 1968): 74 – 75.

Stone, B. K., and N. C. Hill. "Cash Transfer Scheduling for Efficient Cash Concentration." *Financial Management* (Autumn 1980): 35 – 43.

————. "The Design of a Cash Concentration System." *Journal of Financial and Quantitative Analysis* (September 1981): 301 – 321.

————. "Alternative Cash Transfer Mechanisms and Methods: Evaluation Frameworks." *Journal of Bank Research* (Spring 1982): 7 – 16.

Chapter 8
Minimizing Cash Balances

Archer, S. H. "A Model for the Determination of Firm Cash Balance." *Journal of Financial and Quantitative Analysis* (March 1966): 1 – 11.

Batlin, C. A., and S. Hinko. "Game Theoretic Approach to Cash Management." *Journal of Business* (July 1982): 367 – 381.

Baumol, W. J. "The Transactions Demand for Cash: An Inventory Theoretic Approach." *Quarterly Journal of Economics* (November 1952): 545 – 556.

Daellenbach, H. G. "Are Cash Management Optimization Models Worthwhile?" *Journal of Financial and Quantitative Analysis* (September 1974): 607 – 626.

Eppen, G. D., and E. F. Fama. "Solutions for Cash Balances and Dynamic Portfolio Problems." *Journal of Business* (January 1968): 94 – 112.

Girgis, N. M. "Optimal Cash Balance Levels." *Management Science* (November 1968): 130 – 140.

Miller, M. H., and D. Orr. "A Model of the Demand for Money by Firms." *Quarterly Journal of Economics* (August 1966): 413 – 435.

Mullins, D. W., Jr., and R. B. Homonof. "Applications of Inventory Cash Management Models." In *Modern Developments in Financial Management*, ed. S. C. Myers. New York: Praeger, 1976.

Orgler, Y. E. "An Unequal Period Model for Cash Management Decisions." *Management Science* (October 1969): 77 – 92.

Orr, D. *Cash Management and the Demand for Money.* New York: Praeger, 1970.

Punter, A. "Optimal Cash Management Under Conditions of Uncertainty." *Journal of Business Finance and Accounting* (Autumn 1982): 329 – 340.

Sprenkle, C. M. "The Uselessness of Transactions Demand Models." *Journal of Finance* (December 1969): 835 – 848.

Stone, B. H. "The Use of Forecasts and Smoothing in Control Limit Models for Cash Management." *Financial Management* (Spring 1972): 72 – 84.

Stone, B. H., and T. W. Miller. "Daily Cash Forecasting: A Structuring Framework." *Journal of Cash Management* (October 1981): 35 – 50.

Stone, B. H., and R. A. Wood. "Daily Cash Forecasting: A Simple Method for Implementing the Distribution Approach." *Financial Management* (Fall 1977): 40 – 50.

Chapter 9
Analysis of Credit Terms

Alexander, G. L., and J. M. Gahlon. "An Approach to Determining the Firm's Optimal Cash Discount Policy." *Journal of the Midwest Finance Association* (1980): 40 – 46.

Atkins, J. C., and Y. H. Kim. "Comment and Correction: Opportunity Cost in the Evaluation of Investment in Accounts Receivable." *Financial Management* (Winter 1977): 71 – 74.

Beckman, T. N., and R. S. Foster. *Credits and Collections: Management and Theory.* 8th ed. New York: McGraw-Hill, 1969.

Ben-Horim, M., and H. Levy. "Inflation and the Trade Credit Period." *Management Science* (June 1982): 646 – 651.

Brosky, J. J. *The Implicit Cost of Trade Credit and Theory of Optimal Terms of Sale.* New York: Credit Research Foundation, 1969.

Celec, S. E., and J. D. Icerman. "A Comprehensive Approach to Accounts Receivable Management." *Financial Review* (Spring 1980):23 – 34.

Christie, G. N. "Discount Terms Impact on Cash Inflows." In *Occasional Papers.* Lake Success, N.Y.: Credit Research Foundation, June 1979.

Davis, M. P. "Marginal Analysis of Credit Sales." *Accounting Review* (January 1966): 121 – 126.

Halloran, J. A., and H. P. Lanser. "The Credit Policy Decision in an Inflationary Environment." *Financial Management* (Winter 1981): 31 – 38.

Hill, N. C., and K. D. Riener. "Determining the Cash Discount in the Firm's Credit Policy." *Financial Management* (Spring 1979): 68 – 73.

Johnson, R. W. "Management of Accounts Receivable and Payable." In *Financial Handbook,* 5th ed., ed. E. I. Altman, 1 – 28. New York: 1981.

Kim, Y. H., and J. C. Atkins. "Evaluating Investments in Accounts Receivable: A Maximizing Framework." *Journal of Finance* (May 1978): 403 – 412.

Lewellen, W. G., J. J. McConnell, and J. A. Scott. "Capital Market Influences on Trade Credit Policies." *Journal of Financial Research* (May 1980): 105 – 113.

Lieber, Z., and Y. E. Orgler. "An Integrated Model for Accounts Receivable Management." *Management Science* (October 1975): 212 – 219.

Oh, J. S. "Opportunity Cost in the Evaluation of Investment in Accounts Receivable." *Financial Management* (Summer 1976): 32 – 36.

Pyl, E. A. "Another Look at the Evaluation of Investments in Accounts Receivable." *Financial Management* (Winter 1977): 67 – 70.

Sachdeva, K. S., and L. J. Gitman. "Accounts Receivable Decisions in a Capital Budgeting Framework." *Financial Management* (Winter 1981): 45 – 49.

Sartois, W. L., and N. C. Hill. "Evaluating Credit Policy Alternatives: A Present Value Framework." *Journal of Financial Research* (Spring 1981): 81 – 89.

Schiff, M. "Credit and Inventory Management — Separate or Together." *Financial Executive* (November 1972): 28 – 33.

Shapiro, A. "Optimal Inventory and Credit-Granting Strategies Under Inflation and Devaluation." *Journal of Financial and Quantitative Analysis* (January 1973): 37 – 46.

Walia, T. S. "Explicit and Implicit Cost of Changes in the Level of Accounts Receivable and the Credit Policy Decision of the Firm." *Financial Management* (Winter 1977): 75 – 78.

Welshans, M. T. "Using Credit for Profit Making." *Harvard Business Review* (January – February 1967): 141 – 156.

Weston, J. F., and P. D. Tuan. "Comment on Analysis of Credit Policy Changes " *Financial Management* (Winter 1980): 59 – 63.

Wrightsman, D. "Optimal Credit Terms for Accounts Receivable." *Quarterly Review of Economics and Business* (Summer 1969): 59 – 66.

Chapter 10
Forecasting Accounts Receivable Flows

Beranek, W. *Analysis for Financial Decisions.* Homewood, Ill.: Irwin, 1963, Chapter 10.

Cyert, R. M., H. J. Davidson, and G. L. Thompson. "Estimation of the Allowance for Doubtful Accounts by Markov Chains." *Management Science* (April 1962): 287 – 303.

Kallberg, J. G., and A. Saunders. "Markov Chain Approaches to the Analysis of Payment Behavior of Retail Credit Customers." *Financial Management* (Summer 1983): 5 – 14.

Schwartz, R. A., and D. K. Whitcomb. "The Trade Credit Decision." In *Handbook of Financial Economics,* ed. J. L. Bicksler. New York: North Holland, 1979.

Shim, J. K. "Estimating Cash Collection Rates from Credit Sales: A Lagged Regression Approach." *Financial Management* (Winter 1981): 28 – 30.

———. "Forecasting Cash Inflows for Better Budgeting." *Business Economics* (January 1981): 35 – 38.

Van Kuelen, J. A. M., J. Spronk, and A. W. Corcoran. "On the Cyert-Davidson-Thompson Doubtful Account Model." *Management Science* (January 1981): 108 – 112.

Chapter 11
Credit Selection Models

Barkman, A. I. "Testing the Markov Chain Approach on Accounts Receivable." *Management Accounting* (January 1981): 48 – 50.

Batt, C. D., and T. R. Fowkes. "The Development and Use of Credit Scoring Schemes." In *Applications of Management Science in Banking and Finance,* ed. S. Eilon and T. R. Fowkes, Chapter 13. Epping, England: Gower Press, 1972.

Benishay, H. "Managerial Controls of Accounts Receivable: A Deterministic Approach." *Journal of Accounting Research* (Spring 1965): 114 – 133.

Bierman, H., Jr., and W. H. Hausman. "The Credit Granting Decision." *Management Science* (April 1970): B519 – B532.

Boggess, W. P. "Screen-Test Your Credit Risk." *Harvard Business Review* (November – December 1967): 113 – 122.

Buckley, J. W. "A Systematic Credit Model." *Proceedings of the International Symposium on Model and Computer Based Corporate Planning.* March 1972, 1 – 24.

Churchill, G. A., Jr., J. R. Nevin, and R. R. Watson. "The Role of Credit Scoring in the Credit Decision." *The Credit World* (March 1977).

Copeland, T., and N. Khoury. "A Theory of Credit Extension with Default Risk and Systematic Risk." *Engineering Economist* (Fall 1980): 35 – 52.

Cyert, R. M., and G. L. Thompson. "Selecting a Portfolio of Credit Risks by Markov Chains." *Journal of Business* (January 1968): 39 – 46.

Eisenbeis, R. A. "Selection and Disclosure of Reasons for Adverse Action in Credit-Granting Systems." *Federal Reserve Bulletin* (September 1980): 727 – 736.

Greer, C. C. "The Optimal Credit Acceptance Policy." *Journal of Financial and Quantitative Analysis* (December 1967): 399 – 415.

Hettenhouse, G. W., and J. R. Wentworth. "Credit Analysis Model — A New Look for Credit Scoring." *Journal of Commercial Bank Lending* (December 1971): 26 – 32.

Lane, S. "Submarginal Credit Risk Classification." *Journal of Financial and Quantitative Analysis* (January 1972): 1379 – 1385.

Levy, F. K. "An Application of Heuristic Problem Solving to Accounts Receivable Management." *Management Science* (February 1966): 236 – 244.

Long, M. S. "Credit Screening System Selection." *Journal of Financial and Quantitative Analysis* (June 1976): 313 – 328.

Mao, J. C. T., and C. E. Sarndal. "Controlling Risk in Accounts Receivable Management." *Journal of Business Finance and Accounting* (Autumn 1974): 395 – 403.

Mehta, D. "The Formulation of Credit Policy Models." *Management Science* (October 1968): B30 – B50.

O'Connor, W. J., Jr. "The Equal Credit Opportunity Act and Business Credit — Some Problems Reconsidered." *Journal of Commercial Bank Lending* (January 1979): 20 – 36.

Chapter 12
Monitoring Accounts Receivable

Carpenter, M.D., and J. E. Miller. "A Reliable Framework for Monitoring Accounts Receivable." *Financial Management* (Winter 1979): 37 – 40.

Freitas, L. P. "Monitoring Accounts Receivable." *Management Accounting* (Autumn 1976): 18 – 21.

Gallinger, G. W., and A. J. Ifflander. "Monitoring Accounts Receivable Using Variance Analysis." *Financial Management* (forthcoming).

Gentry, J. A., and J. De La Garza. "Monitoring Accounts Receivable: Revisited." *Financial Management* (Winter 1985): 28 – 38.

Harknett, D. H. "Aging by DSO: The Role of Future Datings." *Credit & Financial Management* (October 1982): 24 – 25.

Lewellen, W. G., and R. O. Edmister. "A General Model for Accounts Receivable Analysis and Control." *Journal of Financial and Quantitative Analysis* (March 1973): 195 – 206.

Lewellen, W. G., and R. W. Johnson. "Better Way to Monitor Accounts Receivable." *Harvard Business Review* (May – June 1972): 101 – 109.

Stone, B. K. "The Payments Pattern Approach to the Forecasting and Control of Accounts Receivable." *Financial Management* (Autumn 1976): 65 – 82.

Wemple, W. B. "Troubleshooting Accounts Receivable." *Financial Executive* (November 1980): 46 – 54.

Chapter 13
Inventory Accounting and Cash Flow Effects

Jannis, C. P., C. H. Poedtke, Jr., and D. R. Ziegler. *Managing and Accounting for Inventories.* New York: Wiley, 1980.

Smith, S. L. "Re-Examining Inventory Profits." *Financial Executive* (June 1982): 22 – 28.

Warner, S. E., and F. D. Whitehurst. "Graphical Approach to Lower of Cost or Market." *Accounting Review* (July 1982): 631 – 637.

Chapter 14
Inventory Investment: How Much?

Arvan, L., and L. N. Moses. "Inventory Management and the Theory of the Firm." *American Economic Review* (March 1982): 186 – 193.

Beranek, W. "Financial Implications of Lot-Size Inventory Models." *Management Science* (April 1967): 401 – 408.

Bock, R. H. "Measuring Cost Parameters in Inventory Models." *Management Technology* (June 1964).

Brennan, J. M. "Up Your Inventory Control." *Journal of Systems Management* (January 1977): 39 – 45.

Brooks, L. D. "Risk-Return Criteria and Optimal Inventory Stocks." *Engineering Economist* (Summer 1980): 275 – 299.

Brooks, W. A., and W. S. Alexander. "Two Emerging Methods of Inventory Control." *Journal of Purchasing and Materials Management* (Summer 1977): 3 – 9.

Bunch, R. G. "The Effect of Payment Terms on Economic Order Quantity Determination." *Management Accounting* (January 1967): 53 – 63.

Dickie, H. F. "ABC Inventory Analysis Shoots for Dollars, Not Pennies." *Factory Management & Maintenance* (July 1951).

Dudick, T. S., and R. Cornell. *Inventory Control for the Financial Executive.* New York: Wiley, 1979.

Flowers, A. D., and J. B. O'Neill. "An Application of Classical Inventory Analysis to a Spare Parts Inventory." *Interfaces* (February 1978): 76 – 79.

Haley, C. W., and R. C. Higgins. "Inventory Control Theory and Trade Credit Financing." *Management Science* (December 1973): 464 – 471.

Haley, G., and T. W. Whitin. *Analysis of Inventory Systems.* Englewood Cliffs, N.J.: Prentice-Hall, 1963.

Horngren, C. T. *Accounting for Management Control.* 3rd ed. Englewood Cliffs, N.J.: Prentice-Hall, 1965.

Magee, J. F. "Guides to Inventory Policy," Parts I – III. *Harvard Business Review* (January – February 1956): 49 – 60; (March – April 1956): 103 – 116; (May – June 1956): 57 – 70.

Morse, W. J., and J. H. Scheiner. "Cost Minimization, Return on Investment, Residual Income: Alternative Criteria for Inventory Models." *Accounting and Business Research* (Autumn 1979): 320 – 324.

Parks, W. H. "Simplified Inventory Control for Computer." *Financial Executive,* 36 (May 1968): 86 – 93.

Saunders, G., and J. Taylor. "Evaluating the Effect of Stockouts and Reorder Points on the EOQ." *Cost and Management* (March – April 1982): 38 – 41.

Shaughnessy, T. E. "Aggregate Inventory Management: Measurement and Control." *Journal of Purchasing and Materials Management* (Fall 1980): 18 – 24.

Snyder, A. "Principles of Inventory Management." *Financial Executive* (April 1964): 13 – 22.

Trippi, R. R., and D. E. Lewin. "A Present Value Formulation of the Classical EOQ Problem." *Decision Sciences* (January 1974): 30 – 35.

Chapter 15
Monitoring Inventory Balances

Chumachenko, N. G. "Once Again: The Volume-Mix-Price/Cost Budget Variance Analysis." *Accounting Review* (October 1968): 753 – 762.

Demski, J. S. "Analyzing the Effectiveness of the Traditional Standard Cost Variance Model." *Management Accounting* (October 1967): 9 – 19.

Owens, R. W. "Cash Flow Variance Analysis." *Accounting Review* (January 1980): 111 – 116.

Chapter 16
Accounts Payable Management

Brandon, M. B. "Contemporary Disbursing Practices and Products: A Survey." *Journal of Cash Management* (March 1982): 26 – 39.

Budin, M., and V. Handel. "Managing Your Accounts Payable." *Management Accounting* (May 1982): 53 – 61.

Ferguson, D. M., and S. F. Maier. "By Any Other Name . . . Controlled Disbursing in the New Environment." *Cashflow* (May 1981): 31 – 35.

Gitman, L. J., D. K. Forrester, and J. R. Forrester, Jr. "Maximizing Cash Disbursement Float." *Financial Management* (Summer 1976): 15 – 24.

Herbst, A. F. "Some Empirical Evidence on the Determinants of Trade Credit at the Industry Level of Aggregation." *Journal of Financial and Quantitative Analysis* (June 1974): 377 – 394.

Johnson, T. O. "Credit Terms Policy and Corporate Payment Practices." *Journal of Cash Management* (September 1982): 14 – 21.

Maier, S. F. "Insulated Controlled Disbursing: A Technique for Coping with Noon Presentment and Other Possible Clearing System Changes." *Journal of Cash Management* (November 1982): 32 – 36.

Maier, S. F., and D. M. Ferguson. "Disbursement System Design for the 1980s." *Journal of Cash Management* (November 1982): 56 – 69.

Maier, S. F., D. W. Robinson, and J. H. Vander Weide. "A Short-Term Disbursement Forecasting Model." *Financial Management* (Spring 1981): 9 – 20.

Phillips, T., and D. Strickland. "Controlled Disbursement Eases Middle-Market Firms' Cash Flow." *Cashflow* (December 1982): 34 – 37.

Schwartz, R. A. "An Economic Analysis of Trade Credit." *Journal of Financial and Quantitative Analysis* (September 1974): 643 – 658.

Chapter 17
Asset-Based Financing

Abraham, A. B. "Factoring: The New Frontier for Commercial Banks." *Journal of Commercial Bank Lending* (April 1971): 32 – 43.

Adler, M. "Administration of Inventory Loans Under the Uniform Commercial Code." *Journal of Commercial Bank Lending* (April 1970): 55 – 60.

Berger, P. D., and W. K. Harper. "Determination of an Optimal Revolving Credit Agreement." *Journal of Financial and Quantitative Analysis* (June 1973): 491 – 497.

Bibler, R. S. "What Bankers Need to Know About Asset-Based Lending." *ABA Banking Journal* (March 1982): 68 – 70.

Boullianne, E. C. "Factoring — A Financing Alternative for Clients." *Journal of Accountancy* (December 1980): 22, 24, 26 – 28.

Chrystie, T. L., and F. J. Fabozzi. *Left-Hand Financing: An Emerging Field of Corporate Finance.* Homewood, Ill.: Dow Jones – Irwin, 1983.

Clemente, H. A. "Innovative Financing." *Financial Executive* (April 1982): 14 – 19.

Daniel, F., S. Legg, and E. C. Yueille. "Accounts Receivable and Related Inventory Financing." *Journal of Commercial Bank Lending* (July 1970): 38 – 53.

Diamond, S. C. "Asset-Based Lending — The Role of the Bank and the Finance Company." *Journal of Commercial Bank Lending* (September 1978): 38 – 44.

———. "Asset-Based Lending in a Changing Environment." *Journal of Commercial Bank Lending* (May 1981): 42 – 47.

Fisher, D. J. "Factoring — An Industry on the Move." *The Conference Board Record* (April 1972): 42 – 45.

Gilbert, F. S., Jr. "The Asset-Based Acquisition: How to Maintain Working Capital and Financial Leverage." *Financial Executive* (December 1982): 54 – 57.

Goldman, R. I. "Look to Receivables and Other Assets to Obtain Working Capital." *Harvard Business Review* (November – December 1979): 206 – 216.

Holmes, W. "The Market Value of Inventories — Perils and Pitfalls." *Journal of Commercial Bank Lending* (April 1973): 30 – 36.

Kerr, A. J. "Secured Financing for Improved Cash Flow." *Credit and Financial Management* (September 1975): 30 – 38.

Koe, R. E. "When Good Credits Are Scarce, Look to Asset-Based Lending." *ABA Banking Journal* (March 1983): 89 – 90.

Logan, J. B. "Clearing Up the Confusion About Asset-Based Lending." *Journal of Commercial Bank Lending* (May 1982): 11 – 17.

Mazirow, A. "The Sale-Leaseback: Raising Capital Without Going Broke." *Financial Executive* (September 1982): 32 – 36.

Middleton, J. W. "Term Lending — Practical and Profitable." *Journal of Commercial Bank Lending* (August 1968): 31 – 43.

Naitove, I. *Modern Factoring.* New York: American Management Association, 1969.

Oppenheimer, A. M. "Selecting an Asset Financing Alternative." *Financial Executive* (May 1980): 16 – 23.

Quarles, J. C. "The Floating Lien." *Journal of Commercial Bank Lending* (November 1970): 51 – 58.

Quill, G. D., J. C. Cresci, and B. D. Shuter. "Some Considerations About Secured Lending." *Journal of Commercial Bank Lending* (April 1977): 41 – 56.

Robinson, D. A. "Are Receivables Good Security for a Loan?" *Journal of Commercial Bank Lending* (December 1978): 47 – 51.

Rogers, R. W. "Warehouse Receipts and Their Use in Financing." *Bulletin of the Robert Morris Associates* (April 1964): 317 – 327.

Sandler, L. "The Tenacious Appeal of Asset-Based Financing." *Institutional Investor* (March 1983): 69 – 74.

Shay, R. P., and C. C. Greer. "Banks Move into High Risk Commercial Financing." *Harvard Business Review* (November – December 1968): 149 – 153, 156 – 161.

Simione, D. A., Jr. "A Positive Approach to Accounts Receivable Financing." *Journal of Commercial Bank Lending* (May 1973): 13 – 17.

Stock, K. L. "Asset-Based Financing: Borrower and Lender Perspectives." *Journal of Commercial Bank Lending* (December 1980): 31 – 47.

Stone, B. K. "How Secure Is Secured Financing Under the Code?" *Burroughs Clearing House* (March 1965): 302 – 312.

Chapter 18
Hedging with Futures and Options

Arak, M., and C. J. McCurdy. "Interest Rate Futures." *Quarterly Review, Federal Reserve Bank of New York* (Winter 1979 – 1980): 33 – 46.

Bacon, P. W., and R. Williams. "Interest Rate Futures: New Tool for the Financial Manager." *Financial Management* (Spring 1976): 32 – 38.

Bonen, T. K., and P. B. Kolber. "Hedging Can Reduce Corporate Rate Imbalance." *Financial Executive* (February 1983): 20 – 30.

Ederington, L. H. "The Hedging Performance of the New Futures Market." *Journal of Finance* (March 1979): 157 – 170.

––––––. "Living with Inflation: A Proposal for New Futures and Options Markets." *Financial Analysts Journal* (January – February 1980): 42 – 47.

Gay, G. D., and S. Manaster. "Hedging Against Commodity Price Inflation: Stocks and Bills as Substitutes for Futures Contracts." *Journal of Business* (July 1982): 317 – 344.

Johnson, L. L. "The Theory of Hedging and Speculation in Commodity Futures." *Review of Economic Studies* (June 1960): 139 – 151.

Keen, H., Jr. "Interest Rate Futures: A Challenge for Bankers." *Business Review of the Federal Reserve Bank of Philadelphia* (November – December 1980): 13 – 22.

Kolb, R. W. *Interest Rate Futures: A Comprehensive Introduction.* Richmond, Va.: Dame, 1982.

––––––. *Understanding Futures Markets.* Glenview, Ill.: Scott, Foresman, 1985.

McEnally, R. W., and M. L. Rice. "Hedging Possibilities in the Flotation of Debt Securities." *Financial Management* (Winter 1979): 12 – 18.

Marks, K. R., and W. A. Laws. "Hedging Against Inflation with Floating-Rate Notes." *Harvard Business Review* (March – April 1980): 106 – 112.

Picou, G. C. "Interest Rate Futures." *Financial Executive* (August 1980): 30 – 36.

Snider, T. E. "Using the Futures Market to Hedge: Some Basic Concepts." *Monthly Review of the Federal Reserve Bank of Richmond* (August 1973): 2 – 7.

Snyder, L. "How to Speculate in the World's Safest Investment." *Fortune* (July 1977): 49 – 51.

Speakes, J. K. "Reduce Interest Risk Through a Synthetic Fixed-Rate Loan." *Financial Executive* (December 1982): 50 – 53.

Telser, L., and H. Higinbotham. "Organized Futures Markets: Costs and Benefits." *Journal of Political Economy* (October 1977): 969 – 1000.

Walgren, R. E. "Managing Interest Expense with Futures Contracts." *Financial Executive* (December 1982): 46 – 48.

Chapter 19
Corporate Distress: Signals, Reorganization, and Liquidation

Aharony, J., C. P. Jones, and I. Swary. "An Analysis of Risk and Return Characteristics of Corporate Bankruptcy Using Capital Market Data." *Journal of Finance* (September 1980): 1001 – 1016.

Altman, E. I. "Financial Ratios, Discriminant Analysis, and the Prediction of Corporate Bankruptcy." *Journal of Finance* (September 1968): 589 – 610.

Altman, E. I., and M. Brenner. "Information Effects and Stock Market Response to Signs of Firm Deterioration." *Journal of Financial and Quantitative Analysis* (March 1981): 35 – 52.

Altman, E. I., R. Haldeman, and P. Narayaman. "ZETA Analysis: A New Model for Identifying Bankruptcy Risk." *Journal of Banking and Finance* (June 1977): 29 – 54.

Argenti, J. *Corporate Collapse: The Causes and Symptoms.* New York: Halsted Press, 1976.

Beaver, W. H. "Financial Ratios as Predictors of Failure." *Empirical Research in Accounting: Selected Studies,* supplement to *Journal of Accounting Research* (1966): 77 – 111.

———. "Market Prices, Financial Ratios, and the Prediction of Failure." *Journal of Accounting Research* (Autumn 1968): 179 – 192.

Blum, W. J. "Full Priority and Full Compensation in Corporate Reorganization: A Reappraisal." *University of Chicago Law Review* (Spring 1958): 417 – 444.

Bulow, J. I., and J. B. Shoven. "The Bankruptcy Decision." *Bell Journal of Economics* (Autumn 1978): 437 – 456.

Collins, R. A. "An Empirical Comparison of Bankruptcy Prediction Models." *Financial Management* (Summer 1980): 52 – 57.

Cowans, D. R. *Bankruptcy Law and Practice.* St. Paul, Minn.: West, 1978.

Dambolena, I. G., and S. J. Khoury. "Ratio Stability and Corporate Failure." *Journal of Finance* (September 1980): 1017 – 1026.

Eisenbeis, R. A. "Pitfalls in the Application of Discriminant Analysis in Business, Finance, and Economics." *Journal of Finance* (June 1977): 875 – 900.

Giroux, G., and C. E. Wiggins, Jr. "Chapter XI and Corporate Resuscitation." *Financial Executive* (December 1983): 37 – 41.

Gordon, M. J. "Towards a Theory of Financial Distress." *Journal of Finance* (May 1971): 347 – 356.

Healy, C. R., and V. H. Atrill. "Objective Economics: Will the Real Laffer Curve Please Stand Up?" *Financial Analysts Journal* (March – April 1983): 15 – 25.

Heath, L. *Financial Reporting and the Evaluation of Solvency.* New York: AICPA, 1978.

Hughes, H. "Waivering Between the Profit and the Loss — Operating a Business During Reorganization Under Chapter 11 of the New Bankruptcy Code." *American Bankruptcy Law Journal* (1980): 45 – 94.

Joy, O. M., and J. O. Tollefson. "On the Financial Applications of Discriminant Analysis." *Journal of Financial and Quantitative Analysis* (December 1975): 723 – 739.

Klee, K. N. "All You Ever Wanted to Know About Cram Down Under the New Bankruptcy Code." *American Bankruptcy Law Journal* (1979): 133 – 171.

Kurger, L., and A. M. Quittner. *Bankruptcy Practice and Procedure Under the New Bankruptcy Act.* New York: Practising Law Institute, 1979.

Libby, R. "Accounting Ratios and the Prediction of Failure: Some Behavioral Evidence." *Journal of Accounting Research* (Spring 1975): 150 – 161.

Mapother, W. R. *Creditors and the New Bankruptcy Code.* Louisville, Ky.: Creditors Law Center, 1982.

Moyer, R. C. "Forecasting Financial Failure: A Re-examination." *Financial Management* (Spring 1977): 11 – 17.

Murray, R. F. "The Penn-Central Debacle: Lessons for Financial Analysis." *Journal of Finance* (May 1971): 327 – 332.

Ohlson, J. A. "Financial Ratios and the Probabilistic Prediction of Bankruptcy." *Journal of Accounting Research* (Spring 1980): 109 – 131.

Roy, A. D. "Safety First and the Holding of Assets." *Econometrica* (July 1952): 431 – 449.

Stanley, D. T., and M. Irth. *Bankruptcy — Problems, Process, Reform.* Washington, D.C.: The Brookings Institution, 1971.

Sulmeyer, I., D. M. Lynn, and M. R. Rochelle. *Collier Handbook for Trustees and Debtors in Possession.* New York: Bender, 1982.

Thompson, C. J. "Danger Signs of Corporate Insolvency." *Financial Executive* (June 1982): 47 – 51.

Trost, J. R. "Business Reorganizations Under Chapter 11 of the New Bankruptcy Code." *Business Lawyer* (April 1979): 1309 – 1346.

Van Horne, J. C. "Optimal Initiation of Bankruptcy Proceedings by Debt Holders." *Journal of Finance* (June 1976): 897 – 910.

Vinso, J. "A Determination of the Risk of Ruin." *Journal of Financial and Quantitative Analysis* (March 1979): 77 – 100.

Walter, J. E. "Determination of Technical Solvency." *Journal of Business* (January 1959): 30 – 43.

Wilcox, J. "A Prediction of Business Failure Using Accounting Data." *Empirical Research in Accounting: Selected Studies,* supplement to *Journal of Accounting Research* (1973): 163 – 190.

Chapter 20
A Summary

Bhattacharya, A. K. "The Influence of Liquidity on Corporate Valuation." Ph.D. dissertation, Arizona State University, 1984.

Crum, R. L., D. D. Klingman, and L. A. Tavis. "An Operational Approach to Integrated Working Capital Planning." *Journal of Economics and Business* (August 1983): 343 – 378.

Lifson, K. A., and B. R. Blackmarr. "Simulation and Optimization Models for Asset Deployment and Funds Sources Balancing Profit, Liquidity and Growth." *Journal of Bank Research* (Autumn 1973): 239 – 255.

Mao, J. C. T. "Application of Linear Programming to Short-Term Financing Decisions." *Engineering Economist* (July – August 1968): 222 – 241.

Pappas, J. L., and G. P. Huber. "Probablistic Short-Term Financial Planning." *Financial Management* (Autumn 1973): 36 – 44.

Pogue, G. A., and R. N. Bussard. "A Linear Programming Model for Short-Term Financial Planning Under Uncertainty." *Sloan Management Review* (Spring 1972): 69 – 99.

Sartois, W. L., and M. L. Spruill. "Goal Programming and Working Capital Management." *Financial Management* (Spring 1974): 57 – 64.

Smith, K. V. *Readings on the Management of Working Capital.* 2nd ed. St. Paul, Minn.: West, 1980.

Wagner, J., and L. J. Pryor. "Simulation and the Budget: An Integrated Model." *Sloan Management Review* (Winter 1971): 45 – 58.

Merville, L. J., and L. A. Tavis. "Optimal Working Capital Policies: A Chance-Constrained Programming Approach." *Journal of Financial and Quantitative Analysis* (January 1973): 47 – 60.

Answers to Problems

Chapter 1

1. Residual income = $1421.70
2. Residual income = $500

Chapter 2

1. (b) 20, 1.0
   (d) 56, 14, 2.8
2. Marginal cost for total output of 40 units = $1.88
3. Profit maximized at $522.50 sales
4. (a) Efficient output level = 147 units
   (b) Profit maximization = 147 units
   (c) Profit maximization = 105 units
5. (a) 1392 units
   (b) Current ratio = 2.78
   (c) Reduce current assets and liabilities by $540

Chapter 3

1. Year 1985:
   Current ratio = 1.50
   Quick ratio = 0.83
   Defensive interval = 113 days
   Accounts receivable turnover = 4.44
   Inventory turnover = 2.13
   Net fixed-asset turnover = 2
   Total debt-equity = 0.90
   Fixed coverage = 1.09
   Simple interest coverage = 3.44
   Degree of financial leverage = 1.41

Book value per share = $5.00
Cash flow per share = $1.58
Return on assets = 0.21 (using EBIT)
Return on assets = 0.15 (using net income)
Return on equity = 0.215
Breakeven sales = $260.870
Margin of safety = 0.53

3. Many different answers are possible.

4. Profit = $25.63
   Total assets = $358.75
   Total current assets = $172.77

Chapter 4

1. (a) Deficit = $258,839
   (b) Surplus = $862,081 at 7%
       Deficit = $935,699 at 4%

3. (a) Year 1's borrow option: net income = $24,900
       Year 2's capital lease: net income = $24,866
       Year 3's operating lease: net income = $25,439
   (b) Total assets:
       Borrow option = $206,357
       Capital lease = $204,518
       Operating lease = $180,040
   (c) Debt-equity = 0.97 under the borrow option
       Times interest earned = 3.93 under the capital lease
       Total asset turnover = 1.56 under the operating lease
       Return on assets = 0.288 under the borrow option
       Return on equity = 0.248 under the capital lease

4. (a) Rate = 12%
   (b) Present value = $30,198,158

5. Must capitalize; capitalized value equals market price.

6. Segregate $17,725,527.94; gain = $2,274,472.06

7. Conventional ratio = 0.27; adjusted ratio = 0.31

8. $447,207.48

9. $97,991.02

10. (a) Operating lease cash outflow = $367,466.40
        Capital lease cash outflow = $411,562.00
    (b) Financial (capital) lease; $2,782.68
    (c) IRR = 9% – 10%

Chapter 5

1. Last year, current assets = 0.105 of total assets
   Last year, profit = 0.098 of total sales

2. Last year, ROE = 0.198

3. ROE = 0.267

4. $g_s = 0.265$; $g_a = 0.143$

5. Last year's cash conversion cycle = −44.3 days

6. Traditional breakeven (case 2 type) = $1,282,983
   Cash breakeven sales level = $1,410,400

8. 1985 current assets = 0.474 of total assets
   1985 net income = 0.107 of total sales

9. 1985 debt-equity = 2.39

10. g_s = 0.02

11. 1985 cash conversion cycle = 219 days

12. 1985 cash breakeven sales level = $399.1

Chapter 6

1. August receipts minus disbursement = −$500

2. June receipts minus disbursements = $41,750

3. Month 6's receipts minus disbursements = $24,029

4. July cumulative cash balance = $5

5. Ending cash balance = $120,000

6. Total operating income = $14,202,000
   Total cash receipts = $20,065,000
   Total cash disbursements = $13,515,000

7. Decrease in net working capital = $15

8. Cash flow from operations = $240.4

9. Forecast LFI = 1.05

10. (a) Budget RLI = 3.33
    (b) $39.72

Chapter 7

2. (a) $100,000
   (b) $120,000
   (c) $90,000

3. (a) $1,375,000
   (b) $705,000
   (c) $52,500
   (d) $32,100

4. (a) $497,333
   (b) $25,200
   (c) 5.07%
   (d) $24,533

5. (a) $1,133,333
   (b) $200,000
   (c) −$86,667

6. (a) Cash conversion cycle = 69.7 days
   (b) Net working capital = $8,451,000

7. (a) Ledger = −$200,000
   (b) $600,000 on day 4
   (c) Gain = $120,000

8. (a) Day 3 = $0
   (b) 3 days
   (c) −$1,200,000

9. Sales = $20,100,000

10. (a) Daily sales = $42,500
    (b) 21.5%

Chapter 8

1. *Pro forma* cash balance = $284,750

2. (a) $52,000
   (b) $208,333.33

3. (a) $60,000
   (b) $30,000
   (c) 33.33
   (d) $6000
   (e) $M^* = $44,721.36 and $70,710.68

4. (a) $R = 1004.15; $h = 3012.45; average = $1338.87

5. Ending cash balance on day 3:
   3-day forecast = $14,295
   No forecast = $27,405

6. (a) $10,392.30
   (b) $5196.15
   (c) 41%

7. Tuesday's $d_i^* = −0.002$

8. Day 3's budget = −$4137.93

9. Buy $12,550 of securities.

10. (a) $10,200 securities bought on day 4
    (b) $25,200 securities bought on day 4
    (c) Residual income (forecast) = $210.98
    (d) Residual income (no forecast) = $175.15

Chapter 9

1. When terms are 3/15, n/45
   (a) 0.371
   (b) 0.441

2. (a) 7.963
   (c) 0.276
   (e) 0.157

3. Residual income = $164,750

4. Residual income
   (a) $33,792
   (b) $14,675
   (c) $20,442

5. Turnover
   (a) 19.2
   (b) 24.0
   (c) 12.0

6. Breakeven sales = $60,000
7. Breakeven sales increase
   (a) 1.1%
   (b) 10%
   (c) 52.5%
8. (a) Incremental profit = $145.73
   (b) Day 11's cash flow = $111.38
       Day 26's cash flow = $207.25
9. Residual income = $3662.94
10. (a) $3949.37
    (b) 10%

Chapter 10

1. (a) Element in row 1, column 1 = 1.78571
   (b) State 0 = 2.05 months
       State 1 = 2.27 months
       State 2 = 2.05 months
   (c) State 0 = 0.7%
       State 1 = 3.9%
       State 2 = 29.2%
   (d) Value of accounts receivable:
       State 0 = $3571.42
       State 1 = $681.82
       State 2 = $129.87
   (e) Monthly cash flows = $2097.40
       Monthly bad debts = $25.97
2. (a) The following amounts represent the row values for state 2: 0.380, 0.093, 0.263, 0.065, 0.199
   (b) Incremental investment = $4617.27
   (c) Monthly cash flow = $1963.41
       Monthly bad debts = $42.59
3. Incremental receivables = $805.43 at the new steady state
4. (a) Presently in state 0 = 5.37 periods
       Presently in state 1 = 6.55 periods
       Presently in state 2 = 6.41 periods
   (b) Probability of bad debts:
       State 0 = 9.7%
       State 1 = 14.3%
       State 2 = 22.9%
   (c) Aging: State 0 = $64.92
              State 1 = $38.73
              State 2 = $18.29
   (d) Monthly cash flow = $20.52
       Monthly bad debts = $2.19
5. (b) Row 1 = 1.65644, 0.490798, 0.0613497
6. Probability of collection for policy A:
   State 0 = 85%
   State 1 = 69%

Appendix A

1. (a) Row 1, column 1 = 23
   (b) Row 2, column 2 = 216
   (c) Row 1, column 1 = −0.5 for the first matrix

Appendix C

1. (a) Probability = 18%
   (b) $1327.50
   (c) Probability of less than $1000 = 17%
2. (a) Joint probability of both discounting = 0.455
   (b) New policy's expected cash flow = $4067.19
   (c) Joint probability of not paying by 10th day = 0.105

Chapter 11

2. Indifference value:
   State 0 = 0.1520
   State 1 = 0.3859
   State 2 = 1.179
3. (a) Due date = 65%
   One month late = 69%
   Two months late = 74%
   (b) (i) Due date = 70%
        One month late = 74.4%
        Two months late = 78.9%
        (ii) Due date = 65%
        One month late = 68%
        Two months late = 70.9%
        (iii) Due date = 65%
        One month late = 70.9%
        Two months late = 76.9%
        (iv) Due date = 65%
        One month late = 72.4%
        Two months late = 79.8%
4. State 2's breakeven probabilities:
   Sales of $30 = 85%
   Sales of $85 = 74%
   Sales of $285 = 70%
5. (a) $Z = 1.2005C + 0.0783T$
6. (a) $45
   (b) 2 months
7. (a) 30 days from point of sale for all sales levels
   (b) 30 days from point of sale for sales of $50 and $90; 60 days from point of sale for sales of $145
8. (a) Index value for account 2 = −0.26
   (b) Index value for firm 8 = −0.29

Chapter 12

1. (a) June = $12,000
   (b) July, 30 days or less = 74.8%
   (c) May, 60-day average = 50.3 DSO

2. Collection experience variance = $5467.64, unfavorable
   Sales pattern variance = $732.36, unfavorable
   Sales quantity variance = $2494.66, unfavorable

3. (a) $304
   (b) Period 6's expected margin = −$609

4. (a) Collections in month 5 = $239
      Accounts receivable balance for month 5 = $387.75
   (b) Month 5, 90-day average = 44.56 DSO

5. (a) Month 3 = $524
   (b) Month 3's aging schedule:
         30 days = 0.565
         60 days = 0.355
         90 days = 0.072
         120 days = 0.008
      Month 3's balance proportions:
      End of month 3 = 0.789
      End of month 4 = 0.552
      End of month 5 = 0.141
      End of month 6 = 0.016

7. Collection experience variance = $53.50, favorable
   Sales pattern variance = $19.50, unfavorable

Chapter 13

1. Cost of sales: LIFO = $41,200; FIFO = $39,900

2. Item S: Original = $2700
           Present = $2800
           LCM = $2700

3. Cost of sales:
   Specific = $250
   FIFO = $245
   LIFO = $260

4. Year 3's gross margin (inventory at cost) = $100,000

5. (d) $2000 lower

6. (a) Variable costing = $11,844.90
      Absorption costing = $12,816.90
   (b) $680.40
   (c) Net cash flow: Variable = $2402.28
                      Absorption = $2110.68

7. (a) $3150
   (b) $4350
   (c) $5850

8. Year 1's profit after tax: Year 1's cash flow:
   Selling price = $1200   Selling price = −$10,800
   Conventional = −$600   Conventional = −$9600

9. (a) Period 3's inventory value: FIFO = $54; LIFO = $60
   (b) Period 3's cost of sales: FIFO = $547; LIFO = $531
   (c) Profit difference, period 3: FIFO $16 less than LIFO

Chapter 14

1. EOQ = 4000 units

2. Discount > 3.05%

3. 2-point average turnover ratio = 12
   13-point average turnover ratio = 6.87

4. (a) 3333.33
   (b) $12,910
   (c) $6455

5. (a) $223,607
   (b) $250,000

6. (a) 4.95
   (b) 0.202

7. EOQ = 1414.21
   Total inventory cost = $1,000,707.10
   Average inventory = $7071.05

8. (a) (i) EOQ = 1581
   (b) 5000 units

9. (a) 417 units
   (b) 277 units
   (c) 0 units

10. (a) $3,001,500
    (b) $299,900
    (c) 2.5
    (d) $1,350,800

Chapter 15

1. −$63,750

2. Price variance = $18,000, unfavorable

3. Total cost of sales price variance = $8750, unfavorable

4. Total price variance = $562.50, unfavorable

5. Total price variance = $20,000, unfavorable

6. (a) Gross margin price variance = $80, favorable
   (b) Gross margin cash flow variance = $172.50, favorable

7. Gross margin variance = $0

8. Sales volume variance = $50,000, unfavorable

9. Closing inventory price variance = $17,500, favorable

10. Gross margin volume variance = $44,500, unfavorable

11. Turnover volume variance = 0.1389, unfavorable

Chapter 16

1. For terms 1.5/20, $n/36$, AIC = 0.199
2. AIC = 0.80 for terms of 4/15, $n/30$ and 30 days acceleration
3. (a) AIC = 0.1994
   (b) AIC = 0.2743
4. Breakeven occurs between 40 and 50 days past the discount date.
5. April payment ratio = 0.896
   April's DSO (based on 60 days sales) = 28.9
6. (b) April's purchases discounted = 0.461
   (c) April's cumulative payments: 0.461 by discount date; 0.563 by day 30;
       0.929 by day 60
7. Payment experience variance = $410,000
   Purchase mix variance = $12,000
   Purchase quantity variance = $378,000
8. (a) May's aging schedule:
       Current = 0.82
       31 – 60 days = 0.12
       Over 60 days = 0.06
   (b) May's purchases discounted = 0.51
9. January: Discounts offered = $116
            Discounts taken = $56
10. Payment experience variance = $1562.20
    Purchase mix variance = $336.08
    Purchase quantity variance = $1548.88

Chapter 17

1. (a) $14,375
   (b) $11,250
   (c) $10,833
2. (a) 0.855
   (b) $58,480
   (c) $925.44
   (d) $467.04
   (e) Residual income if pledge = −$5133.61
       Residual income if borrow = −$2298.94
3. (a) Present total assets = $12,900,000
       Recasted total assets = $9,895,325
   (b) Recasted current ratio = 2.06
       Recasted debt-equity ratio = 1.49
   (c) Net cash outflow:
       Without leaseback = $169,980
       With leaseback = $281,888
4. (a) $332,578.28
   (b) $369,531.42
   (c) 28% annually
5. (a) $3723.96
   (b) 13.75% annually
   (c) $386,734.07

6. (a) High: $3,863,399.22
   (b) Low: $145,430.61

7. Total cost = $141,562.50
   Annual effective rate = 18.88%

8. (a) No
   (b) Year 2's before-tax profits will be $19,034.83 higher by owning; after-tax cash flows will be $73,877.28 higher in year 2 by leasing.

9. Debt-equity ratio:
   Loan = 4.33
   Lease = 2.33

Chapter 18

1. Table 3's discounted equity = $31.75
   Table 4's nondiscounted future's equity = −$28.47
   Table 5's discounted equity = $4.57

2. (a) Short hedge
   (b) Basis declines to −0.10 = 0.05 profit
       Basis declines to −0.20 = 0.05 loss

3. Profit = $146,312

4. (a) $18/ounce loss
   (b) $15/ounce loss

5. (a) Long hedge
   (b) −0.25
   (c) −0.50
   (d) Profit = 0.25

6. 1.08 treasury bonds for each corporate bond

7. Buys 0.907 treasury bond for each corporate bond

8. Profit = $0.03 yen per dollar

9. (a) Long hedge
   (b) Buy call options
   (c) Buy futures and buy put options

10. (a) $3
    (b) $1

11. Intrinsic value:
    March = $5/64$
    June = $14/64$
    September = $23/64$

Chapter 19

1. Z = 3.2252

Appendix

1. Partially secured receive 69%

2. Unsecured creditors deficiency = $51,000

Index